Ireland

CÍAN BYRNE

IRELAND
SCOTLAND
ATLANTIC OCEAN
North Channel
Irish Sea
NORTHERN IRELAND
Malin Head
Rathlin Island
The Causeway Coast
Tory Island
Horn Head
Lough Swilly
Inishowen Peninsula
Portrush
Ballycastle
Bushmills
Portstewart
Coleraine
Downings
Bloody Foreland
Gweedore
Glenveagh National Park
Derry
Letterkenny
Glens of Antrim
LONDONDERRY
ANTRIM
Larne
Ballymena
DONEGAL
Lifford
International Appalachian Trail
Bangor
Newtownards
Belfast
Lisburn
Strangford Lough
Lough Neagh
TYRONE
Sliabh Liag
Killybegs
Donegal
Donegal Bay
Mullaghmore Head
Ballyshannon
Bundoran
Lower Lough Erne
Enniskillen
Armagh
DOWN
Banbridge
Downpatrick
Rosses Point
Strandhill
Sligo
LEITRIM
FERMANAGH
ARMAGH
Newcastle
Erris Head
SLIGO
Lough Allen
MONAGHAN
Newry
The Mournes
Carlingford
Greenore
Achill Island
Ballycroy
Wild Nephin National Park
Lough Conn
Mulranny
MAYO
Dundalk
CAVAN
LOUTH
Clew Bay
Clare Island
Westport
Murrisk
ROSCOMMON
LONGFORD
Drogheda
Letterfrack
Leenaun
Lough Mask
Clifden
Connemara National Park
WESTMEATH
Lough Ree
MEATH
DUBLIN
A1
A2
A5
A6
A26
A29
A32
A505
N1
N2
N3
N4
N5
N15
N16
N17
M1
M2
M3

REPUBLIC OF IRELAND
Dublin
Howth
Dún Laoghaire
Sandycove
Killiney
Bray
Greystones
Wicklow
Dundrum
Wicklow Mountains National Park
Wicklow Mtns
Wicklow Way
Clonegal
WICKLOW
KILDARE
OFFALY
LAOIS
CARLOW
WEXFORD
Wexford
Ramsgrange
Hook Head
Waterford
WATERFORD
KILKENNY
Kilkenny
TIPPERARY
Dungarvan
Athlone
Clonmacnoise
River Shannon
Lough Derg
GALWAY
Galway
Galway Bay
Connemara
Roundstone
Aran Islands
The Burren
Doolin
Kilfenora
Burren National Park
Cliffs of Moher
Lahinch
Spanish Point
CLARE
Killaloe
Kilkee
Kilrush
Loop Head
Mouth of the Shannon
Limerick
LIMERICK
Tralee
Dingle Peninsula
Dingle
Slea Head
Dunquin
Ventry
Blasket Islands
Inch Strand
Killorglin
KERRY
Killarney
Killarney National Park
Valentia Island
Cahersiveen
Iveragh Peninsula
Portmagee
Waterville
Kerry Seas National Park
Ballinskelligs
Skellig Michael
Caherdaniel
Kenmare
Glengarriff
Beara Peninsula
Castletownbere
Schull
Mizen Head
Baltimore
Sherkin Island
Cape Clear Island
CORK
Cork
Midleton
Fota Island
Cobh
Kinsale
Celtic Sea
St. George's Channel
M4
M6
M7
M8
M9
M11
M17
M18
N7
N11
N20
N21
N22
N24
N25
N70
0
25 mi
0
25 km
Wild Atlantic Way
© MOON.COM

Contents

THE TEMPLE BAR
THE TEMPLE BAR
TOBACCO
GUINNESS

Cliffs of Moher

WELCOME TO

Ireland

Welcome to the Emerald Isle, a rocky outcrop in the North Atlantic that's been shaped by the elements and history into a truly gorgeous island that enthralls with its endless stories, scenery, and craic.

Ireland and Northern Ireland are small countries, about the same size as the state of Indiana, but they squeeze in a ferocious amount of places to see and things to do. I often find myself on the trails in the Cooley Mountains, taking a dip in the chilly sea afterward, and settling in for a pint and a chat in a traditional pub as the sun finally sets on a long summer's evening—my ideal Irish day.

You're never too far from a slow pace of life in Ireland. In rural areas by the sea, high in the mountains, or hidden among rolling fields, there are places where time has stood still for decades. But it's not all stone walls and flocks of sheep blocking traffic on narrow country roads; there are great cities too. In Galway's outstanding foodie scene, Belfast's indie spirit, and Dublin's go-go-go atmosphere, city-loving folks will feel right at home.

The good weather is hard to predict, even in summer, but one ever-present element is the welcoming people. The Irish go out of their way to help you, and if you find yourself in a rural pub in the back of beyond, people will chat with you as if you've lived around the corner for years. Pubs are part of our culture in Ireland, but we do things a little differently. Think of them as our town squares, where we meet to chat about the local goings-on, where we meet to listen to live music and keep our culture alive, and where we meet with old friends and family.

Ireland is a choose-your-own-adventure place. Step inside ancient structures in the beautiful countryside, or immerse yourself in Irish crafts and language. Whatever your loves are, you'll find them here, and you'll have a bit of craic along the way.

Fáilte go hÉireann.

Glendalough, along the Wicklow Way

10 TOP EXPERIENCES

1 Enjoying a pint of Ireland's iconic drink, Guinness, at one of the many iconic **Dublin pubs,** all with their own story to tell (page 78).

2 Hiking the **Wicklow Way** from Dublin to Clonegall through Wicklow Mountains National Park in short manageable sections—and admiring the brilliant views throughout (page 120).

3 Standing atop the **Cliffs of Moher** at the edge of the world as the sun drops below the horizon and lights up the Atlantic Ocean (page 272).

4 Getting "the gift of the gab" when you kiss the Blarney Stone at **Blarney Castle,** a huge draw for visitors for decades (page 185).

5 Seeing the story of both sides of the Troubles through large **murals** across Belfast and on a tour with **Black Taxi Tours** (page 404).

6 Hopping on a ferry to the **Aran Islands** (page 318), where Irish is still spoken and the tide dictates life, and visiting the prehistoric cliff-top fort of **Dún Aonghasa** (page 321).

7 Summiting the challenging **Carrauntoohil,** Ireland's tallest mountain, for unbeatable views of the MacGillycuddy Reeks (page 241).

8 Taming the mighty Atlantic Ocean by learning how to surf at the **National Surf Centre** in Strandhill (page 360).

9 Tucking into some of the **best Irish dishes and delicacies** that make the most of our amazing farm produce (page 28).

10 Joining in on an impromptu **traditional music session** at a pub where incredible musicians perform and crowd participation is encouraged (page 26).

Planning Your Trip

WHERE TO GO

Dublin

As the capital and the most cosmopolitan city, Dublin is Ireland's most visited destination. On the cobbled streets and narrow laneways, you'll find stories through the ages, traditional pubs where Guinness flows endlessly, and some of the country's best restaurants and chefs.

Around Dublin

Discover the best of the mountains and the coast without traveling far from Dublin. Gaze down on the city from the hills in the Wicklow Mountains National Park and uncover hidden landscapes while hiking the stunning Wicklow Way. Or venture farther along the coast to unforgettable natural scenery and ancient structures that most visitors don't know about.

The Southeast

Get your teeth into history in this sunny region that's a must for history buffs to learn about Ireland's lesser-known past. Hear how the Vikings raided the coast before founding cities, climb the world's oldest functioning lighthouse, and trace the Irish heritage of a US president to his ancestral family farm.

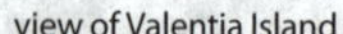
view of Valentia Island

Cork

There's a reason locals call the republic's second-largest city "the People's Republic of Cork." Known for its mighty craic, Cork deserves its residents' pride. The Wild Atlantic Way begins in West Cork and takes you through idyllic villages and towns to some of the most remote and spectacular coast. This part of the country is known for its passionate love of food and fantastic local produce—you'll eat well at every stop.

Kerry

If you close your eyes and think of Ireland, it's likely Kerry that you're daydreaming about. Visitors flock here to explore the rolling hills, Ireland's tallest mountain, wildlife, and historic sights in Killarney National Park. You'll find warm welcomes from people who love visitors. During summer, these quiet towns are abuzz with craic agus ceol (music and fun).

Clare and Limerick

Breathe in the sea air from the top of the Cliffs of Moher as the waves crash below, then leave the crowds behind to explore the remote parts of the West Clare coast and otherworldly rocky landscapes in Burren National Park. Nearby Limerick City, at the mouth of the River Shannon, boasts a thriving food and drink scene as well as a huge passion for rugby.

Galway and Mayo

Enjoy the good life in Galway City, where amazing restaurants and lively pubs create a year-round party atmosphere. You'll hear Irish spoken on the Aran Islands off the coast and throughout Connemara, as well as live trad music in famous pubs in Westport.

The Northwest

Discover an overlooked part of the Wild Atlantic Way that's perfect for surfers to improve their skills. In Glenveagh National Park, hikers can get away from the crowds. Bring your dancing shoes, especially for Ballyshannon, which hosts a number of blues and traditional music festivals every year.

Northern Ireland

Learn about the conflicts that have plagued this country on fascinating tours in the capital, Belfast, and see how the cities of Northern Ireland have become creative hubs brimming with events, venues, and top-quality food. See sights like the Giant's Causeway, and after walking one of the

many great trails, treat yourself to a famous Northern Irish whiskey.

WHEN TO GO

When to visit Ireland depends on what you plan to do. The peak season is summer, when you'll find the most activities and excitement, but if you're here for the outdoors, fall and spring may be even more rewarding.

Summer

It's hard to predict the weather in Ireland, but it's often pleasant June-August. The days are long in June, when the sun rises before 5am and sets just before 10pm, to fit as many sights or trails as possible into your day. Irish summers are mild, with average highs of 15-20°C (59-68°F) and lows of 10-13°C (50-55°F), with a mix of sun, clouds, and occasional showers. Dublin and the east coast tend to be slightly warmer and drier than the west. Summer is the busiest time for visitors, so book attractions and lodging in advance, and expect crowds at popular spots.

Fall

Fall is often the best time to visit Ireland, particularly September. The weather can be surprisingly good, with warmer weather becoming more common, with highs averaging 14-18°C (57-64°F) and lows of 9-11°C (48-52°F) that can extend into mid-October, when most visitors have gone home, making lodging easier to find. Rainfall increases as fall progresses; layering is essential, and a waterproof jacket is a must. The days are still long but begin to shorten as Halloween draws near. This event originated in Ireland as Samhain and is celebrated across the country, blending ancient traditions with modern celebrations through bonfires, festivals, and fireworks.

Winter

Winter can be tough in Ireland. It rains 25 days a month and the days are short, with as little as 8 hours of daylight. While the temperatures don't get too low, averaging 3-8°C (37-46°F), the humidity makes winter feel far colder. November and January are quiet months, and many rural tourism businesses close for the season, but the social scene ramps up in December with Christmas drinks, parties, and nightly trad

If You Have . . .

- **Three Days:** Take your time exploring Dublin, immersing yourself in its rich history, lively culture, and scenic surroundings. Begin with a stop at Trinity College to admire the Book of Kells, then explore Irish history at the Guinness Storehouse and Glasnevin Cemetery. Enjoy a day trip to Howth, a charming seaside village where you can hike the cliff walk, taste fresh seafood, visit the James Joyce Tower and Museum, or try sea swimming.
- **One Week:** From Dublin, drive south to Wicklow Mountains National Park and leave the city behind as you take in the views along the Old Military Road and at the old monastic city of Glendalough. Head southwest to Cork City and see why Corkonians are so proud of their home. Drop by the English Market for tasty treats and foodie gifts, then choose your own adventure: Visit Blarney Castle to kiss the Blarney Stone or, for a more coastal option, head to nearby Kinsale and enjoy the scenic Scilly Walk.
- **Two Weeks:** From Cork, follow the west coast north on the Wild Atlantic Way. Take the very scenic route to Killarney via the Ring of Kerry. Dedicate a day to Killarney National Park, where you can get your bearings at Muckross House before choosing from gentle lakeside walks and short hikes to Torc Waterfall. Continue driving north to the Cliffs of Moher for incredible coastal views. Detour through the Burren National Park on the way to Galway, famous for its party atmosphere, festivals, and amazing food. Head back to Dublin to spend your last couple of days in the area, or, if you have time, take the train from Dublin to Belfast to tour its famed murals and explore the historic Cathedral Quarter.

sessions filling pubs in the cities. Many pubs have open fireplaces, wooden interiors, and soft lighting, creating a welcoming retreat from the chilly weather.

Spring

As Ireland reawakens in spring, the landscapes bloom again, and newborn livestock find their feet in the green fields. Days can be dark and the weather unpredictable, with highs averaging 11-15°C (52-59°F) and lows of 4-7°C (39-45°F), but it's hard to beat an early-morning hike on a fresh and crisp spring morning. St. Patrick's Day (Mar. 17) sees festivities in every city, town, and village. Spring is a great time to travel before the peak summer crowds arrive.

Cathedral Quarter, Belfast

KNOW BEFORE YOU GO

Passports and Visas

It's important to remember that the Republic of Ireland and Northern Ireland are two separate countries, and this may impact your travel plans. The Republic of Ireland is part of the European Union and not part of the United Kingdom. Northern Ireland is part of the United Kingdom and not part of the European Union.

Ireland is also not part of the Schengen Area, so Schengen visas cannot be used for entry. Additionally, having a UK visa does not grant entry to Ireland, and vice versa. All travelers should ensure their passports remain valid for the duration of their stay. People from outside the European Economic Area may face additional immigration checks upon arrival in both the Republic of Ireland and Northern Ireland.

Republic of Ireland

For US and Canadian citizens, no visa is required to enter the Republic of Ireland for stays up to 90 days, but a valid passport is necessary. EU and Schengen Area citizens can enter Ireland without a visa and may use either a national identity card or a passport. Australian and New Zealand citizens don't need a visa for stays up to 90 days in Ireland, but they must have a valid passport. South African citizens must obtain a visa before traveling to Ireland and must present a valid passport.

Northern Ireland

When visiting Northern Ireland, US and Canadian citizens can stay for up to six months without a visa, but must have a valid passport. EU and Schengen Area citizens don't need a visa for Northern Ireland, but they must have a passport, as national ID cards are no longer accepted. Australian and New Zealand citizens can enter Northern Ireland visa-free for up to six months with a valid passport, but they must obtain an Electronic Travel Authorisation (ETA). South African citizens require both a valid passport and a visa to enter Northern Ireland.

ETIAS Registration

ETIAS is an electronic travel authorization system for visa-exempt travelers planning to visit Schengen Area countries in Europe. ETIAS is not required for visitors to Ireland, as Ireland is not part of the Schengen Area and does not participate in the ETIAS system. For visitors to

Northern Ireland, especially if arriving by air, a UK Electronic Travel Authorisation (ETA; www.gov.uk/guidance/apply-for-an-electronic-travel-authorisation-eta) is required, as Northern Ireland is part of the United Kingdom.

Reservations

While many attractions in Ireland allow walk-ins, some popular experiences require or strongly advise advance booking, especially during peak seasons. In Dublin, timed-entry tickets for the **Book of Kells** at **Trinity College** sell out fast, particularly in summer. Also book ahead at the **Guinness Storehouse** to ensure your preferred time slot. Access to **Brú na Bóinne** and **Newgrange** is restricted to small numbers to protect the structures, so book your tour as far in advance as possible.

Access to **Skellig Michael** is extremely limited, with most tour operators offering cruises around the island. Tours that land on the island sell out well in advance, so book as early as you can. You can drive the **Ring of Kerry** or visit the **Cliffs of Moher** on your own, but if you're planning to take a guided tour at either place, book ahead to secure a spot.

What to Pack

With such unpredictable weather, you should pack a lightweight rain jacket and waterproof walking shoes for the frequent rain. Bring layers, such as a fleece or sweater, as temperatures can drop quickly, even in summer, and pack a hat, gloves, and scarf just in case. Ireland is one of the most expensive countries in Europe; although you'll find weather-appropriate clothing here, it can be quite expensive. We dress casually in Ireland, so there's no need for formal clothing in pubs or most restaurants, but if you plan to visit upmarket restaurants and trendy city bars, a smart-casual outfit is appropriate.

Ireland uses Type G electrical plugs, the same as in the UK, which have three rectangular prongs. Electric sockets are 230 V at 50 Hz. If

1: Trinity College 2: view of Skellig Michael 3: Cork City

you're traveling from the United States, you will need a plug adapter and possibly a voltage converter for devices that are not dual voltage.

Transportation

If you're planning to visit rural Ireland, a car is a must.

Air

Dublin Airport (DUB) is where most travelers land in the Republic of Ireland. Cork Airport (ORK) is smaller but serves many European destinations, while Shannon Airport (SNN) in County Clare is a key gateway to the west, known for its proximity to the Wild Atlantic Way and US preclearance facilities. Ireland West Airport (NOC), near Knock, serves regional travelers with flights to the UK and some European locations. In Northern Ireland, Belfast International Airport (BFS) is the largest, connecting to numerous UK and European destinations, while Belfast City Airport (BHD) focuses on domestic and short-haul flights.

Car

We drive on the left side of the road, and most visitors find driving on the major roads quite easy. Expect traffic congestion in and around the cities during commuting hours, and be warned that some country roads are very narrow, and locals tend to drive fast on them.

Train and Bus

Despite being one of the wealthiest countries in the world, Ireland's public transport systems are lagging far behind what many people would expect. The major cities are connected by bus and rail, but not to the standard of continental Europe, with limited services and routes. Attempts are being made to improve this, but if you're planning to visit rural Ireland, a car is a must.

The most convenient areas to travel by train or bus:

- **Dublin and Dublin Bay:** Dublin has the best public transport in the country, including DART (Dublin Area Rapid Transit) to coastal towns like Howth, Malahide, Bray, and Greystones. Intercity trains and buses connect Dublin to major cities across Ireland.
- **Cork:** Cork City is well connected by train and bus to Dublin, Limerick, Galway, and Waterford. Local trains and buses serve Blarney Castle, Cobh, and Kinsale.
- **Galway and Mayo:** Galway has good bus and train links to Dublin and Limerick, plus regional buses to the Cliffs of Moher, Connemara, and Aran Islands ferries.
- **Belfast and Northern Ireland:** Belfast has frequent trains and buses to Dublin (the *Enterprise* train), Derry, and the Causeway Coast as well as excellent local transport.

BEST OF Ireland

This all-encompassing trip through Ireland pairs the well-known must-see attractions with worthwhile lesser-known spots. It's mainly a driving itinerary with some car-free days in Dublin. Covering buzzing towns, the craic, and the great outdoors, you'll laugh, eat, and drink your way around this wonderful island.

Dublin

Day 1

Make a flying start with a tour of the city's highlights. Wander the grounds of **Trinity College** before walking across the city to the **Guinness Storehouse.** Spend some time in the **Liberties** and soak up some true Dublin character. You're never too far from a **pub with live music** in Dublin, so finish your night with some singing before returning to your hotel.

Day 2

After a city-center breakfast, take a short 15-minute bus ride north to Glasnevin to walk the beautiful grounds of the **National Botanical Gardens** and learn about the famous residents of **Glasnevin Cemetery.** No trip to Glasnevin is complete without a visit to **The Gravediggers** for one of the best pints of Guinness in Dublin. If you don't fancy a bowl of coddle, pop back into the city and enjoy some modern Irish cuisine instead.

Day 3

Spend your last day in Dublin immersed in arts and culture and hop on the Luas tram to the **Irish Museum of Modern Art,** housed in a 17th-century hospital in Kilmainham. Book a tour at **Kilmainham Gaol** to fully understand the area. Walk back into the city via Thomas Street and see the vast collection of artifacts at the **Chester Beatty Library.** Go shopping at **Kilkenny Design** and the **Powerscourt Townhouse Centre** and pick up some souvenirs.

Day 4

32 KM (20 MI); 45 MINUTES

Leave the city behind and drive south to **Wicklow Mountains National Park** to take in the views along the scenic **Old Military Road.**

See the thundering **Powerscourt Waterfall** before stopping at **Powerscourt House** for a light lunch and a regal experience. Continue south to **Glendalough** and take a relaxing stroll along **Miners Road** from the old monastic city. Return to the city for the night.

Cork

Day 5

250 KM (155 MI); 3 HOURS

Leave Dublin behind and drive south to Cork City to see why Corkonians are so proud of their home. Wander the bustling streets and stop at **Nano Nagle Place** for insight into the local legend and a delicious lunch. Spend time in the famous **Crawford Art Gallery** and drop by the **English Market** for tasty treats and foodie gifts. Before returning to your hotel for the night, enjoy a local stout like Beamish or Murphy's in one of the many great pubs—you're spoiled for choice in Cork.

Day 6

27 KM (17 MI); 30 MINUTES

Take a short drive to foodie heaven in **Kinsale** and spend your day hopping from cute cafés to unforgettable restaurants on the narrow and colorful streets. Enjoy the **Scilly Walk** along the water to the **Bulman Bar** for a drink, and a quick swim in the water if you're feeling brave. Watch the sun set on **Kinsale Harbour** as you walk back into town and book into one of the top-tier restaurants for dinner before driving back to Cork City.

The Ring of Kerry and Killarney National Park

Day 7

265 KM (165 MI); 4-5 HOURS

Taking the scenic route to Killarney via the **Ring of Kerry,** today has a lot of driving but more than enough beautiful landscapes. Make **Kenmare** your first stop and have morning coffee at the **Park Hotel Kenmare.** Get onto the **Ring of Kerry** here and see the wonderful views at **Moll's Gap** before continuing along the coast,

Muckross House & Gardens

TOP EXPERIENCE

How to Enjoy "The Craic"

"The craic" is hard to pin down. It's an atmosphere; it's a buzz; it's a feeling in a moment, and it's something that's incredibly important to Irish people. I've had great craic out on mountain bike trails by myself and I've also had unreal craic in pubs so full they're busting at the seams, so it's a loose term, like so many in Ireland, that depends on each person's definition. What's great craic to me might be no craic at all to someone else.

CRAIC AGUS CEOL

That said, ceol (music in Irish) goes hand in hand with the craic, and you're never too far from finding both in a traditional pub anywhere across the country.

Trad music sessions are informal musical get-togethers that spring up in pubs all across the country. They're usually very loosely organized around a certain time on a certain day, and whoever turns up is welcome to join in. They've remained popular in many rural places where pubs have remained key venues to local communities, but there's a resurgence in cities nowadays too.

You're likely to see a wide mix of instruments that may include a fiddle, bódhran, concertina, tin whistle, accordion, banjo, guitar, and flute. Traditional Irish songs are shared and passed on through the generations, so expect to hear rousing tunes made popular by The Dubliners, ballads sung in Irish, and classics like "The Parting Glass." Everyone is welcome to join, and if you want to sing a song by yourself, just have a quiet word with whoever in the group seems in charge between songs.

A PROPER PINT

Pouring a pint is an art form in Ireland. This only applies to stout, like Guinness and Beamish, which have a two-part pour that helps create a creamy head. Pint aficionados have their own way of judging whether a pint will be a good one or not, factoring in the cleanliness of the glass, how many pints are being poured, the temperature of the keg room, and a host of others. The ideal pint has about a thumb's width of a head with no bubbles in it, is served in a branded glass that matches the beer, and has a smooth transition from creamy head to beer.

Armed with one of these, you'll be ready to live like an Irish person and enjoy some music or strike up a chat with a stranger in the pub.

BEST PUBS

Any given day, any pub in Ireland can be the best pub in the country, but some standouts are consistently brilliant:

The Cobblestone, Dublin

Craic agus ceol is living its best life at the Cobblestone. In a time when parts of old Dublin are being replaced with a more modern, less authentic version, the Cobblestone is a refuge for live music, a chat over a drink, and a singsong or two (page 78).

Crane Bar, Galway City

In a city known for great craic, the Crane Bar stands out as a bastion of traditional Irish music. The atmosphere starts as a quiet trickle during the day and begins to simmer as the evening rolls on, coming to a boil at night when local musicians pick up their instruments and play late into the night (page 315).

Matt Molloy's, Wesport

Westport is a lively spot, even on a quiet day, and Matt Molloy's is central to it all. Matt was once a member of the legendary group the Chieftains, where he became known as one of the greatest flautists of all time. His pub is a safe bet for a bit of craic (page 339).

Above: Mother Macs, Limerick City

where you'll see **Valentia Island,** the mighty **Carrauntoohil,** and endless beaches. Arrive in **Killarney** for the night.

Day 8

6 KM (4 MI); 10 MINUTES

Get up early and take a short drive into **Killarney National Park.** Start at **Muckross House** to get your bearings and learn about the history of the park, then choose a gentle lakeside walk, a short hike to **Torc Waterfall,** or one of the challenging trails. Keep an eye out for wildlife: The park is home to red deer, birds of prey, foxes, otters, squirrels, and more. Finish your day back at **John M. Reidy's** in Killarney, where the music and craic go into the wee hours.

The Cliffs of Moher

Day 9

177 KM (109 MI); 2.5 HOURS

Swap the forests for the coast and drive west toward County Clare. The **Cliffs of Moher** are a must, and you can walk along the cliff tops. Stay in either **Lahinch** or **Doolin** for the night, but make sure to visit both for incredible coastal views, beautiful beaches, and pubs with strong traditional music.

Galway

Day 10

104 KM (65 MI); 1.5 HOURS

Detour through **Burren National Park** on the way to Galway and get ready for the electric buzz of the city, a place famous for its party atmosphere, festivals, and amazing food. Stay in and around the **Latin Quarter** to be in the center of it all, and plan a day around eating in much loved restaurants like **Kai** and **The Dough Bros.** Spend the rest of the day and the evening pub-hopping in the Latin Quarter.

Day 11

190 KM (118 MI); 3.5 HOURS

Drive west toward **Connemara National Park,** making pit stops to take in the views along the way to **Kylemore Abbey.** Stop for food in **Letterfrack** for a remote setting or **Clifden** for somewhere a bit livelier. Return to Galway City via **Roundstone** and watch the sun set on the calm waters of the spectacular **Dog's Bay.** Cross the River Corrib to the **West End** for a quieter night of casual food and drink in Galway City.

Back to Dublin

Day 12

265 KM (165 MI); 4 HOURS

Have an early breakfast in Galway and start the cross-country journey to **Dublin** with another day of driving. Break up the journey with views of the River Shannon in Athlone and at least one stop in the ancient **Boyne Valley.** Choose from **Newgrange** and **Knowth** for a look into the Stone Age past or the **Battle of the Boyne Visitor Centre** for more recent history. From here, it's less than an hour back to **Malahide** or **Howth** for a scenic stay by the coast close to **Dublin Airport.**

With More Time: Belfast City and the Giant's Causeway

Day 13

If you have more time, take the train from Dublin to Belfast and treat yourself to brunch in one of the trendy cafés in the **Cathedral Quarter.** Learn about the history of the *Titanic* at **Titanic Belfast** and see how the ship helped shape the city. Go on a tour to see **Belfast's murals,** which tell the story of the Troubles, or spend the afternoon strolling the shops and independent businesses in the Cathedral Quarter. Stay in the **Queen's Quarter.**

Day 14

209 KM (130 MI); 4 HOURS

From Belfast, take the train to the **Causeway Coast** and jump out at **Portrush** for a late breakfast watching surfers catch waves. Walk along **Whiterocks Beach** and look through the souvenir shops near the water. Hop on a bus for 15 minutes to the **Giant's Causeway** and see this legendary geological wonder. Return to Belfast on the train for a relaxing car-free day.

Best Irish Dishes

Most believe Irish cuisine to be steak and Guinness pies and hearty stews; that's partly true, but there's more to it. We've quickly gone from being a poor society making meals to survive to a modern European country with global influences. This change has created a varied food culture that's still developing.

TRADITIONAL IRISH DISHES

Boxty

You'll find some traditional Irish restaurants where the menu has a strong focus on the potato. No other dish sums this up more than boxty, a potato pancake, which can be eaten as a side or as part of a main. Try it at:

- **Gallagher's Boxty House,** Dublin (page 72)
- **Bricín,** Killarney (page 231)

Coddle

Coddle is a clear stew or soup that uses leftovers and is most commonly served with sausage and potates. Try it at:

- **The Gravediggers,** Dublin (page 79)

Black Pudding

You're likely to find black pudding in most full Irish breakfasts. It's made with a mix of oatmeal, pork fat, and pork blood. Try it at:

- **The SpitJack,** Cork City (page 189)
- **Achill Island Kitchen,** Achill Island (page 344)

Soda Bread

If you'd rather try a less adventurous option than black pudding, try soda bread. It's a quick-to-make bread that uses baking soda instead of yeast for leavening. This creates a denser, more crumbly texture compared to regular bread. You'll find it served alongside soup, and it's best eaten when slathered in butter and dunked into hot soup. Try it at:

- **Bushes Bar,** Baltimore (page 208)
- **Kenny's Bar,** Lahinch (page 282)

STREET FOOD

Irish street food is where you're likely to find the most surprising dishes in surprising places. A lot of grab-and-go food comes from the deli in convenience shops like Spar, Centra, Londis, and takeaways. Here are some of the best things to try:

Chips

You'll notice that most chippers (takeaway chip shops) have Italian names, and they've perfected the chip—which are better known as French fries or fries to North Americans. Irish chippers serve fat, thick-cut chips, finish them with salt and vinegar, then serve them in a brown paper bag. Try it at:

- **The Roma,** Dundalk (page 140)

Spice Bag

Chinese food in Ireland is an inauthentic version, and this dish sums up the fusion with local cuisine. Chips are cooked with onions and mildly spicy spices alongside chunks of crispy breaded chicken. Enjoy it straight from the bag with a fork. Try it at:

- **Xi'An Street Food,** Dublin(page 73)

Chicken Fillet Roll

If there was a competition to name the most uniquely Irish dish, my money would be on chicken fillet roll, the cornerstone of every deli in the country. A baguette is filled with your choice of lettuce, onion, tomato, cheese, and any type of salad and sauce you'd like, then finished with slices of hot chicken fillet. Try it at:

- You'll get these in almost any petrol station, corner shop, and convenience shops like Centra and Spar.

Above: coddle

The Wild Atlantic Way: Northwest Road Trip

On this stunning coastal road trip you'll experience the ferocious power of the Atlantic Ocean and the gentle welcome of picturesque seaside villages. The main focus is incredible landscapes. Journey from national parks to rugged headlands and cozy up in a traditional pub at night to hear local stories and songs.

Day 1: Derry City

67 KM (41 MI); 1.25 HOURS

Begin your road trip on the Wild Atlantic Way with a prologue in Northern Ireland's second city, where its **historic walls** have repelled attacks and can now be walked for incredible views across the River Foyle. Learn how the Troubles started here and see the impact of the conflict at the **Museum of Free Derry.** Drive out of the city in the evening and stay in Downings for the night.

Day 2: Glenveagh National Park

108 KM (67 MI); 2 HOURS

Surround yourself in Donegal's peaceful nature at **Ards Forest Park** or **Murder Hole Beach** at the very start of the Wild Atlantic Way. Drive south to **Glenveagh National Park** and stretch your legs on any of several walks. Make sure you visit **Glenveagh Castle** to learn about the many different owners. Continue south to **Donegal Town** for the night and stay on the **Diamond,** close to the pubs and restaurants.

Day 3: Sliabh Liag

92 KM (57 MI); 1.5 HOURS

Begin your day with a coastal drive to **Sliabh Liag** and take in the amazing views and sea air from the lookout platform or walking trails. Treat yourself to lunch in **Lough Eske Castle** afterward. This corner of Donegal is a hotbed of live music, and you'll find songs aplenty in the pubs and venues in town before returning to your lodging.

Day 4: Mullaghmore Head

63 KM (39 MI); 1 HOUR

Stand on the edge of the world on **Mullaghmore Head** and feel the ferocious power of the ocean where towering waves devour the coast. Look for the brave **big-wave surfers** in the water. Take a walk along the head and enjoy **Classiebawn Castle** from a distance. Continue on to **Sligo Town** for many food and lodging options.

Day 5: Westport and Achill Island

165 KM (102 MI); 3 HOURS

Take the scenic route to **Westport** via **Wild Nephin Ballycroy National Park,** where the open expanses are astounding, before driving to **Achill Island** to see the clear waters of **Keem Bay.** Finish the day in Westport and enjoy the local food and famous pubs with musical owners.

Day 6: Connemara National Park

52 KM (32 MI); 1 HOUR

Drive south and stop in **Leenaun** for breakfast, then take a stroll along **Killary Harbour** with its incredible views. Once you reach **Connemara National Park,** choose walking the grounds of **Kylemore Abbey** or any of the rewarding nearby hikes. Book a room in **Clifden** for the night and follow your ears to the liveliest pub.

Day 7: Galway City

78 KM (38 MI); 1.25 HOURS

Finish this leg of the Wild Atlantic Way in **Galway City,** which seems to spring from the wilderness of the national park. Keep your plans loose for the evening, especially on the weekend in summer, as you never know what the food and drink in the **Latin Quarter** has in store for you.

Classiebawn Castle, Mullaghmore Head

Best of the Wild Atlantic Way

The Wild Atlantic Way is one of the biggest draws to Ireland nowadays, and it's easy to see why. It's a 2,500-km (1,550-mi) coastal route from Kinsale in the south to Malin Head in the north. The drive mostly follows country roads and links incredible surfing beaches with buzzing cities and remote parts of the Gaeltacht with vibrant foodie towns.

The Wild Atlantic Way has regions filled with rugged windswept peninsulas and colorful towns. You'll find brilliant landscapes, food, and activities in all of them:

CORK

- **Mizen Head:** The most southerly point of mainland Ireland (page 213).

KERRY

- **Killarney National Park:** See wild animals living in natural landscapes (page 233).
- **Skellig Michael:** A famous island once inhabited by monks (page 248).

CLARE AND LIMERICK

- **The Cliffs of Moher:** Stand atop these iconic cliffs with a sheer drop into the ocean (page 272).
- **The Burren:** Take in views of otherworldly rocky landscapes that are home to rare plants (page 278).

GALWAY AND MAYO

- **Connemara National Park:** Find beauty in the wide-open expanses of wilderness (page 329).
- **Achill Island:** Explore this peaceful island and enjoy a swim at Keem Bay (page 343).

THE NORTHWEST

- **National Surf Centre:** Learn how to surf on beginner-friendly waves with expert coaching (page 360).
- **Benbulben:** Gaze up at the unique flat-topped mountain that's linked to local folklore (page 362).
- **Sliabh Liag Cliffs:** Look out from the top of Europe's tallest sea cliffs (page 376).
- **Fanad Lighthouse:** See this striking lighthouse perched on a cliff above the ocean (page 384).
- **Malin Head:** The most northernly point of mainland Ireland (page 387).

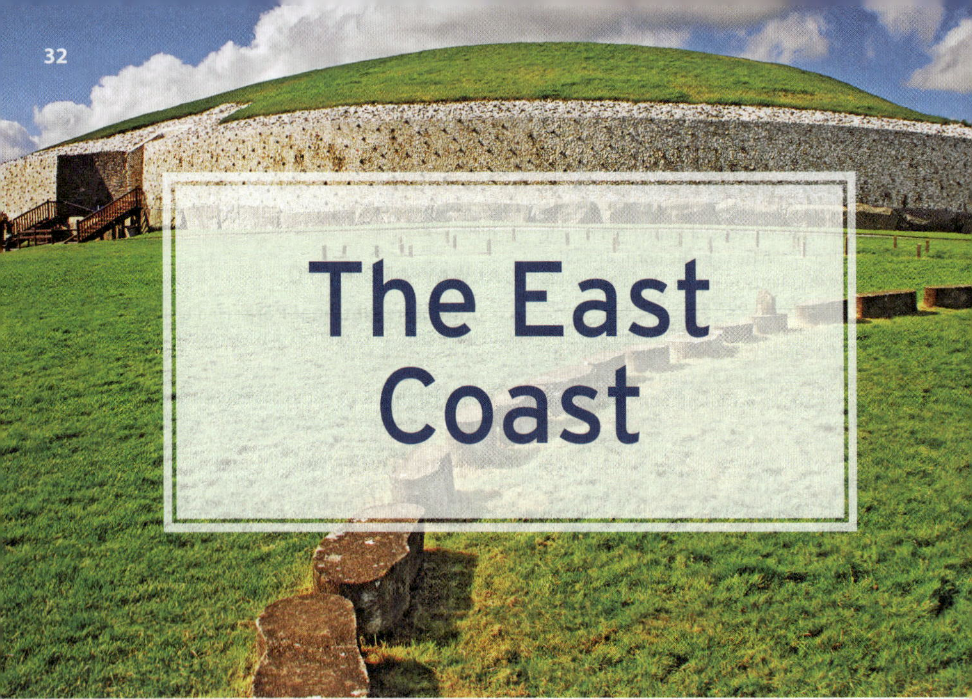

The East Coast

This outdoorsy road trip links the best places on the East Coast for hikes in the mountains and walks by the sea. You'll spend six days staying in lesser visited locations for an authentic experience. Less traveled doesn't mean sacrificing quality; some of the sights and activities mentioned below are among the best in Ireland.

Day 1: Howth and Malahide

18 KM (11 MI); 45 MINUTES

Set off from Dublin City and drive to the affluent seaside suburbs of **Howth** and **Malahide.** Walk the stunning **Howth Cliff Walk** and pop into one of the seafood restaurants for lunch. Wander the grounds of nearby **Malahide Castle** and stay the night in Malahide and before waking to sea views.

Day 2: Cooley Peninsula

102 KM (63 MI); 1.25 HOURS

Head north to the **Cooley Peninsula** and base yourself in the lively town of **Carlingford.** Adventurous types can climb **Slieve Foye,** or take a gentler stroll along the **Carlingford Omeath Greenway.** Both have amazing views of **Carlingford Lough** and the **Mourne Mountains.** Find a restaurant on the narrow streets and try some **Carlingford oysters.**

Day 3: The Mourne Mountains

70 KM (44 MI); 1.25 HOURS

Cross the border into **Northern Ireland** and drive along the coast to **Newcastle.** Treat yourself to a stay at the **Slieve Donard Hotel** and spend your day wandering **Tollymore Forest Park;** *Game of Thrones* fans might recognize the scenery. Experienced hikers can climb Northern Ireland's highest mountain, **Slieve Donard,** instead.

Day 4: The Boyne Valley

104 KM (65 MI); 1.25 HOURS

Take a drive through ancient history in the **Boyne Valley** and step inside the Megalithic tomb at **Newgrange.** Discover Ireland's more recent but still distant past at the **Battle of the Boyne Visitor Centre.** Book a hotel in **Slane** for the night and walk the ramparts before finding a trad music session in one of the pubs.

Day 5: Waterford City

208 KM (129 MI); 2.25 HOURS

After a drive south to the city that Vikings founded, have an easy day strolling the **Medieval Mile,** popping into the **museums** that tell the story of these fierce founders. Swap your mucky walking shoes for something classier and attend a show at the **Theatre Royal Waterford.** Have post-show drinks in a local pub and stay the night in the city.

Day 6: Dunmore East

17 KM (11 MI); 20 MINUTES

Have a blaa with your breakfast and drive the short distance to the quaint seaside village of **Dunmore East,** famous for its stunning beach and cliff walk. Stroll the streets and look across the water to **Hook Head.** When the sun sets, drive back to your lodging in Waterford City.

1: Howth Cliff Walk 2: Malahide Castle 3: the Viking Triangle in Waterford City

St. Patrick's Day

Saint Patrick is our patron saint and probably the best-known person associated with Ireland, even though he was actually Welsh and was captured by Irish pirates and brought to Ireland as a slave. He's credited with bringing Christianity to Ireland and for banishing the snakes, which many interpret as getting rid of paganism, as there have never been snakes in Ireland.

He supposedly used a shamrock to explain to people that its three leaves make up one plant, much like how the Holy Trinity is made up of the Father, Son, and Holy Spirit. Thus, the plant and the color green have been closely associated with him since.

The day is celebrated quite differently here than it is in the United States. While cities do light up notable buildings in green, we don't dye rivers green and there's no pinching or "Kiss Me I'm Irish" T-shirts. It's mainly a day off where people go to the parade in the morning and the pub in the afternoon.

ST. PATRICK'S DAY PARADES

St. Patrick's Day (Mar. 17) centers around the parades that showcase local communities. They are held around the country, from tiny villages where tractors drive down the main street with the local football team on a trailer, to cities where celebrities lead marching bands and every type of group you can imagine. People line the streets to watch the parades.

The parade in Dublin is the biggest, but for a more authentic experience with fewer tourists, try a smaller city or town, such as Dingle (where the parade starts at 6am), Cork City, or Galway City.

Best of the Outdoors

Adventure tourism in Ireland is in its early days and firmly qualifies as soft adventure, giving great numbers of people the opportunity to get outside and enjoy the landscape. There are fewer options for advanced adventurers, but there are long-distance trails and high summits.

Best Short Walks

South Wall Walk

DUBLIN

10 km (6 mi) round-trip; 2.5 hours; easy

Get great views of the city and the port along a cobbled path out to sea that ends at the bright-red Poolbeg Lighthouse. You'll also see South Dublin's most cult landmark—the Poolbeg Towers (page 62).

Ross Island Walk

KERRY

6.1 km (3.8 mi) round-trip; 1.5 hours; easy-moderate

Enjoy peaceful views and historic sights along the edge of Lough Leane, away from the crowds, on this gorgeous walk through Killarney National Park (page 237).

Salthill Promenade

GALWAY AND MAYO

3.2 km (2 mi) one-way; 1.5 hours; easy

This scenic coastal walk takes you from Galway City to the upscale suburb of Salthill and its famous promenade. Watch people leap from the diving tower, kick the wall at the turning back point like the locals, and stop at one of the cafés in Salthill at the halfway point (page 308).

Best Day Hikes

Lugnaquilla

AROUND DUBLIN

16 km (10 mi) round-trip; 6 hours; difficult

Best suited to experienced hikers, this trail in Wicklow Mountains National Park leads through

mountain biking around Dublin

the Glen of Imaal and ends with the best view of all—a traditional rural Irish pub (page 117).

Old Kenmare Road

KERRY

16.9 km (10.5 mi) one-way; 5.5 hours; difficult

This trail is part of the Kerry Way and links the popular sights of cascading Torc Waterfall and Kenmare with a remote hike through the incredible beauty of Killarney National Park (page 237).

Croagh Patrick

GALWAY AND MAYO

7.1 km (4.4 mi) round-trip; 4 hours; difficult

Possibly the most scenic hike in Ireland, this trail follows Saint Patrick's hike to the summit, where he fasted for 40 days and 40 nights. Thankfully your time on the mountain will be much shorter, and there's plenty of great food in Westport afterward (page 334).

Best Long-Distance Trails

The Wicklow Way

AROUND DUBLIN

131 km (81 mi) one-way; 7-10 days; difficult

This bucket-list hike begins in the leafy suburbs of Dublin and runs through Wicklow Mountains National Park. It's Ireland's oldest purpose-built hiking trail and has lots of official dispersed camping spots (page 120).

The Beara Way

CORK

152 km (94 mi) one-way; 8-10 days; difficult

This amazing trail takes you to isolated points along the Beara Peninsula with the option to stay in characterful towns for proper food and a bed (page 214).

The Burren Way

CLARE AND LIMERICK

114 km (71 mi) one-way; 5-6 days; difficult

Walk through a dreamlike landscape in the Burren, where the rock formations, desolate beauty, and rare flora make every step a pleasure (page 280).

Best Cycling Routes

The GAP

DUBLIN

Glencullen Adventure Park; easy-difficult

As Ireland's only uplift bike park, the trails are popular with all levels of mountain bikers. The range of trails are for first-timers and pros who hit the big jump lines (page 100).

The Sally Gap

AROUND DUBLIN

43 km (27 mi) round-trip; 2 hours; difficult

This route is for regular cyclists who aren't afraid of climbing. Once you reach the Sally Gap, you'll have incredible views and a long swooping descent back to the starting point (page 119).

Doolin Cycle Hub

CLARE AND LIMERICK

18-47 km (11-29 mi) round-trip; easy-moderate

Choose from four road routes that begin in Doolin to pedal to the magnificent Cliffs of Moher, the Burren, or the rural countryside (page 276).

Ireland's National Parks

Ireland is blessed with seven national parks, including the well-known classic landscapes, lesser-known places that you'll have to yourself, and parks with scenery that feels alien to Ireland. The national parks are best experienced on foot, and there are plenty of trails to get immersed in gorgeous natural surroundings with the chance to spot wildlife.

AROUND DUBLIN

- **Wicklow Mountains National Park:** Not many capital cities have a national park on the doorstep, making Dublin unique. This park has windswept hills with never-ending mountain and sea views. It's also a great spot for scenic drives (page 114).

KERRY

- **Killarney National Park:** A true wonder brimming with views that'll stop you in your tracks, captivating stories of the families that lived here, and easy hikes to beautiful waterfalls, this jewel of a park has it all, just a stone's throw from one of the liveliest towns in the country (page 233).
- **Kerry Seas National Park:** Ireland's newest and most unconventional park is a collection of land and sea, protected because they're important ecosystems and habitats for marine life. The park includes limestone reefs, rare mussels, iconic beaches, and famous mountain passes (page 250).

CLARE AND LIMERICK

- **The Burren National Park:** This park has to be seen to be believed. Rare geological features feel like another planet, with enormous rock mounds in a sparse landscape dotted with alpine flowers and Mediterranean plants that are unexpected in Ireland (page 278).

GALWAY AND MAYO

- **Connemara National Park:** The vast open expanses feel more impactful here. Winds roar through valleys and across boglands while flocks of sheep clamber up the Twelve Bens mountains (page 329).
- **Wild Nephin Ballycroy National Park:** Unknown to many Irish people, Wild Nephin is a gently rolling park in the middle of nowhere. Long-distance trails run through, with only wildlife, flowing rivers, and remote mountain shelters. This is the place to escape the hubbub of Westport (page 345).

THE NORTHWEST

- **Glenveagh National Park:** A national park with a castle might seem like something from a fairy tale, but in Donegal, the castle beside Lough Beagh is surrounded by wooded slopes. Plenty of facilities make this an accessible choice (page 378).

1
2

SPOTLIGHT ON

Historical Ireland

You're spoiled for choice when it comes to history in Ireland. There are so many eras and stories to discover, including world-class Stone Age wonders, the Troubles, the Vikings, the Normans, the Victorians, and a multitude of others. It's impossible to avoid history in Ireland, and you'll see its layers wherever you go.

Best Ancient History Sites

Monasterboice

AROUND DUBLIN

Two structures symbolize the medieval period in Ireland: round towers and Celtic crosses. You'll see fine examples of both in Monasterboice. Muirdeach's High Cross is believed to be the best example of a Celtic Cross in the world (page 128).

Brú na Bóinne

AROUND DUBLIN

This outstanding burial tomb at Newgrange is an ancient marvel, built in 3200 BCE, that allows light to flood the chamber on the winter solstice. Step inside the tomb on a guided tour (page 132).

Skellig Michael

KERRY

Early Christians in Ireland went to great efforts to show their devotion to their god by going on pilgrimages to harsh places for extended periods. This is one of those places, famous for the beehive huts that the monks built, and more recently for being in the *Star Wars* movies (page 248).

Dún Aonghasa

GALWAY AND MAYO

Ancient sites are rarely more striking than this defensive structure, built on the edge of a 100-m (330-ft) cliff around 1100 BCE. It's a fascinating insight into the dangers people faced and the lengths they went to protect themselves (page 321).

Best Castles

Malahide Castle

DUBLIN

This 12th-century castle is surrounded by lush parklands that make for a leisurely day of strolling. Pop inside on a tour to hear about the family who owned it for almost 800 years (page 90).

Blarney Castle

CORK

Ireland's most famous castle is best known for the Blarney Stone. Kissing it imparts "the gift of the gab." You won't see many Irish people, but it's a rite of passage for visitors (page 185).

Ross Castle

KERRY

See this historic castle set amid the natural beauty of Killarney National Park. It was the last place in Munster to hold out against the Cromwellian invasion (page 235).

King John's Castle

CLARE AND LIMERICK

Visit this impressive Norman structure on the banks of the River Shannon and hear all about the important role it played during the Siege of Limerick (page 290).

1: Ross Castle 2: Skellig Michael

Best Museums

The National Museum of Ireland–Archaeology

DUBLIN

See the Bog Bodies, the remains of people who died over 1,500 years ago and were preserved by the unique conditions of the bog. This is also where you'll find the Ardagh Chalice (page 55).

EPIC Emigration Museum

DUBLIN

Ireland is a nation of emigrants, and you can see the impact they've had on the world at this extensive and interactive museum. EPIC covers politics, industry, sports, and the arts (page 59).

The Hunt Museum

CLARE AND LIMERICK

Inside this museum by the River Shannon is the enormous personal art collection of John Hunt and Gertrude Hartman. Pieces document 10,000 years of Irish history (page 292).

Titanic Belfast

NORTHERN IRELAND

Hear the story of the most famous ship ever in the city where it was built. This brilliant museum goes into great detail on every aspect of the ship's construction, passengers, and fate (page 401).

1: Blarney Castle 2: Titanic Belfast

Dublin

On the cobbled streets of Dublin, music flows

out of pubs, drinks are raised in celebration, and signs of the past live on. A walk through the city reveals plenty of characters and buildings that tell the story of this much loved city.

As you explore, you'll see layers of Dublin's history. Walk through Temple Bar and imagine what it was like when the Vikings arrived by boat to empty land. Relive the glamour of Georgian and Victorian times by shopping for antique jewelry in the Powerscourt Townhouse Centre. Learn about the leaders of the 1916 Easter Rising at the General Post Office (GPO) and look for the bullet holes in the columns. Sit down for a drink or a meal on South William Street or Capel Street and get a feel for what life is like for Dubliners nowadays. In recent times

Highlights

Look for ★ to find recommended sights, activities, dining, and lodging.

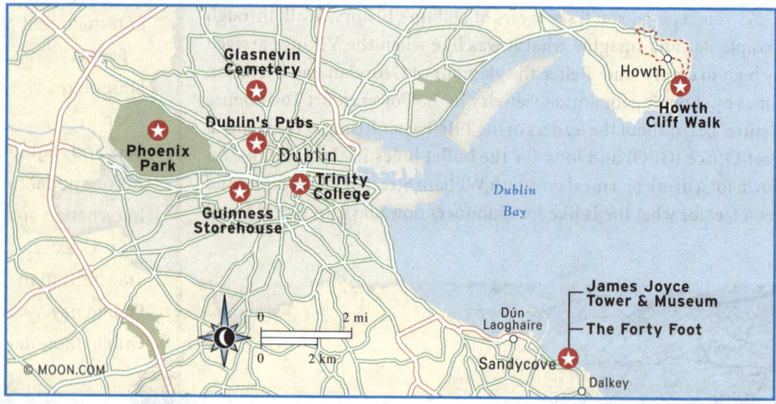

★ **Trinity College:** Walk through the courtyard of this famous university and look at the Book of Kells, one of the most beautiful manuscripts ever created (page 50).

★ **Guinness Storehouse:** Visit the home of the black stuff and get a taste of the story behind the beer that's synonymous with Ireland. Order your pint at the rooftop Gravity Bar and drink in the view (page 56).

★ **Glasnevin Cemetery:** See the final resting place of some of Ireland's best-known names, with revolutionary leaders, famous writers, and cultural icons all buried here (page 59).

★ **Phoenix Park:** Explore the largest enclosed park in any European capital to see wild deer, historic monuments, and mature trees (page 61).

★ **Dublin's Pubs:** You can't come to Dublin and not visit a pub. Thankfully there's an endless number of fantastic ones across the city (page 78).

★ **Howth Cliff Walk:** Escape the crowds and walk to the top of the cliffs beside this picturesque seaside town. See birds nesting in the rocks, smell the wildflowers and gorse, and spot divers jumping into the sea (page 86).

★ **James Joyce Tower and Museum:** Learn about one of the great Irish writers in the Martello tower that he once called home. See exhibits about his work and a re-creation of his quarters (page 93).

★ **The Forty Foot:** Take a run and jump into the Irish Sea at this beloved swimming spot on the affluent South Dublin coastline. Yes, it's always cold, but a sea swim is always worth it (page 94).

the city has become a tech hub, with companies like Meta and Apple headquartered here. The vibe of Dublin these days is an international city with people from every corner of the planet.

The people of Dublin are friendly, and the accents you hear differ depending on whether you're north or south of the River Liffey. The Northside is considered more working-class, while people with money tend to live on the Southside. No matter where you find yourself in Dublin, you'll find friendly locals who are happy to help a visitor.

The city center is busy on evenings and weekends with people out for coffee and drinks long into the night. Dublin is an ever-moving and changing city where so many stories have been told, so plan your visit and get ready to write your own.

ORIENTATION

One of the joys of Dublin is how compact it is. You can go from city streets to mountain trails and sandy beaches all in a day. Dublin City is split by the **River Liffey,** which meets the Irish Sea in **the Docklands** near the **Samuel Beckett Bridge.** The area north of the river is called the **Northside,** and the **Southside** is opposite. Dublin doesn't really have neighborhoods the way US cities do. Instead, it is divided by postcodes, like Dublin 1, Dublin 4, Dublin 7, and so on. Odd numbers are on the Northside and even numbers are on the Southside. Dublin 1 is the main part of the Northside, where you'll see the Spire on O'Connell Street, and the Four Courts is in Dublin 7, farther west along the river. The area of Temple Bar is in Dublin 2 on the southern edge of the Liffey. The distinctly Dublin area known as **the Liberties** is in Dublin 8, a historic working-class area west of the Southside, where you'll find the **Guinness Storehouse** and **Heuston Station.**

Dublin has a walkable city center that you can cross in 10-15 minutes on foot, although lots of backstreets and shortcuts might confuse you if you're used to cities with grid layouts. If you're venturing farther out from the city center or don't want to walk, there are **Dublin Bus** stops across the city and two tram lines, operated by **Luas,** with the **red line** mainly serving the Northside and the **green line** mainly on the Southside. The edge of the Northside of the city is marked by the Royal Canal and the Southside by the Grand Canal.

Southside

The Southside, where you'll spot enormous Land Rovers navigating the narrow city streets, is Dublin's swankier area, where the rugby-loving public speak with the D4 accent—an upper-class, almost British-sounding dialect named after the Dublin 4 area. The main shopping areas of Dublin are on this side of the Liffey, with a great selection of boutiques and international brands. To avoid all that, head to **St. Stephen's Green** for a walk in nature. Although the Southside is more affluent, **the Liberties** is a working-class stronghold on this side of the river, where you'll find attractions like the **Guinness Storehouse** and the **Golden Triangle.**

On the Southside, you'll find **Temple Bar** and **Trinity College.** Walking from **Dame Street** to **St. Stephen's Green** at the top of **Grafton Street** via Trinity College will give you a good sense of the area.

Northside

Dublin's Northside was where the gentry lived in Georgian and Victorian times, so you'll find wonderful period architecture in places like **Henrietta Street.** The neoclassical **Four Courts**—Ireland's main courthouse, housing the Supreme Court, the Court of Appeal, the High Court, and the Dublin Circuit Court—is also here on the Northside. During the 1740s, people with money moved south of the Liffey, and the Northside saw working-class families

Previous: the River Liffey; Trinity College; Guinness Storehouse.

Dublin

National Famine Way Trail
ASHTOWN
R147
R135
National Botanical Gardens
Castleknock
Broombridge
GLASNEVIN CEMETERY
THE GRAVEDIGGERS
CABRA
FARMLEIGH HOUSE
Cabra
PHIBSBOROUGH
Phibsborough
TWO BOYS BREW
R805
R806
CHESTERFIELD AVE
PHOENIX PARK
STONEYBATTER
R805
Heuston Station
R109
R148
The River Liffey
R148
CITY
KILMAINHAM GAOL
GUINNESS STOREHOUSE
THE LIBERTIES
KILMAINHAM
Suir Road
Drimnagh
Goldenbridge
RIALTO
R110
Blackhorse
See "Southside" Map
R111
R137
Bluebell
R110
Kylemore
R110
R139
M50
R137
0
0.5 mi
0
0.5 km
Bushy Park
© MOON.COM

To
HOWTH CLIFF WALK
R105
R107
R132
M50
DRUMCONDRA
Drumcondra DART Station
SHOUK
CROKE PARK
MATER HOSPITAL
CLONTARF
R807
See "Northside" Map
R105
NORTHSIDE
EAST WALL
Connolly Station
NORTH WALL
SAMUEL BECKETT BRIDGE
The River Liffey
Tara Street Station
CENTER
DUBLIN FERRY PORT
Dublin Bay
SURFDOCK
RINGSEND
SOUTH WALL WALK
TRINITY COLLEGE
Pearse Station
SOUTHSIDE
IRISHTOWN
St. Stephen's Green Park
AVIVA STADIUM
R111
SANDYMOUNT
PORTOBELLO
Charlemont
US EMBASSY
PORTOBELLO ADVENTURE
BALLSBRIDGE
R131
BLACKBIRD
Ranelagh
RATHMINES
RANELAGH
R138
BRITISH EMBASSY
R118
Beechwood
Cowper
Milltown
UNIVERSITY COLLEGE DUBLIN
R118
Windy Arbour
R138
To
JAMES JOYCE TOWER & MUSEUM
and THE FORTY FOOT

Dublin's Viking Past

Dublin Castle

Dublin is an outlier in Ireland, as its English name isn't derived from Irish; its original name, Dyflin, came from the Vikings who first settled here in 841. The Old Norse name then became Dubh Linn (black pool) in Irish, then anglicized to Dublin in the 12th century.

Stories and quirks like this give the city layers that take time to be discovered and enjoyed. The Vikings settled in what's known as Temple Bar these days and stayed for over 100 years, until 988, when Máel Sechnaill mac Domnaill conquered Dublin. It wasn't until 1171 that the last Viking king in Ireland was killed during the Norman invasion.

Learn more about Dublin's Viking past at these sights:

- **Temple Bar:** The first Viking settlement in Dublin is now the center of nightlife in the city for visitors (page 54).
- **The National Museum of Ireland—Archaeology:** See artifacts and relics from the time of the Vikings in Dublin (page 55).
- **Dublin Castle:** This landmark was built on an old Viking settlement beside the water that gave Dublin its name (page 55).
- **Christ Church Cathedral:** A striking building founded by the Viking king Sitric in 1030 (page 57).

move in. There's an undeniable charm here—you'll find people at their wittiest, and there's no air of pretense.

On the Northside, use **O'Connell Street** to guide you to **Connolly Station, the GPO,** and the shops on **Henry Street.** Farther north are the residential areas of **Phibsborough** and **Glasnevin.**

Vicinity of Dublin

The **DART** (Dublin Area Rapid Transit) is your best bet to reach areas just outside the city, including **Howth** and **Malahide** to the north in County Dublin, and **Dún Laoghaire, Sandycove, Dalkey,** and **Killiney** to the south. DART runs from Dublin's **Connolly, Tara Street,** and **Pearse Street Stations.** To visit the **Dublin Mountains,** south of the city, it's best to drive.

PLANNING YOUR TIME

Dublin City is easy to cover geographically in a day, but it takes far longer to experience it. For sights and attractions, plan ahead and book tickets for popular places like the **Guinness Storehouse** and the Book of Kells at **Trinity College.** That will give your day some structure and allow you to ramble and stop in cafés and pubs in busy areas like **South William Street, George's Street,** and **Capel Street.** Depending on your interest in history, 2-4 days in the city will give you a proper feel for it.

Given how easy it is to get around, most people use the city as a base and take day trips to areas around Dublin. Breakfast by the sea in Howth or Dún Laoghaire and lunch in the city is very doable. The DART runs until 11:30pm, so if the coast wins you over, you can spend the day and make it back to your bed in the city. If you want to see more of Ireland, it's not uncommon for visitors to travel as far as the Boyne Valley, Cooley Mountains, or Wicklow Mountains National Park and return the same day.

Itinerary Ideas

Three days are a good amount of time to see the best of the city and escape to the coast. These itineraries play the hits as well as some of the lesser-known B-sides.

DAY 1

Keep things central on a leisurely day walking through the city.

1 First, coffee: Stop into **Kaph** on South William Street and bring your drink to the bench outside to people-watch.

2 Make your way a few steps to the **Powerscourt Townhouse Centre** and peruse the boutique clothing and fine jewelry shops.

3 Arrive at **Trinity College** well before your reservation for the Book of Kells Experience to soak up the atmosphere of this famous university. Afterward, have lunch on campus at either The Dining Hall or The 1592.

4 Visit the multi-story **Hodges Figgis** bookshop and pick up a novel by the latest Irish writer.

5 Walk west toward Dublin Castle and **Chester Beatty Library** to see the fascinating collection of books and manuscripts on display.

6 Book a table at **Uno Mas** for a dinner of small bites like the padrón peppers for a Spanish-style meal.

7 Finish your day by pulling up a stool at the ornate bar in **The Long Hall** and ordering a pint of Guinness.

DAY 2

Today is all about the Northside and seaside villages north of the city.

1 Grab a seat at **Two Boys Brew** in Phibsborough. Tuck into avocado toast for breakfast and perk up with a coffee.

2 Walk 15 minutes to the **National Botanical Gardens** and see the beautiful Victorian greenhouses of exotic plants.

Itinerary Ideas

Howth
Howth DART Station
SOUTHSIDE
Trinity
Dawson
St. Stephen's Green
St. Stephen's Green Park
0 200 yds
0 200 m
Dublin Bay
DAY 1
1 Kaph
2 Powerscourt Townhouse Centre
3 Trinity College
4 Hodges Figgis
5 Chester Beatty Library
6 Uno Mas
7 The Long Hall
DAY 2
1 Two Boys Brew
2 National Botanical Gardens
3 Glasnevin Cemetery
4 The Gravediggers
5 Howth
6 Mamó
7 The Harbour Bar
DAY 3
1 Bread 41
2 James Joyce Tower and Museum
3 Forty Foot
4 Cavistons
5 Killiney Hill Walk Loop
6 The Dalkey Duck
7 Bar 1661
0 1 mi
0 1 km
Seapoint Beach
Dún Laoghaire DART Station
Dún Laoghaire
Sandycove DART Station
Sandycove
Dalkey
Dalkey DART Station
Dalkey Island
Killiney Hill Park

3 Make your way to **Glasnevin Cemetery** for your pre-booked guided tour to learn about this place.

4 When you're in Glasnevin, having a pint at **The Gravediggers** is essential. The Guinness is legendary, with many saying it's the best in Dublin. You can also try coddle, a sausage stew.

5 It's time to leave the city behind. Jump on the DART at Drumcondra Station, a 20-minute walk, and head toward **Howth** for some fresh sea air with a walk along the cliffs.

6 Book a table at **Mamó,** as far in advance as you can, and let the staff talk you through their menu of contemporary Irish dishes.

7 Make the climb up the hill behind the harbor afterward to **The Harbour Bar** for live music in a cozy setting before catching the DART back to the city.

DAY 3

Your last day in Dublin focuses on the highlights of the towns and villages along the south coast of County Dublin.

1 Join the fast-moving queue at **Bread 41** for an incredible freshly baked almond croissant before going to Pearse Street Station.

2 Take the DART south to Sandycove and walk over to the **James Joyce Tower and Museum** to learn about the great Irish writer.

3 After you're done at the museum, put your swimming togs on for a refreshing dip in the sea at the **Forty Foot** nearby.

4 Warm up after your swim with a hot drink at Hatch Coffee. If you need lunch, stop at **Cavistons.**

5 Hop back on the DART and keep going south to Dalkey. Head to Killiney Hill and enjoy views of Dalkey Island and Dublin Bay on the **Killiney Hill Walk Loop.**

6 For an early dinner, visit **The Dalkey Duck** and order pub grub like fish-and-chips. If the weather is good, get a seat out in the beer garden.

7 Make your way back to Pearse Street Station in the city on the DART and finish your day by the sea with a cocktail made with poitín at **Bar 1661,** just off Capel Street.

Sights

SOUTHSIDE

Grand Canal Square

Grand Canal Dock; www.dublindocklands.ie; free

Grand Canal Square is one of the newest parks in Dublin, designed by renowned landscape architect Martha Schwartz and completed in 2007. It's a busy thoroughfare with commuting office workers, but lots of seating is built into the angular raised flowerbeds, making it a nice place to relax. Come at night to see the towering red light poles create a moody futuristic scene.

★ Trinity College

College Green; tel. 1/896-1000; www.tcd.ie; Mon.-Sat. 8:30am-7pm; grounds free

Home to the Book of Kells, Trinity College is the closest thing you'll find in Ireland to

1: Trinity College **2:** Book of Kells Experience

1
2
Book
of Kells
Exhibition
www.bookofkells.ie

Southside

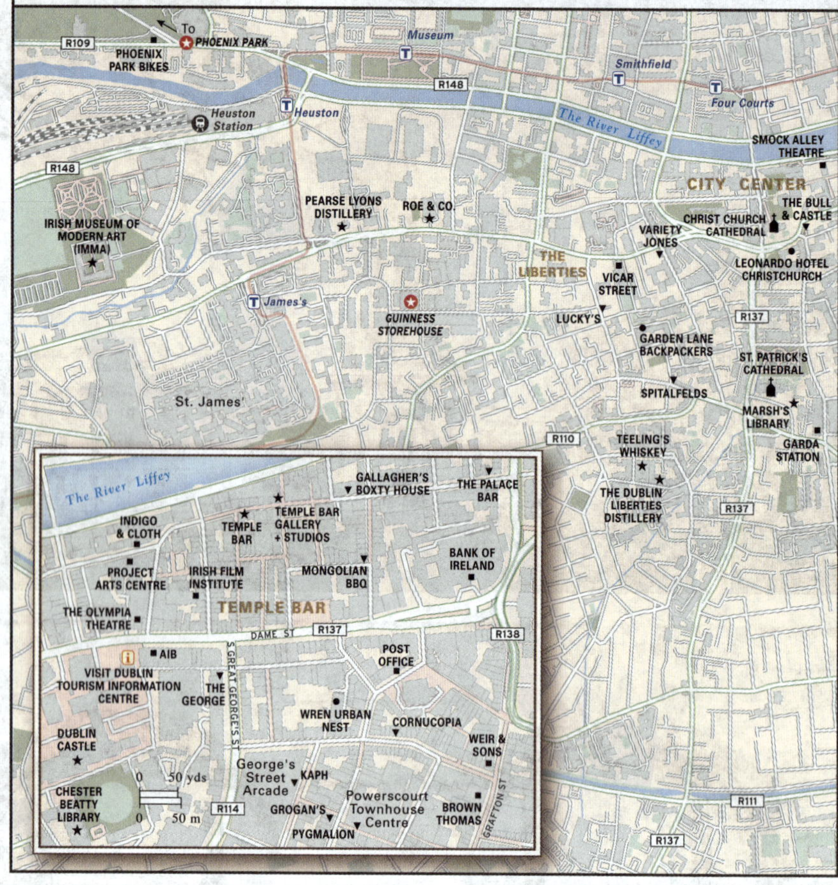

Hogwarts. Ireland's oldest and most prestigious university, its central location makes it a key part of the city. There are several ways to enter the grounds, but the **Front Gate** on College Green is the most dramatic. Walk through the doorway onto the cobblestone square flanked by gray stone buildings with ornate decorations and meticulously manicured lawns.

The Book of Kells

College Green; www.visittrinity.ie; daily 9:30am-4:30pm; from €25

The star attraction is the Book of Kells, a medieval religious manuscript created by Celtic monks in a Columban monastery on Iona, off the west coast of Scotland. The pages are written in Latin and adorned with majestic designs and gold intricacies, making it a Celtic masterpiece. The book is stored in a protective glass case, and a different page is displayed each day, ensuring that each visit offers a new view of the book. To see it, advance booking for the **Book of Kells Experience** is a must, as the limited access fills quickly. On the extremely popular self-guided (€25)

and guided (€65) tours, you may have to wait to get a close view of it. The book is housed in the 65-m (213-ft) Long Room of Trinity College Library, with a vaulted wooden ceiling and towering bookshelves filled with rare and historic volumes. Walk through the Long Room after viewing the manuscript to see other notable items, like a rare copy of the 1916 Proclamation of the Irish Republic and a 15th-century harp.

Campus Tours

Trinity Trails guided tours of the campus are a great way to get an understanding of the university and its buildings. Hear how famous names like Samuel Beckett and Edmund Burke studied here before going on to achieve great things. Tours are often led by students and highlight the architectural history of Trinity College, hidden gardens, and the Museum Building. Guided walking tours (€16) and self-guided tours (€5) are available and can be booked online (www.visittrinity.ie) in advance.

Temple Bar

Temple Bar

Temple Bar is one of Dublin's best-known areas, and its settlement dates to the Viking Age. The name is believed to derive from the Temple family, who lived here in the 17th century, when the area was home to merchants and taverns. The Temple Bar district today is bounded by Westmoreland Street to the east, Dame Street to the south, the River Liffey to the north, and Fishamble Street to the west. It came about in the 1980s when there was public outrage over plans to demolish the area's historic walls and buildings to create a bus depot. The city council changed its mind, repaired the buildings, and revitalized the area as a cultural and artistic hub for Dubliners.

Food

Beyond the historical aspects, the campus is a lively place, with student life adding vibrant energy. There are six restaurants on campus, ranging from the fine-dining seasonal menu at **The 1592** (Dining Hall; tel. 1/896-1592; Mon.-Fri. noon-2:30pm; €20) to budget-friendly options in **The Dining Hall** (Dining Hall; Mon.-Fri. noon-3pm; €10). **The Pavillion Bar** (College Green; tel. 1/896-1279; www.pavilionbar.ie; Mon.-Fri. 9am-11pm; €7), known as The Pav, is a popular spot beside the campus cricket grounds where people meet for a drink on sunny days.

National Gallery of Ireland

Merrion Square W.; tel. 1/661-5133; www.nationalgallery.ie; Tues.-Wed. and Fri.-Sat. 9:15am-5:30pm, Thurs. 9:15am-8:30pm, Sun.-Mon. 11am-5:30pm; free

Dublin's city center art scene revolves around the National Gallery beside Trinity College. The 16,000 artworks are housed in a Victorian building from 1864 that was extended in 2002 with the modern Millennium Wing. Varied permanent collections and exhibitions include masterpieces by Caravaggio, Vermeer, and Monet alongside iconic Irish artists like Jack B. Yeats and Paul Henry. There's plenty for kids to do, with interactive displays and workshops for all ages. Entry is free, and private tours (€100) are available. A café and a gift shop are on-site.

In a way, not much has changed since the early days of Temple Bar, as it is home to many pubs and restaurants. Groups of visitors pose for photos outside a pub called the Temple Bar, and the area has a reputation among locals as a tourist trap. That's not to say there aren't great places, but some are charging over-the-odds prices.

ARTISTIC VENUES

One way to experience Temple Bar in a nontouristy way is to visit some of the art spaces made possible by revitalization.

- **Project Arts Centre:** See exhibitions and shows that celebrate Dublin's contemporary art scene across a variety of mediums (page 65).
- **Irish Film Institute:** Catch the latest arthouse flick or Irish movie in this beloved cinema (page 65).
- **Temple Bar Gallery + Studio** (5 Temple Bar; tel. 1/671-0073; www.templebargallery.com; free): Catch exhibitions in this vibrant space that has a constant flow of exhibitions from Irish and international artists.

PUBS AND RESTAURANTS

To avoid the touristy pubs the area is notorious for, explore the edges of Temple Bar.

- **The Palace Bar:** Get the Dublin pub experience at this spot with strong literary connections and fantastic pints of Guinness at reasonable prices (page 76).
- **Mongolian BBQ** (7 Anglesea St.; tel. 1/670-4154; www.mongolianbbq.ie; €14): At one of the cheapest lunch deals in Temple Bar, you pick your veggies, meat, spices, and herbs for the chefs to cook.

The National Museum of Ireland—Archaeology

Kildare St.; tel. 1/677-7444; www.museum.ie; Tues.-Sat. 10am-5pm, Sun.-Mon. 1pm-5pm; free

Get up close to some famous and fascinating artifacts at the National Museum of Ireland—Archaeology. In a Victorian building on Kildare Street, this museum tells the story of Ireland's Christian, Viking, and prehistoric past. **The Treasury** is a permanent exhibit that celebrates a golden age of Irish art from the late 7th to early 9th centuries, summed up by the bejeweled Ardagh Chalice. The **Viking Ireland** exhibit has a vast collection of jewelry and metalwork from when Dublin was a Viking city. The most interesting piece in the museum's collections is surely the **Bog Bodies.** These people died around 400 BCE, and their bodies have been exquisitely preserved by the conditions in peat bogs. The skin has a leathery look, and you can still clearly see fingernails and fingerprints.

Dublin Castle

Dame St.; tel. 46/942-2213; www.dublincastle.ie; daily 9:45am-5:15pm; €8

A historic landmark in the heart of the city, Dublin Castle has been a center of power in Ireland for over 800 years. Originally built as a medieval fortress on an old Viking settlement under King John of England, it later served as the seat of British rule until Irish independence in 1922. Today, visitors can explore its elegant State Apartments, the medieval undercroft, and the Chapel Royal on a self-guided tour that you can book online. Guided tours are available, but you have to come in person on the day and ask for a space.

Chester Beatty Library

Dublin Castle; tel. 1/407-0750; www.chesterbeatty.ie; Mon.-Tues. and Thurs.-Sat. 9:45am-5:30pm, Wed. 9:45am-8pm, Sun. noon-5:30pm; free

Although it's called the Chester Beatty Library, this building is better known as a museum that houses artistic and religious collections from around the world. The museum started as the private collection of Sir Alfred Chester Beatty, an American-born mining magnate who collected rare manuscripts and books. He opened the collection to the public in 1950. Get insights from the experts on a free hour-long tour (Wed. 5:30pm, Sat. 2pm, Sun. 3pm).

The Liberties

www.libertiesdublin.ie

The Liberties is where Dublin is at its most Dublin. It's a busy area a short walk west of the city center that has regular markets, greasy-spoon cafés, and inner-city pubs filled with laughter. As areas of Dublin have been gentrified over the past few decades, the Liberties has maintained its working-class roots while keeping locally owned businesses open. Walk along Meath Street and James Street to feel how vibrant and strong the community is. The area is home to the **Guinness Storehouse,** the whiskey distilleries of the **Golden Triangle,** and **St. Patrick's Cathedral** beside **Christ Church Cathedral,** all easily walkable.

★ Guinness Storehouse

St. James's Gate; tel. 1/408-4800; www.guinness-storehouse.com; Sun.-Thurs. 9:30am-5pm, Fri.-Sat. 9:30am-6pm; €20

Considered the most popular attraction in Dublin, the tour at the Guinness Storehouse provides an understanding of the impact the Guinness family has had on Dublin and why Guinness is synonymous with Ireland. Arthur Guinness, who first created the famous stout, negotiated a 9,000-year lease for the land where the storehouse stands, and this is where the self-guided tour begins.

Learn how roasted barley, malted barley, hops, yeast, and water are used to create the black stuff in powerful displays that overwhelm the senses. Hear the water flowing, smell the hops being roasted, and feel the texture of the grain. As you move upstairs, you'll see some unforgettable Guinness advertising through the ages, including the iconic surfing ad. The tour finishes at the top of the building at the **Gravity Bar.** Circular, it has windows for 360-degree views of the city and the Dublin Mountains. This is where you get your included pint of Guinness—expertly poured, of course. The bar staff will talk you through the pouring process, why it happens in two stages, and the importance of letting it settle. Be warned that you can only get one drink per person.

If you want to go beyond the normal experience, you can get a **Stoutie** (€8), a picture of yourself printed on the head of a pint, or go to the **Guinness Academy** (€12) on the 4th floor to learn how to pour the perfect pint. There's also a café and a choice of three restaurants on-site once you come down from the Gravity Bar.

St. Patrick's Cathedral

St. Patrick's Close; tel. 1/453-9472; www.stpatrickscathedral.ie; daily 9:30am-5pm; €11

St. Patrick's Cathedral is Dublin's largest church and one of the most impressive. Built in the 13th century on the site where St. Patrick supposedly baptized converts, it's now a Protestant church that had the author of *Gulliver's Travels,* Jonathan Swift, as the dean 1713-1745. Inside you'll see the tall stone arches and stained glass that create an atmospheric setting. If you come for a service (check their website for times; free), you'll hear the choir sing.

Marsh's Library

St. Patrick's Close; tel. 1/454-3511; https://marshlibrary.ie; Tues.-Sat. 9:30am-5pm; €7

Marsh's Library is Dublin's oldest public library, hidden down a winding laneway beside St. Patrick's Cathedral. Opened in 1707, it has barely changed, with rows of dark oak

Dublin's Golden Triangle

The Golden Triangle is an area that had a high concentration of top-class whiskey distillers in the 18th-19th centuries. Today the area is seeing a resurgence with small-batch distillers. Historically the area covered both sides of the Liffey, and big names like Jameson, Powers, and George Roe were the favorite distillers of the time. The revival of the Golden Triangle today is mainly in the Liberties.

Dublin's whiskey district

BEST WHISKEY DISTILLERS

- **Teeling's Whiskey** (13 Newmarket; tel. 1/531-0888; www.teelingdistillery.com; daily 11am-6pm; €20): The return to whiskey production in the city was hard to ignore when Teeling's opened the first distillery in Dublin in over 150 years. Distillery tours and tastings attract connoisseurs of Irish whiskey.
- **Roe & Co.** (92 James St.; tel. 1/643-5999; www.roeandcowhiskey.com; Sun.-Wed. noon-7pm, Thurs.-Sat. noon-9pm; €25): Roe & Co. was one of the area's main players in the 19th century, and it's open again for visits and tastings.
- **Pearse Lyons Distillery** (122 James St.; tel. 1/691-6000; www.pearselyonsdistillery.com; daily 10:30am-6pm; €22): Visit the Pearse Lyons Distillery inside the Church of St. James to taste whiskey in a unique setting.
- **The Dublin Liberties Distillery** (33 Mill St.; tel. 1/410-0380; www.thedld.com; daily 11am-5pm; €20): Try whiskey named for the neighborhood.

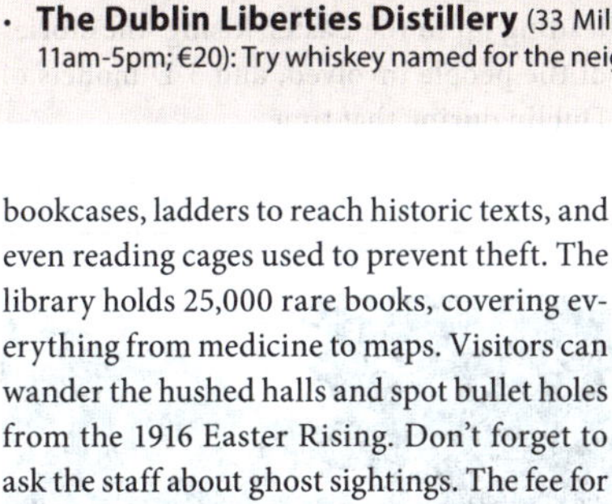

bookcases, ladders to reach historic texts, and even reading cages used to prevent theft. The library holds 25,000 rare books, covering everything from medicine to maps. Visitors can wander the hushed halls and spot bullet holes from the 1916 Easter Rising. Don't forget to ask the staff about ghost sightings. The fee for the self-guided tour can be paid online or on arrival.

Christ Church Cathedral

Christchurch Place; tel. 1/677-8099; https://christchurchcathedral.ie; Mon.-Sat. 9:30am-5:30pm, Sun. 12:30pm-3pm and 4:30pm-6pm; €12

Christ Church Cathedral is a striking landmark, with 1,000 years of history from its origins as a Viking church. It was rebuilt by the Normans in 1185 and is known today for its eye-catching arches, historic crypt, and brilliantly preserved medieval architectural details. One of the most popular attractions is the mummified cat and rat that ran into the pipe organ and died 200 years ago. On a self-guided tour you can see most of the cathedral, but to go up the bell tower, you have to book the guided tour. Times and tickets are available online, and advance booking is advised.

Irish Museum of Modern Art (IMMA)

Royal Hospital Kilmainham, Military Rd.; tel. 1/612-9900; www.imma.ie; Tues.-Sat. 10am-5:30pm, Sat. noon-5pm; free

Considered the country's leading destination for contemporary and modern art, IMMA has an extensive collection of 3,500 works by Irish and international artists that span painting, sculpture, photography, film, digital mediums, and more. The permanent collection is joined by temporary exhibitions from diverse artists. Part of the appeal of IMMA is its fantastic setting in the 17th-century Royal Hospital Kilmainham, brilliantly juxtaposing modern art with historical features. The grounds have formal gardens you can wander after your visit.

Kilmainham Gaol

Inchicore Rd.; tel. 1/453-5984; www.kilmainhamgaolmuseum.ie; daily 9:30am-5:30pm; €8

Kilmainham Gaol is a harrowing place, as it shows the brutality of war and how difficult it was to free ourselves of British rule. First opened in 1796, the gaol became infamous when it housed the leaders of the 1916 Easter Rising. On the guided tour, which must be booked in advance, you'll step inside the cramped cells and hear about the people who were incarcerated here in 1916 and during the famine. The tour ends in the prison yard known as **Stonebreaker's Yard,** where 14 of the leaders of 1916, including Padraig Pearse and James Connolly, were lined up against the wall and shot by a British firing squad. Their killings went on to fuel a strong drive for independence.

NORTHSIDE

The GPO

O'Connell St. Lower; tel. 1/705-7600; daily 8:30am-6pm; free

The General Post Office (GPO) is one of Ireland's most iconic buildings. Completed in 1818, it was designed by architect Francis Johnston in Greek Revival style, but the more significant story of the GPO is its role in the 1916 Easter Rising, in which a group of Irish freedom fighters, led by Padraig Pearse of the Irish Volunteers and James Connolly of the Irish Citizen Army, used the building as their headquarters to launch attacks on the ruling British Army. This conflict was one of the key moments in creating the Ireland we know today.

The building was heavily damaged during the revolutionary period, and bullet holes can still be seen in the columns outside. Through restoration efforts, the GPO today is a working post office, and a look inside is enough for most visitors. If you're a history buff, the **GPO Museum** (€17) has a permanent exhibit that explains the events leading up to the Easter Rising, the stories of the people involved, and 3-D models of Dublin during that time.

Glasnevin Cemetery

14 Henrietta Street

14 Henrietta St.; tel. 1/524-0383; www.14henriettastreet.ie; Wed.-Sat. 10am-4pm; €10

A remarkably well-preserved Georgian building, 14 Henrietta Street offers a rare glimpse into the social history of the city over 300 years. Henrietta Street was upscale when wealthy Dubliners lived on the Northside, with No. 14 reflecting the opulence of the time. As Dublin's fortunes changed, so did the building, and in the mid-1800s it was turned into a tenement. The years after the famine saw a population boom in Ireland, and buildings like these were divided into low-income flats. At one point over 100 people lived in extremely cramped conditions in the 19 flats on the building's five floors.

Today, 14 Henrietta Street is a museum that tells the stories of people who lived here, from wealthy aristocrats to struggling tenement dwellers. On the guided tour, you walk through carefully restored rooms, hear personal testimonies, and see interactive exhibits. Other tours include a walking tour (€10) that covers the history of the building and the surrounding area as well as musical tours (€10) that run once a month, where the history of the building is brought to life through song.

EPIC Emigration Museum

CHQ Bldg., Custom House Quay; tel. 1/906-0861; www.epicchq.com; daily 10am-5pm; €23

Retrace your roots and learn how emigration from this small island has impacted the world at EPIC Emigration Museum on the edge of the Liffey. The museum covers different eras, including when people were shipped to prisoner colonies in Australia, mass emigration to the United States during the famine, and the modern day as Irish people leave these shores in search of a better life. Through interactive displays, short videos, and artifacts, you get a sense of how important emigration has been to Irish people. Toward the end of the museum walkthrough, smaller exhibits cover industries such as music, design, and sport that Irish emigrants have influenced across the world.

The *Jeanie Johnston*

Custom House Quay; tel. 1/473-0111; www.jeaniejohnston.ie; daily 10am-4:30pm; €15

On board the *Jeanie Johnston,* get a glimpse into the lives of thousands of people who sailed from Ireland and never returned because of the famine. Moored at Custom House Quay on the River Liffey, this is a meticulously crafted replica of the 19th-century ship, originally built in Quebec in 1847. Ships that made transatlantic crossings during the famine were often called coffin ships due to the number of people who died on the journey, often quoted at 100,000 overall; somehow not a single person died on this ship.

This version of the *Jeanie Johnston* is a museum and a monument to a tragic period of Irish history. Climb aboard on a 50-minute guided tour to see the impressive masts before heading below deck to see where the 250 passengers lived and slept on the sail to America.

National Botanical Gardens

Glasnevin; tel. 1/804-0300; www.botanicgardens.ie; Mon.-Fri. 9am-5pm, Sat.-Sun. 10am-6pm; free

The National Botanic Gardens is a 20-ha (50-acre) site with a huge variety of plants and gardens. Opened in 1795, it is home to over 15,000 species from around the world, including native Irish flora like oak and ash trees. The gardens are best known for their stunning white Victorian greenhouse, the **Palm House,** which houses succulents, cacti, and tropical plants.

Explore the theme gardens, including the **Rose Garden,** the **Rockery,** and the **Arboretum,** each displaying different species and landscape design. Grab a quick snack at **Acton Café,** with hot drinks and pastries, or **The Garden Tearoom,** with similar offerings plus hot meals. The gardens are wheelchair-friendly, with most accessible via a paved footpath.

★ Glasnevin Cemetery

Finglas Rd.; tel. 1/882-6500; www.dctrust.ie; daily 9:30am-5pm; free

Glasnevin Cemetery is one of Ireland's most

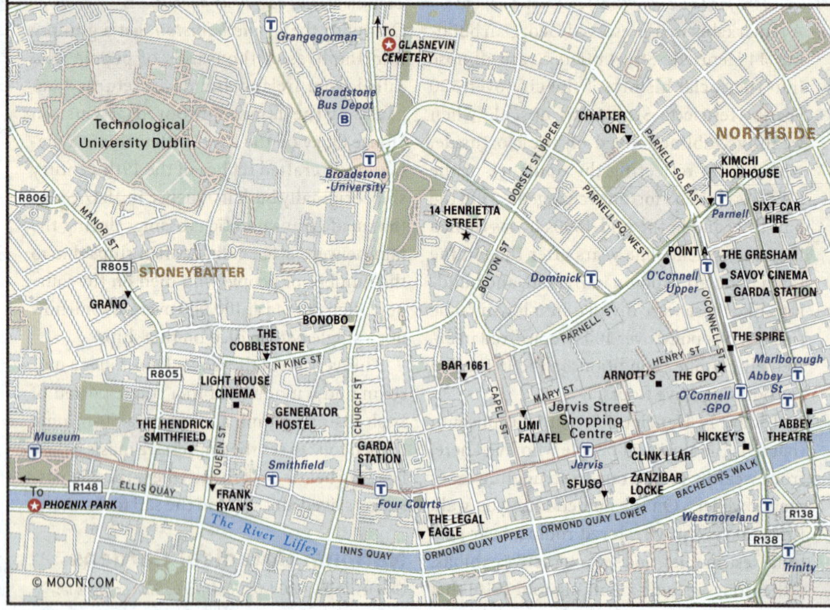

significant historical sites, the final resting place of our biggest stars, writers, and soldiers. First opened in 1832 by the political leader Daniel O'Connell, it covers over 50 ha (120 acres) where 1.5 million people are buried. Think of Glasnevin Cemetery as a burial ground and also an outdoor museum with the most important Irish stories ever told.

Most enter at the visitor center, where the grounds and graves are well maintained with manicured lawns and plantings. Exploring farther and seeing the sheer size of the place, you'll discover other areas that have a more natural and unkempt feel. The graves of the best-known residents are kept in top condition, including political leaders like Michael Collins, Éamon de Valera, and Charles Stewart Parnell as well as cultural icons like playwright Brendan Behan and comedian Dermot Morgan. These graves dot the cemetery rather than being concentrated in one area.

Glasnevin is a serious attraction for anyone interested in the 1916 Easter Rising, as many people involved are buried here. The **Irish History Tour** (€14) focuses on those who played key roles in Irish independence. The **Dead Interesting Tour** (€14) delves into lesser-known stories and the secrets of Dublin's more colorful and unusual characters. As you walk the cemetery, you'll see the round **O'Connell Tower,** with 198 steps up to fantastic views of the city. It can only be accessed on the tower tour (€10). Book tickets in advance on the website.

One of the modern touches at Glasnevin is also one of the most fascinating—the cemetery's genealogy records, a resource for anyone interested in tracing their Irish roots. This enormous collection of records goes back to the cemetery's opening in 1832 and includes burial registers, headstone transcriptions, and grave plot maps. You can research the graveyard's records on the website, and once you arrive, staff can help you find the grave that you're looking for.

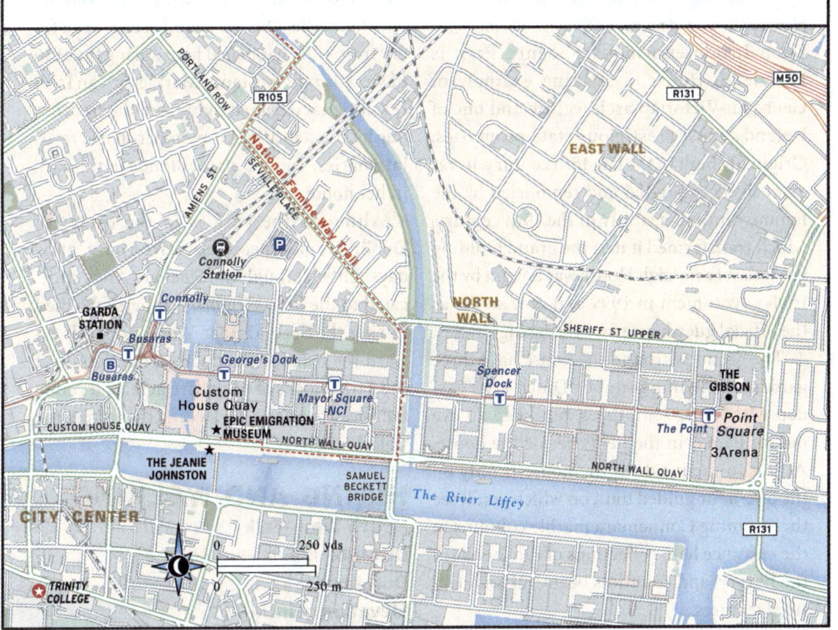

Activities and Recreation

PARKS

★ Phoenix Park

tel. 87/228-9688; www.phoenixpark.ie; daily 24 hours; free

At almost 7 sq km (2.7 sq mi), Phoenix Park is the largest walled park in any European capital. This sprawling urban oasis has wide expanses of grasslands, wetlands, and mature broadleaf trees as well as an impressive number of attractions. Some, like **Dublin Zoo,** require a ticket, but the park is free to walk or cycle.

In the center of the park, off Chesterfield Avenue, climb the steps to the **Papal Cross,** built to mark the arrival of Pope John Paul II in 1979, and take in sweeping views of the park and the Dublin Mountains. Stroll by **Áras an Uachtaráin,** where the Irish president lives, and try to get a glimpse of him walking his dogs. Pose for a photo with the **Wellington Monument,** a 62-m (203-ft) stone obelisk near the Conyngham Road entrance. If you can't decide where to go, start at the visitor center in **Ashtown Castle** to get your bearings.

There are no established walking or cycling routes in the park; pick the sights you want to see and link them up. There are lots of cycle lanes, footpaths, and walkways separated from traffic on the busy main thoroughfare, **Chesterfield Avenue.** In the quieter corners of the park, especially in wooded areas, you can see the 600 deer that call the park home. They're used to being around people, so they won't run away, but don't try to pet them or feed them.

Farmleigh House

White's Rd., Phoenix Park; tel. 1/815-5914; www.farmleigh.ie; daily 10am-5pm; €8

Deep inside enormous Phoenix Park is Farmleigh House, a striking example of Georgian-Victorian architecture and one of Ireland's most prestigious state properties. Originally built in the late 18th century, it was extensively expanded and remodeled by the famous Guinness family in the 19th century, which transformed it into the grand building it is today. Farmleigh House was bought by the Irish government in 1999 and now serves as the official guesthouse for visiting dignitaries.

The grounds around the house have three gardens, including a sunken Dutch-style garden with stone sculptures, but keep an eye out for llamas in the fields beside the house. Access to the inside of the house is only on the one-hour guided tour, on which you'll see the stunning Connemara marble columns in the entrance hall, collections of rare books in the library, and countless beautiful architectural features.

St. Stephen's Green Park

end of Grafton St., St. Stephen's Green; www.ststephensgreenpark.ie; daily from 7:30am; free

St. Stephen's Green is a picturesque park with a historic past. Designed in Victorian style with traditional flowerbeds, ponds, and ornate fountains, these tranquil scenes are a far cry from what happened here during the 1916 Easter Rising. Constance Markievicz, an Irish revolutionary, helped fight from the trenches dug here as a British Army sniper shot at revolutionaries. Today a statue stands in the park in her honor.

Although the park is in the center of Dublin, it's quite peaceful, even on busy sunny days. Enter through the Fusiliers Arch, dedicated to the Royal Dublin Fusiliers who died during the Second Boer War, and stroll toward the ornamental pond in the middle of the park. Flocks of ducks live here, and young families are often seen feeding them from the water's edge.

HIKING AND WALKING

South Wall Walk

Distance: *10 km (6 mi) round-trip*
Duration: *2.5 hours*
Elevation gain: *Negligible*
Effort: *Easy*
Trailhead: *Sandymount Strand*

South Wall is one of the longest seawalls in Europe, built in the 18th century to create a safe passage into Dublin Port. The coastal

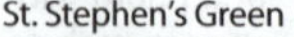

St. Stephen's Green

walk from one end to the other is a refreshing stroll with the wind from the Irish Sea. Start on Sandymount Strand and walk toward the towering **Poolbeg Towers.** Though not in use anymore, these chimneys have become an icon of Dublin. As you turn from the sandy shore onto the South Wall, the views are open sea vistas with lapping waves. The walkway has paved and cobbled sections that take you to the red **lighthouse** at the end. It once played an important role at the dock, but these days it's better known as a backdrop for photos. The walk follows the same route back. Returning via Pigeon House Road is not advised, as it has vehicular traffic and goes past wastewater treatment facilities.

National Famine Way Trail: EPIC Museum to Castleknock

Distance: *20 km (12 mi) round-trip*
Duration: *4-5 hours*
Elevation gain: *Negligible*
Effort: *Moderate*
Trailhead: *EPIC The Irish Emigration Museum*

The National Famine Way Trail is a long-distance walking trail that tells the sad story of those who left the Irish countryside during the famine and walked to the coffin ships in Dublin to sail to America. Thirty pairs of bronze children's shoes commemorate those who died on the journey. The full walk is 165 km (102 mi) one-way; it begins at the National Famine Museum at Strokestown House in County Roscommon and ends at EPIC, The Irish Emigration Museum in Dublin's Docklands. For a taste of the trail, walk the last leg in the opposite direction, from the EPIC Museum to Castleknock, a residential village on the outskirts of the city, and return to the city via Phoenix Park for a 20-km (12-mi) round-trip half-day walk. For more information and maps, visit www.nationalfamineway.ie.

CYCLING

Phoenix Park Bikes

Chesterfield Ave.; tel. 87/379-9946; www.phoenixparkbikes.com; daily 9am-5pm

Zip around Phoenix Park and the city with a rental bike from Phoenix Park Bikes. Located at the park entrance at Conyngham Road, this bike rental place has options for adults and kids, including trailers and tandem bikes. They organize cycling tours of the park, and if you're feeling more adventurous, join them on a cycling tour to Howth, where you'll ride on bike lanes to the seaside village.

Dublinbikes

various locations; www.dublinbikes.ie

This citywide bike-sharing scheme has standard bikes with baskets available for rent at 115 Dublinbikes stations. Rent a bike for 30 minutes to 3 days using your credit card to unlock the bike. Use it again to drop it off when you're finished.

KAYAKING

Portobello Adventure

Lennox Place; tel. 858-313-400; www.portobelloadventure.ie; daily 9am-5pm

Get onto the Grand Canal in the popular Portobello neighborhood with a kayak or stand-up paddleboard (SUP) rental from Portobello Adventure. This is a great place for beginners to get into the sport, as the water is gentle and you're always close to the banks. Double kayaks are available. The rental shop organizes day trips to Howth, Dalkey, and Bray to kayak on the sea.

STAND-UP PADDLEBOARDING

Surfdock

Grand Canal Dockyard; tel. 1/668-3945; www.surfdock.com; Tues.-Sat. 10am-5pm

Learn how to master a SUP on the sheltered water of the Grand Canal, which runs 144 km (89 mi) from the River Shannon to Dublin City, with a lesson by Surfdock, the watersport masters in the city. You'll learn how to find your balance, turn the board, and paddle through the water. You'll also get great views of Grand Canal Square and the Bord Gáis Energy Theatre. Lessons (€45 pp) are suited to beginners and last 90 minutes.

ROCK CLIMBING

Awesome Walls

North Rd., Finglas; tel. 1/880-0088; www.awesomewalls.ie; daily 10am-10pm

For the best climbing walls in Dublin, go to Awesome Walls in Finglas. The journey from the city center is worth it, as the bouldering and roped climbing routes will challenge all levels. There are taster classes (from €32 pp) for those just getting into the sport, and if you're ready to scale the 13-m (43-ft) wall, pick up a punch card online (11 visits €155) and get going.

GOLF

St. Anne's Golf Course

North Bull Island Nature Reserve; tel. 1/833-6471; www.stanneslinksgolf.com; daily from 7am; €140-170

Teeing off in a UNESCO biosphere reserve is a rare experience, but you can at St. Anne's Golf Course on Bull Island, just north of the city. Over 100 years old, this 18-hole course is known for challenging conditions thanks to the coastal winds that ensure no two rounds are the same. Visitor rates are available for nonmembers, and there's a pro shop on-site with clubs, balls, and clothing.

SPECTATOR SPORTS

The four main sports in Ireland are Gaelic football, hurling, rugby, and soccer, all popular in Dublin. The Dublin Gaelic football and hurling teams have been successful in recent years and play major games in Croke Park from early in the year through the finals in summer. For international sports, the Irish rugby and soccer teams play in Aviva Stadium, with the Rugby Six Nations games the highlight in February-March. Other games are held sporadically throughout the year.

Gaelic Football and Hurling

Croke Park

Jones Rd.; tel. 1/819-2300; www.crokepark.ie; from €20

This 82,300-seat stadium is the largest in the country, but even more impressive is that it's owned by the GAA, an amateur sports association for Gaelic football and hurling. Major international games are played in this fantastic atmosphere. GAA sports make great family outings, but if you want to be in the most boisterous part of the stadium, get a ticket for the standing-only Hill 16 stand. Tickets can be bought online but sell out quickly for big games. Outside match days, you can go on a stadium tour (€18) to see the dressing rooms, walk alongside the pitch, and visit the museum.

Rugby and Soccer

Aviva Stadium

Landsdowne Rd.; tel. 1/238-2300; www.avivastadium.ie; from €60

The Irish international rugby and soccer teams play at this modern 51,700-seat stadium, previously called Landsdowne Road. It sells out anytime the rugby team is playing, as Ireland is a top-three side in the world. Conversely the soccer team has fallen on hard times recently and attendance has diminished. Tickets for rugby games are sold through rugby clubs across the country and are hard to obtain. Soccer tickets are sold in packages, so it's common to find resellers outside the stadium on match day. No tours are available.

Entertainment and Events

CINEMA AND THEATER

Southside

Smock Alley Theatre and Boys School Theatre

6-7 Exchange St. Lower; tel. 1/677-0014; www.smockalley.com; from €15

Smock Alley, a 177-seat theater, was established in 1662 on the edge of modern-day Temple Bar. It was the first purpose-built theater in Dublin and one of the earliest in Europe. Over the years it has hosted a wide range of events and nowadays focuses on diverse plays, musicals, and comedians. Smaller shows are hosted in the more intimate 75-seat Boys School Theatre.

Gaiety Theatre

S. King St.; tel. 1/646-8600; www.gaietytheatre.ie; from €25

The ornate Victorian styling of the Gaiety Theatre, with its lush red seating for 1,145 and golden balconies, sets the scene for incredible performances in the heart of Dublin. Loved by Dubliners for its Christmas pantomime performances, there's also a strong heritage of musical performances and Irish plays. Before going in, have a look at the bronze handprints of Italian opera tenor Luciano Pavarotti and Irish writer Brian Friel on the ground outside.

Bord Gáis Energy Theatre

Grand Canal Square; tel. 1/677-7999; www.bordgaisenergytheatre.ie; from €25

Designed by world-famous architect Daniel Libeskind, who also designed One World Trade Center in New York, the Bord Gáis Energy Theatre is one of the most memorable buildings in Dublin. Opened in 2010, this 2,111-seat venue attracts big shows to the Docklands, including *The Book of Mormon*, *Wicked*, and *The Lion King*. Give yourself time before the show to wander around Grand Canal Square and take nighttime photos with the iconic red light poles.

Project Arts Centre

39 E. Essex St.; tel. 1/881-9613; www.projectartscentre.ie; from €10

For a more grassroots theater experience, the Project Arts Centre in the middle of Temple Bar is a fantastic choice. Nurturing the arts and promoting shows by artists from diverse backgrounds, including race, class, gender, and sexuality, this art center has become an important venue. The small theater seats 130 and the gallery space hosts rotating exhibitions.

Irish Film Institute

6 Eustace St.; tel. 1/679-3477; https://ifi.ie; €10

The Irish Film Institute (IFI) is Dublin's home for independent, classic, and international cinema. Tucked away in Temple Bar, it has three screens with seating for 246, 106, and 58 and shows a mix of new releases, Irish films, and indie flicks. It's a center of culture that hosts festivals, Q&A sessions, and special screenings year-round. The archive preserves Ireland's film heritage, while the café-bar is a classy spot to grab a drink before a film.

Northside

Abbey Theatre

26-27 Abbey St. Lower; tel. 1/887-2200; www.abbeytheatre.ie; from €15

Not many theaters make the lofty claim of being founded by a legendary playwright, but the Abbey Theatre was founded by W. B. Yeats and Lady Augusta Gregory in 1904, instantly becoming vital to Dublin's arts scene. In its early days, it hosted performances of *The Playboy of the Western World* and *The Plough and the Stars*. Today it has added contemporary shows to its lineup of classics in the 500-seat space.

Savoy Cinema

17 O'Connell St.; tel. 1/874-8822; https://imc.ie; €14

The Savoy Cinema is Dublin's oldest, dating

to 1929. It has hosted countless Irish film premieres at its famous 2,800-seat Screen 1. The cinema has 13 screens showing a mix of blockbusters and Irish films.

Light House Cinema

Market St.; tel. 1/872-8006; www.lighthousecinema.ie; €13

The indie Light House Cinema has a trendy interior with colorful seating at each of the four screens that seat 67 to 277. It's known for arthouse, classic, and cult films as well as special events like festivals, director Q&As, and themed screenings.

LIVE MUSIC

Southside

Whelan's

25 Wexford St.; tel. 1/478-0766; www.whelanslive.com; from €15

Whelan's is a cornerstone of live rock music and has been the launchpad of many Irish acts. The pub has a live venue in the rear with room for 450. The likes of Arctic Monkeys, Hozier, and Nick Cave have played at Whelan's, but the regular gigs focus on acts before they become household names. Arrive before the show starts and have a drink in the cozy wood-clad pub.

Vicar Street

58-59 Thomas St.; tel. 1/775-5800; www.vicarstreet.com; from €25

Few other music venues in Dublin have such a special hold over Dubliners. Playing this venue is seen as a coming-of-age for Irish acts, often selling out shows here before going on to worldwide fame. Irish acts have included Lankum, Damien Dempsey, and Planxty, along with international acts like Bob Dylan and Kendrick Lamar. Vicar Street is also a popular spot for comedy gigs.

The Olympia Theatre

72 Dame St.; tel. 1/679-3323; www.3olympia.ie; from €20

For a memorable gig where the intimate setting can outshine the performer, get a ticket to the Olympia Theatre. A Dublin favorite for 150 years, this architecturally stunning Victorian building, with a capacity of 1,200, has red fabric seats in intricately carved balconies overlooking the ground-floor standing area. Big-name acts like Radiohead, R.E.M., and Hall & Oates have played here, and it can sell out quickly.

Northside

3Arena

North Wall Quay; tel. 1/819-8888; www.3arena.ie; from €40

The 3Arena is Ireland's biggest indoor concert venue, with 13,000 people regularly attending the most popular acts in the world. Originally known as the Point Depot, it has exceptional acoustics for its size; since the revamp in 2008, it added state-of-the-art facilities. Concerts often sell out well in advance, particularly mega names like Olivia Rodrigo, Coldplay, and Beyoncé, so plan ahead if you want to see a show.

FESTIVALS AND EVENTS

Spring

St. Patrick's Day Parade

O'Connell St.; tel. 1/604-0090; www.stpatricksfestival.ie; Mar. 17; free

Is there any event more synonymous with Ireland than St. Patrick's Day? Ireland's patron saint brought Christianity to the island and is credited with ridding Ireland of snakes. The main draw is the St. Patrick's Day Parade, from Parnell Square down O'Connell Street and ending on Cuffe Street. The parade comprises musical groups, sports teams, artistic performers, and just about anything else. Expect the entire city to be abuzz with celebration.

International Literature Festival

www.ilfdublin.com; mid-May; €5-30

For such a small island, we've managed to

1: statue of James Joyce **2:** Dublin Pride
3: St. Patrick's Day in Dublin

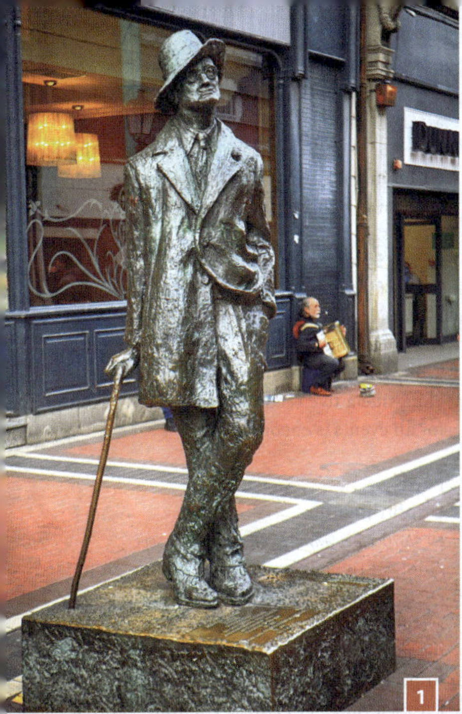

1

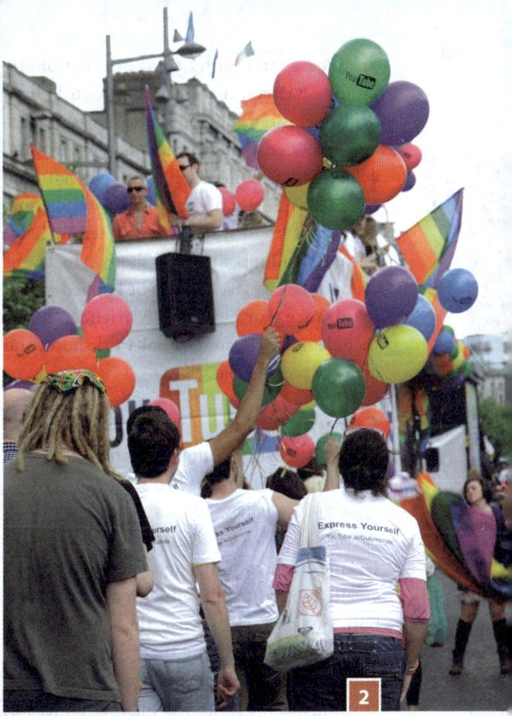

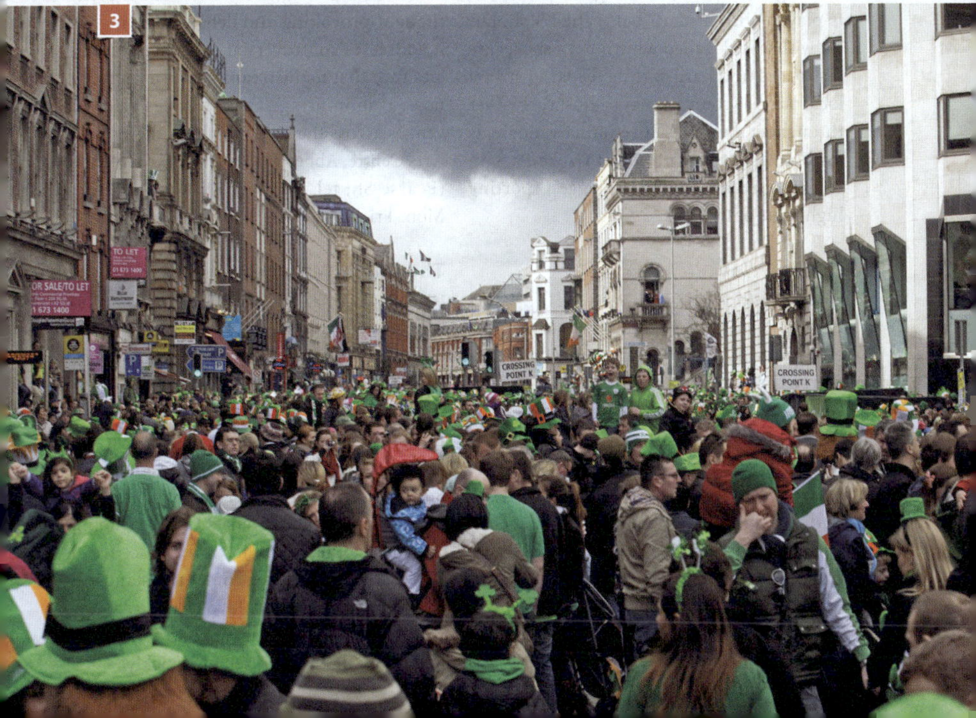

2

3

produce a large number of internationally famous writers, including Brendan Behan, W. B. Yeats, and James Joyce. This heritage has spawned generations of new authors, celebrated at Dublin's 10-day International Literature Festival. The lineup of writers, poets, playwrights, and screenwriters includes debates, readings, and workshops at locations around the city. Tickets can be booked online in advance. For kids, family-friendly events include readings, comic book workshops, and creative writing classes.

Summer

The All Ireland Football and Hurling Championship

Croke Park; tel. 1/819-2300; www.crokepark.ie; throughout summer; from €40

Ireland has two indigenous national sports. Gaelic football is played with a soccer-style ball, but players can use their hands, and score points by kicking the ball over the bar and through the tall posts or by scoring goals. Hurling has the same scoring mechanics but is played with a small ball called a sliotar, hit with a stick called a hurl. Both sports are fast-paced and hard-hitting, evoking strong local pride as counties play against each other throughout the year. The semifinals and finals for both sports are played at Croke Park in summer and are among the biggest sporting highlights of the year.

Dublin Pride

www.dublinpride.ie; June; free

Dublin Pride is a weeklong festival that celebrates the LGBTQ+ community with numerous events across the city, including film screenings, bottomless brunches hosted by drag queens, and talks by the community's most prominent voices. The parade is where most people get involved. This lively and family-friendly event takes place on O'Connell Street and moves toward Merrion Square on the Southside.

Bloomsday Festival

tel. 1/878-8547; www.bloomsdayfestival.ie; June 16; free

Celebrating James Joyce's most famous work, *Ulysses,* the Bloomsday Festival is named after its protagonist, Leopold Bloom. On June 16, people celebrate the book and the writer in public readings, live performances, and walking tours of Dublin inspired by *Ulysses.* One of the highlights is the readings at **Sweny's Pharmacy** in the Liberties, which features in the book. Another is the Bloomsday Breakfast at **Belvedere College** (Denmark St.; €20), where you'll have the kidney breakfast mentioned in the book alongside a live reading. Advance booking for all events is encouraged.

Fall

Dublin Fringe

tel. 1/670-6106; www.fringefest.com; mid-Sept.

Dublin Fringe is an arts festival known for contemporary theater, drag, comedy, and cabaret that push the boundary of art and performance. It gives a platform to emerging artists to perform alongside better-known names across a range of genres. The work is often thought-provoking and debate-sparking, as it addresses controversial areas of sexuality and race that mainstream events usually ignore. Dublin Fringe Festival takes place in venues across the city, mainly in the Project Arts Centre, Abbey Theatre, and **Lír Theatre** (Pearse St.; tel. 1/896-2559; www.thelir.ie; Mon.-Fri. 9am-5pm).

The Dublin Marathon

Leeson St. Lower; tel. 1/623-2250; www.irishlifedublinmarathon.ie; late Oct.

The Dublin Marathon is known for its friendly atmosphere that encourages first-time marathoners and supporters to cheer on the runners. The 42-km (26-mi) race is the last Sunday of October and ends near Merrion Square after taking in Phoenix Park, the Grand Canal, and University College Dublin. The most popular spots to view the race are in Phoenix Park. The area comes to a standstill to cheer the runners on. If you plan to run the race, register as far in advance as possible, as entries are limited and sell out quickly.

Bram Stoker Festival

tel. 1/518-0599; www.bramstokerfestival.com; late Oct.; free-€20

You might be surprised to learn that the famous book *Dracula* was written in Dublin by Bram Stoker, an Irishman. His macabre tale set in Transylvania is celebrated during the Bram Stoker Festival in various places around the city that influenced his work or have an eerie feel. Attend a talk with Bram's great-grandnephew, hear spooky stories at the haunted Marsh's Library, and watch a horror movie in a church after dark. Most events are ticketed.

Winter

Dublin International Film Festival

tel. 1/687-7974; www.diff.ie; late Feb.-early Mar.; from €15

With films from across the globe, expect to see features, documentaries, shorts, and animations from established and new filmmakers. DIFF is held in cinemas throughout the city, including the Savoy, Light House Cinema, and the Irish Film Institute, with talks and Q&As often organized around the big premieres.

Winter Lights

www.dublinwinterlights.ie; Dec.; free

During this illuminating event, some of Dublin's most iconic buildings are lit up with light art shows. Famous landmarks like the GPO, the Spire, Trinity College, and Samuel Beckett Bridge take on a new look during the festival. Along with the large-scale displays, smaller installations are interactive, allowing you to control the art. This is a family-friendly festival, with a lot of the attractions geared toward young families. Irish winters can be gray, so this festival is a welcome way to brighten up the day.

Shopping

Dublin is the best choice for a shopping trip in Ireland. The wide variety of shops includes department stores with designer brands and boutiques stocking local crafts. Most of the action is on the Southside, where you'll find the majority of interesting shops.

SOUTHSIDE

Shopping Areas

Grafton Street

Grafton Street is the most popular shopping street in Dublin, if not the entire country, thanks to the designer stores that line this pedestrianized street. Longtime luxury stores like the jewelers Weir & Sons sit alongside international brands like the North Face, Disney, and Canada Goose. Grafton Street is also where you'll find Brown Thomas, a high-end department store.

Powerscourt Townhouse Centre

59 William St. S.; tel. 1/679-4144; www.powerscourtcentre.ie; Mon.-Sat. 10am-6pm, Sun. 12:30pm-6:30pm

For a unique piece of clothing or jewelry, Powerscourt Townhouse Centre should be on your list. This Georgian building from 1774 houses 25 shops ranging from the large French Connection to far more interesting boutiques. Find antique jewelry at Courtville Antiques, handmade Mongolian sweaters at Daria Cashmere, and Irish perfumes at Cloon Keen.

Department Stores

Brown Thomas

88 Grafton St.; tel. 1/605-6666; www.brownthomas.com; Mon.-Wed. and Fri. 10am-8pm, Thurs. 10am-9pm, Sat. 9am-8pm, Sun. 11am-7pm

Brown Thomas is a staple of the Irish shopping scene, known for stocking top-end luxury brands on four levels. Womenswear and cosmetics dominate this spacious store, but there is some menswear in the basement and homewares on the top floor. Expect brands like Chanel, Alexander McQueen, and Northern Irish designer JW Anderson. A personal shopping service is available to help you find the perfect pieces.

Clothing and Accessories

Weir & Sons

99 Grafton St.; tel. 1/677-9678; http://weirandsons.ie; Mon.-Sat. 9:30am-6pm, Sun. noon-6pm

To splurge on a luxury piece of jewelry or a watch, visit Weir & Sons, selling their wares since 1869. It's a family-run business for landmark purchases like engagement rings and fine Swiss watches from brands that include Rolex, Patek Philippe, and Tag Heuer.

Indigo & Cloth

9 Essex St. E.; tel. 1/670-6403; www.indigoandcloth.com; Mon.-Sat. 10am-6pm, Sun. 10am-5pm

Dublin's shopping scene skews toward womenswear, but Indigo & Cloth in Temple Bar is easily the best menswear shop in the city. A great collection of big names in the contemporary scene includes A Kind of Guise, Norse Projects, and Oliver Spencer, all perfecting the basics of menswear. They've also recently begun to stock womenswear pieces that follow the shop's timeless and understated style.

Books

Hodges Figgis

56-58 Dawson St.; tel. 1/677-4754; www.hodgesfiggis.ie; Mon.-Wed. and Fri. 9am-7pm, Thurs. 9am-8pm, Sat. 9am-6pm, Sun. 10:30am-6pm

With Dublin known for its literary prowess, it's no surprise that there are a number of bookshops to pick up the latest international best seller or a novel from Irish writers. Hodges Figgis is the pick of the bunch, an enormous shop spread over four floors and believed to be the third-oldest functioning bookshop in the world.

Sweny's Pharmacy

1 Lincoln Place; tel. 83/457-9688; www.sweny.ie; daily 11am-6pm

James Joyce turned this pharmacy into a literary landmark in his book *Ulysses*. It was a chemist at the time, and the book's main character came to buy his lemon soap, but today it's a bookshop. The window is decorated as if it were still a Victorian chemist, but inside you'll find a treasure trove of used books from Irish and international writers. Check the website for readings and events around Bloomsday (June 16).

Crafts

Kilkenny Design

6 Nassau St.; tel. 1/677-7066; www.kilkennydesign.com; Mon.-Sat. 9:30am-6pm, Sun. 10am-6pm

Pick up a souvenir or gift made by Irish artisans at Kilkenny Design in a modern store across from Trinity College. The shop is well stocked with blankets and clothing, but it really shines in homewares, especially pottery. Find works from studios like Beleek, Diem Pottery, and Nicholas Mosse. For more travel-friendly gifts, there's a great choice of beauty products from Irish brands like VOYA and the Handmade Soap Company.

NORTHSIDE

Shopping Areas

Henry Street

Henry Street is the main shopping street on the Northside and home to the large department store Arnott's, international chain stores like Zara and H&M, and the **Jervis Street Shopping Centre** (125 Abbey St.; tel. 1/878-1323; www.jervis.ie; Mon.-Wed. 9am-6:30pm, Thurs. 9am-9pm, Fri.-Sat. 9am-7pm, Sun. 11am-6:30pm). There aren't many independent retailers, but it's useful if you've forgotten to pack anything.

1: Anne Street South, off Grafton Street **2:** Henry Street at Christmas

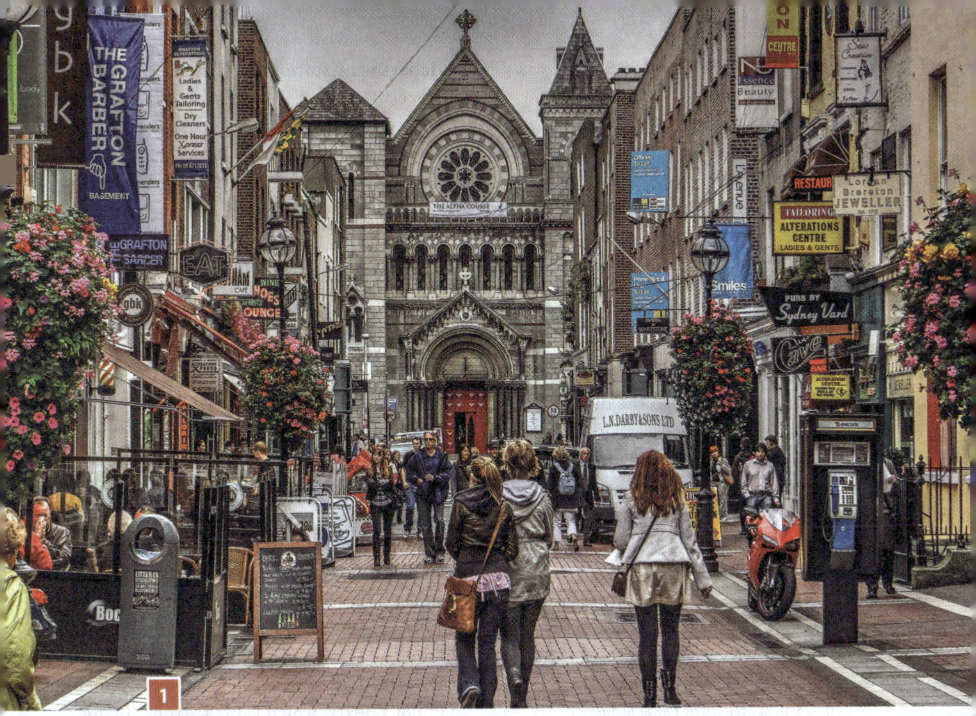
THE GRAFTON BARBER
BASEMENT
EAT
THE ALPHA COURSE
L.N.DARBY&SONS LTD
TAILORING
ALTERATIONS CENTRE
LADIES & GENTS
JEWELLER
Sydney Vard
Smiles
RESTAUR
1

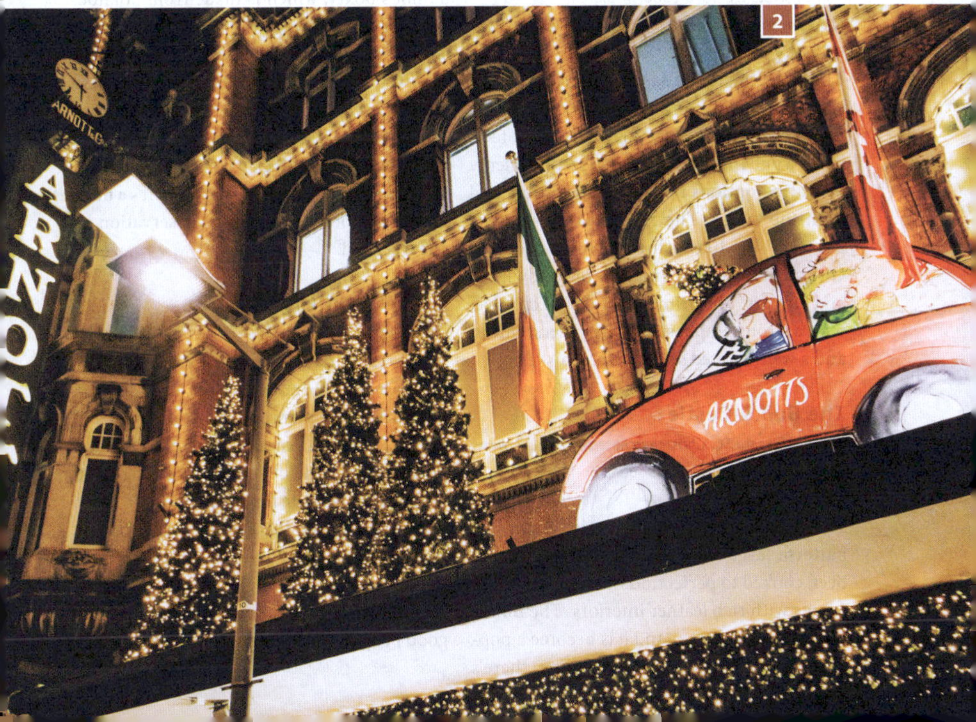
ARNOTTS
2

Department Stores

Arnott's

12 Henry St.; tel. 1/805-0400; www.arnotts.ie; Mon.-Wed. and Fri. 10am-7pm, Thurs. 10am-8pm, Sat. 9am-7pm, Sun. 11am-7pm

Arnott's is the Northside's premier department store and a fixture of Dublin since 1843. They sell everything from home furnishings to cosmetics and designer clothing for men and women across four floors. There are six places to eat and drink inside this landmark building.

Food

Dining out in Dublin is popular for locals and visitors thanks to the diverse offerings available. Most new restaurants focus on high-quality casual dining, with older establishments holding on to the fine-dining approach. There aren't many cheap meals in Dublin, but there are great venues and plenty of talented chefs.

SOUTHSIDE

Pub Grub

The Gingerman Pub

40 Fenian St.; tel. 1/676-6388; Instagram @thegingermanpub; Tues.-Thurs. and Sun. 4pm-11:30pm, Fri.-Sat. noon-12:30am; from €15

The Gingerman Pub, just off Merrion Square, is a cozy and inviting gastropub on multiple levels. The small space means it often feels lively, a pub first and gastropub second. Plenty of seating options include snug corners and high-top tables. The menu features classic pub fare like like fish-and-chips, beef and Guinness stew, and an array of sandwiches and burgers. The drink selection is extensive, with a strong emphasis on Irish beers, ciders, and a well-curated selection of whiskeys.

The Bull & Castle

5-7 Lord Edward St., Christchurch; tel. 1/475-1122; www.thebuckleycollection.ie; Mon.-Sat. noon-10pm, Sun. 12:30pm-9pm; from €25

Steak houses tend to follow a tried and tested pattern: large servings of properly sourced beef, cooked to perfection in dimly lit dining rooms with rich leather interiors. The Bull & Castle is no different and has become a popular choice. With 10 steak options, there's enough choice for any steak connoisseur. On Sunday, they have a roast available, served with potatoes and vegetables.

Gallagher's Boxty House

Temple Bar; www.boxtyhouse.ie; tel. 1/677-2762; Mon.-Sat. 9am-10pm, Sun. 10am-10pm; from €27

Gallagher's Boxty House has stood the test of time in Temple Bar, having been open since 1988, which is a testament to the quality of food and service. The chefs make the majority of dishes from scratch, including their famous boxty, which is made from potatoes and served with a choice of different meats and toppings, and their own Jack Smyth beer, which they brew in Dublin. There's also an inventive cocktail menu that focuses on Irish spirits. The Grace O'Malley is the top pick here, made with Black's spiced rum, strawberry, lemonade, and vanilla foam. It's a busy, bustling spot that warrants a reservation on the weekend.

Cafés and Light Bites

★ Kaph

31 Drury St.; tel. 1/613-9030; www.kaph.ie; Mon.-Sat. 8am-6pm, Sun. 10am-6pm; from €4

Dublin's coffee scene has come on leaps and bounds in recent years, and there's a constant battle for the title of the best coffee shop in Dublin. My favorite for a while now has been Kaph, a busy shop that mainly sells takeaway coffee, but it's worth the wait. There's seating upstairs and a slightly cramped waiting area downstairs beside the pastries. For good people-watching on one of the trendiest streets in the city, try to get a seat on the bench outside.

Bread 41

41 Pearse St.; tel. 1/633-6877; www.bread41.ie; Tues.-Sat. 8am-4pm, Sun. 9am-4pm; from €5

We don't have a culture of lining up for food in Ireland, so when you see people waiting outside a bakery on a weekend morning, you know they have to be making something special. Once inside Bread 41, you're greeted with mountains of fresh, perfectly baked treats like flaky almond croissants, decadent custard tarts, and pain au chocolat dusted in icing sugar. Grab whatever catches your eye with a coffee to go and cross the street to Trinity College to enjoy your treats.

Bambino

37 Stephen St.; tel. 1/567-7387; www.bambino.ie; Mon.-Sat. noon-10pm, Sun. 1pm-9pm; from €5

New York-style pizza slices are popping up across Dublin, but it's hard to beat the pies at Bambino. The menu has classics like cheese, hot pep, and marinara, with slices huge enough that one will be enough for most people. You can also get a full 20-inch pizza (from €30). This is a takeaway restaurant, although there are some ledges to rest on for a quick bite.

Books Upstairs

17 D'Olier St.; tel. 1/677-8566; www.booksupstairs.ie/café; Mon.-Sat. 10am-6pm, Sun. noon-6pm; from €8

Books Upstairs is a delightful little coffee shop above a bookshop. The bay window with sections of stained glass makes this place inviting as light floods in. The menu is small, mainly coffees and pastries, but the atmosphere is relaxed, with no laptops allowed, making it a small pocket of calm. Buy a book in the shop below and unwind with a coffee.

★ Cake Café

Daintree Bldg., 8 Pleasants Place; tel. 1/478-9394; www.thecakecafe.ie; Mon.-Sat. 10am-5pm; from €10

The term *hidden gem* is despised among travel writers, but it's undeniable that Cake Café is well hidden and a gem. You can enter through Pleasants Place, but the best way to visit is through **The Last Bookshop** (61 Camden St.; tel. 86/851-7419; Instagram @thelastbookshopdublin; Mon.-Sat. 10am-5pm). Once you've stepped through to the courtyard surrounded by hanging plants and lights, order from the brunch menu (the mixed nut rayu is a highlight) or try one of the freshly baked treats.

International

Xi'An Street Food

Anne St. South; www.xianstreetfooddublin.ie; tel. 1/677-8953; daily noon-midnight; from €9

Xi'An Street Food is an extremely popular restaurant that is more popular with takeaways, though there is seating for roughly 20 people inside. The menu has a choice of authentic Asian dishes as well as some Irish creations. This spot is often cited as having the best spice bag in the city, and it's hard to argue against it. This fusion dish combines crispy chicken, chips, onions, and a spice blend that's perfect for a quick snack on the way home after a day in the city.

Tang

23 Dawson St.; tel. 1/873-3672; www.tang.ie; Mon.-Fri. 8am-3:30pm, Sat. 9:30am-4pm; from €10

Putting sustainability first on their menu, the team at Tang creates tasty and considered breakfast, brunch and lunch. The offerings of shakshuka, DIY flatbreads, and Turkish eggs are not groundbreaking, but the quality sets them apart. The minimally styled space feels like it's halfway between fast food and a restaurant, making it a good choice for a quick healthy bite.

★ BIGFAN

60 Aungier St.; tel. 1/598-5368; www.bigfan.ie; Wed.-Sun. 5pm-10pm; from €10

BIGFAN does a lot of things and does them all well. It's a lively modern Chinese restaurant that serves interesting small plates, like wagyu cheeseburger jiaozi, rare feather blade steak, and corn ribs. They take pride in hand-making their gyoza and bringing traditional Chinese flavors to Dublin. The interior is stunning—don't miss the terrazzo floor, neon lights, and fully golden toilet. There's always a party atmosphere, making it a good fit for birthday parties or somewhere to start a night out.

Uno Mas

6 Aungier St.; tel. 1/563-9496; www.unomas.ie; Tues.-Sat. noon-9:30pm; from €27

This Spanish restaurant has a reputation in Dublin for serving exceptionally tasty dishes in a relaxed yet refined dining room. The menu focuses on small plates influenced by Spain's tapas dishes, great for sharing. Fill your table with Ibérico ham, potato, and onion tortillas, and rabbit rice with aged Manchego. The wine list is ever-changing and has lots of Spanish wines, alcohol-free options, and even orange wines.

Vegetarian and Vegan

★ Brother Hubbard

46 Harrington St.; tel. 1/441-1112; www.brotherhubbard.ie; Mon.-Fri. 8am-3pm, Sat.-Sun. 10am-4pm; from €13

Brother Hubbard is a popular café known for flavorful Middle-Eastern dishes. One location is on Capel Street, and the original is on Harrington Street, my pick of the two. They focus on breakfast, brunch, and lunch, so plan to arrive early. Signature dishes include shakshuka, a richly spiced tomato and pepper stew with eggs, and mezze plates with a variety of dips, salads, and freshly baked bread. There are plenty of vegan and vegetarian options that will win over the most dedicated meat eater, and meat options are also available.

Cornucopia

19-20 Wicklow St.; tel. 1/677-7583; www.cornucopia.ie; daily 8:30am-9pm; from €15

This vegan restaurant in the center of the city has been serving tasty and affordable meals for 35 years. On three floors inside a Georgian building, the owners make all the healthy dishes fresh on-site each day, including scrambled tofu, sweet potato ragout, and Keralan curry made with cauliflower and sugar snaps. The green ethos goes beyond the food, as they serve everything in compostable packaging and use a range of zero-waste products.

Glas

17-18 Chatham St.; tel. 1/569-4111; www.glasrestaurant.ie; Mon.-Thurs. 5pm-10pm, Fri.-Sun. noon-10pm; from €45

Aiming to attract meat eaters to the world of vegan and vegetarian dining, the chefs at Glas use seasonal ingredients to create beautifully plated dishes akin to fine-dining. The vibe is more relaxed, with large leafy plants adorning the colorful dining room. The two-course dinner menu consists of a starter like a chestnut parfait paired with a main like glazed eggplant. The three-course menu includes a dessert. On weekends Glas has a small brunch menu with dishes like potato waffles with cashew ricotta, gorse honey, and poached pears, available from midday.

Fine Dining

★ Spitalfields

25 The Coombe; tel. 1/454-3482; www.spitalfields.ie; Tues.-Sat. 5pm-9pm; from €25

The Liberties is the heart of working-class Dublin, but in recent years business owners have been moving into old buildings and creating spaces that link the past and present. Spitalfields is a great example, as it looks like a traditional neighborhood pub covered in colorful hanging baskets. Inside, much of the pub infrastructure remains, but the kitchen has been upgraded to produce modern Irish dishes that are artistically plated. There's a three-dish minimum per person including a main course, but with hand-harvested scallops, beef cheek and oxtail, and cock-a-leekie pie, there's no shortage of great options.

Variety Jones

78 Thomas St.; tel. 1/551-7845; www.varietyjones.ie; Wed.-Sat. 5pm-10pm; from €65

Sometimes it's best to defer to the experts, and that's what you do at Variety Jones. The menu is a chef's choice sharing menu of six courses that have included satay monkfish, jalapeño and grape salad, and octopus tempura. The restaurant is tiny, with only 10 tables, so it's an intimate experience. They can cater to pescatarians with advance notice but cannot cater to vegetarians or vegans.

NORTHSIDE

Pub Grub

The Legal Eagle

1-2 Chancery Place; tel. 1/555-2971; www.thelegaleagle.ie; Wed.-Thurs. 5pm-9:30pm, Fri.-Sat. 5pm-10pm, Sun. noon-7pm; from €25

This pub's proximity to the legal goings-on at the Four Courts has provided its name, but the food has given this swanky spot its reputation as one of the finest gastropubs in Dublin. The menu has modern takes on hearty dishes like pork chops served with charred hispi cabbage. Don't forget to order the crisps, made in house. On Sunday they have roast dinner specials of pork, chicken, or beef and also a vegetarian option.

Cafés and Light Bites

Two Boys Brew

375 N. Circular Rd., Phibsborough; www.twoboysbrew.ie; Mon.-Fri. 7:30am-3:30pm, Sat.-Sun. 9am-4pm; from €15

Café culture has made its way north to the suburb of Phibsborough in the form of Two Boys Brew. The brunch menu has a nice mix of café favorites like avocado toast and overnight oats as well as more unusual offerings like ricotta hotcakes with roasted strawberries. The food is served alongside specialty coffee from around the world. They operate on a first come, first served basis but can take reservations for groups of six or more.

International

Kimchi Hophouse

160-161 Parnell St.; tel. 1/872-8318; www.kimchihophouse.ie; Mon.-Thurs. noon-10pm, Fri.-Sat. noon-10:30pm, Sun. noon-11pm; from €13

With a combination unlikely to be reproduced anywhere else, informal Kimchi Hophouse is a Korean restaurant in an Irish pub. Somehow it works, with bulgogi served over purple rice, fresh kimchi, and colorful bowls of bibimbap, among other Korean favorites. For drinks, the varied selection includes Guinness and soju cocktails. Reservations are not required but are advised on weekends.

Sfuso

Bloom Lane; tel. 1/888-0834; www.sfuso.ie; Tues.-Thurs. and Sun. 11am-10pm, Fri.-Sat. 11am-10:30pm; from €12

Bloom Lane is Dublin's unofficial tiny Little Italy. Among the handful of Italian restaurants, Sfuso is the pick, as it sells food by weight, allowing you to choose how much you want to eat. Traditional Italian picks like lasagna, parmigiana, and arancino are accompanied by a wine list with 250 options from big-name producers and small-scale wineries. The restaurant is cozy, with space for 25 inside and 8 outside if the weather is good.

Vegetarian and Vegan

Umi Falafel

4 Mary St.; tel. 1/445-4344; www.umifalafel.ie; daily noon-9pm; from €10

Fast food doesn't get better in Dublin than Umi Falafel, with 100 percent vegetarian Middle Eastern cuisine. Meal deals are the way to go, with a wrap, salad or soup, and a drink for €13.50—great value for Dublin. The other must-try on the menu is the hummus, made in house each day. There are three other Umi Falafel locations on the Southside.

Shouk

40 Drumcondra Rd. Lower; tel. 1/532-2114; www.shouk.ie; Wed.-Thurs. and Sun. noon-10pm, Fri.-Sat. noon-10:30pm; from €15

Enter through the doorway of this Victorian redbrick building in Drumcondra and get ready for a Middle Eastern feast. The setting is fantastic, with a large outdoor dining area covered to create a bustling atmosphere where mezze plates are shared and bread is dunked into tasty servings of shakshuka. For something different, try the Moroccan fish made with fried sea bass fillets cooked in a spicy tomato sauce.

Fine Dining

★ Grano

Manor St., Stoneybatter; tel. 1/538-2003; www.grano.ie; Tues.-Fri. 5pm-10pm, Sat.-Sun. 12:30pm-10pm; from €18

Stoneybatter's Grano is an in-demand Italian restaurant that only serves pasta mains. Served in rustic bowls in a minimalist dining room, the house-made pasta is incredible. Simplicity is the key focus, with dishes like spaghettoni ai tre pomodori made with three types of seasonal tomatoes, showcasing the talents of the chef. The starters are more varied, with mackerel, burrata, and artichoke. Since making it into the Michelin Guide, this neighborhood restaurant has exploded in popularity; book ahead if you can.

Chapter One

18-19 Parnell Square N.; tel. 1/873-2266; www.chapteronerestaurant.com; Tues.-Wed. 6:30pm-9:30pm, Thurs.-Sat. noon-2pm and 6:30pm-9:30pm; from €85

As one of Dublin's most popular fine-dining restaurants, Chapter One combines the formality of a two-star Michelin restaurant with an inspiring menu that turns rarely used Irish ingredients into unforgettable dishes. There is a three-course lunch menu (€85), a four-course dinner menu (€160), and a tasting menu (€190). Dishes change seasonally but expect sika deer, lobster rice, and Swiss mountain vinegar among the ingredients. Enjoy these delicately plated dishes in a bright and airy dining room with subtle touches of luxury like heavy pristine tablecloths, delicate lighting, and high-quality tableware.

Bars and Nightlife

Dublin is known for its pubs, and it lives up to the hype. Traditional pubs (we call them "old man pubs") are places that have been around for years and offer a quiet shelter to enjoy a pint. The majority have no TVs or recorded music; these are places for conversation and trad sessions.

SOUTHSIDE

Traditional Pubs

The Palace Bar

21 Fleet St.; tel. 1/671-7388; www.thepalacebardublin.com; Sun.-Thurs. noon-11:30pm, Fri.-Sat. noon-12:30am; from €6

Temple Bar is known as an unapologetic tourist trap, but one pub bucks that trend: the Palace Bar. On the edge of Temple Bar by Westmoreland Street, this traditional pub has a small seating area out front, low tables and snugs inside, and an open, almost communal space at the back where it's easy to meet new people. The pub has a strong literary heritage, as Robert M. Smyllie, the editor of the *Irish Times*, drank here in the 1930s; writers and journalists visited hoping to meet him. This led to writers Brendan Behan, Patrick Kavanagh, and Flann O'Brien becoming regulars.

★ Grogan's

15 S. William St.; tel. 1/677-9320; www.groganspub.ie; Mon.-Thurs. 10:30am-11:30pm, Fri.-Sat. 10:30am-12:30am, Sun. 12:30pm-11pm; from €6

On a sunny day, there's no better place to be seen in Dublin than outside Grogan's. An extremely popular spot with Dubliners, it's common to see local celebrities. Guinness is what most people are drinking, so grab a table as soon as you see one and settle in. Watch people in one of the busiest pedestrian areas in the city to get a feel for Dublin. Inside is much calmer, with a mixed collection of art hanging over the regulars at the bar.

The Long Hall

51 S. Great George's St.; tel. 1/475-1590; Instagram @thelonghalldublin; Mon.-Thurs. noon-11:30pm, Fri.-Sat. noon-12:30am, Sun. 12:30pm-11pm; from €6

When Bruce Springsteen plays one of his epic gigs in Dublin, he often pops into The Long Hall for a beer afterward. This pub has a reputation as an everyman pub that celebrities of that level can come to and not be pestered. The pub is decorated floor to ceiling in elaborate rich red furnishings, giving it an old-world feel. High stools at the bar are the only option at the front, with low tables with stools and sofas to the rear for larger groups.

Bars

Blackbird

82 Rathmines Rd. Lower; tel. 83/330-4001; www.blackbirdrathmines.com; Sun.-Thurs. 4pm-midnight, Fri.-Sat. 4pm-1am; from €7

Blackbird is Rathmines's go-to pub for people in the music scene. There's no live music but always a solid rock playlist blasting through the speakers. The spacious bar is dimly lit with candles and filled with wooden tables and chairs; it can fill quickly on weekends with large groups and parties. The beer garden outside is a nice spot to catch some sun and meet new people as you share the covered picnic tables. Craft beers from across the country are the specialty.

Lucky's

78 Meath St.; tel. 1/556-2397; www.luckys.ie; Mon.-Thurs. 4pm-midnight, Fri. 4pm-1am, Sat. 1pm-1am, Sun. 1pm-11:30pm; from €7

This trendy spot in the Liberties is known for its colorful beer garden, where you can tuck into a pizza, cooked fresh on-site by Coke Lane Pizza, at the long banquet-style table. Inside, Lucky's has a late-night feel, with a deep-green interior, soft lighting, and a DJ booth. There's always something on, including daytime markets out back, DJ sets, and even occasional exhibitions; check the website or social media. The bar is stocked with canned and bottled craft Irish beers, wine on tap, and five local whiskeys that all originate within 850 m (2,800 ft) of the bar.

Nightclubs

The George

89 S. Great George's St.; tel. 1/478-2983; www.thegeorge.ie; Mon.-Fri. 2pm-2:30am, Sat. 12:30pm-2:30am, Sun. 12:30pm-1:30am; from €7

The George is the biggest gay bar in the city and has been the nightclub home for the queer community for decades. There's always an exciting DJ playing or a drag show happening. The main bar area is where the action is, and when the night progresses, this turns into a dance floor, where a mix of pop, dance, and classic club anthems keeps the crowd on their feet into the wee hours.

Pygmalion

59 S. William St.; www.pyg.ie; Mon.-Sat. noon-3am, Sun. noon-1:30am; from €7

In the vaults of the Powerscourt Townhouse is the late-night club Pygmalion. Hard-hitting music fills this popular venue, with the bar to the rear opening to the grandeur of the Georgian shopping center above. If you're not in the mood for dancing, there are leather sofas to relax on as you take in the atmosphere. You can experience this venue from midday as a bar, with the busy outdoor seating area often full of people drinking Aperol spritzes and people-watching.

Copper Face Jacks

29-30 Harcourt St.; tel. 1/425-5300; www.copperfacejacks.ie; daily 10am-late; from €7

Copper Face Jacks is a late-night institution in Dublin. This multistory nightclub is busy every weekend, particularly when there are big Gaelic football or hurling matches, as it's a favorite of people from outside Dublin. The music is standard chart hits and classic anthems. There are seven areas, including the large dance floor, smoking areas, and a cocktail bar.

TOP EXPERIENCE

☆ Dublin's Pubs

Dublin's main draw is arguably its pubs. Ireland has mastered the art of creating inviting places to meet with people and enjoy a pint of beer, and there's nowhere with a greater density of fantastic pubs than Dublin. The atmosphere makes these places special, and it's common to see historic buildings host quiet drinks in the early afternoon and then become a roaring hive of activity come evening. Find one that takes your fancy, pull up a stool, and order a pint to experience it for yourself.

Grogan's

PUB NAMES

Pub names in Ireland can be tricky. If I were to ask you to meet me at **Grogan's** in Dublin, you'd get there and see that the sign sticking out of the building says "The Castle Lounge," while the one above the door says "Grogan's." This isn't done to confuse people; pubs in Ireland are often old and have gone through different owners over the years, with regulars and locals using the old names instead of the new ones. Another example is **The Gravediggers** in Glasnevin. There's no sign with that name on the pub; instead, the sign reads "John Kavanagh," with The Gravediggers name given to the pub because of the work of the people who drank here.

DUBLIN'S BEST PUBS

- **Best Craic:** The craic at **Grogan's,** also called the Castle Lounge, is unbeatable, especially outside on a summer's evening (page 76).
- **Best Pint:** Picking the best pint of Guinness in Dublin is like being forced to pick your favorite child, but if I had to choose, it's **The Long Hall** (page 76).
- **Best for Food: Lucky's** complements their craft beer offering with pizzas from a food truck in the beer garden (page 77).
- **Best Trad Session:** Hands-down the best place to go in Dublin for live trad music is **The Cobblestone** (page 78).
- **Best Name: The Gravediggers** got its moniker by being the pub of choice for workers in Glasnevin Cemetery (page 79).

NORTHSIDE

Traditional Pubs

★ The Cobblestone

77 King St. N.; tel. 1/872-1799; www.cobblestonepub.ie; Mon.-Thurs. 4pm-11:30pm, Fri.-Sat. 1:30pm-12:30am, Sun. 1:30pm-11pm; from €6

The Cobblestone is a much loved pub considered the center of traditional Irish music in Dublin. Recently it was saved from demolition by public protests, which further cemented its legendary status. Don't expect pomp or grandeur; the rickety seats and warped wooden bars show its age and set the scene for the performances. There are some scheduled events, but most sessions start organically by people who bring their instruments. No two visits are the same, but they're always enjoyable.

Frank Ryan's

5 Queen St.; tel. 89/217-3073; www.frankryans.com; Mon.-Sat. 4pm-11:30pm, Sun. 6pm-11pm; from €6

The old cliché of the Irish pub with a cantankerous barman rings true at Frank Ryan's. Oddly it's part of the charm, but do as you're told by the staff or you might be asked to leave. This pub is best suited for a cozy drink on a wintery day, as the interior is very dark and dimly lit, which makes it a popular date spot. If the weather is good, there's a small outdoor seating area to the rear. The bar is lined with the usual Guinness and the latest craft creations from Dublin breweries.

★ The Gravediggers

1 Prospect Square; Instagram @gravediggers2; Mon. 11:30am-10:30pm, Tues.-Wed. 10:30am-10:30pm, Thurs.-Sat. 10:30am-11:30pm, Sun. 12:30pm-10:30pm; from €6

As the closest pub to Glasnevin Cemetery, The Gravediggers got its name from the workers who used to come for a pint after their work was done. Legend has it that the gravediggers knocked on the wall that separated the cemetery from the pub using their shovels and then reached through a hole in the wall to grab their pints. Thankfully you don't have to go through this rigmarole to get your drink. Most people in this pub, covered floor to ceiling in wood, drink Guinness, and The Gravediggers is known for pouring one of the best pints of the black stuff in the city.

Bars

Bar 1661

1-5 Green St.; tel. 1/878-8706; www.bar1661.ie; Mon.-Thurs. 5pm-11:30pm, Fri. 5pm-12:30am, Sat.-Sun. 2pm-12:30am; from €10

Bar 1661 is a creative cocktail bar just off Capel Street. The menu is a timeline of cocktails through the ages, with each drink dated and given a backstory. There are 15 cocktails and 2 nonalcoholic concoctions. The fresh flavors of rhubarb, hibiscus, and lemon in the Y2K are great on a sunny day, and if you're settling in on a winter day, their Belfast Coffee, made with cold brew, poitín (a traditional Irish spirit), and cream, is a longtime favorite. Once you order, you'll get a small poitín-based drink while you wait.

Bonobo

119 Church St. Upper; Instagram @bonobo_smithfield; Mon.-Thurs. 4pm-midnight, Fri. 4pm-1am, Sat.-Sun. 1pm-midnight; from €7

Bonobo is a sprawling bar on Dublin's Northside that always has a buzzing atmosphere. The main bar is dark and moody, and it turns into a dance floor in later hours. The bar is surrounded by smaller seating areas. To the rear is a covered outdoor area with long picnic tables, where they serve Neapolitan-style pizza. Craft IPAs and stouts are on tap, with a sizeable 15-cocktail menu and a good selection of whiskeys. Reservations are possible and are advised if you're a large group.

Accommodations

Generally speaking, the Northside is cheaper to stay in than the Southside, but keep in mind that hotels across Dublin are generally quite expensive. Most attractions are on the Southside, so it's best to stay here, but if you're OK with walking, the Northside has places away from the bustle.

SOUTHSIDE

Under €100

Garden Lane Backpackers

8 Garden Lane; tel. 1/551-5733; www.canbe.ie; €40

Garden Lane Backpackers is in the middle of the Liberties and is a great place to experience day-to-day Dublin. Walk through the nearby Liberty Market, stop for a coffee on Meath Street, and visit the nearby Christ Church Cathedral or Guinness Storehouse. The dorms sleep 4-8, with female-only dorms available as well as private rooms. They offer a discount for stays longer than a week.

€100-200

★ Wren Urban Nest

St. Andrew's Lane; tel. 1/223-4555; www.wrenhotel.ie; €170

This new eco-friendly boutique pod hotel is tucked between some of Dublin's busiest streets and is Ireland's first that is net carbon-neutral. Don't expect a lot of space in the 137 rooms, but touches like the rooftop garden and bar made from reclaimed wood are well-considered and shout Scandi-chic. The zero-waste kitchen serves seasonal food, the ALT bar furniture is made from repurposed wood, and the entire hotel runs on 100 percent renewable energy. The eco-endeavors don't make things rough around the edges; Wren Urban Nest is extremely well polished.

Leonardo Hotel Christchurch

Christchurch Place; tel. 1/454-0000; www.leonardo-hotels.com; €185

Leonardo Hotel Dublin Christchurch, formerly known as Jurys Inn, is centrally located across from the iconic Christ Church Cathedral. The 182 rooms have DREAM beds, included Wi-Fi, and flat-screen TVs in both standard and superior rooms. There are a bar and a restaurant, but given its setting in the city, there are better food and drink options a short walk away on Dame Street or the Liberties.

Stauntons on the Green

83 St. Stephen's Green; tel. 1/478-2300; www.stauntonsonthegreen.ie; €200

Overlooking the mature trees in St. Stephens Green is Stauntons on the Green, an elegant Georgian townhouse that epitomizes 18th-century charm. Beautifully restored, the boutique hotel retains the style of the time with rich wooden furnishings, glittering chandeliers, and cabinets of antiques. The 54 rooms are each unique and all have modern touches like Wi-Fi, TVs, and a kettle. There's a small walled garden where the hotel can organize a picnic of finger food and champagne.

Over €200

★ The Dylan

Eastmoreland Place; tel. 1/660-3000; www.dylan.ie; €330

The Dylan is a modern five-star boutique hotel that showcases the best of contemporary Ireland. Each of the 72 rooms is individually decorated. Design fans will feel at home thanks to the bespoke furniture, Irish art, and the great use of color and patterns; you'll be snapping pics. There are four places to eat and drink, with **The Edison** serving modern Irish cuisine, wines from around the world at **The Dylan Bar,** casual bites at the **Nurserie Terrace,** and craft cocktails at **The Ruby Room.**

The Westbury

Balfe St.; tel. 1/679-1122; www.doylecollection.com; €400

The five-star Westbury is in the thick of it, just steps away from Grafton Street, and a lavish urban retreat in some of the swankiest surroundings in the city. The 205 rooms combine luxurious design touches like four-poster beds and open fireplaces with modern amenities. Although it's close to great bars and restaurants, it would be a mistake not to dine on Irish food at award-winning **WILDE** or have brunch at **Balfe's.**

★ The Shelbourne

27 St. Stephen's Green; tel. 1/663-4500; www.theshelbourne.com; €550

The Shelbourne is one of Dublin's most beloved hotels, and timeless elegance has made it the go-to spot for Dubliners celebrating milestones. First opened in 1824, the 265-room five-star hotel has hosted its share of celebrities, and it's common to see the Irish rugby team after a big win. The classically styled rooms come in nine types in the newer section or the heritage wing. For food and drink, **The Saddle Room,** the hotel's flagship restaurant, focuses on Irish seafood and steak; **The Lord Mayor's Lounge** is well known for its elegant afternoon tea; and **The Horseshoe Bar** offers a lively setting for cocktails. History lovers will want to visit the Constitution Room, where the Irish Constitution was drafted in 1922.

The Merrion

21-24 Merrion St. Upper; tel. 1/603-0600; www.merrionhotel.com; €600

The five-star, 142-room Merrion Hotel is in a meticulously restored collection of four Georgian townhouses dating to the 1760s. The rooms and suites, each individually designed, are an ode to its heritage but don't forgo the modern comforts of a luxury hotel. Rooms are spacious and decadently furnished, with period details like high ceilings, sash windows, and antique furniture complemented by plush bedding, marble baths, included Wi-Fi, and flat-screen TVs. Enjoy a pocket of nature in the city with garden-facing rooms and suites that overlook the landscaped grounds. Keep an eye out for art by famous Irish painters like Jack B. Yeats, and try to get a reservation at **Restaurant Patrick Guilbaud,** the first in Ireland to be awarded two Michelin stars.

NORTHSIDE

Under €100

Clink i Lár

35-36 Abbey St.; tel. 1/963-9050; www.clinkhostels.com; €45

Clink i Lár does a lot of what a hostel needs to do. It's centrally located, making it a short walk from attractions like Trinity College, Grafton Street, and the GPO. It offers a range of rooms from wallet-friendly 12-bed dorms to quieter private rooms, and female-only dorms are available. There's a bar and café on-site that serve quick bites, bottled beer, and coffee.

Generator Hostel

Smithfield Square; tel. 1/901-0222; www.staygenerator.com; €85

Generator is a large chain of hostels, and this is one of the city's largest, with beds for 540. There are four types of private rooms and dorms with 4-8 beds. Large groups can book the private 10-bed dorm with a jetted tub. There's a 24-hour reception desk, a bar that regularly has live music, and a cinema room.

The Shelbourne

€100-200

The Gibson

Point Square; tel. 1/681-5000; www.thegibsonhotel.ie; €160

This four-star hotel is a good choice if you're going to the 3Arena or want to stay somewhere quieter. The Point Luas tram stop is right outside the hotel, so you can zip into O'Connell Street in 10 minutes. The modern glass structure has 252 rooms in seven types. The Superior Double Room is the most affordable, with an en suite bath and Wi-Fi included, while the most expensive room, the Gibson Suite, is a penthouse with a king bed and a separate lounge.

★ The Hendrick Smithfield

11 Hendrick St.; tel. 1/482-6500; www.hendrickdublin.ie; €175

The Hendrick is a trendy hotel in Smithfield with small rooms that are comfortable to sleep in but too small to hang out in; it's best for people who plan to be out and about. There are four room types on six floors, ranging from the snug 12-sq-m (130-sq-ft) double to the 18-sq-m (195-sq-ft) accessible double with a king bed. There's a solid art collection from Irish artists on the walls.

Point A

17 Moore Lane; tel. 1/221-0400; www.pointahotels.com; €180

Point A is a modern and stylish hotel just steps from Henry Street and O'Connell Street. The 141 rooms are on the small side, but the layout is well thought out, so they feel comfortable for a short stay thanks to the mood lighting, power shower, and smart TVs. The hotel doesn't have a restaurant but offers continental breakfast. There are great dining options a short walk away.

Zanzibar Locke

34-37 Ormond Quay; tel. 1/436-3700; www.lockeliving.com; €200

Overlooking the River Liffey, Zanzibar Locke is a chic apartment hotel that puts a big emphasis on style. The 160 rooms in five types come with fully equipped kitchens and are bright, floral, and bold; they are dog-friendly and have Wi-Fi and double or twin beds. The property also has a coworking space, a fitness center, and a café and bar where they serve artisanal coffee and cocktails.

Over €200

The Gresham

23 O'Connell St.; tel. 1/874-6881; www.riu.com; €250

The iconic four-star Gresham has welcomed guests since 1817 in a landmark building in the heart of the city, close to the attractions on the Northside and a 5-minute walk to the Southside. The bright marble lobby welcomes you, and the 400 rooms, refurbished in 2024, have old-world charm and modern comforts. **Toddy's Brasserie** is the in-house dining option, with crowd-pleasing steaks and seafood as well as a smaller lunch menu with soups and sandwiches.

Information and Services

VISITOR INFORMATION

The **Visit Dublin Tourism Information Centre** (Barnardo Square, Dame St.; tel. 1/265-5634; www.visitdublin.com; daily 9am-5pm) is the newest in the city and happy to help. All the information is free and the staff know the city inside out, so they can assist in planning your ideal day. There's also information about other parts of Ireland.

HOSPITALS

The two main hospitals for emergencies are **St. James** (James St.; tel. 1/410-3000; www.stjames.ie) and the **Mater Hospital** (Eccles St.; tel. 1/803-2000; www.mater.ie).

PHARMACIES

There's no shortage of pharmacies in Dublin, with chain stores like Boots as well as family-run pharmacies. For a late-night pharmacy, try **Hickey's** (55 O'Connell St.; tel. 1/873-0427; www.hickeyspharmacies.ie; daily 9am-11pm).

POLICE

The police, called Garda in Ireland, can be called in an emergency by dialing 999. You'll find Garda stations on O'Connell Street, Store Street, and Chancery Street on the Northside, and on the Southside, stations on Pearse Street, Kevin Street, and Harcourt Street.

POST OFFICES

There are two major **post offices** (www.anpost.ie) in the center of Dublin. The Grand Post Office (GPO) is on O'Connell Street, with another on St. Andrew's Street.

BANKS AND ATMS

ATMs are widespread throughout the city. Most banks have them outside, and corner shops like SPAR and Centra have ATMs inside. Dame Street has two large banks, with a **Bank of Ireland** opposite the entrance to Trinity College and an **AIB** branch toward Dublin Castle.

EMBASSIES

The majority of embassies are in the suburbs of the Southside.

- **US Embassy** (42 Elgin Rd.; tel. 1/668-8777; https://ie.usembassy.gov; daily 8:30am-5pm)
- **Canadian Embassy** (7 Wilton Terrace; tel. 1/234-4000; www.international.gc.ca; Mon.-Fri. 9am-4:30pm)
- **British Embassy** (29 Merrion Rd.; tel. 1/205-3700; www.gov.uk; daily 24 hours)
- **Australian Embassy** (49 St. Stephen's Green; tel. 1/664-5300; https://ireland.embassy.gov.au; Mon.-Fri. 8:30am-4:30pm)
- **New Zealand Embassy** (2 Merrion Row; tel. 1/567-7680; www.mfat.govt.nz; by appointment)
- **Embassy of the Republic of South Africa** (Alexandra House; tel. 1/661-5523; https://dirco1.azurewebsites.net; Mon.-Fri. 9am-noon)

LUGGAGE STORAGE

Use a service like **Radical Storage** (www.radicalstorage.com) to find places to leave your luggage at locations in or near major sights like Temple Bar, Connolly Station, and O'Connell Street. Your bags are insured for damage up to €3,000.

Transportation

GETTING THERE

Air

With multiple direct routes to the United States and low-fare options to Europe, **Dublin Airport** (DUB) is one of the busiest in Europe and where most visitors to Ireland arrive.

Dublin Airport is 10 km (6 mi) from the city center, and for an airport of its size and importance, its connections to the city are an embarrassment. There is no rail service; your options are bus or taxi, both found outside the arrival halls. A taxi (€25-30) takes roughly 30 minutes, and there is sometimes a short wait for them. Route 16 and Route 41 **Dublin Bus** (www.dublinbus.ie; €2.60) takes 45-60 minutes. Private buses **Aircoach** (www.aircoach.ie) and **Dublin Express** (www.dublinexpress.ie) charge €10 to the city center. Tickets can be bought on arrival or online.

Car

The M50 motorway is a ring road around the capital that connects to other motorways that span the country. You'll likely be on this road at some point, but be warned that traffic comes to a standstill during rush hour. Drive to or from Cork on the M7 motorway, to Galway on the M8, and to Limerick on the M4; these journeys take 2-3 hours. From Belfast, the M1 motorway runs directly to Dublin and takes 1.5-2 hours.

Train

Traveling to Dublin by train is convenient and scenic. The two main railway stations are **Heuston Station** (St. John's Rd., Dublin 8) and **Connolly Station** (Amiens St., Dublin 1). From the west or south, including Galway, Limerick, Cork, and Killarney, you'll arrive at Heuston Station. Journey times are 2.5 hours from Cork and 2 hours from Galway. Trains are operated by **Iarnród Éireann** (www.irishrail.ie). From the north or east, including Belfast and the northeast coast, you'll arrive at Connolly Station. *The Enterprise* between Belfast and Dublin offers a scenic 2-hour journey and terminates at Connolly Station.

Both stations are well connected to Dublin's public transport network, including buses and trams. Booking rail tickets online in advance is advised, especially during peak travel times or on weekends, as trains can fill quickly.

Bus

Dublin is connected with towns and cities across Ireland by **Bus Éireann** (www.buseireann.ie), which operates services to and from Busáras (Store St.). Tickets can be bought online or in person at the station. There are regular, direct, and express buses with few stops between Dublin and major destinations like Cork, Galway, and Belfast.

GETTING AROUND

On Foot

Dublin is very walkable, and it's the quickest way to get around. Some footpaths are narrow, but streets that have recently been renovated, like O'Connell Street, and pedestrianized streets like Grafton Street and Drury Street, are easy to walk.

Bus

The most convenient way to explore the city is by bus. Run by **Dublin Bus** (www.dublinbus.ie), the network is extensive and covers the city. The most cost-effective way to pay is a **Leap Card** (www.about.leapcard.ie), a prepaid travel card that you can buy in most convenience stores; it can be replenished as needed. Tap the card when you get on, and again when you get off. Fares range €1.60-3.10 depending on the distance traveled. You can also pay with cash, but exact change is required.

Buses generally operate 5:30am-11:30pm, with less frequent service in the evenings and on weekends. For late-night travel, Nitelink buses run until around 4am on weekends, with slightly higher fares and reduced routes. To plan your journey, the **Dublin Bus app** and website offer real-time information on arrivals, routes, and schedules, although it's not always accurate. Stops are well-marked with yellow poles, and buses typically have digital displays and audio announcements. For tourists, **Hop-On, Hop-Off** bus tours provide a flexible and informative way to see the city's major attractions.

Avoid traveling during rush hours if possible, as buses can get crowded and slowed by traffic.

Tram

Getting around Dublin by **Luas** (www.luas.ie), the city's tram system, is quick and efficient, especially for exploring areas beyond the city center. The two lines are the **Red Line,** from Tallaght to the Point in the Docklands, and the **Green Line,** from Brides Glen to Broombridge, passing through St. Stephen's Green and Dundrum. Fares vary by distance and range €2.10-3.30, with the Leap Card offering the most cost-effective option. Tickets can be purchased from machines at Luas stops, and you must have a valid ticket before boarding, as there are regular ticket checks.

The Luas operates Monday-Friday 5:30am-12:30am, with slightly reduced hours on weekends. Trams are frequent, especially during peak hours, and the service is known for its punctuality. The trams are modern, clean, and fully accessible, with low floors for easy boarding with strollers and wheelchairs. Stops are well-marked, and electronic displays provide real-time information on the next tram. There have been reports of antisocial behavior on the Luas, but by and large it's a safe and pleasant experience.

Train

The **DART** (Dublin Area Rapid Transit) rail service is fast and often scenic to travel to the coastal suburbs. Running along the coast from Malahide and Howth in the north to Greystones in the south, the DART provides access to some of Dublin's most picturesque areas. It operates from three stations in the city: **Connolly Station** (Amiens St., Dublin 1), **Tara Street Station** (Tara St., Dublin 2), and **Pearse Street Station** (Westland Row, Dublin 2). Slightly farther away is **Drumcondra Station** (Drumcondra Rd., Dublin 9). Fares vary by distance and range €2.50-5 one-way. Using a Leap Card gives you the cheapest fare, and tickets can also be purchased from machines at DART stations.

Cycling

Lots of bike lanes in Dublin are shared with bus lanes, so cycling might give you a shock at first. You can also stick to vehicle-free cycle paths along the Grand Canal and Royal Canal. **Dublinbikes** (www.dublinbikes.ie) has cheap and easy bike rentals for visitors. Bike thieves are common in Dublin, so lock it up properly in a visible location.

Car

In the city, be prepared for congested traffic on tight streets that share space with bus and cycle lanes, although it's nowhere nearly as panic-inducing as driving in places like Italy. Cars can be rented from multiple companies at Dublin Airport, such as **NewWay** (Terminals 1 and 2; tel. 1/605-7588; www.newway.ie; daily 5am-12:15am), and in the city from companies that include **Sixt** (Marlborough Place; tel. 1/235-2030; www.sixt.ie; Mon.-Fri. 8am-6pm, Sat.-Sun. 8am-3pm).

Don't forget, we drive on the left in Ireland. Paid street parking is available in most areas in Dublin. Tickets must be bought at payment terminals on the street with cash or a card.

Taxi

Dublin's taxis have gotten a bad reputation in recent years, as there's a shortage of drivers. This has led to lots of reported cases of drivers refusing fares or refusing to take card payment, both illegal. On a busy night, you may be waiting a long time for a taxi and may not get one.

Apps like **FreeNow** (www.free-now.com) and **Bolt** (www.bolt.eu) work well to book taxis outside busy periods on weekends. To estimate your fare, head to the **Transport for Ireland** website (www.transportforireland.ie).

Dublin Bay

Dublin is on Dublin Bay and near the foothills of the Dublin Mountains, providing easy, quick escapes to experience life in picturesque villages. Many are along the DART line and are very popular on summer days in good weather, when people head to the beach. Expect brilliant views of the sea, cute streets, and plenty of places to eat and drink.

ORIENTATION

North of the city is **Howth,** on a headland jutting into the sea, and farther north is **Malahide.** Both are on the DART line from the city, making them easy to reach. South of the city is **Dún Laoghaire** and **Sandycove,** separated by a 30-minute walk or one stop on the DART. Beyond these seaside villages are **Dalkey** and **Killiney,** also separated by a 30-minute walk.

HOWTH

Howth is a fishing village on a headland surrounded by the Irish Sea and protected by cliffs along its edge. At the working harbor you'll see fishing boats unloading their catch as visitors walk the pier. There's a nice balance of locals and day visitors in the pubs and restaurants. Seafood tends to dominate menus, and there are options for every budget.

Sights

Howth Pier

Harbour Rd.

Howth Pier flanks both sides of Howth Harbour and offers a lot for visitors. The West Pier is a popular place to eat and drink, with four seafood restaurants and fishmongers selling the local catch. The East Pier is great for walking, as it's wide and well maintained, with brilliant views of the boats in the harbor. At the end of East Pier is **Howth Lighthouse,** where you can look across the water to Ireland's Eye, a small island just off the coast, or look at West Pier to see fishers casting lines into the sea. On the shore between the piers is linear **Howth Pier Park,** with some picnic benches, green space, and a playground.

Hiking and Walking

★ Howth Cliff Walk

Distance: *7.8 km (4.8 mi) round-trip*
Duration: *2 hours*
Elevation gain: *130 m (425 ft)*
Effort: *Easy-moderate*
Trailhead: *Howth DART Station*

The Howth Cliff Walk is a vista-packed stroll that takes in sea views, crumbling cliffs that protect the village from the Irish Sea, and meandering trails through gorse and wildflowers. Part of the appeal is the easy access from public transport. From the Howth DART Station, you quickly reach the hills behind the harbor, with most of the ascent on the first 2 km (1.2 mi). The views are teased as you climb, with the full panorama when you reach the gentle summit. As the trail winds along the cliffs, look over Dublin Bay to the south and toward the Cooley Mountains in the north; between the two views is Ireland's Eye and Lambay Island. Keep an eye out for people diving into the sea from the lower reaches of the cliffs, as well as seabirds like guillemots and razorbills overhead.

Dublin Bay

THAT'S AMORE
THE GREEDY GOOSE
STRAND ST
THE GREEN
OLD STREET RESTAURANT
OLD ST
TOWNYARD LN
Malahide
Malahide DART Station
NEOLA
THE MALL
MAIN ST
Malahide Bus Stop
CHURCH RD
0 100 yds
0 100 m
Portrane Beach
Tower Bay Beach
CORBALLIS FARM
M1
See Detail
Malahide
GRAND HOTEL MALAHIDE
MALAHIDE CASTLE & GARDENS
NEWWAY
DUBLIN AIRPORT
M2
DUBLIN COUNTY
Portmarnock Beach
M50
AWESOME WALLS
HOWTH PIER
MAMÓ
THE HARBOUR BAR
Howth DART Station
Howth
N3
See "Dublin" Map
GLASNEVIN CEMETERY
ST. ANNE'S GOLF COURSE
MARTELLO TOWER SUTTON
HOWTH CLIFF WALK
PHOENIX PARK
Dublin
TRINITY COLLEGE
GUINNESS STOREHOUSE
Dublin Bay
See "Dún Laoghaire to Killiney" Map
N7
JAMES JOYCE TOWER & MUSEUM
THE FORTY FOOT
Dún Laoghaire
Dundrum
N11
Sandycove
Dalkey
Marlay Park
THE MERRY PLOUGHBOY
BIKING.IE
Killiney
BOHERNABREENA RESERVOIR LOOP
HELLFIRE CLUB
THREE ROCK LOOP
Ticknock Forest
Bohernabreena Reservoir
GLENCULLEN ADVENTURE PARK (THE GAP)
Dublin Mountains
0 2 mi
0 2 km
Bray
© MOON.COM

Shopping

Howth Market

3A Harbour Rd.; tel. 1/839-4141; www.howthmarket.ie; Mon.-Fri. 7am-6pm, Sat.-Sun. 8am-7pm

Howth Market is busy and popular, with up to 25 stalls on weekends and in summer. Expect a good mix of artisanal jewelry, art from local designers, and freshly baked treats like cupcakes and crepes. There is a small covered seating area and the stalls are covered, but the market is outdoors and not fully protected from rain.

Food

Mamó

Harbour House; tel. 1/839-7096; www.mamorestaurant.ie; Sun.-Mon. 1pm-7pm, Thurs.-Sat. 12:30pm-3pm and 6pm-9:15pm; from €35

Creating modern Irish dishes with locally sourced ingredients in a beautiful waterfront setting has given Mamó a great reputation among foodies. The menu changes frequently, but given its location, you can expect fresh seafood like langoustines, sea scallops, and monkfish. Vegetarians can dine on grilled fennel served with house ricotta and Howth honey, while carnivores can tuck into dishes like dry-aged hogget with leeks and dark kale.

Bars and Nightlife

The Harbour Bar

18 Church St.; tel. 1/564-5891; Instagram @theharbourbar_howth; Sun.-Thurs. 12:30pm-11:30pm, Fri.-Sat. 12:30pm-12:30am; from €6

The walk up the hill behind the harbor is worth it for the incredibly cozy Harbour Bar. Step through the door and walk across the dark wooden floor to find a comfy nook to settle into with a pint of craft beer or a cocktail. There's often live music, mostly impromptu, but scheduled events sometimes take over a corner of the pub or the outdoor beer garden.

Accommodations

Martello Tower Sutton

Red Rock; tel. 86/164-2671; www.martellotowersutton.com; €525 for 2 nights

Sleeping in this Martello tower is a stay that you're unlikely to forget. The tower has been converted to self-catering with two bedrooms to sleep 4, a large living area, and views of Dublin Bay from the windows and balcony. There are quiet walks along the coast that start just outside, making it a great choice for a secluded escape.

Howth Cliffs

Martello Towers

tower on Dalkey Island

Martello towers were built in the early 1800s as defensive structures to repel potential attacks by Napoleon. The stout round buildings are found along the coast of Ireland, with 28 in Dublin and 22 in the rest of the country. Some towers have been repurposed as museums, like the James Joyce Museum in Sandycove, or lodging, but most are empty.

NOTABLE MARTELLO TOWERS AROUND DUBLIN

- **Martello Tower Sutton:** See this tower on the southern edge of Howth Head (page 88).
- **James Joyce Tower and Museum:** Learn about the famous writer in the tower that he once called home (page 93).
- **Seapoint Beach:** Take a dip in the sea beside this tower in South County Dublin (page 94).
- **Dalkey Island:** Walk around the base of this tower on scenic Dalkey Island (page 96).

Getting There and Around

The most popular and convenient way to get to Howth is the DART from any of Dublin's central stations, including Connolly, Tara Street, and Pearse Street. The journey takes 25-30 minutes and offers scenic coastal views as you approach **Howth DART Station** (Howth Rd). Trains run frequently, typically every 15-20 minutes.

You can also take Dublin Bus Route H3 from the city center, which departs from Lower Abbey Street. The journey takes 45-50 minutes, depending on traffic, and drops you off at Howth DART Station. By car, Howth is a 30-minute drive from the city center via the R105 coastal road. Paid parking is available in the village, but it can get busy on weekends and holidays, so this should be your last option.

Once you're in Howth, it's easiest to get around on foot. It's small, and the places you'll want to go are close to one another.

MALAHIDE

The promenade along the waterfront and buzzing streets filled with pubs and restaurants make Malahide a good choice for a day out from the city. There's plenty of history and

Day Trips from Dublin

Destination	Why Go	Travel Time	How Long to Stay
Howth (page 86)	Visit this coastal fishing town and walk the Howth Cliff Walk for amazing views.	30 minutes on the DART from Connolly Station	Half day
Malahide (page 89)	See the amazing Malahide Castle and stroll along the waterfront.	30 minutes on the DART from Connolly Station	Half day
Dún Laoghaire and Sandycove (page 93)	Take a dip in the sea at the Forty Foot and enjoy a coffee by the sea from Hatch Coffee afterward.	30 minutes on the DART from Pearse Street Station	Half day
Dalkey and Killiney (page 96)	Dive into the water at Vico Baths and stop for a quick lunch at Mug's Café before making the short crossing to Dalkey Island.	30 minutes on the DART from Pearse Street Station	Full day
Wicklow Mountains National Park (page 114)	Drive the Old Military Road into the park and go on a hike up Djouce Mountain. Stop in Enniskerry afterward for lunch, then visit Powerscourt Estate and Waterfall.	1.5-hour drive from Dublin City	Full Day

nature thanks to Malahide Castle and some of north County Dublin's finest beaches.

Sights

Malahide Castle and Gardens

Malahide Demesne; www.malahidecastleandgardens.ie; daily 9:30am-5:30pm; €16

Malahide Castle and Gardens is an enticing historic site that gives a fascinating glimpse into Ireland's past with a backdrop of beautifully landscaped gardens. The castle dates to the 12th century and is where the Talbot family lived for 800 years, until 1975, making it one of the longest continually inhabited castles in Ireland. The last remaining member, Rose Talbot, sold it to the Irish state. Experience the centuries of history on a guided tour. Over the years, the castle adopted different architectural styles, including Gothic revival and Tudor, which you'll see in beautiful details on the exterior and in wonderfully preserved rooms like the Great Hall. Afterward, stop by the visitor center, with detailed exhibits of the castle's history and stories about the Talbot family.

Surrounding the castle, the 105-ha (260-acre) estate includes the landscaped Malahide Gardens, which rival the castle's

Destination	Why Go	Travel Time	How Long to Stay
Bray and Greystones (page 109)	Enjoy a leisurely day by the sea, walking the promenade in Bray and having lunch at the Happy Pear or a coffee at Fat Fox in Greystones.	45 minutes on the DART from Pearse Street Station	Half day
Glendalough (page 122)	Head to the old monastic city in the mountains and spend a few hours exploring the ruins and walking the trails.	1.5-hour drive from Dublin City	Half day
Battle of the Boyne Site (page 128)	Drive north to visit the battleground, learn about the battle at the visitor center, and walk the parklands around it.	45-minute drive from Dublin City	Half day
Brú na Bóinne (page 132)	Learn about the ancient wonders at Newgrange, Knowth, and Dowth.	1-hour drive from Dublin City	Half day

grandeur. The variety of themed areas include the **Walled Garden** and the **Butterfly House,** where you can stroll among exotic plants and colorful butterflies. The gardens also house the **West Lawn,** a perfect spot for a picnic or leisurely ramble when the weather is good.

Beaches

Portmarnock Beach

Portmarnock Beach is an 8-km (5-mi) stretch of open sand that's popular with walkers, sea swimmers, and even volleyball players when the weather is good. At low tide, the sea retreats a sizeable distance, making the large beach feel even bigger.

Portrane Beach

Portrane is a smaller beach, at 2 km (1.2 mi) long, protected by sand dunes at the mouth of the Rogerstown Estuary. The beach ends at a headland to the south, but for a more secluded spot, continue south over the headland to **Tower Bay Beach,** popular with sea swimmers and people exploring the sea caves at low tide.

Horse Trekking

Corballis Farm

Corballis Cottages; tel. 86/860-0578; www.corballis-horsetrekking-therapeutic.com; Tues.-Sun. 9am-8pm; €30

Ride on horseback through leafy woodlands or a sandy beach at this 49-ha (120-acre) farm. If you're a beginner, you can stay near the stables and take a group or private lesson in the gated pen. People of all abilities are welcome, as they offer therapeutic riding sessions to those with physical, cognitive, emotional, and developmental disabilities. Phone to make a reservation, as there is no online booking system.

Shopping

Neola

Main St.; tel. 1/846-0000; www.neola.ie; Mon.-Sat. 10am-6pm

Neola is a popular women's boutique serving the area for 20 years. They sell eye-catching pieces from 40 brands, including a choice of Irish pieces and a range of price points.

Food and Accommodations

That's Amore

12 Townyard Lane; tel. 1/845-6278; www.thatsamoremalahide.com; Wed.-Sun. 12:30pm-9:30pm; €14

Owned and operated by Enzo from Naples, That's Amore is an authentic Italian restaurant that focuses on pasta, pizza, and fresh seafood using locally sourced ingredients. It's a favorite with locals thanks to the casual atmosphere and consistently tasty food.

Old Street Restaurant

Old St.; tel. 1/845-5614; www.oldstreet.ie; Tues.-Thurs. 5pm-9pm, Fri. noon-2:30pm and 5pm-9pm, Sat. 1pm-9pm, Sun. 1pm-7pm; from €25

This neighborhood-style place in the center of Malahide champions contemporary Irish cuisine rooted in comfort food. The menu changes with the seasons and depends on availability from Irish suppliers. The large eight-seat tables and varied menu of fish, meat, and some veggie options make it a good choice for a group night out. Finish with a tipple from the extensive drinks menu of aperitifs like Aperol spritzes, ginger whiskey sour cocktails, or a glass of vino from the 12-page wine list.

The Greedy Goose

15 Townyard Lane; tel. 1/845-1299; www.greedygoose.ie; Mon.-Fri. 5pm-10pm, Sat.-Sun. 1pm-10pm; €35 pp

The Greedy Goose is a tapas restaurant that serves a diverse range of dishes and cuisines. Some menu highlights are the seared scallops, duck spring rolls, and chana masala, which you'll enjoy with views of the marina. The dining room is bright and airy with tables dressed in crisp white tablecloths. It's not overly fancy, but it has a classy feel.

Grand Hotel Malahide

Grove Rd.; tel. 1/845-0000; www.thegrand.ie; €185

First opened in 1835, the historic Grand Hotel is on the waterfront and has 203 updated rooms. It feels modern throughout. The view is the star, particularly for sunrise, with many rooms overlooking the sea. A close second is the 21-m (69-ft) swimming pool, sauna, steam room, and jetted tub that wouldn't look out of place in ancient Rome. For food and drink there's the semiformal **Coast Restaurant,** with seafood and steaks, and the **Matt Ryan Bar** for light bites throughout the day.

Getting There and Around

The DART is the easiest way to get to Malahide from Dublin. Trains run frequently from city center stations like Connolly, Tara Street, and Pearse Street, with the journey taking 25 minutes. The **Malahide DART Station** (Main St.) is a 5-minute walk from the waterfront. Dublin Bus Route H2 runs from Gardiner Street in Dublin and drops you off at a stop on Malahide Road. It can take over an hour, depending on traffic. The DART is a far better choice.

Driving to Malahide from Dublin City takes 30-45 minutes via the M1 motorway and the R106 road. There's lots of on-street parking, but it fills quickly on weekends.

DÚN LAOGHAIRE AND SANDYCOVE

Dún Laoghaire is a large coastal town south of Dublin that's home to many who commute to the city. That doesn't make it a ghost town during the day, however. For a quieter time, head farther south to Sandycove, where there are fewer crowds.

Sights

★ James Joyce Tower and Museum

Sandycove Point; tel. 1/280-9265; www.joycetower.ie; Tues.-Sun. 10am-4pm; donation

Located in Sandycove, just steps from the Forty Foot, the literary great is celebrated at the James Joyce Tower and Museum, housed inside a Martello tower. First built as a defense against a potential attack by Napoleon in the 19th century, it appeared in Joyce's most famous novel, *Ulysses*. Joyce fell in love with the building when he visited his friend and fellow writer Oliver St. John Gogarty, making it his home for six days in 1904, and it has become synonymous with his legacy since becoming a museum in 1962.

Visitors can explore the tower's two levels,

filled with fascinating exhibits and memorabilia related to Joyce. The first floor contains original letters, photographs, first editions of Joyce's works, and personal items belonging to the author. The second floor is a reconstructed living space and gives a sense of what life was like during Joyce's stay. From the top of the tower, you can look out over stunning panoramic views of Dublin Bay, where you'll likely see sea swimmers preparing for a dip. Tours are self-guided, and there are occasionally events.

Beaches and Sea Swimming

★ The Forty Foot

Sandycove Point

The Forty Foot is Dublin's go-to spot for sea swimming. Regardless of the temperature or weather, there are always hardy swimmers braving the Irish Sea. In summer the water is 14.5-15°C (58-59°F) on average, and in winter it drops to 4-8°C (39-46°F). During the COVID-19 pandemic, sea swimming became popular in Ireland, and the Forty Foot was among the most popular thanks to its scenic setting and proximity to the city. There's no beach; instead, steps are cut into the rocks to walk down to the water and take the plunge. If you're a more cautious swimmer, there is a space beside the steps protected from the swell, often the calmest water at the Forty Foot. If you're feeling adventurous, you can walk up the rocks behind the outdoor changing area and leap into the water from a height of 5 m (16 ft), depending on the tide. Jumping is safe, as the water is deep, but be careful on the rocks because they can be slippery.

The changing area is a concrete bench with a small overhang that protects your belongings from rain, but you may want to plan ahead to keep your gear dry. There's nowhere to change in private, so be prepared for some nudity. If this is your first time swimming in the sea, you will likely want to stay on dry land, as the water is deep and there are no lifeguards.

Sandycove Beach

Sandycove Point

A good option for your first sea swim is around the corner from the Forty Foot at Sandycove Beach, where the water is shallow and calm. The small changing area is similar to the Forty Foot. There's a limited amount of parking, but most people park in Sandycove town and walk 5 minutes.

Seapoint Beach

Seapoint Ave.

Seapoint Beach is a popular sea swimming spot along the south Dublin coastline. A Martello tower acts as a marker for the beach as you approach the swimmers taking the plunge alongside it. At low tide, you can walk across the concreted shoreline, down the steps, and into the sea, where most people can keep their feet on the bottom and head above the water. At high tide, the sea swallows most of this area, so you need to be a confident swimmer. There's an outdoor changing area and very limited parking.

Food and Accommodations

Hatch Coffee

4 Glasthule Terrace, Sandycove; Instagram @hatchcoffee; Mon.-Fri. 7am-5pm, Sat.-Sun. 8am-5pm; from €4

On sunny days around high tide, Hatch Coffee usually has a line of sea swimmers looking to warm up with a coffee. This sleek modern shop whips up 240-ml (8-oz) flat whites, iced coffees, and pour-over brews from their machines beside the exposed redbrick wall. There's seating inside for 20, but if the weather is good, grab a seat on the bench outside. Don't forget the pastries—the cinnamon buns are great.

Cavistons

56 Glasthule Rd., Sandycove; tel. 1/280-9245; www.cavistons.com; Wed.-Thurs. noon-9pm, Fri.-Sat. noon-9:30pm, Sun. 1pm-8pm; from €25

Cavistons has two strings to its bow: Firstly, it's a refined seafood restaurant that uses freshly caught produce from the waters around Dublin. This reliance on local

Sea Swimming

sea swimming at the Forty Foot

Sea swimming has become incredibly popular in Ireland, and not just during summer—you'll regularly see people wading into the water in the depths of winter. The benefits are irrefutable, with lots of people building their day (and personality) around tide times to get their cold-water fix. Take the plunge and warm up with a coffee afterward, or if you're lucky, there might be a sauna nearby.

BEST PLACES TO SEA SWIM

We're an island nation, so thankfully there are endless amounts of places to go for a swim. But there are some standout spots:

- **The Forty Foot, Dublin:** This spot is arguably the most well-known sea swimming spot in the country thanks to its close location to the city, stairs down into the sheltered water, and rocks to dive in from (page 94).
- **Pollock Holes, Clare:** The might Atlantic Ocean might be roaring, but the water in the Pollock Holes is always calm. These natural pools have been carved out of the reef and fill at high tide to create beautiful pools for relaxing dips (page 287).
- **Salthill, Galway:** Leap into the sea from the iconic diving tower here and join the army of brave locals who swim in the Atlantic. Or, if you'd rather keep your feet dry, grab a seat along the promenade and watch others splash into the water (page 307).

SAFETY TIPS

Sea swimming can be dangerous, especially if you've never tried it before. The water is always cold; even on the hottest summer day you'll be lucky if the temperature gets above 15°C (59°F). It's important to take your time and ease yourself into the water to prevent the shock you get from diving in. Although there are a dizzying array of beaches to swim at, few are regularly patrolled by lifeguards. If you do decide to swim at a spot without lifeguards, choose a place where locals are also swimming—tides and currents can be very strong here.

fishing means the menu can change day to day. Expect dishes like shellfish tagliatelle and wild cod with shiitake mushrooms. Cavistons is also an upscale grocery store that focuses on local producers. Find freshly filleted fish, artisanal cheese, and seasonal vegetables. There's also a deli to grab a sandwich, soup, or salad to go and enjoy by the sea.

Hartley's

1 Harbour Rd., Dún Laoghaire; tel. 1/280-6767; www.hartleys.ie; Tues.-Thurs. 12:30pm-10pm, Fri.-Sat. 12:30pm-10:30pm, Sun. 12:30pm-9pm; from €25

In a beautifully restored Victorian railway station building on the Dún Laoghaire waterfront, it's easy to see why Hartley's always has a crowd. With views of Dún Laoghaire Harbour and a menu that focuses on local produce, Hartley's is connected with its locality. The beer-battered fish-and-chips served with pea puree is one of the most popular dishes. Plan your visit Tuesday-Friday 5pm-7pm and you can enjoy 2-for-1 on the 10 house cocktails.

Haddington House

9-12 Haddington Terrace, Dún Laoghaire; tel. 1/280-1810; www.haddingtonhouse.ie; €175

In a Victorian townhouse that overlooks the sea, Haddington House is a luxury boutique hotel that surpasses its three-star rating. The building has been renovated and upgraded over the years but retains its heritage with large sash windows, a wrought-iron fence, and detailed wood paneling. It stands out because of the staff's hands-on approach: They organize walking tours of Dún Laoghaire, can bring you down to the Forty Foot and show you the best place to get in, and even join you on a run along their favorite 5-km (3-mi) route.

Getting There and Around

The easiest and quickest way to get to Dún Laoghaire or Sandycove from Dublin is taking the DART. Trains run frequently from Connolly, Tara Street, and Pearse Street Stations. The journey to **Dún Laoghaire DART Station** (Crofton Rd.) takes 20 minutes; stay on for one more stop to reach **Sandycove DART Station** (Summerhill Rd.). Several Dublin Bus routes, including Route 7 and Route 46a, run from the city center to Dún Laoghaire. The journey can take 40-60 minutes, depending on traffic.

By car, head southeast from Dublin City via the N11 or R118 roads, then follow signs for Dún Laoghaire. The drive takes 25-35 minutes, but parking can be limited in busy areas, particularly on sunny weekends.

DALKEY AND KILLINEY

It's hard to describe the adjacent villages of Dalkey and Killiney as anything other than upscale. These villages have an old-money feel that's on full display on the main streets, home to premium artisanal shops and expensive restaurants. Nature is another reason why people live and visit here, with brilliant sea swimming spots and parks just a short stroll from the villages.

Sights

Dalkey Island

The 9-ha (22-acre) island, just off the coast from Dalkey, has history, wildlife, and amazing views that make people want to sail or kayak over. This grassy lump of a rock is a fantastic place to visit for a few hours to explore the rolling hills, ruins, and sea cliffs.

There's evidence that the island was inhabited as far back as 6,000 years ago, as axes and pots have been found. It became a religious hot spot during the early Christian period, when St. Begnet's Church was built, and the crossing was seen as a mini pilgrimage. The ruins of the church are still here. In more recent times, a Martello tower was built as a defensive structure against a potential invasion by Napoleon. You can admire the tower from the outside, but it's not open to visit.

Wildlife lovers will be spoiled. Wandering the island and munching on grass is a trip of wild goats that are quite friendly, although

1: views from Dalkey Island **2:** swimming at Vico Baths

1

2

they can be unpredictable, so keep your distance. The island's rabbits can be hard to spot. Seabirds like gulls, cormorants, and guillemots take advantage of the small rugged cliffs to nest and scour for food. In the water, it's common to see dolphins and porpoises, and between the island and the mainland, seals often play with kayakers and paddleboarders.

Access to Dalkey Island is by boat or kayaking the 300 m (990 ft) from the mainland. Guided kayaking tours (3 hours; €78 pp) from **Kayaking.ie** (www.kayaking.ie) run three times daily. Another option is a boat ride over from Coliemore Harbour (€10 adults, €5 children round-trip); get in touch with **Ken the Ferryman** (www.kentheferryman.ie; daily 10am-6pm). There are no services on Dalkey Island, so bring everything you'll need, and use the restroom before you go.

Hiking and Walking

Killiney Hill Walk Loop

Distance: *2.7 km (1.7 mi) loop*
Duration: *1 hour*
Elevation gain: *111 m (365 ft)*
Effort: *Easy*
Trailhead: *Killiney Hill Car Park*

For a short, sweet walk in nature, you can't go wrong with this loop trail. The route can be walked in either direction from the car park, but most go counterclockwise so that the majority of the climb is up front and the views from the top of Killiney Hill appear sooner. The well-marked paths are a mix of tarmac lower down and earth toward the top, and they lead through sections of woodland and open grassy areas. From the top, beside the 18th-century obelisk, the views stretch across the Irish Sea, north toward the city, and southwest toward the Wicklow Mountains.

Beaches and Sea Swimming

Vico Baths

Vico Rd.

Imagine performing the perfect dive into the Irish Sea as yachts sail beyond and the DART passes in the hills above. That's sea swimming at Vico Baths. Walk through the small entrance in the wall along Vico Road, down the steps, and along the trail to the small changing area in the rocky cliffs. The water is deep but manages to remain calm in good weather, which makes it a good choice for confident swimmers. There's a diving area, ladders and stairs to get out of the water, and sometimes tide pools in the rocks after high tide. There's no parking, so you have to find a spot on the nearby street.

Coliemore Harbour

Coliemore Rd.

Coliemore Harbour is a good option for swimmers to walk into the sea rather than jump, although that's an option here also. When the tide retreats, a small sandy beach is revealed in the harbor, and as it's south-facing, it acts as a sun-trap. When the tide is in, people jump from the stone walls of the harbor into the water. Be careful, though, as it's a working harbor with boats constantly coming in and out. On-street parking is available but not in abundance.

Shopping

hark.

42 Castle St.; http://hark.ie; Mon.-Sat. 10am-5:30pm

hark. is a family-run business that sells timeless homeware and lifestyle pieces with a focus on lasting quality. Most pieces are large and not suitcase-friendly, but the stationery section has a good choice of notepads and pens that make nice mementos.

The Gutter Bookshop

20 Railway Rd.; tel. 1/285-9633; http://gutterbookshop.com; Mon.-Sat. 10am-6pm, Sun. noon-5pm

Owned by passionate bookworms, the Gutter Bookshop is much loved and has a cozy feel. The original shop opened in Temple Bar in 2009, and the Dalkey store opened in 2013, where they celebrate Irish authors and have a wide range of books for all interests.

Food and Accommodations

Mug's Café

61A Castle St.; Instagram @mugscafedalkey; Mon.-Fri. 6:30am-6pm, Sat.-Sun. 7:30am-6pm; from €7

Mug's Café sums up the Dalkey lifestyle with its beachy vibe, proper coffees, and piping-hot toasties that are perfect after a swim in the sea. Food specials change regularly, but the bacon and cream cheese bagel and turkey with brie sandwich are staples. Seating inside is limited, especially on weekends, but there is plenty of public seating outside.

The Dalkey Duck

Castle St.; tel. 1/552-8605; Instagram @dalkeyduck; Sat. noon-12:30am, Sun. noon-11pm, Mon.-Thurs. 2pm-11:30pm, Fri. 2pm-12:30am; from €17

The Dalkey Duck is a busy pub in the heart of Dalkey, known for its food, bustling atmosphere, and live music. The interior is what you'd expect from an Irish pub in an old building with lots of wooden furniture, comfy seating, and carpeted floors. The menu follows this theme with classic pub fare like fish-and-chips, beef burgers, and chicken wings. Outside, the large open beer garden, surrounded by plants, feels like a park. Live music is played outside on weekends, with other performances inside.

Fitzpatrick Castle Hotel

Killiney Hill Rd.; tel. 1/230-5400; www.fitzpatrickcastle.com; €220

Fitzpatrick Castle Hotel in Killiney is an 18th-century castle that offers a historic stay in the stunning surrounds of Killiney Hill. The castle's luxurious past is the inspiration for the interiors, with plush golden furniture, an ornate bar stocked with fine spirits, and four-poster beds in the pricier rooms. There are 113 rooms and a leisure center with a 20-m (66-ft) spa-like swimming pool lit with soft mood lighting. Pop into any of the three restaurants and two bars on-site.

Getting There and Around

Dalkey and Killiney are on the DART line, the easiest and best way to get here from Connolly, Tara Street, and Pearse Street Stations in Dublin. The ride to **Dalkey DART Station** (Ardeevin Rd.) takes 25 minutes and **Killiney** (Station Rd.), the next stop, 28 minutes. Dublin Bus Route 59 and Route 111 go to Dalkey and Killiney, but the traffic can get congested, taking much longer than the DART, often around 1 hour.

To drive, take the N11 southbound from Dublin and exit at the R118 road for Dalkey, or continue to the R119 for Killiney, which should take 1 hour.

Dublin Mountains

The Dublin Mountains are sometimes overlooked for the Wicklow Mountains, but in reality, they're the same mountains in a different county. There are no major towns or villages with pubs and restaurants; come instead for the outdoor activities, forests, and trails.

MARLAY PARK

Grange Rd.; www.dlrcoco.ie; daily 9am-9pm; free

Rivaling Phoenix Park in the city for the best park in Dublin, Marlay Park is a tranquil 120-ha (300-acre) park that spreads from the suburb of Rathfarnham to the base of the Dublin Mountains. Throughout are beautifully maintained lawns, mature woodlands with leafy walking trails, manicured gardens, and sports fields.

One of the park's highlights is Marlay House, an 18th-century Georgian mansion that adds a touch of historical allure. Marlay Park is well suited to families thanks to two playgrounds, a summertime miniature railway, and a weekend farmers market with local produce.

The park is also well known for hosting concerts during summer, with bands like

Radiohead, Hozier, and the Red Hot Chili Peppers having played here. If you'd rather spend time in nature, the famous Wicklow Way trailhead starts in the park.

Getting There

You can get a Dublin Bus to Marlay Park on Routes 16, 116, or 161.

TICKNOCK FOREST

Ticknock Rd.; www.coillte.ie

Find 10 km (6 mi) of walking trails and 15 km (9 mi) of mountain bike trails in Ticknock, made memorable by stunning views of Dublin City, Dublin Bay, and the Wicklow Mountains. The forest features the iconic Three Rock Mountain and Two Rock Mountain, topped by the Fairy Castle, a Neolithic passage tomb. Given its proximity to the city and Marlay Park, Ticknock is a popular spot with outdoorsy people.

Hiking and Walking

Three Rock Loop

Distance: *3.5 km (2.2 mi) loop*
Duration: *1 hour*
Elevation gain: *135 m (440 ft)*
Effort: *Easy-moderate*
Trailhead: *Ticknock Forest*

There's parking at the trailhead, and as you start the climb up the hillside on the paved surface, you'll spot mountain bikers on trails in the woods. Toward the top you can stay on the smooth surface or take a singletrack trail to the summit. This is where you'll see the granite formations that give Three Rock its name, along with views over the city. From here, the route loops back down to the trailhead at the car park.

Mountain Biking

Ticknock MTB Trails

Ticknock Forest

The mountain bike trails at Ticknock have come on leaps and bounds in recent years, with six long sanctioned trails as well as a number of trails made by riders. The sanctioned trails are great for beginners, as most are wide and don't have tricky technical features. The climbing is all on a paved road, so there's no grueling off-road pedal to the top. Rentals and a bike wash are available at Biking.ie at the trailhead.

Biking.ie

Ticknock Forest; tel. 1/206-3919; www.biking.ie; daily 9:30am-4:30pm

Found at the trailhead in Ticknock, Biking.ie is the launchpad to riding the trails. Guided lessons for beginners and advanced riders are available (from €115). Lessons are two hours, and although rentals are not included, they will help you set up your suspension. Full-suspension bikes are recommended, and if you don't have a bike, rentals are available (from €45, e-bikes from €80).

Getting There

Ticknock is easily accessible by car from the city. Drive south on the N11, then turn right for Sandyford and cross over the M50. Finally, turn right onto Blackglen Road, which leads to Ticknock. The drive is 15 km (9 mi) and takes 45 minutes. Parking is available on-site.

GLENCULLEN ADVENTURE PARK (THE GAP)

Glencullen Adventure Park; tel. 1/294-2782; www.thegap.ie; Wed. and Fri.-Sun. 9am-5pm, Thurs. 9am-9pm; from €25

The GAP, also known as Glencullen Adventure Park, is the closest thing you'll find to a bike park in the Dublin Mountains. There's the option to get lifts to the top in the van (half-day €25, full day €40) to ride the 35 downhill trails, a good mix of wide, flowy, jump trails and technical trails with tricky root sections and gnarly rock gardens. The GAP is best suited to intermediate riders, although there are trails for beginners and advanced riders. You can rent a full-suspension mountain bike (€40). When you're finished for the day, stop by the Kitchen Café for a burger, a hot drink, or a sweet treat.

Getting There

The GAP is a 45-minute, 35-km (22-mi) drive south on the M50 to exit 14, then west on the R113, which merges with the Ballyedmonduff Road to the GAP.

HELLFIRE CLUB

Mountpelier Hill, Killakee Rd.; free

The mysterious and spooky Hellfire Club in the Dublin Mountains is home to myriad intriguing stories that attract walkers to the Dublin Mountains. It was originally built as a hunting lodge in the 18th century by William Conolly, a powerful politician who quickly brought an infamous reputation to the stone building he originally named Mount Pelier.

The building became associated with the Hellfire Club, a group of wealthy young men known for their debauchery, hedonism, and interest in the occult. Soon stories of devil worship, black masses, and the supernatural began to circulate. The most famous story is about a stranger who turned up unannounced to a poker game at the lodge. During the game, a member dropped his cards, and when he bent down to pick them up, saw the stranger had hooves instead of feet, revealing him to be the devil. The building is named after the group to this day.

There's parking for 70 cars on-site and a coffee truck (daily 7:30am-5pm) selling hot drinks and treats.

Hiking and Walking

Today, the Hellfire Club is a popular destination for walkers of all ages, with two loop walks.

Forest Loop Trail

Distance: *5.5 km (3.4 mi) loop*
Duration: *1.5 hours*
Elevation gain: *205 m (672 ft)*
Effort: *Moderate*
Trailhead: *Hellfire Car Park*

The Forest Loop Trail is a loop of the whole forest and gives you a good stretch of the legs.

Mountpelier Loop Trail

Distance: *4 km (2.5 mi) loop*
Duration: *1 hour*
Elevation gain: *157 m (515 ft)*
Effort: *Moderate*
Trailhead: *Hellfire Car Park*

The Mountpelier Loop Trail leads past the Hellfire Club and to the top of Mountpelier Hill, where there are views over the city and Dublin Bay.

Food

The Merry Ploughboy

Edmondstown Rd.; tel. 1/493-1495; www.mpbpub.com; Mon.-Thurs. 12:30pm-11:30pm, Fri.-Sat. 12:30pm-12:30am, Sun. 12:30pm-11pm; from €18

Inside the cottage-like Merry Ploughboy is a lively and traditional gastropub with amazing views over Dublin and live music every Friday-Saturday night. They host an Irish Night Show from time to time where the owners play trad music with Irish dancers performing. The menu is steaks, burgers, and vegetarian salads served in the restaurant or the bar.

Getting There

Take the M50 south and follow exit 12 onto Ballycullen Road, which leads into the mountains to the Hellfire Club. It's a 24-km (15-mi) drive that takes 45 minutes.

BOHERNABREENA RESERVOIR

The Bohernabreena Reservoir was built in the late 19th century to provide water for local mills and to control flooding. Today, it supplies drinking water to parts of Dublin. If you don't fancy the full loop walk, you can walk to the dam from the car park in 5 minutes.

Hiking and Walking

Bohernabreena Reservoir Loop

Distance: *8.5 km (5.3 mi) loop*
Duration: *1.5 hours*
Elevation gain: *Negligible*
Effort: *Easy*
Trailhead: *Ballinascorney Rd.*

1

2

This walk takes you through a stunning and serene area of natural beauty between Wicklow Mountains National Park and the Dublin Mountains. The walk starts and ends at the small car parks and follows the paved path alongside the River Dodder, passing the reservoir, which is surrounded by lush woodlands. A slight detour lets you walk on top of the dam, which has amazing views across the water to the mountains. Dogs must be kept on a leash.

Getting There

Drive south on the M50 to exit 12, then west on the R113 road, continuing on the R114 to the reservoir. This 26-km (16-mi) drive takes 45 minutes.

1: Fairy Castle atop Ticknock Forest **2:** Hellfire Club in winter

Around Dublin

You don't have to go far from Dublin to find history, landscapes, and food that rivals anywhere else in the country, if not the world. The mountains and valleys surrounding the capital aren't as well-known as some of the sights on the west coast, but you'll be missing a trick if you overlook the Wicklow Mountains, Boyne Valley, and Cooley Peninsula on the way elsewhere.

History is what defines these parts of Ireland. The mythological epic Táin Bó Cúailnge battle in the Cooley Mountains, the mystifying tombs in the Boyne Valley, and the monastic city in Glendalough have stories from every era of Ireland's past to be discovered. The best way to learn about what happened here is by getting outside and onto any of the great trails and greenways. The Wicklow Mountains and Cooley

Highlights

Look for ★ to find recommended sights, activities, dining, and lodging.

★ **Wicklow Mountains National Park:** Plan outdoor adventures on the hiking trails and visit historic religious sites in this national park, easily reached from Dublin city center (page 114).

★ **Glendalough:** Visit the stunning lakes, trails, and St. Kevin's monastic city in the idyllic surroundings of Glendalough, high in the Wicklow Mountains (page 122).

★ **Battle of the Boyne Site:** Walk the grounds of Oldbridge House, site of the epic Battle of the Boyne, and discover how the battle was won—and how it still shapes life in Ireland today (page 128).

★ **Brú na Bóinne:** Older than the Pyramids of Giza and home to ancient mysteries from the megalithic era, the tombs at Brú na Bóinne are truly astounding (page 132).

★ **Slane Castle and Distillery:** Find out what world-famous rock bands have taken to the stage at this gorgeous riverside castle and reserve a tour of their whiskey distillery (page 134).

★ **Emerald Park:** Feel the thrill of riding Ireland's only wooden roller coaster in a rural Irish theme park that you'll share with exotic animals in the zoo (page 137).

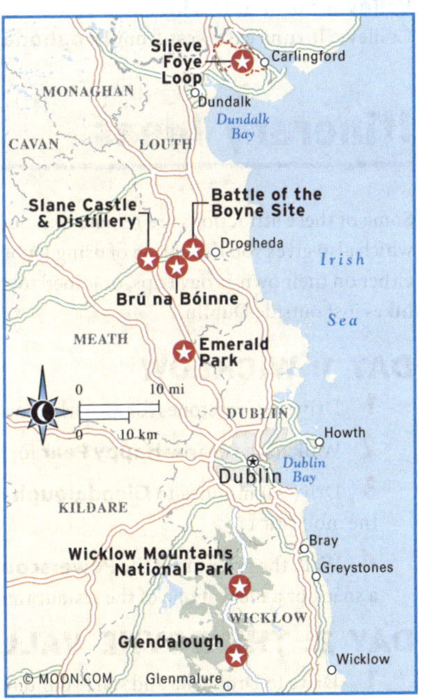

★ **Slieve Foye Loop:** Hike up Slieve Foye, the tallest peak in the Cooley Mountains, and get unbelievable views of Carlingford Lough, the Cooley Peninsula, and the Mourne Mountains in Northern Ireland (page 143).

Mountains are best for experienced hikers, as the land can be quite steep and trails can be challenging. Casual walkers and families will find easier routes along the waterfront in Bray and on the banks of the Boyne in Drogheda and Slane.

In such a compact area, a two-hour drive from Carlingford in the north to the southernmost hub in Greystones, you can see three vastly different regions without the effort you might normally expect for so much reward.

ORIENTATION

The areas of interest around Dublin run from the gorgeous **Cooley Mountains,** in the north in County Louth, on the border with Northern Ireland, to County Wicklow in the south, where you'll find the **Wicklow Mountains National Park** and the seaside towns of **Bray** and **Greystones.** The **Boyne Valley** is north of Dublin but south of the Cooleys. It runs east-west from **Drogheda** in County Louth to **Slane** in County Meath and beyond.

PLANNING YOUR TIME

The amount of time you spend in this region depends on how active you plan to be. A lot of the hikes and walks can easily fill a day. Two days in each of the three areas give enough time to combine some historical sights and hikes and visit the best restaurants. Day trips from Dublin to **Wicklow** are popular, but these trips are quite busy, and you miss out on experiencing peaceful evenings in the mountains or by the coast. It's possible to visit **Carlingford** for a day and squeeze in a hike and a meal, but at a slower pace you can soak up the atmosphere. If you're pressed for time, you can prioritize visiting **Newgrange** at the **Brú na Bóinne Visitor Centre** on a day trip from Dublin, but history lovers should plan to spend a night or two to see all the important sites in **Slane** and **Drogheda.**

Itinerary Ideas

Some of these attractions are remote and not served by public transport, so it's best to drive, which also gives you the option of using Dublin as your base. These suggested itineraries work either on their own as day trips, or joined together to see some of the best historical sights and hikes just outside Dublin.

DAY 1: WICKLOW

1 Drive to Greystones for an early morning swim at **Greystones South Beach.**

2 Walk to the nearby **Happy Pear** for a healthy vegan smoothie bowl for breakfast.

3 Drive 40 minutes to **Glendalough** in the Wicklow Mountains and wander around the monastic city.

4 Walk the grounds of the **Powerscourt Estate** and see their extensive gardens. Have a snack or a meal at one of the restaurants before heading back.

DAY 2: THE BOYNE VALLEY

1 Drive to Drogheda and start your day with the American pancake stack at **Five Good Things.**

Previous: sheep in the Cooley Mountains; Brú na Bóinne; Glendalough.

Around Dublin

Itinerary Ideas

2 Wander across the town to **St. Peter's Church** and see the head of Saint Oliver.

3 Drive 15 minutes to the **Brú na Bóinne** and enter a megalithic tomb that's over 5,000 years old. Make sure to book your ticket online in advance.

4 Continue the drive another 10 minutes to Slane and visit the famous **Slane Castle and Distillery.**

5 Stop into **Boyle's of Slane** and see live bands and trad music sessions.

DAY 3: DUNDALK AND COOLEY PENINSULA

1 Drive to Dundalk and see the large-scale **murals** that world-renowned street artists have painted.

2 Stop by **Strandfield** on the way to Carlingford and have an egg stack sandwich for lunch.

3 Lace up you hiking boots in Carlingford and set off on the **Slieve Foye Loop** for a 3-4-hour hike that shows off the best views on the peninsula.

4 Book a table at **Ghan House** for dinner and order from their ever-changing menu that uses fresh ingredients from their garden.

5 Experience the craic agus ceol (music and fun) at **PJ O'Hare's** and enjoy a pint of Guinness in this very lively pub.

Wicklow

Mountains, the sea, historic sights, and a national park all within easy access from Dublin—it's no wonder Wicklow is such a good place to visit. There's a good chance that you've seen Wicklow on TV or at the movies, as production crews make the most of the stunning backdrops for their sets. Hikers, walkers, and cyclists take full advantage of the impressive trail network in Wicklow Mountains National Park. If you're more a coastal person, there are a host of beach towns like Bray, with groups of sea swimmers braving the chilly waters throughout the year. Given that it's such a sought-after county, Wicklow has a bougie feel in parts, where the culinary scene and prices of Dublin have made their way south to towns like Greystones and Enniskerry. Lots of places try to offer visitors the best of everything, and thanks to the natural landscapes, food scene, and proximity to the capital, Wicklow does a far better job than most.

ORIENTATION

County Wicklow lies to the south of Dublin, where the Dublin Mountains turn into the Wicklow Mountains and affluent seaside towns like **Bray** and **Greystones** continue down the Wicklow coast. The **M11** road runs almost parallel to the coast, with the sea on one side and the **Wicklow Mountains National Park** on the other, where you'll find gateway towns like **Enniskerry, Roundwood,** and **Ballinastoe.** Toward the southern end of the county is where you'll find **Glendalough.**

BRAY AND GREYSTONES

Bray and Greystones feel like two cousins, each with their own personalities, but there's an undeniable link between the two. Greystones is the more affluent town, with the main thoroughfare filled with vegan cafés, flat white-drinking sea swimmers, and boutiques.

Bray is the older cousin, more traditional with waterfront pubs, a bandstand on the promenade, and a feeling that most of the residents have lived here for generations. The towns are only a 12-minute train ride apart, so check them both out.

Sights

Bray Seafront Promenade

The Bray Seafront Promenade was built during the Victorian era when it was decided that Bray should be a seaside resort, and that Victorian influence is still seen today. On the 1.6-km (1-mi) stretch alongside **Bray Beach,** which starts at James Joyce's childhood home and ends at the foot of **Bray Head,** you'll see plenty of historic ironwork as well as a large bandstand. Walking the promenade is a good way to get your bearings in Bray, as the majority of the pubs, restaurants, and sights can be seen.

Kilruddery House & Gardens

Southern Cross, Bray; tel. 1/286-3405; www.killruddery.com; Tues.-Sun. 9:30am-5pm

This historic house in the Wicklow countryside has been home to nobility since it was built in the 17th century. The current iteration was built in the Tudor revival style and has some fascinating architectural features, including the orangery in the garden where exotic plants grow. The garden also has sprawling woodlands among its 320 ha (800 acres) and formal terraced gardens to explore. Lunch is served at the **Grain Store,** and there's a grab-and-go coffee shop as well as the **Pizza Shed.** There are three tours daily (Tues.-Sun.; €6) with tickets are sold on a first come, first served basis.

Hiking and Walking

Bray Head Cross Walk

Distance: *10 km (6.2 mi) round-trip*
Duration: *2 hours*
Elevation gain: *240 m (790 ft)*
Effort: *Moderate*
Trailhead: *Bray Seafront Promenade*

This popular coastal trail starts at the picturesque **Bray Seafront Promenade** and winds up to the summit of **Bray Head,** a prominent hill with a tall cross at the top. You're treated to wide-open views of the Irish Sea, the Wicklow Mountains, and the town of Bray below. The path is well-marked and suitable for various fitness levels, making it a good choice for active families and casual walkers. Along the route you'll see green hills, rugged cliffs, and the iconic **Bray Head cross,** a prominent landmark that has stood on the summit since 1950.

The Great Sugarloaf Loop

Distance: *6.5 km (4 mi) round-trip*
Duration: *2.5 hours*
Elevation gain: *390 m (1,280 ft)*
Effort: *Moderate*
Trailhead: *Kilmacanogue GAA grounds*

The Sugarloaf is an easily recognizable peak thanks to its pointed top among gently rolling mountains. Early on, the trail turns upward, where small trees hang over and shrubs line the side. Eventually the trees end and the shrubs take over, providing expansive views of the Wicklow countryside. The rocky trail continues toward the peak, where it turns into an open mountain scramble rather than a clearly defined trail. There are some sections where you'll be climbing small rock features rather than hiking. From the top you'll see Dublin, Wicklow Mountains National Park, and enormous views of the Irish Sea. When you're ready to return, take the same route down.

Beaches and Water Sports

Bray Beach South Promenade

This stretch of beach runs from Bray Head to Bray Harbour and spans the length of Bray Promenade. Expect a typical Victorian seafront experience, with people sunning themselves when the weather is good, kids playing in the playground, and ice cream vans selling treats. The beach is a mix of stone and sand, and you can swim in the sea with lifeguards on duty during summer.

Greystones South Beach

Sea swimming began to boom in Ireland during the pandemic, but it's been a popular activity at some beaches, like Greystones South Beach, for far longer. There's a strong sea swimming community bolstered by local celebrity chefs from the Happy Pear joining sunrise swims. The beach itself is a mix of sand and stones and runs for 1 km (0.6 mi) from the south side of the town. There are public toilets and a children's playground nearby, but dogs are not allowed on the beach during summer.

Bray Adventures

Strand Rd.; tel. 87/366-9999; www.brayadventures.ie

Making the most of their seaside location, Bray Adventures has a great choice of water-based activities. First-timers can take things

1
2
3
4

easy with gentle kayaking or stand-up paddleboard (SUP) tours that teach the basics. For a more thrilling day out, the coasteering tour sees you clambering along the cliffs by the sea and jumping into the water below. Or if you'd rather keep your feet dry, they also run hill walking and rock climbing trips as well.

Festivals and Events

The Bray Jazz Festival

tel. 1/272-4030; www.brayjazz.com; weekend of the 1st Mon. in May

Taking place over the May Bank Holiday weekend, the Bray Jazz Festival brings a diverse lineup of international acts to Wicklow. There's a nice mix of events at the festival, with small shows in the informal setting of **The Harbour Bar** and better-known acts on stage at the Mermaid Arts Center. Tickets can be bought online in advance or at the door.

Shopping

JuJu

3 La Touche Place, Greystones; tel. 1/201-6723; www.juju.ie; Mon.-Sat. 10am-6pm

This small women's wear boutique focuses on finding offbeat creations from the international fashion world, and it has become a destination on the shopping scene. The bold garments sit alongside more timeless pieces that can be worn every day.

Halfway Up the Stairs

Malvern, La Touche Place, Greystones; tel. 1/287-3002; https://halfwayupthestairs.ie; Mon.-Sat. 10am-5:30pm

This children's bookshop is stocked with a diverse range of books sure to stoke the imagination in young readers. There's a good choice of books from Irish authors as well as some Irish-language books. It was voted Bookshop of the Year in 2023, and the staff are willing to help you find the right book.

1: Bray Seafront Promenade **2:** Bray Beach **3:** Bray Head Cross Walk **4:** Kilruddery House & Gardens

Food

The Fat Fox

1 Trafalgar Rd., Greystones; 87/933-5093; www.thefatfox.ie; Mon.-Fri. 7am-4pm, Sat. 8am-5pm, Sun. 8am-4pm; from €4

It's hard to miss the bright-green exterior of the Fat Fox near South Beach in Greystones. The large spacious café has a trendy white and pink interior where they serve house-roasted coffee and homemade cakes. Treat highlights include the tiramisu pots, apple brioche, and enormous almond croissants. Visiting after a dip in the sea is a dream Greystones combo.

Pizza Shed at Kilruddery

Southern Cross, Bray; tel. 1/286-3405; www.pizza.killruddery.com; daily noon-6pm; from €14

The historic Kilruddery House has a modern pizza restaurant housed in an old stone building on its grounds. The Pizza Shed is an informal place to eat, with large rustic wooden tables great for families. They serve half pizzas for kids. The menu is small, with seven pizzas, including the classics and a vegan special.

The Happy Pear

Church Rd., Greystones; tel. 1/287-3655; www.thehappypear.ie; daily 9am-5pm; from €15

Twin brothers David and Stephen Flynn are the poster boys for the active vegan lifestyle in Ireland thanks to their café and media presence. The café has been open over 20 years and serves tasty, healthy vegan dishes for brunch and lunch. Top picks include the lentil lasagna, Buddha bowl, and sweet potato curry. There's also a fruit and veg shop on the premises that stocks grab-and-go lunches. If you've been won over by the Happy Pear, you can book a spot on any of their vegan cooking or baking courses.

Chakra by Jaipur

Church Rd., Greystones; tel. 1/201-7228; www.chakra.ie; Tues.-Thurs. 5pm-10pm, Fri.-Sat. 5pm-10:30pm, Sun. 2pm-9pm; from €26

Don't let the shopping center setting of Chakra by Jaipur put you off; the food is of fine-dining standard. This restaurant has received widespread praise for serving beautifully plated meals from all regions of India in a bright modern dining room with colorful furniture. There are six vegetarian choices along with familiar dishes with a twist.

Bars and Nightlife

The Harbour Bar

1 Strand Rd., Bray; tel. 1/286-2274; www.theharbourbar.ie; Tues.-Thurs. and Sun.-Mon. noon-11:30pm, Fri.-Sat. noon-12:30am

The Harbour Bar is a proper local pub on the northern end of the promenade near the harbor. Inside is a rambling series of small rooms clad in dark wood. They serve popular beers on tap as well as some from the local Wicklow Wolf Brewery. There's a large covered outdoor area where you can order from the small pub grub menu. Check out the event listings, as there's music four nights a week and regular comedy shows.

The Beach House

The Harbour, Greystones; tel. 1/287-4623; www.beachhousepub.ie; Tues.-Thurs. and Sun.-Mon. noon-11:30pm, Fri.-Sat. noon-12:30am

The Beach House in Greystones comprises five quite different areas, giving you the choice to find the spot that's right for you. Through the front doors is the lounge, with a large circular bar and tables where you can order from their seafood-inspired pub grub menu. Dann's Bar feels like a trip back in time with its stone floor and private snug, while Fisherman's Bar is a small space reminiscent of country bars from days gone by. On a sunny day, there's a beer garden out back, but you'll really want to be on the front terrace, where you can smell the sea air and watch boats come into the harbor.

Accommodations

The Martello Hotel

47 Strand Rd., Bray; tel. 1/286-8000; www.themartello.ie; €115

The Martello Hotel, beside the bandstand on the Bray Promenade, is a good choice for self-catering. As well as having 30 en suite rooms, there are 17 one-bedroom apartments that can sleep four and have fully-equipped kitchens. If you don't want to cook, pop down to the gastropub for breakfast, lunch, or dinner made with local and seasonal ingredients. The Martello Hotel welcomes group bookings.

The Palm

Strand Rd., Bray; tel. 1/286-0668; www.thepalmbray.ie; €175

Better known as a gastropub in Bray, The Palm is also a small boutique hotel with 12 rooms decorated with wooden parquet floors, exposed brick walls, and modern tasteful furnishings. There are standard and deluxe double rooms available, some with sea views. As it's a small hotel, the amenities are limited, but the lively cocktail bar and bottomless brunches in the restaurant downstairs should keep you busy.

Getting There and Around

Bray and Greystones are well connected towns, and the most popular transport from Dublin is the DART. This rail service to **Bray DART Station** (Florence Rd.) runs every 10-20 minutes during peak hours and 15-30 minutes off-peak. **Greystones DART Station** (Church Rd.) has fewer trains, every 15-30 minutes throughout the day. Round-trip journeys from Pearse Station in Dublin cost €5 to Bray and €7.50 to Greystones. There's also the Route 155 Dublin Bus, which ends at Bray DART Station.

Driving is straightforward, as you take the M50 south to exit 5 for Bray. For Greystones, continue south to the N11, where you'll see signs for the town.

★ WICKLOW MOUNTAINS NATIONAL PARK

Wicklow Mountains National Park is a beautiful and wild area of 210 sq km (80 sq mi) that begins at the Dublin-Wicklow border and runs south to the peak of Lugnaquilla. The park draws an enormous number of people from Dublin and surrounding areas to hike the trails and mountain bike at the trail

Wicklow Mountains National Park

To Marlay Park
Enniskerry
POWERSCOURT HOTEL
POWERSCOURT ESTATE
OLD MILITARY RD
WICKLOW MOUNTAINS NATIONAL PARK
Wicklow Way
Djouce Wood
Powerscourt Waterfall
DJOUCE WOOD LAKE CAR PARK
DJOUCE MOUNTAIN
The Sally Gap
Djouce Mountain
Wicklow Mountains National Park
Wicklow Mtns
JB MALONE MEMORIAL
Lough Tay
Ballinastoe Wood
BIKING.IE
THE SALLY GAP
VARTRY TRAILS CAR PARK
WICKLOW
ROUNDWOOD INN
THE COACH HOUSE
Roundwood
Glenmacnass Waterfall
0 1 mi
0 1 km
Scenic Route
OLD MILITARY RD
Way
Wicklow
SPINC & GLENEALO VALLEY
MINER'S ROAD WALK
GREEN ROAD WALK
See Detail
GLENDALOUGH CAFÉ
Glendalough Upper Lake
GLENDALOUGH
Laragh
Poulanass Waterfall
To Glenmalure Lodge

To Upper Car Park
THE GLENDALOUGH HOTEL
ST. KEVIN'S KITCHEN
Glendalough Bus Stop
ST. KEVIN'S WAY-PILGRIM PATH
GLENDALOUGH
GLENDALOUGH INTERNATIONAL HOSTEL
GLENDALOUGH VISITOR CENTRE
ST. KEVIN'S MONASTIC CITY
Wicklow Way
0 100 yds
0 100 m

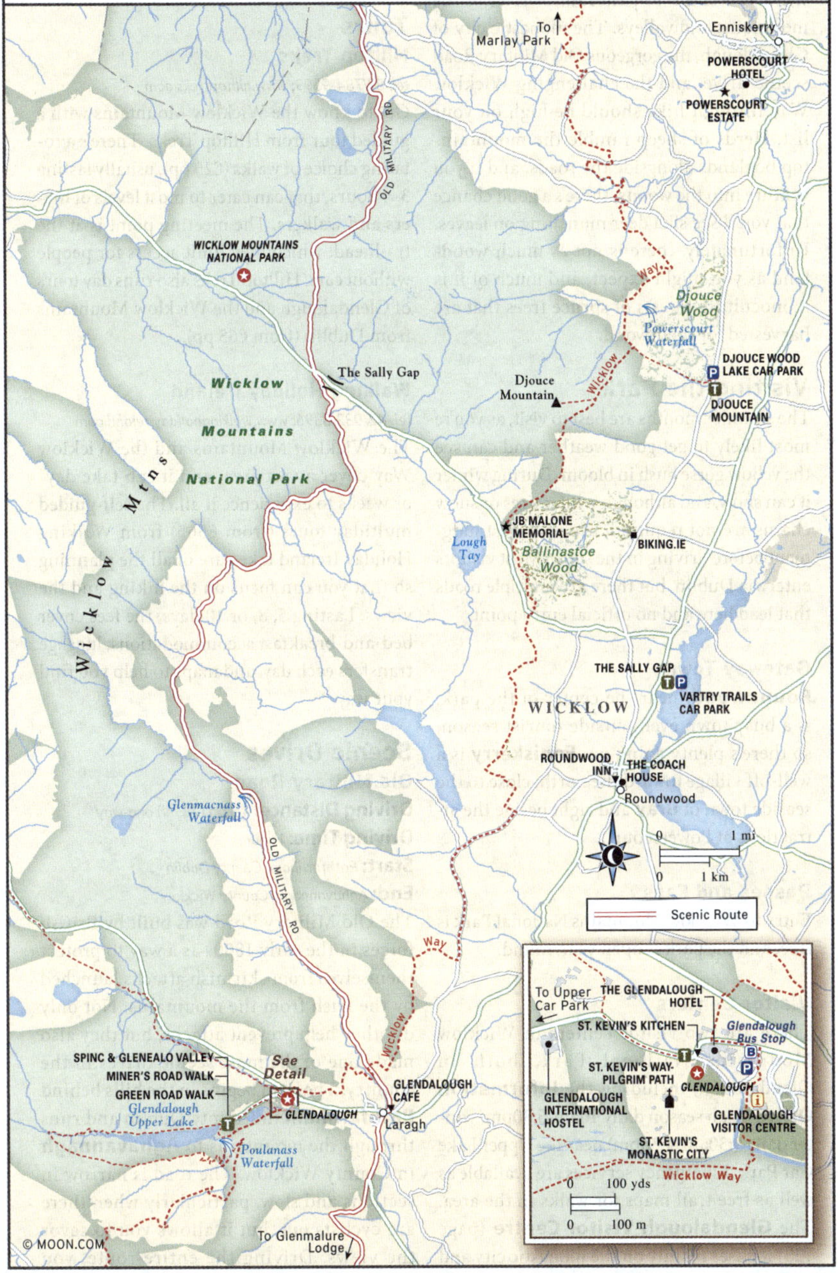

centers. Driving through the park is a memorable experience, as the narrow country roads wind and climb to panoramic views of the mountains and valleys. The monastic city of Glendalough, the gorgeous Old Military Road scenic drive, and the challenging Wicklow Way through-hike should be high on your list. Herds of sheep ramble the mountaintop boglands alongside the roads, and if you venture into the woods, there's a good chance that you'll see sika deer munching on leaves. Unfortunately, there is not as much woodland as you might expect, and much of it is monoculture forests of spruce trees that are harvested for their wood.

Visiting the Park

The summer months are best to visit, as you're most likely to get good weather and can see the yellow gorse bush in bloom. During winter it can snow, and although winter tires or snow chains are not required, use your best judgment before driving in the snow. Most visitors enter via Dublin, but there are multiple roads that lead here and no official entry point.

Gateway Towns

Roundwood, near the center of the park, is a busy town even outside tourist season, so there's plenty going on. **Enniskerry** is a well-off village toward the north, close to the seaside town of **Bray** and right beside the attractions at Powerscourt.

Passes and Fees

Entry to Wicklow Mountains National Park is free, and the park is open year-round.

Visitor Centers

There are two visitor centers in Wicklow Mountains National Park, both in Glendalough, including the **Information Office** (high season daily 10am-5:30pm, winter daily 9:30am-4:30pm) near the Upper Lake Car Park. Emergency services are available as well as free trail maps for walks in the area. The **Glendalough Visitor Centre** (page 125) focuses mainly on the monastic city and lakes, but there is some information available on the wider park.

Tours

Hilltop Treks

tel. 87/784-9599; www.hilltoptreks.com

Get to know the Wicklow Mountains with a guided tour from Hilltop Treks. There's a rotating choice of walks (€25 pp), usually lasting 3-4 hours, that can cater to most levels of hikers and walkers. The meeting point is at the trailhead, which may limit access for people without cars. Hilltop Treks also runs day tours of Glendalough and the Wicklow Mountains from Dublin (from €65 pp).

Walking Holiday Ireland

tel. 42/932-3396; www.walkingholidayireland.com

The Wicklow Mountains and the Wicklow Way cover a vast area, and it can take days or weeks to experience it all. The self-guided multiday tours (from €565) from Walking Holiday Ireland take care of all the planning so that you can focus on the hiking and the views. Lasting 5, 8, or 10 days, the fees cover bed-and-breakfast accommodations, luggage transfers each day, and maps to help you find your way.

Scenic Drives

Old Military Road

Driving Distance: *45 km (28 mi) one-way*
Driving Time: *1 hour*
Start: *Rathfarnham, County Dublin*
End: *Aghavannagh, County Wicklow*

The Old Military Road was built by British forces in the early 1800s as a way to protect themselves from skirmish attacks launched by the Irish from the mountains. Not only did they help prevent attacks, but they also made one of the most scenic drives in the country. The road begins in the hills behind **Rathfarnham** in County Dublin and runs through the mountains to **Aghavannagh** in County Wicklow. The road is narrow in sections and slow, particularly when there are cyclists out, but it allows you to savor the views. Driving the entire route, you pass through the **Sally Gap** and drive past **Glendalough.**

Sights

JB Malone Memorial

JB Malone Car Park

J. B. Malone is credited with being one of the most important people in Ireland's hill walking and hiking world. Working as a TV host and author, he promoted walking in the mountains and helped develop some of the country's most popular routes, including the Wicklow Way. His work also helped gain public access to land that was previously blocked off. The memorial to Malone overlooks **Lough Tay,** sometimes called Guinness Lake due to its dark water and white-sand beach, on the Wicklow Way. It is a place to stop, catch your breath, and enjoy the spoils of his efforts.

Powerscourt Estate

tel. 1/204-6000; www.powerscourt.com; daily 9:30am-5pm; €14

Powerscourt Estate is one of the premier attractions in the Wicklow Mountains and manages to squeeze many things to see and do into 19 ha (47 acres). Powerscourt House has existed for over 800 years, but the current Palladian-style building was built in the 18th century and survived a fire in 1974. Wander the halls of the house and imagine what it was like to live here. You can access the famous gardens and see the **Italian Garden** and **Pet Cemetery.** There's a gift shop and a café in the main building, but if you want something stronger, book in for a tour and tasting at the **Powerscourt Distillery.**

Powerscourt Waterfall

Powerscourt Estate; tel. 1/204-6000; www.powerscourt.com; daily 9:30am-5pm; €8

At 121 m (397 ft), Powerscourt Waterfall is Ireland's tallest waterfall, cascading down a jutting rock face. When heavy rains come, the water thunders down. The waterfall is on the private Powerscourt Estate, so there are open hours and entry fees. Once past the gates on the grounds of the waterfall, there are large green spaces to wander through, barbecue areas, a refreshment kiosk, and the sensory trail, a family-friendly stroll lined with plants that have interesting smells, textures, and colors. Admission to Powerscourt Gardens does not include access to the waterfall.

Hiking and Walking

Djouce Mountain

Distance: *13 km (8 mi) round-trip*
Duration: *4 hours*
Elevation gain: *570 m (1,870 ft)*
Effort: *Difficult*
Trailhead: *Djouce Wood Car Park*

Starting in **Djouce Woods,** this hike starts with a steady 4-km (2.5-mi) climb that has most of the elevation gain. The hike leads up behind the Powerscourt Waterfall, giving you a unique view of Ireland's tallest waterfall and a handy way to avoid paying the entry fee. Keep an eye out for the wild sika deer that live in the hills; these sprightly animals are often seen on the trails munching on the plants. Because the route climbs to the peak of Djouce Mountain, the return route includes some extended boardwalk sections to help prevent the ground from getting damaged. Be careful in wet conditions as these can get slippery.

Lugnaquilla

Distance: *16 km (10 mi) round-trip*
Duration: *6 hours*
Elevation gain: *770 m (2,530 ft)*
Effort: *Difficult*
Trailhead: *Fenton's Pub, Glen of Imaal*

Lugnaquilla is one of the more challenging day hikes in the Wicklow Mountains. The terrain is rough, the hike is long, and the signage could be improved. However, the views of the national park are worth the effort. There are a few ways to hike up Lugnaquilla, but the route that starts at Fenton's Pub in the Glen of Imaal is the shortest and most popular with visitors. The weather can be unpredictable, even for Ireland. Wet weather is known to arrive quickly and without warning, so be prepared for all conditions. There's also an

1

2

active artillery range beside the hike, so don't be alarmed if you hear gunshots.

Cycling

Ballinastoe Mountain Bike Trails

Ballinastoe Woods; www.biking.ie

Purpose-built mountain bike trail centers are becoming more popular in Ireland, and Ballinastoe was one of the first. There are 25 km (16 mi) of maintained trails made up of 5 blue (beginner), 11 red (intermediate), and 5 black (advanced) trails—plenty to keep you busy for a full day of biking. As these are trail center trails, expect the flow tracks to be wide, with tabletop jumps and no mandatory gaps or drops, with the tech trails being mainly made up of rock. There's no lift access here, so it's about pedaling up the 150-m (492-ft) climb on the 3-km (1.8-mi) access road to get to the trails.

The Sally Gap

Distance: *43 km (27 mi) round-trip*
Duration: *2 hours*
Elevation gain: *710 m (2,350 ft)*
Effort: *Difficult*
Trailhead: *Vartry Trails Car Park*

The Sally Gap is a famous mountain pass in the Wicklow Mountains that's best experienced on two wheels rather than four. There are no easy routes; all have some steep climbs, making this area best suited to experienced cyclists. The majority of the climbing is done by the time you reach the Sally Gap, 12 km (7.4 mi) from the start point. This means the remaining 31 km (19 mi) is full of sweeping descents on mountain roads with expansive views and a visit to **Glenmacnass Waterfall** on the **Old Military Road.** Roughly 13 km (8 mi) before the end, the route passes through Laragh, where you can get a coffee at the **Glendalough Café.**

Biking.ie

Ballinastoe Woods; tel. 83/434-6992; www.biking.ie; Wed.-Sun. 9am-4:30pm; from €35

Biking.ie manage the mountain bike trails in Ballinastoe as well as other places across the country, so they're experienced. You are welcome to bring your own mountain bike and ride the trails for free, or you can rent a bike here. Full suspension, hardtails, and e-bikes are available, and if you'd like a lesson, there are experienced bike guides on-site. After your ride, refuel with a coffee, sandwich, and sweet treat at the on-site café.

Food and Accommodations

Roundwood Inn

Main St., Roundwood; tel. 1/281-8107; daily noon-8:45pm; from €15

This old hunting lodge has been developed into a pub and restaurant. The menu has a mix of Irish and continental dishes, but the real reason to come here is the atmosphere. Acting almost as a refuge for hikers, bikers, and locals, the Roundwood Inn is a bustling spot to enjoy some food and drink in a beautiful mountain setting.

The Coach House

Main St., Roundwood; tel. 1/233-6010; www.thecoachhouse.ie; €225

This 1820s coach house has recently been refurbished to create tastefully decorated, traditional-style rooms in the beautiful setting of Roundwood. The rooms are on the small side, but they fit a king bed and all have an en suite bath, although some have twin beds. Downstairs is a gorgeous pub, and the restaurant oozes that country pub charm. The menu elevates itself above others in the area with ever-changing options that have included a Wagyu cheeseburger, Donegal squid, and Glenmalure lamb koftas. Private dining rooms are available for group bookings.

Powerscourt Hotel

Powerscourt Estate; tel. 1/274-8888; www.powerscourthotel.com; €315

The five-star Powerscourt Hotel with its 198 rooms is the most luxurious stay in the Wicklow Mountains. There are a staggering 14 room types, and you can choose a

1: Wicklow Mountains **2:** Powerscourt Estate

TOP EXPERIENCE

The Wicklow Way

Lough Tay

Distance: *131 km (81 mi) one-way*
Duration: *7-10 days*
Elevation gain: *3,200 m (10,500 ft)*
Effort: *Difficult*
Trailhead: *Marlay Park, Dublin*

The Wicklow Way (www.wicklowway.com) is the best-known long-distance hiking trail in the country and also the oldest, formally established in 1980 by J. B. Malone. The route starts in Marlay Park in County Dublin and links some of the best parts of the Wicklow Mountains before ending in Clonegall, County Carlow. Most people take 7-10 days; some days have more elevation gain and are more challenging than others. It's possible to make it to lodging in towns each night to rest and refuel, as well as plenty of official dispersed camping spots if you bring your tent. If hiking the full route isn't feasible, hiking the first half of the north-south route from Marlay Park to Glenmalure is the most popular option.

Marlay Park is easily reached by car from Dublin City, or you can take the Route 16 or Route 74 Dublin Bus from various stops in the city to the park. There are transportation and luggage services available locally that can help make things easier.

HIGHLIGHTS OF THE WICKLOW WAY

- **JB Malone Memorial:** Pause for a moment at this scenic memorial to the man who created this incredible trail (page 117).
- **Lough Tay:** Gaze down onto the dark waters and white sand to see why some people call this Guinness Lake (page 117).
- **Powerscourt Waterfall:** See this magical waterfall cascading down the rock face either from above on the trail or on a short detour to the base (page 117).

- **Roundwood:** Refuel and refresh in this charming mountain village that's got some great food and lodging options (page 119).
- **Glendalough:** Journey to this old monastic city along the same route pilgrims took hundreds of years ago (page 122).

SAMPLE SEVEN-DAY HIKE

Here's one of the ways to hike the Wicklow Way in seven days. Depending on your fitness level and lodging preferences, your itinerary may differ.

- **Day 1: Marlay Park to Knockree (21 km/13 mi):** Stroll through the lush parklands of Marlay Park before the climbing begins in the Dublin Mountains. Continue through the Glencree Valley to Knockree.
- **Day 2: Knockree to Roundwood (18 km/11 mi):** See the magnificent Powerscourt Waterfall and climb Djouce Mountain for amazing views. Follow the boardwalk trail down and finish in Roundwood for a big meal.
- **Day 3: Roundwood to Glendalough (14 km/9 mi):** Continue onward to the monastic city, take in the incredible views of the lakes, and learn all about the historical importance of these buildings.
- **Day 4: Glendalough to Glenmalure (11 km/7 mi):** Climb Spinc, look back on more great views of Glendalough, and venture through Glenealo Valley and into Glenmalure.
- **Day 5: Glenmalure to Moyne (21 km/13 mi):** Hike along quieter parts of the trail and see Lugnaquilla, Wicklow's highest peak, in the distance, and cross into rural farmland signaling the final stages of the trail.
- **Day 6: Moyne to Shillelagh (21 km/13 mi):** The verdant countryside scenes continue and extend well into County Carlow. Cross the county border from Wicklow and finish in Shillelagh, a traditional market village.
- **Day 7: Shillelagh to Clonegall (21 km/13 mi):** The final day is a gentle route to the finishing point in Clonegall, letting you reflect on your incredible achievement.

BEST DAY HIKES

- **Djouce Mountain:** Making up part of the Wicklow Way, you'll take in wonderful views of the Wicklow Mountains and the Irish Sea from the top of this mountain. The boardwalk sections are great for taking photos as you descend toward Lough Tay (page 117).
- **Lugnaquilla:** This challenging hike up Wicklow's tallest mountain is a tough day out that requires good levels of fitness and orienteering. Finish your hike with a beer at the pub at the end (page 117).
- **Spinc and Glenealo Valley:** This scenic hike offers picturesque views of Poulanass Waterfall and the lakes below (page 124).

mountain or garden view. All are decked out with the luxurious touches that you'd expect from a top-tier hotel. **Sika** and its contemporary Irish menu is the culinary highlight, but there are more relaxed options as well. To keep you entertained and pampered, there's a 20-m (66-ft) Swarovski crystal-lit swimming pool, falconry demonstrations, and an extensive spa.

Getting There and Around

The easiest way to access the gateway towns of Roundwood, Ballinastoe, and Enniskerry is by driving. From Dublin, get on the M50 and drive south to the N11. Continuing south, take exit 7 for Enniskerry and exit 8 for Ballinastoe and Roundwood. There is no rail service to these towns, but you can get the Route 44 Dublin Bus from O'Connell Street to Enniskerry (€2.60 cash).

★ GLENDALOUGH

High in the Wicklow Mountains is Glendalough, famous for its monastic city founded by Saint Kevin in the 6th or 7th century. The ruins are quite well preserved, with the round tower, St. Kevin's Church, and the cathedral making for spots to feel what life was like for monks back then. The visitor center has detailed exhibits and a huge amount of information on the history of the area and the buildings. The natural setting of Glendalough is also a big part of what makes it special. *Lough* means lake in Irish, so no surprise that there's a lake here. There are nine walks, all including time by the water or views of Poulanass Waterfall, ranging from 30-minute strolls to half-day hikes. The €5 admission covers the visitor center, the monastic city, lakes, and trails as well as parking. Bring the camera; the views are spectacular even if the weather isn't.

Sights

St. Kevin's Monastic City

Seven Churches; tel. 404/45-325; www.heritageireland.ie; daily 9am-5:30pm; €5

St. Kevin's monastic city is a brilliantly well-preserved and densely packed valley in the Wicklow Mountains where you can wander the grounds and see the buildings up close. When you arrive, you enter via the visitor center and pay the entry fee. There are toilets and snacks available; I'd recommend using both, as it may be a few hours before you return. The architectural and historical highlights of the monastic city are the 30-m-tall (100-ft) **round tower,** built as a defensive structure to ward off Viking attacks; the Irish Romanesque **St. Kevin's Church;** and **St. Kevin's Cross,** believed to have the power to make your wishes come true.

Glendalough Upper Lake

Glendalough Upper Lake Car Park; www.glendalough.ie; €5 paid at the monastic city

There are two lakes in the Glendalough Valley, with Glendalough Upper Lake the most popular, thanks to its stunning views and location. Formed by glacial movement, the lake sits in a lush green valley a short stroll from the monastic city. The Spinc is a busy walking route that gives easy access to the best views of the lake as you look across to the old miners' village. You can bring your swimming gear and take a dip at the eastern end of the lake. You can fish here also, but the fish are small and must be returned to the water.

Poulanass Waterfall

Glendalough Upper Lake Car Park; www.glendalough.ie; €5 paid at the monastic city

Though Powerscourt Waterfall is the biggest and best-known in Ireland, Poulanass Waterfall has it matched for beauty. The narrow stepped waterfall has carved out a path through the dense forest and dark rock to tumble down the hills beside Glendalough Upper Lake. To get the best views of the waterfall, take the 1.6-km (1-mi) walk from the car park.

1: St. Kevin's monastic city **2:** the lakes of Glendalough

1

2

Hiking and Walking

Spinc and Glenealo Valley

Distance: *9.5 km (6 mi) round-trip*
Duration: *3 hours*
Elevation gain: *380 m (1,250 ft)*
Effort: *Moderate*
Trailhead: *Glendalough Upper Lake Car Park*

Spinc and Glenealo Valley is a popular route in Glendalough, as the looped hike takes in some of the best scenery in County Wicklow. *Spinc* means "pointed hill" in Irish, so the route is steep in parts, particularly at the start, when you leave the car park and make your way up to Poulanass Waterfall. The trail is a mix of woodland single track, wooden boardwalks, and a series of 600 steps that bring you to a viewpoint over the lake. The hike continues down around the back of the lake, where you'll see the ruins of the miners' village before walking the gravel road back to the car park.

Miners Road Walk

Distance: *5 km (3 mi) round-trip*
Duration: *1 hour*
Elevation gain: *20 m (65 ft)*
Effort: *Easy*
Trailhead: *Glendalough Upper Lake Car Park*

This out-and-back route along the northern shore of the Upper Lake is an easy walk on mainly gravel tracks under mature trees. At the halfway mark is an abandoned miners' village, which gives the walk its name, where workers mined lead, zinc, and silver until the 1790s. It's a fantastic trail that gives you a rare view from the lake toward the monastic city. On the way back, look for St. Kevin's Bed, a cave where it is believed Saint Kevin lived as a hermit.

Green Road Walk

Distance: *3 km (2 mi) round-trip*
Duration: *45 minutes*
Elevation gain: *20 m (65 ft)*
Effort: *Easy*
Trailhead: *Upper Lake Car Park*

This is one of the easiest walks in Glendalough, as it's a gentle ramble down relatively flat ground around Lower Lake. From the car park, walk through the oak forest until you reach the wetlands on the edge of the lake. This part of Glendalough is a haven for wildlife, including frogs, dragonflies, and surprisingly, small lizards who warm themselves in the sunny spots of the trail. As you reach the halfway point, you'll see the buildings of the monastic city before returning to the start point.

St. Kevin's Way–Pilgrim Path

Distance: *30 km (19 mi) one-way*
Duration: *7-8 hours*
Elevation gain: *580 m (1,900 ft)*
Effort: *Moderate*
Trailhead: *St. Kevin's Church, Hollywood*

Retracing the pilgrimage that Saint Kevin undertook, this trail is a long route through idyllic mountain scenery to picturesque viewpoints. Despite the distance it's not that difficult a walk, so if you have a decent level of fitness, this could be a great option. The trail begins in Hollywood at St. Kevin's Church and follows a remote route to Glendalough. Pack all that you'll need for a full day out, as there are no shops along the way. The trail is mostly a single-track hiking trail. Make sure you plan your arrival time to get the bus back from Glendalough.

Food and Accommodations

St. Kevin's Kitchen

R757; daily 9am-6pm; from €5

Food options in Glendalough are few, with most, except St. Kevin's Kitchen, having a reputation as tourist traps. Thankfully, this outdoor café serves coffee and snacks alongside daily hot specials like fish-and-chips, burgers, and chicken nuggets. There are good views from the area, covered by umbrellas so that you'll stay dry if it rains.

Glendalough Café

Laragh; tel. 404/45-151; Instagram @glendalough_cafe; Tues.-Sun. 9am-5pm; €5

This quirky café is uniquely decorated and well placed near the entrance to Glendalough

Visitor Centre. Offerings include light bites like salads and sandwiches and freshly baked goods. On a sunny day, find a seat outside among the colorful flowers, and if the weather is poor, move inside and sit beside the fire.

Glendalough International Hostel

R757; tel. 404/45-342; www.anoige.ie; €40

Well located for an overnight stay on the Wicklow Way or as a base to explore Glendalough, this hostel is in a scenic spot near the Glendalough Visitor Centre. There are 5-10-bed male, female, and mixed dorms. You'll likely spend most of your time outdoors, but the hostel has a pool table, internet access, and table tennis.

The Glendalough Hotel

R757; tel. 404/45-135; www.glendaloughhotel.com; €150

Accommodations are hard to come by in Glendalough. The three-star Glendalough Hotel is the only hotel in the area, having first opened in 1830. Five rooms include a single and a quad room with a double bed and two singles. The dining options are a barbecue-style spot called **The Barn** and **Casey's Bar and Bistro,** where you can replace all those burned-off calories with pasta dishes and burgers.

Information and Services

Glendalough Visitor Centre

R757; tel. 404/45-325; www.heritageireland.ie; daily 9am-5:30pm; €5

The visitor center has all the info you need about Glendalough, St. Kevin, the monastic city, and the lakes. Displays showing the area's past alongside artifacts from the time of Saint Kevin give insight into the lives of monks at the time. There are guided tours in English, French, German, and Spanish, and if you have questions, the staff are willing and knowledgeable. Prebooking of tours is advised.

There's also a small information office beside the Upper Lake Car Park (high season daily 10am-5:30pm, winter daily 9:30am-4:30pm).

Getting There and Around

Driving from Dublin, take the M50 south and then the N11 southbound. Continue to exit 8, where you turn off for Glendalough, and follow the signs. Alternatively, the St. Kevin's Bus service (€23 round-trip) runs twice a day from St. Stephen's Green to Glendalough, with plenty of stops in south Dublin and north Wicklow en route.

GLENMALURE

The longest glacial valley in Ireland, Glenmalure stretches 20 km (12 mi) into the Wicklow Mountains and is the halfway point along the Wicklow Way. There's nothing here except Glenmalure Lodge, but if you're hiking the long-distance trail, you'll be glad to stop in for a pint.

Food and Accommodations

Glenmalure Lodge

Wicklow Way; tel. 404/46-188; www.glenmalurelodge.ie; food from €6, rooms from €100

Glenmalure Lodge is a charming, historic mountain lodge nestled in the heart of Glenmalure Valley. Ideally located halfway along the Wicklow Way, it's a great stop for those exploring the valley and the nearby Lugnaquilla mountain. Fuel up for the day ahead with a hearty breakfast, or refuel on your arrival with their gastro pub menu made with local produce. To make life easier for hikers, you can buy a packed lunch for €8 that comes with a sandwich, fruit, snacks, and water. There are 14 rooms here, 3 of which are family rooms that can sleep up to 4 people, which is great for groups that are hiking on a budget.

Getting There

Driving south from Glendalough, take the R756 for 1.7 km (1.1 mi), then turn right on R755. Continue another 1.4 km (0.9 mi) before turning right onto the L2083, following the winding valley road for 7.4 km (4.6 mi) to Glenmalure Lodge. The drive takes about 20 minutes. The hike is 11 km (6.8 mi) and takes 304 hours.

CLONEGALL

Clonegall is a small village of 250 people known as the endpoint of the Wicklow Way, a gentle ending in a soft rural landscape after days in the mountains. Some argue the trail should end in a different place, as there aren't many services in Clonegall.

Food and Accommodations

Sha-Roe Bistro

tel. 53/937-5636; https://sha-roe.ie; Thurs.-Sat. 7pm-9:30pm, Sun. 12:30pm-2:30pm; from €25

Sha-Roe Bistro is a surprising find in this rural village that serves contemporary Irish cuisine with a focus on seasonal produce in a moody dining room with soft lighting. What sets Sha-Roe Bistro apart is the incredibly pleasing plating of dishes like the slow-roasted shoulder of lamb, wild garlic risotto, or John Dory with peas, asparagus, and butter sauce.

Huntington Castle

tel. 53/937-7160; https://huntingtoncastle.com; €260

This grand castle is set among the green rolling hills of County Carlow and is a treat for weary hikers who have conquered the trail. The rooms are fantastically decorated in a traditional style with four-poster beds, antique furnishings, and original windows. Wander the castle gardens and see the well-maintained seasonal flowerbeds and an atmospheric avenue of yew trees.

Getting There

Drive south from Glendalough on the R756 and R755 roads before turning onto the R747 toward Tinahely. Continue on this road to Clonegall. The drive is 55 km (34 mi) and takes 1 hour. It's also possible to hike from Glendalough on the Wicklow Way. The hike is 62 km (39 mi) and takes three days.

The Boyne Valley

The Boyne Valley is where you'll see Ireland at its oldest, where ancient civilizations decoded the stars and seasons to create monuments along the River Boyne that still astound. Rich folklore that inspired legends and myths is still told today. History defines this area, from prehistoric sites to castles from the Norman invasions, battlegrounds of history-defining wars, and leftovers from the Cromwellian conquest of Ireland. Put the Boyne Valley in your plans if you want to take a trip to the Neolithic era in the green Irish countryside.

ORIENTATION

Drogheda and **Slane** are the two main hubs. Drogheda is a previously walled town with a gruesome history of battles and invasions, while Slane is centered around Slane Castle, deep in the County Meath countryside. The Boyne Valley starts in the east in Drogheda, near the Irish Sea. Moving west and following the **River Boyne** is **Newgrange** and the famous monuments at **Brú na Bóinne,** roughly the halfway point to Slane. The region ends at Trim but is densely packed with things to see, so you can return via a different route.

DROGHEDA

Drogheda is a historic town that has one foot in County Louth and one in Country Meath as it straddles the River Boyne. The most important story in Drogheda's history is how Oliver Cromwell attacked the town and brutally killed large numbers of residents. Scarlet Street in Drogheda got its name when Cromwell's soldiers killed so many people that the street ran red with blood. These days, many see Drogheda as a commuter town for people working in Dublin, and unfortunately poor planning has seen the town center become less popular with locals. It's a shame because Drogheda is a visually attractive town with plenty of independent places to eat, drink, and shop.

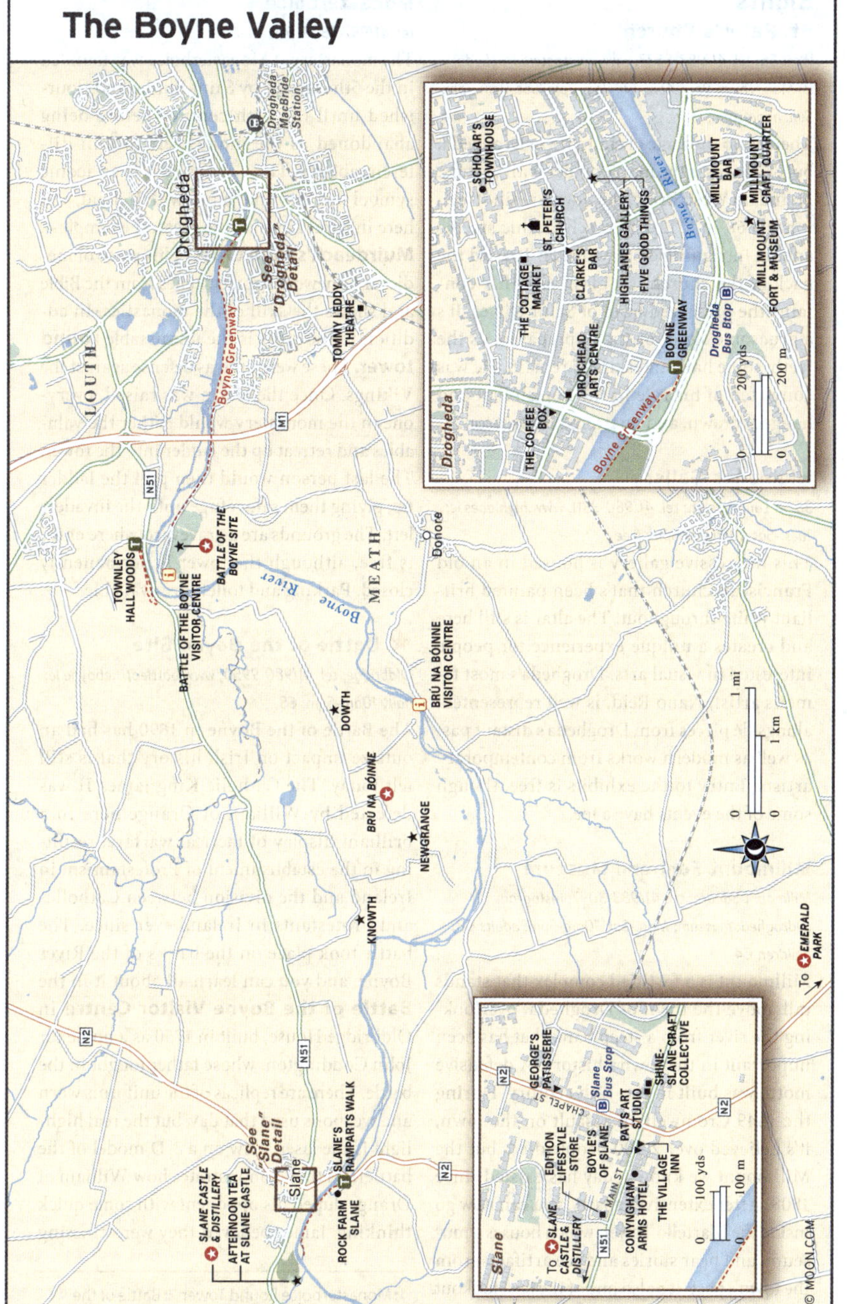
The Boyne Valley
Drogheda
Drogheda MacBride Station
See "Drogheda" Detail
Boyne Greenway
TOMMY LEDDY THEATRE
LOUTH
MEATH
M1
N51
N2
TOWNLEY HALL WOODS
BATTLE OF THE BOYNE SITE
BATTLE OF THE BOYNE VISITOR CENTRE
Boyne River
Donore
BRÚ NA BÓINNE VISITOR CENTRE
DOWTH
BRÚ NA BÓINNE
NEWGRANGE
KNOWTH
To EMERALD PARK
See "Slane" Detail
Slane
SLANE'S RAMPARTS WALK
ROCK FARM SLANE
SLANE CASTLE & DISTILLERY
AFTERNOON TEA AT SLANE CASTLE
0 1 mi
0 1 km
Drogheda
SCHOLAR'S TOWNHOUSE
ST. PETER'S CHURCH
THE COTTAGE MARKET
CLARKE'S BAR
HIGHLANES GALLERY
FIVE GOOD THINGS
DROICHEAD ARTS CENTRE
THE COFFEE BOX
BOYNE GREENWAY
Boyne River
MILLMOUNT BAR
MILLMOUNT CRAFT QUARTER
MILLMOUNT FORT & MUSEUM
Drogheda Bus Btop
0 200 yds
0 200 m
Slane
To SLANE CASTLE & DISTILLERY
EDITION LIFESTYLE STORE
BOYLE'S OF SLANE
GEORGE'S PATISSERIE
Slane Bus Stop
CHAPEL ST
MAIN ST
PAT'S ART STUDIO
SHINE-SLANE CRAFT COLLECTIVE
CONYNGHAM ARMS HOTEL
THE VILLAGE INN
0 100 yds
0 100 m
© MOON.COM

Sights

St. Peter's Church

West St.; tel. 41/983-8537; www.saintpetersdrogheda.ie; Mon.-Thurs. 9am-4pm, Fri. 9am-2pm, Sat. 9am-7pm, Sun. noon-4pm; free

There is no shortage of churches in Drogheda, but St. Peter's is the most popular with visitors. Found on West Street, the town's main street, it has a 68-m (222-ft) French Gothic steeple and an intriguing display inside: Toward the back of the church is a glass case that contains the preserved head of Saint Oliver. It's a gruesome sight for the unprepared, as the teeth, some hair, and skin all remain. He was convicted of his role in the Popish Plot and hanged, drawn, and quartered for treason.

Highlanes Gallery

36 St. Laurence St.; tel. 41/980-3311; www.highlanes.ie; Tues.-Sat. 10:30am-5pm; free

This impressive gallery is housed in an old Franciscan church that's been painted brilliant white throughout. The altar is still here and creates a unique experience for people interested in visual arts. Drogheda's most famous artist, Nano Reid, is well represented, alongside pieces from Drogheda's distant past as well as modern works from contemporary artists. Entry to the exhibits is free, though some of the events have a fee.

Millmount Fort and Museum

Millmount Square; tel. 41/983-3097; Instagram @droghedamuseum; Mon.-Sat. 10am-5pm; adults €8, children €4

Millmount is a fortified complex that stands tall above the town of Drogheda, overlooking the river from a steep bank that has been important in the town's history. A defensive motte was built in the 12th century. During the 1649 Cromwellian assault on the town, it's believed over 2,500 people died, but the Millmount we know today has existed since 1808. After extensive repairs, you can now go inside the Martello Tower, which houses a museum, and hear stories and see artifacts from the town's past. It's also one of the best lookout points in town.

Monasterboice

tel. 41/987-2843; free

The monastery at Monasterboice was founded in the 5th century by Saint Buithe and flourished until the 12th century before being abandoned as the monks left to join different abbeys. The Celtic Cross is an iconic symbol that is synonymous with Ireland, and here in rural Louth is the greatest example—**Muirdeach's High Cross.** This piece of medieval stonework depicts scenes from the Bible and shows the skill of the monastics. In addition to the cross is the unmissable **round tower.** These were built as defense against the Vikings. Once the alarm was raised, everyone in the monastery would gather the valuables and retreat up the ladder into the tower. The last person would then pull the ladder up, giving them safe refuge until the invaders left. The grounds are a graveyard where entry is free, although the tower is permanently closed. Parking and toilets are available.

★ Battle of the Boyne Site

Oldbridge; tel. 41/980-9950; www.battleoftheboyne.ie; daily 10am-5pm; €5

The Battle of the Boyne in 1690 has had an outsize impact on Irish history that is still felt today. The Catholic King James II was defeated by William of Orange here in a brilliant display of tactical warfare, resulting in the establishment of Protestantism in Ireland and the division between Catholics and Protestants in Ireland ever since. The battle took place on the banks of the River Boyne, and you can learn all about it in the **Battle of the Boyne Visitor Centre** in Oldbridge House, built in 1750 as a home for John Coddington, whose father fought in the battle. There are replicas of the uniforms worn and weapons used that day, but the real highlight is the laser show on a 3-D model of the battlefield that demonstrates how William of Orange duped his opponent with some quick thinking. James believed they were crossing

1: Monasterboice Round Tower **2:** Battle of the Boyne Site

1

2

the river at Oldbridge but were actually crossing farther upstream, flanking the Catholic troops. The visitor center takes a neutral and fact-driven approach, giving insights into both sides. Access to the grounds is free. The tour is self-guided and should take no more than an hour.

There are five walks around the grounds, with the **Canal Towpath Walk** (5 km/3 mi; 1 hour; easy) being my pick, as you get to spend time along the River Boyne and see more of the outbuildings around the house. The other routes take you across parklands and up short grassy hills where you'll see the **Mary McAlesse Bridge** and the steeples of churches in Drogheda. There's a map in front of the house with details on the walks. The walled gardens offer a leisurely ramble, particularly on a sunny day, but dogs are not permitted in the walled gardens.

There's a **café** with standard offerings of sandwiches, hot drinks, and baked goods. It's pricey compared to others in the region, but the views from the patio make up for it. There's plenty of free parking on-site, but if you're feeling active, you can walk the 4.5-km (2.8-mi) **Boyne Greenway** from Drogheda.

Hiking and Walking

Townley Hall Woods

Distance: *1.6 km (1 mi) round-trip*
Duration: *30 minutes*
Elevation gain: *30 m (100 ft)*
Effort: *Easy-moderate*
Trailhead: *Townley Hall Forest car park*

This is an easy short hike that rewards your effort up one steep pitch with great views of the River Boyne and the Battle of the Boyne site. The route starts with stairs that account for most of the elevation gain, with flat and undulating forest paths on the rest of the route. It's not wheelchair-accessible but is suitable for kids thanks to its short length and flat sections. You'll walk under mature trees, see small waterfalls, and wander through a small meadow. Parking is available at the trailhead; the gates close in summer daily at 4:30pm and in winter daily at 3:30pm.

Boyne Greenway

Distance: *4.5 km (2.8 mi) one-way*
Duration: *1 hour*
Elevation gain: *Negligible*
Effort: *Easy*
Trailhead: *St. Dominic's Bridge, Drogheda*

The Boyne Greenway runs from Drogheda to the Battle of the Boyne Visitor Center at Oldbridge House. Fully pedestrianized, it hugs the River Boyne for the full route, making it scenic and good for all ages. The trail's surface is mainly asphalt, with some boardwalk sections, so it's wheelchair and stroller accessible. There's no noticeable elevation change, and you can continue on the five walks at the Battle of the Boyne grounds. The return leg follows the same route.

Entertainment and Events

Tommy Leddy Theatre

East Coast Business Park, Matthew's Lane; tel. 41/987-8560; www.thetlt.ie; from €30

The Tommy Leddy Theatre, also known as the TLT, is Drogheda's premier music venue, although its location in an industrial estate on the outskirts of the town is not ideal. The modern purpose-built building makes the acoustics fantastic, and the busy events schedule has a number of impressive performers.

Droichead Arts Centre

Stockwell St. and Narrow West St.; tel. 41/983-3946; www.droichead.com; from €5

The Droichead Arts Centre is a busy hub of performing arts in the Boyne Valley that helps up-and-coming acts as well as locally established ones. With two locations in Drogheda, Stockwell Street and Narrow West Street, there's a good mix of theater, comedy, songwriting, music, and more. There's no dedicated parking at either location but plenty of on-street parking and car parks in the town.

Shopping

Millmount Craft Quarter

Millmount Square; Instagram @millmountcraftquarter

Inside the walled grounds of Millmount is a small collection of independent studios selling everything from jewelry and ceramics to art and knitwear. The goods are all artisanal and high quality; it's a great place for gifts and souvenirs you won't find anywhere else.

The Cottage Market

Scotch Hall; Instagram @cottagemarketdrogheda; 1st Sat. of the month

On the ground floor of Scotch Hall, Drogheda's biggest shopping center, is the monthly Cottage Market. The stalls are a motley collection of food producers, artists, and more. A lot of these businesses are small, so it's a good idea to bring cash, as not everyone takes card payments.

Food and Accommodations

The Coffee Box

George's St.; Instagram @thecoffeeboxireland; Mon.-Sat. 7:30am-6:30pm, Sun. 9am-5pm; from €5

Drogheda's coffee options aren't as plentiful as nearby Dublin or Dundalk, leaving the Coffee Box as the town's only real option. It's a busy little spot that serves reasonably priced toasted sandwiches alongside the coffee. There's a covered outdoor seating area as well as a grab-and-go coffee bar and a small indoor seating area with seven tables and a sofa.

Five Good Things

36 St. Laurence St.; www.fivegoodthings.ie; Mon.-Sat. 9am-4pm, Sun. 10am-3pm; from €10

This bright spacious café adjoins the Highlanes Gallery and is a great spot for a lazy brunch. The menu has breakfast favorites like a full Irish alongside modern picks like potato hash and avocado toast. Vegan and veggie options are available in the dining room, which comfortably holds 40 people.

Scholar's Townhouse and Restaurant

King St.; tel. 41/983-5410; www.scholarshotel.com; daily noon-9pm; restaurant from €18, hotel €160

The 16 rooms of this boutique hotel in a revamped 150-year-old monastery are a staple in Drogheda. Five room types include singles and a family room for four. There's a nice mix of old meets new with four-poster beds and rich wooden furniture alongside modern touches like flat-screen TVs and Wi-Fi. The formal setting of Scholar's Townhouse sets the tone for Scholar's Restaurant, which embraces traditional luxury with its large golden curtains, deep red seats, and soft lighting. The pan-seared scallops and catch of the day make the most of the location, with plenty of beef and chicken dishes also. There are some vegetarian options, but vegans will want to go elsewhere.

Bars and Nightlife

Clarke's Bar

1 Fair St.; tel. 41/983-6724; www.clarkesofdrogheda.com; Mon.-Thurs. 1pm-11:30pm, Fri.-Sat. noon-12:30am, Sun. 12:30pm-11pm

Stepping into Clarke's Bar is like stepping into a time machine. The wooden interiors and bottles of beer left out on the shelves are reminiscent of a pub 100 years ago. There are two snugs and plenty of nooks and crannies to tuck into while you enjoy your drinks. The pub is no stranger to live music, but it's often off the cuff rather than planned events.

Millmount Bar

Samson's Lane; tel. 41/983-6449; Mon.-Thurs. noon-11:30pm, Fri.-Sat. noon-12:30am, Sun. noon-11pm

Millmount Bar is Drogheda's oldest pub and has a storied past. It famously remained open in 1922 when Millmount Fort, just steps across the street, came under attack during the Civil War. The bar today has some memorabilia from its past, but the real attraction is the view from the seats outside that look down the river into the Boyne Valley.

Information and Services

For banks and ATMs, there is an **AIB** (www.aib.ie) on Dyer Street and a **Bank of Ireland** (www.bankofireland.com) on St. Laurence Street.

Drogheda Tourist Information Office

West St.; tel. 41/987-2843; www.drogheda.ie; daily 9:30am-5:30pm

Sea Louth Trail

fishermen catching fresh seafood

Drogheda is the southern endpoint of the Sea Louth Trail (www.sealouth.ie), a foodie trail that links 70 km (43 mi) of the Louth coastline to promote the amazing seafood on offer in County Louth. Pick up a **Sea Louth Passport** in the Drogheda, Dundalk, or Carlingford Tourist Office and make your way to the 14 coastal scenic viewpoints where you can get your passport stamped. Of course, there's plenty of food along the way.

BEST VIEWPOINTS

- **Blackrock:** Enjoy a strong brew along the water in this popular seaside village with some great pubs and cafés (page 138).

Drogheda Tourist Information Office is easy to spot, in the Tholsel municipal building on West Street. Staff will help you find things to do and can plan a trip along the coast or into the Boyne Valley.

Getting There and Around

Drogheda is well connected and easy to get to from Dublin. Driving, go north on the M1 motorway to Drogheda, which takes about 40 minutes and 55 km (34 mi). **Drogheda MacBride Station** (Dublin Rd.) is regularly served by trains from Connolly Station in Dublin (€20 round-trip). The *Enterprise* is the express train service that runs once per hour during busy periods and takes 30 minutes; there's also the commuter train that runs more frequently but makes more stops. **Bus Éireann** (www.buseireann.ie) operates 19 buses a day on Route 100X from Busáras in Dublin to **Drogheda Bus Station** (Donore Rd.) via the airport (€18 round-trip).

Drogheda itself is compact and walkable. There is a local bus service but it serves residential areas outside the town center.

★ BRÚ NA BÓINNE

Having grown up in the area, sometimes the sights here get lost on me, but never Newgrange at Brú na Bóinne. Thought to be an ancient city, this is the epicenter of the Boyne Valley, and the prehistoric tombs still amaze today. Newgrange is the main

- **Salterstown Pier:** Take a dip in the sea here or admire the views across Dundalk Bay from the comfort of dry land (page 139).
- **Slieve Foye:** Climb this rewarding route to the top of the Cooley Mountains to gaze down on the lough below (page 143).

BEST FOOD STOPS

Visit producers to see where the food comes from and stop into any of the seafood restaurants along the coast. Carlingford, Clogherhead, and Dundalk have the most restaurants serving up quality local seafood.

- **PJ O'Hare's:** This lively pub is well-known for hosting parties on the weekend, but it's also a great spot to stop for freshly caught local seafood and Carlingford oysters (page 146).
- **Carlingford Oyster Company** (Mullatee; tel. 42/937-3800; Mon.-Fri. 7:30am-5pm): Ireland's west coast tends to get the plaudits for great food, but there's one delicacy where Cooley has them all beat—oysters. The tidal setting and clean water of Carlingford Lough make ideal conditions for oysters that can be eaten straight from the water.
- **Oriel Sea Salt** (Port Oriel; tel. 41/988-9624; https://magnesiumstore.com; Mon.-Fri. 9am-4pm): This salt is made by extracting deep seawater outside Clogherhead, filtered to create an organic and sustainable product. You can buy direct from them or in shops in the area.
- **Dunany Crab** (www.dunanycrab.wordpress.com): This family business supplies locally caught crab to restaurants along the east coast. They're caught using traditional crab pots, and the meat is known to be sweet and delicate. Check local restaurants to see if they have fresh Dunany crab on the menu.

attraction, along with the nearby tombs of Knowth and Dowth. You can only visit Newgrange or Knowth via the Brú na Bóinne Visitor Centre. You can access Dowth for free, but it has collapsed and is a ruins.

Sights

Brú na Bóinne Visitor Centre

Glebe; tel. 41/988-0300; www.heritageireland.ie; daily 9:30am-4:45pm; from €5

The Brú na Bóinne Visitor Centre is your first stop. The modern building sits alongside the river, and inside you'll find exhibits, a café, and a choice of three tours. It's important to book your tour as far in advance as possible, particularly in summer, as this is one of the most popular attractions in the country, and access is restricted to small numbers to protect the structures.

Newgrange

Newgrange, a large circular mound with a stone passageway and chambers inside, was built around 3200 BCE, making it older than the Pyramids of Giza. Part of the Brú na Bóinne complex, the passage tomb, clad in stone and capped with grass, is a marvel. As you squeeze through the entrance and into the narrow passageway, you leave the world outside. A small slit in the wall high above is the only light source, and at sunrise on the winter solstice, the sun aligns perfectly with the slit, lighting up the entire tomb for 15 minutes. The site is a marvel of ancient engineering and astronomical knowledge. The purpose of Newgrange is believed to be both a tomb and a ceremonial site, and it likely held great significance for the prehistoric people who built it. Today, Newgrange is a UNESCO World Heritage Site and attracts visitors with its incredible story and ancient mysteries.

Knowth

This Neolithic passage tomb dates to around 3200 BCE and consists of a large central mound, 12 m (39 ft) high and 67 m (219 ft) in diameter, surrounded by 17 smaller satellite tombs. The main mound contains two separate passages that lead to burial chambers.

Dowth

Dowth, another significant Neolithic passage tomb in Ireland's Boyne Valley, dates to around 3200 BCE. It's in quite bad condition, as efforts to explore it have caused it to collapse, but you can walk up the sides of the tomb, which you cannot do at Newgrange or Knowth.

Getting There

From Drogheda, take the Donore Road through Donore village, then continue on to the visitor center on the right side. This route is about 9 km (5.6 mi) and takes 15-20 minutes to drive. The Local Link Route 163 bus (40 minutes; €3 one-way) connects Drogheda to Brú na Bóinne Visitor Centre, departing from both Drogheda MacBride train station and the Spar opposite the bus station on the Donore Road. There are five daily departures from Drogheda to Brú na Bóinne daily.

From Slane, take the N2 south across the River Boyne and follow signs for Brú na Bóinne. This drive covers 9 km (5.6 mi) and takes 10-15 minutes. There is no bus service between Slane and Brú na Bóinne.

SLANE

The hilltop town of Slane is another major hub in the Boyne Valley, with enough lodging, pubs, and restaurants to make it a base for many visitors. The ancient River Boyne flows past Slane, connecting the town with the mythological stories of the Salmon of Knowledge, which was said to have been caught here, and providing the distillery at Slane Castle with fresh water for fantastic whiskeys. Slane is a well-connected town, with the tombs at Brú na Bóinne just a 10-minute drive. If you fancy venturing deeper into the Boyne Valley, it's easy to drive to less frequented sights like the Hill of Tara and Trim Castle.

Sights

★ Slane Castle and Distillery

Slane Castle Demense; tel. 41/988-4477; www.slanecastle.ie; Sat.-Sun. 11am-5pm; €14

This 120-year-old castle on a 610-ha (1,500-acre) estate is mainly known in Ireland for hosting some of the biggest concerts. U2, Queen, the Rolling Stones, and Madonna have all performed at the natural amphitheater, although these events are rare nowadays. Instead, people visit to see the castle, walk the grounds, and tour the distillery. On a public or private tour of the castle, you'll learn about its architectural importance and historical stories, with a few mysteries about hidden passages and ghosts thrown in. If the weather is on your side, walk the grounds, where you'll see woodlands on the river's edge and the concert venue. After your walk, reserve the **afternoon tea** in the ballroom, where you'll be served prosecco, tea, and sweet and savory treats.

If you're a whiskey fan, you'll already know about Slane Distillery, and if you don't, you can learn about it on a 75-150-minute tour, where you'll learn how to make whiskey-based cocktails, taste all the flavors in the whiskey, and sip on Irish coffee. After your tour, you can visit **Browne's Bar,** open in summer, and try more of the whiskey while surrounded by memorabilia from the concerts held here over the years.

Hiking and Walking

Slane's Ramparts Walk

Distance: *5 km (3 mi) round-trip*

Duration: *1 hour*
Elevation gain: *Negligible*
Effort: *Easy*
Trailhead: *Slane Town Center*

This gentle ramble along the edge of the meandering River Boyne is an enjoyable stroll through the heart of Slane. Starting in the center, the walk turns toward the river and onto a single track that weaves toward mature trees and views of Slane Castle, 2.5 km (1.6 mi) down the trail. Caution is needed when you get close to the river, as there's no guardrail, and the river can be dangerous. While it's suitable for kids and people of all ages, it's not accessible to wheelchairs. Once you reach the viewpoint, the way back follows the same path back to Slane.

Shopping

Pat's Art Studio

Main St.; tel. 87/244-5246; www.patsartstudio.ie; Mon.-Sat. 10am-6pm

Stop by the studio of local artist Pat Doyle and see his colorful oil paintings of the Boyne Valley and his travels in Central and South America and the Middle East. His work is available for purchase, and Pat also paints commissioned pieces.

Shine-Slane Craft Collective

Main St.; Instagram @shineinslane; Tues.-Sat. 11am-5pm

This spot in the center of Slane is well stocked with craft gifts that are inspired by the local area. Selling artworks, ceramics, textiles, and more from Irish makers that have embraced the beauty of the Boyne Valley, Shine is the place to find something a bit different.

Edition Lifestyle Store

Main St.; www.editionslane.ie; Wed.-Sat. 10:30am-5pm

Billing itself as a lifestyle store, Edition adds gifts, jewelry, and kids wear to its curated collection of contemporary women's wear. Expect to find colorful prints and bold patterns from boutique brands rather than the usual fare.

Food

George's Patisserie

Chapel St.; Instagram @georges_patisserie; Mon. 9am-3pm, Wed.-Sun. 9am-4pm; from €5

Serving traditional breakfasts and light lunches in a busy dining room, George's Patisserie is a popular spot with a mix of locals, visitors, and cyclists. The baked goods are brilliant, so stock up on fresh bread and cakes.

Slane Castle and Distillery

The Salmon of Knowledge

River Boyne

The Salmon of Knowledge is one of Irish mythology's best-known stories. The salmon lived in the River Boyne, named after the Irish goddess Boann, and gained all the world's knowledge by eating the nuts that fell from the nine hazel trees surrounding the Well of Wisdom. It was believed that whoever ate the salmon would gain all its knowledge.

The druid Finegas spent seven years trying to catch it. Finally, he succeeded, and asked his young apprentice, Fionn Mac Cumhaill, to cook the fish, but told him not to eat any of it. While cooking, Fionn burned his thumb on the fish and instinctively put his thumb in his mouth to soothe the burn. In doing so, he gained the salmon's knowledge. When Finegas learned what had happened, he realized the prophecy had been fulfilled.

Fionn went on to become one of the greatest and wisest leaders of the Fianna, a band of warriors in Irish mythology who fought the Tuatha Dé Danann, a supernatural race of warriors. Whenever Fionn needed to access the salmon's knowledge, he would simply suck his thumb.

Afternoon Tea at Slane Castle

Slane Castle; tel. 41/988-4477; www.slanecastle.ie; Sat.-Sun. 11am-5pm; €58

Get treated like royalty for a few hours at Afternoon Tea at Slane Castle. The experience runs once a month and includes a short tour of the castle. You'll dine in the ballroom, noted for its Gothic Revival architecture, as prosecco, cakes, and savory snacks are served. During summer, it is sometimes held outside under a canopy. Pre-booking is essential.

Bars and Nightlife

Boyle's of Slane

Main St.; tel. 89/491-9265; Instagram @boyles_of_slane; daily 9am-midnight

This traditional pub comes alive when the live music starts. Most pubs organize traditional music, but Boyle's isn't afraid of contemporary musicians or letting people bring their own instruments for an impromptu set. There's a small covered beer garden out back as well as the indoor space, with high tables, a bar, and benches.

The Village Inn

8 Main St.; tel. 87/744-6730; Instagram @hardingsslane; daily 9am-midnight

The Village Inn is a family-run pub with a nice community feel, with locals stopping by throughout the day for traditional breakfasts in the morning and lunch with drinks later on. It's a popular spot when there are important soccer or rugby matches on TV. They don't take reservations, but between the bar seating and the tables, it's often possible to find a seat.

Accommodations

Rock Farm Slane

Rock Farm; tel. 41/988-4861; www.rockfarmslane.ie; €100

On a small hill on the bank of the Boyne, Rock Farm is a peaceful site for a glamping getaway. Three houses can be booked for large groups, but the yurts, bell tents, and shepherd huts let you get the full experience of the beautiful setting. Rock Farm is open year-round, but the yurts are only available March 17-October, and the bell tents June-August. There's a farm shop on-site where you can pre-book supplies for a barbecue; farm tours and kayaking tours are also available.

Conyngham Arms Hotel

Main St.; tel. 41/988-4444; www.conynghamarms.ie; €110

This traditional stone-clad hotel in the middle of Slane has quintessential countryside charm. A coach inn in the 18th century, the hotel has 11 standard and 4 luxury rooms, complete with four-poster beds. The restaurant is open breakfast to dinner with a mix of cuisines and a special Sunday menu with roast dinners and steaks.

Getting There and Around

To get from Drogheda to Slane, you can take bus Route 190 from **Bus Éireann** (www.buseireann.ie), which takes about 25 minutes. Driving, head west on the N51 for 20 minutes. On-street parking is available. From Dublin, you can take the M1 north to Drogheda and then the N51, or take the N2 from Dublin if you don't want to drive on the motorway. Slane doesn't have a train station, so if you're relying on public transport, take the bus with **Collins Coaches** (https://collinscoaches.ie; 45 minutes; €19 round-trip, €13 Leap Card), which drops you off at the **Slane bus stop** on Chapel Street. There are multiple departure points in Dublin.

★ EMERALD PARK

Kilbrew; tel. 1/835-1999; www.emeraldpark.ie; hours vary; €18-52

Emerald Park is where you'll find Cú Chulainn, one of Europe's largest wooden roller coasters, family-friendly attractions, and exotic animals in the zoo area. It's Ireland's only theme park and zoo, and they've got a great selection of things to do. Adventurous kids will want to go on thrill rides like the Rotator, the Quest, and Power Surge, while younger kids have age-appropriate rides like the Grand Carousel and Leap Frogs. The zoo is home to 46 types of animals, including an amur tiger, silvery marmosets, meerkats, mountain lions, and birds of prey. Get up close to some animals at the petting farm and bird demonstrations. There are 36 attractions, and the latest is the world of Tír na nÓg, which delves into the mythological stores of Ireland with two roller coasters and a spinning swing. Don't leave without trying Dunk! ice cream, where they coat ice cream with all manner of sweet and colorful toppings of your choice. An All Access ticket costs €43-52, depending on when you book; tickets to the Junior Zone cost €39-47; and After Dark tickets cost €18-20. Opening hours change regularly; check the website.

Getting There

To reach Emerald Park from Drogheda, drive south on the M1 motorway toward Dublin for 30 minutes. Take exit 4 onto the R136 and follow signs for Emerald Park. The total journey is approximately 45 km (28 mi) and takes 40 minutes.

From Dublin city center, you can drive to Emerald Park by taking the M50 motorway north and exiting onto the N2 toward Ashbourne. Follow signs for Emerald Park, with the total journey being 28 km (17 mi) and taking 30-40 minutes, depending on traffic. There are no direct public transport options to the park.

Dundalk and Cooley Peninsula

It's lazy to call this part of Ireland a hidden gem, as it's halfway between Dublin and Belfast along one of the busiest motorways in the country. It's overlooked rather than hidden, a great place for visitors to go somewhere different but not too far from Dublin. This part of Ireland is best-known because of the Troubles, due to its location on the border, but that time is gone, and the restaurants and pubs now match the trails and landscapes that have always been popular. Fans of folklore will find the Cooley Mountains are home to the story of the Táin Bó Cúailnge and the exploits of Queen Medb. Venture north toward Slieve Foye and experience a part of Ireland that many mistakenly dismiss.

ORIENTATION

From Dublin, your first glimpse of the Cooley Mountains is past Drogheda. They hug the coast and disappear into the Irish Sea. **Slieve Foye** is the highest peak but is easily confused with the taller Slieve Donard, part of the Mourne Mountains in Northern Ireland. **Dundalk** is to the east of the **Cooley Peninsula,** between the M1 to the west and Dundalk Bay to the east.

DUNDALK AND BLACKROCK

Dundalk's reputation has taken a turn upward over the past few decades since the 1998 signing of the Good Friday Agreement. It has always marched to the beat of its own drum, which has helped the local music scene punch above its weight. This creative spirit has crossed into the world of pubs and restaurants, with the town now home to places that are worth visiting on their own. The seaside suburb of Blackrock is popular thanks to the wonderful sea views and cafés.

Sights

County Louth Museum

8 Jocelyn St., Dundalk; tel. 42/939-2999; Instagram @county_museum_dundalk; Tues.-Sat. 10am-5pm; free

The County Louth Museum manages to pack in an impressive amount of history into three floors. Exhibits go back to the Stone Age and show how Viking invasions impacted the area. Learn about Dundalk's industrial past and how the town was once a beer-brewing and cigarette-making hub. The highlight is the exhibition on the visionary engineer Peter Rice. See how he helped to create iconic buildings like Paris's Centre Pompidou, the Sydney Opera House, and the Louvre Pyramid. The museum may close over lunchtime, and there's an elevator to access all floors.

Hiking and Walking

Navvy Bank Walk

Distance: *9 km (5.6 mi) round-trip*
Duration: *2 hours*
Elevation gain: *Negligible*
Effort: *Easy-moderate*
Trailhead: *Point Rd.*

The Navvy Bank Walk is an easy but lengthy stroll along the Castletown River as it flows into Dundalk Bay. The route begins and ends on the Point Road beside the memorial for the victims of the SS *Dundalk,* torpedoed by a German U-boat in 1918. As you walk along the footpath you'll get great views of the Cooley Mountains across the water. After 3 km (1.8 mi) you pass the **Spirit Store** pub, walk through **St. Helena's Park,** and on to the **Riverside Walk.** This is the halfway point, where you turn back toward the sea. You'll be facing the Cooley Peninsula on this half of the walk, looking up at the peaks and ridges. There is limited on-street parking available.

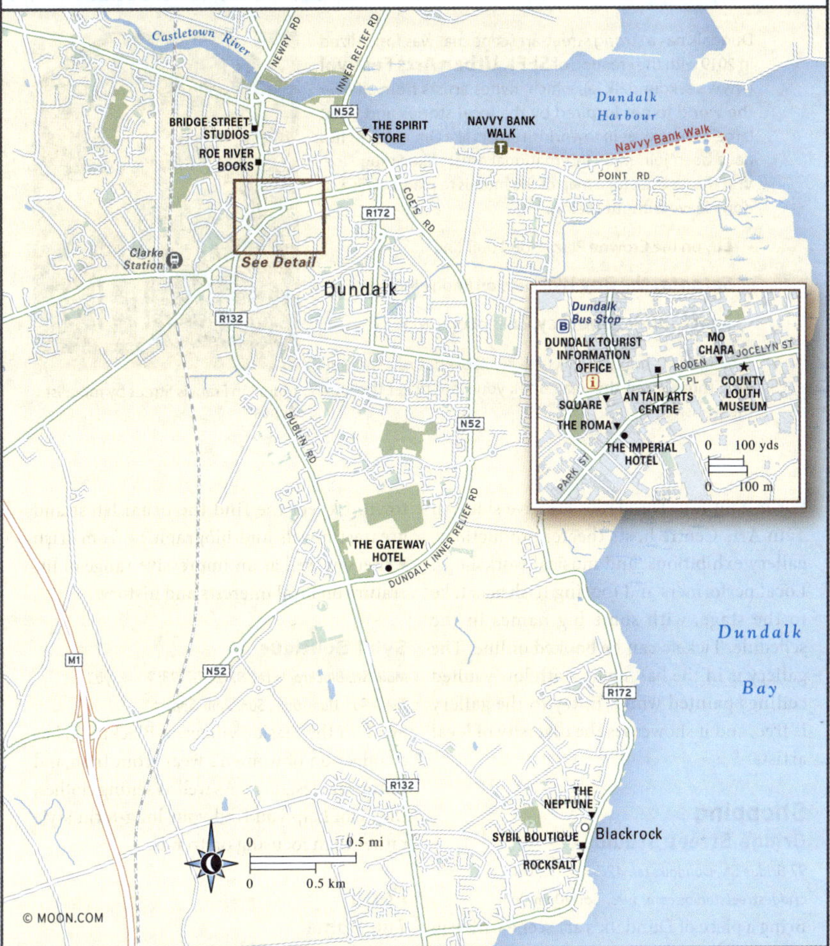

Sea Swimming

Salterstown Pier

Strand Rd.

Sea swimming is a popular hobby in the northeast, and Salterstown Pier near Annagassan is one of the best places for a dip. Parking can be tight on the country lane that leads to the pier, but when you see the views, you'll see why it's always busy at high tide. The pier slips into the sea, giving you an easy way to wade into the water of Dundalk Bay. As you swim, you'll get a panoramic view of the Cooley Peninsula and mountains across the water. It's a rough-and-ready spot, so don't expect lifeguards, changing rooms, or showers.

Entertainment and Events

An Táin Arts Centre

Crowe St., Dundalk; tel. 42/933-2332; www.antain.ie; Tues.-Sat. 10am-4pm; free-€30

Dundalk Murals

Dundalk has a strong street-art scene that was formalized in 2019 with the creation of **SEEK Urban Arts Festival** (www.seekdundalk.ie), which invites artists from all over the world to get inspired by the local stories and paint large-scale pieces in town. Irish artists like Omin and Aches have been joined by international artists like Smug One. Visit the website for a map of the murals to plan a walk, but don't leave without seeing:

- ***Lú,*** on the Crowne Plaza Hotel building
- ***Setanta, the Boy Warrior,*** on Bridge Street
- ***Tom "Sailor" Sharkey,*** on the Long Walk

Guided 90-minute walks are available but run sporadically throughout the year. Book your free ticket through the website.

mural on Francis Street by muralist Aches

For insight into Dundalk's creative side, An Táin Arts Centre hosts theater productions, gallery exhibitions, and musical workshops. Local performers and touring Irish acts take to the stage, with some big names in the schedule. Tickets can be booked online. The gallery is in the basement, with low vaulted ceilings painted white. Entry to the gallery is free, and it showcases the diversity of local artists.

Shopping

Bridge Street Studios

97 Bridge St., Dundalk; tel. 42/935-1712; www.bridgestreetstudios.com; Tues.-Sat. 10am-5pm

Bring a piece of Dundalk's art scene with you after a visit to Bridge Street Studios, home to artists working in textiles, ceramics, and paint, with a gallery and shop stocked with handmade items. You can find out all there is to know about the pieces.

Roe River Books

60 Clanbrassil St., Dundalk; tel. 42/933-4359; www.roeriverbooks.ie; Mon.-Sat. 10am-6pm

As Dundalk's only independent book shop, Roe River Books is an important part of the town. Expect the find the usual latest and greatest novels and biographies from Irish writers as well as an impressive range of literature on local interests and history.

Sybil Boutique

Main St., Blackrock; tel. 87/207-7193; www.sybil.ie; Tues.-Sat. 11am-6pm, Sun. 2pm-5pm

Sybil, in the seaside village of Blackrock, has a collection of women's wear from Irish and European designers. As well as selling clothes, they can help you find your long-term style rather than focusing on trends.

Food

The Roma

7 Park St., Dundalk; tel. 42/933-4928; daily 11am-8pm; from €5, cash only

The Roma is a Dundalk institution. You'll be hard-pressed to find a chipper in Ireland more beloved by locals than this place. Good-quality food at a great price in a clean environment is what it's all about. Try some Irish chipper classics like a battered sausage or spice burger with your thick-cut chips. You can get your food to go or sit in one of the booths.

Square

6 Market Square, Dundalk; tel. 42/933-7969; www.squarerestaurant.ie; Thurs. 5pm-9pm, Fri. 5pm-10pm, Sat. 4pm-10pm, Sun. 4pm-8pm; from €10

Serving modern Irish cuisine using local suppliers and seasonal ingredients, Square is the type of restaurant people travel for. Order a few small plates and nibbles (the homemade cheese and onion crisps are fantastic) with a glass of wine, or make an evening of it with a perfectly plated monkfish main or sirloin steak. The dining room is small, with space for 20, creating an intimate relaxed atmosphere.

Strandfield

Ballymascanlon; tel. 42/937-1856; www.strandfield.com; daily 8am-6pm; from €10

This gorgeous destination café, a short drive from Dundalk toward Cooley, is housed in old farm buildings and a barn. The menu is a mix of sourdough pizzas, sandwiches, and salads served on mixed tableware in a spacious dining area that seats over 50. For after, grab one of the freshly baked and beautifully decorated sweet treats. Strandfield is possibly the busiest place in Dundalk, and bookings are not accepted, but don't let the long lines put you off; they move quickly, and the food is worth the wait.

Rocksalt

Main St., Blackrock; tel. 87/912-7174; www.rocksaltcafe.ie; daily 9am-5pm; from €13

Rocksalt put Blackrock on the foodie map when it opened in 2018. The café serves modern brunch and lunch favorites like a sweet pancake stack, huevos rancheros, and veggie Buddha bowls in a tastefully decorated space that uses salvaged wood and tiles. On a sunny day, grab one of the four outdoor tables at the front of the café and look out at the mountains as you eat. There are plenty of veggie options and a number of vegan ones. The coffee is good, with their sister business, Little Rocksalt, next door doing coffee and treats to go.

Bars and Nightlife

The Spirit Store

George's Quay, Dundalk; tel. 42/935-2697; www.spiritstore.ie; Mon.-Wed. 4pm-11:30pm, Thurs. noon-11:30pm, Fri.-Sat. noon-12:30am, Sun. 2pm-11pm

The Spirit Store is an icon of the Irish music scene, as the pub's upstairs venue has hosted some of the country's biggest names and international acts before they hit it big. The harbor setting is also a draw, as you can sit outside and watch the fishing boats unload. The Spirit Store was initially a house that served drinks to the fishermen and then grew into a pub. Most of the quirkiness of a house-turned-pub was lost during a recent renovation, though some still remains at the front.

Mo Chara

19 Roden Place, Dundalk; www.mo-chara.ie; Mon. noon-12:30am, Wed.-Thurs. 12:30pm-11:30pm, Fri. noon-12:30am, Sat. 11am-12:30am, Sun. 11am-11:30pm

Run by three young friends, Mo Chara (which means "my friends" in Irish) is quickly becoming one of Ireland's most talked about pubs. The tap list is Irish craft breweries alongside their own lager, and the food menu has creative dishes like the curry chips pizza. This dog-friendly and youthful pub has large banquet-style seating in the main room with a quieter seating area upstairs. There's a large beer garden that can get busy, particularly when there's live music.

The Neptune

Main St., Blackrock; tel. 42/932-1506; Instagram @the_neptune_blackrock; Mon.-Fri. 4pm-11:30pm, Sat. 2pm-12:30am, Sun. 2pm-11:30pm

The Neptune is the place to be in Blackrock when the sun is shining. The recently renovated beer garden has ample seating, an extensive bar, and plenty of buzz. If there's an important game on TV, there's always a crowd. Inside the pub is much quieter, particularly at the front bar, where the dark wooden furnishings and low lighting make it a cozy spot for a drink. There's also hot food, with pizzas the majority of the menu options.

The Glyde Inn

Main St., Annagassan; tel. 42/937-2350; www.theglydeinn.ie; Wed.-Sun. noon-8pm

The Glyde Inn is well geared to serving visitors, as it leans into its history and serves traditional Irish pub grub. On the site where the Vikings first tried to establish their capital, you can learn the story of Annagassan through the ages. The front bar keeps its old-world charm with decorations and memorabilia on the walls and shelves, while the more modern touches are in the back bar and on the patio, perched on the edge of Dundalk Bay.

Accommodations

The Gateway Hotel

Inner Relief Rd., Dundalk; tel. 42/939-4900; www.gatewayhotel.ie; €150

Gateway by name and by nature, the main draw of this hotel is its location. It's easily reachable from the M1 motorway, only a short drive from the center of Dundalk, and on the way to the Cooley Peninsula. The modern 14-story building has 129 standard, double, and executive rooms, some wheelchair-accessible. Get a room with a mountain view if possible. On-site restaurant **54 Degrees** serves dishes from around the world for lunch and dinner.

The Imperial Hotel

95 Park St., Dundalk; tel. 42/933-2241; www.thehotelimperial.ie; €170

Stay in the heart of the action in Dundalk at the four-star Imperial Hotel, just steps from great restaurants and pubs. The 49 rooms in four types are comfortable and modern enough to spend your evening in. There is a contemporary bar and restaurant in the lobby.

Information and Services

Dundalk Tourist Information Office

Magnet Rd.; tel. 42/935-2111; www.visitlouth.ie; Mon.-Fri. 10am-4pm

In the middle of the town, this tourist office has useful information on local businesses and historical sites.

Getting There and Around

From Dublin or Drogheda, the same transport options are available. Taking the M1 north toward Belfast, exits 16, 17, and 18 all lead to Dundalk. The Route 100X bus (€20 round-trip) from **Bus Éireann** (www.buseireann.ie) runs 19 times daily from Dublin via Drogheda. **Matthews Coaches** (www.matthews.ie) runs 21 buses daily from Dublin (€20 round-trip) but does not accept card payments. Buses drop off at the stop on the **Long Walk.** Trains run throughout the day from Connolly Station in Dublin to Dundalk's **Clarke Station** (Carrickmacross Rd.; €25 round-trip), with direct trains available.

RAVENSDALE FOREST RECREATION AREA

Ravensdale Forest Recreation Area is a great place for hiking. The forest is mainly monoculture evergreens, but older parts have a better ecological mix toward the hills on the northern edge. Parking is available at the car park and sometimes overflows onto the road, but make sure not to block any emergency access gates. Dogs are welcome but must be kept under control.

Hiking and Walking

Ravensdale Forest Loop

Distance: *8.5 km (5.3 mi) round-trip*
Duration: *3 hours*
Elevation gain: *450 m (1,480 ft)*
Effort: *Moderate*
Trailhead: *Ravensdale Forest car park*

The Ravensdale Forest Loop is mainly on gravel logging roads from the car park up to the mast on **Black Mountain.** At the top are great views down the mountains and over **Carlingford Lough,** but don't leave without taking a short detour to see **Clermont Cairn,** a megalithic tomb at the summit. The trail is signposted throughout. On the way back down, the views of the Louth countryside and stone circle folly make the hike well worth it.

Getting There

From Dundalk, take the M1 north to exit 18

and follow the signs for Ravensdale. Turn left once you reach the forest; the car park is toward the end of the road. The drive is 13 km (8 mi) and takes 15 minutes. From Carlingford, take the R173 to Jenkinstown and turn onto the R174, which brings you to the car park. This route is 24 km (15 mi) and takes 30 minutes. There is no bus service to the forest.

CARLINGFORD AND THE COOLEY PENINSULA

The Cooley Peninsula is a rural part of the northeast whose spirit and way of life are defined by the Cooley Mountains. With an interesting mix of farmers, hill walkers, and wedding parties, the town of Carlingford and villages like Greenore and Ravensdale always have something going on. The two ridges of the Cooley Mountains have generations of stories and folklore, and the best way to experience it is to get out on the trails.

Sights

Carlingford Lough

Carlingford Lough is a glacial fjord that has shore in both Northern Ireland and the Republic of Ireland. You can sit by the water in Carlingford and take in the views of the lough, but it's best enjoyed by walking or cycling the Carlingford Omeath Greenway, which runs 10 km (6 mi) along the water's edge. Keep your eyes peeled for protected geese and terns and the occasional dolphin. Boat tours from the Carlingford Marina take you out to **Haulbowline Lighthouse,** which guided ships into the harbor in the 1800s.

The Long Woman's Grave

Corrakit

The story goes that a Cooley man named Lorcan O'Hanlon sailed to Spain, where he met a woman named Cauthleen, and they fell in love. She was hesitant to return with him to Ireland, preferring her life in Spain, but Lorcan convinced her by telling her that he inherited land on the Cooley Peninsula from his father. Technically, this wasn't a lie, but he didn't tell her that his brother had tricked him into only getting a small sliver of land. When they returned to Ireland, she saw the paltry land that he owned and died on the spot from the shock. Today, her grave still stands in the mountain hollow. There is parking nearby for visitors.

Greenore Railway & Maritime Museum

22 Euston St., Greenore; tel. 42/937-3822; Wed.-Sat. 9:30am-4:30pm; free

This unique business in the ex-railway town of Greenore is part museum and part coffee shop. It is housed in the old co-op building, where you'll learn all about the role that the railway played before it was removed and how local people have worked with the sea and the lough in the last 200 years. The hot drinks served are quite basic, but the afternoon tea events, run sporadically, are worth visiting for, and come with hats and shawls from the Victorian era so you can look the part.

Hiking and Walking

★ Slieve Foye Loop

Distance: *8.5 km (5.3 mi) round-trip*
Duration: *3 hours*
Elevation gain: *340 m (1,120 ft)*
Effort: *Moderate*
Trailhead: *Carlingford Tourist Office car park*

Slieve Foye is the tallest of the Cooley Mountains, and the loop to the top is a rewarding hike. It can be done in either direction, but the clockwise option is the most popular, as you get to enjoy the open mountain scramble to the peak. The hike begins and ends at the tourist office car park by the playground and follows part of the **Táin Way** on narrow country roads before turning onto a single-track trail. There are challenging sections toward the top, especially after bad weather, but at the summit you'll have unbeatable views across Carlingford Lough to the Mourne Mountains in the north and rolling green fields to the south.

Táin Way

Distance: *41 km (25 mi) round-trip*

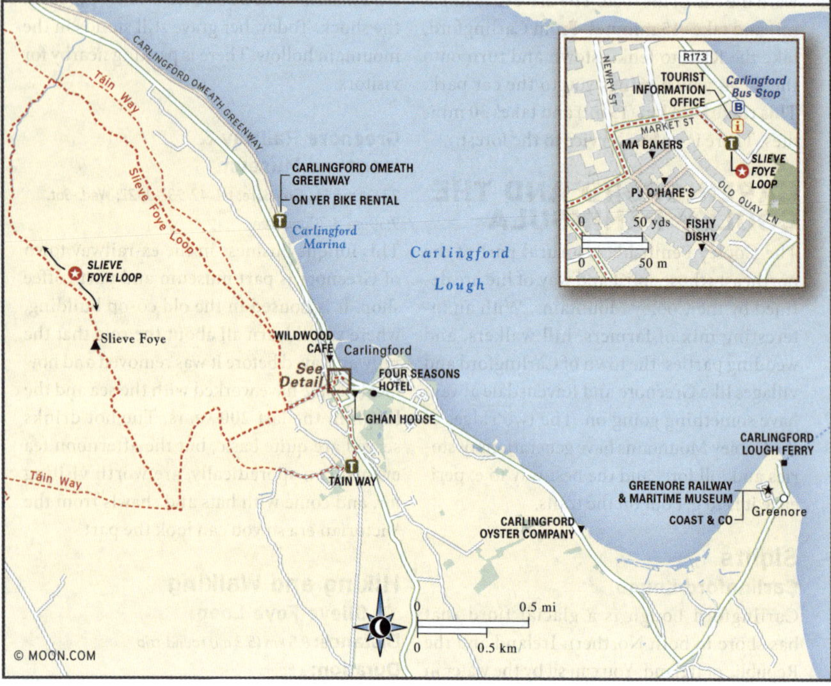

Duration: *12-15 hours*
Elevation gain: *1,440 m (4,720 ft)*
Effort: *Difficult*
Trailhead: *Station House, Carlingford*

This mammoth hike takes in all sides of the Cooley Peninsula and is a challenge for any hiker. Start in Carlingford and stock up on supplies at the only shop in town before you leave, as there is no resupply point on the trail. Hiking alongside the lough, you cross up and over into **Ravensdale Forest** before taking on a 350-m (1,150-ft) climb over 7 km (4.3 mi) up **Annaloughan** mountain. The trail then turns toward **Slieve Foye** before you begin your final descent into Carlingford. There's no lodging or campgrounds on the trail, so dispersed camping is your only option. This is a difficult trail and should only be attempted by experienced hikers and hill walkers.

Cycling

Carlingford Omeath Greenway

Distance: *11 km (7 mi) round-trip*
Duration: *1-2 hours*
Elevation gain: *50 m (160 ft)*
Effort: *Easy*
Trailhead: *Carlingford Marina*

Cycling the Omeath Carlingford Greenway is a relaxing way to see Carlingford Lough and toward the Mourne Mountains in Northern Ireland. The greenway starts at the Carlingford Marina, where you can also rent bikes, and takes the form of a wide asphalt path with room for cyclists to pass in either direction. This is a multiuse greenway, so cyclists must yield to walkers. Once you leave Carlingford, you ride north to the village of Omeath with only a slight detour from the

1: on top of Slieve Foye **2:** Lily's Finnegans

1
2
LILY FINNEGAN'S
WINE & SPIRIT STORE

Táin Bó Cúailnge

The Táin Bó Cúailnge (the Cattle Raid of Cooley) tells of the 1st century CE Queen Medb and King Ailill of Connaught attempting to steal the legendary bull Donn Cuailnge from Ulster. Despite warnings of doom, they march to the Cooley Mountains, where the Ulstermen are cursed and unable to fight—except for the mighty Cú Chulainn. After three days of fierce battles, Cú Chulainn triumphs, but Medb still manages to steal the bull. The story is often described as Ireland's version of the *Iliad* by Homer. You can get a great understanding of the story today on the **Táin Way,** a 41-km (26-mi) hiking trail that follows part of the route of Queen Medb.

water along the way. Once you reach Omeath and take in the views, turn around and follow the same route back to Carlingford Marina.

On Yer Bike Rental

Carlingford Marina; tel. 87/992-1559; www.onyerbike.ie; Fri.-Wed. 10am-6pm; from €14

On Yer Bike rents basic and affordable bikes suitable to ride the Carlingford Omeath Greenway. There are e-bikes, cruisers, mountain bikes, and kids' bikes as well as trailers and kids' seats. Bikes can be rented for 2 hours to multiple days.

Boating

Carlingford Lough Ferry

The Harbour; tel. 800/938-004; www.carlingfordferry.com; seasonally Mar.-Oct.; from €8

Carlingford Lough is so scenic that the ferry locals use as part of their commute is also an attraction for visitors. The ferry runs from Greenore in the Republic of Ireland to Greencastle in Northern Ireland, and there's room on board for a limited number of cars. There's one crossing per hour 9am-8pm daily with more services during summer. For an even more memorable time, book a ticket on the Sunset Cruise, Lough of Legends tour, or Twilight Cruise with live music.

Food

Coast & Co

Euston St.; tel. 85/730-1741; www.coastandco.ie; Mon.-Fri. 9:30am-4pm, Sat.-Sun. 10am-4pm; from €9

Mixing coffee with wine and home interiors, Coast & Co is a passion project for the owners, who welcome you for shopping, drinking, or just browsing. The breakfast menu has US influences with a breakfast hash, a pancake stack, and a breakfast burrito. The lunch menu has a more European feel with pasta dishes and fresh salads. The building is an old schoolhouse with a small outdoor seating area to take in the tranquil terraced street.

Wildwood Café

Newry St.; Instagram @wildwoodstreetfoodbox; Wed.-Fri. and Mon. 10am-3pm, Sat.-Sun. 10am-5pm; from €10

Serving coffee, tacos, and burgers, Wildwood Café is a popular place in Carlingford, particularly with cyclists stopping in to refuel. The business started as a food truck, but they've kept the relaxed and informal appeal. All the food is made to go, but there are covered picnic tables if you'd like to stay.

★ PJ O'Hare's

Tholsel St.; tel. 42/937-3106; www.pjoharescarlingford.ie; daily noon-9pm; from €14

Known locally as PJ's, this buzzing pub is a very lively venue that attracts stag dos and hen parties (bachelor and bachelorette parties) to the large covered beer garden. It's more than just a place for big parties, as the interior of the pub has traditional charm alongside a seafood menu with shellfish from Carlingford Lough, including the famous oysters. During summer they have a busy schedule of live music.

Fishy Dishy

Tholsel St.; tel. 87/980-7774; Instagram @FishyDishyCarlingford; Wed.-Sun. 5pm-9pm; from €18

Fishy Dishy is a family-run restaurant on the medieval streets of Carlingford. The cozy dining room creates a comfortable dining experience. Fishy Dishy specializes in fresh fish and shellfish, making it a great place to try Carlingford oysters. There's a small seating area outside, and there are also meat and vegetarian choices available.

Bars and Nightlife

Lily's Finnegans

Whitestown; tel. 42/937-3730; www.lilyfinnegans.com; Thurs. 5pm-11:30pm, Fri. 5pm-12:30am, Sat. 12:30pm-12:30am, Sun. 1pm-11pm

Lily's Finnegans isn't the easiest pub to find, but it's worth the short drive from Carlingford. Located in Whitestown, one of the ancestral homes of Joe Biden, this pub is like having a drink in someone's house thanks to the warm welcome and low ceilings. In summer they have live music out back, and when the weather is bad they light the fire.

Ma Bakers

Market St.; tel. 87/449-3654; www.mabakershenandstag.com; Mon.-Sat. 11am-midnight, Sun. 12:30pm-midnight

You'll find Ma Bakers in the medieval part of Carlingford, among the narrow streets. They have live music six nights a week and twice on Sunday. You'll find trad sessions and singer-songwriters as well as plenty of parties and groups dancing. The bartenders pour pints, wine, and highballs in this busy down-to-earth pub.

The Carlingford Brewing Co.

Dundalk Rd.; tel. 42/939-7519; www.carlingfordbrewing.ie; Thurs.-Fri. 5pm-12:30am, Sat. 1pm-12:30am, Sun. 1pm-11pm

Embracing its setting along the old railway line, the Carlingford Brewing Co. encourages people to sit outside on the deck to see the old railway carriages. The terrace has space for 40 with more seating inside. With a brewery on-site, they serve their own beer, including the Long Woman session IPA, as well as pizza, fries, and chicken wings. The owner runs brewery tours (90 minutes), and you can rent the Old Mill and Táin Taproom.

Accommodations

Ballymascanlon Hotel & Golf Resort

Carlingford Rd.; tel. 42/935-8200; www.ballymascanlon.com; €150

As a four-star hotel with a golf course and famous guests like the Beatles, the Ballymascanlon Hotel, or Ballymac as locals call it, is a staple in the northeast. The quiet drive from the entrance to the hotel past the golf course sets the tone for this classy place. Once a Victorian house, expect to find touches of classic luxury across the 53-ha (130-acre) site. Among the 97 double, twin, and family rooms are 6 rooms that still use the original 19th-century interior design. Take a dip in the 20-m (65-ft) pool, play a round on the 18-hole course, or have some food and drink in the **Proleek Restaurant** or **Terrace Bar.**

Ghan House

Old Quay Lane; tel. 42/937-3682; www.ghanhouse.com; restaurant from €63 pp; hotel €210

Ghan House is a restored Georgian from the early 1700s tucked into the foothills of the Cooley Mountains. A quiet refuge from the bustle of Carlingford, this award-winning hotel has 12 rooms decorated with antique furniture with views of Slieve Foye or Carlingford Harbour. Modern touches include Wi-Fi and power showers. Dining at Ghan House is not to be missed, with dishes made with ingredients from the garden and local shellfish, served in the drawing room. The menu changes seasonally but you can expect interesting choices like pigeon, scallops, and venison; they also accommodate vegans with advanced notice. The dining room feels formal but the dress code is smart casual, which gives it a more leisurely feel.

Four Seasons Hotel

Greenore Rd.; tel. 42/937-3530; www.4seasonshotelcarlingford.ie; €300

This four-star 58-room hotel at the foot of the Cooley Mountains lets you experience the mountains and peninsula in the comfort of a quality hotel. Plenty of parking is available, and the **4FIT Leisure Club** has an 18-m (60-ft) swimming pool, a sauna, a steam room, and a jetted tub. If you don't want to walk into Carlingford for food, the **Lough Lounge** in the lobby is open for lunch and dinner.

Information and Services

There's an **ATM** in the Centra (https://centra.ie) on Newry Street.

Carlingford Tourist Information Office

Liberties of Carlingford; tel. 42/937-3650; www.carlingford.ie; daily 11am-5pm

Find out about all the restaurants and the various hikes and walks from the staff.

Getting There and Around

To get to Carlingford from Dublin, take the M1 north and drive past Dundalk to exit 18 for Carlingford. From here it's a 15-minute drive along Dundalk Bay on the Cooley Peninsula before turning left into Carlingford. **Bus Éireann** (www.buseireann.ie) operates the Route 161 bus from Dundalk to Carlingford (€10 round-trip), which runs six times a day and drops off at the **Liberties of Carlingford.**

The Southeast

Take a journey to the sunny southeast, where the natural beauty of the endless beaches and stunning islands tells a story of Viking invasions and regal families. This part of Ireland is home to lesser visited counties Wexford, Waterford, and Kilkenny, and it rewards visitors with tranquil holidays and world-class sights.

The Vikings left an impression on most of Ireland's east coast, but their impact is felt most in the southeast. They created settlements here in the Middle Ages, and we still use their names for places like Waterford and Wexford. Kilkenny City and Waterford City both have a Medieval Mile that tells their stories, while Wexford has the Irish National Heritage Park, where you can see how people lived in the 10th century.

Highlights

Look for ★ to find recommended sights, activities, dining, and lodging.

★ **Medieval Mile:** Discover Kilkenny's Viking past on the cobbled streets of the Medieval Mile, home to museums, preserved buildings, and lively pubs (page 157).

★ **Kilkenny Castle:** Stroll the grounds of this impressive castle by the river and visit the gallery to see portraits of the family that owned it for 500 years (page 158).

★ **Saltee Islands:** Sail to these small islands off the coast of Wexford to spot puffins taking flight from the cliffs and hear about the eccentric owners (page 165).

★ **Hook Lighthouse:** Climb to the top of this 800-year-old structure in Wexford, the oldest operational lighthouse in the world (page 167).

★ **The Kennedy Homestead:** Find out about the Kennedy family's connection to rural Wexford and see how they went from Irish emigrants to the White House (page 168).

★ **Waterford Greenway:** Cycle the foothills of the Comeragh Mountains on this traffic-free 46-km (29-mi) greenway from the city to the coast, with historical sights and tasty cafés along the way (page 170).

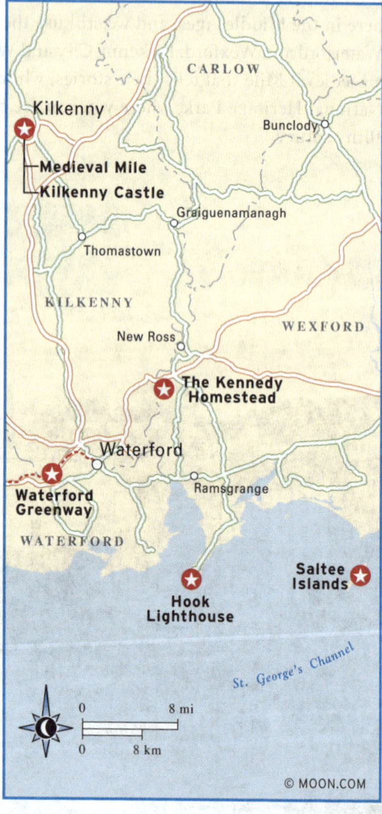

During the 19th-century famine, people left Ireland en masse and sailed to America on vessels like the *Dunbrody*. One such man was Patrick Kennedy, great-grandfather of US President John F. Kennedy, who emigrated to Boston.

People in this part of the country have a reputation for being fierce hurlers. This is the heartland of this skillful and blazingly fast Irish sport that has to be seen to be believed. It's also an area with great craftspeople, with crystal-making at Waterford, great potters at Kilkenny, and wonderful textiles at Wexford.

ORIENTATION

Three counties make up the sunny southeast, with more sunshine than other parts of Ireland. **Wexford** is on the east coast, with **Waterford** to its west, where it is part of the south coast. Landlocked **Kilkenny** borders both counties with its northern edge stretching into the midlands.

The major towns and cities here are all by the water. **Waterford City** is on the River Suir, **Kilkenny City** is on the River Nore, and **Wexford Town** is at the mouth of the River Slaney and the Irish Sea. These places are close to each other, with no journey between these places taking more than an hour by car.

PLANNING YOUR TIME

These cities are small and can easily be seen in one day each. Part of the attraction of the sunny southeast is that there isn't a list of must-see places; instead, it's a place to slow things down, see some sights, and spend time strolling the beaches. Give Waterford City, Kilkenny City, and Wexford Town three days in total, with two nights in Waterford City and one in Kilkenny City; this allows you to explore the entire area from a lively base. If you only have enough time to visit one place, then it comes down to choosing between the Norman history in Kilkenny City or the Viking history in Waterford City.

Itinerary Ideas

A visit to this relaxed part of the country generally doesn't involve a strict schedule, with the majority of sights not requiring advance booking outside summer. In the peak months, try to book tickets to Hook Lighthouse and Kilkenny Castle in advance. You can visit Kilkenny, Wexford, or Waterford on their own, on the way from Dublin to Cork, or stitch them together for a three-day trip to the region. If you visit all three, go to Waterford direct from Kilkenny, then head to County Wexford.

ONE DAY IN KILKENNY CITY

1. Check into **Hotel Kilkenny** for a relaxing start with a visit to the pool and spa before walking into the city.
2. Book your tickets for a tour of **Kilkenny Castle** to hear about the Butler family and see the extensive art collection in the Long Gallery. Wander the parkland trail toward the center of the city.
3. Stop at the **Yard Café** for lunch and try a summer salad or bacon sandwich.

Previous: Kilkenny; Kilkenny Castle; puffins on the Saltee Islands.

The Southeast

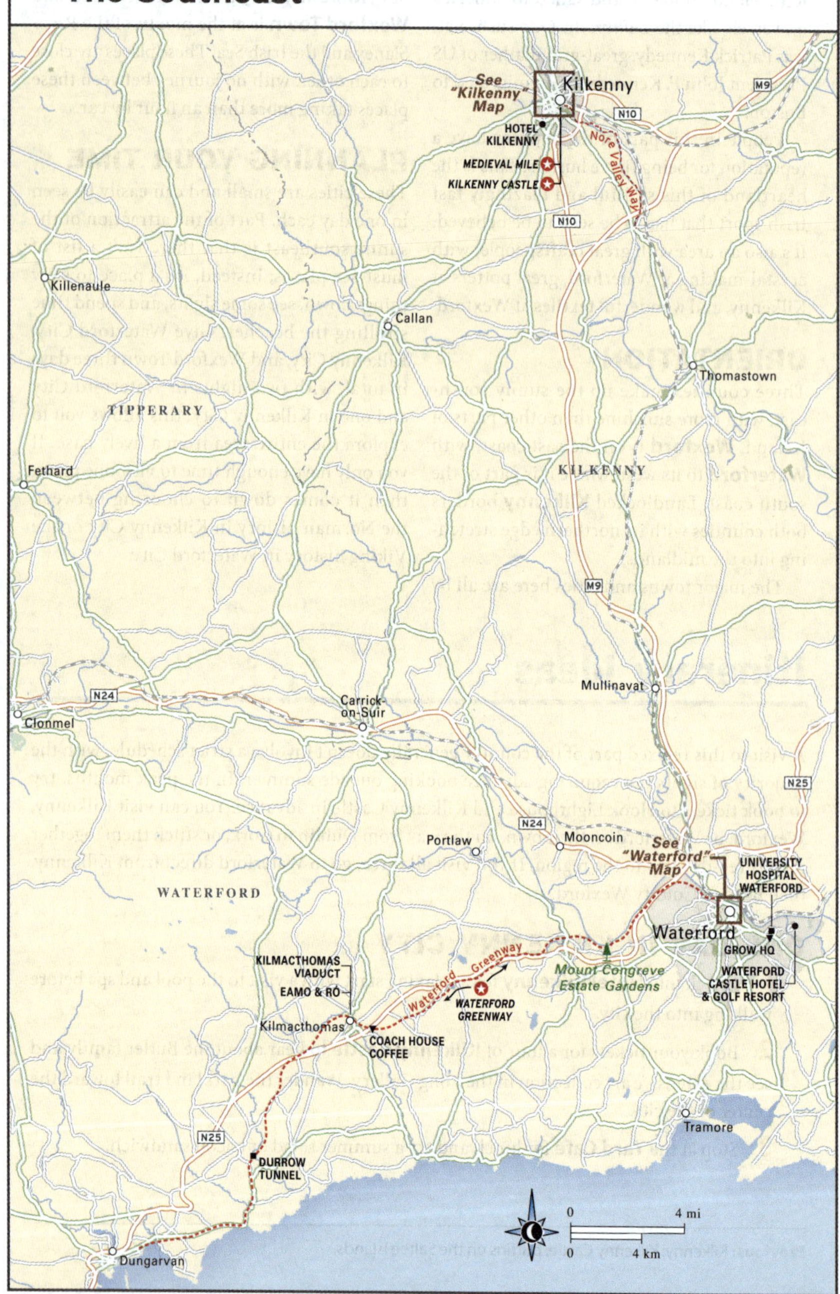

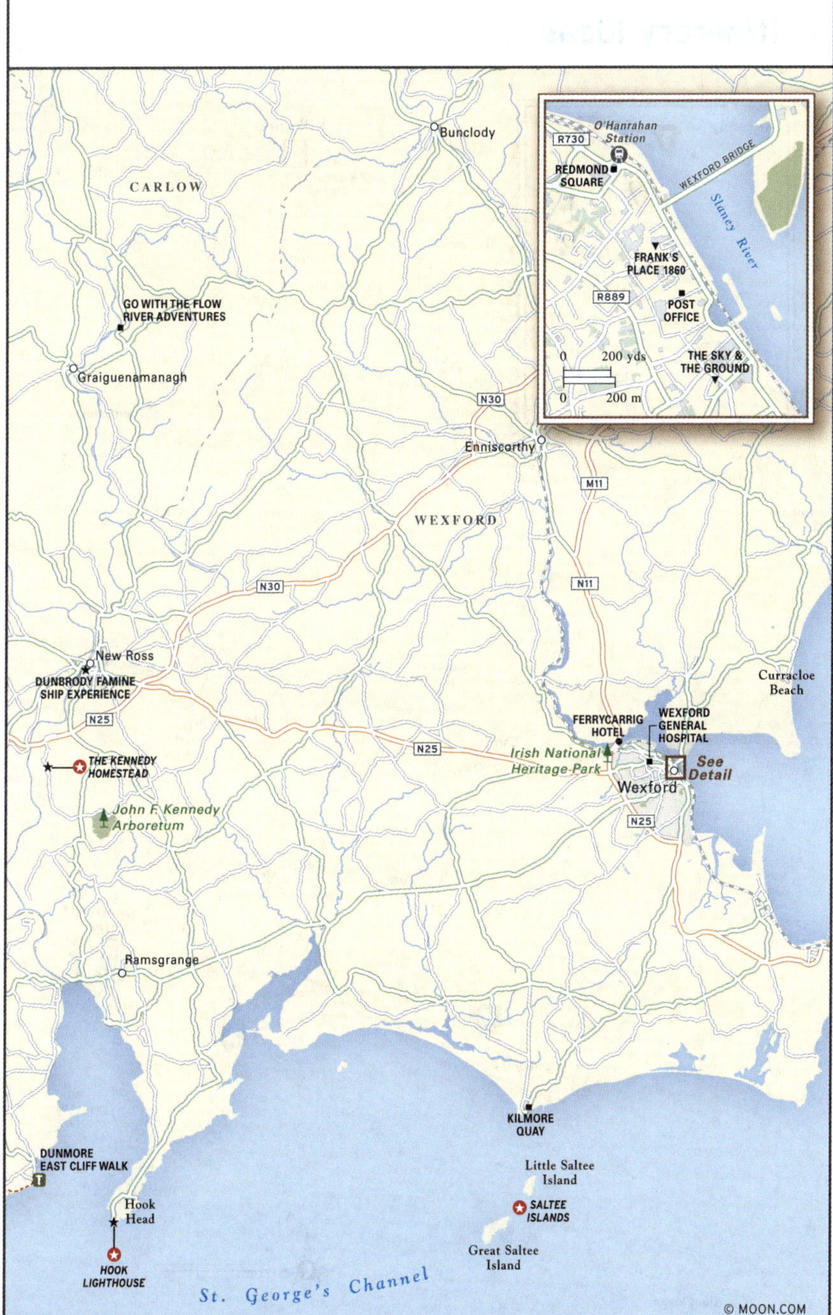

Bunclody
CARLOW
GO WITH THE FLOW RIVER ADVENTURES
Graiguenamanagh
N30
Enniscorthy
M11
WEXFORD
N30
N11
New Ross
DUNBRODY FAMINE SHIP EXPERIENCE
N25
THE KENNEDY HOMESTEAD
John F. Kennedy Arboretum
N25
FERRYCARRIG HOTEL
WEXFORD GENERAL HOSPITAL
Irish National Heritage Park
See Detail
Wexford
N25
Curracloe Beach
Ramsgrange
KILMORE QUAY
DUNMORE EAST CLIFF WALK
Hook Head
HOOK LIGHTHOUSE
Little Saltee Island
SALTEE ISLANDS
Great Saltee Island
St. George's Channel
© MOON.COM
O'Hanrahan Station
R730
REDMOND SQUARE
WEXFORD BRIDGE
Slaney River
FRANK'S PLACE 1860
R889
POST OFFICE
0 200 yds
0 200 m
THE SKY & THE GROUND

Itinerary Ideas

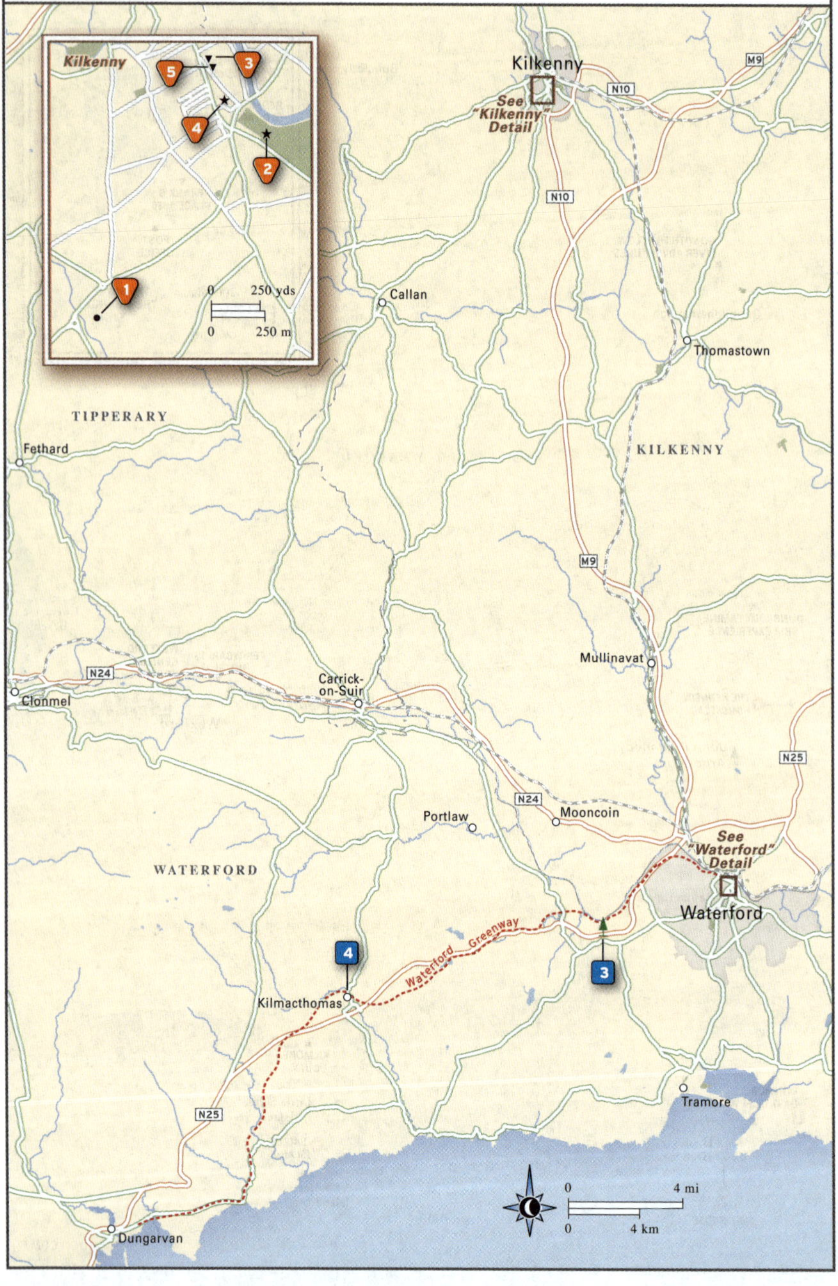
Kilkenny
5
3
4
2
1
0
250 yds
0
250 m
Kilkenny
See "Kilkenny" Detail
M9
N10
N10
Callan
Thomastown
TIPPERARY
KILKENNY
Fethard
M9
Mullinavat
N24
Clonmel
Carrick-on-Suir
N25
N24
Mooncoin
Portlaw
See "Waterford" Detail
WATERFORD
Waterford
Waterford Greenway
4
3
Kilmacthomas
Tramore
N25
0
4 mi
0
4 km
Dungarvan

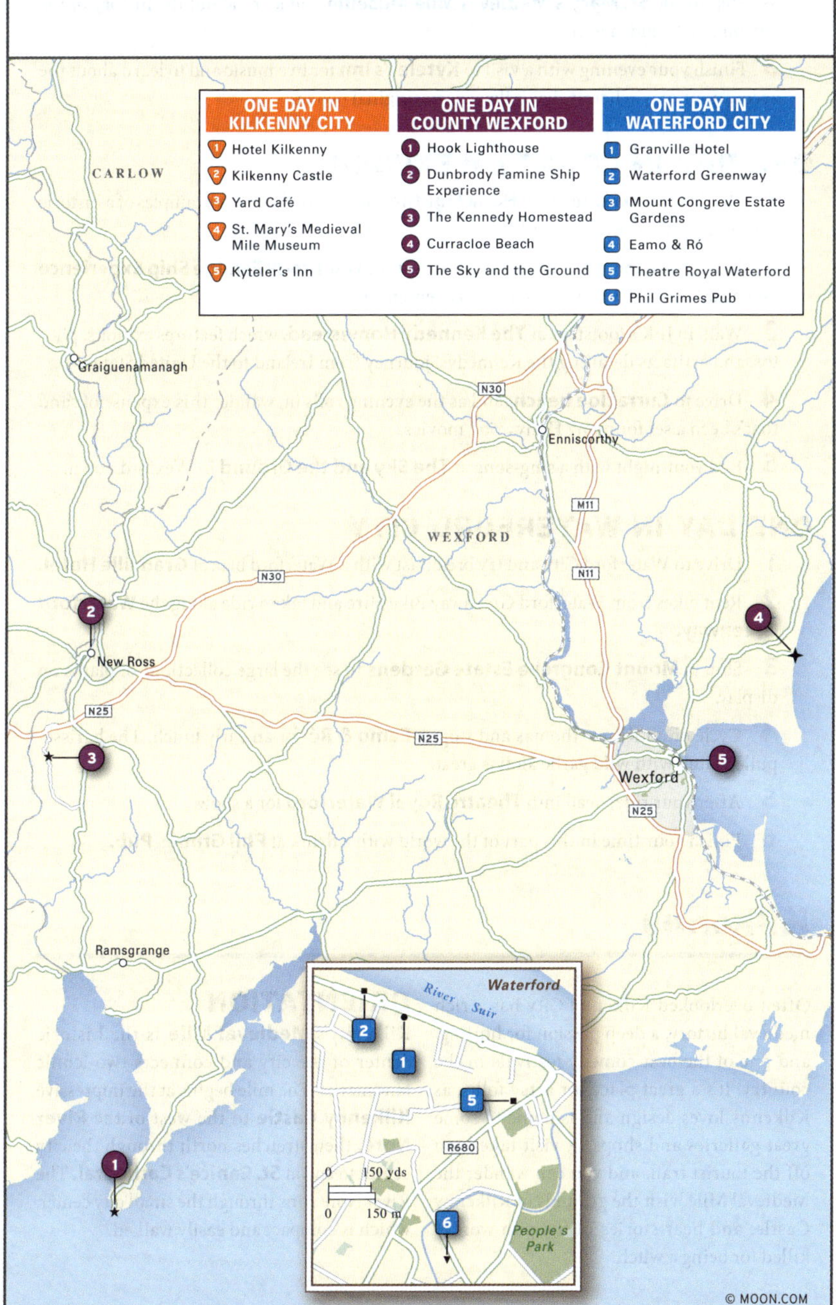
ONE DAY IN KILKENNY CITY
1 Hotel Kilkenny
2 Kilkenny Castle
3 Yard Café
4 St. Mary's Medieval Mile Museum
5 Kyteler's Inn
ONE DAY IN COUNTY WEXFORD
1 Hook Lighthouse
2 Dunbrody Famine Ship Experience
3 The Kennedy Homestead
4 Curracloe Beach
5 The Sky and the Ground
ONE DAY IN WATERFORD CITY
1 Granville Hotel
2 Waterford Greenway
3 Mount Congreve Estate Gardens
4 Eamo & Ró
5 Theatre Royal Waterford
6 Phil Grimes Pub
CARLOW
Graiguenamanagh
N30
Enniscorthy
M11
WEXFORD
N30
N11
New Ross
N25
N25
Wexford
N25
Ramsgrange
Waterford
River Suir
R680
0 150 yds
0 150 m
People's Park
© MOON.COM

4 Step inside **St. Mary's Medieval Mile Museum** and learn about the history of the city on a self-guided tour.

5 Finish your evening with a visit to **Kyteler's Inn** for live music and to learn about the accusations of witchcraft that followed the original owner.

ONE DAY IN COUNTY WEXFORD

1 Head for the coast and visit **Hook Lighthouse,** one of the finest examples of a historic working lighthouse in the world.

2 Learn more about the history of the area at the **Dunbrody Famine Ship Experience** and hear how it played a key role in Irish emigration.

3 Walk in JFK's footsteps at **The Kennedy Homestead,** which features exhibits, photos, and artifacts detailing the Kennedys' journey from Ireland to the United States.

4 Drive to **Curracloe Beach,** and as the evening rolls in, wander this expanse of sand that's been a set for many Hollywood movies.

5 End your night with a sing-song at **The Sky and the Ground** in Wexford Town.

ONE DAY IN WATERFORD CITY

1 Drive to Waterford City and try breakfast with a Waterford blaa at **Granville Hotel.**

2 Rent bikes from Waterford Greenway Bike Hire and take a ride along the **Waterford Greenway.**

3 Stop at **Mount Congreve Estate Gardens** to see the large collections of plants on display.

4 Cycle on to Kilmacthomas and stop at **Eamo & Ró** for an early lunch. The harissa-pulled lamb with wild garlic aioli is great.

5 After your ride, head into **Theatre Royal Waterford** for a show.

6 Finish your time in this part of the world with a drink at **Phil Grimes Pub.**

Kilkenny

Often overlooked Kilkenny City has a rich medieval history, a deep passion for hurling, and one of the best comedy festivals in the country. It's a great place for artsy folks, as Kilkenny loves design and is home to some great galleries and shops. A visit takes you off the tourist trail, and you can wander the Medieval Mile, visit the grounds of Kilkenny Castle, and hear stories of the pub worker killed for being a witch.

ORIENTATION

Kilkenny's **Medieval Mile** is the historic center of the city and connects two iconic landmarks. The mile begins at the impressive **Kilkenny Castle** to the west of the **River Nore,** then stretches north through the city center to end at **St. Canice's Cathedral.** The River Nore runs through the small city center, which is compact and easily walked.

Kilkenny

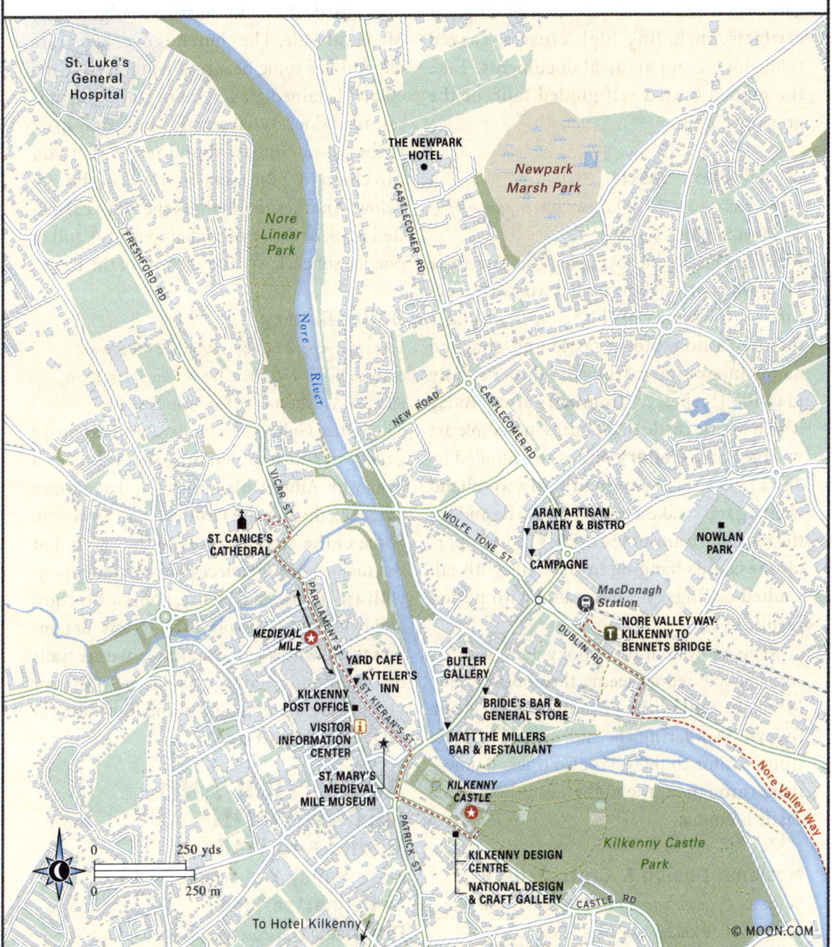

SIGHTS

★ Medieval Mile

The cobblestone streets of Kilkenny's Medieval Mile are the historic heart of the city, with the narrow streets and stone buildings home to fascinating stories about its past. The area was developed during the Norman invasion when Richard "Strongbow" de Clare, the Earl of Pembroke, built Kilkenny Castle. The area is home to many major attractions, including Kyteler's Inn and St. Canice's Cathedral, but spend some time just wandering the area to soak up the atmosphere.

St. Mary's Medieval Mile Museum

2 St. Mary's Lane, High St.; tel. 56/781-7022; www.medievalmilemuseum.ie; daily 9:30am-4:30pm; from €9

Kilkenny's main draw is this museum, a brilliantly modern renovation of the 13th-century St. Mary's Church. Many of the original features remain, surrounded by sleek white finishings reminiscent of a contemporary art gallery. There's a vast collection of religious artifacts, including high crosses, carved tombstones, and archival documents. Take the guided tour, a self-guided tour, or the graveyard tour.

★ Kilkenny Castle

The Parade; tel. 56/770-4100; www.kilkennycastle.ie; daily 9am-5:30pm; from €8

Kilkenny Castle has occupied this site since 1195, when Strongbow built a wooden structure on the banks of the river. It was later fortified into a stone castle and changed hands many times, from the Butler family to Catholic rebels to Cromwell's army. Today it's a majestic castle that houses incredible art in **The Long Gallery** and is surrounded by 20 ha (50 acres) of parkland with a woodland walking trail. Take a tour of the castle and see the regal portraits of the castle's most important residents hanging in the halls with tall vaulted ceilings and decorated with period furniture.

Keep an eye out for spooky goings-on, as some people report seeing the ghost of Lady Margaret Butler, the grandmother of Anne Boleyn, wandering the hallways. The electronic visitor counter has also tracked movement throughout the night, even though the castle is empty.

National Design & Craft Gallery

Castle Yard, The Parade; tel. 83/090-8264; www.ndcg.ie; Tues.-Sat. 10am-5:30pm; free

Design is a huge passion in the city, and you'll get an understanding of it at this gallery in the stables at Kilkenny Castle. This is the only gallery in the country dedicated to design and crafts, and it hosts exhibits of textiles, glass, ceramics, and more from Irish designers. It's a great addition to a visit to the castle, especially on rainy days.

St. Canice's Cathedral

Coach Rd.; tel. 56/776-4971; www.stcanicescathedral.ie; Mon.-Sat. 9am-6pm, Sun. 1pm-6pm; from €7

Not many cities have a patron saint, but Kilkenny's is Saint Canice, and you can visit his cathedral on the northern edge of the Medieval Mile. The church is over 800 years old and has some beautiful features, like the colorful stained glass windows and the mosaic tiled floor. What sets this cathedral apart is the 30-m (100-ft) round tower that you can climb (€7) for fantastic views of the city below. Another highlight is the 700-year-old Red Book of Ossory (guided tour €10), full of poems, songs, laws, and records of the time.

Butler Gallery

Evans Home, John's Quay; tel. 56/776-1106; www.butlergallery.ie; Tues.-Wed. 10am-5pm, Thurs. 10am-8pm, Fri.-Sat. 10am-5pm, Sun. 11am-5pm; free

The Butler Gallery is a modern and extensive gallery in a historic building that was once a priory for Augustinian priests and a military barracks during the Cromwellian invasion. Some of the artwork dates to the 1800s, but the majority of the pieces are contemporary, with artists like Paul Henry, Louis le Brocquy, and Evie Hone on display. There's lots for families to do, with a kid's play space, nature trails on the grounds, and regular events. After your visit, enjoy a coffee and some light bites at **MUSE Coffee + Food.**

ACTIVITIES AND RECREATION

Hiking and Walking

Nore Valley Way: Kilkenny to Bennettsbridge

Distance: *10 km (6 mi) one-way*
Duration: *2 hours*
Elevation gain: *130 m (430 ft)*
Effort: *Easy-moderate*
Trailhead: *MacDonagh Train Station*

The Nore Valley Way is split into three unconnected stages that follow the river: Kilkenny to Bennettsbridge, Thomastown to Inistioge, and Bennettsbridge to Thomastown. This section starts on the eastern side of the river,

1: Kilkenny's medieval streets **2:** St. Canice's Cathedral **3:** Kilkenny Castle

1
2
3

Hurling

the Kilkenny hurling team in action

Hurling is one of those sports that has to be seen to be believed. It's like a mix between the power and roughness of rugby with the speed and skill of ice hockey. The women's version of the sport is called camogie and is essentially the same with some minor rule tweaks. Kilkenny has won the most hurling championships, with 36, and Cork has the most successful camogie team, with 29 wins.

RULES OF THE GAME

Each team has 15 players. They use a stick called a hurl to hit a ball called a sliotar. Hurls are made from ash, and the sliotar is cork wrapped in leather. A point is scored if a player hits the sliotar

with great views of Kilkenny Castle and the parklands. Walk the natural trail that gently undulates as you go south through beautiful riverside scenes with mature trees and bustling with wildlife. Watch for the mill, the church, and the limestone quarry as you approach Maddockstown, and when you get to the endpoint in Bennettsbridge, pop into **Crafted** (Main St.; Instagram @CraftedBennettsbridge; Mon.-Sat. 10am-3:30pm; from €10) for soup and a sandwich.

Water Sports

Go with the Flow River Adventures

Lock House; tel. 87/252-9700; https://gowiththeflow.ie; daily 9am-6pm; from €29

The family-focused company has been bringing people of all ages on river adventures for 30 years. The main offerings are canoe and kayak tours on your own or with a guide. Book a 3-hour trip down the River Barrow, where you'll hear stories of the history and folklore of the area. If you're feeling brave, paddle down the mini rapids that form at the weirs, or divert around them. Book a multiday canoe trip (from €95 pp) to spend full days on the river and sleep in unique glamping cabins in the countryside.

FESTIVALS AND EVENTS

Cat Laughs Comedy Festival

https://thecatlaughs.com; June

The Cat Laughs Comedy Festival is a knee-slapping annual event that's been making people laugh since 1994 at various venues

between the posts and over the bar. A goal, worth three points, is scored if the ball goes in under the bar.

SIGNIFICANCE OF THE GAME

The sport is ancient and dates to the time of the demigod Sétanta, a fierce player. These days, hurling is a local sport played for the "pride of the parish," the village teams. The best players advance to play for the county and compete in the All-Ireland Championship. If you get a chance to see the sport live, you'll be blown away by the skill of players running with the sliotar on their hurl and thundering shots at the goal.

HOW TO WATCH THE GAME

The men's hurling season begins in late January and culminates with the All-Ireland Hurling Final in July in Croke Park in Dublin. The camogie season follows a similar timeline, beginning in February and ending in August. Hurling and Gaelic football share the same pitches, and each county has a stadium that ranges from the smallest in Drogheda, with a capacity of 3,500, to the 82,300-capacity Croke Park.

- **Croke Park, Dublin:** This stadium hosts the All-Ireland semifinals and finals in both hurling and Gaelic football (page 64).
- **Nowlan Park, Kilkenny:** Hurling is a way of life in Kilkenny, and you can see the county teams play at the 27,000-capacity Nowlan Park.
- **Páirc Uí Chaoimh, Cork:** This 45,000-capacity stadium is the largest in Munster and hosts the Munster provincial finals as well as Cork's home games.
- **TV and streaming options:** The latter games of the championship are televised on RTÉ and TG4. You'll find the majority of games streamed on the paid platform **GAAGO** (www.gaggo.ie; €12/month).

across the city, including pubs, theaters, and hotels. Irish and international comedians perform over the holiday weekend before the first Monday in June. Tickets are sold for individual events. Over the years big names like Bill Murray, Stephen Fry, and Peter Kay have played this festival. It's extremely popular, so plan as far ahead as possible, as tickets and lodging sell out well in advance.

SHOPPING

Kilkenny Design Centre

Castle Yard, The Parade; tel. 56/772-2118; https://kilkennydesign.com; Mon.-Sat. 10am-6pm, Sun. 11am-6pm

Set on the beautiful grounds of Kilkenny Castle, this high-quality crafts and design shop stocks pieces by some of the biggest Irish names. This store is their flagship among 18 across the country. Find new home furnishings like glassware from Killarney Crystal, skin-care products from VOYA, and knitwear from Kilkenny Design. The shop is high-end, with premium products that stand the test of time.

FOOD

Cafés and Light Bites

Arán Artisan Bakery & Bistro

8 Barrack St.; tel. 56/775-6297; www.arankilkenny.ie; Mon. and Wed.-Thurs. 9:30am-3:30pm, Fri.-Sun. 9am-3:30pm; from €15

This chic little bakery and bistro is well worth the stroll east of the River Nore. The bright yellow and green interiors pop, and the food is just as attractive. Every bakery needs a good sourdough, and the one here is top-notch, made using local flour and a 48-hour fermentation process. The menu can change daily, but expect all-day brunch with items like the Irish breakfast sandwich, made with in-house bread and local sausage, bacon, and eggs. If you like spice, try their Korean-inspired Magic Sauce.

Casual Dining

The Yard Café

27 St. Kieran's St.; tel. 89/237-4033; Facebook @theyardcafe1; daily 8:30am-6pm; from €12

This cozy café with a nice outdoor seating area is tucked away in the Market Yard in the old part of the city. The menu focuses on fresh and healthy food like summer salads and falafel, though there are still some more gluttonous choices available, such as bacon sandwiches. The Yard Café is a good choice for vegans and vegetarians, too, with a number of choices on the menu as well as baked treats. When the weather is dry, nab yourself a seat outside and the friendly staff will take care of you.

Fine Dining

Campagne

The Arches, 5 Gas House Lane; tel. 56/777-2858; www.campagne.ie; Wed.-Thurs. 5:30pm-9pm, Fri.-Sat. 5pm-9:30pm, Sun. 12:30pm-2:30pm; 3 courses €80

For French dining, book a table at this 70-seat restaurant, awarded a Michelin star seven times. The dining room is classy yet more casual than most restaurants of this caliber, making it easy to settle in. The menu changes seasonally, with hand-picked shellfish and wild game in dishes like woodpigeon served with pickled grapes or roast monkfish with octopus and seaweed butter sauce. The three-course dinner menu (€80) is priced fairly, but the real deal is the three-course early-bird menu (€50), also available on the weekend.

BARS AND NIGHTLIFE

Kyteler's Inn

St Kieran's St.; tel. 56/772-1064; www.kytelersinn.com; Mon.-Thurs. 11:30am-11:30pm, Fri.-Sun. noon-11:30pm; from €6

In the heart of the Medieval Mile, this historic pub tells a gruesome story. Dame Alice Kyteler was married four times to wealthy husbands who all died in mysterious circumstances. With her fortune she bought this pub, and all was well until one of her stepchildren accused her of being a witch, forcing her to flee Ireland. Her servant, Petronilla de Meath, was accused of helping her and was burned at the stake.

Today the pub bears Alice's name, and thankfully there have been no more murders. The building is very old, and you'll walk through original stone archways on your way to the bar. There's live music every night during summer, with trad musicians taking to the small stage.

Bridie's Bar & General Store

72 John St. Lower; tel. 56/776-5133; Instagram @bridies_bar; Mon.-Fri. 8:30am-5pm, Sat. 9am-12:30am, Sun. 10am-5pm; from €6

If this is your first time in Ireland, you might be surprised to see bars that sell drinks alongside groceries and tools, but places like this were once a one-stop shop for everything you'd need. The front of the building is a beautifully renovated shop, but for old-world charm, step through the doors at the back to the bar. It has a speakeasy vibe, with jars of sweets on the shelves alongside bottles of whiskey. If it's a nice day, take your drink out back to the walled garden, where there's a small amount of seating among the shrubs.

Matt the Millers Bar & Restaurant

1 John St. Lower; tel. 56/776-1696; www.mattthemillers.com; Mon. and Thurs.-Sat. noon-2am, Tues.-Wed. noon-11:30pm, Sun. noon-11:30pm; from €6

This is a quintessential traditional pub with worn wooden floors and a rich wooden bar surrounded by wooden barstools. On a quiet day in the city, this is a great option to relax with a drink. In the evening, that changes as Matt the Millers (named because it was a 19th-century flour mill) roars to life with live music and craic across its five floors. Traditional pub grub like beef and Guinness stew and seafood chowder are served from noon, with the live music continuing into the wee hours with bands and DJs.

ACCOMMODATIONS

Hotel Kilkenny

College Rd.; tel. 56/776-2000; www.hotelkilkenny.ie; €150

Book at four-star Hotel Kilkenny for a relaxing getaway. With 138 rooms just 20 minutes' walk from Kilkenny Castle, it might be hard to drag yourself away from the 20-m (66-ft) pool, jetted tub, steam room, and spa. Rooms are stylish yet understated, and in the lobby is the **Rosehill 1831 Bar** to enjoy a pre-dinner cocktail.

The Newpark Hotel

Castlecomer Rd.; tel. 56/776-0500; www.newparkhotelkilkenny.com; €200

Set on 10 ha (25 acres) of parkland north of the city, but still within walking distance, this four-star 132-room hotel is a great choice for families. Deluxe family rooms come with a double bed and two singles, while the superior family rooms have two doubles and one single. There's plenty to do, with a kids club to let parents escape to the spa and pool, but the main attraction is **Jurassic Newpark,** Ireland's only dinosaur-themed park, with 17 life-size moving dinosaurs, walking trails, and a go-kart track.

INFORMATION AND SERVICES

The **visitor information center** (79 High St.; Mon.-Sat. 9am-5pm) is in the Medieval Mile. The main hospital in the area is **St. Luke's General Hospital** (Freshford Rd.; www.hse.ie), north of the city. **Kilkenny Post Office** (High St.; www.anpost.com) is in the Medieval Mile, close to the **AIB** (High St.; www.aib.ie) bank branch.

GETTING THERE AND AROUND

To get to Kilkenny City from Waterford City by car, take the M9 north and then the N10 just outside Kilkenny, a 40-minute, 50-km (30-mi) drive. **Dublin Coach** (www.dublincoach.ie) operates Route 600 buses (40 minutes; €7 one-way) between the two cities 10 times daily. The pickup point in Waterford is on Merchant's Quay, and the drop-off in Kilkenny is at **MacDonagh Station.** There's also the train from Plunkett Station on Waterford's Terminus Street to MacDonagh Station seven times daily.

Matt the Millers

The 130-km (80-mi) drive to Kilkenny from Dublin takes 1.5 hours. Head west on the N7 and then take the M9 outside Newbridge. The Route 600 bus with Dublin Coach also links Kilkenny with the capital. The bus leaves Dublin from Bachelor's Walk and arrives at MacDonagh Station in Kilkenny in under 2 hours. By rail, go to Dublin's Heuston Station (St. John's Rd. W.) and take one of the hourly trains to MacDonagh Station in Kilkenny.

Wexford

Known for beautiful natural landscapes and Viking invasions, County Wexford today is famous for Ireland's best strawberries. The sun shines on the long gentle beaches where the Viking and Norman invasions landed. In recent times, Hollywood directors have invaded the beaches to film historical blockbusters. The coastline plays a huge role in this part of Ireland, with major landmarks like Hook Lighthouse, Curracloe Beach, and the Saltee Islands.

ORIENTATION

Most of the action in County Wexford happens in the southeast and south. **Wexford Town** is in the southeast on the banks of the **River Slaney** where it meets the sea. Farther south is **Kilmore Quay,** with the ferry to the **Saltee Islands.** Farther along the southern shore is **Hook Head,** near the border with County Waterford, which runs north along the **River Barrow** inland to **New Ross.**

WEXFORD TOWN

Wexford Town is the county's largest and was first raided and settled in the 9th century by the Vikings, who named it Waesfjord. The town developed through the medieval period, and by the river you can still explore the narrow alleyways that were common at the time. The Vikings built a temple dedicated to Odin, but when Christianity came to Ireland and the Vikings fled, it became Selskar Abbey. Much later, more churches were built, and they still tower over the town. Most of Wexford Town's attractions are outside town, but there are enough good food and lodging options to warrant making it a base.

Sights

Irish National Heritage Park

tel. 53/912-0733; www.irishheritage.ie; daily 9:30am-5:30pm; €14

Just outside town, this 14-ha (35-acre) park portrays different eras of Wexford history, including the Viking and Norman invasions, the early Christian period, and even the Stone Age. In its woods and shoreline are 16 re-creations of historical sites where you can envision how the Vikings lived in longhouses and what prehistoric funerals were like at megalithic tombs. The three guided tours are suitable for kids: Prehistoric Ireland, Early Christian, and the Age of Invasion. Tour times vary but there are at least two of each per day.

Beaches

Curracloe Beach

This beautiful beach runs 11 km (7 mi) from Raven Point in the south to Ballyconnigar Beach in the north. It was awarded Blue Flag status for its cleanliness, and swimming is allowed, with lifeguards on duty during summer. The Raven Point Nature Reserve Walk starts at the Raven Wood Car Park and leads through the sand dunes into the forest, where you'll have the rare opportunity to see red squirrels in the trees on one side and seals on the shore on the other. The beach was used as a set for the D-Day landings in the movie *Saving Private Ryan* and also in the movie *Brooklyn.*

Food and Accommodations

The Sky and the Ground

112 S Main St.; tel. 53/912-1273; Instagram @TheSkyAndTheGround; Tues.-Thurs. 4pm-11:30pm, Fri.-Sat. 3pm-12:30am, Sun. 3pm-11pm; €6

This traditional pub in the middle of town is a lively spot with regular live music. It should be on your itinerary for a good night out. The bar in front was rebuilt in 1995 after a fire, but they've managed to maintain the traditional feel, with wooden floors and furnishings lit with candles. This part of the pub hosts trad sessions on Sunday evenings. To the rear, a modern beer garden hosts bigger performances.

Frank's Place 1860

Main St.; tel. 53/918-9109; www.franksplace1860.ie; Mon.-Thurs. 9am-6pm, Fri.-Sat. 9am-8pm, Sun. 10am-5pm; from €13

Given the name, it's no surprise that this building has been around since the late 1800s, when it first opened as a bakery. These days it's a chic lunch spot and wine bar that serves breakfast, brunch, lunch, and tapas. The food is contemporary, with roasted mango and edamame salad as well as coconut prawn scampi, all well presented on dark plates. The wine list is mainly European varieties with 10 available by the glass and over 50 by the bottle. There's also a small grocer to pick up condiments and wine.

Ferrycarrig Hotel

Ferrycarrig; tel. 53/912-0999; www.ferrycarrighotel.ie; €130

The four-star, 102-room Ferrycarrig Hotel has a wonderful riverside setting just outside Wexford Town. Its wellness offerings are strong thanks to its tranquil setting, the option to dine by the river, and the on-site spa with extensive facials, body scrubs, and massages. The 20-m (66-ft) pool and kids pool keep the family entertained, and there's a sauna. For food, visit **Reeds Restaurant,** regularly voted the best hotel restaurant in Wexford thanks to its local produce in dishes like guinea fowl with a morel mushroom sauce and a terrine of sole, salmon, and cod.

Information and Services

Wexford General Hospital (Newtown Rd.; www.hse.ie) is in the north part of town and offers inpatient, outpatient, and emergency services. There are three banks in Wexford: **PTSB** (The Bushels; www.ptsb.ie), **Bank of Ireland** (Church Lane; www.bankofireland.com), and **AIB** (Main St.; www.aib.ie). The **post office** is on Anne Street.

Getting There and Around

To drive to Wexford Town from Dublin, take the N11 out of the city south. It turns into the M11 and then reverts to the N11 outside Enniscorthy. It's a 155-km (96-mi), 2-hour journey. Irish Rail trains run roughly every 3 hours during the day from Dublin's Pearse Street Station to Wexford **O'Hanrahan Station** (www.irishrail.ie; 2.5 hours; €15 one-way). Bus Éireann Route 2 (€15 one-way) stops at Busáras in the city and drops off at O'Hanrahan Station in Wexford 11 times daily. **Wexford Bus** (www.wexfordbus.com) Route 740 (€15 one-way) departs the city every 30 minutes from Lesson Street Upper and drops off at **Redmond Square.** Once you're in Wexford Town, everywhere is easily reached on foot.

★ SALTEE ISLANDS

The Saltee Islands lie off the coast of **Kilmore Quay** and comprise **Little Saltee Island** and **Great Saltee Island.** Today they are an idyllic escape from the bustle of the mainland, but they've had a colorful past. Christian hermits settled the islands to repent their sins and show their dedication to their god. After that came Viking raids and even pirates. In the 1940s, an Irishman by the name of Michael Neale bought the islands and crowned himself Prince Michael I of the Principality of the Saltee Islands. Of course, this is all in fun, but his family has created a coat of arms and shipped a throne from the mainland.

The islands have always been popular

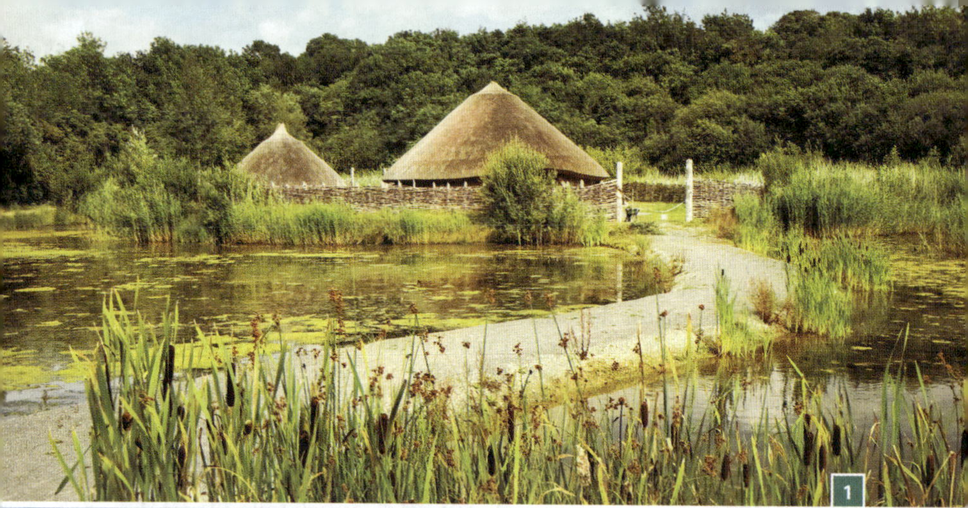

1

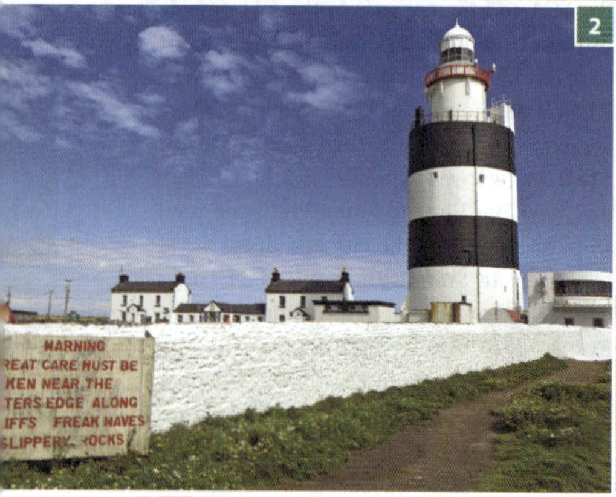
WARNING
REAT CARE MUST BE
KEN NEAR THE
TERS EDGE ALONG
IFFS FREAK WAVES
SLIPPERY ROCKS

2

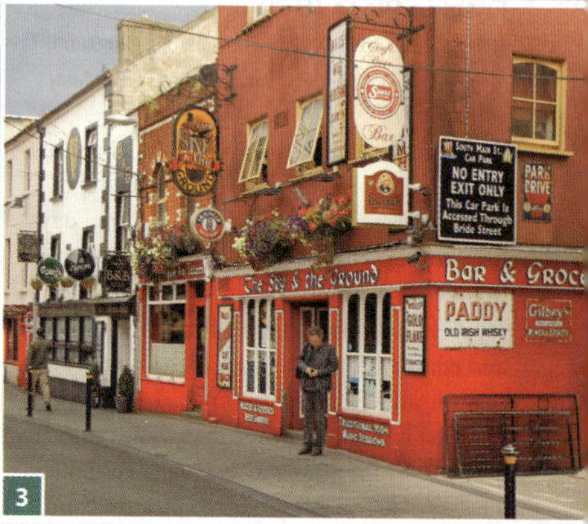
NO ENTRY
EXIT ONLY
This Car Park Is Accessed Through Bride Street
PARK DRIVE
The Sky & the Ground
Bar & Groc
PADDY
OLD IRISH WHISKY

3

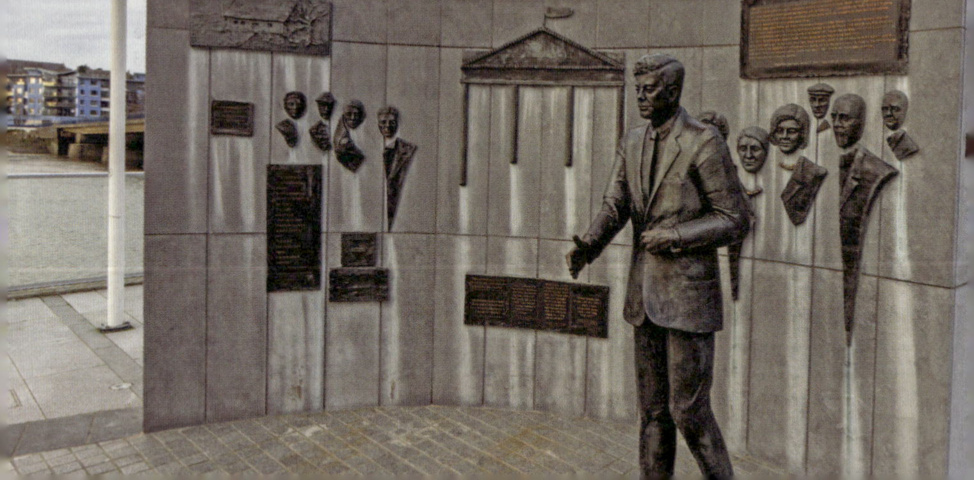

4

with bird watchers who come to see the puffins nesting in the cliffs and razorbills taking flight. There are no tour operators on the island, so visits are self-guided. There are also no facilities at all, not even a pier. You change from the ferry to a small boat that lands on the shore. It's not the easiest trip, and it requires physical effort, but it's well worth it.

Getting There

Getting to the Saltee Islands requires some effort. From Wexford Town, take the N25 south for 3 km (1.9 miles). At the Rosslare Rd roundabout, take the 1st exit onto the R739. Continue for 16 km (10 miles) to Kilmore Quay. Free parking is available in the village or behind the harbor. **Wexford Bus** (www.wexfordbus.ie) also provides daily bus service between Wexford Town and Kilmore Quay.

The ferry (20 minutes; €40 round-trip) departs Kilmore Quay, and the last stretch is in a smaller boat, which you have to transfer into at sea. The small boat lands on the beach on Great Saltee Island and you hop out. The landing might be slippery because of seaweed, and you might have to walk a few steps in the water. June-August there are four departures daily, and April-May and September one departure daily Monday-Friday and four departures daily Saturday-Sunday. There are no ferries October-March.

★ HOOK LIGHTHOUSE

Hook Head; tel. 51/397-055; https://hookheritage.ie; daily 9:30am-5pm; guided tours from €14

Hook Lighthouse is a historic structure on a historic headland. Hook Head is the origin of the phrase "by hook or by crook," supposedly spoken by Cromwell in the 17th century when he was planning an attack on Waterford, that he would take it by Hook Head or by nearby Crooke. The story of the lighthouse dates back even farther. In the 5th century, a monk named Dubhán set up a monastery on the headland and burned a coal fire here to warn passing ships. The lighthouse that stands today was built over 800 years ago by the Earl of Pembroke, making it the oldest intact and operational lighthouse in the world.

Access to the lighthouse is by guided tour only. On the guided tour, you can climb the 115 steps to the top of the tower and look out at brilliant sea views. It's not uncommon to see dolphins here, and if you're lucky, you might spot whales far offshore in winter. Sunrise and sunset tour experiences are available from €60. The tours can be booked online.

1: Irish National Heritage Park **2:** Hook Lighthouse **3:** The Sky and The Ground pub **4:** memorial to John F. Kennedy in New Ross

Getting There

The drive from Wexford Town to Hook Lighthouse is 47 km (29 mi) and takes 50 minutes. Head west on the R733 road and turn left on the R737. **TFI Local Link** (www.transportforireland.ie) runs Route 370 buses from Wexford Town to **Ramsgrange,** where you change to the Route 399 bus to Hook Head. There are only four buses per day, so it's not an easy way to get here.

NEW ROSS

The small town of New Ross is a quiet place on the edge of the River Barrow, which borders County Kilkenny. The town has had a huge impact on the world through the ships that left the port during the famine. This emigration runs through the generations in the UK, Australia, and the United States, with the Kennedy family tracing its roots here. Most visitors to New Ross tend to stay in Wexford Town, Waterford City, or Kilkenny City.

Sights

Dunbrody Famine Ship Experience

The Quay; tel. 51/425-239; www.dunbrody.com; Mon.-Fri. 9am-5pm, Sat.-Sun. 9am-5:30pm; from €14

This famous famine ship was originally built in Quebec, Canada, to carry cargo, but when the famine hit in 1845, it began to transport people from the challenges in Ireland to new lives. The *Dunbrody* sailed from New Ross and docked mainly in Quebec City in Canada and New York in the United States. Conditions were cramped, with 160-300 passengers crowding into the sleeping quarters, which you can see on the tour, led by guides dressed as period passengers. A new exhibit of letters and records of the time adds layers to the stories. The tour lasts 1 hour and ends at the Irish America Hall of Fame, which celebrates Irish immigrants who played a part in the story of the United States.

On the first floor of the visitor center, the **Captain's Table** (Apr.-Sept. daily 9am-6pm, Oct.-Mar. daily 9am-5pm) serves breakfast, lunch, and dinner, with a Sunday Special Menu offered from noon to 5pm. The restaurant overlooks the River Barrow with views of the ship and the town of New Ross.

★ The Kennedy Homestead

tel. 51/388-264; www.kennedyhomestead.ie; daily 9:30am-5:30pm; €10

One of America's most famous sons can trace his heritage back to the farmlands around New Ross. In 1848, at the height of the famine, Patrick Kennedy packed up what few belongings he had, said good-bye to his home forever, and boarded a ship to the United States. In 1917 his great-grandson John F. Kennedy was born and went on to become the 35th US president.

Patrick's home is now a state-of-the-art cultural museum in the family's old farm buildings. It tells the story of the family's rise to greatness and documents it with archival material from the Kennedy Library in Boston. The homestead was visited by JFK himself in 1963, just months before he was assassinated in Texas.

Tickets can be bought online, and you can buy a combined ticket that includes a tour of the Dunbrody Famine Ship. The homestead closes down December-March, but tours can still be booked with 48 hours' notice.

John F. Kennedy Arboretum

tel. 46/942-3490; https://heritageireland.ie; daily 10am-6:30pm; €5

This arboretum (a garden dedicated solely to trees) is an interesting link between Ireland and the United States. The trees were planted to commemorate JFK's visit to New Ross, and it's now home to over 5,000 species of trees and shrubs, with 22 countries donating plants. There are easy walks around the site and free guided tours March-October. The trees are grouped by the continents they're native to. There are over 500 varieties of rhododendrons and an impressive collection of azaleas.

Getting There and Around

The drive from Wexford Town to New Ross is 35 km (22 mi) and 30 minutes. Follow the N30 south and follow signs for the R714 and New Ross. From Dublin, take the N7 to Naas, then the M7 and M9 toward Carlow Town, and turn onto the R448 for New Ross. This route is 147 km (91 mi) and takes 2 hours.

Bus Éireann (www.buseireann.ie) and **Wexford Bus** (www.wexfordbus.com) operate buses from Dublin, but you have to change in Enniscorthy or Wexford Town to get to New Ross. Expect a journey time of over 3 hours. From Wexford Town, there are regular buses with both Bus Éireann and Wexford Bus.

Waterford City

Like other major towns in the area, Waterford City began as a Viking stronghold in 914 CE, making it the oldest urban settlement in the country. Learn about how Ragnall, the grandson of Ivar the Boneless, developed the city at the Viking Triangle and Waterford Treasures. Today people in Waterford love hurling, are skilled crystal makers, and explore the outdoors as much as possible. Waterford City is one of the smallest cities in the country but has many layers and stories to discover.

Waterford

ORIENTATION

The **Viking Triangle** is in the heart of the city and forms the historic core next to the **River Suir.** The **Waterford Greenway** starts along the quays of the river and runs into the countryside to the west. **Dunmore East** is a 20-minute drive south along the coast.

SIGHTS

The Viking Triangle

The Viking Triangle is an open expanse in the heart of the city where you'll find many of Waterford's attractions. The area was once surrounded by 1,000-year-old walls and is now dominated by **Reginald's Tower** (Bailey's New St.; www.waterfordtreasures.com), Ireland's oldest civic building, with exhibits on the city's past. It's a good place to relax and soak up centuries of history before going to one of the museums nearby.

Waterford Treasures: Medieval Museum

Cathedral Square; tel. 51/849-501; www.waterfordtreasures.com; Mon.-Fri. 9:15am-5pm, Sat. 9:30am-5pm, Sun. 11am-5pm; from €10

This historic museum is a fascinating place to visit, as it houses two authentic medieval structures: the 13th-century Choristers' Hall and the 15th-century Mayor's Wine Vault. Discover medieval artifacts like the Great Charter Roll, which depicts the earliest known view of the city, and the cloth-of-gold vestments, made of Italian silk and embroidered in Belgium. Join the guided tour to hear the details. Alongside these permanent exhibits are events like talks by historians and Halloween tours.

House of Waterford

28 The Mall; tel. 51/317-000; www.waterfordvisitorcentre.com; daily 9:30am-4:15pm; €18

Waterford Crystal was once one of the most sought-after crafts in the world thanks to the distinctive polishing technique and the Lismore pattern, perfected over 200 years. The House of Waterford showcases the famous crystal brand alongside a working manufacturing site where you can see the pieces being made. The tour lasts 1 hour, and you'll see mold-making, glass-blowing, cutting, and engraving. After the tour, pop by the gift shop to pick up a souvenir and have a coffee at the on-site café.

Waterford Treasures: The Bishop's Palace

The Mall; tel. 51/849-650; www.waterfordtreasures.com; Mon.-Fri. 9:15am-5pm, Sat. 10am-5pm, Sun. 11am-5pm; from €10

Most of Waterford City's historical attractions center on the Viking era, but the Bishop's Palace offers insight into the upper class during the more genteel Georgian period. The building houses 250 years of history in beautifully preserved rooms decorated with period furniture and captivating paintings. The guide on the tour plays the part of the housekeeper or the butler to show you the highlights, including the Penrose decanter, the oldest surviving piece of Waterford Crystal.

ACTIVITIES AND RECREATION

Hiking and Walking

Dunmore East Cliff Walk

Distance: *14 km (9 mi) round-trip*
Duration: *4 hours*
Elevation gain: *220 m (720 ft)*
Effort: *Difficult*
Trailhead: *Harbour Rd., Dunmore East*

This out-and-back hike along the coast takes in amazing views of the sea alongside steep climbs for a challenging day out. The route follows a single-track trail to the popular swimming spot at Portally Cove. The next section, to Rathmoylan Cove, has most of the elevation change along the route. Take a break at the White Lady, a standing stone that looks out on the coast. The trail ends by stunning Ballymacaw Cove, where you can turn around and hike the trail back to Dunmore East.

Cycling

★ Waterford Greenway

Distance: *46 km (29 mi) one-way*
Duration: *2-4 hours*
Elevation gain: *594 m (1,948 ft)*
Effort: *Moderate*
Trailhead: *Grattan Quay*

The Waterford Greenway is one of the highlights of the outdoors in Ireland. The 46-km (29-mi) route is a traffic-free path on a former rail line from the banks of the river in Waterford City through the lush foothills of the Comeragh Mountains, past historic sights to Dungarvan on the coast. The route doesn't have any steep sections, but its length may make it challenging for those who aren't used to riding bikes.

The first stop-off point on the greenway is **Mount Congreve Estate Gardens** (Mount Congreve; tel. 51/384-115; www.

mountcongreve.com; daily 10am-4pm; €13), a tranquil and colorful part of the countryside with a striking 18th-century house. Ride underneath the towering arches of the **Kilmacthomas Viaduct** that marks the halfway point of the ride, and stop at **Coach House Coffee** (Union Rd.; tel. 51/295-654; www.coachhousecoffee.ie; daily 9am-5pm; from €10). The menu of burgers, curries, and sandwiches hits the spot for hungry cyclists. As you pedal toward the end of the greenway, you'll pass through the **Durrow Tunnel** and into Dungarvan.

It's a fantastic ride that's a nice day out for keen cyclists and a great achievement for those who aren't. Most bike rental companies in the area offer a pickup service in Dungarvan to save you the ride back to the city.

Waterford Greenway Bike Hire

Hanover St.; tel. 51/295-955; www.waterfordgreenwaybikehire.com; Feb.-Oct. daily 9am-6pm

With three locations along the Waterford Greenway, this is a convenient option to ride shorter sections. The bikes are family-focused, with two sizes of bikes for kids, a tag-along carrier, a bike with a buggy, and kids seats available. The adult bikes are modern Giant bikes with 21 gears to make going uphill easier. If you want to take all the effort out of cycling the greenway, they rent e-bikes. Bicycles can be reserved online.

ENTERTAINMENT AND EVENTS

Theatre Royal Waterford

The Mall; tel. 51/874-402; https://theatreroyal.ie; from €18

Step into Ireland's oldest continually operating theater and enjoy wonderful live performances in the historic heart of the city. The theater has a good mix of live music and plays, with acts in recent years like Damien Dempsey, Mary Black, and Gilbert O'Sullivan. A 2009 renovation turned it into a modern space with 430 seats along with a strong link with its location: a Waterford Crystal chandelier overhead.

SHOPPING

Nest Waterford

127 The Quay; tel. 87/205-0074; Instagram @lovenest; Thurs.-Sat. 10am-4pm

This cute homeware shop sells a mix of vintage pieces and new works from crafters and makers. The shop is stocked floor-to-ceiling with statement pieces like brightly colored flowerpots, vibrant lampshades, and stylish mirrors. Browse for artwork and candles, which make for great gifts. Keep an eye on their social media accounts for sporadic events, which often include light bites and drinks.

FOOD

Modern Irish

Everett's

22 High St.; tel. 51/325-174; www.everetts.ie; Tues.-Thurs. 5:30pm-9:30pm, Fri.-Sat. 12:30pm-2pm and 5:30pm-9:30pm; 2 courses from €41

Modern Irish cuisine is a trend in Ireland that takes much-loved ingredients like beef, potatoes, and other vegetables and reinvents traditional dishes with more flair and creativity. Stepping into Everett's dining room, which seats 30, feels like going back to the medieval era thanks to the dark wooden floors and wooden beams; some of the features date to the 1400s. The food is much more contemporary. The menu changes seasonally, but expect generous portions of dishes like Irish venison with smoked black pudding and braised beef with creamed kale.

Cafés and Light Bites

Phoenix Yard Market

39 O'Connell St.; tel. 85/180-0755; https://phoenixyard.ie; Wed. 11:30am-9pm, Thurs.-Sun. 11am-9pm; from €7

The small outdoor Phoenix Yard Market has five vendors selling grab-and-go street food. The Crazy Vegetable sells vegan fast-food items like the sizzling seitan shawarma and loaded mushroom rings. Socafro Kitchen serves a fusion of African and Caribbean dishes like beef dodo and Jamaican jerk chicken. Another standout is Chingon, a Tex-Mex vendor who whips up classics like

MEDIEVAL MUSEUM
MEDIEVAL MUSEUM
1
THEATRE ROYAL
BUS
2
3

breakfast burritos and chikki con carne. Once you get your food, grab one of the outdoor seats or walk around the corner to the Quay and sit by the water.

No. 9 Café

9 Barronstrand St.; tel. 51/857-706; www.thestableyard.ie; Mon.-Thurs. 9am-4pm, Fri. 8:30am-4:30pm, Sat. 9am-4:30pm, Sun. 10am-4pm; from €10

If a full Irish breakfast isn't your cup of tea, then you'll want to pop into No. 9 Café, located in the Stable Yard Food Hall, where the brunch menu is inspired by North America and includes eggs Benedict and pancakes served with fried chicken. Beyond the brunch items, the staff here use local ingredients to make pizzas, sandwiches served on blaa, and burgers—all served in a bright and modern space with a mix of high tables and sofa seating areas.

GROW HQ

Dunmore Rd.; tel. 51/584-422; https://giy.ie/grow-hq; Wed.-Sun. 9am-5pm; from €13

GROW HQ is all about GIY (grow it yourself). Part café, part educational venue, part cookery school, this is where you can learn about where your food comes from. Most of it is aimed at kids, but everyone gets a kick out of seeing food being grown in the garden and then used on the menu. This zero-waste café is heavily focused on being environmentally friendly, with ingredients from local producers. The HQ blaa is a must if you've yet to try this famous Waterford bread, which they layer with pulled pork, applesauce, and fermented celeriac.

Eamo & Ró

Main St., Kilmacthomas; tel. 87/714-2176; Instagram @eamo_and_ro; Wed.-Thurs. 9am-4pm, Fri.-Sat. 9am-4pm and 7pm-11pm, Sun. 9am-3pm; from €18

If you're cycling the Waterford Greenway, pop into this refined café in the sleepy village of Kilmacthomas; it might just be the highlight of your ride. The menu doesn't have any headline-grabbing items. Instead, they've gone for tried-and-tested classics like an all-day breakfast and pork chops, but have elevated each ingredient with a touch of care and craft to make fantastic dishes. It's a small space with seating for 20, with breakfast from 9am and lunch from 12:30pm.

BARS AND NIGHTLIFE

Uisce Beatha

8 Merchants Quay; Instagram @anuisce; Mon.-Thurs. 1pm-midnight, Fri.-Sat. 1pm-1am, Sun. 1pm-11pm; from €6

Uisce beatha means whiskey in Irish, so it's no surprise that this traditional pub on the quays has a fantastic selection of the spirit. Most are Irish whiskeys, but if you're a stickler for scotch or bourbon, you'll also find them. The pub is intimate, ideal for a chat with friends, and come evening it's a venue for impromptu traditional Irish music.

Phil Grimes Pub

60 Johnstown; tel. 51/875-759; daily 5pm-midnight; from €6

Cozy up beside the fire in this friendly pub that has a good collection of craft beers on tap, including Rye River Brewing Co. from Kildare and Delirium from Belgium. Phil Grimes is known as a cultural hub in Waterford thanks to its upstairs space, where indie musicians, budding poets, and DJs play. There's a small courtyard out back for sunny days.

Itty Bittys

Bank Lane; tel. 51/347-303; www.ittybittys.ie; Fri.-Sat. 5pm-1am; from €6

Itty Bittys is a mix of traditional Irish pub and modern cocktails that creates an interesting space to spend an evening. The menu highlights are the spicy margarita, made with agave, fresh lime, mango, and a chili rim, and the Solero, made using vanilla vodka, Malibu, passion fruit, lime juice, and orange juice. On a nice day, grab a seat on the small rooftop terrace. The bar caters to groups and can arrange

1: Waterford Treasures: Medieval Museum
2: Theatre Royal Waterford **3:** the Waterford Greenway

Waterford Blaa

Waterford blaa sandwich

Blaa is a bread bun that's a Waterford specialty, and it's adored by locals here. Its origins date back to the late 17th century, when bakeries used leftover dough to make more bread, which ended up being softer and doughier than other breads. Blaa is mainly eaten in the morning as part of a breakfast sandwich that's loaded with sausage, bacon, and eggs.

Like French champagne, the Waterford blaa has a Protected Geographic Indication from the European Commission. Other places might make a soft, doughy, white bread roll, but unless it's made in Waterford, it can't be called a blaa.

WHERE TO TRY IT

- **No. 9 Café:** The brunch blaa here is a typical way to enjoy this specialty. It comes with eggs, bacon, sausage, and caramelized onions and apples (page 173).
- **Granville Hotel:** Order the traditional breakfast blaa in the on-site Thomas Francis Meagher Bar. It sticks to the basics and comes with sausage, bacon, and tomato relish (page 174).

entertainment like bingo, a cocktail masterclass, and a cabaret show.

ACCOMMODATIONS

Granville Hotel

Meagher's Quay; tel. 51/305-555; www.granvillehotel.ie; €155

This 98-room, four-star hotel along the river has classic rooms in 18th-century style, king rooms, and balcony rooms, all decorated individually. Dating to the 1700s, it is one of the oldest hotels in the country. You can see historic elements in the stained-glass entrance and the facade. There are two restaurants on site: the **Thomas Francis Meagher Bar** and the **Bianconi Restaurant.** The Bianconi Restaurant is a treat, particularly the breakfast, which has options like smoked Irish kippers and a Waterford take on eggs Benedict made with Waterford blaa.

Waterford Castle Hotel & Golf Resort

The Island; tel. 51/878-203; www.waterfordcastleresort.com; €290

On a private 125-ha (310-acre) island in the

Suir River east of the city, this luxury castle-hotel dates to the 6th century. The 19 rooms are each decorated in classic style fit for history's upper class. The 18-hole golf course is a major attraction, with nonmembers able to book tee times for as little as €40, even if they're not staying at the hotel. If golf isn't your game, there are tennis courts and walking trails with views of the city.

INFORMATION AND SERVICES

The **Waterford Tourist Information Centre** (Cathedral Square; www.visitwaterford.com; summer) is in the Viking Triangle. The nearest hospital is **University Hospital Waterford** (Dunmore Rd.; www.hse.ie), which has an emergency department. **Merchant's Quay** has two banks: a **Bank of Ireland** (www.bankofireland.com) and an **AIB** (www.aib.ie). The main post office is the **Waterford General Post Office** (www.anpost.com) on Custom House Quay.

GETTING THERE AND AROUND

The 170-km (105-mi) drive from Dublin takes 2 hours on the N7 toward Naas, then the M9, which takes you into the city. Bus Éireann operates Route 4 from Busáras to **Waterford Bus Station** (2 hours; €12 one-way) 11 times daily.

Waterford City is a 57-km (35-mi), 1-hour drive from Wexford Town on the N25 and R711 roads. The Route 340 Wexford Bus (www.wexfordbus.com; 1 hour; €12 one-way) departs from Redmond Square and arrives at the **Clock Tower** in Waterford. There are eight buses daily.

Cork

County Cork on the southwest coast of Ireland is one of those rare places that gives the best of both worlds without compromising. Cork City, though small, with a population under 125,000, is a buzzing urban hub that's been hugely influential on Irish culture and history. The city marches to the beat of its own drum with a strong independent spirit, best seen in the pubs and restaurants that aren't afraid to do things differently.

Once you leave the city for West Cork, however, the counterculture fades. Out here it feels like the rest of the world has disappeared. It has an entirely different way of living, where waves pummel the coast, the tide dictates life in the villages, and people eat with the seasons. Artists

Highlights

Look for ★ to find recommended sights, activities, dining, and lodging.

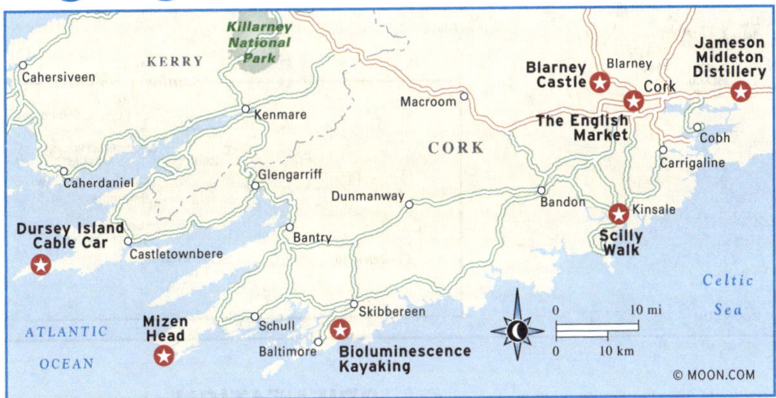

★ **Blarney Castle:** High on the list of most visitors, Blarney Castle is home to the famous Blarney Stone. Will you kiss it (page 185)?

★ **The English Market:** Enjoy food and produce from local makers in this famous market that opened in 1788 (page 189).

★ **Jameson Midleton Distillery:** Whiskey is synonymous with Ireland, and in Midleton you can become a whiskey expert on a series of tours (page 200).

★ **Scilly Walk:** There are few walks to the pub that can be as scenic as this one in Kinsale that takes in gorgeous views of West Cork (page 203).

★ **Bioluminescence Kayaking:** Kayak through the bioluminescent waters of Lough Hyne or Castlehaven Bay and watch as each paddle stroke turns the night into a surreal shimmering adventure (page 208).

★ **Mizen Head:** Stand on the southernmost point of mainland Ireland on this raw and rugged headland on the Mizen Peninsula (page 212).

★ **Dursey Island Cable Car:** Ride Ireland's only cable car to Dursey Island and watch the waves crash on the coast below (page 217).

Cork

visit and never leave, off-grid communes have formed, and West Cork is where Irish people go to see the real Ireland.

The scenery changes as you go from drinking a flat white in Cork City to sipping a pint of Beamish in Baltimore, but the pride Corkonians have for their home never wavers. Spend as much time as you can here; the magic is in the journey as well as the destination.

ORIENTATION

Cork City is in the center of County Cork and serves as a central hub for the region. **East Cork** includes areas like **Cobh** and **Fota Island,** southeast of Cork City. **West Cork** is a broader region that includes **Kinsale, Baltimore,** and **Cape Clear Island,** part of West Cork's southwestern coast. The **Beara Peninsula** stretches southwest, bordering County Kerry, and includes **Glengarriff,**

Previous: West Cork; the English Market; Blarney Castle.

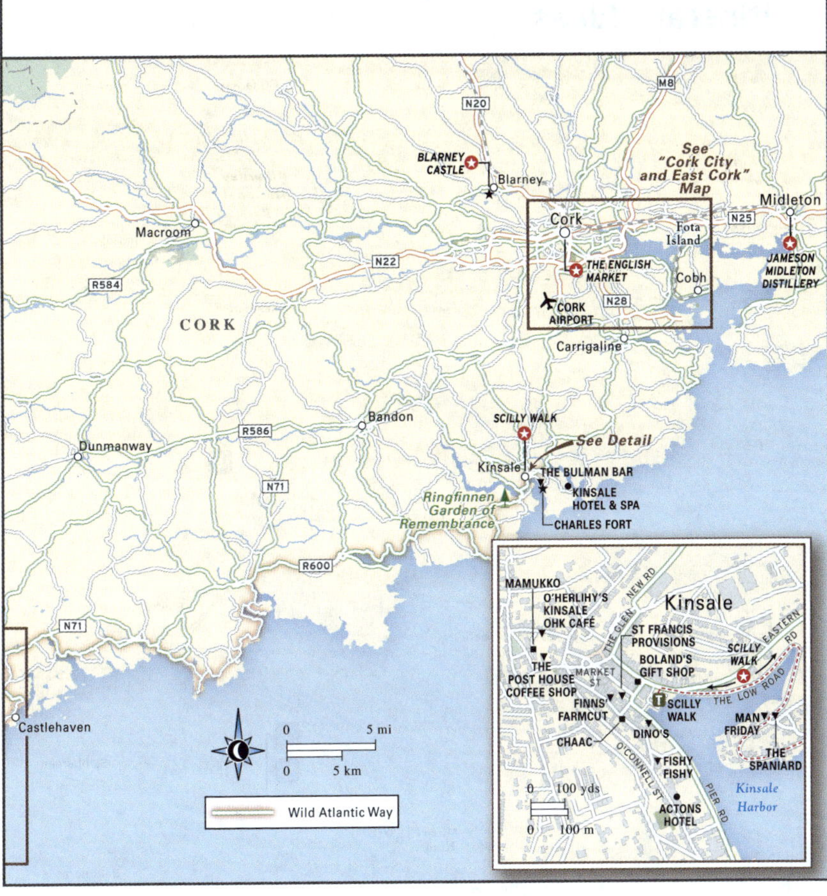

Dursey Island, and **Mizen Head,** Ireland's most southerly point.

Parts of West Cork are remote, but that makes them special. Don't be afraid to go off the beaten track. You'll need a car; public transport in these rural areas is limited.

PLANNING YOUR TIME

Five days is an ideal amount of time to spend in County Cork. You can see it in less time, but I recommend at least three days up to a week to soak up more atmosphere along the coast. Give Cork City at least a full day and night, and the same for Kinsale—there are so many good places to eat. Day-tripping from Cork City to Cobh and Fota is a manageable option. West Cork is about going slowly, so take your time and get out to some of the islands. Cork City, Kinsale, and Schull are good places to base yourself while you explore.

Itinerary Ideas

M8
N20
Blarney
Cork
N25
Macroom
N22
See "Cork" Detail
Cobh
2
R584
N28
CORK
Carrigaline
3
Bandon
See "Kinsale" Detail
R586
Dunmanway
Kinsale
N71
N71
Castlehaven
Celtic
Sea
Cork
River Lee
7
N20
N8
5
N22
N22
6
1
4
0 200 yds
0 200 m
Kinsale
NEW RD
1
3
2
4
5
0 100 yds
0 100 m
To Charles Fort

Itinerary Ideas

DAY 1: CORK CITY AND COBH

1 Wake up and have a fry for breakfast at **The SpitJack** in the city center.

2 Enjoy a leisurely 20-minute walk across town to Kent Station, where you can hop on a train to **Cobh.** Take in the views of the coast during the 30-minute ride.

3 Get the ferry to **Spike Island** from Kennedy Pier, just a 5-minute walk from the train station on Westbourne Place, and explore over 1,300 years of history on this old prison island. Book your tickets online in advance.

4 Return to Cork City and have a late lunch at **Good Day Deli** at Nano Nagle Place—the kimchi fried eggs are a great choice.

5 Walk the **Shandon Mile** to get a good feel for the city and check out the local independent shops.

6 Book in for dinner at **Goldie** and try the incredible seafood dishes. Don't forget to make a reservation in advance.

7 See out the day at **Sin É** with an Irish whiskey and live music in this spot that's a firm local favorite.

DAY 2: KINSALE

1 Drive west to the foodie haven of Kinsale for breakfast at **O'Herlihy's Kinsale OHK Café** for their Turkish egg flatbread.

2 Wander around the colorful town and support the local independent businesses by getting a coffee at **The Post House Coffee Shop** and browsing the shops on Main Street.

3 Enjoy a stroll on the **Scilly Walk** and bring your swimming gear for a dip at the halfway point, or continue on to Charles Fort. Pack all you'll need if you plan to swim, as there are no changing rooms.

4 Grab a table at **St. Francis Provisions** for an early dinner—this spot is in high demand, so book ahead.

5 Watch the sunset from the harbor, and if you're still hungry, get a bag of chips from **Dino's.**

DAY 3: MIZEN AND BEARA PENINSULAS

1 Stop in Schull on your drive to Mizen Head and pick up a gift at **Worm Books,** part of the small town's buzzing shopping scene.

2 Book in for a weekend brunch at **Nico's Food and Wine.** When it's sunny, the best spot to be is at one of their outdoor tables.

3 Drive south toward Mizen Head and stop for a stroll on the incredible **Barley Cove Beach.**

4 Get a ticket to the **Mizen Head Signal Station & Visitor Centre** and walk across the bridge to mainland Ireland's southernmost point.

5 Head back to your car and drive 2 hours to the **Dursey Island Cable Car,** which you can take to visit one of Ireland's most spectacular islands.

6 Make your way back to the mainland and drive to Glengarriff. Check in to **Eccles Hotel & Spa Glengarriff** and unwind with a massage.

Cork City

Cork City, capital of the self-proclaimed People's Republic of Cork, is staunchly proud and feels more like a village thanks to the number of pedestrian streets and the laid-back approach of Corkonians. The city is built on a series of islands, making it an interesting place to wander and explore. The independent spirit of the people is seen in the businesses, with plenty of independently owned shops, restaurants, and bars. Cork might also be Ireland's festival capital, with a schedule packed with small and niche events throughout the year.

ORIENTATION

Cork City is easy to navigate on foot thanks to the **River Lee** splitting it in two and providing a constant point of reference. South of the river is the **city center,** with a number of pedestrianized areas. **St. Patrick's Street** and car-free **Plunkett Street** are the main thoroughfares among plenty of side streets. On the other side of the Lee's South Channel is **South Parish,** where you'll find **Nano Nagle Place.** North of the river is the historic **Shandon** neighborhood and **The VQ,** with **MacCurtain Street** as the main road. Outside the city center, you'll find **Cork City Gaol** and **Blarney Castle,** 10 km (6 mi) northwest of the city along the N20 road.

SIGHTS

City Center

Crawford Art Gallery

Emmet Place; tel. 21/480-5042; www.crawfordartgallery.ie; Mon.-Wed. and Fri. 10am-5pm, Thurs. 10am-8pm, Sun. 11am-4pm; free

Designated a National Cultural Institution,

the Butter Museum

Cork City

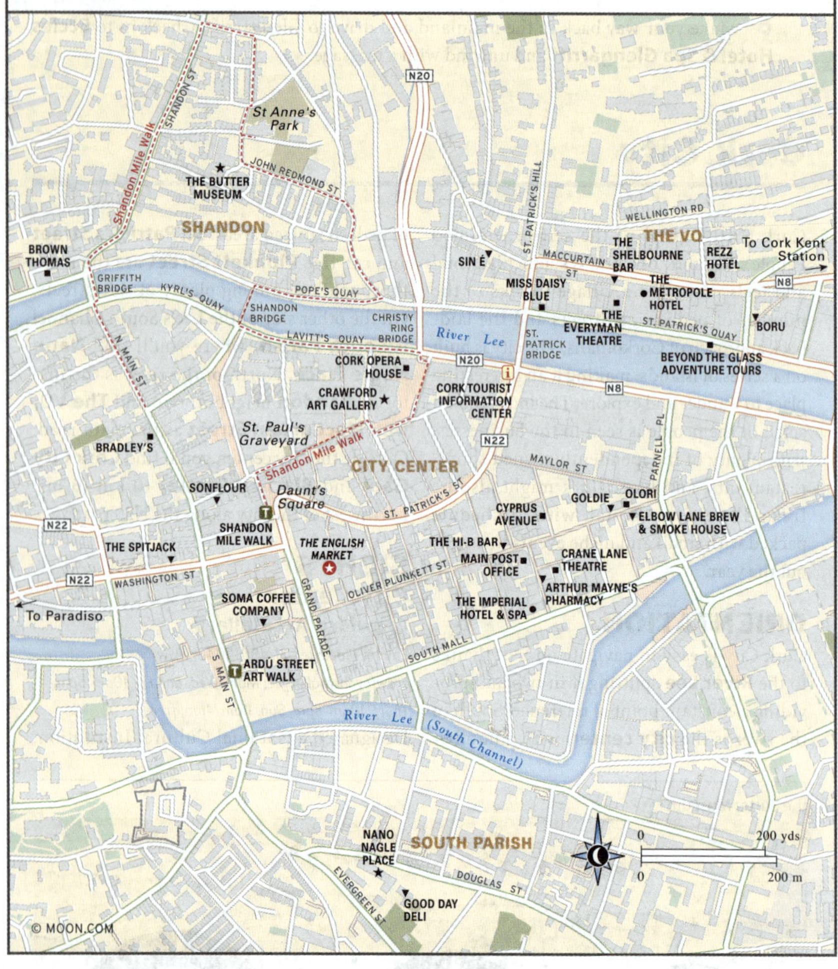

the Crawford Art Gallery is a must for art lovers. Over 3,000 pieces are in the former Custom House building, with the permanent collection of Roman and Greek sculptures a serious draw. Temporary exhibitions tend to focus on Irish art. Lots of talks and workshops are on the events schedule.

Shandon

The Butter Museum

O'Connell Square, Shandon; tel. 21/430-0600; https://thebuttermuseum.com; June-Sept. Mon.-Sat. 10am-4pm, Sun. 11am-4pm, Oct.-Nov. Wed.-Sat. 10am-4pm, Sun. 11am-4pm; €5

Butter might not seem worthy of its own museum, but the people of Cork would disagree. The golden spread played an important part in this merchant city, as butter was bought and sold here before being loaded onto ships to be exported. The Butter Museum is in the old Cork Butter Exchange, the largest butter market in the world in the 18th century. Admission covers everything from butter-making demonstrations to the bog butter exhibit. If you're looking for something different to do, you've found it.

The VQ

This area on the north side of Cork City was previously called the Victorian Quarter due to its architecture. It was renamed the VQ in 2022 to distance it from Queen Victoria, whom many blame for the famine.

South Parish

Nano Nagle Place

Douglas St.; tel. 21/419-3580; https://nanonagleplace.ie; Mon.-Sat. 10am-5pm, Sun. noon-5pm; free

Named after a nun who dedicated her life to educating poor people, Nano Nagle Place is a hub of history, wildlife, and design on the south side of Cork City. See what life was like during the 18th century and the challenges faced by Nano Nagle as she formed a religious order called the Presentation Sisters. Wander the vibrant urban park and visit her grave before having lunch at **Good Day Deli** or picking up some Irish gifts in the design shop. Entry is free but there is a fee for the museum and self-guided tour (€11).

Outside City Center

Cork City Gaol

Convent Ave., Sunday's Well; tel. 21/430-5022; https://corkcitygaol.com; daily 10am-5pm; €11

Some of Cork's most fascinating stories lie within the walls of Cork City Gaol, which housed prisoners 1824-1923. The castle-like structure was the temporary home of some notable figures in Ireland's history, including Countess Markievicz, who said it was the most comfortable jail she had ever visited. On the guided or self-guided tours, you'll hear how it became Ireland's only female prison before housing people involved in the Irish Civil War. The jail is a 2-km (1.2-mi) walk from the city center, and there is on-site parking.

TOP EXPERIENCE

★ Blarney Castle

Blarney; tel. 21/438-5252; https://blarneycastle.ie; daily 9am-4pm; €22 adults, €10 children

There are more impressive castles in Ireland, but I doubt any are more famous than this 600-year-old structure. The Blarney Stone is the main attraction, with people believing that if you kiss it, you'll get the "gift of the gab." I'm not sure how valid that is, but you'll have a story to tell your friends. To kiss the stone, you have to lie on your back and bridge the small gap at the top of the tower. Don't worry, you won't fall; the guide will be holding you the entire time.

There's more to see than the Blarney Stone, as the castle was home to Chief Cormac McCarthy and the rooms are still in good condition, complete with furnishings from its past. Step into the banquet hall where chiefs hosted guests to see if you can still hear the screams of people locked in the dungeons. Outside the castle are extensive gardens where you'll see the Great Trees, which include evergreen oaks over 300 years old. The tree-lined walks lead around the grounds to the Fern Garden and Vietnamese Woodlands, but the most interesting is the Poison Garden. The diminutive plants here look harmless, but all are poisonous and can cause great discomfort if eaten.

You should spend 3 hours here to see everything. All the tours are all self-guided.

The easiest way to get to Blarney Castle is driving 17 minutes on the N20 road northwest from the city. Bus Éireann operates the Route 215 bus from St. Patrick's Street in Cork City to Blarney Church, a 4-minute walk from the castle, making a trip from the city to Blarney Castle about 30 minutes one-way.

ACTIVITIES AND RECREATION

Hiking and Walking

Ardú Street Art Walk

Distance: *3.5 km (2.2 mi) round-trip*
Duration: *1 hour*
Elevation gain: *Negligible*
Effort: *Easy*
Trailhead: *35 S. Main St.*

The street art scene in Ireland has been gathering pace in recent years and is now seen as an art form rather than graffiti. Most cities have large bodies of work on public view, and this street art walk, organized by Ardú, Cork's contemporary street art project, is a leisurely stroll around the city that shows off work by some of Ireland's most prominent street artists, including Maser, Aches, and James Earley. The self-guided walk has audio descriptions and maps on the website (www.arducork.ie). The works are all inspired by the burning of Cork, when British forces set the city alight in 1920. The walk is a ramble through the city rather than an active day out, and you can stop for coffee and lunch along the way.

Shandon Mile Walk

Distance: *2.5 km (1.5 mi) one-way*
Duration: *45 minutes*
Elevation gain: *20 m (66 ft)*
Effort: *Easy*
Trailhead: *Daunt's Square*

An easy stroll through the city brings you to some of the most notable sights along a signposted route. Starting by St. Paul's graveyard in Daunt's Square, you'll soon come across the Crawford Gallery and Christy Ring Bridge, named after Cork's most famous hurler. The walk leads into the Shandon part of Cork and then returns to the city center. The most notable highlights are No. 2 Rowland's Lane, home of Annie Moore, the first person processed at Ellis Island in 1892; the birthplace of Jack Lynch, a famous politician and sportsman, on Bob and Joan's Walk; and the medieval part of the city.

Cycling

Beyond the Glass Adventure Tours

34 St. Patrick's Quay; tel. 86/385-0398; www.beyondtheglass.ie; €47

Choose to explore Cork City by bike or e-bike with Beyond the Glass, experts on the streets and stories of the city. Hear all about the Norman and Viking invasions as you ride from lush parks to riverside paths and university grounds. The tours take 3 hours and bike rentals are included in the price.

ENTERTAINMENT AND EVENTS

Performing Arts

Cork Opera House

Emmet Place; tel. 21/427-0022; www.corkoperahouse.ie; from €15

Despite its name, the Cork Opera House is home to more than just opera; it also hosts theater, dance, and comedy. Known as a cultural institution for over 165 years, it continues to attract big names to its stage, where 1,000 people can enjoy the shows.

Everyman Theatre

15 MacCurtain St.; tel. 21/450-1673; https://everymancork.com; from €15

Diversity of performers and shows is at the heart of Everyman Theatre. Expect talks, performances, and plays from people of all walks of life. The venue is also an attraction because of its stunning Victorian interiors, golden ceiling, and 650 deep-red seats.

Live Music

Cyprus Avenue

Caroline St.; tel. 21/427-6165; www.cyprusavenue.ie; daily from 7pm; from €10

For over 20 years Cyprus Avenue has been the epicenter of the Cork City music scene. With a capacity of 500, the space attracts up-and-coming bands as well as established names. Snow Patrol, Fun Lovin' Criminals, and GZA have all played here. A second, more intimate venue called **Winthrop Avenue** (Winthrop Ave.; tel. 21/427-6165; www.cyprusavenue.ie;

daily 7:30pm-2am; from €10) has a capacity of 80.

Crane Lane Theatre

Phoenix Place; tel. 21/427-8487; www.cranelanetheatre.ie; daily from 2pm

For jazz, blues, and burlesque, the Crane Lane Theatre is the place. This small and intimate venue has a capacity of 350 standing and is known for alternative acts that sync with the creative side of Cork. The rich velvety red interiors set the scene for shows that are more frequent toward the weekend.

Cinemas

Cameo Cinema

Glanmire Rd.; tel. 21/453-0050; www.themontenottehotel.com; €60

This cinema in the Montenotte is usually only open to hotel guests, but nonguests can do the Dinner & Movie Experience (Sun. 5:30pm, Mon.-Thurs. 6:30pm; €60 pp), a three-course meal alongside a classic movie. You can order drinks to your seat in the cinema at extra cost.

Festivals and Events

Cork World Book Festival

City Library, Grand Parade; https://corkworldbookfest.com; Apr.; free

Settle in for a reading from a world-class author at the Cork World Book Festival, running for over 20 years. Hear from acclaimed children's authors, fiction writers, and upcoming talent at free events held mainly at the City Library.

Quarter Block Party

multiple venues; www.quarterblockparty.com; usually July; some events free

The Quarter Block Party is an eclectic festival that celebrates local arts and culture, featuring a mix of music, theater, and visual arts at various venues. Many events with emerging artists are free, while events with established artists begin at €10.

Oyster Shucking Championship

Metropole Hotel; www.themetropolehotel.ie; Sept.; €30

As one of Cork's more niche events, the Oyster Shucking Championship has cult status in the city. Hosted at the fancy Metropole Hotel, it has seen world record holders open oysters and remove the meat at unbelievable speeds. Expect plenty of oysters paired with glasses of prosecco.

Sounds from a Safe Harbour

multiple venues; www.soundsfromasafeharbour.com; Sept. in odd-numbered years; from €15

Sounds from a Safe Harbour is a biennial festival, celebrating its 10th anniversary in 2025. It combines music, dance, and talks, featuring appearances by artists like Bon Iver and Feist. It takes place in in venues across the city; tickets are separate for each event.

Guinness Cork Jazz Festival

multiple venues; https://guinnesscorkjazz.com; Oct.; from €30

Given the size of the city, you might be surprised by the acts an event like this can attract. Spread across some of the city's best venues, the festival has been running for 45 years around the October public holiday, the last Monday in October. Plan ahead and book tickets for the bigger acts, or hop around the smaller venues to catch acts who have yet to hit it big.

SHOPPING

Cork City isn't a renowned shopping destination, but there are some interesting shops and name brands. The main areas are St. Patrick's Street, with department stores like Brown Thomas, and Opera Lane, with well-known fashion outlets like H&M and River Island.

Clothing and Accessories

Olori

131 Oliver Plunkett St.; tel. 21/424-8932; www.olori.ie; Mon.-Sat. 10am-6pm

Clean lines and classic designs with a modern take are at this womenswear shop. The light and airy interior suits the garments, and they offer a complimentary personal shopping service.

ENGLISH MARKET
CORK
Serving the City
for 230 Years
NACHOS
EVERYTHING IS GLUTEN FREE + VEGAN!
BLACK BEAN CHIPOTLE €8
TEMPEH CHILLI, NOTCHO CHEEZE, KIMCHI PICO,
CORN CHIPS RICE, CURTIDO,
SALSA ROJA, SOUR CREAM
Moynihan
Rose
STEPHEN'S BACON
BACON AND PORK SPECIALIST
1
2
3
4

Miss Daisy Blue

1-2 St. Patrick's Quay; tel. 87/650-4186; Instagram @missdaisyblue; Wed. 11am-3:30pm, Thurs.-Sat. 10am-4pm, Fri. 10am-5pm, Sun. 12:30pm-3pm

This boutique has a strong focus on timeless pieces from the 1930s through the 1990s. Dresses lean toward formal, but some options are for more relaxed settings.

Brown Thomas

18 St. Patrick's St.; tel. 21/480-5555; www.brownthomas.com; Sun.-Thurs. 10am-7pm, Fri. 10am-8pm, Sat. 9am-7pm

Ireland's high-end department store, Brown Thomas has an outlet in Cork where you can treat yourself to designer brands and premium beauty products. Gift wrapping is available, and in the run-up to Christmas, there's always a great selection of decorations for sale.

Artisanal Food and Markets

Bradley's

81/82 N. Main St.; tel. 21/427-0845; www.bradleysofflicence.ie; Mon.-Sat. 8am-8pm

For a nice bottle of Irish whiskey or a gift for a wine lover, Bradley's should be on your list. Stocking 150 whiskeys, 300 wines, and 200 craft beers, you'll find something that suits. Although it opens at 8am, you won't be able to buy alcohol until after 10:30am due to Irish law, but you can buy the artisanal food items.

★ The English Market

Grand Parade; tel. 21/327-4407; www.corkcity.ie/en/english-market; Mon.-Sat. 8am-6pm

The English Market is probably the most famous in Ireland. Opened in 1788, it has been described as the "stomach and soul" of Cork. Roughly 50 indoor stalls include small bakeries and well-stocked fishmongers and butchers. It's a busy spot, but there are places to sit and get coffee to soak up the buzz, so give yourself an hour to experience it. If you're gift shopping, you'll find lots of beautifully packaged artisanal products.

1: the English Market **2:** Blarney Castle **3:** Good Day Deli **4:** Cork Opera House

FOOD

City Center

Sonflour

9 Castle St.; tel. 21/427-4216; www.sonflour.ie; Fri.-Sat. 1pm-10pm, Tues.-Thurs. 5pm-10pm; from €11

Sonflour has that "neighborhood favorite" feel more often found in cities like Paris thanks to its busy dining room that all can see through the large windows. The chefs serve vegetarian or vegan sustainable Italian street food with Irish produce. Don't leave without trying their Pratai-Pratai-Pratai, a three-layer potato pizza that's surprisingly fantastic.

★ Elbow Lane Brew and Smoke House

4 Oliver Plunkett St.; tel. 21/239-0479; https://elbowlane.ie; daily 5pm-9:30pm; from €22

Elbow Lane's combination of a brewery and smokehouse makes for a rare experience. Take a seat at the polished stone bar and order one of five beers, also available as part of a tasting tray. Stay at the bar for your meal or move to one of the candlelit tables for more intimate dining. The menu changes based on local suppliers, but it's mainly beef and pork with at least one vegetarian option for the starter and main course.

★ Goldie

128 Oliver Plunkett St.; tel. 21/239-8720; https://goldie.ie; Wed.-Sat. 5pm-10pm; €10-35

You might stroll past Goldie and not notice this discreet restaurant, as there's no sign above the door. Book a table at this popular spot, which leans heavily on local seafood. There are vegetarian and meat options available also. Chef Aisling Moore, who has written a book on sustainable seafood, takes parts of fish that are often discarded and turns them into magnificent dishes like monkfish cheeks.

The SpitJack

34 Washington St.; tel. 21/239-0613; www.thespitjack.com; Mon.-Wed. 9am-3:30pm and 5pm-9pm, Thurs. 9am-3:30pm and 5pm-9:30pm, Fri.-Sat. 9am-3:30pm and 5pm-10pm, Sun. 10am-3:30pm and 5pm-9pm; from €25

The husband-and-wife team behind The SpitJack have a simple goal: make incredible dishes using Irish meat cooked in a rotisserie oven. This method is popular in France and Spain, whose influence can be seen on the dinner menu. The SpitJack is open for breakfast, brunch, lunch, and dinner, but don't let the meat-heavy menu put you off; there's a full vegan menu available. Stop by for their Sunday lunch three-course set menu.

Paradiso

16 Lancaster Quay; tel. 21/427-7939; https://paradiso.restaurant; Tues.-Sat. 5pm-10pm; set menu €68 pp

Vegetarian cuisine meets fine dining at Paradiso, by the River Lee. The creativity and the plating make this place stand out, as they take often overlooked ingredients like red kuri squash and make them the focal point. Paradiso is vegetarian, but they have a full vegan menu available that stays close to the regular menu.

SOMA Coffee Company

23 Tuckey St.; tel. 21/203-9316; https://somacoffeecompany.ie; Mon.-Fri. 7:30am-7pm, Sat.-Sun. 8:30am-6:30pm; from €4

Sometimes you need a break from the bustle, and SOMA is a great escape to recharge with a coffee. The black interior sets the tone for this quiet coffee shop a few steps from St. Patrick's Street and the English Market. Grab a cake or pastry and sit at the large shared table, sofa, or high stools.

The VQ

Boru

Brian Boru St.; Instagram @borucoffeeshop; Mon.-Fri. 7:30am-4pm; from €4

This small coffee shop is ideal for quick grab-and-go thanks to its location in the VQ beside the River Lee. As well as tasty excellent coffee, there are some hefty pastries and take-away granola pots.

South Parish

★ Good Day Deli

Nano Nagle Place; tel. 21/432-2107; www.gooddaydeli.ie; Tues.-Fri. 10am-4pm, Sat.-Sun. 9:30am-5pm; from €17

Good Day Deli focuses on sustainably sourced food in a gorgeous setting, a combo that has won the café multiple awards. With a large glass wall and an intimate dining room, it's hidden behind tall wildflowers and under leafy trees in Nano Nagle Place. Dishes use local cheese and eggs to create breakfast and lunch options with American, European, and Middle Eastern influences. There's a solid natural wine menu as well as some sweet treats.

Marina Market

Centre Park Rd.; www.marinamarket.ie; daily 8am-8pm

Marina Market is Cork's answer to the Time Out Markets chain, with 35 food and drink vendors packing the warehouse on the south side of the River Lee. Find savory snacks or sit down with a slap-up meal. Don't be afraid to take your time; the market has generous open hours. With such a wide choice of food and a relaxed atmosphere, it works for a quick bite or a family-friendly meal out.

BARS AND NIGHTLIFE

If you've fallen in love with Guinness, you might be disappointed in Cork City, as the Dublin-made stout is hard to come by. Instead you'll find Cork's brilliant stouts, Murphy's or Beamish, in every pub.

City Center

The Hi-B Bar

108 Oliver Plunkett St.; tel. 21/427-2758; Mon.-Thurs. 4pm-11:30pm, Fri.-Sat. 2pm-12:30am, Sun. 1:30pm-11:30pm

Technically named the Hibernian Bar, the Hi-B Bar is Cork's smallest and one of the quirkiest. Phones are banned, except to pay, to encourage people to chat like in the olden days. In a pub as snug as this one, it's easy to meet new people.

Arthur Mayne's Pharmacy

7 Pembroke St.; tel. 21/427-9449; Instagram @arthurmaynes; Sun.-Thurs. 10am-2am, Fri.-Sat. 10am-2:30am

A wine bar in a Victorian pharmacy? Arthur Mayne's is a brilliant spot for a memorable evening out. Look for the neon sign and step inside to see the cabinets stocked with fine wines and medicine from the building's last 120 years. Pull up a chair and leaf through the wine menu. There's also a tapas menu.

The VQ

Sin É

8 Coburg St.; tel. 21/450-2266; Instagram @sin_ebarcork; Mon.-Thurs. 12:30pm-11:30pm, Fri.-Sat. 12:30pm-12:30am, Sun. 12:30pm-11pm

Open since 1889, Sin É is an incredible example of a traditional Irish pub. The place lives and breathes craic agus ceol with live trad sessions happening every evening. The ceiling is covered in memorabilia that celebrates the pub's musical past, but you'll find modern touches behind the bar, with local craft beer on tap alongside stouts and ales from the big Irish breweries.

The Shelbourne Bar

17 MacCurtain St.; tel. 21/450-9615; Mon.-Thurs. 11am-11:30pm, Fri.-Sat. 11am-12:30am, Sun. 12:30pm-11:30pm

Whiskey bars are intimidating if you're not a knowledgeable drinker, but the Shelbourne Bar is inviting and surprisingly spacious, with walls lined with cabinets of rare and discontinued whiskeys from across the country. They claim to have the largest selection of Irish whiskeys of any bar. Flights are available if you want to try a few different whiskeys, or ask the staff for recommendations. If whiskey isn't your thing, they have Beamish, Murphy's, and local craft beers on tap.

South Parish

The River Club

Western Rd.; tel. 21/493-2700; www.theriverclubcork.ie; daily noon-10pm; €15

For a little slice of New York in Cork City, visit the River Club. Its art deco-inspired interior is paired with a Mediterranean-style riverside terrace, perfect for a meal on a sunny day. Menus have an international feel with eggs Florentine in the morning and prawn curry in the evening. Each dish is beautifully presented, and the atmosphere is always relaxed.

ACCOMMODATIONS

The VQ is ideal to enjoy the historic architecture with a more laid-back vibe that's still within walking distance to the city center and its restaurants and attractions. For a nightlife-focused trip, stay in the city center, particularly around St. Patrick's Street, near vibrant pubs and bars. For a peaceful stay away from the bustle, look at South Parish or just outside the city.

City Center

The Imperial Hotel & Spa

76 South Mall St.; tel. 21/427-4040; www.imperialhotelcork.com; €200

Treat yourself to an indulgent stay at this city center spa hotel. Billed as a sanctuary, the spa focuses on facials, massages, and treatments for pregnant people. Even if the spa isn't your thing, the Imperial is worth a stay in its 125 rooms and penthouse suite. You can book afternoon tea in the ornate Romanesque surroundings of **Lafayette's** (Mon.-Fri. 8:30am-4:30pm; €13).

The VQ

Rezz Hotel

55 MacCurtain St.; tel. 21/455-1149; www.rezz.ie; €90

This micro-hotel aims to be a happy medium between the rates of a hostel and the privacy of a hotel. The 70 rooms are small but have the essentials, making Rezz a good base to explore the city rather than spend time in your room when you're not sleeping. There are communal areas and a bar in the lobby, so not much in the way of amenities, but the rates are extremely attractive.

★ The Metropole Hotel

MacCurtain St.; tel. 21/464-3700; www.themetropolehotel.ie; €200

Opened in 1897, the 112-room Metropole is a Cork icon and was renovated in 2025. As one of the most glamorous buildings in the VQ, it has hosted celebrities and big events. **The MET** in the lobby covers food and drink from breakfast to dinner, while the five room types, from standard doubles to suites, cover quick stays to luxurious getaways. The hotel has a small fitness center with limited equipment for a quick workout.

★ The Montenotte

Middle Glanmire Rd.; tel. 21/453-0050; www.themontenottehotel.com; €215

You'll find the luxury Montenotte a 30-minute walk east of the city center. Tranquility is made the most of in 91 uniquely designed boutique rooms and suites along with the Woodland Suite Experience. These rooms blend indoors and outdoors with large windows, the forest setting, and airy yet classy interiors. There are three places to eat, and for a unique experience, make your way to the in-house Cameo Cinema, where movies from the 1920s play.

South Parish

River Lee Hotel

Western Rd.; tel. 21/425-2700; www.doylecollection.com; €215

With 182 rooms on six floors, the River Lee Hotel is one of the largest in the city and one of the most modern. Making the most of the riverside setting, the hotel's bar the **River Club** has a large outdoor terrace with gorgeous views. When the sun sets, make your way to the **Cocktail Bar** for a nightcap made with rare whiskeys. The 20-m (66-ft) pool and fitness studio provide plenty of ways to keep fit.

INFORMATION AND SERVICES

Visitor Information

Cork Tourist Information Center

125 St. Patrick's St.; tel. 1/265-5634; www.discoverireland.ie; daily 9am-5pm

The Cork Tourist Information Center provides maps, brochures, and expert local advice.

Hospitals

For emergencies, dial 112 or 999. The main hospital is **Cork University Hospital** (Bishopstown Rd.; tel. 21/492-2000; www.cuh.hse.ie).

Post Offices

The **main post office** is at 30 Oliver Plunkett Street, and various courier services like FedEx and DHL are available.

Banks and ATMs

AIB (https://aib.ie) and **Bank of Ireland** (www.bankofireland.com) branches are citywide; for currency exchange after hours, use ATMs.

GETTING THERE

Air

Cork Airport (ORK; Kinsale Rd.; tel. 21/431-3131; www.corkairport.com) is handily 7 km (4.3 mi) south of the city center. Major airlines like Aer Lingus, Ryanair, and KLM provide connections to European destinations, including London, Amsterdam, and Paris. Reach the city center via the Route 225 or Route 226 buses (20-30 minutes; €5 one-way) operated by Bus Éireann. Taxis (15-20 minutes; €15-20) are available outside the arrivals hall. You can rent a car at the airport, with advance booking advised for the best rates.

Car

From Dublin, Cork City is 260 km (160 mi) southwest. Take the M8 motorway to Cork, a well-signposted straightforward route. The journey takes 2.5-3 hours. From Galway, the drive is 200 km (125 mi) south on the N20 via Limerick and takes 2.5-3 hours. From Limerick City, Cork is 100 km (60 mi) south along the N20, which takes about 1.5 hours.

Train

Irish Rail (tel. 1/836-6222; www.irishrail.ie) trains run every hour from Heuston Station in Dublin to Cork (2.5 hours; €20-40 one-way). There is no direct train between Galway and Cork, but you can travel via Limerick Junction (4 hours; €30 one-way). Trains run from Limerick to Cork (2 hours; €20 one-way). **Cork Kent Station** (Glanmire Rd.; tel. 818/294-015; www.irishrail.ie) is north of the River Lee and east of the city center, a 10-minute walk.

Bus

Bus Éireann (www.buseireann.ie) runs buses from Busáras in Dublin to Parnell Place in Cork (3.5 hours; from €12 one-way). Buses run frequently throughout the day, and tickets can be purchased online or at the bus station. Bus Éireann also runs buses from Galway Coach Station to Parnell Place in Cork (3.5-4 hours; €15 one-way). Buses also run from Limerick (2 hours; from €10 one-way). The bus station at Parnell Place in Cork is on the edge of the city center, a 5-minute walk into the city.

Transport App

Download the **Transport for Ireland** (TFI) app for schedules and ticket purchases. Buying tickets in advance online can often secure the best fares and seat reservations.

GETTING AROUND

On Foot

Cork City is compact and pedestrian-friendly. Many main attractions, shopping areas, and dining spots are within walking distance of each other. The city center has well-maintained sidewalks and pedestrian crossings, making walking safe and convenient.

Bus

Cork City is well-served by **Bus Éireann,** with extensive routes throughout the city. Fares start at €2 one-way. Buses typically run daily 6am-11:30pm, every 10-15 minutes during peak hours and with reduced frequency evenings and weekends. The **Leap Card** (www.leapcard.ie) offers discounted fares on buses, trains, and trams and can be purchased at various outlets and online. Daily, weekly, and monthly passes are available.

Cycling

Cork City has a good number of bike lanes, some part of the bus lane, as well as dedicated cycle paths. **Cork City Bikes** (www.bikeshare.ie), a public bike-sharing scheme, offers a convenient option for short trips. Rates start at €3 for a three-day membership. The first 30 minutes of each ride are included, and additional time is charged at €0.50 per hour.

Car

Traffic in Cork City is reasonable, which makes getting around by car an option. Multistory car parks are available in the city, but driving should be your last resort, as Cork City is easy to navigate on foot or public transport. Street parking is hard to find, with a lot of it reserved for residents.

Taxi

You can hail a taxi on the street, find them at taxi ranks, or book one through apps like **Uber** and **FreeNow.** Fares start around €4 with additional charges based on distance and time.

East Cork

Cork is the Ireland's largest county and has endless reasons to visit. Most travelers arrive in Cork City and go west, but they're missing the beautiful and quieter East Cork. The area extends from the Glashaboy River outside Cork City to Youghal in the east and down to the gorgeous beaches in Ballycotton and Inch. A strong connection to the sea is seen in sailing, shipbuilding, and fishing, which shaped the culture and way of life for generations. A trip in East Cork can include a visit to Ireland's Alcatraz, tasting sessions of world-famous whiskey, and a chance to see animals that normally call the Serengeti home. If you're looking for a slower pace away from the traditional highlights, East Cork might be the place for you.

ORIENTATION

East Cork, naturally enough, lies east of the city. By train or by car, you'll come first to **Fota Island,** which leads to **Cobh** on Great Island. Looking south from Cobh, you'll see **Spike Island** and ferries heading out. **Midleton** is farther east and inland along the N25 road, which links Cork City with East Cork and continues to Dungarvan, Waterford City, and Wexford.

FOTA ISLAND

Tucked between Little Island and Great Island, just a 20-minute drive from Cork City, is Fota Island, known for a luxury resort hotel as well as an enormous wildlife park with exotic animals. Outside these two, there's not many places to eat and drink; nearby Cork City and Cobh have far more options.

Sights

Fota Island Wildlife Park

Fota Island; tel. 21/481-2678; www.fotawildlife.ie; daily 9:30am-6pm; €22 adults, €14 children, free under age 3

You might not expect Asiatic lions, Brazilian tapirs, or Indian rhinoceroses in the Irish countryside, but you'll see these and more at Fota Island Wildlife Park. Across 40 ha (100 acres) are 54 different types of animals and plants, from tall giraffes to small red squirrels. The giraffes are among the most popular, but the real treat is the free-roaming areas, where you can see different animals mixing as they would in the wild.

Family tickets (from €61 for 2 adults and 2 children) are available. Book online for a small discount. Wildlife talks and feeding demonstrations take place throughout the day for little ones who want to know more about the animals. Half a day is more than enough to see the park and visit your favorites again.

The VIP package (2 hours; from €135) has a park ranger as your private tour guide, letting you go behind the scenes and feed the animals. There's on-site parking (€3), or take the train to Fota Station, where an entrance to the park is only steps away.

Fota Island Adventure

Fota Island; tel. 21/465-2004; www.fotaadventure.com; daily 9:30am-4:30pm; from €20 pp

On the grounds of the Fota Resort are plenty of opportunities for family fun at the adventure center. Six activities last 1-4 hours and include stand-alone kayaking, orienteering, the escape room-style Cabin Fever, and Adventure Camp, with archery, an obstacle course, and teamwork games. There are even weeklong camps for kids. Adrenaline junkies may want to go elsewhere, as Fota Island Adventure focuses on making the outdoors accessible.

Food and Accommodations

Fota Resort

Fota Island; tel. 21/488-3700; www.fotaisland.ie; €250

This five-star resort and spa is in a peaceful area, with a 1-km (0.6-mi) drive from Cork Road through the forest to the hotel. Expect traditional luxury with plush interiors and

Cork City and East Cork

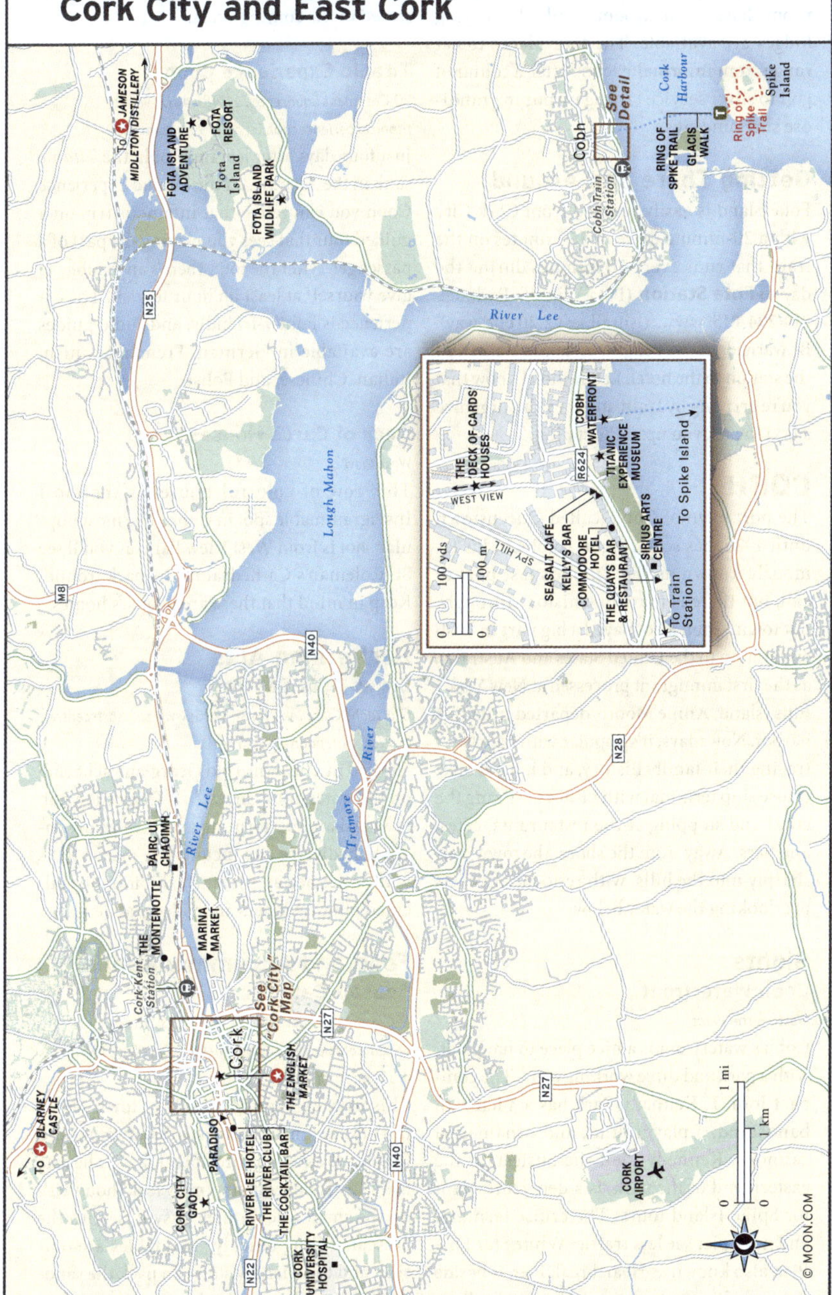

staff wearing formal shirts and ties. The 131 rooms have 2-4 bedrooms, and self-catering lodges are available. The four places to eat range from informal nachos after a round of golf to silver service tasting menus in grandiose surroundings.

Getting There and Around

Fota Island is easily reached from Cork City with a 20-minute drive or 15 minutes on the train that runs every 30 minutes during the day to **Fota Station** (Fota Wildlife Park; tel. 818/294-015; www.irishrail.ie; €2.20 one-way). Be warned that it's roughly an hour's walk from the station to the hotel. Let the hotel know that you're arriving by train and they can organize a taxi to pick you up at the station.

COBH

The port town of Cobh, called Queenstown until 1920, has seafaring in its blood. It's famously known as the *Titanic*'s last port of call, but there is maritime history throughout town. Cobh also played a big part in Irish emigration to the United States and Australia, as the first immigrant processed at New York's Ellis Island, Annie Moore, departed from this harbor. Nowadays, it's popular with people retracing their family history, and it has a busy cruise ship terminal with visitors walking the coast and stopping at the restaurants, cafés, and bars. Away from the shore, the town rises sharply into the hills, with residential streets overlooking the water below.

Sights

Cobh Waterfront

Westbourne Place

Cobh's waterfront is a nice place to hang out, with a park and three working piers. The compact John F. Kennedy Park has a Victorian bandstand, a playground, and ornamental cannons. Kennedy Pier, the busiest, at the eastern end of the park, is a departure point for Spike Island tours. The cruise terminal and navy pier see less traffic. White Star Line Pier, also known as Heartbreak Pier, is beside Kennedy Pier and was the last port of call for the *Titanic* before it sank. It is due to be restored in the coming years.

Titanic Experience Cobh

20 Casement Square; tel. 21/481-4412; www.titanicexperiencecobh.ie; daily 9am-6pm; €11

Just four days after leaving Cobh, the *Titanic* sank in the Atlantic. At the Titanic Experience Cobh you can relive that infamous trip on a guided tour that sees you playing the part of a passenger. After the tour, there's an exhibit, so give yourself at least an hour to visit. The experience is family-friendly, and audio guides are available in German, French, Spanish, Italian, Chinese, and Polish.

Deck of Cards Houses

West View

This row of colorful houses is the most Instagrammable spot in Cobh. The most popular shot is from West View Park, as you'll see St. Coleman's Cathedral in the background. Keep in mind that these are people's homes.

Performing Arts

Sirius Arts Centre

Old Yacht Club; tel. 21/481-3790; www.siriusartscentre.ie; Wed.-Sat. noon-5pm; free

Housed in a beautiful old Georgian yacht club on the waterfront, Sirius Arts Centre is a hub of visual and performing arts. Events are incredibly diverse and include live music, talks with acclaimed artists, and exhibitions by talented photographers and videographers.

Food and Accommodations

Seasalt Café

17 Casement Square; tel. 21/481-3383; https://seasaltcobh.ie; Mon.-Fri. 9am-4pm, Sat.-Sun. 10am-4:30pm; from €10

This busy café in the middle of town serves tasty quick lunches of toasted sandwiches and flatbreads as well as fired breakfasts. The café has a rustic but contemporary feel, though it's on the small side for how busy it is, with the 20 seats filling quickly. Two tables are outside, and the friendly staff can pack the sandwiches, baked goods, and coffee to go.

The *Titanic*

The *Titanic's* last port of call was in Cobh.

The *Titanic*, the world's best-known ship, was built in Belfast at the Harland and Wolff Shipyard and launched on May 31, 1911, in front of a massive crowd. The plan was to sail from Southampton in England to New York City, but before its ill-fated trip across the Atlantic, it made a final stop in Queenstown, Ireland, nowadays called Cobh. The first-class passengers on board were mainly American and English, with most Irish people traveling third class on the well-trodden route to a better life in the United States.

The connection to the infamous ship is best seen in both Belfast and Cobh.

- **Titanic Experience Cobh** in Cork delves into the people who died on April 14, 1912, when the Titanic hit an iceberg in the North Atlantic Ocean and sank almost 700 km (435 mi) off the coast of Newfoundland (page 196).
- **Titanic Belfast** takes you back to the origins of the ship in the city where it was designed, built, and launched (page 401).

The Quays Bar and Restaurant

17 Westbourne Place; tel. 21/481-3539; www.thequays.ie; Thurs.-Mon. noon-9pm; from €19

Every good seaside town has a restaurant on the water, and this is Cobh's. The large modern dining area has plenty of seating, but sit outside on the patio, especially if the sun's shining. The menu has a mix of modern staples like burgers and steaks, but the seafood is the way to go. The clam chowder, prawn pilpil, and slow-roasted scallops are popular choices. Vegetarian options are also available.

Kelly's Bar

19 Casement Square; tel. 86/601-5954; daily 10am-1:30am

Kelly's feels like a haven for sailors returning from sea with a cozy bar that pours Beamish and Murphy's, two of Cork's favorite beers. Framed memorabilia from the *Titanic* and nautical maps are on the walls. This quiet pub picks up speed in the evening with regular live music sessions throughout summer.

Commodore Hotel

4 Westbourne Place; tel. 21/481-1277; www.commodorehotel.ie; €150

Claiming to be the first purpose-built hotel

in Ireland, back when Cobh was called Queenstown, it opened under the name Queen's Hotel after Queen Victoria. Eight room types include spacious suites and affordable single rooms, all with a great blend of historic features and modern amenities, particularly in the sea-facing rooms. Food and drink are at **O'Shea's Bistro,** with dishes like chicken curry, steak sandwiches, and chicken wings.

Getting There and Around

The best, and most scenic, way to get to Cobh from Cork City is by train (€3.45 one-way). The 30-minute trip crosses the water and runs along Fota Island before the views of the River Lee. Trains run up to every 30 minutes. Driving takes 30 minutes, while **Cobh Connect** (tel. 21/455-1720; www.corkconnect.ie; €4 one-way) runs two buses per hour. Once you're in Cobh, it's best to get around by foot, as it's small and public transport options are limited.

SPIKE ISLAND

ferry from Kennedy Pier; tel. 21/237-3455; www.spikeislandcork.ie; Apr.-Oct. daily, Nov.-Mar. Sat.-Sun.; €27 adults, €14 children

Known as Ireland's Alcatraz, 42-ha (104-acre) Spike Island has lived many lives since it was first inhabited in the 7th century, when Saint Mochuda ran a monastery here. Others noticed that Spike Island has a strategic location in Cork Harbour just off Cobh. During the 17th-century invasion, Cromwell used the island to house Irish people who rose up against him. A number of fortresses were built on the island in the 1700s and 1800s, including the famous star-shaped fortress, which the British believed could dissuade an attack on their empire via Cork. During the famine, Spike Island was the largest prison in the world; it remains the largest prison ever on the British Isles. Things are more relaxed now, and the island opened for tourism in 2016 with a permanent exhibit, a café, and events. The exhibit covers the history of the island; check the website for temporary exhibitions. Most people take about 4 hours to visit Spike Island, including the ferry trip. Admission includes the ferry, a guided tour, and a visitors guide to help you find the most interesting places.

After Dark Tours

Two-hour Spike Island After Dark Tours offer a spine-tingling experience of the island's dark history. Guided by storytellers who bring the past to life, you'll explore candlelit corridors, spooky tunnels, and old prison cells off-limits to daytime visitors. This is for ages 16 and older and runs sporadically year-round; check the website.

Hiking and Walking

Glacis Walk

Distance: *1.4 km (0.9 mi) round-trip*
Duration: *20-30 minutes*
Elevation gain: *Negligible*
Effort: *Easy*
Trailhead: *Main entrance*

Glacis Walk is a family-friendly stroll around the exterior walls of the fortress, with sea views the whole way. Seeing the walls from this vantage, you'll know what it was like for invaders who tried to attack Spike Island.

Ring of Spike Trail

Distance: *2.4 km (1.5 mi) loop*
Duration: *35-45 minutes*
Elevation gain: *Negligible*
Effort: *Easy*
Trailhead: *Spike Island pier*

The Ring of Spike trail loops around the island along the shoreline. The edge of the island is dotted with lookout points, benches, and the old sergeants quarters. At the southern edge you'll find the convicts cemetery among trees by the water.

Getting There and Around

To get to Spike Island, take the ferry from **Kennedy Pier** in Cobh. In summer several sailings run daily 10am-2:30pm. In other

1: Deck of Cards Houses **2:** Cobh's waterfront **3:** Spike Island **4:** Jameson Midleton Distillery

1

seasons the trip is daily at noon and 1pm. The ferry takes 15 minutes to cross. You can drive to Cobh and park by the Cobh Heritage Centre, or take the train to Cobh. From **Cobh Train Station** (Westbourne Place; tel. 21/48-116-55; www.irishrail.ie) it's a 5-minute walk to the ferry terminal.

Spike Island is accessible to wheelchair users thanks to the pontoons at both piers. Once on the island, a wheelchair-friendly walkway leads to the fortress and around the inner fortress, but there is one short steep section up from the pier. Ten of the 12 exhibits, the gift shop, and the café are wheelchair-friendly.

★ JAMESON MIDLETON DISTILLERY

Distillery Walk; tel. 21/461-3594; www.jamesonwhiskey.com; daily 10am-6pm

Think about Irish whiskey and you likely picture a bottle of Jameson. This behemoth is drunk around the world, but every drop originates in Cork. First established in Dublin's famous Golden Triangle, the distillers moved production to Midleton in the 1970s to keep up with demand.

Tours, Tastings, and Classes

Seven experience tours focus on different aspects of whiskey, from making it to enjoying it. If you can't choose, my recommendations are:

- The **Midleton Distillery Experience & Premium Whiskey Tasting** (2 hours; €56) combines the story behind the drink with four tastings of top-shelf whiskeys.
- If you fancy yourself a bartender, in the **Midleton Cocktail Class** (1 hour; €60) you'll learn to make three different cocktails.
- For serious whiskey connoisseurs, in the **Discoverer Academy** (full day; €350) you'll learn the full grain-to-glass process as well as take part in cask sampling and tasting sessions.

Getting There

Take the N8 road north from the city and cross the River Lee before merging with the N25. Stay on this road and follow signs for Midleton. The drive is 24 km (15 mi) and takes 30 minutes. On public transport, take the train from Kent Station to Midleton Station and walk 10 minutes down Main Street to the distillery.

Southwestern Coast

West Cork is one of Ireland's bucket-list destinations. It has the charm of rural seaside towns, with unbelievable views and landscapes, yet it never feels sleepy. This faraway part of Ireland has always attracted creatives and alternative lifestyles, meaning the towns and villages don't lose their character. You won't find a Starbucks out here, but what you will find is far better. West Cork is beloved for its fresh produce, which passionate chefs serve in high-quality but unpretentious restaurants. Pack your walking boots, as West Cork is best enjoyed in the sun, when you're making your way to lunch by the harbor.

ORIENTATION

Kinsale is 29 km (18 mi) south of Cork City, a gateway to the Southwestern Coast. **Baltimore** is 85 km (52 mi) west of Kinsale and serves as the main access to **Sherkin Island,** just off the coast of Baltimore, and **Cape Clear Island,** 13 km (8 mi) away by ferry. **Schull** is 16 km (10 mi) west of Baltimore. This region ends on the **Mizen Peninsula,** where you'll find **Barley Cove Beach** 21 km (13 mi) west of Schull and

1: Charles Fort **2:** view of the sea on the Scilly Walk **3:** colorful streets of Kinsale

1

2

3

Southwestern Coast

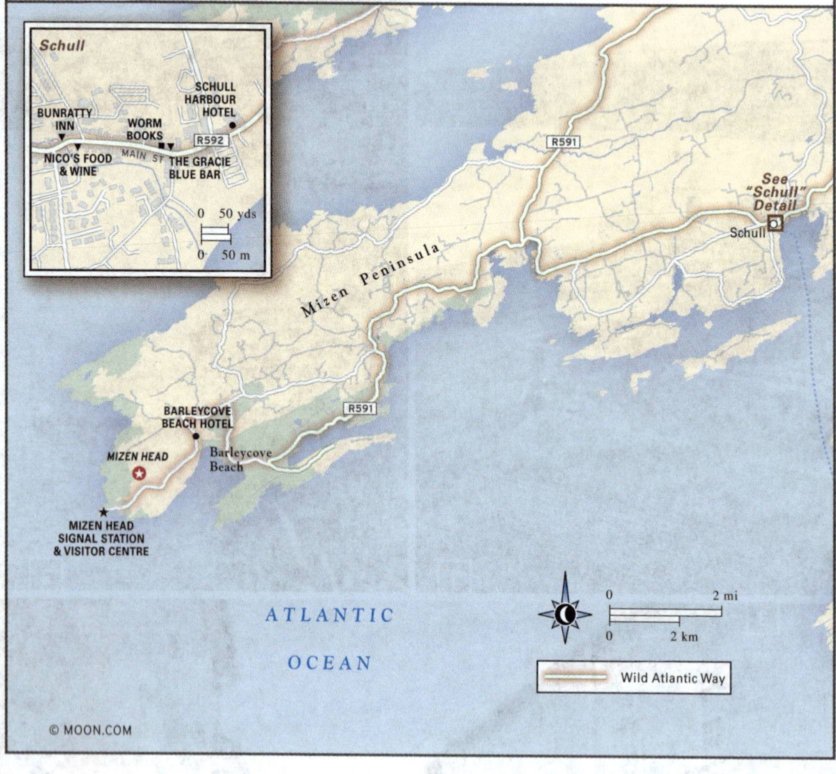

Mizen Head, the southernmost point of the mainland.

KINSALE

Cork has a number of colorful towns, but Kinsale may be the most colorful, with narrow twisty streets lined with independent businesses. In Ireland, Kinsale is known as a foodie town thanks to the surprisingly wide choice of brilliant restaurants. It's a busy little spot, as the Wild Atlantic Way starts here, but it doesn't feel like a tourist trap, with locals in the pubs and restaurants. If you're a foodie, you may decide to stay longer than you initially planned.

Sights

Charles Fort

Summercove; tel. 21/477-2263; https://heritageireland.ie; Mar.-Oct. daily 10am-6pm, Nov.-Feb. daily 10am-5pm; €5

Impressive star-shaped Charles Fort was built into the cliffs on the far side of Kinsale Harbour in 1682 to protect the town from attack. Later it served as a barracks for the British army, and today you can take a self-guided tour. Parking is free, but if you want to make it part of a longer trip, you can hike the **Scilly Walk** from the center of Kinsale in 40 minutes. If you're on a tight budget, you can see lots of the fort without going inside. There's a small café on-site.

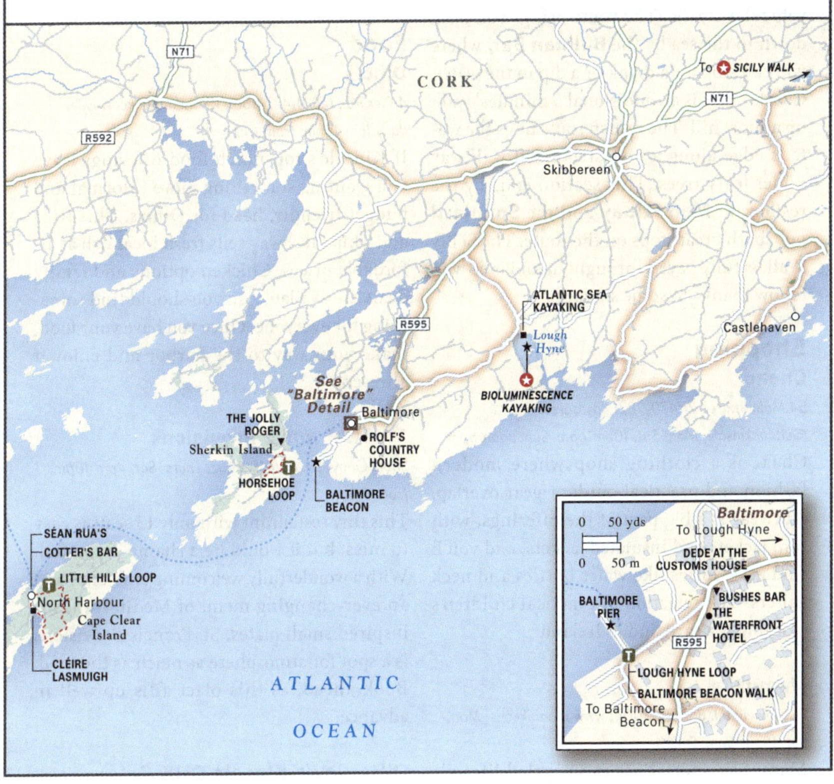

Ringfinnan Garden of Remembrance

Ringfinnan; tel. 86/864-7028; daily 7am-10pm; free

You might think it odd to find a 9/11 memorial in West Cork, but that shows that the people in this part of the world don't fit the norms. This garden has 343 trees for each of the firefighters and the chaplain lost that day. First started by Kathleen Murphy, a Kinsale woman who spent 30 years in New York, the project was completed in 2002 thanks to the help of her friends and family.

Kinsale Harbour

Pier Rd.

Kinsale is a seafaring town, so the harbor is an important place. The marina is popular with yachts, and you're likely to find people sitting on the wall on a sunny day, taking in the views across the water to the Scilly Walk.

Hiking and Walking

★ Scilly Walk

Distance: *6 km (3.7 mi) round-trip*
Duration: *1 hour*
Elevation gain: *50 m (165 ft)*
Effort: *Easy-moderate*
Trailhead: *The Low Rd.*

The Scilly Walk is a brilliant way to see the quieter side of Kinsale without a car and to get views of the harbor and town. The trail starts on the Low Road by the harbor and quickly leaves the bustle, with a couple of short sharp inclines at the start. The effort is rewarded when you get onto High Road and can see out to sea. There's no footpath on this section, but it's a low-speed residential road without much vehicular traffic. The route brings you back down to the sea by the **Bulman Bar,** where you can stop for a drink or a dip in the water. Charles Fort is an additional 5 minutes' walk up a short hill. The return route hugs the water's edge along a pedestrianized walkway under leafy trees. This section ends by the restaurant **Man Friday** and the **Spaniard** pub, both great stops on the route. The Scilly Walk is fully paved throughout and is easy to follow thanks to some signage.

Shopping

Chaac

54 Main St.; tel. 21/470-9821; Instagram @chaackinsale; Mon.-Sat. 10am-6pm, Sun. noon-5pm

Chaac is a clothing shop where modern fashion and practical outdoor gear overlap. Outwear is a big part of the offerings, with rain jackets and insulated jackets, and you'll find accessories like water bottles and neck gaiters. The selection of practical children's clothing is a rare find in Ireland.

Mamukko

Guardwell; tel. 85/734-2004; www.mamukko.ie; Mon.-Sat. 10am-5pm, Sun. 11am-6pm

Mamukko specializes in upcycled lifestyle bags and accessories and has a loyal following across the world. Founded by husband-and-wife team Nora and Attila Magyar, they combine Hungarian leather crafting heritage with sustainable practices. They use old materials like ocean race sails and airplane parts to create unique eco-friendly tote bags, messenger bags, duffle bags, and more.

Boland's Gift Shop

Pearse St.; tel. 21/477-2161; wwwbolandkinsale.ie; Mon.-Sat. 9am-6pm, Sun. 10am-6pm

Stock up on gifts at this large shop inside a heritage building in the heart of the town. Boland's has been open for 40 years and has amassed a varied selection of crafts, jewelry, and homewares, many Irish made. The pick of the bunch is the knitted hats by Erin Knitwear, which come in useful if the weather is bad.

Food

Dino's

4 Pier Rd.; tel. 21/477-4561; www.dinostakeaway.ie; daily 1pm-10pm; from €10

If Kinsale's top-notch food offerings leave you wanting something more informal and budget-friendly, head for Dino's. This fish-and-chip takeaway sells fresh local fish at affordable prices. Chicken options and family deals are available, so you should find something for everyone. Once you have your food, make your way to the harbor and enjoy it alfresco.

★ St. Francis Provisions

Short Quay; tel. 83/016-8652; Thurs.-Sat. 4pm-10pm; from €12

This tiny restaurant with only 13 seats is easy to miss, but it would be a shame if you did. With a wonderfully welcoming ambiance and an ever-changing menu of Mediterranean-inspired small plates, St. Francis Provisions is a spot for atmosphere as much as the food. Book ahead, as this place fills up well in advance.

O'Herlihy's Kinsale OHK Café

The Glen; www.oherlihyskinsale.com; Thurs.-Mon. 8:30am-3pm; from €14

O'Herlihy's is a small cozy café that focuses on breakfast and brunch. The menu is refined but small; the Turkish egg flatbread and breakfast sandwiches are the most popular items. The interior is colorful, with mismatched colors on the walls and mismatched furniture, although the limited seating means this isn't a place for large groups. There's a takeaway coffee hatch at the front.

Fishy Fishy

Crowleys Quay; tel. 21/470-0415; https://fishyfishy.ie; Thurs. noon-9pm; from €22

Fresh fish caught locally and prepared by an award-winning husband-and-wife team: It's easy to see why Fishy Fishy has become

Kinsale's most popular seafood restaurant. The baked local lobster and pan-seared yellowfin tuna are consistent favorites. For small plates instead of a full meal, grab a seat in the Blue Room, their relaxed wine bar. Reservations are advised for both.

Finn's Farmcut

6 Main St.; tel. 21/470-9636; www.finnsfarmcut.com; Tues.-Sat. 6pm-9pm; from €22

In a town like Kinsale that focuses on seafood, Finn's Farmcut and its charcoal-fired beef and lamb-heavy menu is a tasty outlier. The meat comes from the Finn's family farm, an hour away in Mitchelstown, creating a true farm-to-table experience that makes it a hit. The dining room has some formal touches, but overall this is a relaxed space to enjoy a steak.

★ Man Friday

Scilly; tel. 21/477-2260; https://manfridaykinsale.ie; Tues.-Sat. 5pm-11pm; from €24

Man Friday is a cornerstone of Kinsale's culinary scene for almost 50 years. The interior has a beachy vibe with light wooden furniture and whitewashed walls. The menu changes often but always has meat and seafood options with a couple for vegetarians and vegans.

The Post House Coffee Shop

23 Main St.; tel. 85/146-3217; Instagram @posthousecoffeeshop; daily 8am-4pm

The Post House Coffee Shop is a charming spot for coffee and pastry thanks to the exposed brick walls and comfy seating. When the weather is good, grab a seat in the courtyard out back or at the table out front. They don't serve meals, but keep an eye on their social media, as they open late some evenings to host pop-up events like wine-and-cheese nights and book launches.

Bars and Nightlife

The Bulman Bar

Summercove; tel. 21/477-2131; www.thebulman.ie; Mon.-Tues. 4pm-11:30pm, Wed.-Sat. 2:30pm-12:30am

This charming maritime pub and restaurant by the water at the end of the Scilly Walk has a cozy atmosphere and stunning views across the harbor. It's busy with locals thanks to its seafood, like fresh lobster, oysters, and monkfish, served in the restaurant upstairs. Booking is advised, especially during summer. The pub downstairs is decorated with fishing artifacts and has a mix of bar seating and comfy nooks by the window. The limited food menu downstairs has more casual dishes like chowder and sandwiches.

The Spaniard

Scilly; tel. 21/477-2436; www.thespaniard.ie; Mon.-Thurs. 11am-11:30pm, Fri.-Sat. 11am-12:30am, Sun. 12:30pm-11pm

Built on the foundations of an old castle on the opposite side of the harbor from Kinsale, the Spaniard has a welcoming vibe with rustic decor and warm wooden furniture. It gets even more inviting when the flickering candles are lit. The pub springs to life with live music in the evening on weekends, and if the sun is shining, head outside to the patio to take in views of the water.

Accommodations

★ Actons Hotel

Pier Rd.; tel. 21/477-9900; www.actonshotelkinsale.com; €160

Overlooking Kinsale Harbour and beside some of the best places to eat and drink, Actons Hotel is in the thick of the action. With options from standard doubles to family rooms and seven spacious luxurious suites, there's a wide choice of rooms and rates. There's a 15-m (50-ft) pool, a sauna, a steam room, a bar with a patio, and a relaxed restaurant.

Kinsale Hotel & Spa

Rathmore; tel. 21/470-6000; www.kinsalehotelandspa.ie; €200

A destination hotel on the far side of the harbor, Kinsale Hotel & Spa is a 10-minute drive from the center of town. The setting by the Atlantic and the River Stick gives the 71 harbor or waterfall rooms a relaxing feel away from the busy Wild Atlantic Way. The spa menu is extensive, with 26 treatments in an award-winning setting, and the calm extends to the guest rooms.

Getting There and Around

The Cork rail network doesn't reach West Cork, so your options are driving or the bus. From Cork City, the drive is 30 minutes on main roads and country roads. The bus (45 minutes; €11 round-trip) runs roughly twice hourly during daytime with **West Cork Connect** (tel. 21/701-1288; https://westcorkconnect.ie) or **Bus Éireann** (www.buseireann.ie), who drop off at Kinsale Bus Station (Pearse St.).

BALTIMORE

Not many Irish villages have a story as unexpected as West Cork's Baltimore. In 1631 pirates sailed from Algeria, and with the help of the Ottoman Empire, captured almost every inhabitant of the town and sold them into slavery in Africa. These days the waters are friendlier, with a sailing club and fishing. South-facing pubs and restaurants pack the waterfront, which also marks the start of the walk to the famous Baltimore Beacon.

Sights

Baltimore Beacon

Beacon Rd.

One of Cork's most iconic landmarks, the Baltimore Beacon is a serious draw. This standing stone beacon is painted bright white in stark contrast to the green hills, deep-blue sea, and dark cliffs that surround it. The waters around Baltimore Harbour are deep and treacherous, and the beacon was built to guide ships home. Now that navigation technology has improved, the beacon only guides visitors to the cliff for incredible views. Be careful on windy days, as the drop into the ocean is severe. There's parking for three cars and a short rambling hike to the beacon itself.

Lough Hyne

Lough Hyne, 6 km (4 mi) east of Baltimore, is a unique lough connected to the sea via a narrow channel. In 1981 it became Ireland's first Marine Nature Reserve and is now known for stunning views and as a destination for cycling and kayaking. On the northern edge of the lough is a small forest called Knockomagh Wood with a 3.5-km (2.2-mi) out-and-back walk to the top of the hill.

Hiking and Walking

Baltimore Beacon Walk

Distance: *3.8 km (2.3 mi) round-trip*
Duration: *1 hour*
Elevation gain: *30 m (100 ft)*
Effort: *Easy*
Trailhead: *Baltimore Pier*

There are parking spaces close to Baltimore Beacon, but it's more enjoyable to stroll along the country lanes and the short hiking trail to the beacon instead, as you can see the beacon from various angles and are rewarded with the strong sea wind when you reach the endpoint. The walk starts at the harbor and quickly turns onto very quiet roads. There are no footpaths, so watch for traffic, although most vehicles are moving slowly. Once you've walked up the short hill, you'll see a trail on the left side that brings you to the beacon via a couple of small rolling hills. The walk returns along the same route and handily ends in front of a collection of pubs and restaurants.

Cycling

Lough Hyne Loop

Distance: *15.5 km (10 mi) loop*
Duration: *1 hour*
Elevation gain: *243 m (797 ft)*
Effort: *Moderate*
Trailhead: *Baltimore Pier*

This bicycle loop runs from the water at the harbor through green countryside to the shore of Lough Hyne, Ireland's only saltwater lake. The route is accessible to casual cyclists, but there are two sizeable climbs. There are no bike lanes, so cycle with the traffic and make sure you have lights, as some sections are heavily covered by trees. Stop for a stroll in

1: Baltimore **2:** Baltimore Beacon

1

2

Lough Hyne Forest when you reach the halfway point for even more time outdoors.

Cycle West Cork

Market St.; tel. 87/392-1894; http://cyclewestcork.com; from €20 per day

Cycle West Cork will drop your rental bike off at your lodging, making it easy to get out and explore Baltimore by bike. The bikes are quite basic and best suited to leisurely days on quiet laneways rather than epic bike rides. They also offer guided and self-guided tours.

★ Bioluminescence Kayaking

Atlantic Sea Kayaking

Reen; tel. 282/1058; www.atlanticseakayaking.com; from €50 pp

For an unforgettable night on the water, book a bioluminescence kayaking tour and see the water light up as you paddle. The tour begins after dark, and you'll paddle across the water with your guide as they explain how each paddle stroke causes the sparkling colors. Most common April-October, this natural phenomenon can be experienced at Lough Hyne or Castlehaven Bay, 15 km (9 mi) east of the lough. Daytime tours along the rugged coast and family-friendly options are also offered.

Food and Accommodations

Bushes Bar

Baltimore; tel. 28/20-125; www.bushesbar.com; Mon.-Thurs. 9:30am-11:30pm, Fri.-Sat. 9:30am-12:30am, Sun. 12:30pm-11:30pm; from €5

Bushes is a proper harbor bar, with an interior decorated with coastal paraphernalia, and looks like it hasn't changed much since the 1980s. The patio outside is the place to be on sunny days, looking over the water. The food is classic pub fare centered around sandwiches, so keep an eye out for the daily special or go for the much loved crab sandwich. The beer taps have the Cork classics Beamish and Murphy's, and gin drinkers can try creations from Cape Clear Distillery.

Dede at the Customs House

Customs House; tel. 28/48-248; www.customshousebaltimore.com; Thurs.-Fri. 5:30pm-8:30pm, Sat. 12:30pm-8:30pm, Sun. 12:30pm-2:30pm; tasting menu from €100

As one of only five restaurants in Ireland with two Michelin stars, Dede is extremely sought-after and has gained accolades for culinary works of art inspired by the chef's Turkish roots. Vegetarian and pescetarian menus are available, while the standard menu takes advantage of the seaside location to include lobster, razor clams, and haddock options. Advanced booking is essential.

Rolf's Country House

The Hill; tel. 28/20-289; https://rolfscountryhouse.com; €160

This intimate guesthouse, a 10-minute walk from the center of Baltimore, is surrounded by beautiful gardens and has an award-winning restaurant on its grounds. Choose from eight courtyard rooms, two deluxe garden rooms, and for extra space, one of the cottages.

The Waterfront Hotel

The Square; tel. 28/20-600; www.waterfrontbaltimore.ie; €160

This family-run three-star hotel has 12 clean modern rooms, many beside the water with large windows and great sea views. The hotel is in the thick of the action in Baltimore, with pubs and restaurants on the street below. There's no swimming pool, but the hotel will give you a pass to use the community pool, a 5-minute walk away.

Getting There and Around

You have to take a bus or drive to Baltimore from Cork City. **Bus Éireann** (www.buseireann.ie) operates on this route, but you have to change in Skibbereen before getting off at the stop at Baltimore Pier. Depending on the schedules, it can take 2-3 hours. Driving is quicker at 1.25 hours. The roads are in good condition. Parking in Baltimore is ample and free.

SHERKIN ISLAND

Home to 100 people, Sherkin Island is a rugged 5-km-long (3-mi) island off the coast of Baltimore. Despite the small population there is a busy year-round schedule of festivals and arts events that create an artsy feel. Walk the 2-km (1.2-mi) Horseshoe Loop, where you might even see a lizard, and stop by the Jolly Roger for a drink before getting the Sherkin Island Ferry back to the mainland.

Hiking and Walking

Horseshoe Loop

Distance: *2 km (1.2 mi) loop*
Duration: *30-45 minutes*
Elevation gain: *40 m (130 ft)*
Effort: *Easy*
Trailhead: *Sherkin Island Pier*

This short walk is a mix of quiet roads and off-road trails that begins with a stretch toward the western coast of the island and returns along hills that surround Horseshoe Harbour. The loop route returns you to Sherkin Island Pier.

Festivals and Events

Open Ear Music Festival

www.openear.ie; June; €245

The Open Ear Music Festival on Sherkin Island showcases experimental, ambient, and electronic music. You'll discover lesser-known cutting-edge Irish artists and international acts who play in outdoor settings by the water, creating magical shows. The festival takes place over the June holiday weekend, before the 1st Monday in June, when revelers camp out in the sunshine.

Summer on the Islands

www.westcorkislands.com; May-Sept.

The Summer on the Islands Festival celebrates West Cork's island life with art exhibitions, storytelling, and music events across several islands, including Sherkin. Most events take place May-September, though some are hosted in other months. Tickets can be bought online, and some events are free; check the website.

Food and Nightlife

The Jolly Roger

Farranacoush; tel. 85/141-2503; Instagram @TheJollyRogerPub; Mar. 17-Sept. Sun.-Thurs. 11am-11:30pm, Fri.-Sat. 11am-12:30am

The Jolly Roger on Sherkin Island is a traditional seaside pub and restaurant that serves fresh local seafood and quality pints. A short walk from the pier, you'll enjoy stunning views of the channel between the island and the mainland. The pub is loved for its warm atmosphere, spontaneous music sessions, and lobster dishes, often caught fresh near the island. Note that it's open seasonally.

Getting There and Around

To get to Sherkin Island from Baltimore, take **Sherkin Island Ferries** (www.sherkinferry.ie; 10 minutes; €12 adults, €4 children). Ferries run every few hours throughout the day, and the timetable varies by season, but typical departures from Baltimore include 7:45am, 9am, 10:30am, noon, 2pm, and 4pm.

CAPE CLEAR ISLAND

Cape Clear Island is Ireland's southernmost Gaeltacht (Irish speaking region). Located 13 km (8 mi) off the mainland, Cape, as the locals call it, is like stepping back in time. The island is covered in a blanket of peacefulness where people's lives center around the tide and the sun. Walking and bird-watching are the main activities, and if you're feeling more adventurous, try kayaking and keep an eye out for dolphins and whales.

Hiking and Walking

Little Hills Loop

Distance: *4 km (2.5 mi) loop*
Duration: *1-1.5 hours*
Elevation gain: *200 m (655 ft)*
Effort: *Easy*
Trailhead: *Cape Clear Pier*

This relaxing walk follows quiet country roads and grassy trails along the rugged coastline that's a haven for birds. The trail rambles over small hills, and around the halfway point, you'll reach the old Signal Tower once used to communicate with ships at sea. The route brings you back to the starting point at the pier.

Bird-Watching

Despite its size, this small island is a big hit on the bird-watching scene, particularly at the Cape Clear Bird Observatory, which opened in 1959 beside the harbor. You'll learn about seabird migrations and rare species sightings. Weekend-long bird-watching courses are available through BirdWatch Ireland (www.birdwatchireland.ie; €160), which lets you explore the island's diverse birdlife, where you're likely to see species like Manx shearwaters and peregrine falcons.

Kayaking

Cléire Lasmuigh

Cape Clear Island; www.lasmuigh.ie

During summer, it's possible to go on a kayaking tour with Cléire Lasmuigh. You'll explore the caves and coves on the island and likely see some wildlife. Birds nest in the rocks and dolphins are known to pass through. If you're extremely lucky, you might even see a basking shark; they swim through in May-June. Group bookings are welcome, and the guide has plenty of experience.

Food

Sean Rua's Restaurant

North Harbour; tel. 28/39-099; Instagram @siopabeagandseanruas; hours vary; €12

This restaurant, right by the water on Cape Clear, serves a mix of traditional homemade Irish dishes and pizzas every day, but opening hours vary week by week, with the sign in the door the best way to find out. It's a friendly and casual affair, which makes it great for people traveling with kids.

Cotter's Bar

Cape Clear Island; daily noon-11:30pm; from €16

On a remote island like Cape Clear, the local pub has to wear many hats. Cotter's is a place for a drink or a meal, to sit out in the sun, to meet locals, and much more. Lunch and dinner is standard pub fare like chicken curry and steak, but the atmosphere makes it special. Order at the bar, head out to the large outdoor seating area, and watch the last ferry leave as the sun begins to set, knowing you're on the island for the night.

Getting There

Cape Clear Island is easily reached from Baltimore or Schull with **Cape Clear Ferries** (tel. 28/39-159; www.capeclearferries.com; 40 minutes; €18 round-trip). The ferry from Baltimore departs from Baltimore Pier up to three times a day during summer. The ferry from Schull departs Schull Pier (25 minutes; €25 round-trip).

SCHULL

Although it's rural and remote, Schull is lively in summer, with fantastic independent restaurants and shops instead of the usual chains. People out this way are a creative bunch, with the Fastnet Film Festival, named after the offshore Fastnet Lighthouse, attracting big names.

Festivals and Events

Fastnet Film Festival

www.fastnetfilmfestival.com; May; from €5

The small town of Schull hosts one of Ireland's best film festivals, which shows over 500 films from 40 countries. Although it's centered in Schull, the Fastnet Film Festival has screenings as far away as Cape Clear Island. The venues are part of what makes it so interesting, with screenings in pubs, GAA halls, and cafés.

Shopping

Worm Books

Main St.; tel. 89/204-3327; www.wormbooks.ie; Tues.-Sat. 10am-5pm, Sat. 11am-3pm

This small bookshop has floor-to-ceiling shelves stocked with the latest and greatest Irish books. Fans of fiction will find something to enjoy, and there's a good young adult section and a strong music section. Worm

1: Sherkin Island **2:** Cape Clear Island

1
2

Books fits brilliantly with the strong independent shopping scene in Schull.

Food and Accommodations

Nico's Food and Wine

Main St.; tel. 85/218-0484; Wed.-Fri. 5pm-11pm, Sat.-Sun. 1pm-11pm; from €10

Calling themselves a garden restaurant, it's no surprise that the alfresco dining area at Nico's is a highlight. With some covered outdoor seating, this gorgeous space is a hit year-round. The menu is a mix of seafood and meat with influences from around the world.

The Gracie Blue Bar

Main St.; tel. 28/28-801; www.schullharbourhotel.ie; Sun.-Thurs. noon-midnight, Fri.-Sat. noon-1am; from €15

The Gracie Blue Bar at the Schull Harbour Hotel is a stylish spot with a modern interior just a short stroll from the water. Expect a sophisticated experience with an elevated seafood menu—the pan-fried West Cork hake, served with parsley mash and tender-stem broccoli, is my top pick.

Bunratty Inn

Main St.; tel. 28/28-341; Tues.-Thurs. noon-6pm, Fri.-Sat. noon-8pm, Sun. 12:30pm-4pm; from €16

This traditional pub has an exterior fit for a postcard thanks to the ornate sign and hanging flowering plants. Inside the traditional atmosphere continues with a wooden interior and wood-burning stove. The food is hearty with a strong seaside influence in the crab claws and fish-and-chips. Behind the bar is a good selection of Irish whiskeys and gin.

Schull Harbour Hotel

Main St.; tel. 28/28-801; www.schullharbourhotel.ie; €130

Just a few minutes' walk from Schull Pier and Main Street is the Schull Harbour Hotel, with 30 rooms and self-catering apartments. Grab a seat in the Gracie Blue Bar for dinner and a drink in the evening. There's a strong seafood presence on the menu as well as some vegetarian options. There's an 18-m (60-ft) swimming pool, a sauna, and a steam room.

Getting There and Around

It's possible to get to Schull from Kinsale by bus, but departures are infrequent and involve a layover of over an hour in Bandon. It's really only feasible to drive the 90-km (56-mi) route. Take the N71 road to avoid the narrow winding country roads. From Cork City, there's one direct bus daily with **Bus Éireann** (2 hours; €12 one-way). Otherwise, it's a 90-minute drive. Schull is a small rural town, so walking is the best way to get around.

BARLEY COVE BEACH

The expansive Barley Cove Beach, tucked between rolling green hills on the farthest reaches of the Mizen Peninsula, is truly stunning. Take your time and wander, or go for a swim on summer weekends when the lifeguards are on duty.

Food and Accommodations

Beach Bar & Restaurant at Barley Cove Beach Hotel

Barley Cove Beach; tel. 28/35-874; www.barleycovebeachhotel.com; daily 12:30pm-8:30pm; €15

The dining at the Barley Cove Beach Hotel is highly regarded, with lunch and dinner drawing people from the surrounding area. They specialize in seafood with strong focus on local produce and a catch-of-the-day special. At lunch, try the fish-and-chips, which you can order to go and enjoy on the beach. Dinner is served from 5pm; daily specials like monkfish in kataifi pastry are always highly recommended. Reservations are advised for dinner, and for lunch on a sunny day, try get a seat on the deck.

Getting There

From Kinsale, drive west on the N71 road toward Clonakilty, then continuing on the R592 toward Schull and then Barley Cove, a distance of 95 km (59 mi) that takes 1.25 hours. The journey from Schull is 21 km (13 mi) and takes 20 minutes.

★ MIZEN HEAD

Mizen Peninsula is a remote part of Ireland that stretches into the Atlantic. The ocean batters the coast, creating rugged cliffs and jaw-dropping beaches. Stand at the southernmost point of mainland Ireland at Mizen Head and look south over the water as the wind thunders past—the next landmass is Africa.

Sights

Mizen Head Signal Station & Visitor Centre

Mizen Rd.; tel. 28/35-000; https://mizenhead.ie; July-Aug. daily 10am-6pm, Sept.-Oct. and Apr.-June daily 10:30am-5pm, Nov.-Mar. daily 11am-4pm; €8

Unfortunately Mizen Head is on private land, so to get to the edge you have to go through the Mizen Head Signal Station & Visitor Centre. The upside is that the experience is worth the entrance fee, mainly due to the Mizen Head Bridge, which crosses a corner of the Atlantic. There's a shop and a café serving sandwiches and snacks.

Getting There

To drive from Kinsale to Mizen Head, take the N71 road toward Clonakilty. Continue on the N71 to Ballydehob, then the R592 through Schull and Toormore, and finally the R591 to Goleen, and follow signs to Mizen Head. This journey covers 120 km (75 mi) and takes 2 hours. From Schull the journey is 25 km (16 mi) and takes 30 minutes.

Beara Peninsula

Time seems to move slower on the Beara Peninsula as you traverse the landscape to rocky outcrops that feel like the edge of the world. The peninsula is mainly in County Cork and partly in County Kerry. Towns and villages like **Glengarriff** and Castletown-Bearhaven are on the shore, with the center of the peninsula home to the Miskish and Caha Mountains. Outdoor activities like walks and hikes are popular. **Sheep's Head** has several short but jaw-dropping hikes, while keen hikers will want to walk part of the **Beara-Breifne Way,** which runs 500 km (310 mi). If you're into plants, the gardens on **Garinish**

Mizen Head

Island are a must; the peninsula's microclimate allows for flora you'd usually see in far warmer places. Off the coast of the Beara Peninsula is **Dursey Island,** which you can take a cable car to, but be warned you may be sharing the ride with a farmer and his sheep.

GLENGARRIFF

Surrounded by natural beauty, Glengarriff marks the beginning of the Beara Peninsula. Most importantly, it's the access point to Garinish Island.

Sights

Garinish Island

One of Ireland's idyllic escapes, Garinish Island is loved for its horticulture. Often dubbed "Ireland's Garden Island," this green oasis has breathtaking gardens that wouldn't look out of place in far warmer countries thanks to its unique microclimate. From the tranquil Japanese garden to the vibrant Italianate terraces, every corner is an explosion of color. Climb the Martello tower for panoramic views of the island and sea or simply relax and soak up the peaceful atmosphere. Garinish Island is a hit with wildlife, with seals often seen on the boat journey from the mainland, and a variety of birdlife calling the island home. History buffs will want to head to Bryce House, a charming residence filled with art and artifacts where you'll find out how the house and gardens came to be.

To reach this peaceful island, take a ferry from Glengarriff with one of the local companies. They work independently of Garinish Island, so the fare (from €13 round-trip) is not included in the €5 admission fee. This scenic journey takes about 10 minutes, and you should give yourself 2 hours to see everything. If you're a gardening enthusiast, nature lover, or just want a tranquil retreat, Garinish Island is for you.

Hiking and Walking

The **Beara Way** is a difficult multiday hike that makes up part of the lengthy 500-km (310-mi) Beara-Breifne Way. The route starts in Glengarriff but can be walked in sections. It's easy to refuel along the way and make it to a proper bed most nights. As well as seeing the peninsula, you'll make your way to Dursey Island in Cork and into County Kerry and the town of Kenmare. The route is a mix of single-track trail, crushed-gravel paths, and country roads, which keeps things interesting. Here's a section of the Beara Way that you could hike in a day.

Glengarriff to Kenmare

Distance: *19 km (12 mi) one-way*
Duration: *5-6 hours*
Elevation gain: *350 m (1,150 ft)*
Effort: *Moderate*
Trailhead: *Glengarriff Woods*

This section of the Beara Way can be done in either direction, to start or finish in Glengarriff. From Glengarriff, it begins at Glengarriff Woods and follows old tracks and trails into the countryside. This route is a stage of the Beara Way, so it's challenging in parts, particularly the steeper sections as you approach the Caha Mountains, but you're rewarded with great sea views. The route then follows country roads before ending in Kenmare.

Food and Accommodations

Coasties

Main St.; Instagram @coastieswestcork; Sat.-Sun. noon-5pm; €7

Only open on the weekend, Coasties is worth the wait, as their crispy, gooey, and tasty toasted sandwiches hit the spot every time. This food truck elevates the standard cheese toastie with some gourmet touches and unexpected combinations. Beside the truck there's seating shared with other businesses.

Garnish Restaurant

Harbour; tel. 27/63-003; www.eccleshotel.com; Mon.-Sat. dinner, Sun. lunch and dinner; €24

Complementing the views of Bantry Bay are the wonderful dishes served at Garnish Restaurant in the Eccles Hotel. It's a refined experience with a chef who has worked in

Ring of Beara Drive

Ring of Beara

The Ring of Beara is a spectacular 140-km (90-mi) coastal drive that loops around the rugged Beara Peninsula. It's less well known than the Ring of Kerry but equally beautiful and less intimidating to drive during the busy summer months. The drive takes you through rural villages, alongside unforgettable seascapes, and through remote foothills. Most people begin the drive either at Glengarriff in County Cork or at Kenmare in County Kerry.

THE BEST STOPS ON THE RING OF BEARA DRIVE

There are plenty of great sights, villages, and places to eat along the drive. Five of the best:

- **Glengarriff:** As one of the largest villages on the drive, it's the gateway to the peninsula.
- **Healy Pass:** This twisty narrow road is challenging but has brilliant views of rural Cork and Kerry.
- **Dursey Island Cable Car:** Hop on this famous cable car to Dursey Island.
- **Harrington's Ardgroom:** Part post office, part grocer, part café, this spot does it all, and their sandwiches are delicious.
- **An Síbín:** Enjoy a mix of traditional Irish food and global wines at this spot outside Lauragh.

Michelin-starred restaurants plating feather blade steak and monkfish scampi in textured earthenware dishes.

Eccles Hotel & Spa Glengarriff

Harbour; tel. 27/63-003; www.eccleshotel.com; €200

Perched by the water, this is a beautiful place to stay. The 59 rooms are traditional but not dated, and the bay view rooms are worth the added expense. The on-site Garnish Restaurant is well regarded in foodie circles as it uses the best of West Cork produce. There's no pool, but you can take a dip in the sea outside and pamper yourself at the spa afterward.

Getting There and Around

If you're driving from Cork City to Glengarriff, the journey is 91 km (57 mi) and takes 1.25 hours via the N22 and R585 roads. From Kinsale, it's 91 km (57 mi) and 1.5 hours on the R600 and N71. From Schull, the distance is 42 km (26 mi) and takes 40 minutes via the R591 and N71. From Cork City, **Bus Éireann** (www.buseireann.ie) has a direct bus, Route 236, from the Parnell Place bus station to the stop outside the pharmacy in Glengarriff.

SHEEP'S HEAD

Sheep's Head is a popular spot with informed hikers who have heard about the fantastic trails. The landscape is steep and surrounded by views of the ocean. You're likely to see sheep grazing on the headland. The 88-km (55-mi) Sheep's Head Way runs through, but there are shorter day hikes as well.

Hiking and Walking

Seefin Loop

Distance: *12.8 km (8 mi) loop*
Duration: *4 hours*
Elevation gain: *345 m (1,130 ft)*
Effort: *Difficult*
Trailhead: *Ahakista Pier*

Explore this scenic route that gives a snapshot of Irish folklore. Beginning at the car park at Ahakista Pier, follow the blue arrows to St. Patrick's Church and then to the summit of Seefin, a lengthy and steep climb. Seefin is the anglicization of the hill's Irish name, which means "the seat of Finn," a legendary Irish warrior. Once at the top, you'll get views along Sheep's Head and out to sea. The way down is a steep descent onto a country road, where you'll return to the start point at the pier.

Lighthouse Loop

Distance: *3.7 km (2.3 mi) loop*
Duration: *2 hours*
Elevation gain: *190 m (625 ft)*
Effort: *Moderate*
Trailhead: *Tooreen Point Car Park*

This coastal trail is a fantastic way to see crashing waves, idyllic views of Bantry Bay, and Sheep's Head Lighthouse. The route is exposed in places, steep in sections, and tricky underfoot in others, so care is required throughout, particularly on top of the cliffs. The lighthouse marks the halfway point, and the trail loops back to the car park.

Getting There

Take the N71 road east from Glengarriff, then turn right once you've passed through Bantry to stay by the ocean.

Dursey Island Cable Car

DURSEY ISLAND

This isolated island is famous for its cable car that connects it with the mainland. It's a peaceful place where sheep roam the hills and waves crash on the rocky cliffs. At Dursey Point, on the southernmost tip, you can look across to Bull Rock, an impressive rock formation with a lighthouse on top.

★ Cable Car

Ballaghboy; www.durseyisland.ie; Nov.-Feb. daily 9:30am-4:30pm, Mar.-Oct. daily 9:30am-7:30pm; €10

On the remotest part of the Beara Peninsula is Ireland's only cable car, linking the mainland with Dursey Island. The journey takes 10 minutes and is the only cable car in Europe that crosses open sea. Note that the cable car runs continuously but pauses for lunch. The current cars look dated, with wooden doors and small windows, but there's an undeniable charm, and they've recently been upgraded to ensure safety.

Hiking and Walking

Dursey Island Loop

Distance: *14 km (8.7 mi) loop*
Duration: *4 hours*
Elevation gain: *400 m (1,310 ft)*
Effort: *Moderate*
Trailhead: *Dursey Island Cable Car*

This loop walk can be split into smaller chunks, or take 4 hours to walk the whole route. There are few places to refuel, so bring all the supplies you'll need. The loop begins at the cable car and passes through three very small villages as you make your way to the old signal tower, then loops back through gorgeous green hills.

Bird-Watching

The main bird-watching site is on the northern shore of the island, with black redstarts, lesser whitethroats, yellow-browed warblers, and pied flycatchers the main draws to the island.

Bull Rock Boat Tour

The Pier; tel. 83/898-9999; https://durseyboattrips.com; Apr.-Sept. daily; €60

Get up close to Ireland's biggest gannet colony on this boat tour around Bull Rock. The birds blanket this incredible rock formation that's been battered by the ocean into a rugged and striking scene. Bull Rock Lighthouse stands atop the rock, but the real attraction is what's below. Known as the "Entrance to the Underworld," this passageway runs from one side of Bull Rock to the other. You can sail through it on this 90-minute tour.

Getting There

Take the R572 road southwest from Glengarriff for 55 km (34 mi) and 1 hour until you reach the cable car.

Kerry

The saying goes, "There are only two kingdoms, the Kingdom of God and the Kingdom of Kerry." So it's safe to presume that the people of Kerry are immensely fond of their county. Kerry is hard-core in Gaelic football (one of our national sports) with both the men's and women's teams the most successful in the country. Kerry is where you'll find nature in full swing, with Ireland's tallest mountain, Killarney National Park, and remote beaches that you'll have to yourself. If you close your eyes and think of Ireland, it's likely Kerry that you're daydreaming about.

The Kingdom of Kerry is Ireland's fifth largest county, but Killarney, the main base for visitors, has a population of just 14,000. The jagged coastlines, mountains, and green valleys are smattered with towns

Highlights

Look for ★ to find recommended sights, activities, dining, and lodging.

★ **The Ring of Kerry:** More than just a drive, this 179-km (111-mi) route is a journey through the best-known parts of County Kerry, with incredible views and picturesque towns (page 226).

★ **Killarney National Park:** With endless mountain views and unforgettable scenic drives, Killarney National Park is vast and outstandingly rewarding (page 233).

★ **Carrauntoohil:** Gaze up at the highest peak in Ireland—which stands at 1,038 m (3,406 ft) tall—and if you're an adventurous hiker, climb to the top (page 241).

★ **Skellig Michael:** Sail to a galaxy not so far away at this otherworldly island, home to a monastery before featuring in two *Star Wars* movies (page 248).

★ **Valentia Island:** Walk in the footsteps of a tetrapod on a rocky outcrop on Valentia Island and see the footprints that mark the water mammal's move to land 380 million years ago (page 250).

★ **The Blasket Islands:** This remote uninhabited island gives insight into the hardships of life in a jaw-droppingly beautiful place that inspired incredible writers (page 260).

Kerry

Brandon Point
Brandon
The Dingle Way
R550
See "Slea Head Drive and the Dingle Peninsula" Maop
Mount Brandon
R560
Glanteenassig Forest Park
Mount Brandon SAC
Dingle
R549
Conor Pass
R559
The Kerry Camino
Slea Head
Dingle
Annascaul
Ventry
N86
Dunquin
HEAD DRIVE
Kinard Beach
R559
SLEA
Kerry Seas National Park
THE BLASKET ISLANDS
Dingle Bay
N70
RING OF KERRY
ATLANTIC OCEAN
DINOSAUR FOOTPRINTS
VALENTIA ISLAND LIGHTHOUSE
Cahersiveen
VALENTIA ISLAND
THE ROYAL VALENTIA HOTEL
THE RING LYNE BAR & RESTAURANT
R565
Iveragh
Portmagee
N70
Kerry International Gold Tier Dark Sky Reserve (Core Area)
R567
R566
Waterville
CHARLIE CHAPLIN STATUE
Ballinskelligs
Kerry Seas National Park
0 4 mi
0 4 km
SKELLIG MICHAEL
DERRYNANE MASS PATH
Caherdaniel
Derrynane Beach
DERRYNANE HOUSE
Wild Atlantic Way
Scenic Route
© MOON.COM

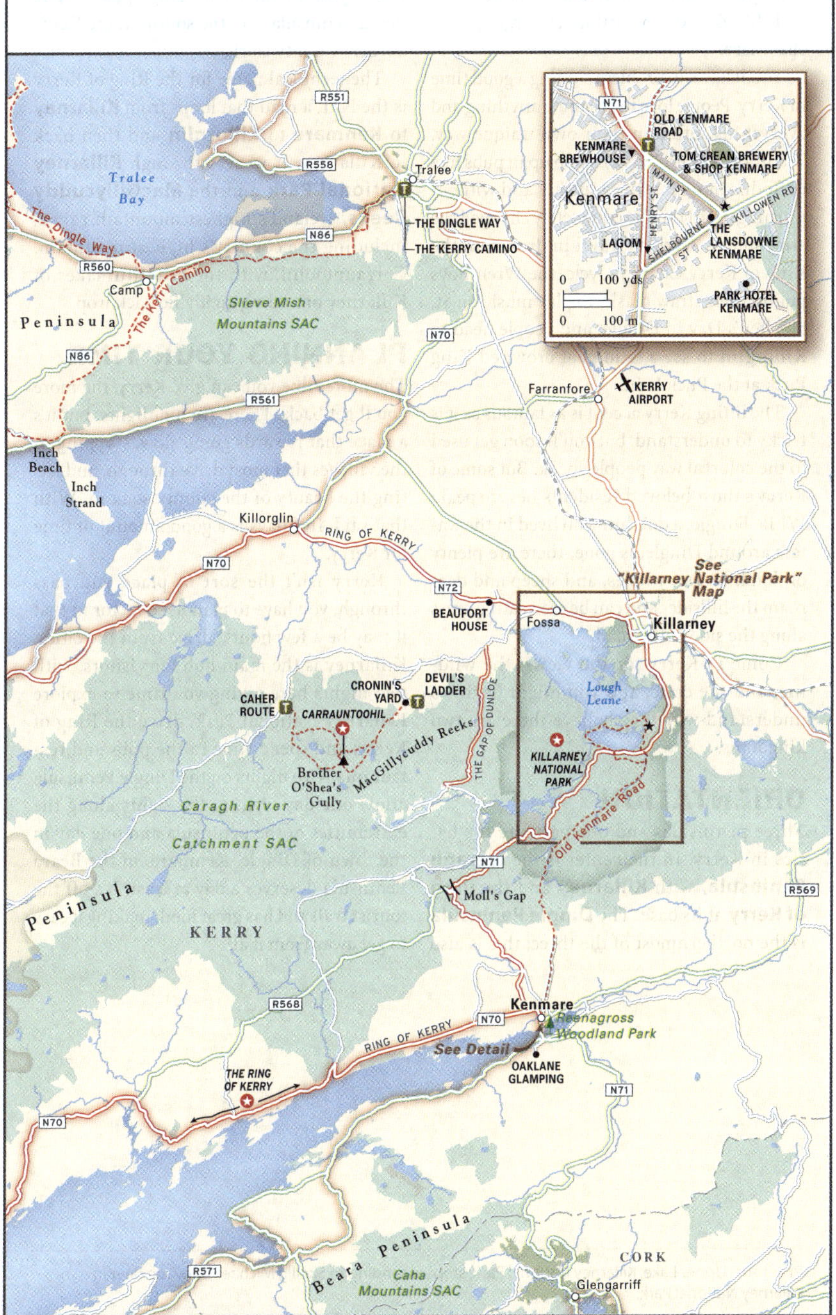
Tralee Bay
The Dingle Way
The Kerry Camino
R551
R558
Tralee
THE DINGLE WAY
THE KERRY CAMINO
N86
R560
Camp
Peninsula
Slieve Mish
Mountains SAC
N70
N86
R561
Farranfore
KERRY AIRPORT
Inch Beach
Inch Strand
Killorglin
RING OF KERRY
N70
N72
See "Killarney National Park" Map
BEAUFORT HOUSE
Fossa
Killarney
Lough Leane
CAHER ROUTE
CRONIN'S YARD
DEVIL'S LADDER
CARRAUNTOOHIL
THE GAP OF DUNLOE
MacGillycuddy Reeks
Brother O'Shea's Gully
KILLARNEY NATIONAL PARK
Old Kenmare Road
Caragh River
Catchment SAC
N71
Moll's Gap
R569
Peninsula
KERRY
R568
Kenmare
N70
Reenagross Woodland Park
RING OF KERRY
See Detail
OAKLANE GLAMPING
THE RING OF KERRY
N71
N70
Beara Peninsula
Caha Mountains SAC
CORK
R571
Glengarriff
N71
OLD KENMARE ROAD
KENMARE BREWHOUSE
TOM CREAN BREWERY & SHOP KENMARE
MAIN ST
Kenmare
HENRY ST
KILLOWEN RD
THE LANSDOWNE KENMARE
LAGOM
SHELBOURNE ST
0 100 yds
0 100 m
PARK HOTEL KENMARE

and villages that have amazing places to eat and things to do to rival much larger places elsewhere.

You'll have no problem finding a good time in Kerry. People love to celebrate anything and everything, often in their own unique way. Traditional music sessions pop up in pubs like daffodils in springtime, quickly and without warning, until they've completely changed the atmosphere. Cyclists travel in droves on the Ring of Kerry Charity Cycle, the Wren Boys put on their straw masks to play music on St. Stephen's Day in Dingle, and people head to Killorglin to see a wild goat crowned King Puck at the Puck Fair.

The lilting Kerry accent is as famous as it is tricky to understand, but you'll soon get used to the colorful way people speak. But some of Kerry's most beloved residents never speak: While Fungie, a dolphin who lived in the waters around Dingle, is gone, there are plenty of dolphins and whales, and sheep and deer roam the hillsides and can be seen eating grass along the side of the road.

Come to Kerry for the views, the wildlife, and the craic, and you might begin to understand why they believe there are two kingdoms.

ORIENTATION

Three peninsulas and one park are the basics in Kerry. In the center is the **Iveragh Peninsula,** with **Killarney** and the **Ring of Kerry** at its base. The **Dingle Peninsula** is the northernmost of the three; this is also where you'll hear Irish being spoken. The Beara Peninsula is in the south, where Kerry borders County Cork.

The technical name for the Ring of Kerry is the N71, a road that loops from **Killarney** to **Kenmare** to **Killorglin** and then back to Killarney. It weaves through **Killarney National Park** and the **MacGillycuddy Reeks,** Ireland's highest mountain range, including the country's highest mountain, Carrauntoohil, with the beautiful lakes of Killarney providing an idyllic backdrop.

PLANNING YOUR TIME

The more time you can give Kerry, the more you'll get back. There are highlights, but it's a place that rewards going slow, stopping in the villages that most drive through, and letting the beauty of the county soak in. With that said, five days is a good amount of time for Kerry.

Kerry isn't the sort of place you pass through; you have to plan it, so factor in that it may be a few hours' drive from the cities. Killarney is the main hub for visitors, with two nights here giving you time to explore Killarney National Park, drive the Ring of Kerry, and spend time in the pubs and restaurants. Two nights on the Dingle Peninsula allow one day visiting the sights along the extremities of the peninsula and one day in the town of Dingle. Kenmare on the Beara Peninsula deserves a day at least. It's off the tourist trail and has great food, making it easy to get away from it all.

Previous: Upper Lake, Killarney National Park; steps ascending to Skellig Michael; baby roe deer in Killarney National Park.

Itinerary Ideas

DAY 1: KILLARNEY

1 Fuel up for the day with a healthy acai bowl for breakfast and tasty coffee at **Luna Coffee + Wine.**

2 Walk across the street to the **Killarney House & Gardens,** learn about the history at the free exhibit, and walk the manicured grounds.

3 See even more of the beautiful gardens in a horse-drawn **jaunting car** and trot your way around Killarney.

4 Get a taste of traditional Irish food at **Bricín** and try the boxty, an Irish potato pancake.

5 Sleep out under the stars at **Killarney Glamping at the Grove** and wake up to stunning lake views.

DAY 2: THE DINGLE PENINSULA

1 Embark on the sometimes challenging but always rewarding drive up **Conor Pass** to the northern edge of the peninsula to Brandon.

2 Put on your hiking boots and go for a short walk in the foothills of **Mount Brandon** for incredible views across the peninsulas and ocean.

3 Get back in the car and make your way to **Dunquin Pier** and get photos of the coast and the striking pier.

4 Sail to the **Blasket Islands** for a journey to Ireland's past and keep an eye out for dolphins and whales at sea.

5 Drive the **Slea Head Drive** to Dingle.

6 Have a well-earned nightcap in **Dick Mack's Pub.**

DAY 3: DINGLE TOWN

1 Take in that fresh sea air on the **Dingle Harbour Walk** to get a good feel for the town.

2 Get your caffeine fix at **Bean in Dingle** and people-watch from one of the seats by the window.

3 Head for **Púca Café** for lunch and get a seat in the garden if it's sunny, before checking out the independent shops in town.

4 Order fish for dinner in either **Reel Dingle Fish Co** if you want something quick and cheap or **Out of the Blue** if you want to splurge.

5 Finish the night in **O'Sullivan's Courthouse Pub,** where there's live music seven days a week.

Killarney to Kenmare

Even in Ireland, where we're surrounded by natural beauty, this part of the country still manages to amaze. Yes, it does get busy; the Ring of Kerry is firmly established on the tourist trail, but that doesn't mean that it's been spoiled. There are plenty of places to get well off the beaten track and find isolation, even during the height of summer. So lace up your hiking boots and get into the landscape. There'll be plenty of music, food, and drinks waiting in Killarney and Kenmare when you return.

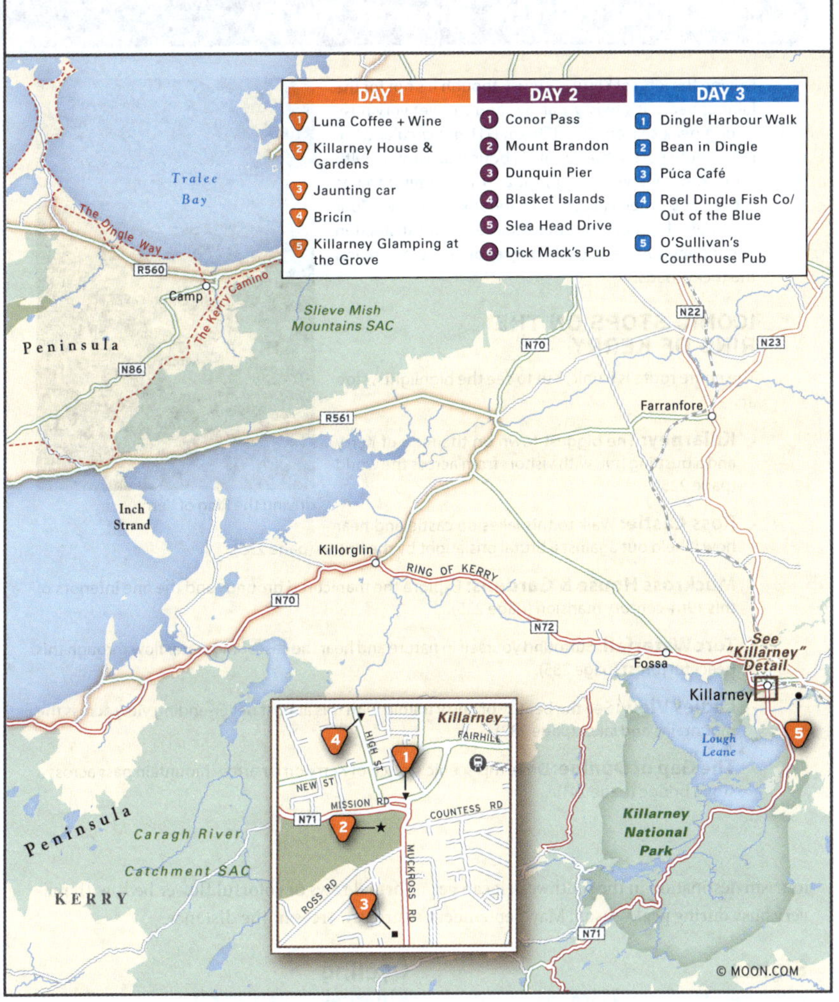

ORIENTATION

Killarney sits at the heart of the Ring of Kerry, surrounded by **Killarney National Park,** where Lough Leane lies at the base of the **MacGillycuddy Reeks** to the west, where you'll spot **Carrauntoohil.** South of Killarney is **Kenmare,** a busy town on the edge of Kenmare Bay.

KILLARNEY

Killarney is an energetic nonstop town that most visitors to Kerry visit thanks to its airport and proximity to the area's attractions. There's no end to the traditional pubs, modern restaurants, and narrow Irish streets, and it's the gateway to the wilderness of Killarney National Park, including scenic Moll's Gap and Ladies View. Kerry people are friendly and helpful, and tourism is part of daily life. As the major

☆ Exploring the Ring of Kerry

Driving the Ring of Kerry is a must, though it's not for the faint of heart. It's twisty, narrow, and can get very busy during peak season. This 179-km (111-mi) circular drive in a remote part of the county is bound to astound with remarkable views throughout and welcoming towns tucked into green valleys and overlooking the sea. Tour buses ply the route, but there's a sense of satisfaction and independence you can only experience by driving the tricky roads.

driving the Ring of Kerry

ICONIC STOPS ON THE RING OF KERRY

The entire route is iconic, but to see the highlights, stop at:

- **Killarney:** The biggest town on the Ring of Kerry and a bustling hub with visitors from across the world (page 225).
- **Ross Castle:** Walk to this lakeside castle and hear how it held out against a brutal onslaught by the British (page 235).
- **Muckross House & Gardens:** Explore the manicured grounds and the fine interiors of this 19th-century mansion (page 235).
- **Torc Waterfall:** Surround yourself in nature and hear the cascading water flow through this peaceful forest (page 235).
- **Ladies View:** See the beauty of Kerry unfold with this almost never-ending view across the mountains and lakes (page 237).
- **The Gap of Dunloe:** Drive this scenic stretch of Kerry on a narrow mountain pass across a stone bridge (page 241).

tourism destination in the southwest, it can get very busy during peak season, May-September.

Sights

Killarney House & Gardens

Demense; www.killarneynationalpark.ie; daily 9:15am-1pm and 2pm-5:15pm; free

Think of Killarney House & Gardens, located in the center of town, as a teaser to the wilder reaches of the national park. Both the house and gardens are free, and it's worthwhile stopping by for the visitor center with plenty of information. The house has exhibits on the geographical history of the area, the wildlife, and the people who live in and around the park. The wide manicured gardens have formal rows of colorful flower beds with mature yew trees in the distance.

Cycling

Killarney Bike Rental

Muckross Rd.; tel. 87/236-3044; www.killarneybikerental.com; €20 per day

The no-fuss bikes at Killarney Bike Rental, suited to riding on pavement and well-maintained gravel paths, are good for exploring the relaxed routes in the area. Some kids' bikes are available. For a sportier ride, rent a touring bike, or let the bike do the work with an e-bike. The staff are able to recommend routes around the town and in the national park for your fitness level.

- **Moll's Gap:** Wind your way along an exposed mountain pass in the park from tight country roads into an open expanse of wilderness (page 242).
- **Kenmare:** Embrace the slower pace of life and amazing food in this charming village away from the crowds in Killarney (page 242).
- **Derrynane House:** Visit the home of Daniel O'Connell, known as "the Liberator" for his role in helping Catholics gain equal rights (page 246).
- **Skellig Michael:** Sail to this striking pyramid-shaped island where devout monks made pilgrimages and built beehive huts (page 248).
- **Valentia Island:** Journey back millions of years and see footprints that mark a pivotal point in evolution (page 250).

READY TO DRIVE

The Ring of Kerry can be driven in either direction on the N71, though most go clockwise, as you get right into the action at Muckross as soon as you leave Killarney. This route takes you to Kenmare, then Killorglin, before arriving back in Killarney. It's best to start in the morning, especially during summer, to experience the drive at its quietest. It takes around four hours to drive the route, but give yourself a full day so that you can take it slow and soak up all the views.

Remember to slow down and drive safely. Locals and tour bus drivers are well accustomed to the roads, so their confidence may come as a shock.

TOUR OPTIONS

If you don't feel comfortable driving the narrow winding roads, you can still experience the Ring of Kerry on a bus tour. Local providers include **O'Connor's of Kerry** (https://oconnorsofkerry.ie) and **Wild Kerry Days** (https://wildkerrydaytours.com), offering day tours (€35-40). **Killarney Executive Tour Co.** (https://killarneytour.com; from €15) offers hop-on, hop-off buses with five stops.

Jaunting

Killarney Jaunting Cars

Gilhuys 10B Close, Muckross Rd.; tel. 64/663-3358; https://killarneyjauntingcars.com; Mon.-Sat. 8:30am-6pm, Sun. 9am-6pm; €65 pp

Jaunting cars are synonymous with Killarney, and the team at Killarney Jaunting Cars have a brilliant choice of tours. These horse-drawn cars are driven by a jarvey (driver) with the passengers sitting in the covered section at the back. Listen to the jarvey's stories and history of Killarney as you take in the sights. The tours around Muckross House & Gardens and lakes in Killarney National Park are the most popular, but if you're a fan of whiskey, book a spot on the Whiskey & Wonders in Killarney Tour, which runs through the park and ends at a pub in town for a whiskey tasting session from Irish distillers, paired with a cheese board.

Food

Luna Coffee + Wine

1 Brewery Lane; www.lunacoffeewine.ie; daily 7:30am-7pm; from €5

It's hard to miss the bold blue exterior of this modern coffee shop on the corner of Brewery Lane. The blue is swapped for pink and chic wooden furnishings inside, making this medium-size café, with room for about 30, feel big-city. There's also a large covered outdoor seating area in front of all the businesses on

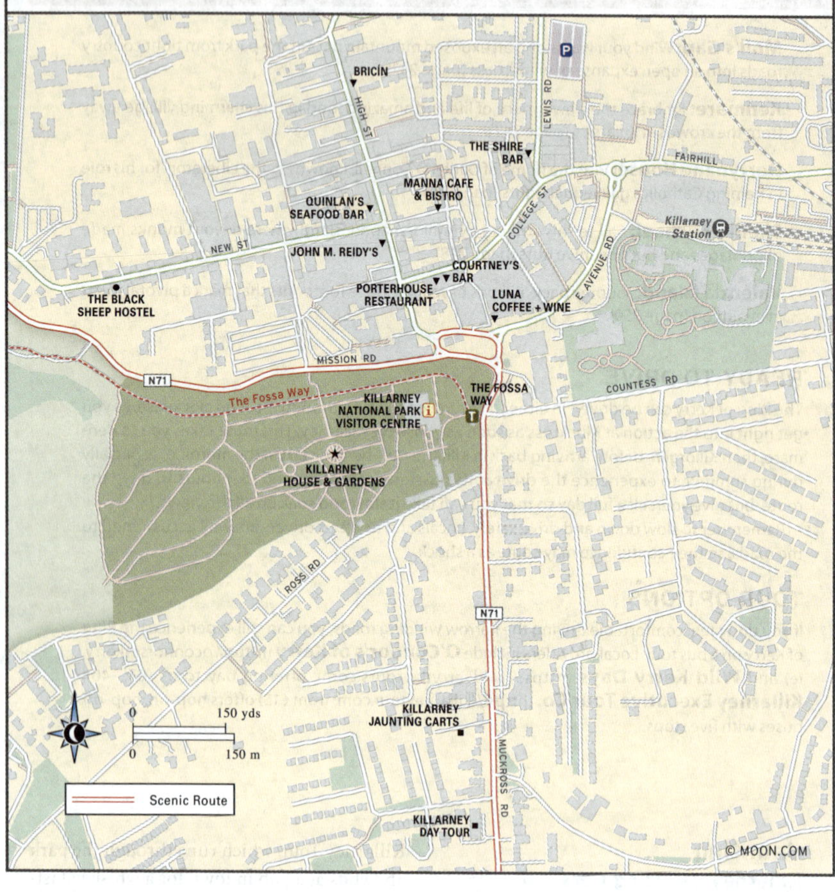

Kenmare Place, perfect for people-watching on a warm day. Complementing the coffee menu are focaccia sandwiches, artisanal sausage rolls, and freshly baked pastries. In the afternoon, the space turns into a wine bar, with smoked almonds served alongside chili and garlic olives.

Manna Cafe & Bistro

5 Old Market Lane; tel. 64/663-1596; Instagram @mannacafekillarney; Mon.-Sat. 9am-5pm, Sun. 10am-4pm; from €12

Good-quality grub and plenty of it at good prices, particularly for Killarney, make Manna Café & Bistro worth seeking out. They serve breakfast until midday, then lunch until 4:30pm in the bright airy space that has four-seat tables as well as the high-tops you'd usually find in pubs. The menu has Irish favorites; the Big is their take on a full Irish breakfast and will feed the hungriest. The lunch menu includes a club sandwich, caesar salad, a chicken burger, and plenty of other classics.

Ring of Kerry Charity Cycle

Gap of Dunloe, Ring of Kerry

The Ring of Kerry Charity Cycle (www.ringofkerrycycle.ie) has been a popular event since 1984. Held the 1st Saturday of July, it attracts thousands of cyclists from all over. Riders cycle 170 km (106 mi) around the Ring of Kerry to raise funds for a range of local and national charities. Over €190 million has been raised for 160 groups.

THE ROUTE AND RIDE

The expert-level ride follows the Ring of Kerry, starting and ending in Killarney, with four tough climbs and an elevation gain of 1,490 m (4,890 ft) in total. Lots of road closures are in place, leaving long stretches car-free. The atmosphere is part of the experience: This isn't a race; it's an enormous group cycle where people go at their own pace and stop in villages to refuel and chat with other cyclists. Some fit riders finish the route in just a few hours, but most take 6-10 hours.

HOW TO PREPARE

Given the length and challenging nature of the route, riders train in advance. Prepare for varying weather conditions, even in July, and you must have a suitable bike and helmet to join. Registration usually opens in March.

Quinlan's Seafood Bar

77 High St.; tel. 64/662-0666; https://seafoodbar.ie/killarney; Sun.-Thurs. 12:30pm-8:30pm, Fri.-Sat. 12:30pm-9pm; from €20

Operating on a "tide to table" principle, Quinlan's Seafood Bar builds their menu around fresh local seafood cooked without fuss. It feels like the big brother to the fish-and-chips places you normally find in Ireland—everything is more considered on the extended menu, including crab claws and local craft beers. It can get quite busy during peak times. Quinlan's also has a seafood shop on the edge of town in Deerpark, where you can pick up fresh fish and tips on how to cook it.

Porterhouse Restaurant

26 Plunkett St.; tel. 64/667-1130; http://theporterhousekillarney.com; daily 5pm-10:30pm; from €25

Porterhouse Restaurant brings a refined touch to casual dining by plating Instagram-worthy dishes in a pub-style setting elevated with

1

2

3

tasteful Irish furnishings and soft lighting. The menu isn't groundbreaking, but there is a strong focus on local suppliers and produce. The lamb stew uses lambs from the Ring of Kerry. For vegetarians they have three starters and three mains, with the House Korean Tacos the smart choice.

Bricín

26 High St.; tel. 64/663-4902; www.bricin.ie; Tues.-Sat. 6pm-9:30pm; from €25

Ireland doesn't really have its own distinct cuisine, but some dishes are uniquely Irish, and you'll find them at Bricín. You know you're in for a traditional Irish experience as soon as you set foot inside, with dark wooden floors, wood paneling, and deep red walls. Irish comfort food includes rack of Kerry lamb and wild Atlantic hake, both good choices, but you're missing a trick if you overlook the boxty. This potato pancake is traditionally served with chicken or lamb, or as a vegetarian option with ratatouille.

Bars and Nightlife

John M. Reidy's

4 Main St.; https://reidyskillarney.com; daily 8am-11pm

Traditional pubs don't get bigger or better in Killarney than John M. Reidy's. In the 1870s the front bar acted as a bakery, hardware shop, and sweets shop. This part of Reidy's hasn't changed a lot, and it's a great spot to grab a drink at the old wooden bar. There are also informal dining areas, booths, and small rooms tucked away. The cobbled courtyard regularly hosts live music, the menu is a solid collection of pub classics, and mornings you can grab a scone from the bakery just like in the 1870s.

The Shire Bar

Michael Collins Place, Lewis Rd.; tel. 64/667-1605; http://theshirekillarney.com; Mon.-Thurs. 8am-11:30pm, Fri.-Sat. 8am-12:30am, Sun. 8am-11:30pm

The Shire offers something different from the traditional pubs in Killarney. It's part pub, part restaurant, part café, and also what I'd call *Lord of the Rings*-ish. The toilets are signposted "Hobbits," and the style of the pub resembles houses in the books. But they haven't gone all-in on the theme. You can't go wrong with the bacon- and cheese-loaded fries topped with jalapeños, and local craft beers are on tap, including the Shire Red Ale.

Courtney's Bar

24 Plunkett St.; tel. 64/663-2689; www.courtneysbar.com; Mon.-Thurs. 2pm-11:30pm, Fri. noon-12:30am, Sat. 10:30am-12:30am, Sun. 12:30pm-11:30pm

"Pulling pints in three centuries" is the motto of Courtney's Bar, and you'd be forgiven for not knowing what century you're in once you step inside. It feels like hardly anything has changed since they opened in 1891, with the dark wooden interior, glasses of warming whiskey, and a roaring fireplace offering comfort from the weather. The walls of the bar are decorated with money donated by travelers from all over the world, a sign that visitors are embraced. Despite its motto, Courtney's is known as a whiskey bar, and you'll find a fantastic collection from mainly Irish distilleries and a couple from Scotland.

Accommodations

The Black Sheep Hostel

68 New St.; tel. 64/663-8746; www.blacksheephostel.ie; €70

The eco-friendly Black Sheep Hostel feels like it's custom-made for outdoorsy people looking for a sustainable budget-friendly place, with six- and eight-bed mixed dorms as well as a female-only six-bed dorm, private doubles, and a one-bedroom apartment. In the morning, the coffee shop downstairs has single-origin coffee; learn about their sustainable practices like growing their own vegetables and solar panels.

Cronin's Yard

Mealis; tel. 64/662-4044; https://croninsyard.com; €120

Cronin's Yard offers a range of lodging options

1: Killarney jaunting cars **2:** Courtney's Bar and restaurants in downtown Killarney **3:** Killarney House & Gardens

for hikers exploring the MacGillycuddy Reeks and Carrauntoohil. The site has timber-built insulated camping pods, including the Big Gun Pod for two, the Corrán Tuathail Pod for three, and the Cruach Mhór Pod for two. These cozy pods are equipped with electric heating, double-glazed windows, and sheep's wool insulation. For a more traditional option, Paddy Ninth's Mountain Cottage is a self-catering stone cottage. Tent camping is also possible on-site if you bring your own tent.

Beaufort House

Beaufort; tel. 64/664-4764; www.beaufortireland.com; €140

Set on 16 ha (40 acres) of private grounds, Beaufort House is a serene escape surrounded by stunning gardens, woodlands, and mountain views just 10 km (6 mi) from Killarney. Enjoy strolls through the gardens or relax in the peaceful countryside at this boutique country house. There are 13 rooms in the main house and cottages, making it great for large groups. No dining options are on-site, but there is a space that can be set up for 24 people to be catered. There are nearby pubs and restaurants within walking distance to dine without going into Killarney.

Killarney Glamping at the Grove

Ballycasheen; tel. 87/975-0110; www.killarneyglamping.com; €165

Located 2 km (1.2 mi) outside Killarney is Killarney Glamping, a couples-only spot that mixes the outdoors and comfort. Choose the romantic glamping suite or the luxury lodge, both resembling A-frame style houses, or the cabins, wooden-clad tastefully designed tiny homes complete with amenities. Once you've settled in, make your way to the riverside sauna, where you can get your sweat on before cooling off with a dip in the river.

Hotel Killarney

Cork Rd.; tel. 64/662-6200; www.hotelkillarney.ie; €175

Refurbished in 2024, Hotel Killarney is a 188-room, family-friendly hotel away from the bustle of the town center. Leisure facilities include an 18-m (60-ft) indoor swimming pool, a toddler pool, a fully equipped gym, a sauna, a steam room, and a whirlpool. There is also an on-site spa for wellness treatments. For families, the hotel has a dedicated kids club for 3-12-year-olds and a teen zone for age 13 and up with games, a soft play area, and mini golf. Dining options include the **Strawberry Tree Restaurant** (6:30pm-9:30pm; €25) and **Sloe Berry Bar** (12:30pm-late; €15), where there are dedicated extensive kids menus.

The Europe Hotel & Resort

Fossa; tel. 64/667-1300; www.theeurope.com; €355

On the shores of Lough Léin, the stunning Europe Hotel & Resort is a luxurious five-star retreat overlooking Killarney National Park, with 180 elegant rooms and suites, each with views of the lakes or gardens. World-class amenities include the ESPA spa, three exquisite restaurants, and two bars. Active guests enjoy complimentary horseback riding, indoor tennis, and access to the hotel's extensive leisure facilities.

Aghadoe Heights Hotel & Spa

Lakes of Killarney; tel. 64/663-1766; www.aghadoeheights.com; €475

Aghadoe Heights Hotel & Spa is renowned for its stunning views and has 74 spacious modern rooms in eight types, from kings to the penthouse suite. Many feature private balconies or floor-to-ceiling windows. A highlight is the spa, with a range of reviving treatments, a thermal suite, an indoor swimming pool, and an outdoor hot tub overlooking the lakes. Dining is top-notch, with the **Lake Room** (6:30pm-9:30pm; €32) offering seasonal locally sourced fine-dining and an extensive wine list. The **Heights Lounge & Piano Bar** (12:30pm-late; €15) is all about the views across the lakes while you sip on your drink.

Information and Services

Services are limited in these rural areas, but you'll find most in towns like Killarney, Kenmare, and Cahersiveen. Petrol stations are common, from basic fuel to modern ones that have toilets, ATMs, and delis serving hot food. Before you start your drive, pop into the Killarney National Park Visitor Centre to pick up free maps and get an understanding of the area.

Getting There

Air

Kerry Airport (KIR), located in Farranfore, is a gateway to County Kerry, with flights to Dublin, London, Frankfurt, Alicante in Spain, and Faro in Portugal. Amenities include a restaurant, a bar, a gift shop, and free Wi-Fi. About 15 minutes from Killarney, it's an ideal starting point for the Ring of Kerry and the Dingle Peninsula.

Car

The drive from **Dublin** to Killarney takes 3.5-4 hours, depending on traffic. Take the M7 motorway southwest toward Limerick. At Portlaoise, continue on the M7 to the M8, toward Cork. Then take exit 12 for the N72, which leads directly to Killarney.

From **Cork,** the drive is 1.5 hours, following the N22 road west toward Killarney. From **Limerick,** take the N21 southwest through Adare, where traffic can be quite heavy, and Newcastle West until you reach Castleisland, where you take the N23, then the N22 to Killarney. The drive takes 1.5-2 hours.

Train

Trains to Killarney station (The Avenue) depart from **Dublin Heuston Station** (3.5 hours; €60 round-trip) with a change of trains in Mallow for most riders, although there are some direct trains. Direct trains run from **Cork Kent Station** to Killarney (1.5 hours; €15 one-way). Check **Irish Rail's** (www.irishrail.ie) schedule for departure times. There are no direct trains between Limerick and Killarney, as you'll have to transfer in Mallow, with a travel time of around 2 hours.

Bus

Dublin Coach (www.dublincoach.ie) operates buses from Dublin to Killarney (4.5 hours; €57 round-trip). Buses depart from Bachelors Walk and go via Limerick. Or take a bus with Flight Link (www.flightlink.ie) from Dublin Airport to Killarney (€70 round-trip).

Bus Éireann (www.buseireann.ie) provides direct buses between Western Road in Cork City and **Killarney Bus Station** (1.5 hours; €10 one-way). Bus Éireann also runs a direct route from Limerick to Killarney (1.5 hours; €20), which departs from Arthur's Quay.

Getting Around

Once in Killarney, it's easy to get around town on foot. To get to the national park, you will need private transport as there are no public transport options. **Flemings Taxis** (tel. 87/238-3592) is a reputable local company that can drive you to nearby attractions like Torc Waterfall. There are also jaunting cars and bus tours from the town with **Killarney Tours** (www.killarneytour.com).

★ KILLARNEY NATIONAL PARK

Killarney National Park is one of Ireland's most ecologically diverse and historically rich natural areas. It's one of the most popular, too, with 1.5 million visitors a year. Established in 1932, it was Ireland's first national park, created to protect its ecosystems and historic landmarks. On the Iveragh Peninsula, the park is just outside Killarney, covering over 10,500 ha (26,000 acres), and nestled between the MacGillycuddy Reeks and the famous Lakes of Killarney. It's home to diverse landscapes, from the lowlands surrounding the lakes to the rugged peaks of Carrauntoohil, Ireland's highest mountain at 1,038 m (3,406 ft).

Visiting the Park

Entrance to the park is free, though some attractions, like Muckross House and boat tours, have a fee. The park is open year-round, though some of the hikes and outdoor attractions may be challenging in wet weather, so pack your hiking boots and wet-weather

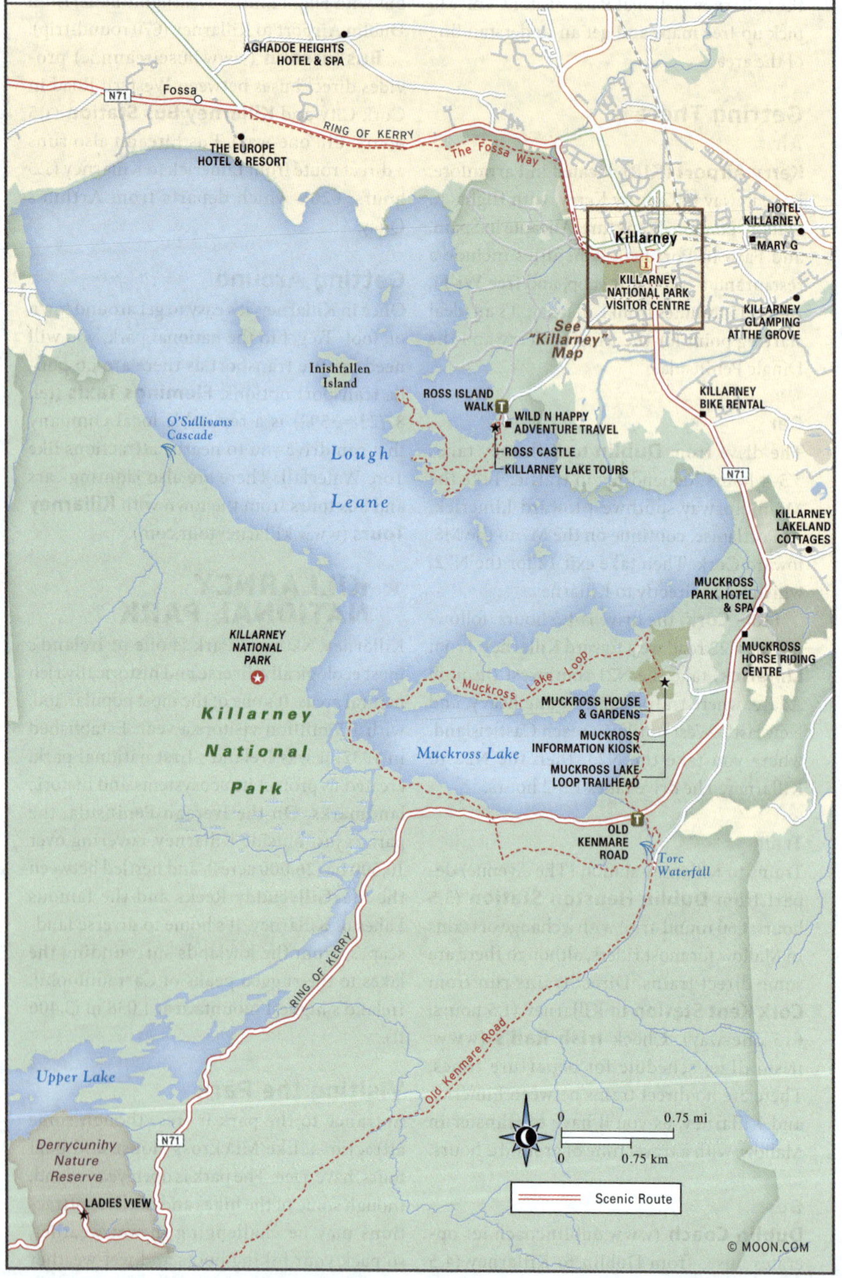
Killarney National Park
AGHADOE HEIGHTS HOTEL & SPA
N71
Fossa
RING OF KERRY
THE EUROPE HOTEL & RESORT
The Fossa Way
HOTEL KILLARNEY
Killarney
MARY G
KILLARNEY NATIONAL PARK VISITOR CENTRE
KILLARNEY GLAMPING AT THE GROVE
See "Killarney" Map
Inishfallen Island
ROSS ISLAND WALK
WILD N HAPPY ADVENTURE TRAVEL
KILLARNEY BIKE RENTAL
O'Sullivans Cascade
Lough Leane
ROSS CASTLE
KILLARNEY LAKE TOURS
N71
KILLARNEY LAKELAND COTTAGES
MUCKROSS PARK HOTEL & SPA
MUCKROSS HORSE RIDING CENTRE
KILLARNEY NATIONAL PARK
Muckross Lake Loop
MUCKROSS HOUSE & GARDENS
Killarney National Park
MUCKROSS INFORMATION KIOSK
Muckross Lake
MUCKROSS LAKE LOOP TRAILHEAD
OLD KENMARE ROAD
Torc Waterfall
RING OF KERRY
Old Kenmare Road
Upper Lake
0
0.75 mi
0
0.75 km
N71
Derrycunihy Nature Reserve
Scenic Route
LADIES VIEW
© MOON.COM

gear. Phone reception is nonexistent in remote areas, so plan ahead and let people know when you expect to return if you venture beyond the busy spots.

Visitor Centers

Killarney National Park Visitor Centre (Killarney House & Gardens, Muckross Rd.; tel. 1/539-3620; www.killarneynationalpark.ie; daily 9:15am-5:15pm; free) is the largest in the park with a wealth of information at the desk. The staff can recommend the best places to go on the day you're visiting. Ask about the nearby walking and hiking trails. Beyond the information desk, numerous exhibits in the house cover the geography and history of the park.

Muckross Information Kiosk (Muckross House & Gardens, N71; tel. 64/667-0144; www.muckross-house.ie; free) is a small information kiosk that operates during summer.

Tours

If you'd rather leave all the planning to somebody else, guided tours are available that cater to different interests, budgets, and times. **Killarney Day Tour** (Lahard, Beaufort; tel. 87/261-7967; www.killarneydaytour.com; €45) is a six-hour tour on buses, boats, and carriages to see the highlights of the park around Lough Leane. For a private guided tour of the park, go with **Mary G** (65 Park Dr.; tel. 87/240-7986; www.marygtours.ie; from €400), a woman-owned private chauffeur company that will show you the best of the park.

Sights

Ross Castle

Ross Rd.; tel. 64/663-5851; https://heritageireland.ie; Mar.-Oct. daily 9:30am-5:45pm; €5

The 15th-century Ross Castle was built by the O'Donoghue chieftains and remains a prime example of the defensive structures that dotted the countryside of medieval Ireland. During the Cromwellian invasion of Ireland in the 1650s, Ross Castle was the last place in Munster to hold out. Ross Castle has been carefully restored since then, and you can get a taste of medieval life behind these walls. Around the grounds are walking paths through wooded areas. The entrance fee covers a guided tour that provides detailed historical context, explaining how people lived and defended themselves in the castle centuries ago.

O'Sullivans Cascade

O'Sullivans Cascade is a picturesque series of waterfalls on the Owengarriff River. This natural beauty flows through ancient oak and yew woodland, creating a host of stunning scenes. The waterfall gets its name from the O'Sullivan clan, who were once prominent in the area. You can walk to the cascade on a scenic trail.

Muckross House & Gardens

Muckross; tel. 64/667-0144; www.muckross-house.ie; daily 9am-6pm; gardens free, tours from €9

The Victorian Muckross House & Gardens was completed by the Herbert family in 1843 and is a fantastic example of how the gentry lived during the mid-19th century. It's so fancy that even Queen Victoria stayed here when she visited in 1861. It's still as opulent as then, and you can see the furniture and art on the guided tour. The large gardens are equally impressive, with meticulously landscaped lawns, flowerbeds, and tree-lined walkways. Paths wind through the gardens and offer scenic views of the nearby lakes and mountains. If it starts to rain during, there is a **café** and **craft shop** to shelter in.

Torc Waterfall

Torc; www.killarneynationalpark.ie/visit/torc-waterfall; free

Sometimes you don't have to work that hard for an incredible view. Torc Waterfall is only a short 200-m (660-ft) walk from the car park along a gently sloping accessible trail. The 20-m-high (66-ft) waterfall doesn't sound that impressive on paper, but it's how the waterfall descends the densely wooded hillside into the pool below. If you want to spend more time in the woods, there are two walking routes

1
2
3
4

around the waterfall that take 40-60 minutes. If you'd rather make a short visit and don't want to miss out on photos, go down the small trail below the main viewing point.

Upper Lake

Upper Lake is the smallest and southernmost of Killarney's three lakes. Upper Lake is connected to Lough Leane by the winding Long Range River, famous for its picturesque Old Weir Bridge. A small offshoot of this river connects Upper Lake with Muckross Lake at the Meeting of the Waters.

Muckross Lake

Muckross Lake, also known as Middle Lake, is the deepest of Killarney's three lakes at 75 m (246 ft). Well known for its scenery and surrounded by woodlands and mountains, it's a popular spot for boating, fishing, and wildlife watching. Muckross Lake is connected to Lough Leane by the Long Range River and to the Upper Lake at the offshoot of the river called the Meeting of the Waters.

Lough Leane

Lough Leane is the largest of Killarney's three lakes, with a surface area of 1,900 ha (4,700 acres) and a depth of 66 m (216 ft). It's a haven for wildlife and water activities like fishing and boating. The lake is steeped in history and legend, featuring islands like Innisfallen, with its ancient monastery ruins.

Innisfallen Island

Innisfallen Island, on Lough Leane, is home to the ruins of Innisfallen Abbey, founded in the 7th century by Saint Finian the Leper. The abbey was a renowned center of learning for over 950 years, producing the historically significant *Annals of Innisfallen*. Explore the ruins and see the 12th-century Romanesque church while out in nature.

1: Ross Castle **2:** Torc Waterfall **3:** hiking Killarney National Park **4:** Muckross House & Gardens

Ladies View

Ladies View is a stunning viewpoint with a breathtaking panorama of the Killarney Lakes and the surrounding mountains. The spot got its name in 1861 when Queen Victoria's ladies-in-waiting expressed their admiration for the view during a visit. Today, it's a popular stop for visitors and has a café and a craft shop. The view is particularly incredible at sunset.

Hiking and Walking

Ross Island Walk

Distance: *6.1 km (3.8 mi) round-trip*
Duration: *1.5 hours*
Elevation gain: *40 m (130 ft)*
Effort: *Easy-moderate*
Trailhead: *Ross Castle Car Park*

Starting at Ross Castle, the Ross Island Walk is an easy loop through some wonderful landscapes along the edge of Lough Leane, where you'll see old-growth oaks and yews. Keep your eyes peeled for deer in this area. You'll get a feel for what it felt like here when Cromwell invaded and also see the ruins of the Ross Island Copper Mine that nature has slowly been reclaiming. There's evidence that people have been using the natural resources here since the Bronze Age. The walk is a leisurely one, with no tricky sections along the gravel path. For great photos, come for sunset.

Old Kenmare Road

Distance: *16.9 km (10.5 mi) one-way*
Duration: *5.5 hours*
Elevation gain: *590 m (1,940 ft)*
Effort: *Difficult*
Trailhead: *Torc Waterfall*

The Old Kenmare Road is a rewarding hike from Torc Waterfall to Kenmare and makes up part of the Kerry Way. The trail runs through valleys of the MacGillycuddy Reeks, including along the foothills of Torc Mountain. Although relatively short for a remote hike, the out-and-back route is full of varied views, with ancient forests, sparse valleys, gentle streams, and mighty lakes. It's hard to pick one highlight, but the passage through Esknamucky Glen and its megalithic

Our First National Park

Killarney National Park

The history of Killarney National Park begins with Muckross Estate, the heart of the park. In 1932, Senator Arthur Vincent and his parents-in-law donated Muckross House and its surrounding 10,000 ha (24,700 acres) to the Irish state in memory of Vincent's wife, Maud, marking the foundation of the park and intended to preserve the estate's natural beauty and cultural heritage. Over the years the park expanded to include the MacGillycuddy Reeks mountain range and the Lakes of Killarney. At the forefront of conservation in Ireland, the park focuses on preserving ancient woodlands, rare species, and historical sites. In 1981 it was designated a UNESCO Biosphere Reserve, recognizing its importance for conservation.

PACKED WITH SIGHTS AND SITES

Killarney National Park is all about scenic beauty and historical landmarks. The three main lakes, Lough Leane, Muckross Lake, and Upper Lake, make up almost a quarter of the park's area and have outstanding views. An itinerary with visits to Muckross House, Ross Castle, and Torc Waterfall is a good way to get a feel for the park without traveling too far.

CERTIFIED SPECIAL

Killarney National Park is a designated Special Area of Conservation (SAC). Its diverse flora includes oak and yew woodlands, wetlands, and heathlands home to beautiful animals, including Ireland's only remaining herd of native red deer. It also contains rare plant species such as the Kerry lily. Conservation efforts focus on protecting habitats and educating people about their importance.

OUT AND ABOUT IN THE PARK

The park has an expansive and easily accessible network of trails for all levels of fitness, from gentle strolls around Muckross Gardens to more challenging hikes up Carrauntoohil and beyond.

tombs is a treat. You'll likely be on the trail for at least half a day, and while you're likely to meet other experienced hikers on the route, you will need to be fully self-sufficient, as there are no towns or villages along the way.

Muckross Lake Loop

Distance: *16.7 km (10.4 mi) round-trip*
Duration: *5 hours*
Elevation gain: *523 m (1,715 ft)*
Effort: *Moderate-challenging*

Trailhead: *Muckross House & Gardens*

This scenic hike is a full tour around Muckross Lake that begins and ends at the entrance to Muckross House & Gardens on the N71. Through ancient woodlands, you'll have almost constant lake views. Around the halfway point, the Meeting of the Waters and Old Weir Bridge make for scenic resting spots. There aren't many challenging sections, but be aware of the length and the one serious climb up Torc Mountain. The remainder of the elevation gain is on undulating terrain with no other major ascents. The loop is well-marked, and for an easier walk, follow the route as far as Dinis Cottage and return the same way, avoiding the main climb.

Cycling

The Fossa Way

Distance: *22 km (14 mi) round-trip*
Duration: *2.5 hours*
Elevation gain: *149 m (488 ft)*
Effort: *Easy-moderate*
Trailhead: *Killarney House & Gardens*

Starting at Killarney House & Gardens, this out-and-back traffic-free route ends at the Europe Hotel & Resort, where you can stop for refreshments before heading back to Killarney on the same trail. Take in views of Lough Leane and the MacGillycuddy Reeks on the route away from busy Killarney. Short punchy climbs make the route feel more challenging than the length and overall elevation gain would lead you to believe. Back in Killarney is a wealth of food and drink options to refuel.

Horse Riding

Muckross Horse Riding Centre

Muckross Rd.; tel. 87/057-6703; www.muckrosshorseriding.com; €85 pp

If the jaunting cars sound too pedestrian, you can get your adrenaline fix while enjoying the magnificent views of Killarney National Park from horseback on a private guided tour at Muckross Horse Riding Centre. Tours can be catered to your level, and most last 1-2 hours on a mix of woodland trails and views across the lakes. The guides are experienced and can help people of all ages ride for the first time or help advanced riders increase their skills.

Boating

Killarney Lake Tours

Ross Castle; tel. 64/663-2638; www.killarneylaketours.ie; daily 9am-5pm; €15 pp

Set sail from Ross Castle in a waterbus to see all of Lough Leane. Most visitors to Killarney National Park only see the lake from Muckross House & Gardens, but you'll get a deeper understanding of the lake and its surrounds as you sail past O'Sullivans Cascade and the monastic ruins of Innisfallen Island. The 50-minute tour is suitable for all ages, but keep in mind there are no toilets on board. They also run a longer tour that combines the boat ride with a jaunting car ride.

Wild N Happy Adventure Travel

Ross Castle Lower Car Park; tel. 86/389-0171; https://wildnhappytravel.com; Tues.-Sun. 8am-6pm; €40 pp

Paddle your way around the gorgeous Lough Leane on a kayak tour with Wild N Happy. The 2-hour tour around Ross Castle covers the history of the structure as you navigate a two-seat sit-on-top kayak. The Innisfallen Island Tour is 2.5 hours and takes you to lesser-seen parts of the lake, where you'll hear about Innisfallen Abbey and the monks. Both tours are suitable for beginners but require a decent level of fitness.

Food and Accommodations

Colgan's

Muckross Rd.; tel. 64/662-3400; www.muckrosspark.com/colgans; Mon.-Thurs. 3pm-9:30pm, Fri.-Sun. 12:30pm-9:30pm; from €20

Colgan's is part of the swanky Muckross Park Hotel & Spa, but it feels more relaxed than other parts of the hotel. It's a traditional-style gastropub with slate floors, wooden barstools, and a roaring open fire that serves hearty food at acceptable prices, given the location. The menu has the usual gastropub offerings like Irish lamb stew alongside a good choice of vegetarian options like the

Irish Wildlife

As you explore Ireland, you'll undoubtedly see some amazing wildlife. From giants in the ocean to delicate insects, there's a brilliant array of fauna.

red deer stag

BIRDS: COASTAL CLIFFS TO INLAND WETLANDS

Bird-watchers will find a wealth of attractions, with many notable spots for sighting rare birds.

- The **Saltee Islands,** off the coast of County Wexford, are a must for seabird enthusiasts, as they are home to colonies of puffins, razorbills, and gannets (page 165).
- For a glimpse of majestic birds of prey, head to **Killarney National Park,** where white-tailed eagles, recently reintroduced to Ireland, now soar (page 233).
- The cliffs of **Skellig Michael,** off the coast of County Kerry, are also home to puffins during the breeding season (page 248).

mushroom risotto, but after a long day outdoors, it's hard to go wrong with their burger and beer deal (€25).

Muckross Park Hotel & Spa

Muckross Park Hotel; tel. 64/662-3400; www.muckrosspark.com; €200

The five-star Muckross Park Hotel & Spa is the swankiest spot in the national park and a welcome sight if you've just spent the day hiking on trails that start from the door or boating on the nearby lakes. The 70 rooms in four room types are each indulgently decorated with a timeless elegant design. The **Yew Tree Restaurant** (Tues.-Sat. 6pm-9:30pm; €25) is the main restaurant, with a seasonal and sustainable menu in a white-tablecloth formal setting. Even if you're not staying, it's worth reserving afternoon tea in **Monk's Lounge** (12:30pm-9:30pm; €18), where you'll be able to taste their top-tier scones. The Gothic-inspired spa has a vitality pool, a spa garden walk, an outdoor hot tub, and a full offering of massage treatments.

Killarney Lakeland Cottages

Muckross; tel. 64/663-3290; https://killarneycottages.com; €225

Choose from 19 holiday homes in three different styles across 5 ha (12 acres) of countryside ideally placed between Killarney and the national park. Great for families, the cottages sleep 4-8, and a playground, a tennis court, and a games room are available. The cottage interiors are a bit dated, but they have the usual amenities like a washing machine and a fully equipped kitchen. If you're staying here, you'll most likely be spending most of your time outside.

Getting There

Unless you're coming from the Iveragh Peninsula west of the national park, you'll reach the park via Killarney. From the center of town, you can easily walk to Killarney House & Gardens, one of the access points to the park. Driving, head 5 minutes south from town to the entry to the park at Muckross House & Gardens. You can cycle to the park from Killarney in 20 minutes along this road,

MAMMALS: DEER, SEALS, AND WHALES

Ireland's range of mammals, though not extensive, is still notable.

- **Killarney National Park** is not only a haven for birdlife but also a refuge for the country's native red deer. These impressive animals roam freely in the park's woodlands and mountains. Smaller sika deer can also be found here, often mingling in the same areas (page 233).
- The west coast, particularly around **Dingle Bay** (page 258) in County Kerry, is famous for sightings of dolphins, and the waters around **Baltimore** (page 206) and **Cape Clear** (page 209) in County Cork are excellent for whale-watching. Here, visitors may encounter minkes and humpbacks, particularly June-September.
- For seal sightings, the **Blasket Islands** (page 260) and **Howth** (page 86) in County Dublin are prime locations. Both the gray seal and the common seal breed in these areas, and it's common to see them basking on rocks or swimming near shore.

INSECTS: HIDDEN TREASURES

Ireland's meadows and gardens are alive with insect life, particularly in summer.

- Keep your eyes peeled in **The Burren,** a unique limestone landscape in County Clare, where you might spot native butterflies such as the peacock and the orange-tip (page 278).

but there are no dedicated cycle lanes, and it's a very busy road. Walking this route takes over an hour, which is time and energy better spent exploring the park itself.

THE GAP OF DUNLOE

The Gap of Dunloe is a breathtaking narrow mountain pass carved by glaciers over 25,000 years ago. Stretching 11 km (7 mi) between the MacGillycuddy Reeks and Purple Mountain, this scenic route showcases Ireland's rugged beauty. The pass has five picturesque lakes connected by the River Loe, with the famous Wishing Bridge said to grant wishes to those who cross it. Explore the Gap on foot, by bicycle, or in a traditional jaunting car, but watch for the free-roaming sheep.

Getting There

Exploring the Gap of Dunloe typically begins at Kate Kearney's Cottage and winds through the valley. From Killarney, follow the N72 west for 12 km (7.5 mi) and 30 minutes, turning left at the Gap of Dunloe sign. From Kenmare, it takes about an hour; follow the N71 north to Moll's Gap, then follow the R568 through the Black Valley to the Gap's southern entrance.

TOP EXPERIENCE

★ CARRAUNTOOHIL

Carrauntoohil, at 1,038 m (3,406 ft), is Ireland's highest peak. It is part of the **MacGillycuddy Reeks,** a rugged mountain range that runs from the Dingle Peninsula in the west into Killarney National Park to the east. The mountain is known for its challenging and sometimes deadly terrain, which draws hikers for a tough yet rewarding outdoor challenge.

Hiking and Walking

Devil's Ladder

Distance: *13 km (8 mi) round-trip*
Duration: *7 hours*
Elevation gain: *840 m (2,760 ft)*
Effort: *Very strenuous*
Trailhead: *Cronin's Yard*

The most popular route to Carrauntoohil's summit is via the ominously named Devil's Ladder, a steep and rocky path. The route winds through **Hag's Glen** before the ascent becomes more intense, with climbers scrambling over loose stones and scree. The descent comes down **Brother O'Shea's Gully.** On a clear day, climbers are rewarded with panoramic vistas across the Iveragh Peninsula and the Dingle Peninsula. The region's dramatic landscapes were shaped by glacial activity, with deep, sharp ridges and stunning valleys. The region is also rich in Irish mythology, with Fionn Mac Cumhaill and his warriors said to have hunted here. Wildlife is abundant in the mountains, with red deer commonly seen grazing in the foothills. Birdlife includes ravens and peregrine falcons, while golden eagles are occasionally spotted soaring above the peaks. The flora is equally beautiful, with wildflowers like heather and gorse adding splashes of color to the otherwise sparse rocky landscape.

Despite its popularity, the Devil's Ladder can be difficult, especially in wet conditions, and should be approached with caution. Climbing Carrauntoohil requires a lot of preparation. Weather conditions in Kerry are notoriously unpredictable, with rain, fog, and strong winds often sweeping across the mountains. Even in summer, it's essential to bring warm waterproof clothing, sturdy boots, navigation equipment, and a fully charged phone.

Caher Route

Distance: *12 km (7.5 mi) round-trip*

Duration: *6 hours*

Elevation gain: *981 m (3,218 ft)*

Effort: *Very strenuous*

Trailhead: *Carrauntoohil Parking Hydro Rd. car park*

This strenuous trail ascends via Ireland's third-highest mountain, Caher, and follows the southern rim of Coomloughra, with breathtaking views of the Kerry landscape. After conquering Caher's summit, descend slightly before tackling the final push to Carrauntoohil's peak. This route is recommended for experienced hikers with good fitness levels.

Getting There

To reach Cronin's Yard from Killarney, take the N72 toward Killorglin and turn left for the Gap of Dunloe after Fossa Village. Continue about 8 km (5 mi) to Kissane's Shop, then cross a small bridge and take the next left, following signs for Cronin's Yard. This 18 km (11 mi) journey typically takes 25 minutes.

For the Hydro Road car park, follow the same route but continue past the Cronin's Yard turnoff, following signs for the car park. This slightly longer drive is 25 km (16 mi) and takes around 30 minutes.

MOLL'S GAP

Moll's Gap is a scenic mountain pass on the Ring of Kerry. It's named after Moll Kissane, who ran a shebeen (a house that illegally sold alcohol) during the 1820s when the road was being built. Views from the road are breathtaking, with the MacGillycuddy Reeks dominating the landscape. Formed by glacial activity during the last ice age, the area has distinctive old red sandstone rocks with unique green staining. The road through the pass is narrow, winding, and not for the faint of heart.

Getting There

From Killarney, drive the N71 southwest through the national park and past Ladies View for 30 minutes to Moll's Gap. It's a shorter drive from Kenmare, at 15 minutes. Take the N71 north toward Killarney and follow the signs.

KENMARE

If the buzz and crowds of Dingle and Killarney get to be too much, head south toward Kenmare. This compact town was created as an estate for the Lansdowne family in the 1650s and today is a slightly off-the-beaten-track destination in County Kerry. Though

1: Carrauntoohil **2:** Moll's Gap

1
2

it is quieter than Dingle and Killarney, in no way is Kenmare dull. You'll get a feel for day-to-day life in a place that loves good food, craft beer, and unspoiled views of the great outdoors.

Sights

Reenagross Woodland Park

Killowen Rd.; daily 24 hours; free

On a small wooded peninsula, just a short walk from the town and surrounded by old-growth trees, gorgeous Reenagross Woodland Park springs to life when the pink leaves of the Japanese maple trees appear. Every Halloween the park hosts a spooky event (€5) when the park is turned into an open-air haunted house. When the ghosts and ghouls aren't here, the park has 3 km (2 mi) of walking routes, picnic tables, and beautiful views of the river.

Tom Crean Brewery & Shop Kenmare

Killowen Rd.; tel. 86/042-2307; www.tomcreanbrewerykenmare.ie; Mon.-Thurs. 10am-5pm, Sat.-Sun. 10am-7pm

Tom Crean Brewery & Shop tells the story of Antarctic exploration with local craft beer. Founded in 2019 by explorer Tom Crean's granddaughter, Aileen Crean O'Brien, and Bill Sheppard, this family-run brewery honors Crean's legacy through sustainably brewed beers like the award-winning Six Magpies Stout and seaweed-infused Kerry Surf & Turf. Visitors can tour the solar-powered facility, sample pours in the memorabilia-filled taproom, and hear firsthand accounts of Crean's polar expeditions on a tour (€20).

Food and Accommodations

Kenmare Brewhouse

The Square; tel. 64/664-2357; www.kenmarebrewhouse.com; Mon.-Tues. 9:30am-11:30pm, Wed.-Thurs. noon-11:30pm, Fri.-Sat. 9:30am-2am, Sun. 9:30am-11pm; from €16

Kenmare Brewhouse has great-value pub grub, particularly notable if you've just come from Dingle or Killarney. It includes American dishes like meatloaf and sticky barbecue ribs served in a large modern gastropub-style bar with high-top seats and a small area with tables outside. Although *brewhouse* is in the name, they don't brew their own beer. There's a mix of local beer from the Tom Crean Brewery and national brewers like Guinness.

Lagom

36 Henry St.; tel. 64/664-8423; www.pfskenmare.com; Tues.-Thurs. 6pm-8:30pm, Fri.-Sat. 6pm-9pm; from €26

In a town with plenty of traditional dining options, Lagom serves the same great local produce with a contemporary take instead. Vegetarians have good choices, with the wild garlic gnocchi with smoked cauliflower and local mushrooms a standout choice. Meat lovers fear not; the short rib is a great chunk of beef that melts in your mouth. Contemporary doesn't mean costly: The early bird menu (6pm-7pm) has two (€35) or three (€41) courses.

Oaklane Glamping

Mucksna; tel. 86/854-1645; www.oaklaneglamping.com; €160

Oaklane Glamping is an absolute treat in a modern cabin in a rural setting where you'll have nonstop views of the Kenmare River flowing into Kenmare Bay. Two beautiful compact cabins are fantastically well-designed and packed with features like a premium Nespresso machine, coffee-table books on the locality, and a generously sized bath with a waterfall shower. The cabins sleep up to two, and you'll wake to unforgettable views of the fog lifting off the water in the distance as the sheep in the field beside you wake up for the day.

The Lansdowne Kenmare

Main St.; tel. 64/664-0200; www.lansdownekenmare.com; €250

The Lansdowne Kenmare is a modern mid-range boutique hotel in the center of town, built in the 1790s and named after the Lansdowne family, the landlords of the area at the time. The 28 rooms are trendy, with natural light and bright colors, making the historic building pop. **Shelburne Street** is the on-site restaurant with a gastropub-style menu, and you can retreat to the **Poet's Bar** (3pm-11pm; €7) for a cocktail after dinner. In the morning, the **Nead** (8am-5pm; €12) serves light breakfasts in a spacious well-lit room, and there are cozy seating nooks in the lobby with board games and books.

Park Hotel Kenmare

Shelbourne St.; tel. 64/664-1200; www.parkkenmare.com; €450

The Park Hotel Kenmare is a well-regarded five-star luxury hotel that balances its traditional architecture with modern furnishings and art, including work by Sean Scully. Each of the 46 elegant rooms is individually designed, and the superior rooms have a private garden or balcony. Although it's in the middle of the town, it feels like a place to escape thanks to the manicured grounds to the rear that lead to the banks of the Kenmare River. Fully commit to the relaxing feel here at the **SÁMAS Spa** (tel. 64/664-1413; daily 10am-5pm; €145) and look over the water from the outdoor heated pool. It's also the only place in Europe where you'll find the fantastic Blue Bottle Coffee, although it's pricey (€6).

Getting There and Around

The drive from Killarney to Kenmare is 35 km (22 mi) and takes 35-40 minutes. Take the N71 road, which winds through scenic Killarney National Park, passing by the viewpoint Moll's Gap along the way. There's also the direct Route 270 bus (€8 one-way) toward Skibbereen, which runs every two hours, but this bus does not take the scenic drive.

The journey from Cork to Kenmare is 95 km (59 mi) and takes about 1.5 hours. Take the N22 road west from Cork toward Macroom. Continue on the N22 and then take the R569 to Kenmare. Driving from Dublin to Kenmare is about 350 km (220 mi) and takes 4 hours; take the M7 motorway southwest from Dublin toward Limerick, then follow the signs for the N21 toward Castleisland, and the N22 toward Killarney. Just before Killarney is the turnoff for the R569, which leads to Kenmare. There are no direct public transport routes from Dublin or Cork to Kenmare.

Once you're in Kenmare, you can get around easily on foot.

Kenmare to Killorglin

West of Killarney and Kenmare is the Iveragh Peninsula, the largest in the southwest, comprising rural regions with small vibrant towns that reward your travel instincts. This part of the country is best explored by car, with rural roads through mountain valleys and along epic oceanside cliffs. It's easy to get away from it all out here. Even the biggest towns are quite small, and people are always happy to point you in the right direction or toward the best place for lunch. Have a rough plan before you go, but don't be beholden to it, as you never know: You might just fall in love with the next view and never want to leave.

ORIENTATION

From Kenmare, you first reach **Caherdaniel** on the southern coast, followed by **Waterville** on the western shore. Farther north, **Ballinskelligs, Portmagee,** and **Valentia Island** cluster together, offering access to **Skellig Michael** just off the coast. **Killorglin** is at the northeastern edge of the Iveragh Peninsula, a gateway to the Ring of Kerry.

CAHERDANIEL

Caherdaniel's claim to fame is Derrynane House, offering a combination of nature and history. The area boasts excellent trails, beautiful beaches, and panoramic views of Derrynane Bay and the Atlantic Ocean.

Sights

Derrynane House

tel. 66/947-5113; http://derrynanehouse.ie; daily 10am-4:45pm; €5

Derrynane House, located in Caherdaniel, is the ancestral home of Daniel O'Connell, one of Ireland's most significant historical figures, known as "the Liberator," a 19th-century political leader who championed Catholic emancipation and fought for the rights of the Irish people.

Now a museum, the house provides a glimpse into O'Connell's life and his contributions to Irish history. Explore the rooms where O'Connell lived and worked to view historical artifacts, including the chariot he was gifted a few years before his death, and learn more about his legacy. Set within beautiful Derrynane National Historic Park, the estate also features stunning gardens, the 6-km (3.7-mi) Derrynane Mass Path walking trail, and access to Derrynane Beach.

Hiking and Walking

Derrynane Mass Path

Distance: *6.8 km (4.2 mi) round-trip*
Duration: *90 minutes*
Elevation gain: *170 m (560 ft)*
Effort: *Easy*
Trailhead: *Derrynane Beach Car Park*

The Derrynane Mass Path holds deep historical significance. During the Penal Laws era, when Catholic mass was illegal, this path led worshippers to secret mass rocks. Starting at Derrynane House, the trail has views of Derrynane Bay and the Atlantic Ocean. It's also part of the Kerry Way walking route.

Beaches

Derrynane Beach

Derrynane More

Derrynane Beach is a pristine Blue Flag beach renowned for its golden sands and crystal-clear waters. Part of Derrynane National Historic Park, it offers stunning views of the Skellig Islands. It's a popular spot for swimming, windsurfing, and kayaking, but most visitors walk the beach and view the islands just off shore.

Getting There and Around

To reach Derrynane from Kenmare by car, follow the N70 Ring of Kerry road southwest for 49 km (30 mi) and 40 minutes. The rural route passes through Sneem, with views of

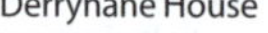

Derrynane House

Kenmare Bay and the Beara Peninsula. The **Local Link** (www.transportforireland.ie/tfi-local-link) Route 281 bus runs four times daily from Tom Crean Brewery & Shop in Kenmare to Caherdaniel Village Cross (€4 round-trip). Derrynane Harbour is a departure point for Skellig Michael tours.

WATERVILLE

Waterville is a charming coastal village that captured the heart of one of Hollywood's first superstars, Charlie Chaplin. Today a bronze statue, surrounded by the coastal views he loved so much, honors him.

Sights

Charlie Chaplin Statue

You might be surprised to find out about the link between the remote village of Waterville and one of the biggest stars of the silver screen. Charlie Chaplin was a regular visitor to the area and often stayed at the nearby Butler Arms Hotel. To commemorate the actor, there's a life-size bronze statue of him near the water, and the village once hosted the annual Charlie Chaplin Comedy Film Festival, which unfortunately no longer runs.

Getting There

From Kenmare, follow the N70 Ring of Kerry road west for 60 km (37 mi). The scenic drive typically takes 1.25 hours, passing through picturesque towns like Sneem and Caherdaniel. There are no direct public transport links.

KERRY INTERNATIONAL GOLD TIER DARK SKY RESERVE

tel. 87/784-5688; www.kerrydarkskytourism.com; free

Stargazing by the ocean under clear dark skies in the Kerry International Gold Tier Dark Sky Reserve is an incredible way to connect with the landscape after dark. In an area that covers a lot of the south of the Iveragh Peninsula, where there is very little light pollution, the stars and planets appear as they did for millennia. The reserve covers much of South Kerry, offering numerous stargazing spots like Ballinskelligs Beach and Hogs Head Golf Club, many with convenient parking. Throughout the year, the reserve hosts public events, including the Dark Sky Festival each spring. There are also 1.5-2-hour guided stargazing tours. These tours introduce visitors to the concept of star-hopping and, on clear nights, feature stargazing with an expert. In poor weather, the tour still happens but moves indoors to a building in Caherdaniel for an informative presentation. Keep in mind that summer nights are shorter with brighter skies, while winter provides longer, darker nights ideal for stargazing.

Getting There

Drive 35 km (22 mi) and 40 minutes northwest via the N70 Ring of Kerry road. Pass Waterville and turn left onto the R567 toward Kells, entering the reserve's core near Kells Bay. Park at designated stargazing areas like Kells Harbour or St. Finian's Bay.

From Portmagee, take the N70 east for 18 km (11 mi) and 25 minutes to Cahersiveen, then follow signs for Kells via the R566. The reserve spans this rural area. Optimal viewing spots are near Kerry Cliffs or Foilmore, accessible via minor roads marked with dark-sky signage. Keep in mind that these roads are twisty and unlit at night.

PORTMAGEE

Portmagee is a vibrant fishing village with colorful waterfront houses that line a natural harbor. Use it as a base to explore Valentia Island and the dark sky park, or relax in the pubs, known for fresh seafood.

Sights

Portmagee Marina

This sheltered harbor offers modern berthing facilities and easy access to the Atlantic. It's also a departure point for Skellig Michael tours, making it a bustling spot during the summer months. The harbor provides stunning views of Valentia Island and the surrounding Kerry coastline.

Food and Accommodations

The Bridge Bar

Main St.; tel. 66/947-7108; www.moorings.ie; Sun.-Thurs. 8am-11:30pm, Fri.-Sat. 8am-12:30am; €6

The Bridge Bar, part of the Moorings, is a lively traditional Irish pub known for its warm atmosphere and live traditional Irish music sessions. There's a wide selection of local craft beers, whiskeys, and spirits alongside award-winning fresh seafood. The bar's walls are decorated with maritime memorabilia, telling the story of Portmagee's rich fishing heritage.

The Moorings

Main St.; tel. 66/947-7108; www.moorings.ie; €130

Overlooking the busy harbor, The Moorings has 16 elegantly furnished rooms, some with king beds and spa tubs and all with marble baths, TVs, and tea and coffee. The hotel boasts a renowned seafood restaurant and bar, and it serves as an ideal base for Skellig Michael tours, with the pier a 30-second walk away.

Getting There

To reach Portmagee from Caherdaniel, drive the N70 Ring of Kerry road northwest for about 50 km (30 mi) and 1 hour, passing through Waterville and Cahersiveen. From Kenmare to Portmagee, follow the N70 west for 90 km (55 mi) and 1.75 hours. This route passes through Sneem, Caherdaniel, and Waterville before reaching Cahersiveen, where you turn onto the R565 to Portmagee.

★ SKELLIG MICHAEL

Skellig Michael, also known as Great Skellig, is 12 km (7.5 mi) off the southwest coast of County Kerry and makes up part of the Kerry Seas National Park. The jagged, almost pyramid-like natural rock formation is a striking part of the Irish landscape and undoubtedly one of its most iconic landmarks. Skellig Michael sprung to international fame when it was featured in the movies *Star Wars: The Last Jedi* and *Star Wars: The Force Awakens*.

In the 6th century, Christian monks established a monastery on the island and built beehive-shaped stone huts, known in Irish as clocháns, which provided shelter from the harsh Atlantic weather and served as an oratory. Isolation was the main draw for the monks, to dedicate themselves fully to prayer and manual labor in the remote and inhospitable environment. The island remained a monastic center for over 600 years. The monks abandoned it likely due to fierce storms, raids by the Vikings, and changes in the structure of the church, though the exact reason is unknown. In 1996, Skellig Michael was recognized as a UNESCO World Heritage site for its cultural and religious significance.

Remote and uninhabited, Skellig Michael has no toilets, shelters, or amenities. The stone buildings are as advanced as life got on the island. Once you arrive, there are 618 steps up to the monastery, so the island tour is best suited for people with a decent level of fitness and proper walking or hiking gear.

Tours

Casey's Skellig Islands Tours

Portmagee Marina; tel. 1/443-3718; http://skelligislands.com; €45

One of the many tour operators is Casey's Skellig Islands Tours, offering the Skellig Michael Eco Tour, which sails around the island but does not land on it. You'll learn about the wildlife in the area and possibly see puffins on the cliffs. They also offer the Skellig Michael Landing Tour, which lands once a day and covers the history of the island and the people who inhabited it. Tours depart from Portmagee; ask for Brendan Casey when you arrive.

Skellig Tours

Derrynane; https://skelligtours.com; €120

Tours of Skellig Michael with Skellig Tours depart from Derrynane Harbour, with the journey taking two hours each way.

1: climbing the stairs on Skellig Michael **2:** Valentia Island

1

2

Kerry Seas National Park

Kerry Seas National Park, Ireland's first marine national park and its newest, is a collection of small areas in Kerry joined to protect wildlife, scenery, and history. Scattered across the western part of the county, the park includes the Blasket Islands, where dolphins and whales visit; the sand dunes at Inch Beach, popular with seabirds; and the uplands of Mount Brandon, where heather grows.

This national park exists to protect what's here, and it holds significant cultural importance. Skellig Michael is part of the park and tells the story of Ireland's Christian past. As it was recently established and is not laid out like a typical national park, there are currently no visitor centers or tours.

Getting There

The island is accessible May-September. Tours are weather-dependent and can be canceled at short notice when the sea becomes too rough. Tours depart from Portmagee, Ballinskelligs, and Caherdaniel; early booking is essential due to how popular the island is. Access is extremely limited, with most tour operators offering cruises around the island. Tours that allow access to the island sell out well in advance.

★ VALENTIA ISLAND

Valentia Island, off the Iveragh Peninsula, is one of Ireland's most westerly points. It is easily accessible by a bridge to the mainland at Portmagee. Famous for its stunning natural beauty and some of the world's oldest tetrapod fossils, Valentia played a pivotal role in global communications history as the eastern terminus of the first successful transatlantic telegraph cable, laid in 1866, connecting Europe to North America.

Sights

Dinosaur Footprints

Valentia Island; www.valentiaisland.ie; free

Ireland has its own Jurassic Park on Valentia Island. This remote island might not live up to the excitement of the movie, but there are tetrapod tracks, one of the world's oldest known fossilized footprints, dating back 350 million years. These ancient tracks mark an important point in the evolution of early four-legged creatures from sea to land.

Valentia Island Lighthouse

Valentia Island; www.valentiaisland.ie; €9

An iconic landmark is the Valentia Island Lighthouse at Cromwell Point that has guided ships in the Atlantic for over 200 years. Visitors learn about its history and enjoy stunning views of the ocean and nearby Skellig Islands.

Food and Accommodations

The Ring Lyne Bar & Restaurant

Chapeltown; tel. 66/947-6103; www.theringlyne.com; daily 10am-midnight; from €15

The Ring Lyne Bar & Restaurant has been an institution in these parts since 1889. The recently renovated 60-seat dining room has great views of the coast, and the menu has a strong emphasis on local produce like Valentia Island scallops and Kerry lamb. The bar stocks over 100 Irish whiskeys and hosts regular trad music sessions, making it popular among locals and Skellig boat crews. During summer, reservations are advised for the restaurant, especially for dinner.

The Royal Valentia Hotel

Market St.; tel. 66/947-6144; http://royalvalentia.ie; €100

Each of the 30 rooms in the historic Royal Valentia Hotel has great views of the harbor and Portmagee Channel. First opened in 1833, it blends modern amenities with Victorian details. Facilities include a restaurant serving locally sourced seafood, a cozy bar with music, and a spacious outdoor terrace.

Getting There

From Kenmare, the drive to Valentia Island is 87 km (54 mi) and takes about 1.75 hours on the N70, part of the Ring of Kerry road, heading west out of Kenmare through picturesque towns like Caherdaniel. Continue on the N70 to the R565 toward Portmagee, where you cross the Valentia Bridge to Valentia Island. Alternatively, April-October, you can take the scenic Valentia Island Ferry from Renard Point.

From Killarney, the drive is about 1.5 hours and 80 km (50 mi). Take the N72 west toward Killorglin and then the N70, which takes you on the Ring of Kerry toward Cahersiveen. Follow the R565 to cross the bridge at Portmagee.

KILLORGLIN

Killorglin is a vibrant market town, famous for its annual Puck Fair festival, where a wild goat is crowned king. It's a lively hub that blends the traditions of rural Ireland with modern energy. With a choice of hotels and proximity to Kerry's natural wonders, Killorglin is an ideal base for exploring the surrounding beauty.

Festivals and Events

Puck Fair

The Square; https://puckfair.ie; Aug. 10-12

Dating back to at least 1613, Puck Fair centers around crowning a wild mountain goat as King Puck. The quirky three-day event features a horse fair, street markets, and traditional Irish music. Each day has a theme: Gathering Day, Fair Day, and Scattering Day. Visitors can enjoy free concerts, storytelling, and a carnival atmosphere. The fair's origins are debated, with theories ranging from pagan harvest celebrations to a goat warning of Cromwellian invaders.

Shopping

McCaffrey Crafts

Lower Bridge St.; tel. 87/312-8497; https://mccaffreycrafts.com; Mon.-Fri. 9:30am-noon

This fifth-generation family business has been open since 1847 and specializes in handcrafted blackthorn walking sticks and shillelaghs, a traditional Irish walking stick or club, often used for self-defense. Blackthorn is prized for its durability and distinctive knobbed appearance. The wood's natural strength and resistance to splitting make it ideal for crafting these iconic Irish tools. Visitors can explore a range of authentic Irish crafts and learn about the time-honored tradition of stick making.

Food and Accommodations

Kingston's Townhouse

Market St.; tel. 66/976-1178; https://kingstonstownhouse.com; €120

The 10 modern rooms in this well-appointed townhouse create a home-away-from-home feel in the center of the town. **Kingston's Bar,** on the ground floor, has been open since 1889, today serving Neapolitan-style pizzas in a traditional pub setting.

The Bianconi

Annadale Rd.; tel. 66/976-1146; https://bianconi.ie; €140

The Bianconi Inn is a family-run boutique hotel with 16 comfortable en suite rooms. A popular on-site bar and restaurant serves locally sourced cuisine, including fresh seafood. The hotel's central location makes it an ideal base for attending the Puck Fair.

Getting There

From Killarney to Killorglin, head west on the N72 for 20 km (12 mi) and 20-25 minutes. By bus, Bus Éireann Route 279 (30 minutes) operates every 2 hours. In Killarney, the bus departs from Killarney Bus Station and also stops at Rock Road. In Killorglin, the bus arrives at the main stop in the town center.

To drive from Kenmare to Killorglin, take the N70 north toward Killarney. After 30 km (19 mi), at Moll's Gap, continue on the N71 to Killarney. There are no direct buses between Kenmare and Killorglin.

Dingle Town

Dingle is a bit of a cult hero in Ireland. As the largest outpost on the Dingle Peninsula, it's a bustling hub with a strong, creative, and relaxed spirit with a nice balance between visitors and residents. Paired with the beautiful scenery of the region, it has become a popular spot for holiday homes and people relocating from Dublin. The town is large despite how remote it is. Rather than one main street, Dingle has a labyrinth of streets, laneways, and courtyards that you can easily spend a few hours exploring. The town is also home to plenty of local independent businesses that march to the beat of their own drum when it comes to goods for sale and open hours.

SIGHTS

Dingle Oceanworld Aquarium

The Wood; tel. 66/915-2111; www.dingle-oceanworld.ie; daily 10am-7pm; €20

Dingle Oceanworld Aquarium is known for its volume of marine life and interactive exhibits. Once upon a time, people would visit Dingle to see the resident dolphin Fungi swimming in the bay, but these days, the best sea life is seen in the aquarium, home to an array of creatures, including local species and exotic animals from far-off oceans, such as sharks, rays, and seahorses. One of the highlights is the impressive shark tank, where you can see these majestic creatures up close. Another hit with visitors is the penguin enclosure, home to a charming colony of gentoo penguins, always popular with families. Advance online booking is advised so that you can be here for the feeding times of your favorite animals.

Dingle Distillery

Slea Head Dr., Milltown; tel. 86/777-5551; www.dingledistillery.ie; daily 10am-5:30pm; €22

The three-man team behind Dingle Distillery was ahead of the curve when it came to producing artisanal spirits back in 2012, when most whiskey, gins, and vodkas were made by large-scale producers. Dingle Distillery's whiskey is matured in oak casks, giving it a distinctive complex flavor. Their gin, infused with locally foraged botanicals, has also gained a good reputation by offering a

Dingle Lighthouse

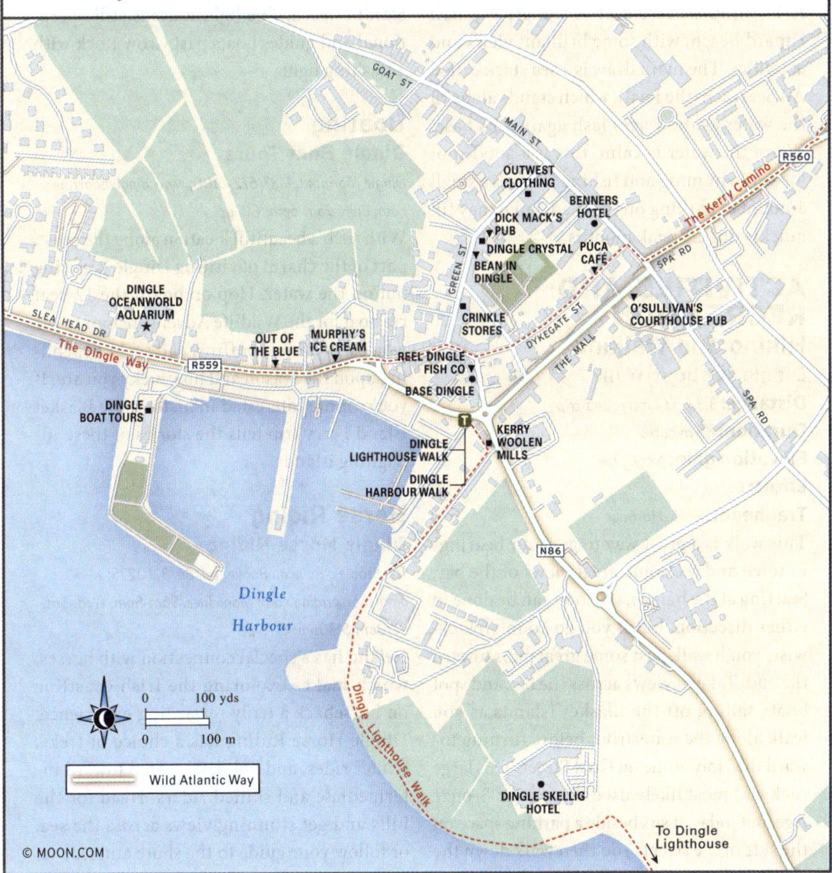

unique taste of the surrounding landscape. The vodka, which follows the high standards the distillery has set themselves, rounds out the impressive lineup. On the 1.25-hour tour, you'll get to see the drinks being made and get to taste the creations.

Dingle Lighthouse

Dingle Lighthouse is a picturesque red and white structure at the entrance to Dingle Harbour. Built in the 1880s, it still guides ships along the rugged Atlantic coast. The structure is not open to visitors, but scenic paths, with brilliant views of the Atlantic Ocean and Dingle Bay, lead to the lighthouse. It's also sometimes possible to spot dolphins in the waters below and seabirds above. The journey to the lighthouse is part of its appeal, with a two-hour walk starting at the harbor and leading along the sea past **Hussey's Folly,** a tower built around the same time. Alternatively, you can park nearby at Beenbane Beach and walk 15 minutes to the lighthouse.

BEACHES

Kinard Beach

A 10-minute drive east of Dingle is small Kinard Beach, with some brilliant views and activities. The main draw is a sea stack called An Searrach (the Foal), which stands alone in the water as the waves lash against its base. When the water is calm, this is a good spot for sea swimming and fishing. There's a small amount of parking on the road, but it may fill quickly during peak months.

ACTIVITIES AND RECREATION

Hiking and Walking

Dingle Harbour Walk

Distance: *3.3 km (2 mi) round-trip*
Duration: *45 minutes*
Elevation gain: *Negligible*
Effort: *Easy*
Trailhead: *Dingle Harbour*

This walk is a great way to get your bearings in town and see some great views of the bay. Starting at the harbor, the loop can be done in either direction, but if you go counterclockwise, you'll walk past some great pubs toward the end. Take in views across the bay and spot boats sailing off the Blasket Islands as you walk along the waterfront before turning toward the Holy Stone on Goat Street. This large rock was most likely used during the Bronze Age, but today, it sits beside a parking space on the side of the street. You then walk down the gentle hill toward St. James Church on Main Street before looping back around to the starting point at the harbor.

Dingle Lighthouse Walk

Distance: *7.9 km (4.9 mi) round-trip*
Duration: *2 hours*
Elevation gain: *110 m (360 ft)*
Effort: *Moderate*
Trailhead: *Dingle Harbour*

Take a "walk out the banks," as the locals say, on this coastal trail that leads to the red and white Dingle Lighthouse. The route starts at Dingle Harbour and passes through green fields with stunning views along a natural trail. You'll encounter Hussey's Folly, a famine-era tower, and the picturesque Sláidín beach. The lighthouse is still operational and guides boats past Crow Rock with a flashing light.

Boating

Dingle Boat Tours

Dingle Marina; tel. 87/672-6100; www.dingleboattours.com; daily 9am-6pm; €15 pp

With such a beautiful location along the coast, part of the charm of visiting Dingle is getting out on the water. Hop on board the 12-seat rib boat for the Wildlife Adventure tour to see whales, dolphins, puffins, and seals, depending upon the season and how lucky you are. If you're more interested in history, the Blasket Island Ferry trip tells the stories of these intriguing islands.

Horse Riding

Dingle Horse Riding

The Stables, Baile na Buaile; tel. 86/821-1225; www.dinglehorseriding.com; Mon.-Tues. 9am-5pm, Wed.-Sat. 9:30am-5:30pm; €175 pp

Ireland has a special connection with horses, which makes exploring the Irish coastline on horseback a truly rewarding experience. Dingle Horse Riding has a choice of treks, winter rides, and holidays geared toward intermediate and skilled riders. Head for the hills and get stunning views across the sea, or follow your guide to the shore and ride on beautiful West Kerry beaches with the mountains in the distance. For even more riding, book in for one of their 3- or 6-day holidays, where you'll get an even deeper understanding of this part of Ireland.

FESTIVALS AND EVENTS

The Dingle Races

Ballintaggart Racecourse; tel. 87/927-255; www.dingleraces.ie; early Aug.

Running for three days at Ballintaggart Racecourse, the Dingle Races are an important date in Ireland's race calendar. The 20 races are on a seven-furlong grass circuit, and its popularity has seen it become the biggest horse and pony meeting in the country. Even if you don't know your fillies from your mares, the atmosphere is worth visiting for, especially if you've packed your glad rags and go on Ladies Day.

Wren Day

Dec. 26

Wren Day in Dingle is celebrated on St. Stephen's Day to keep a unique and ancient tradition alive. Locals known as Wren Boys parade through the town in elaborate straw costumes, colorful attire, and masks, accompanied by drummers and tin whistles. Groups of Wren Boys play songs and ask for money to "bury the wren," which is donated to local worthy causes.

SHOPPING

Crinkle Stores

Green St.; www.crinklestores.ie; Mon.-Sat. 10am-6pm, Sun. 11:30am-5pm

This cozy homeware shop, not far from the harbor, is stocked with plenty of pottery from local artists, including coffee-making accessories like drippers and tampers. Pick up a seaweed face mask made locally, or if you keep a journal when you travel, Crinkle Stores have their own branded notepads. You can grab a cup of barista-made coffee or cacao here too.

Kerry Woolen Mills

Mail Rd.; tel. 66/915-2164; www.kerrywoollenmills.ie; daily 10am-5:30pm

Traditional Irish clothing has never gone out of style in Kerry, and at Kerry Woolen Mills, you'll find fantastic examples made locally as well as modern pieces. The shelves are well stocked with chunky knitted sweaters in a host of colors, including the iconic off-white colorway. Stock up on knitted hats, toasty gloves, and cozy socks for when the weather turns, or for a warmer day, there's a good choice of collarless grandfather shirts.

OUTWEST Clothing

Green St.; www.outwestclothing.ie; Mon.-Sat. 10am-5pm, Sun. 11am-4pm

Even though the weather in Ireland can be unpredictable year-round, we're not great at dressing for it. OUTWEST is one of the few Irish outdoor brands designed to keep people warm and dry. The hoodies, sweatshirts, and T-shirts are all soft and inspired by the colors of the local landscape while also being competitively priced. OUTWEST is B Corp certified, which means they have serious environmentally friendly credentials.

Dingle Crystal

Green St.; tel. 66/915-1550; www.dinglecrystal.ie; daily 10am-5pm

Created by Sean Daly, a master craftsman who learned his trade at the world-famous Waterford Crystal, Dingle Crystal is a boutique crystal shop stocked floor to ceiling with premium products. For wine connoisseurs and whiskey drinkers there's a wide choice of drinkware to elevate your favorite tipple. For a special gift for someone back home, there are elaborate crystal bowls and candles. If Sean's work inspires you, you can visit his workshop just outside town for a 45-minute tour.

FOOD

Bean in Dingle

Green St.; www.beanindingle.com; Mon.-Sat. 8am-4pm; from €4

Bean in Dingle is a busy specialty coffee shop that's open before most others, and they roast their own coffee beans. All the usual suspects are on the menu as well as seasonal drinks, like an iced Spanish latte made with condensed milk. The interior is bright and modern, with contemporary art from Irish artists and eight-seat high-top tables. A small bar-style table is for solo visitors along with two three-seat tables. You can buy beans to go, and they'll grind them for you. There's a good choice of pastries and treats like a breakfast muffin, cinnamon buns, and sweet brioche buns.

Púca Café

Dykegate St.; tel. 85/495-0254; Instagram @puca.dingle; Fri.-Mon. 9am-4pm, Tues. 10am-3pm; from €10

Vegetarian Púca Café is in a small stone cottage with a red metal roof down a back street that matches the earthy vibe of Dingle. The breakfast and lunch menus have plenty of vegan options. For a light breakfast, go with the breakfast bowl, made with local fruits, homemade granola, and Dingle yogurt, or if you're very hungry, try their vegetarian take on the classic full Irish breakfast. The lunch menu kicks in at midday, when you can order a barbecue jackfruit sandwich or a salad. If the sun is shining, grab a spot in the garden to the rear and sit under the hanging branches.

Reel Dingle Fish Co

Bridge St.; tel. 66/915-1713; Instagram @ReelDingleFish; Tues.-Sun. 1pm-10pm; from €10

Dingle has a lot of seafood options, but many are expensive and require reservations. This fish-and-chips takeaway is the opposite: a great value and quick despite everything being made to order. There's a menu above the cash register, but it's only a guide, as they serve the day's locally caught fish. If the boats didn't catch any hake, there's no hake available. Even though it's a takeaway, there's a small bar with four seats, which fill up quickly. A small covered picnic table is across the street, and plenty of covered seating is a short walk away at the harbor.

Out of the Blue

Strand St.; tel. 66/915-0811; www.outoftheblue.ie; daily 4pm-9:30pm; from €29

Don't let the unrefined exterior and signage of Out of the Blue fool you. Inside it's a refined restaurant that only serves seafood. There are no chips, so if you're not a seafood aficionado, you may want to go elsewhere. The menu changes depending on what local produce is available, but expect staples like seafood chowder and freshly caught oysters. The bright dining room has white-painted stone walls, and the team has created a modern Irish seafood restaurant that deserves the many awards they've won.

Murphy's Ice Cream

Strand St.; tel. 66/915-2644; www.murphysicecream.ie; daily 11am-10:30pm; from €6

Murphy's is an institution in ice cream, known for taking Irish ingredients and making them into creations that you're unlikely to find anywhere else. The brown bread ice cream is one of their best-known flavors, and they've managed to make it sweet by caramelizing the bread in the oven. There are also flavors made with Irish gin, sea salt, and local honeycomb. The cost is a bit pricey, but you can mix multiple flavors. Originally from Dingle, you can find Murphy's locations across Kerry as well as in Dublin, Cork, and Galway.

BARS AND NIGHTLIFE

Dick Mack's Pub

47 Green St.; tel. 66/915-1787; www.dickmackspub.com; Wed. 11am-11pm, Thurs.-Tues. noon-11pm

The packed shelves of whiskey bottles seem to be holding up the wooden interior of Dick Mack's, a popular pub at the top of the hill. The wood paneling and dark slate floor give the pub a traditional feel, but the addition of a large communal table in the middle of the front bar gives it a more modern feel. There are also snugs in the front bar and plenty of tables in the rooms to the rear. They brew their own pale ale and IPA next door at Dick Mack's Brewing House, and you can only find it on draft here. They also run tours of the brewery. Enhancing the contemporary feel is the music, with singer-songwriters rather than the trad music normally found in Dingle pubs.

O'Sullivan's Courthouse Pub

The Mall; www.osullivanscourthousepub.com; Mon.-Fri. 6pm-midnight, Sat.-Sun. 3pm-midnight

Mind your head when you enter this traditional music-loving pub, slightly off the beaten track and popular with locals. The low ceiling and low beams create an intimate atmosphere alongside the live music. You'll hear local musicians every night around 9pm. Keep in mind that they don't serve food. There's nothing groundbreaking about the drinks menu, but it's reliable.

ACCOMMODATIONS

Base Dingle

Bridge St.; tel. 66/915-2284; www.basedingle.com; €150

The Base is a 30-room city-style room-only hotel. The modern rooms are available in four varieties, from a 20-sq-m (215-sq-ft) double room to 30-sq-m (325-sq-ft) rooms with one king bed or one king and two singles. There's not much in terms of amenities apart from a place in the lobby to grab a coffee and a co-working space to catch up on emails.

Benners Hotel

Main St.; tel. 66/915-1638; www.dinglebenners.com; €250

Slap-bang in the middle of town, Benners Hotel has others beat if you're looking for a place steps from the lively pubs and great restaurants. The 44 rooms hark back to traditional hotels, with plush seating, ornate lighting, and high ceilings. Although you're close to some great food, there are also good choices in the hotel at **Mrs. Benners Bar,** like the Tournafulla black pudding salad and prawn linguini. For a nightcap, the bar is well stocked with local whiskeys and top-shelf spirits.

Dingle Skellig Hotel

Emlagh West; tel. 66/915-0200; www.dingleskellig.com; €300

The luxurious Dingle Skellig Hotel is a five-minute walk from Main Street on the edge of Dingle Bay. It's one of the largest in the area, with 120 standard and 32 deluxe rooms. It's not cheap, but waking up to fantastic views of the Kerry coast may be worth the outlay. There's a 17-m (56-ft) swimming pool with a eucalyptus steam room, a jetted tub, and a spa.

GETTING THERE

Car

From **Killarney,** take the R563 road west, followed by the N70, and then the R561 to Dingle. This scenic drive takes about 1.25 hours. From **Cork City,** the fastest route by car is the N22 toward Killarney, then the R561 and N86 to Dingle, a journey of 2.25 hours. From **Limerick City,** follow the N21 to Castleisland, then take the R561 and N86 to Dingle. The drive takes around 2 hours.

Murphy's Ice Cream

Bus

From **Killarney,** you have to take two buses, with a change in **Tralee. Bus Éireann** (www.buseireann.ie) runs Route 275 and Route 279 buses on the journey that takes about 2 hours. There are no direct public transport services from **Cork City** or **Limerick City,** so you need to take Bus Éireann to Tralee and transfer to a Dingle-bound bus, with the total journey taking 3-4 hours. The bus drops you at Dingle Harbour.

Train

Though Dingle once had the most westerly railway in Europe, that's long gone, and there are no trains to Dingle. The closest stations are in Killarney, Farranfore, and Tralee.

GETTING AROUND

Dingle is a small town, and you can easily explore on foot. It takes 10 minutes to walk from one edge of the town to the other.

Slea Head Drive and the Dingle Peninsula

Heading west from Dingle, the **R559** road forms a loop known as Slea Head Drive along the dramatic Atlantic coast of the Dingle Peninsula. Remote, rare, and rewarding, this chunk of Ireland is some of the most untouched in the country, which makes it an incredible place to connect with nature. As the waves crash against the shore, it creates scenery unlike anywhere else and habitats for animals that you might not normally associate with Ireland. The harshness of the wilderness is softened by the warm towns and villages where music pours out of pubs and independent restaurants fill with hungry guests.

ORIENTATION

The Dingle Peninsula stretches west from the town of **Tralee,** bordered by **Tralee Bay** to the north and **Dingle Bay** to the south. The main road onto the peninsula is the **N86,** which runs from Tralee to **Dingle.**

West of Dingle, **Slea Head Drive** passes through small villages such as Ventry and Dunquin as it loops around the peninsula back to Dingle. To the north of Dingle, the R560 leads over **Conor Pass,** one of Ireland's highest and most scenic mountain roads. Beyond Conor Pass, the northern coast features quieter areas like **Brandon Point,** with stretches of peaceful countryside and beaches. To the east, the stunning **Inch Beach** sits along the N86. The peninsula is marked by the towering presence of **Mount Brandon,** a key landmark visible from much of the area.

SLEA HEAD DRIVE

Coumeenoole Beach

Coumeenoole Beach is a stunning pocket of coastline a 25-minute drive west of Dingle that's well worth a visit. Steep, sharp cliffs surround the golden sand, a fantastic backdrop for photos, but keep in mind that the majority of the beach is covered by the sea at high tide. As tempting as it may be to dive into the water, it's strongly advised that you don't, as the currents can be treacherous.

Getting There

From Dingle, head west on the R559, also known as Slea Head Drive, a scenic route that follows the coast and is almost as spectacular as your destination. The drive to Coumeenoole Beach takes 25 minutes.

Dunquin Pier

Dunquin Pier is one of the most picturesque and photographed spots along the Wild Atlantic Way. Tucked away at the edge of towering cliffs, this steep and winding pier has brilliant views of the Blasket Islands just off

Slea Head Drive and the Dingle Peninsula

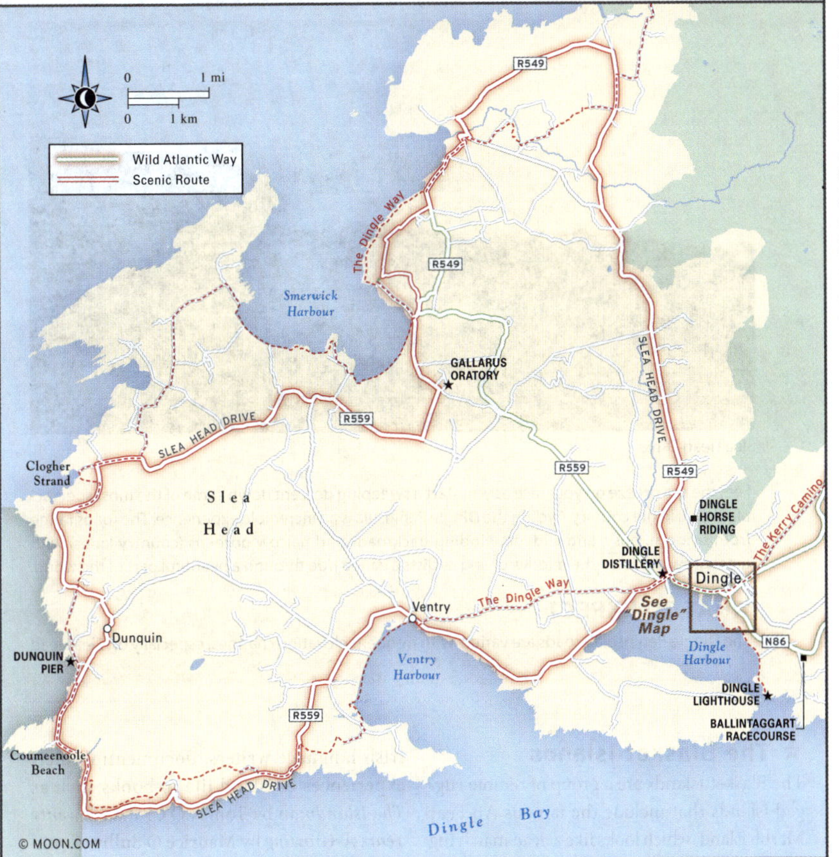

the coast. Dunquin Pier is often thought of as the launchpad to these islands, as it once served as the primary departure point for boats ferrying people and supplies, particularly before the islanders were evacuated in 1953. Nowadays, the ferries that make the journey are for sightseeing trips.

The access road to the pier is narrow and twisty and thus not open to vehicles past the wooden ticket hut. Even with the warnings, some try and inevitably get stuck and damage their cars.

Getting There

From Dingle, head west on the R559, also known as Slea Head Drive, a scenic route that follows the coast and is almost as spectacular as your destination. Dunquin Pier is 5 minutes up the road from Coumeenoole Beach and 30 minutes from Dingle Town, and traffic can back up during summer. There is a **Local Link Bus** (www.transportforireland.ie/tfi-local-link) that runs every four hours from Supervalu (€4 round-trip) that drops you off in Dunquin; from there it's a 20-minute walk to the pier.

Cycling the Dingle Peninsula

Slea Head Drive

Feel the sea breeze on your face as you start a sweeping descent down some of the most spectacular roads in the country. Cycling the Dingle Peninsula is an incredible experience. The roads range from smooth, busy, and wide to winding backroads and narrow boreens (country lanes) with grass growing down the middle, giving cyclists a varied ride through a beautiful part of the world.

WHAT TO EXPECT

The Dingle Peninsula's roads are varied, with frequent elevation changes, especially on Slea Head

★ The Blasket Islands

The Blasket Islands are a group of remote rugged islands that include the famous An Fear Marbh island, which looks like a dead man lying in the sea. The largest of the Blasket Islands, Great Blasket was inhabited until 1953 when the Irish government evacuated the remaining residents due to the harsh living conditions and inability to keep the elderly population safe. Today, the islands are uninhabited but remain a sought-after spot to get a glimpse into Ireland's past and an unspoiled natural environment. Visitors to the Blaskets can explore the ruins of the old village on Great Blasket Island, hike the grassy hills, and enjoy being fully surrounded by the Atlantic Ocean.

The islands are famous for their unique literary history and gorgeous landscapes. Many former residents became renowned Irish-language writers, documenting their experiences of island life in books such as *The Islandman* by Tomas O'Crohan, *Twenty Years A-Growing* by Maurice O'Sullivan, and the stories from the famous seanchaí (Irish storyteller) Máiréad "Peig" Sayers.

It's important to note that Great Blasket Island has no services—no electricity, running water, or shops—so visitors should come prepared with food, water, and appropriate clothing. Day trips are popular, but some visitors choose to stay overnight in the island's rustic self-catering cottages.

Getting There

Boats (40 minutes; €40 round-trip) operate from Dingle, Ventry, and Dunquin during summer, usually April-September, depending on weather conditions.

and Conor Pass. Traffic can be an issue during peak season, particularly around Dingle and the busier towns and sights, so cyclists should stay vigilant. In more remote areas, shops and cafés are sparse, so carry water and snacks. And, of course, you'll need to pack rain gear, even if you're planning a trip during summer; it rains a lot. There are three bike rental shops in Dingle, all offering e-bikes: **Dingle Electric Bike Experience** (www.dinglebikes.com), **Paddy's Bike Shop** (www.paddysbikeshop.com), and **WeWheel** (https://wewheel.com).

ROAD TYPES AND SURFACES

The best roads for cycling on the peninsula are the R (regional) roads, such as the R559, which forms part of the loop around Slea Head. These are typically well-maintained with smooth tarmac surfaces. However, they can be quite narrow and twisty in sections, with poor visibility, particularly along cliff-side stretches, where there is limited space for passing vehicles. The roads tend to be busy during peak season, so stay alert for cars and tour buses.

The smaller L (local) roads are quieter, with less traffic in more remote parts of the countryside. These roads can be rougher in places, especially where tractor traffic is common, but they're often a more peaceful ride through rural villages and farmland. You'll also likely encounter boreens, narrow, often single-lane roads that can be uneven and overgrown. Boreens are great fun to cycle on, especially if you have a gravel bike.

WILD CAMPING WHEN BIKEPACKING

If you're planning a bikepacking trip, there are a few things to consider about dispersed camping. Avoid camping on private land like forests managed by Coillte, and, of course, you must leave no trace and be considerate of others. Pack out all your waste, stay far away from houses, set up your tent late in the day, and get going early the following morning. Thankfully, there are plenty of places on the peninsula that have lodging options for people of all budgets.

Clogher Strand

Get unbeatable views of An Fear Marbh, also known as the Dead Man, the most northerly of the Blasket Islands, from Clogher Strand on the western edge of the Dingle Peninsula. If the weather is rough, Clogher Strand is a dramatic place to be as heavy waves and high winds pummel the shore. If the beach looks familiar, you might recognize it from the 1970s movie *Ryan's Daughter.*

Getting There

Drive the Slea Head Drive westward for 16 km (10 mi) and 20-25 minutes. Continue toward the coast and you'll see signs for Clogher Strand on your right.

Gallarus Oratory

Gallarus; tel. 66/915-5333; www.gallarusoratory.ie; daily 9am-8pm

The small stone Gallarus Oratory is a remarkable example of early Christian architecture and stonemasonry. Dating to the 7th-9th centuries, it was built entirely without mortar. The oratory's carefully cut stones fit closely together, creating a watertight interior that has survived the elements for over 1,000 years. The oratory is shaped like an upturned boat, with sloping sides that form a distinctive, elongated oval shape. It's believed it was used as a place of worship for Christians and a shelter from the elements for pilgrims.

You can enter via the visitor center, with toilets and exhibits, to learn more about the structure, which charges a €4 admission fee. If you'd rather not pay, continue up the road

The Dingle Way and the Kerry Camino

hiking the Dingle Way

THE DINGLE WAY

Distance: *180 km (110 mi) round-trip*
Duration: *8 days*
Elevation gain: *4,025 m (13,200 ft)*
Effort: *Difficult*
Trailhead: *Tralee*

The Dingle Way is a long-distance hiking loop that reaches the most remote parts of the peninsula. It technically starts in the town of Tralee, but you can start anywhere along the route. As you hike the rugged coastline, you'll see spectacular beaches, prehistoric structures, and friendly villages. It's well signposted throughout, and even though its length makes the route difficult, the trail surface is generally in good condition.

THE KERRY CAMINO

Distance: *70 km (43 mi) one-way*
Duration: *3-4 days days*
Elevation gain: *810 m (2,660 ft)*
Effort: *Moderate*
Trailhead: *Tralee*

If you can't commit to hiking the full Dingle Way, there's a shorter hike called the Kerry Camino on part of it. This hike starts in Tralee and gives insight into the life of Saint Brendan, believed to have followed this route to its endpoint in Dingle and then sailed to America almost 1,000 years before Columbus.

to the second car park and you can enter the site for free.

Getting There

Driving is the only realistic option, as there is no direct public transport. Head north on the R559, following the signs for Slea Head Drive for 15-20 minutes. Continue on this road until you see signposts directing you to Gallarus Oratory.

NORTH OF DINGLE TOWN

Conor Pass

High in the mountains, winding and narrow 12-km (7.5-mi) Conor Pass is a country road that links Dingle with Kilmore Cross; on maps it is marked as R560. When you reach the highest point, a pull-off lets you stop to look at the view. Gaze across the fields separated by stone walls and out to the Atlantic Ocean. The drive can be challenging, and lots of drivers on the road may not be accustomed to the tight conditions.

Getting There

Drive north of Dingle on the R560 road for 10 minutes to Conor Pass, 7 km (4.3 mi) away.

Mount Brandon

Mount Brandon draws hikers and walkers to climb to its summit, 952 m (3,123 ft) above sea level, where they're rewarded with panoramic views of the mountains and the Atlantic. If you

1: Conor Pass **2:** Inch Beach

1

2

want to climb, head for Ballynahow car park and take the trail from here. This is the easiest route to the top, though there are other options that link with longer hikes. The trail is grassy in the lower parts and then turns rocky toward the top. The 15-km (9-mi) route from the car park to the summit and back takes about four hours. Given its height, difficulty, and exposure, it's best to skip this hike if there are strong winds.

Getting There

To get to Mount Brandon, take the R549 north from Dingle for 15 km (9 mi) and 20 minutes.

Brandon Point

Brandon Point, on the northern tip of the Dingle Peninsula, is where you'll feel powerful ocean winds as you take in views of Brandon Bay and Mount Brandon. The area is steeped in history, with links to Saint Brendan the Navigator, and has scenic walks and stunning sunsets. There's a small car park that fills quickly when the weather is good.

Getting There

It takes 30 minutes to drive from Dingle. Follow the R560 north from Dingle and through Conor Pass toward Cloghane. Turn for the R550 to Brandon Point.

Glanteenassig Forest Park

It can be tricky to escape the crowds in Kerry, but you should find some tranquility on the trails or by the lakes in Glanteenassig Forest Park near Castlegregory on the R560 road. There are two main walking trails, both easy and well-marked. The 1.5 km (0.9 mi) trail around **Lough Caum** is suitable for all fitness levels, and a longer 6 km (3.7 mi) **loop trail** takes you deeper into the forest.

Getting There

There are two routes to the forest park from Dingle. The narrow, winding R560 through Conor Pass takes 40 minutes to drive the 30 km (18 mi). The other route along the wider N86 road takes 50 minutes for 40 km (25 mi). The park is easy to access by car, with parking available near the entrance and the walking trails beginning just steps away.

EAST OF DINGLE TOWN

Inch Beach

Long, sandy Inch Beach stretches 5 km (3 mi) into Dingle Bay. Known for its wide flat expanse, Inch is a good spot for walking, surfing, and relaxing. The natural beauty comes from its sweeping views of the Atlantic Ocean with the Slieve Mish Mountains in the background. It became popular when it was featured in the 1962 movie *The Playboy of the Western World.*

Getting There

Take the N86 east from Dingle and turn onto the R561 in Annascaul, which leads to Inch Beach. The drive is 22 km (13.6 mi) and takes 20-25 minutes.

Clare and Limerick

Outside a few tourist hot spots, County Clare

and Limerick City are relatively quiet parts of the Wild Atlantic Way that give visitors insight into life in rural Ireland, where the natural landscapes entertain for days on end.

In North Clare, the majestic Cliffs of Moher rise dramatically from the Atlantic, with breathtaking views to the Aran Islands and beyond. Nearby Doolin is known for its traditional Irish music sessions, where you can hear storied ballads and tales recited in the pubs. From here, the landscape transforms into the otherworldly terrain of the Burren, a vast limestone plateau dotted with ancient monuments and rare plants as well as one-of-a-kind experiences like hiking amid stone formations and Neolithic tombs. In West Clare, the Loop Head Peninsula

Highlights

Look for ★ to find recommended sights, activities, dining, and lodging.

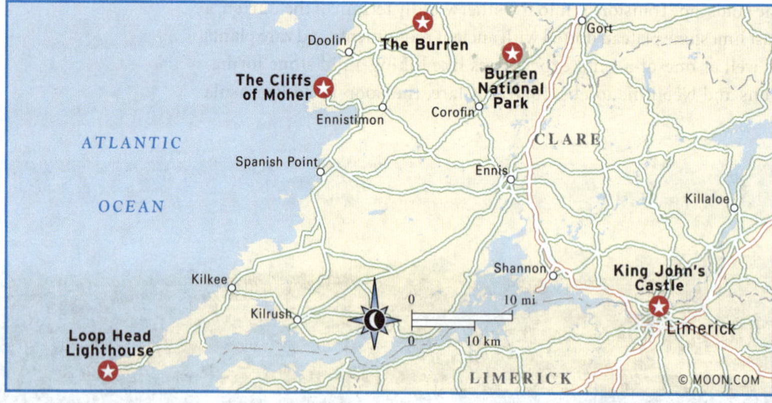

★ **The Cliffs of Moher:** These iconic cliffs are one of Ireland's most spectacular sights. Feel the wind on your face and hear the roar of the Atlantic (page 272).

★ **The Burren and Burren National Park:** Many liken these incredible rocky landscapes to the moon. A unique microclimate means some surprising plants grow (page 278).

★ **Loop Head Lighthouse:** On the farthest reaches of West Clare on Loop Head Peninsula, visit Loop Head Lighthouse, guiding ships since 1854 (page 288).

★ **King John's Castle:** One of the best-preserved Norman castles in Europe played a key role in the Siege of Limerick in 1642. Learn about its fascinating history at its modern museum (page 290).

is a fantastic escape from the tourist trail. Lighthouses stand guard over churning seas, dolphins swim in the Shannon Estuary, and the landscape feels like a sanctuary.

Medieval history is unavoidable in Limerick City, with King John's Castle the top pick, but the city has a creative modern spirit. The foodie scene is eclectic with international influences, centered around producers and sellers at the Milk Market.

ORIENTATION

Waterways mark the physical boundaries of this region. The towns of **Kilkee, Lahinch,** and **Doolin** are on the Atlantic coast, while the eastern border of County Clare is defined by **Lough Derg.** The main attractions of the **Cliffs of Moher** and **Burren National Park** are in **North Clare,** while the **Loop Head Peninsula** in **West Clare** is a more tranquil escape. To the south is the **River Shannon** and the **Shannon Estuary** at **Limerick City.**

PLANNING YOUR TIME

The farther west you go, the slower you'll travel. North Clare deserves two full days, one in Burren National Park and another in either Lahinch or Doolin on your way to the Cliffs of Moher. The remote parts of West Clare should be given a full day also. Plan to spend at least a full day and night in Limerick City, as there are plenty of sights to see and pubs to visit.

Itinerary Ideas

TWO DAYS IN NORTH CLARE AND THE BURREN

Day 1: The Burren and Doolin

1 Check in to Hotel Doolin and grab a quick breakfast at their restaurant **Stonewall,** where they serve healthy smoothies.

2 Drive to the **Burren National Park** visitor center in Corofin and find a walk that suits your mood.

3 Book in for a tour of the **Aillwee Caves** and go underground to see an incredible cave structure and the remains of ancient creatures.

4 Head back to Doolin and visit **Oar Restaurant & Rooms** for dinner, where the beautifully plated dishes look almost too good to eat.

5 Round the evening off with a live traditional music session at **Gus O'Connor's Pub,** where you'll hear great tunes and meet lots of people.

Day 2: The Cliffs of Moher and Lahinch

1 Start your day with a drive to Ennistimon for a coffee at **Unglert's Bakery,** where you can stock up on some nourishing snacks.

2 Stop by **The Salmon Bookshop** and pick up some gifts.

3 Drive to the **Cliffs of Moher,** where you can leave your vehicle at the car park and walk the cliff-top trail to see the legendary views. On your way back, pop into the visitor center to learn how the cliffs came to be.

Previous: Cliffs of Moher; King John's Castle; Loop Head Lighthouse.

Clare and Limerick

To Athlone and Clonmacnoise
N67
N67
Ballyvaughan
R380
GALWAY
R480
M18
Gort
R460
BURREN NATIONAL PARK
Mullaghmore
MULLAGHMORE LOOP
R462
R476
Corofin
R460
Lough Derg
CLARE
N85
Ennis
M18
R462
Killaloe
N68
Newmarket on Fergus
R465
R463
R471
M7
R473
BUNRATTY CASTLE & FOLK PARK
Shannon
SHANNON AIRPORT
KING JOHN'S CASTLE
River Shannon
THOMOND PARK
N18
Limerick
See "Limerick City" Map
UNIVERSITY HOSPITAL LIMERICK
N24
M20
LIMERICK
0
5 mi
0
5 km
N20
N21
Rathkeale
Wild Atlantic Way

Itinerary Ideas

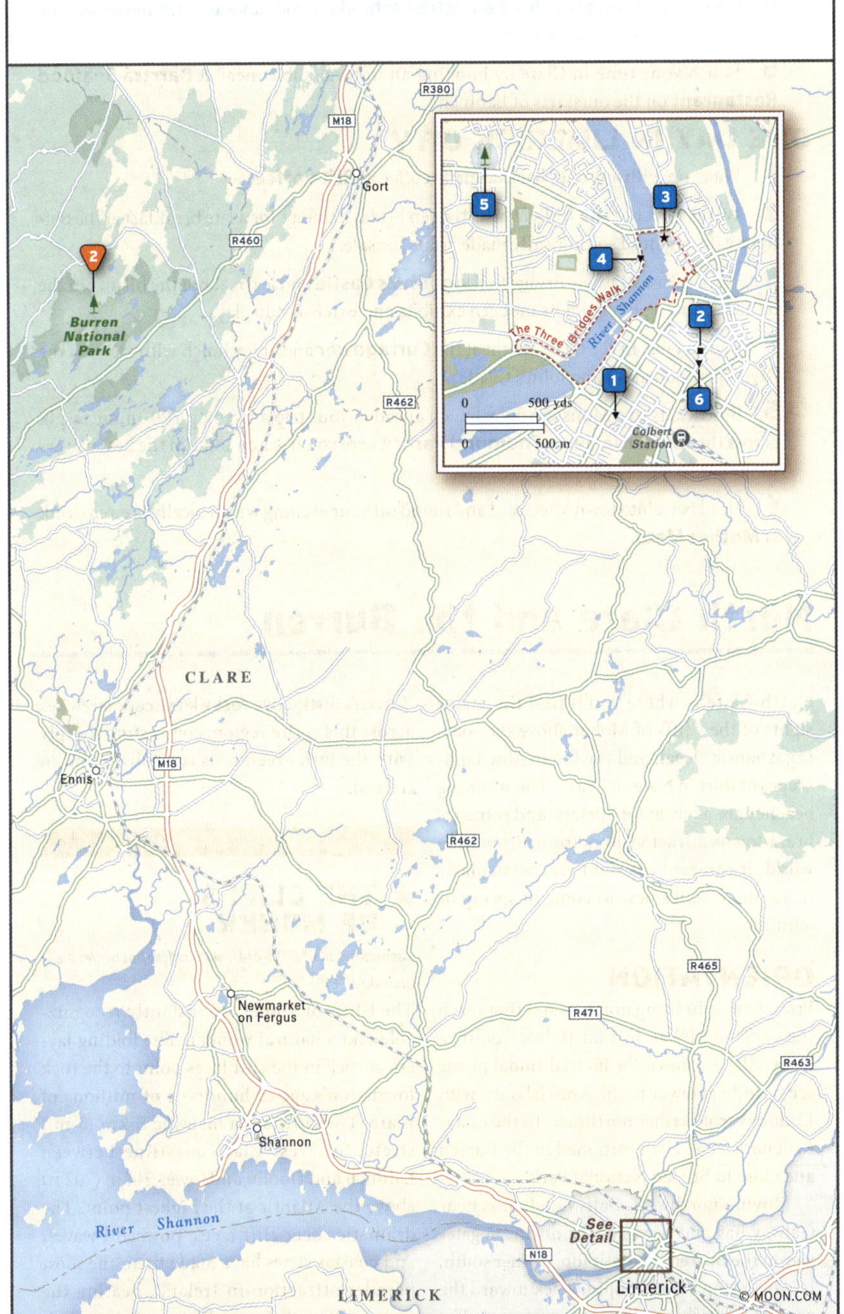
R380
M18
Gort
R460
Burren
National
Park
R462
CLARE
M18
Ennis
R462
R465
R471
R463
Newmarket
on Fergus
Shannon
River Shannon
See
Detail
N18
Limerick
LIMERICK
© MOON.COM
The Three Bridges Walk
River Shannon
0 500 yds
0 500 m
Colbert
Station

4 Come back down to earth at **Lahinch Beach,** where you can walk the sandy shoreline or learn to surf at Ollie's Surf Centre.

5 Finish your time in Clare by booking an unforgettable meal at **Barrtrá Seafood Restaurant** on the outskirts of Lahinch.

ONE DAY IN LIMERICK CITY

1 Wake up with a proper barista-made coffee at **Rift Coffee.**

2 Wander over to **the Milk Market,** open Friday-Sunday, for a late breakfast at the outdoor café, and find some locally made crafts for sale.

3 Walk across Mathew Bridge to **King John's Castle** and learn about the history of the building and region from its modern exhibits and extensive displays.

4 Book a table in the Glass Room at the **Curragower** and enjoy lunch with views of the River Shannon and King John's Castle.

5 Buy tickets to a Munster rugby match ahead of your trip and enjoy a 20-minute walk across the River Shannon to **Thomond Park,** where you'll watch some of the best players in the world take to the pitch.

6 Head back into town afterward and round off your evening with a locally brewed drink at **Mother Macs.**

North Clare and the Burren

North Clare is where you'll find the major sights of the Cliffs of Moher above the roaring Atlantic Ocean and the fascinating landscapes of Burren National Park. The stunning beaches are a haven for surfers, and some vibrant towns attract visitors from around the world. It can get busy out here, particularly in summer, so it's best to come in spring or autumn.

ORIENTATION

From Dingle heading north, you'll first reach the Cliffs of Moher. Just north lies Doolin, a lively village known for its traditional music scene and a gateway to the Aran Islands, with Lisdoonvarna farther northeast. To the east is Kilfenora, centrally positioned in the Burren and close to Burren National Park.

Moving northwest, Ballyvaughan is near Galway Bay and serves as the northern gateway to the Burren. Ennistimon, farther south, is a great stop before looping back toward the coast at Lahinch, a well-known surf town. The Burren's distinctive rocky landscape stretches across this entire region, contrasting sharply with the lush green hills typically found in Ireland.

TOP EXPERIENCE

★ THE CLIFFS OF MOHER

Liscannor; tel. 65/708-6141; www.cliffsofmoher.ie; daily 8am-dusk; €15

The Cliffs of Moher are instantly recognizable and a natural wonder. The folding layers of rock in the cliff faces point to the rock formation's age of hundreds of millions of years. The cliffs are a majestic 8-km (5-mi) stretch of West Clare coastline between Lahinch and Doolin and tower 214 m (702 ft) above the Atlantic at the highest point. The dramatic sheer cliff faces, powerful waves, and coastal views have made them the most popular attraction in Ireland, beating the Guinness Storehouse and Titanic Belfast. This

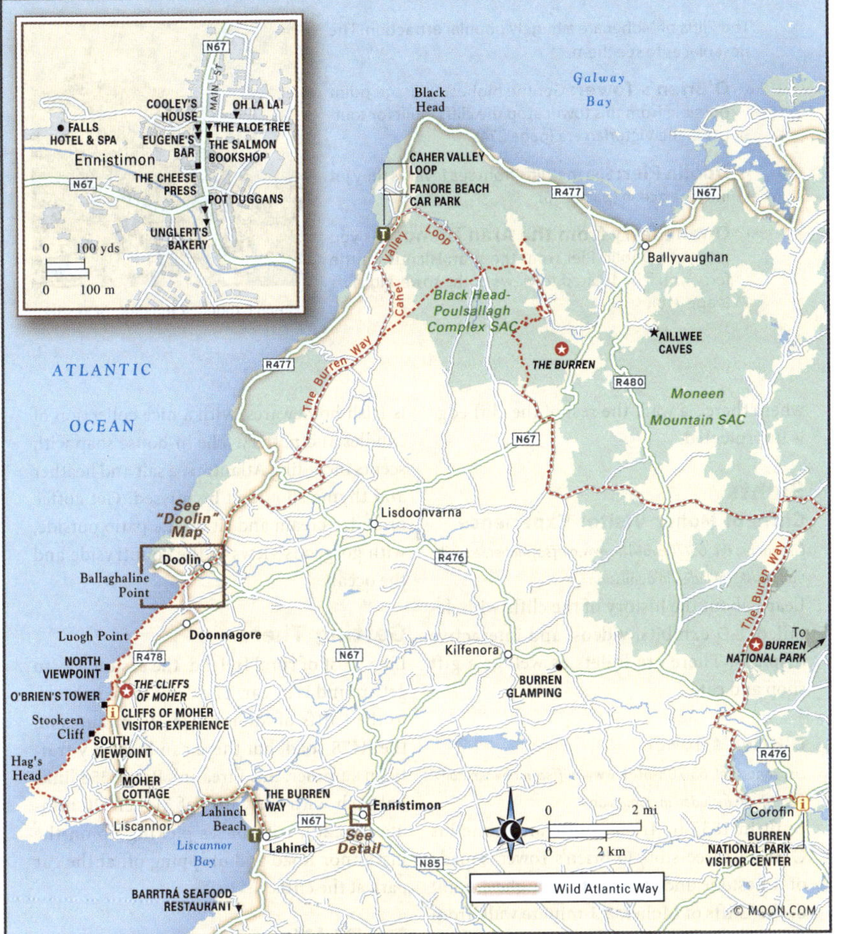

popularity has made it hard to visit for free, as there's only one car park, and it's where you buy your ticket for the cliffs. Expect traffic jams during summer to get into the car park, but once you've parked, the crowds disperse along the cliff tops, so you'll still have some of the cliffs to yourself. **The Burren Way** (page 280), a 114-km (71-mi) hiking trail, passes the cliffs, and without a car you can see them for free.

Walking up the slope from the road toward the edge of the cliff, you'll hear the roar of the ocean and the waves crashing into them. Puffins and guillemots perch on the rocky outcrops, and you might even see dolphins and seals in the water below. To the north is **O'Brien's Tower,** a stone structure built in 1835 for visitors to enjoy the view while sheltered from the elements. Beyond the **main viewing point** outside the visitor center,

Best Views of the Cliffs

The Cliffs of Moher are a hugely popular attraction. The best places to see them:

- **O'Brien's Tower:** Get the highest vantage point possible from this tower atop the cliffs, built for tourists in the Victorian era (page 274).
- **Doolin Pier:** See the cliffs from sea level as they jut into the ocean (page 275).
- **On the ferry from the Aran Islands:** As you return to Doolin Pier from the Aran Islands on the ferry, you'll be treated to views of the towering cliffs (page 318).

O'Brien's Tower at the Cliffs of Moher

where there's a wall, the rest of the cliff edge is unprotected.

Sights

Cliffs of Moher Visitor Experience

Liscannor; tel. 65/708-6141; www.cliffsofmoher.ie; daily 8am-dusk; included in admission

Learn about the history of the cliffs with detailed 3-D exhibits, videos, and interactive displays. There are toilets as well as a gift shop and café.

O'Brien's Tower

Liscannor; tel. 65/708-6141; www.cliffsofmoher.ie; daily 8am-dusk; included in admission

Built in 1835 by Irish politician Cornelius O'Brien, three-story O'Brien's Tower is made of limestone and stands at the highest point of the Cliffs of Moher, a 3-minute walk from the visitor center. O'Brien saw potential in developing tourism in the area and built it as an observation point. You ascend up the tower via a spiral staircase. On clear days you can see the Aran Islands.

Shopping

Moher Cottage

St. Brigid's Well; tel. 87/295-9096; https://mohercottage.com; daily 10am-5pm

This family-run gift shop and coffeeshop is a 3-minute drive from the cliffs. The focus is Irish homewares, with a nice collection of candles and pottery. The in-house soap with scents including Atlantic sea salt and heather and thyme shouldn't be missed. Get coffee or an ice cream and sit on the patio outside, with gorgeous views of the countryside and the ocean.

Getting There

Like most of rural Ireland, the easiest way to get around is by car. The drive from Lahinch to the Cliffs of Moher takes 10 minutes on the R478 road, but there can be heavy traffic in summer. Bus Éireann's Route 350 links Lahinch with the Cliffs of Moher (20 minutes; €3.20), with buses picking up on the Liscannor Road and dropping off at the car park at the cliffs.

DOOLIN

Doolin is a popular small village in North Clare thanks to its location beside the Cliffs of Moher, Burren National Park, and ferries to the Aran Islands. It's also a picturesque rural village with fantastic coastal views, pubs filled with live music, and great dining options. You'll likely meet visitors in Doolin, as it's on the tourist trail, but it is in no way a tourist trap. Enjoy the food and the pubs, and when the weather is good, take a stroll down to the coast to watch the sun set on the Aran Islands.

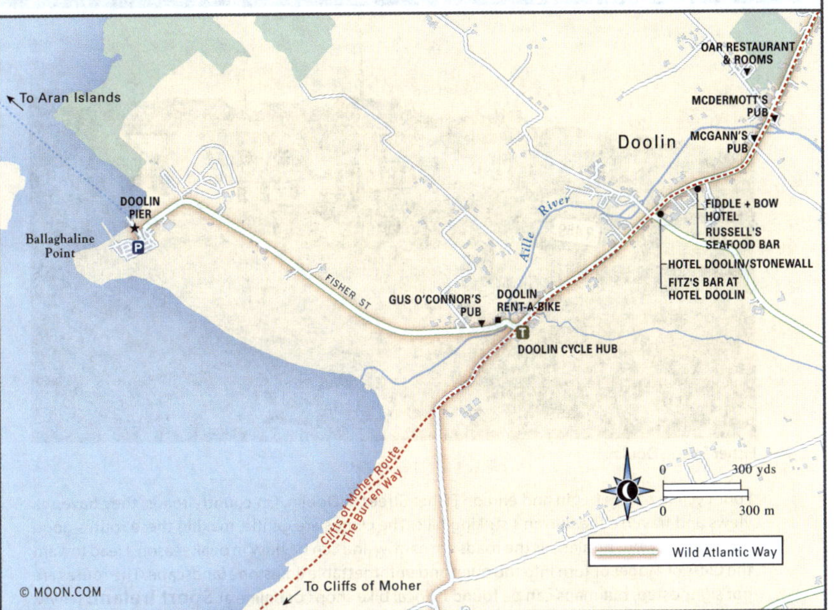

Sights

Doolin Pier

Doolin Pier, on the western edge of Doolin village, is a great spot for stunning coastal views of the Atlantic, the Cliffs of Moher, and the Aran Islands. It serves as a departure point for ferries to the Aran Islands.

Cycling

Doolin Rent-a-Bike

Fisher St.; tel. 87/656-9837; www.doolinrentabike.ie; daily 9am-6pm

A good choice of basic bikes in a range of sizes is aimed at leisurely cycling, but there are no e-bikes. Rentals are hourly, daily, or weekly, and you can arrange to have your bike picked up at your end point.

Festivals and Events

The Burren Slow Food Festival

www.slowfoodclare.com; May

See why locals love the food so much at Slow Food Clare through meals, talks, and farmers markets. Chefs from local restaurants and hotels show how to make their favorite dishes, following the belief that food can be good for you and the planet. A five-course Slow Food Banquet uses the best local produce to create a delicious meal in the heart of the Burren. Tickets to the events are free, but book as far ahead as possible.

Food

Gus O'Connor's Pub

Fisher St.; https://gusoconnorsdoolin.com; Mon.-Fri. 10am-midnight, Sat.-Sun. 9:30am-midnight; from €20

Serving hearty fare for breakfast, lunch, and dinner seven days a week, bustling O'Connor's Pub has an open fireplace and wood-paneled walls decorated with photos and trinkets from the pub's history. The full Irish breakfast is a must on the weekend; later in the day are pub favorites like beef and Guinness stew and a steak sandwich. O'Connor's is also a hub for

Doolin Cycle Hub

Fisher Street, Doolin

Four cycling routes begin and end on Fisher Street in Doolin. On country roads, they have sea views and traverse the Burren's striking hills. The climbs are gentle, making these routes good for beginners, but be alert, as the roads are narrow and can be busy in peak season. Head toward the Cliffs of Moher or turn into the quiet and unforgettable limestone landscape. The routes are not signposted, but maps can be found in local bike shops or online at **Sport Ireland** (www.sportireland.ie) or **Komoot** (www.komoot.com).

- **Cliffs of Moher Route** (18 km/11 mi round-trip): This gentle route takes you from Doolin to the cliffs on country roads. Expect incredible views at the halfway mark, then return to Doolin.
- **Coastal Route** (26 km/16 mi round-trip): Head north to quieter parts of the Clare coast and through the Burren on this loop. Fanore marks the halfway point, and you return via Lisdoonvarna.
- **Burren Route** (43 km/27 mi round-trip): This route brings you inland toward the town of Kilfenora, where you'll see the rocky landscape of the Burren.
- **Town to Town Route** (47 km/29 mi round-trip): Ride to the Cliffs of Moher and then south to the towns of Liscannor, Lahinch, and Ennistimon before taking back roads back to Doolin.

live traditional music seven nights a week, as tin whistle players recite Irish classics alongside the fiddle, flute, and bodhrán.

Russell's Seafood Bar

Teergonean; tel. 65/670-0200; www.fiddleandbow.ie; Mon.-Sat. 5pm-11pm, Sun. 1pm-11pm; from €24

At the Fiddle + Bow Hotel in Doolin, the head chef at Russell's Seafood Bar uses seafood from the Atlantic in mains like steamed Moher lobster and grilled Irish sea bass. There's also a choice of small plates. The dining area has a modern rustic feel, with woven lampshades over light wooden furniture and a bar area with 50 Irish whiskeys, including local creations.

Oar Restaurant & Rooms

Roadford; tel. 65/704-7990; https://oardoolin.ie; Thurs.-Sun. 5:30pm-11pm; from €75 pp

Fine dining has made its way to the Burren at Oar Restaurant, where local products are served in a comfortable dining room. Dishes blur the line between food and art, as delicately sliced and carefully placed ingredients are beautifully presented. Choose a two-course (€75) or three-course (€85) meal and enjoy highlights like the spiced tuna tartare, cod nori, and blackcurrant soufflé. There are also four guest rooms and one suite.

Bars and Nightlife

McGann's Pub

Roadford; https://mcgannsdoolin.com; Mon.-Thurs. noon-11:30pm, Fri. noon-12:30am, Sat. 10am-12:30am, Sun. 10am-11pm; from €15

This traditional pub is a busy and lively spot a short walk from the center of town, the sort of place you could spend the entire night. A mixture of small rooms and spaces spreads across red tile floor, and the walls are lined with nods to its love for music. Live music happens in the front bar with traditional Irish instruments. To the rear of the pub is a more modern area with outdoor covered dining, making long summer evenings last longer. There's a small food menu; Tony's famous beef stew is the most popular dish.

McDermott's Pub

Roadford; tel. 65/707-4328; https://mcdermott-s-pub.com; daily 11am-midnight; €16

McDermott's Pub is a family-run business serving pints since 1867. Large portions of classic pub dishes like fish-and-chips and beef stew are served, and live music is played regularly, ramping up to nightly in summer.

Fitz's Bar at Hotel Doolin

Fitz Cross; tel. 65/707-4111; www.hoteldoolin.ie; noon-11:30pm Tues.-Thurs., noon-12:30am Fri.-Sat., noon-11pm Sun.-Mon.; €18

Fitz's Bar, inside Hotel Doolin, is known for lively trad music sessions and a tasty menu of seafood, meat, and vegetarian dishes. The bar has a cozy front area with an open fire, perfect for warming up after a day out on the cliffs. Behind the bar is a good choice of Irish craft beers and over 100 whiskeys.

Accommodations

Hotel Doolin

Fitz Cross; tel. 65/707-4111; www.hoteldoolin.ie; €200

This four-star boutique hotel has 17 airy eco-conscious rooms with a nice punch of color in the furnishings. Greenwashing is common these days, but Hotel Doolin harvests rainwater (there's a lot), composts waste, and grows vegetables in a 15-m (50-ft) polytunnel to keep their carbon footprint as small as possible. On-site eateries are **Stonewall,** with wood-fired pizzas served with organic wine, and **Glas Restaurant,** with a tapas menu.

Fiddle + Bow Hotel

Teergonean; tel. 65/670-0200; www.fiddleandbow.ie; €250

A top choice for a touch of modern luxury and unique decor, Fiddle + Bow Hotel is in the middle of Doolin with 13 rooms, each styled to reflect the area's heritage. For groups and families, 20 self-catering lodges and 12 cottages are available. There are four places to eat, including a takeaway, a modern coffee shop, and **Russell's Seafood Bar** in the lobby, with a focus on local products.

Getting There and Around

From the Cliffs of Moher, head northeast on the R478 road toward Doolin, a scenic coastal route through the charming village. The R478 curves south to Lahinch. This short drive takes 15 minutes, offering stunning views of the coastline along the way. By bus, Route 350 from Bus Éireann departs five times a day and takes 20 minutes.

From Limerick, drive northwest on the N18 toward Ennis, then the M18 motorway. Take exit 12 toward Ennistimon and merge onto the R458. Follow the R476 to Ennistimon, then the R478, following signs for Doolin. The journey is 80 km (50 mi) and takes about 1 hour. There is no direct bus from Limerick City to Doolin.

★ THE BURREN AND BURREN NATIONAL PARK

The Burren is a 360-sq-km (140-sq-mi) region of County Clare that's defined by its rocky, barren, moon-like landscape. The unique geology of limestone slabs combines with warm microclimates to create habitats for rare flora, and there are sea views you won't find anywhere else. The landscape has created a culture that feels more in tune with nature, as the land is hard to clear and tough to farm on, making people in the Burren proud of what they produce.

The Burren has been inhabited for 6,000 years, with traces of different eras still visible in ancient tombs, Iron Age forts, and remnants of Cromwell's attacks on Ireland. At the heart of the region is Burren National Park, where the most beautiful and sparsest landscapes can be seen. Hiking the Burren Way is a fantastic way to experience the magic of this captivating area. The small towns Lisdoonvarna, Kilfenora, Corofin, and Ballyvaughan are hubs in the area, often filled with music.

Burren National Park is an 1,800-ha (4,450-acre) area that protects a landscape you're unlikely to find anywhere else on the planet. The rocky limestone slabs are made up of small divots and peaks that create tiny microclimates where alpine plants grow near those more often seen in the Mediterranean. The landscape is harsh, and there's no better way to fully experience it than getting on the hiking and walking trails.

You can also drive the Burren Scenic Drive, a 66-km (41-mi) loop through Kilfenora, Lisdoonvarna, and other picturesque villages that gives plenty of opportunities to see the landscape and chances to pull off the road to take it in.

Visiting the Park

The park is free and there are no gated entrances. The staff runs guided walks throughout the year; see www.nationalparks.ie/burren.

Visitor Center

Burren National Park has one visitor center, on the main street in Corofin. Displays cover the flora and fauna in the park. This is where to get of information from the guides about the hiking trails and park highlights.

Sights

Aillwee Caves

tel. 65/707-7036; www.aillweeburrenexperience.ie; daily 10am-5pm; €26

Discovered by chance by a local farmer in 1940, the Aillwee Caves has become Ireland's top underground attraction. Believed to be millions of years old, these caves stretch for 1 km (0.6 mi), and you can see stalactites, stalagmites, and a 6-m-high (20-ft) underground waterfall. On the 45-minute tour, you'll walk deep below ground and peer into hibernation chambers where the remains of European brown bears were found. Back above ground, the fun continues at the **Birds of Prey Centre,** where trained staff put on shows with birds of prey, demonstrating their power and incredible hunting abilities.

Hiking and Walking

Mullaghmore Loop

Distance: *7.5 km (4.6 mi) loop*
Duration: *2 hours*
Elevation gain: *212 m (695 ft)*
Effort: *Moderate*
Trailhead: *Gortlecka Crossroads*

Get out into the amazing landscapes of the Burren on this rocky trail that rewards with panoramic views from the summit of Mullaghmore. You'll see rock formations and flora up close, with the unique Sliabh Rua formation the highlight of this trail. The hike is moderately challenging due to the loose uneven surface throughout.

Caher Valley Loop

Distance: *14.1 km (8.8 mi) loop*
Duration: *3-4 hours*
Elevation gain: *300 m (985 ft)*

1: rock formations in the Burren **2:** Lahinch Beach

1

2

Effort: *Moderate*
Trailhead: *Fanore Beach Car Park*
This loop trail is lengthy but without steep sections. It begins at Fanore Beach and leads through the Caher Valley, where you'll be flanked by the landscapes of the Burren and treated to views of Galway Bay and the Aran Islands from the elevated points. The route follows country roads, some that rarely see traffic, and signs guide you back to Fanore.

The Burren Way

Distance: *114 km (71 mi) one-way*
Duration: *5-6 days*
Elevation gain: *540 m (1,770 ft)*
Effort: *Moderate*
Trailhead: *Lahinch Beach Car Park*
The Burren Way is one of those long-distance hiking trails that takes you to remote places that most only dream about. While Lahinch, Doolin, and the Cliffs of Moher all get lots of visitors, the places between are often empty, which is the best way to see the Burren. That doesn't mean you miss the best of the region on this hike; you'll see it all between Lahinch and Corofin via the national park. The trail is a nice mix of roads, gravel paths, and single-track trails, with no steep parts. You'll have a chance to resupply each day, although in some sections you'll be isolated for hours at a time.

Food and Accommodations

Vaughan's Pub

Main St., Kilfenora; tel. 65/708-8004; https://vaughanspub.ie; daily 11am-midnight; €12

Historic Vaughan's Pub has been open for over 100 years and offers old Irish atmosphere in a recently renovated space. The sprawling venue has a pub with a restaurant attached, a six-bedroom guest house, and a wedding barn. Catch live music on weekends in the pub, and try contemporary twists on classic dishes like beef top rib and chicken supreme.

Burren Glamping

Cahirminnaun, Kilfenora; tel. 65/708-8931; http://burrenglamping.com; €140

Kids will be talking about this cute family-friendly place for years. There's just one room, a tiny house made from a horse truck. The space is decorated like a farm cottage with a Belfast sink and white wooden interiors. The well-thought-out space comes with two permanent beds and two that fold out when needed, along with a wood-burning stove. The owners also run a small pig farm, and you can see the piglets running around the fields.

Getting There and Around

To reach the Burren visitor center in Corofin from Doolin, take the R479 road southeast toward Lisdoonvarna. From Lisdoonvarna, follow the R476 south, heading toward Kilfenora and into Corofin. The visitor center is central in the village. The journey takes 25-30 minutes and is a preview of the landscapes to come.

LAHINCH AND ENNISTIMON

Lahinch (sometimes written Lehinch) is a laid-back surf town that attracts all manner of visitors to the water and those who prefer to watch from the shore. Lahinch Beach is the main attraction, but there's also a solid foodie scene with influences from across the world. Along with Doolin, Lahinch is one of the larger towns near the Cliffs of Moher, making it a natural stop for a few hours.

Most visitors pass through Ennistimon (you'll also see it written as Ennistymon) on the way to the Cliffs of Moher without stopping, but they're missing an interesting little town that's big on health food and independent businesses. The River Cullenagh runs alongside the town, and Main Street and New Road have most of the shops and restaurants. There's not enough here to warrant an overnight stay, but it should be a stop on your way to the coast.

Beaches

Lahinch Beach

Lahinch

In a place that loves surfing, Lahinch Beach

might be the most famous surf spot of all. This 1.5-km (1-mi) Blue Flag beach lines a horseshoe-shaped bay with consistent waves. This makes it ideal for surfing in summer, particularly for beginners, as a lifeguard is on duty. Winter brings bigger swells. There's a designated swimming area, but watch for the strong currents. Toilets and showers are available.

Surfing

Ollie's Surf Centre

Lower Car Park, Lahinch Rd., Lahinch; tel. 86/812-0400; http://ollieslahinchsurfcentre.ie; daily 10am-8pm; €40 pp

Ollie set up his surf school in a brilliant location at Lahinch Beach over 20 years ago. His aim is to make it easy and fun for beginners to try the sport. His wide range of classes includes lessons for kids and adults, groups of up to 40, and stag and hen (bachelor and bachelorette) parties. If you're an experienced surfer, three types of surfboards and wetsuits are for rent.

Shopping

The Salmon Bookshop

Main St., Ennistimon; tel. 85/231-8909; https://thesalmonbookshop.com; Mon.-Sat. 10am-5:30pm

The Salmon Bookshop is a literary hub in County Clare. While some pop in to pick up the latest best seller, most find themselves staying to peruse the large second-hand section and the rare books shelf with first editions from the early 1900s. There's a library-like tranquility with classical music and a reading nook by the window. This space is a literary center, so check the website for readings and workshops. During summer, some events are held in the garden at the rear.

The Cheese Press

Main St., Ennistimon; tel. 65/707-1217; https://cheesepressennistymon.ie; Tues.-Sat. 9am-6pm; from €3

This warm and welcoming cheese shop goes beyond selling delicious products; owner Sinead also sells local crafts and famous toasted sandwiches. The small shop has limited seating, but try the toastie made with mature Irish cheddar and sun-dried tomato pesto on sourdough. Locally made St. Tola goat cheese is a popular choice. There's a strong emphasis on sustainability, with a zero-waste policy and regular events and workshops that make it feel like a cornerstone of the community.

Food

Pot Duggans

New Rd., Ennistimon; tel. 65/707-2212; www.potduggans.com; Tues.-Sat. 9am-6pm; from €9

Straddling a café and a pub, Pot Duggans serves food and drink in a relaxed space in an old building brightened up with punchy artwork, leafy plants, and modern furniture. The venue attracts a young crowd, as the owners made a name for themselves in the nightlife scene in Dublin. Lunch is toasted sandwiches and soup; in the evening there's a pizza menu. The front bar is traditional, with wooden features, large windows, and seating for 15. Downstairs and outside, the space opens up to riverside seating for 50, one of the best beer gardens in the country when the sun is shining.

Joe's Café

Marine Parade, Lahinch; tel. 65/708-6113; daily 9am-5pm; from €10

Joe's Café is a cute offbeat spot with seating for 30, a colorful interior, and a crafty feel to the furnishings for a quick lunch after the beach. The menu is sandwiches, pizzas, and salads with an international approach, like the tasty Moroccan chicken and roasted pepper sandwich. Joe's Café has a healthy breakfast menu, with the top pick the sautéed sweet potato served on a bed of greens with poached eggs and mixed seeds.

Barrtrá Seafood Restaurant

Barrtrá, Lahinch; tel. 65/708-1280; www.barrtra.com; Thurs.-Sat. 12:30pm-9pm, Sun. noon-7pm; from €30

Dining at Barrtrá feels like dinner at a friend's house, as this seafood restaurant is in a house down a country road 4 km (2.5 mi) from

Lahinch. They focus on local Irish ingredients and are happy to cater to dietary restrictions with a bit of notice. What makes this restaurant stand out is its Surprise Menu, when chef Ruben O'Brien finds the best produce available that day. Choose seafood, meat, or vegetarian, then wait to see what arrives.

Unglert's Bakery

New Rd., Ennistimon; tel. 65/707-1217; Instagram @unglerts; Tues.-Sat. 9am-6pm; from €3

Unglert's Bakery has been a staple of Ennistimon for over 40 years. Stephan has been consistently creating delicious baked treats and bread in the small production room in back. There's a strong focus on healthy eating, despite what the apple turnovers might suggest, and he's extended this ethos to health foods and supplements. Everything is handmade, and the shop is a destination for those in the know. The exterior of the shop alone is worth a visit. Many shops in Ennistimon have traditional fronts, but Unglert's is immaculate, with a bright yellow facade and punchy red signage.

Oh La La!

Parliament St., Ennistimon; tel. 65/707-0000; Mon.-Sat. 9:30am-5pm; from €4

You might not expect to find a slice of Brittany in Clare, but that's what you get at Oh La La! Run by Marie from France, this informal café plays jazz music and serves sweet and savory crepes. Pull up a seat in the dining area, with an old stone fireplace, and choose classic toppings like lemon and sugar, or one of the Irish-French fusion options that use Clonakilty black pudding or smoked salmon from the Clare coast.

Bars and Nightlife

Kenny's Bar

Main St., Lahinch; tel. 65/708-1433; www.kennysbar.ie; Thurs. 5pm-11:30pm, Fri. 2pm-12:30am, Sat. 10:30am-12:30am, Sun. 12:30pm-12:30am, Mon. 12:30pm-9pm; €5

Kenny's Bar first opened as a coach house in the 1830s and has managed to retain some of that feel in a space that wears its history on its walls through memorabilia and photos. The pub is cluttered in parts, but that adds to the charm. It's popular with locals, especially in summer, with live music from modern bands. A small seafood-focused menu has mussels and chowder plus some other items.

Eugene's Bar

10 Main St., Ennistimon; tel. 65/707-1777; Mon.-Fri. 5pm-11pm, Sat.-Sun. noon-11pm; €5

Eugene's Bar is a charming pub in the middle of town. During summer there's live music every night in a mix of styles, and Sunday is for traditional music. The stained-glass windows and knickknacks draw visitors in, while the excellent Guinness can see "one quick drink" turn into a night out.

Cooley's House

Main St.; Ennistimon; tel. 65/707-1712; Mon.-Thurs. 10:30am-11:30pm, Fri.-Sat. 10:30am-12:30am, Sun. noon-11pm; €5

Cooley's House, known locally as Cooley's, is a family-run traditional pub with a welcoming atmosphere thanks to the rich wooden interior and slate floor. Every Friday and Wednesday evening the pub hosts Irish music sessions.

Accommodations

Vaughan Lodge Hotel

Ennistimon Rd., Lahinch; tel. 65/708-1111; https://vaughanlodge.ie; Apr.-Nov.; €160

This 30-room boutique hotel in Lahinch is open seasonally and a good choice for a modern room close to the major attractions. The casual **VL Restaurant** serves Irish breakfasts made to order.

Falls Hotel & Spa

Castlequarter, Ennistimon; tel. 65/707-1004; www.fallshotel.ie; €220

This 18th-century mansion beside a meandering river offers a luxury stay and 140 rooms. The River Spa is a big draw, with an indoor pool, a sauna, a steam room, and spa treatments. Dining options are **Cascades,** for more formal evenings, and the more relaxed **Dylan Thomas Bar;** both serve locally sourced ingredients.

Getting There

The drive from Limerick City is 65 km (40 mi) and takes 50-60 minutes. Take the N18 road toward Ennis, which is bypassed, then the N85 to Ennistimon. Lahinch is 3.7 km (2.3 mi) farther west on the N67.

You can take the train from Limerick City's Colbert Station (Prior's-Land) to Ennis Station (Clonroad More) and then the Route 331 bus operated by Local Link from the train station to Ennistimon. There are only three buses daily in each direction, making it not an appealing option. Bus Éireann Route 333 runs from Bellbridge House Hotel in Spanish Point to the Liscannor Road bus stop in Lahinch (€3.80) four times a day. By car, the 13-km (8-mi) drive along the N67 takes 15 minutes, and there's a large car park at Lahinch Beach, but it can get very busy during summer.

West Clare and Loop Head Peninsula

If North Clare feels too busy, and you want the postcard scenes of remote coastline with empty beaches and colorful villages with peaceful pubs, make your way to West Clare. This region is known for its traditional Irish music, and pubs regularly host sessions that can go long into the night. Although it's not as popular as North Clare, there's still plenty of craic to be had.

ORIENTATION

Spanish Point is where North Clare meets West Clare and stretches from the outskirts of **Ennis** to the tip of the **Loop Head Peninsula.** At the base of the peninsula are **Kilrush,** on the Shannon Estuary side, and **Kilkee,** on the Atlantic side. These are the two residential areas, with the rest of the region rural and remote.

SPANISH POINT

Named after the Spanish Armada sailors shipwrecked here in 1588, this small coastal village has a permanent population of 200, but in summer, numbers multiply as holiday home owners and tourists visit for the beaches with stunning views, windswept shores, and reliable surfing. Don't expect a busy main street full of shops and pubs; instead, activity is centered around stand-alone buildings like the Armada Hotel.

Beaches

Spanish Point

This beach is one of the most popular in West Clare thanks to its sweeping dunes, golden sand, and distant cliffs. Its Blue Flag designation means it meets high standards for water quality, cleanliness, and safety. At 1 km (0.6 mi) long, it's a busy spot for walkers and families on sunny days. When the waves are pumping, the water is filled with surfers, as it's a safe and reliable wave for beginners. There are showers, toilets, and parking along with specially adapted Hippocampe wheelchairs, booked through the **lifeguard station** (tel. 87/638-4416).

Surfing

Surfing in Ireland is massively overlooked. If you can brave the cold—the water never truly warms up—you'll experience some of the best waves in Europe. When winter comes, the west coast of Ireland is known as one of the best cold-water surfing destinations in the world.

Whitewater Surf Company

tel. 86/862-5564; www.whitewatersurfco.com; daily 7am-8pm; €35 pp

Family-run Whitewater Surf Company is led by Pat Keane, aware of Ireland's surfing excellence since the 1980s. He'll help surfers of

1

2

all levels, from standing up for the first time to improving their technique. Two-hour lessons for adults (€35 pp) and kids (€25) include wetsuit and surfboard rentals. Families are welcome.

Food and Accommodations

The Armada Hotel

tel. 65/707-9000; www.armadahotel.com; €200

This is as close to sleeping on the beach as you're likely to get. The four-star Armada Hotel is perched on a rocky outcrop facing south over Spanish Point Beach. The 87 rooms feel fresh thanks to clean design, with ocean-view rooms drinking in spectacular views of the coast. Family rooms have play areas and tepees. The Seascape Suite comes with floor-to-ceiling windows with views of the beach along with a freestanding bathtub.

Aileen's Restaurant at The Armada Hotel

tel. 65/707-9000; www.armadahotel.com; daily 5pm-9:30pm; from €25

The main restaurant in the Armada Hotel is worth visiting, even if you're not staying here. The focus is local ingredients, some grown on the hotel's farm, which you can also visit, to create modern Irish dishes paired with international wines. The Atlantic prawns and Flaggy Shore mussels are delicious and sourced locally, but a pro tip is to come for the Sunday roast. They served a dry-aged roast of beef with a Yorkshire pudding, roast potato, seasonal vegetables, and rich gravy 12:30pm-3:45pm. Sit by the floor-to-ceiling windows and watch the tide roll in. Reservations are advised, especially in summer.

Getting There

From Lahinch, head south on the R458 road toward the N67. Drive south on the N67 through Miltown Malbay and continue for 3 km (2 mi). Spanish Point is on the right. Bus Éireann's Route 333 connects Lahinch (Liscannor Rd.) to Spanish Point (R482), passing through Miltown Malbay.

The drive from Kilrush to Spanish Point is an easy 30 minutes south along the N67, passing through Doonbeg and Quilty. Bus Éireann operates Route 333 from the Square in Kilrush to the Bellbridge House Hotel in Spanish Point (30 minutes; €7.60 one-way) four times a day.

KILRUSH AND SCATTERY ISLAND

Kilrush lies off the tourist trail and has a lived-in feel with a strong community. People say hello on the street and visit shops and cafés to check on the latest news. While it lacks the sights and attractions of Doolin and Lahinch, it has plenty to see and do for a day. To get away from the crowds, particularly in summer, and see what life is like in the banner county, Kilrush is a great choice.

Sights

Scattery Island

Beautiful Scattery Island, 2 km (1.2 mi) off the coast of Kilrush, is just 50 ha (120 acres) and full of fascinating history, ruins, and wildlife. In the 6th century, Saint Senan sailed to the island and created a monastery. Lots of the buildings, including an impressive round tower, a cathedral, and several churches, still stand today.

In the early 1800s, the French landed in County Mayo to help the Irish rebels, which made the English realize how exposed they were to threats from the sea. They built a gun battery in the southeast of Scattery Island. Uninhabited today, the island is a peaceful place to relax in nature. Keep an eye out for rabbits and hen harriers in the sky.

Access to Scattery Island is via the 15-minute **Scattery Island Tours** (https://scatteryislandtours.com) ferry trip from Kilrush Marina (€27 round-trip), which operates daily May-September. There's an optional guided walking tour (€35 including round-trip ferry). October-April, the ferry operates intermittently, depending on the weather. The

1: Spanish Point **2:** ruins on Scattery Island

Kilkee and Loop Head Peninsula

ferry ride is a highlight for many thanks to the scenic views of the Shannon Estuary.

Vandeleur Walled Garden

Killimer Rd.; tel. 65/905-1760; www.vandeleurwalledgarden.ie; daily 10am-4pm; €7

Set among mature woodlands, Vandeleur Walled Gardens is a must for gardeners, as its unique microclimate allows a diverse range of plants to thrive. Explore the maze, play a game of giant chess, and visit the Victorian greenhouse. Afterward, visit **The Woodland Bistro** for hot drinks and light bites.

Shopping

Clan

Henry St.; www.clan.studio; Wed.-Sun. 9am-5pm

Furthering Kilrush's contemporary feel is the homewares and lifestyle products at Clan. This earthy and enriching space is stocked with candles, pottery, and coffee-table books from Irish makers and doers as well as some international artists. It's an easy place to find a meaningful gift that will stand the test of time. Gift wrapping is available, and there's an online shop.

Banner Books

Hector St. Mills, Frances St.; tel. 65/908-0745; https://bannerbooks.ie; Sun.-Mon. 11am-5pm, Tues.-Sat. 10am-6pm

Find a new or used book in this clean and bright bookshop that's worth a stop. Pick up a photography book on Irish landscapes for someone back home. Check the website for reading events.

Food

Béag Café

Corner House, Henry St.; tel. 85/106-1083; www.beagfood.com; Thurs.-Sat. 9am-4pm, Sun. 9am-3pm; from €10

Modern Béag Café is run by a husband-and-wife team who have come home after a life as touring musicians in London. Béag is Irish for small, but the café has 20 seats in a spacious old pub from the 1800s, with low bar seating by the window and two-seat tables in the middle. Toasted sandwiches use local ingredients, and the pick is the Tola, made with St. Tola goat cheese and treacle-caramelized onions with thick-cut sourdough. A quick bite might turn into a longer stay once you've had one of the Calendar coffees and homemade baked treats. The small grocery section is stocked with artisanal Irish hot sauces and condiments.

Oileán

26 Henry St.; tel. 65/905-1070; https://oileanrestaurantkilrush.ie; Thurs. 5pm-11:30pm, Fri.-Sat. 1pm-12:30am, Sun. 1pm-11pm; €24

Oileán delivers a relaxed yet refined experience with beautifully plated meals that focus on high-quality locally sourced ingredients. The best seasonal organic produce on the menu changes often, but expect dishes like sea bream served with a prawn bisque and potato, leek, and mushroom pie.

Getting There

Driving is the fastest and most direct way to reach Kilrush from Limerick. The journey is 78 km (48 mi) and takes just over 1 hour. Take the N18 road out of Limerick toward Foynes. Then follow the N85 through Ennis to the N68, which takes you to Kilrush.

On public transport, take a train from Limerick Colbert Station (Parnell St.) to Ennis and change for Bus Éireann Route 336, which stops at Ennis Train Station. This bus drops off in Kilrush. The journey takes 2 hours because of the transfer.

KILKEE

Kilkee is a popular seaside town known for its beautiful horseshoe-shaped bay and sandy beach. It's also home to the famous Pollock Holes, natural tidal pools ideal for swimming at low tide. Kilkee serves as a gateway to the remote parts of the Loop Head Peninsula. It can get very quiet in winter, with many businesses closing for the season.

Hiking and Walking

Kilkee Cliff Walk

Distance: *5.6 km (3.4 mi) loop*
Duration: *1.5 hours*
Elevation gain: *126 m (413 ft)*
Effort: *Easy*
Trailhead: *Kilkee Beach*

The looped Kilkee Cliff Walk takes you on a rewarding ramble along the rugged west coast. The route takes you past the famous Pollock Holes swimming spot before venturing out on an exposed trail as you make your way up to the top of the cliffs on a dirt trail that can get slippery in the wet. The second half of the walk takes you down quiet country roads where you're flanked by stone walls and fields of livestock before returning into Kilkee.

Beaches and Swimming

Kilkee Beach

A sheltered and calm stretch of coastline in a region known for rugged seascapes, Kilkee Beach is crescent-shaped, which protects it from rough waves and makes it one of the safest in the area. Lifeguards are on duty June-August.

Pollock Holes

The Pollock Holes are a series of natural tidal pools in the rocky shoreline that fill with water at high tide and give swimmers places sheltered from the Atlantic. They are on West End, a 10-minute walk west from Kilkee Beach. When the tide retreats, three main pools are revealed, 20-50 m (65-165 ft) long and 1-2.5 m (3-8 ft) deep. Sea life often gets caught in the pools until the next high tide, so bring your snorkel to look in the clear water. To get to the Pollock Holes, you walk across large flagstones that can get slippery. Even if you don't swim, the holes are worth a visit.

Water Sports

Nevsail Watersports

Kilkee Strand Line; tel. 86/330-8236; https://nevsailwatersports.ie; daily 10am-5pm

Get out on the water with Nevsail Watersports to try surfing, scenic paddleboarding, and kayaking for various ages and abilities. Slots can fill ahead of time, particularly during school holidays, so book online. Nevsail also runs activities in Limerick City.

Food

O'Mara's Bar

O'Curry St.; tel. 89/495-7178; Facebook @omaras; Mon.-Thurs. 4pm-11:30pm, Fri.-Sat. 4pm-12:30am, Sun. 4pm-midnight

O'Mara's Bar is a cozy pub with an open fire and a steady flow of locals and a few visitors. In cold months you'll find the fire blazing, warming the tiled floor and the patrons. The beer is the usual and live music only happens in summer, but the atmosphere is fantastic, with locals having a chat, encouraging you to stay for one more drink. In warmer months, there's outdoor seating for 24 at the front in addition to the small bar seating area and five low tables. Dogs are welcome inside.

Getting There

Kilkee is a 15-minute drive from Kilrush on the N67 road. The **Limerick Clare Local Link** (www.locallinklc.ie) Route 339 bus departs Kilrush twice a day outside **Turks Bar** (Frances St.) to Kilkee and Loop Head. The journey to **The Square** in central Kilkee takes 15 minutes. It's 45 minutes farther to Loop Head.

LOOP HEAD PENINSULA

Most visitors stay farther north, making the Loop Head Peninsula a striking and unspoiled part of Ireland's Wild Atlantic Way. Flanked by the Atlantic Ocean on one side and the Shannon Estuary on the other, the peninsula offers breathtaking landscapes of rugged cliffs, a historic lighthouse, and seasonal towns like Kilkee.

Sights

★ Loop Head Lighthouse

www.loopheadlighthouse.ie; daily 10am-5pm; €3

This iconic lighthouse has been guiding ships on the treacherous coast since the 1670s, with the current structure dating to 1854. Still operating, it has been automated since 1991. On the tour (€8) you can climb the spiral staircase

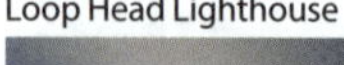

Loop Head Lighthouse

to the top and stand on the 23-m-high (76-ft) balcony. From the viewing platform, take in panoramic views of the surrounding area, including the rugged cliffs, the crashing Atlantic waves, and on clear days, landmarks like the Cliffs of Moher to the north and the Blasket Islands to the south. You can stay overnight in the lighthouse.

Hiking and Walking

Loop Head Loop

Distance: *1.8 km (1.1 mi) round-trip*
Duration: *30 minutes*
Elevation gain: *62 m (203 ft)*
Effort: *Easy*
Trailhead: *Loop Head Lighthouse car park*

Despite the rugged coastline, this walk offers a gentle way to experience the area's natural beauty. Park at the lighthouse car park and follow the path to the coast. Looking due west, the next land is Canada—the ocean feels truly massive. The walk continues past the white and red Loop Head Lighthouse toward a large "EIRE" sign carved into the ground during wartime to let pilots know which country was below. After this point, the trail goes slightly downhill before gently rising again to the car park. It can get very windy, so don't get too close to the edge.

Accommodations

Loop Head Lightkeeper's House

www.irishlandmark.com; €520 for 2 nights

It's not often you get the chance to sleep in a historic lighthouse. Iconic Loop Head Lighthouse has been renovated to sleep six in two double rooms and one twin room. The rooms are unorthodox, and feel a bit cramped, but that's the only downside of staying in a round building. There's a kitchen for self-catering, as there are no local amenities. You can buy supplies at two small groceries stores on the western end of O'Curry Street. Imagine waking up to spectacular views surrounded by natural beauty on a remote part of the Irish coast.

Getting There

From Kilkee, Loop Head Lighthouse is 30 minutes farther south on the R487 road.

Limerick City

Limerick City might not be the first urban destination you think of, but its location near Shannon Airport makes it a gateway to the Wild Atlantic Way and a natural stopping-off point for driving the route.

The River Shannon meets the Atlantic Ocean at this strategic point, and settlements have existed since the days of the Vikings, when they established it as a busy trading port. During the Norman period Limerick gained the name "The Treaty City" when a treaty was signed to give Catholics rights, but it was soon broken. The layers to Limerick's history can be seen on a stroll past medieval landmarks like King John's Castle and the Georgian buildings surrounding People's Park. At Thomond Park, the character and pride of Limerick feels strongest when the Munster rugby team takes to the field.

The atmosphere is arty and creative, with galleries like the Hunt Museum and the local art university producing artists. This creative, sometimes off-beat personality appears in local coffee houses, restaurants, and shops.

ORIENTATION

The **River Shannon** divides the city into distinct areas, with most attractions on the east side. The medieval heart of the city is on **King's Island,** with the River Shannon to the west and the River Abbey to the east. This is where you'll find King John's Castle and Treaty City Brewery. Crossing the **River Abbey,** the city opens into the bustling **Newtown Pery** area, Limerick's primary

retail district, where shopping streets and the lively Milk Market attract crowds. Walk farther south to the **Georgian Quarter,** centered around **Pery Square,** where wide boulevards and elegant townhouses show the city's 18th-century architectural heritage.

West of the River Shannon is **Thomond Park,** home of the Munster Rugby Club. Continue west to the outskirts of Limerick City to **Bunratty Castle & Folk Park,** a 15th-century castle surrounded by a living history village.

SIGHTS

Medieval Quarter and King's Island

★ King John's Castle

Nicholas St.; tel. 61/370-501; www.kingjohnscastle.com; daily 9:30am-5pm; €15

I wonder how many castles have been named for people who never visited them? In Limerick's Medieval Quarter, built on the banks of the River Shannon in the early 13th century, during the Norman period,

1: King John's Castle **2:** the Hunt Museum

1

2

this military stronghold offers intriguing insights. King John of England's interests in Ireland lay elsewhere, but he wasn't the first person to appreciate the strategic benefits of this site; the Vikings had built longhouses 400 years earlier. The castle was a stronghold for the Jacobites, loyal to King James II, during the Siege of Limerick in 1691. It was renovated in 2013 with touch screens and 3-D exhibits, bringing a modern feel to the storied treasures and jewels on display. Explore the castle and its towers, and make sure to wander the large courtyard and try your hand at the medieval games like archery and horseshoes. There's a gift shop and a small café for hot drinks and light refreshments.

Newtown Pery

The Hunt Museum

Rutland St.; tel. 61/312-833; www.huntmuseum.com; Thurs.-Sat. 10am-5pm, Sun. 11am-5pm; €13

The Hunt Museum is an astounding personal collection of works amassed by husband and wife John Hunt and Gertrude Hartmann since the 1930s, on display here since 1996. The permanent collection covers 10,000 years of history, culture, and life across Irish and international arts. Some highlights include works by Pablo Picasso, Pierre Auguste Renoir, Roderic O'Conor, and Jack B. Yeats. Temporary exhibitions often cover contemporary art, fashion, and digital art. Outside is a sculpture garden on the riverbank, and there's a small café.

Georgian Quarter

Limerick City Gallery of Art

Carnegie Bldg., Pery Square; tel. 61/310-633; www.limerick.ie/gallery; Mon.-Sat. 10am-5pm, Sun. noon-5pm; free

See Limerick's love for art in the Limerick City Gallery of Art inside the Carnegie Building. Opened in the 1930s, it has been an important fixture in the Irish art scene since, with a diverse collection of Irish art from notable figures like Jack B. Yeats and Seán Keating. Contemporary art is exhibited as well.

Limerick City Outskirts

Bunratty Castle & Folk Park

Bunratty; tel. 61/711-222; www.bunrattycastle.ie; daily 9am-5:30pm; €10

This historical landmark, 20 minutes west of the city, is well known for its authentic and painstaking restoration, offering a glimpse into the harshness of life in the 1400s when it was built. Large towers protected inhabitants from the frequent attacks, and actors describe farming the land and what it took to survive in medieval Ireland.

Inside, things are more regal. An impressive collection of furniture, tapestries, and art from the 15th-16th centuries showcases what life was like for the upper classes, particularly in the Great Hall, where the nobility are celebrated. You can reserve the Medieval Banquet (€72) to feast on a four-course meal and drink Bunratty mead.

ACTIVITIES AND RECREATION

Parks

People's Park

Prior's-Land; tel. 61/556-000; www.limerick.ie; daily 8am-9pm; free

Flanked by beautiful Georgian buildings, People's Park is a fine example of Victorian landscape architecture thanks to its formal plantings, bandstand, and manicured lawns. First opened in 1877 for the residents of Pery Square, the park is now busy with locals walking their dogs, hurling, and relaxing in the well-kept surroundings. There's a playground for little ones as well as **Zest Café** and the **Limerick City Gallery of Art** at the northern entrance.

Hiking and Walking

The Three Bridges

Distance: *3.6 km (2.2 mi) loop*
Duration: *45 minutes*
Elevation gain: *Negligible*
Effort: *Easy*
Trailhead: *Arthur's Quay Park*

This leisurely urban walk is a fantastic way to

The River Shannon

the River Shannon

Ireland's longest, the River Shannon flows 360 km (225 mi) from the Shannon Pot in north County Cavan, through 11 counties and three large lakes, to the Atlantic Ocean in Limerick City. It's popular for boating holidays, where people cruise down the river in comfortable boats that are easy to maneuver. Numerous places rent boats along the Shannon, but major suppliers **Carrickcraft** (www.carrickcraft.com) and **Emerald Star** (www.emeraldstar.ie) have prices starting at €749 for 3 nights. Known as cruisers, the boats are slow-moving and easy to pilot—no license is required.

Four main journeys take 1-2 days:

CARRICK-ON-SHANNON TO LOUGH KEY

This trip is popular, as Carrick-on-Shannon is the northernmost hub on the river, with plenty of pubs and restaurants. The route slowly winds toward Lough Key Forest Park. Dock your boat at the park's marina to walk in the forest, where you can also zip-line through the treetops.

ATHLONE TO CLONMACNOISE

History lovers will find the supposedly oldest pub on the planet, **Sean's Bar** (13 Main St., Athlone; 90/649-2358; www.seansbar.ie; Mon.-Tues. and Thurs.-Sat. 10:30am-12:30am, Wed. 10:30am-11:30pm, Sun. 12:30pm-11:30pm), as well as a historic monastic site a short sail south at Clonmacnoise. Early Christian monks built round towers, high crosses, and churches by the water.

THE LOUGH REE LOOP

Known for calm water and rich history, Lough Ree is a tranquil spot that's surrounded by small villages perfect to stop and explore, like Lanesborough and the larger town of Athlone. This leg is manageable for first-time sailors, as there are no river sections to navigate.

LOUGH DERG TO LIMERICK VIA KILLALOE

At the end of the river, combine rural views with a mini city break. This route from tranquil Lough Derg to bustling Limerick gives insight into High King Brian Boru in Killaloe before arriving in the city. Start in the north at Portumna or in the south at Killaloe.

get your bearings and see a number of sights. The route can be walked in either direction, but counterclockwise you'll get the best views of King John's Castle across the river. The walk is on footpaths and pedestrianized areas, so it's family-friendly. For a longer day, use this route to visit the Hunt Museum and Treaty Stone, where the treaty that ended the Siege of Limerick was signed, giving Catholics protections and rights. Afterward, pop into the Curragower for a bite. You'll arrive back at Arthur Quay's Park with a deeper understanding of the Treaty City.

Spectator Sports

Thomond Park

Cratloe Rd.; tel. 61/421-100; http://thomondpark.ie; €10

Thomond Park is a cathedral dedicated to **Munster rugby.** In this region it has long been the most popular sport, with legendary players like Ronan O'Gara, Anthony Foley, and Paul O'Connell leading to European Cup glory. The season runs August-May, and tickets can be bought online in advance for the 25,600-seat home stadium. On days with no match, tours take you into the dressing rooms and onto the pitch.

FESTIVALS AND EVENTS

Riverfest

www.limerick.ie/riverfest; May

Riverfest is a celebration of the River Shannon with fun events for all ages. Running over the May holiday weekend (1st Monday in May) you'll find dragon boat races, zip lines across the river, and a carnival-style parade with large sculptures and artworks. There's lots of food, with the national barbecue competition, and when you've eaten your fill, pop over to the big wheel for skyline views of the river and the city. Most activities have fees, but some are free. It's hard to find a more unique festival in Ireland.

SHOPPING

Newtown Pery

O'Connell Street is the busiest shopping street in Limerick; expect big chains covering fashion, groceries, and other necessities.

O'Mahony's

120 O'Connell St.; tel. 61/418-155; www.omahonys.ie; Mon.-Sat. 9:30am-5:30pm

O'Mahony's is a large modern bookshop in the city center with more than 75 categories across three floors, including local interest, engineering, and gardening alongside popular fiction and nonfiction. O'Mahony's is Ireland's largest independent bookshop, with six locations and 120 years of experience. Check their social media for visits by authors on book tours.

The Milk Market

Cornmarket Row; tel. 61/214-782; www.milkmarketlimerick.ie; Fri. and Sun. 11am-3pm, Sat. 8am-3pm

While Cork City has the English Market as its home for food, Limerick City has the Milk Market. It was built in 1852 to centralize sellers and was so successful that it continues today. The market is under a weatherproof shelter that creates a buzz with traders selling goods and produce. Friday and Sunday have an outdoor café, while Saturday has a farmers market and street food. Expect local breads, sweet treats, and vegetables. Regular monthly fairs happen Sunday, dedicated to record sales, antiques, or art.

FOOD

Medieval Quarter and King's Island

The Curragower

Clancy's Strand; tel. 87/701-4723; www.curragower.com; Sun.-Thurs. noon-11:30pm, Fri.-Sat. noon-12:30am; from €18

Old-school pub in front, chic restaurant in back—the Curragower feels like two distinct places on the western bank of the River Shannon. Step inside the compact traditional pub with a worn wooden bar and wooden walls around low seating with people chatting. Walk through the rear of the pub into a large, chic, bright dining room in a glass veranda, called the Glass Room, with space for 100. The white-tiled floor and glossy white tables give the space a modern feel and lifts the mood even on a dull day. The menu straddles modern Irish and international with a strong focus on seafood; my pick is the chicken and waffles elevated with fresh chilies. My tip: Reserve for dinner in the Glass Room by the window and take in views of the river and King John's Castle while you dine, then have a drink in the pub section afterward.

Newtown Pery

The SpitJack

6/7 Bedford Row; tel. 61/781-996; http://thespitjack.com; Thurs.-Fri. 9:30am-8pm, Sat. 9am-9pm, Sun. 10am-8pm; from €20

Serving food morning until evening, the SpitJack is a good choice for the hungry any time of day. The restaurant has two large open areas with a modern feel thanks to the open kitchen and cocktail bar. Seven menus have a safe but pleasing choice of dishes. For breakfast are six types of eggs Benedict; the brunch highlight is huevos rancheros; the West Cork rotisserie chicken is the pick for dinner; and for vegans, the linguine verde with asparagus, peas, and baby spinach. Try the house special cocktail Bramble at 34, made with Brockman's gin, homemade lemon and lime cordial, fresh lemon, and blackberry.

Dasco Deli

2 High St.; tel. 61/599-197; Instagram @dascodeli; Thurs.-Sat. 10am-5pm; from €10

Filipino food and culture are in Limerick City at Dasco Deli, a small busy spot near the Milk Market. People have embraced the new cuisine, with chicken abodo a top pick. A breakfast menu has traditional Irish items as well. It's impossible to miss the colored treats in the display case, including the purple ube cake. There's seating for 20, and a small grocery section sells Filipino goods.

Georgian Quarter

Rift Coffee

30 Upper Mallow St.; tel. 61/312-657; www.riftcoffee.com; Mon.-Fri. 8am-4:30pm, Sat. 9:30am-4:30pm, Sun. 10am-4:30pm; from €5

Making the most of their location on the edge of the city center, Rift Coffee has space for 35 in booths, bar seating at the windows, and two-seat tables. The coffee is done properly in handleless 240-ml (8-oz) cups and presented in theatrical fashion on a stone board. The food menu is small but with a modern Irish twist on breakfast classics with cornbread,

the Curragower

smokey streaked bacon, and poached eggs topped with feta. A selection of pastries is available to grab and go.

Zest Café

Pery Square; tel. 61/319-449; www.zestfood.ie; Mon.-Sat. 8:30am-5:30pm, Sun. 10:30am-5pm; €10

Grab a coffee and pastry to go from Zest Café and enjoy a stroll around People's Park, just outside. If the weather is poor, there are some seats inside.

BARS AND NIGHTLIFE

Medieval Quarter and King's Island

Treaty City Brewery

24-25 Nicholas St.; tel. 87/140-5560; http://treatycitybrewery.ie; Mon.-Thurs. 8am-11:30pm, Fri. 8am-12:30am, Sat. 10am-12:30am, Sun. noon-11pm

This alternative and eclectic brewery is a cult hit right beside King John's Castle. It opens at 8am to serve coffee, pastries, and cheese toasties instead of beer. Later the taps pour Treaty City beer, brewed on-site, and you can join a brewery tour (Tues. and Fri.-Sat.; €23). The music is the Clash, Roxy Music, and the Jam, giving this spot a retro vibe, backed by vintage armchairs surrounding mix-and-match tables. Directly above the bar are five four-seat tables, with an extended seating area open in evenings; alternatively, sit outside at the small tables along the street. Dogs are welcome.

Newtown Pery

Tom Collins' Bar

34 Cecil St.; tel. 61/415-749; Sun.-Thurs. 2pm-11:30pm, Fri. 2pm-12:30am, Sat. 1pm-12:30am

The red and cream traditional exterior of this popular pub stands out in the center of the city. The red theme intensifies inside with the red floor, seats, walls, and ceiling inviting chats with friends. The focus on conversation is furthered by the lack of TVs. The bar has smaller sections at the entrance and opens to the rear with low tables and a covered seating area out back for 25. The drinks on offer aren't extensive but the basics are done well.

Mother Macs

9 High St.; tel. 61/414-900; www.mothermacs.ie; Thurs.-Fri. 1pm-midnight, Sat. 11am-1am, Sun. 12:30pm-11:30pm

This warm and inviting pub is in a landmark corner unit near the Milk Market, where the large windows draw you in. Up front is the buzz of the pub at high tables for groups of four in the middle and low tables for two at the windows. Ten rotating beer taps promote local and national breweries, and the menu is on a chalkboard. For a quieter spot for a chat with your drink, there are semi-private booths to the side of the bar.

The Horse and Hound

1 Mulgrave St.; tel. 61/419-194; Mon.-Thurs. 7:30am-11:30pm, Fri.-Sat. 7:30am-12:30am, Sun. 9am-11pm

Just a stone's throw from Limerick Greyhound Stadium, this aptly named pub is a popular spot for watching sports. Unlike most pubs, it opens early for breakfast and serves food through evening. Expect simple fare like a full Irish breakfast, soup and sandwiches, and bangers and mash. The spacious interior fills on big match days, especially when Munster or Ireland are playing rugby; plan to get here well ahead of kick-off. Overall this is a friendly no-fuss neighborhood pub.

ACCOMMODATIONS

Medieval Quarter and King's Island

Absolute Hotel Limerick

Sir Harry's Mall; tel. 61/463-600; www.absolutehotel.com; €150

This 4-star hotel on King's Island has 99 rooms within easy walking distance of King John's Castle. The modern five-story structure is perched on the River Abbey before it meets the Shannon, offering a strong contrast to the old buildings in the area. Four room types include a family room with a sofa bed plus a double or two singles. Enjoy the riverside setting at **Harry's on the River,** where you can sit outside for a gastropub-style meal. The hake-and-chips, caught nearby in Doonbeg, County Clare, is a standout.

Limerick Strand Hotel

Ennis Rd.; tel. 61/421-800; www.strandhotellimerick.ie; €200

Found on the western shores of the River Shannon, the four-star Limerick Strand has 184 recently refurbished rooms ranging from the Superior to the Presidential, with views over the city. The neighborhood is quiet but within a short walk of King John's Castle and the Hunt Museum. There's a 20-m (66-ft) heated pool, a jetted tub, a sauna, and a steam room as well as the **River Bar & Restaurant,** where the focus is on local artisanal produce.

Georgian Quarter

No. 1 Pery Square

1 Pery Square; tel. 61/402-402; www.oneperysquare.com; €275

This boutique 21-room Michelin Key Award hotel is a slice of historic luxury beside Limerick's Peoples Park. It's all about old-world decadence, with ornate furniture, plush headboards, and gold-framed mirrors in the guest rooms and 2-bedroom suite. Food and drink are at the **Long Room,** with pork belly and steamed mussels served with fine and rare European wines, including picks from Greece and Slovenia. During summer, the outdoor dining area hosts barbecues, and you can reserve afternoon tea indoors.

INFORMATION AND SERVICES

Visitor Information

Limerick City Seasonal Tourist Information

King John's Castle; tel. 1/800-230-330; May-Sept. daily 9:30am-5pm

This seasonal information center is where you'll find free maps and guides as well as help from local experts.

Hospitals

For emergencies, dial 112 or 999. The main hospital in Limerick City is **University Hospital Limerick** (St. Nessan's Rd.; tel. 61/301-111; www.hse.ie).

Post Offices

Four **An Post** (www.anpost.ie) branches are on Lower Cecil Street, Edward Street, William Street, and Mary Street.

Banks and ATMs

There are ATMs from **Bank of Ireland** (www.bankofireland.com), **AIB** (www.aib.ie), and **PTSB** (www.ptsb.ie) throughout the city, with a high concentration on O'Connell Street. Each bank also has a branch on O'Connell Street.

GETTING THERE

Air

Shannon Airport (SNN) is the major international airport on the west coast, 30 minutes west of Limerick City in County Clare. It has direct flights to the United States and Europe with British Airways, Aer Lingus, Delta, United, and Ryanair. To get to the city, take the Route 343 bus from Bus Éireann or Routes 13 or 14 with Expressway (from €6 one-way). Buses run every 30-60 minutes.

Car

From Dublin, take the M7 motorway, a drive of 200 km (125 mi) and 2.5 hours. This is a toll road, with a toll plaza in Portlaoise (€2.30). From Galway City, the best route is the M18 and N18, both toll-free. The 105-km (65-mi) drive takes 1.75 hours.

From the Cliffs of Moher, head southeast toward Lisdoonvarna and continue on the N67, following signs for Ennistimon and Lahinch. From Lahinch, stay on the N67, passing through Ennis, where you merge onto the M18 motorway. Follow the M18 south to junction 1, where you merge onto the N18 to Limerick City. This drive is 80 km (50 mi) and takes 90 minutes.

Train

Most of the 64 daily trains from Dublin's Heuston Station to Limerick's **Colbert Station** (3 hours; from €4.80 one-way) require a change at **Limerick Junction.** Direct trains run from Galway's Ceannt Train

Station to Limerick's Colbert Station (2 hours; €20 round-trip).

Bus

Citylink (www.citylink.ie) runs the Route 712X bus from Dublin Airport to Limerick City (2.5 hours; €30 one-way) 10 times daily. The drop-off in Limerick is **Arthur's Quay.** For buses from the city, Route 300 goes from Dublin's Eden Quay to Arthur's Quay (3 hours; €17 one-way). Departures are every 30 minutes during peak times.

From Galway, Citylink buses depart from Galway Coach Station to **Henry Street** in Limerick (1.5 hours; €11 one-way). Expressway buses depart Ceannt Station in Galway and arrive at **Limerick Bus Station.**

There are no direct buses to Limerick from the Cliffs of Moher, but it is possible to go by bus to Ennis and change for Limerick. Routes and timings depend on the time of day and the day of the week.

GETTING AROUND

On Foot

Like most cities in Ireland, Limerick is very walkable, with the main shopping areas around O'Connell Street having wide footpaths for pedestrians. It's easy to walk between the main sights, shops, and restaurants in a few minutes.

Public Transport

Limerick City has a local bus network of 10 routes to residential areas outside the city rather than in the city. The most useful buses for visitors are Routes 302, 303, and 313, which run to Thomond Park.

Cycling

TFI Bikes (www.bikeshare.ie) rents 215 bikes from 23 stations across the city. Choose an annual subscription (€10) or a 3-day pass (€3), with rental rates of €0.50 per hour.

Car

Limerick is walkable, but to visit sights outside the city, the roads are good and not busy outside peak times.

Taxi

Limerick City taxis can be hailed on the street. You can also book a taxi through apps like **FreeNow** (www.free-now.com) and **Bolt** (www.bolt.eu). To get a fare estimate before your journey, visit the **Transport for Ireland** website (www.transportforireland.ie).

Galway and Mayo

On the rugged shores of Galway and Mayo, the harsh beauty and warm welcome of the west of Ireland are unavoidable. Prepare for a city break that will make you see Irish food in a whole new light, and endless adventures outdoors on bikes, boats, and trails. Some say that the west is the best, and after a few days here you'll see why.

In Galway City, known for its bohemian vibe, you'll find music pouring out of pubs, street performers entertaining visitors, and vibrant festivals like the Galway International Arts Festival and the Galway Races that showcase the town's lively spirit. The university gives the city a youthful and contemporary feel, refreshed every year with new arrivals and new ideas. Connemara begins at the edge of the city and contrasts city life with wide-open spaces, tiny villages, and herds

Highlights

Look for ★ to find recommended sights, activities, dining, and lodging.

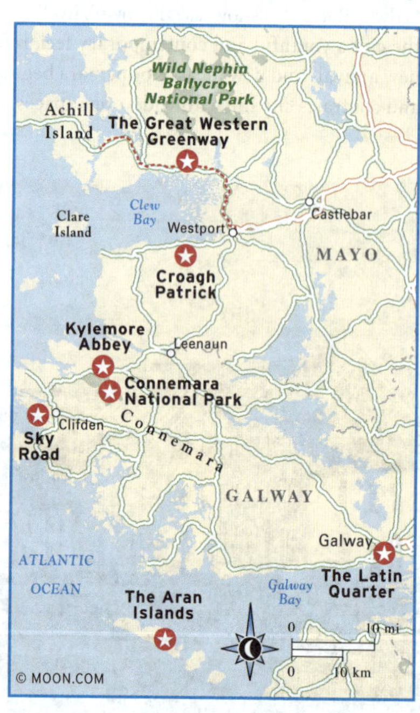

★ **The Latin Quarter:** Feel the buzz of Galway City in this legendary area, filled with buskers and some of the country's favorite pubs (page 305).

★ **The Aran Islands:** Sail back to a forgotten time on these beautiful rugged islands, where Irish is spoken, ancient structures still stand, and life is dictated by the sea (page 318).

★ **Sky Road:** Drive this incredible route to see the stunning coast and mountains that surround Clifden. You can also cycle the Sky Road (page 327).

★ **Connemara National Park:** Discover the beauty of emptiness and escape from it all in this incredible park, where nature is the dominant force (page 329).

★ **Kylemore Abbey:** Like an oasis in the desert, Kylemore Abbey springs from the Connemara wilderness with opulent buildings, Victorian gardens, and chocolate-making nuns (page 331).

★ **Croagh Patrick:** Climb Ireland's holiest mountain and join the pilgrimage to the church at the summit for outstanding views of Clew Bay (page 334).

★ **The Great Western Greenway:** Cycle from Westport to Ireland's largest island with the whole family on this car-free route that takes in views of Clew Bay and the Nephin Beg Mountains (page 335).

Galway and Mayo

of sheep rambling on the roads. These postcard scenes are part of daily life, and while you'd want to be hardy to live and work here, when people meet in pubs and cafés, they're gentle and interested in knowing where you've come from.

This landscape continues north into County Mayo to Westport and Achill Island, which feel like shelters from the power of the nature that surrounds them. The iconic Croagh Patrick stands behind Westport and looks over Clare Island, Achill Island, and the hundreds of uninhabited islands of Clew Bay. Old meets new here, and it's easy to go from sipping a flat white in a trendy coffee shop to touching a tomb that's thousands of years old on a hiking trail. Visit Galway and Mayo and see if it rings true for you.

ORIENTATION

The west coast of Ireland is remote, with huge expanses of tranquil nothingness between the major towns and hubs. This region is anchored by **Galway City** in County Galway in the south and **Westport** in County Mayo in the north. Outside these points, you get into the wilderness.

The **Aran Islands** are southwest of Galway City in the Atlantic; **Connemara** and its **national park** are west of Galway City in the region that runs north toward Westport. Westport is on **Clew Bay** and you can continue west toward **Achill Island.** Marking the entrance to Clew Bay is **Clare Island.**

PLANNING YOUR TIME

This part of Ireland has many layers. The lively city has an incredible food and pub scene that foodies could easily spend three days enjoying. On the other end of the spectrum is spectacular wilderness to immerse yourself in for several days. Staying in Galway City for at least two days allows you to try the best restaurants and escape to the Aran Islands on a day trip. Connemara deserves at least an overnight stay even if you're not outdoorsy. Waking up here is a treat. Base yourself in Westport for two nights, with day trips to Achill Island or Clare Island.

While the distances between destinations in this region may seem small, the roads are often narrow and winding, so expect to drive at slower speeds.

Itinerary Ideas

With Galway City such a foodie destination, restaurant reservations can be hard to find last-minute during peak seasons, so plan ahead. The same goes for lodging in the entire region.

DAY 1: GALWAY CITY

1 Grab a morning coffee at **Coffeewerk + Press.**

2 Stroll down to the **Spanish Arch** for beautiful views across the River Corrib and out to Galway Bay.

3 Walk across the street to the **Galway City Museum** and get a deeper understanding of the history and people of Galway City with the free exhibits.

4 Visit **The Dough Bros** for lunch and see why experts think their pizzas are among the best in the world. The Pep Guardijala is a must if you like spicy food.

Previous: Galway City; Connemara National Park; Kylemore Abbey.

Itinerary Ideas

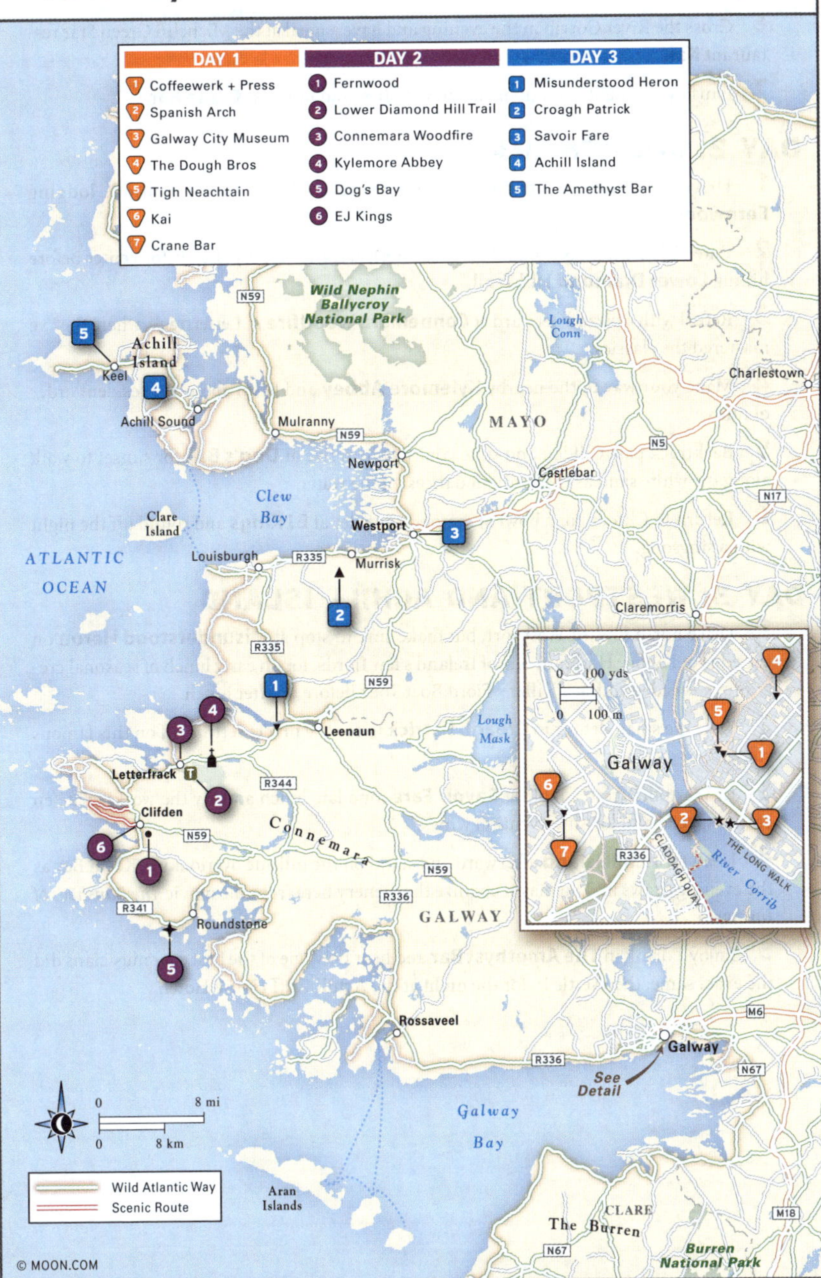

5 Wander through the Latin Quarter to hear the buskers on the streets and stop into **Tigh Neachtain** for a drink in this famous pub.

6 Cross the River Corrib in the evening and have a meal at the Michelin Green Star restaurant **Kai.**

7 Finish your night a few doors down with live trad music at **Crane Bar.**

DAY 2: CONNEMARA

1 Drive to Clifden, the capital of Connemara, and stay in the boutique lodging **Fernwood.**

2 Enter Connemara National Park in Letterfrack and stop by the visitor center before hiking **Lower Diamond Hill Trail.**

3 Refuel with a pizza afterward at **Connemara Woodfire** in Letterfrack, where they've mastered the classics.

4 Make your way to the nearby **Kylemore Abbey** and learn about the resident order of nuns.

5 Backtrack past Clifden and time your day to arrive at **Dog's Bay** for sunset to walk along the white sand as the sunlight dances on the water.

6 Return to Clifden for a bowl of seafood chowder at **EJ Kings** and round off the night with a singsong.

DAY 3: WESTPORT AND ACHILL ISLAND

1 Drive north toward Westport, but make sure to stop at **Misunderstood Heron** on the edge of Killary Harbour, one of Ireland's few fjords, for an early lunch of seasonal creations. Consider taking a Killary Fjord Boat Tour before or after lunch.

2 Take the small detour to **Croagh Patrick** to see the hikers setting off on this famous route.

3 In Westport, grab a table at **Savoir Fare** for a late lunch and try the weekly pâté en croûte special and low-intervention wines.

4 Head for **Achill Island** afterward and stand on the hillside overlooking Keem Bay as the evening draws in. You may recognize the scenery here from the movie *The Banshees of Inisherin*.

5 Enjoy a drink in **The Amethyst Bar** and hear how one of the best ever musicians did the exact same, then settle in for the night at the Achill Cliff House Hotel.

Galway City

Galway City feels like a meeting of the rivers. A steady stream of visitors and students flows over a bedrock of long-term locals known for slightly alternative lifestyles. The streets are lined with independent businesses rather than multinational chains, and unlike places with businesses purely for tourists, there's a feeling that Galway is an authentic, lived-in city. The arts are part of Galway City's identity. Buskers play on the pedestrianized streets lined with pubs flying flags and covered in colorful hanging baskets. With festival season in summer, the place buzzes with energy, celebration, and craic. Though Galway is a city, it feels more like a big town as you go from famous landmarks to quiet residential streets in just a few steps. If you're deciding between cities in Ireland, Galway is the hipster's pick, but not in a pretentious way. It just does things the way it sees fit and often results in something special.

ORIENTATION

Galway is a small city and easy to navigate on foot. The **River Corrib** splits the city, and the eastern side is where visitors spend most of their time, with the **city center** marked by **Eyre Square.** West from the square toward the river is the thick of the action in the **Latin Quarter,** defined by the pedestrianized Shop Street, High Street, and Quay Street, among others. Crossing the river, near the **Spanish Arch,** is the **West End** and **Eglinton Canal.** The area is more peaceful and has a reputation for amazing restaurants and old-school pubs. South of here is the residential area known as the **Claddagh,** which lends its name to the famous ring, and west along the coast 15 minutes is the affluent seaside suburb of **Salthill.** To the east of the city is the suburb of **Mervue,** and 5 km (3 mi) north of the city is **Menlo Castle.**

SIGHTS

City Center

Eyre Square

Eyre Square; tel. 353/91-536-400; www.galwaycity.ie/public-parks

This spacious public square, named after the 19th-century politician Edward Eyre, is a busy park where people come to meet and relax. The large copper-colored sculpture honors the Galway hooker boats that sailed Galway Bay; the metal uprights represent the boat's sails. Footpaths crisscross the square, making it feel lively throughout the day. Around the square are plenty of shops and pubs, with O'Connell's Pub one of the more popular. Eyre Square is a key venue during the Galway International Arts Festival, when the square is reimagined by artists into something spectacular.

★ The Latin Quarter

High St.; www.thelatinquarter.ie

It's hard to miss the Latin Quarter; it's the social hub of the city center that covers a largely pedestrianized area bounded by the **Spanish Arch, O'Brien's Bridge, St. Nicholas' Church,** and **Middle Street.** It's packed with coffee shops, restaurants, and pubs, many housed in medieval buildings, such as Ard Bia at Nimmos near the Spanish Arch. The name Latin Quarter implies historical importance, but it was named only recently. Before 2004 it was called the Left Bank. A good way to experience this part of Galway is walking down busy Shop Street from Eyre Square to the Spanish Arch, which looks over the Claddagh, and then returning via Middle Street. Give yourself time to stop for food and a drink along the way.

The Spanish Arch

2 The Long Walk

The Spanish Arch is a famous meeting place, and on a sunny day you'll see the area thronged with people relaxing well into the

Galway City

evening. The arch was built in 1584 as the entrance to the city, which was once walled. This section was built to protect the boats at the quay. Nowadays, the area is popular for views of the Claddagh across the water and with visitors to the nearby Galway City Museum.

St. Nicholas' Church

Lombard St.; tel. 353/89-489-8084; https://stnicholas.ie; Tues.-Fri. 10am-5:30pm

St. Nicholas' Collegiate Church was founded way back in 1320 and is the largest medieval parish church in continuous use. Named after the patron saint of seafarers, Saint Nicholas of Myra, it has a unique three-roofed profile and carvings of mythical creatures. Learn about the history, including the Crusader's grave and a 400-year-old baptismal font. The church hosts concerts (free-€10) on weekends. Guided tours are available, with the bell-ringing experience a memorable choice.

Galway City Museum

Spanish Parade; tel. 353/91-532-460; www.galwaycitymuseum.ie; Tues.-Sat. 10am-5pm, Sun. noon-5pm; free

The Galway City Museum is a great first stop to get an understanding of the city on three floors of archaeology, history, and science. The ground floor covers the ancient history of County Galway and when the city was established by the O'Connors in 1124. The next level has a replica of a Galway hooker, a 19th-century fishing boat. The history exhibits cover Galway's role in the fight for independence and contain personal items from soldiers involved. On the top floor are temporary science exhibits on topics like marine biology and human physiology. A small space outside the building is for art exhibits. Tours run throughout the day.

West End

Galway Cathedral

Gaol Rd.; tel. 353/91-563-577; www.galwaycathedral.ie; Tues.-Sun. 8:30am-6:30pm, Mon. 8:30am-9pm; free

Galway Cathedral, completed in 1965, is the youngest great stone cathedral in Europe, built on the site of the old city jail. Its architecture blends Renaissance, Romanesque, and Gothic influences. The centerpiece is the enormous octagonal dome that rises 44 m (145 ft), a landmark of Galway's skyline, supported by eight pillars adorned with mosaics of the Beatitudes. Admire the rose windows, coffered wooden ceiling, marble floors, and notable artworks like the intricate statue of the Virgin Mary and a striking Crucifixion mosaic. Visitors are welcome, but be respectful if mass is being held, often on weekend mornings.

University of Galway

University Rd.; tel. 353/91-524-411; www.universityofgalway.ie

The historic University of Galway, founded in 1845, is along the River Corrib and well-known for its iconic Quadrangle building in Tudor Gothic style. Explore the beautiful campus, ranked among Europe's most picturesque thanks to the open green spaces and mature trees. Guided campus tours are available on Saturday (reservation required). Visit the **James Mitchell Geology Museum** in the Quadrangle to view fascinating fossil and mineral collections, and follow the University Trail to discover the modern architecture and sculptures.

Salthill

Blackrock Diving Tower

Salthill Promenade; daily dawn-dusk; free

The Blackrock Diving Tower epitomizes the suburb of Salthill; it's fun, social, and connected to nature. This iconic seaside landmark is a hub for taking a dip in the ocean, and the tower has three diving boards at 1, 3, and 10 m (3, 10, and 33 ft) to add a dash of adrenaline. The tower was built in 1885, demolished in the 1950s, and replaced with the current structure, with changing rooms, showers, and toilets. The water can be very cold, even in summer under 10°C (50°F), so be prepared! If you'd rather stay warm and dry, visit just before sunset for a picturesque and classic Galway scene.

ACTIVITIES AND RECREATION

Hiking and Walking

The Long Walk

Distance: *0.3 km (0.2 mi) one-way*
Duration: *10 minutes*
Elevation gain: *Negligible*
Effort: *Easy*
Trailhead: *The Spanish Arch*

This may just be the shortest walk in the book, but it's worthwhile to get an understanding of Galway City's seaside setting and can easily be linked to other sights. The Long Walk is anything but long at 314 m (1,030 ft). From near the Spanish Arch it leads toward the sea past a row of colorful photogenic houses. A stroll through the Latin Quarter and continuing to Galway Cathedral will add 1 km (0.6 mi) to the route.

Salthill Promenade

Distance: *3.2 km (2 mi) one-way*
Duration: *1.5 hours round-trip*
Elevation gain: *Negligible*
Effort: *Easy*
Trailhead: *Claddagh Quay*

One of the many joys of Galway City is how easy it easy to get from the city into nature. The Salthill Promenade runs from Claddagh Quay to the Blackrock Diving Tower in Salthill, west of the city. The walk has plenty of stopping-off points, like **Coco Café** and **Jungle Beach Break Café,** for coffee or lunch. Enjoy it at a leisurely pace; benches along the seafront offer wonderful views across Galway Bay. Follow the local tradition when you reach the end of the Salthill Promenade by kicking the wall and turning back toward the city.

Cycling

Galway City Canal and River Corrib Trail

Distance: *4.5 km (2.8 mi) round-trip*
Duration: *45 minutes*
Elevation gain: *Negligible*
Effort: *Easy*
Trailhead: *Claddagh Quay*

This gentle cycle from the city takes in great views of the River Corrib and gives a glimpse into everyday life in the city. Starting at the Claddagh, pedal north to Eglinton Canal and the mini waterfall. The route continues up through the University of Galway, where it's worth making a pit stop to see the Quadrangle, based on the University of Oxford's Christ Church. Continuing on a gravel path, you traverse wooded areas and get views across the river to Menlo Castle, slowly being reclaimed by nature. Before heading back, take a detour to **Dangan House Nurseries** (Dangan House; tel. 353/91-524-716; https://galwaygardencentre.ie; Mon.-Sat. 9am-6pm; €5) for a coffee and a treat at the tearooms.

West Cycling Ireland

Fairhill Rd., Claddagh; tel. 353/87-176-8480; https://westirelandcycling.com; daily 9:30am-6pm; from €20

West Cycling Ireland has an extensive fleet of rentals, including city runarounds, e-bikes, and carbon bikepacking bikes. There's also a host of equipment for any type of biking holiday. There are panniers for your gear, bike racks for cars, luggage trailers, child seats, and child trailers. To see the best of Galway by bike, guided and self-guided tours are available.

ENTERTAINMENT AND EVENTS

Performing Arts

Galway Arts Centre

47 Dominick St. Lower; tel. 353/91-565-886; www.galwayartscentre.ie; Mon.-Fri. 10am-5pm, Sat. 10am-1pm and 2pm-5pm

The Galway Arts Centre is one of the main institutions behind Galway's thriving arts scene. One venue is on Dominick Street, with the reception area and art galleries, and the other is the main performance space, on Nun's Island, a short walk away. Exhibitions on Dominick Street see visual artists display their work during residencies, and entry is free. At the Nun's Island Theatre, with seating for 82 inside an old Presbyterian church, performing arts (from €10) span theater, dance, film, and more.

Druid's Theatre

Flood St.; tel. 353/91-568-660; www.druid.ie; Mon.-Fri. 9:30am-5:30pm; from €20

The mission of the touring theater company Druid's Theatre is to take Irish performance to the rest of the world. Anchored here, ambitious new projects and re-created classic pieces keep Irish and Galwegian values central. They perform regularly at the Mick Lally Theatre on Flood Street, with bigger productions in Dublin as well.

1: the Latin Quarter **2:** the Spanish Arch
3: St. Nicholas' Church

1

2

3

1

2

Live Music

Róisin Dubh

8 Dominick St. Upper; www.roisindubh.net; daily 6pm-2am; from €5

Music is part of life in the west of Ireland, but it's not all traditional Irish music. The home for rock, indie, and alternative music in the city is definitely Róisin Dubh, where you'll find bands like Two Door Cinema Club, Franz Ferdinand, and The xx before they make it to the festival circuit. The venue is also a hot spot for comedy, with names like Dylan Moran, Tommy Tiernan, and Dara Ó'Briain. The venue's capacity is 150 with a small amount of unreserved seating available.

Festivals and Events

Galway International Arts Festival

www.giaf.ie; July

For two weeks in summer, the Galway International Arts Festival turns the city into Ireland's most exciting cultural location with a mix of theater, music, visual arts, and street performances. Talent from around the world fills venues across the city and includes public street performances. Key venues are the **Galway City Museum** and the iconic pop-up **Spiegeltent.** Plan ahead for this popular event, and book lodging and tickets as early as possible.

Galway Races

Ballybrit Race Track; tel. 353/91-700-100; www.galwayraces.com; late July-early Aug.

Ireland punches well above its weight in horse racing, and some of the greatest horses, jockeys, and trainers come from these shores. The Galway Races is where they all want to win. People put on their Sunday best and head to the Ballybrit Race Track for an exciting seven days of flat and jump racing. There's entertainment in the stands too, particularly on the Thursday that is Ladies Day, when the races feel more like a fashion show. Betting is allowed, and even if you don't fancy a flutter, you'll be impressed by the bookies shouting their odds out across the crowd. Tickets are available for individual days or the full week, but like most events in Galway, these sell out quickly, so plan ahead.

1: the River Corrib in Galway City **2:** Salthill Promenade with the diving tower

Galway International Oyster and Seafood Festival

tel. 353/91-394-637; www.galwayoysterfestival.com; last weekend of Sept.

The Galway International Oyster and Seafood Festival is the world's longest-running oyster festival and one of Ireland's most internationally recognized events. Since it began in 1954, the festival has drawn huge crowds of seafood lovers. Events run all weekend, but the highlight is the World Oyster Opening Championship, where the world's fastest shuckers compete. The festival is centered around the Long Walk, the Spanish Arch, and Claddagh, with the main events in a large festival tent.

SHOPPING

City Center

Brown Thomas

1-29 William St.; tel. 353/91-565-254; www.brownthomas.com; Mon.-Fri. 10am-7pm, Sat. 9am-7pm, Sun. 11am-6pm

Just steps outside the Latin Quarter's northern edge is Brown Thomas, a luxury department store where you'll find the biggest names of men's and women's wear and cosmetics.

Booley

Eglinton St.; tel. 353/91-562-869; http://booley.ie; Mon.-Fri. 9:30am-7pm, Sat. 9am-6pm, Sun. noon-6pm

Booley is a newcomer to the Irish outdoors scene, with some of the best outdoors brands, including Arc'teryx, Yeti, and Rab, plus plenty more premium options. Hiking is the main activity catered for, with rain jackets, base layers, and insulated coats, but there's also clothing and equipment for surfers and skiers. Check out the sale section upstairs.

The Latin Quarter

As you wander the Latin Quarter, you'll

notice a lack of chain shops and restaurants. The locals prefer to shop and dine with independent businesses, and this ethos results in interesting shops for unique gifts and mementos. The famous Claddagh ring comes from the Claddagh part of Galway, and you'll find local jewelry makers like the **Claddagh Jewelers** (25 Mainguard St.; tel. 353/91-534-494; www.thecladdagh.com; Tues.-Sat. 10am-5:30pm, Sun.-Mon. 1:30pm-5:30pm) selling them. For homewares and clothing with an Irish spin, make your way to **Designs of Ireland** (2 Cross St. Lower; tel. 353/91-539-790; www.designsofireland.ie; Mon.-Sat. 10am-6pm, Sun. 11am-6pm) and **Kilkenny Shop** (6 High St.; tel. 353/91-566-110; https://kilkennydesign.com; Mon.-Fri. 10am-5pm, Sat. 10am-5:30pm).

Charlie Byrne's Bookshop

The Cornstore, Middle St.; tel. 353/91-561-766; http://charliebyrne.ie; Mon.-Sat. 9am-6pm, Fri. 9am-8pm, Sun. noon-6pm

Charlie Byrne's Bookshop is perfect for bookworms who want a personal and immersive experience while shopping for the next great read. The only way to describe this shop is as a sprawling obsession of books, old and new, that's so overpowering it fills floor-to-ceiling shelves in seven rooms and spills onto shelves on the exterior of the shop. There's a strong focus on history, fiction, Irish books, and children's books. The helpful staff even have hand-drawn maps at the counter to help you explore.

Kindf_olk

Unit 10, The Cornstore, Middle St.; tel. 353/91-865-847; https://kindfolkgalway.ie; Mon.-Fri. 10am-6pm, Sat. 9am-6pm, Sun. noon-5pm

Kindf_olk is a lifestyle shop in the center of Galway that caters to modern tastes in men's and women's clothing and homewares. Big name brands include Carhartt WIP, Rains, and Portuguese Flannel, and the shop is well stocked with accessories like wooly hats and gloves. The space is bright and airy, and a barista whips up caffeinated drinks as you browse.

River Deep Mountain High

6 Middle St.; tel. 353/91-563-938; http://rdmh.ie; Mon.-Thurs. 10am-6pm, Fri. 10am-7:30pm, Sat. 10am-6pm, Sun. 1:30pm-5:30pm

Before hiking became mainstream, it was an activity for hardy self-reliant folk. River Deep Mountain High is a favorite for these hikers, as that's what the owners do in their spare time. The gear is all about comfort and survival. But that's not to say that beginners aren't welcome; you'll get brilliant tips on how to start hiking and what local trails might best suit you. Maps on nearby hikes are also available.

Cloon Keen Atelier

21A High St.; tel. 353/91-565-736; www.cloonkeen.com; Mon.-Sat. 10am-6pm, Sun. noon-6pm

This gorgeous perfumery hand-makes all their products and is a guaranteed hit to brighten your day with perfume and scented candles. Fragrances are rooted in Irishness, like Lá Bealtaine, encapsulating spring. Hand lotion and room sprays are also available from this husband-and-wife team.

FOOD

The Latin Quarter

Coffeewerk + Press

4 Quay St.; tel. 353/91-448-667; www.coffeewerkandpress.com; daily 9am-6pm; from €4

Part coffee shop, part design store, Coffeewerk + Press is for coffee purists. The menu is solely coffee, tea, and kombucha, all of which they've perfected. The space is small and tight, and there are no seats downstairs; as you wait for your drink, you can look through the coffee-making paraphernalia and coffee-table books. Take a seat at one of the two-seat tables out front or upstairs in the design store. Seating is informal and very limited, but it's a nice place to sit and look at the artwork.

Cava Bodega

1 Middle St.; tel. 353/91-539-884; www.cavarestaurant.ie; Mon.-Wed. 3pm-10pm, Thurs.-Fri. 3pm-10:30pm, Sat. noon-10:30pm, Sun. noon-9:30pm; from €9

In a city with a landmark called the Spanish Arch, it comes as no surprise that Galway City has some brilliant Spanish cuisine. Cava Bodega is a tapas restaurant on two levels. Upstairs is a compact dining room with a European feel, with legs of jamón hang from the ceiling and seating for 15 cobbled together informally; you have to reserve ahead of time to eat here. Downstairs has room for 30, and it feels more spacious and relaxed. The menu is large, with a range of meat, fish, poultry, and veggies. The fried polenta with Mahón cheese is the pick, but if you need meat, the chorizo in red wine sauce is a close second.

The Dough Bros

Cathedral Bldg., 1 Middle St.; www.thedoughbros.ie; Sun.-Wed. noon-9:30pm, Thurs.-Sat. noon-10pm; from €14

Brothers Ronan and Eugene have garnered a serious following for their Neapolitan pizzas. The menu is a good mix of classics and modern pies like the Can't Banh Mi Love, a take on the Vietnamese dish. Plenty of Irish ingredients include mozzarella made in County Cork. The dining room is informal; order at the counter when you arrive, then sit at the 20 tables in the bright wood-clad dining area. Speed and value make it a top choice for families. The restaurant has been voted the number 15 best pizzeria in the world, and they regularly get recognition from master pizza chefs in Italy.

Rouge

Dominick St.; tel. 353/91-530-681; https://rougegalway.com; Sun.-Tues. 4pm-10:30pm, Sat. 1pm-10:30pm; from €20

Rouge is a charming French restaurant that recreates the Parisian experience with charming decor and warm ambiance. The menu features classic French steak, fish of the day, and vegetarian options, all prepared with high-quality ingredients and traditional techniques. Guests enjoy live piano music while dining, adding to the romantic atmosphere. The restaurant boasts an extensive and exclusive French wine list, with 80 varieties sourced from small vineyards. Reservations are advised, especially for weekend dinner.

Ard Bia at Nimmos

Spanish Arch; tel. 353/91-561-114; www.ardbia.com; Mon. 10am-3pm, Tues.-Sun. 10am-3pm and 6pm-late; from €20

In an old building overlooking the River Corrib by the Spanish Arch, Ard Bia at Nimmos offers a scenic dining experience. Rustic Irish cuisine combines with global influences using locally sourced seasonal ingredients. The eclectic interior features warm wood paneling, soft creamy walls, and aged furniture, creating a cozy atmosphere. Ard Bia serves breakfast, lunch, and dinner, with a popular weekend brunch. The menu changes seasonally, offering creative dishes like buttermilk orange pancakes and innovative dinner options. They also have a carefully curated wine list featuring natural wines.

Rúibín

1 Dock Rd.; tel. 353/91-563-830; www.ruibin.ie; Mon.-Sat. noon-11pm; from €30

On two levels, Rúibín has two different dining experiences. Downstairs feels casual thanks to the bar seating and bar menu, while upstairs is more formal and better suited to celebrating important occasions. Fantastic modern Irish cuisine has influences from abroad, like pan-fried plaice served with nduja butter, braised fennel, roe, and cavolo nero. The cocktail list is inventive, with the usual drinks replaced with creations like the Notorious F.I.G., made with silver tequila, house fig syrup, beetroot, and lime black salt.

West End

John Keogh's Gastropub

22-24 Dominick St. Upper; tel. 353/91-449-431; www.johnkeoghs.ie; Mon.-Thurs. 5pm-11:30pm, Fri. 5pm-midnight, Sat. 3pm-midnight, Sun. 3pm-11:30pm; from €17

Mungo Murphy's Seaweed Co.

seaweed along the Connemara coast

Mungo of **Mungo Murphy's Seaweed** (Keeraunagurk South; tel. 353/85-758-3862; www.mungomurphyseaweed.com) is the most passionate person about seaweed that you're likely to meet. He lives in Connemara and harvests seaweed from the Atlantic to create delicious meals and skin care products. In the shop, you can buy dried seaweed and seasoning made with seaweed; they also sell abalone and sea cucumbers when they can.

TOURS AND TASTINGS

On the tours you can learn about the benefits of seaweed and get insight into how they farm sea creatures.

- **The Connemara Abalone Tasting Tour** (€25 pp): Learn about the abalone, a shelled sea snail that's considered a delicacy thanks to its buttery and salty taste, and see how they raise and farm them.
- **Mungo Murphy's Coastal Walking & Tasting Tour:** Forage along the coast and find seaweed and sea herbs before visiting the abalone farm. Afterward enjoy lunch of seaweed and abalone.

GETTING THERE

Take the R336 road west from Galway City to Inverin, where you pass through An Spidéal and Bearna. The drive is 35 km (22 mi) and takes 45 minutes.

The owners of John Keogh's Gastropub have added fantastic food offerings to a classy traditional pub with rich, warm wooden interiors lit with soft amber lighting that catches the memorabilia on the walls. Rather than reinventing pub grub, they've mastered the cuisine. Highlights include the 6-hour roasted shoulder of lamb, Galway Bay seafood chowder, and locally sourced sirloin steak. The beer taps lean heavily toward Irish breweries, and when the weather gets cold, the bar is a great place to warm up with a hot whiskey.

Kai

22 Sea Rd.; tel. 353/91-526-003; www.kairestaurant.ie; Tues.-Sat. 11am-4pm and 6:15pm-11:30pm; from €28

Chef Jess Murphy moved to Galway from New Zealand in 2003 and has become one of the biggest names in the Irish culinary scene. She is loved for her buzzing personality and sustainable inventive cooking, and a reservation at Kai is one of the most sought-after in Galway. The bright restaurant is relaxed and inviting, with flowers in jugs and jars around the space. On the menu is a tasty choice of seasonal dishes like John Dory with clams and miso hispi, or Roman gnocchi with muhammara and pistachio zhoug. For lunch they serve one course with homemade pastries for walk-ins, but for dinner you need to reserve.

Salthill

Blackrock Cottage

Blackrock House; tel. 353/91-399-280; www.blackrockcottage.ie; Mon. 8am-9pm, Tues.-Wed. 8am-5pm, Thurs.-Sat. 8am-5pm and 6pm-9pm, Sun. 8am-8pm; from €20

This modern restaurant is in a beautiful location along the shore in Salthill and looks over the Atlantic and Galway Bay. It's open for breakfast, brunch, lunch, and dinner with café favorites like lemon and chili avocado on sourdough. In the evening they serve international dishes like Korean chicken poke bowl and plaice Milanese alongside their in-house lager. The building is a restored cottage from the famine era, with exposed stone walls, dark floors, and small windows harking back to that time. On a nice day, try to get a seat outside, where you'll see people jumping off the diving tower.

BARS AND NIGHTLIFE

City Center

Tigh Neachtain

17 Cross St. Upper; tel. 353/91-568-820; www.tighneachtain.com; daily 11am-11pm

From the narrow entrance, Tigh Neachtain unfurls like a warren into one of the finest traditional pubs in the country. Around each corner of the wooden interior are nooks perfect for curling up with a nice drink. If it's sunny, the seating out front sprawls around the perimeter of the pub in a wee sun catch, and it's a good spot for people-watching and listening to buskers. The walls are covered in memorabilia from Galway's art scene and works by local artists. The draft taps are a nice mix of local craft and the usual pub favorites, and there's a bright and airy wine bar upstairs called Kasbah that also serves light bites like bruschetta and cheese boards.

West End

Crane Bar

2 Sea Rd.; tel. 353/91-587-419; www.thecranebar.com; Mon.-Fri. 3pm-11:30pm, Sat. 4pm-11:30pm, Sun. 1pm-11:30pm

The Crane Bar is a bare-bones trad music pub that's equally enjoyable whether quiet or busy. Worn wooden tables and chairs on a slightly uneven floor add to the charm. There's no fuss whatsoever, just a steady flow of regulars chatting with visitors, and the location in the quieter West End makes it feel more like a neighborhood local than a city hot spot. The traditional aspect extends to the drinks on offer; you won't find anybody ordering a cosmopolitan, but plenty of pints of Guinness and Beamish. There's regular live music in the pub with local musicians, and upstairs is a music venue where bigger acts play ticketed events.

ACCOMMODATIONS

City Center

Kinlay Hostel

Merchants Rd., Eyre Square; tel. 353/91-565-244; www.kinlaygalway.ie; €80

On Eyre Square, the Kinlay Hostel is slap-bang in the middle of the city and all the action. It has won numerous awards for its modern design, fun communal spaces, and range of rooms. Choose 8- or 6-bed dorms, a private double, or a 4-bed family room. With pool tables, pianos, and guitars, Kinlay Hostel is best for people who want to mingle with other travelers.

Hyde Hotel

Forster St.; tel. 353/91-564-111; www.hydehotel.ie; €120

This three-star hotel just off Eyre Square is sleek and stylish, with three on-site venues to eat and drink. The contemporary design is apparent, with a large wall of plants making the building stand out on the street. Inside, the finishings are loud, bright, and bold in the lobby and the 69 rooms. The largest is the Jekyll & Hyde Suite, with two bedrooms and a living room.

Mervue

The Connaught

Old Dublin Rd.; tel. 353/91-381-200; www.theconnacht.ie; €115

Staying just outside the city center means there's more space at this family-friendly hotel, still within a 2-km (1.2-mi) walk of the main parts of Galway City. The bunk-bed rooms are great for families without breaking the budget, with a queen, twin, and single beds in a space that doesn't feel cramped. The kids club has a kids swimming pool; at dinner, kids menus are available at the on-site restaurant. On Sunday a family lunch has the kids entertained, giving parents a break.

The G Hotel

Old Dublin Rd.; tel. 353/91-865-200; www.theghotel.ie; €300

This five-star modern spa hotel offers a restful stay a 20-minute walk from the Latin Quarter. Seven room types include standard doubles and a penthouse suite. Go for the deluxe lake-view room to wake up to views of Lough Atalia. The spa is a standout, with the luxurious retreat spread over two floors. There's a long list of spa treatments, but the thermal suite is a must, with the hydro pool, crystal steam room, rain showers, and rock sauna.

Galway City Outskirts

Glenlo Abbey Hotel & Estate

Bushy Park; tel. 353/91-519-600; www.glenloabbeyhotel.ie; €335

The five-star Glenlo Abbey Hotel & Estate feels a world away from Galway City in a stunning setting on the edge of Connemara, but it's only a 15-minute drive from the city center. Five room types include lake views and garden views in 73 rooms, and there are lodges for larger groups. Fill your days with strolls on the serenity walks, the driving range, or the Abbey Movie Theatre. Glenlo Abbey also has a memorable dining experience at the **Pullman Restaurant,** where you can reserve a three-course meal made with Irish produce in two of the original carriages from the *Orient Express.*

INFORMATION AND SERVICES

Visitor Information

Galway Tourist Information Centre

Galway City Museum; tel. 353/1-265-5634; Mon.-Sat. 9am-5pm

The information center has lots of information about things to do in the city as well as maps and recommendations to suit your interests.

Hospitals

For emergencies, dial 112 or 999. The main hospital in Galway City is **University Hospital Galway** (Newcastle Rd.; tel. 353/91-524-222; www.saolta.ie).

Banks

There are a number of **Bank of Ireland** (www.bankofireland.com) branches citywide as well as less numerous **AIB** (www.aib.ie) branches.

Post Offices

The main **post office** (www.anpost.com) in Galway City is on Eglinton Street. There's also a post office on the Upper Salthill Road in Salthill.

GETTING THERE

Air

Shannon Airport (SNN; N19; tel. 353/61-712-000; www.shannonairport.ie) is a major international airport in County Clare, with a wide range of direct flights to Europe, North America, and Asia. As a significant transportation hub, Shannon Airport has convenient connections to various parts of Ireland. **Expressway** (www.expressway.ie) operates the Route 51 and Route X51 buses to Galway City (1.5 hours; €14 one-way) up to 19 times daily in peak season. Driving time from the airport to Galway City is just over 1 hour, and there are lots of car rental companies at the airport.

Knock Airport (NOC; Kilgariff; tel. 353/94-936-8100; www.irelandwestairport.com) is a small regional airport in County Mayo. It has flights on domestic routes and to a few European destinations, with convenient access to the west of Ireland. The Expressway Route 64 bus connects the airport to Galway City with direct service (€15 one-way). The journey by car takes around 1.5 hours, and there are multiple car rental companies located in the airport.

Car

From Dublin, take the M6 motorway westbound, a straightforward 2.5-hour drive of 200 km (125 mi). Along the way, towns like Athlone and Ballinasloe offer convenient stops. The M6 is a fast and efficient route, with well-maintained roads and clear signage.

From Cork City, the journey takes about 3 hours and 210 km (130 mi). Start by taking the N20 northbound toward Limerick, then the M18 after Limerick, heading northwest to Galway.

Bus

From Dublin City, buses depart regularly from Busáras, Crampton Quay, and Dublin Airport, with journeys taking 2.5-3 hours, depending on traffic. Operators like **Expressway** (www.expressway.ie), **Citylink** (www.citylink.ie), and **Bus Éireann** (www.buseireann.ie) provide direct buses along the M6 motorway and come with free Wi-Fi, comfortable seating, and charging points.

From Cork City, direct buses operated by Expressway depart from Parnell Place bus station and take around 4 hours to reach **Galway Coach Station** (Fairgreen Rd.). The route follows the N20 to Limerick and then the M18 motorway.

Train

From Dublin, **Irish Rail** (www.irishrail.ie) direct trains (€17 one-way) depart frequently from Heuston Station, a 2.5-hour trip to Galway's **Ceannt Station** (Station Rd.). From Cork City, there are no direct trains to Galway. You can take a train from Cork's Kent Station to Limerick Junction, which takes about 1 hour, and transfer to a connecting train to Galway, with the total journey taking around 4 hours. The route is scenic.

GETTING AROUND

On Foot

Galway is a safe and walkable city, with lots of pedestrianized streets in the center, particularly in the Latin Quarter. Each street in the city has a sidewalk. From Eyre Square to the West End is 1 km (0.6 mi) or 15 minutes, and there are walking paths along the waterfront by the Long Walk, Claddagh, and Salthill.

Public Transport

The city's bus network, operated by **Bus Éireann** (www.buseireann.ie) and **CityDirect** (www.citydirect.ie), covers major areas, including Salthill, Eyre Square, and the university district. Adult fares are €2.70 one-way, and weekly tickets cost €20. The fare drops to €2.20 when bought with a **Leap Card** (www.leapcard.ie).

Cycling

With its relatively compact layout, Galway is highly accessible by bike and has dedicated cycling lanes on key routes, as well as bike-friendly paths along the coast with stunning views of Galway Bay. **TFI Bikes** (www.bikeshare.ie) operates 23 stations with 195 bikes for short-term rentals. An annual subscription (€10) or a three-day pass (€3) is required, with hourly rentals from €0.50. For longer-term rentals, there are multiple bike shops in the city.

Taxi

Taxi stands operate from Bridge Street and Eyre Square, and taxis can be hailed on the street. You can use apps like **FreeNow** (www.free-now.com) and **Bolt** (www.bolt.eu) to book a taxi, and they are highly reliable outside peak times on weekends. To get an estimate of your fare before starting your trip, visit the **Transport for Ireland** website (www.transportforireland.ie).

Car

Galway City has a traffic problem, particularly when entering the city, so driving is neither advised nor required. It's such a walkable city that driving should be a last resort.

★ The Aran Islands

TOP EXPERIENCE

The remote and rocky Aran Islands—Inis Mór, Inis Meáin, and Inis Oírr—are off the coast of County Galway and County Clare in a shield-like formation that guards Galway Bay from the fierce Atlantic Ocean. The islands are ancient, with forts built by warriors who worked with the landscape at Dún Aonghasa on Inis Mór. Dedicated pilgrims followed in the 5th century CE, determined to prove their dedication to God by traveling to these faraway islands and enduring the harsh environment. In recent history, the Aran Islands are an important part of the Irish-speaking Gaeltacht region, known for its brave fishermen, and, of course, Aran jumpers (sweaters), which were first knitted for the fishermen. These beautiful islands are a short sail from the mainland but feel a world away.

ORIENTATION

The three islands that make up the Aran Islands are Inis Meáin (Inishmaan), Inis Oírr (Inisheer), and Inis Mór (Inishmore). **Inis Mór** is the largest and most westerly, closest to Connemara. **Inis Oírr** is the smallest, off the coast of County Clare, and has a view of the Cliffs of Moher on clear days. **Inis Meáin** is in the middle size-wise and geographically.

GETTING THERE AND AROUND

The two options to reach the Aran Islands are ferry and plane. The most popular, the ferry, operates year-round, although the schedule is reduced in winter. Ferries depart from two locations on the west coast: Rossaveel, with more frequent departures, and Doolin.

From Rossaveel, about 45 minutes from Galway City, **Aran Island Ferries** (www.aranislandferries.com) provides regular service to all three islands (€30 round-trip). Inis Mór, the largest, has the most frequent sailings. During high season (Apr.-Sept.), Rossaveel has multiple daily sailings: to Inis Mór (40 minutes) at 10:30am, 1pm, and 6pm (6:30pm Fri.), and similarly to Inis Meáin and Inis Oírr (1 hour). In July-August, an additional sailing is added to Inis Mór at 11:45am. During winter (Oct.-Mar.), at least one round-trip sailing per day goes to each island, with departures typically at 10:30am and 6pm (6:30pm Fri.).

The drop-off points are **Kilronan Pier** on Inis Mór, **Cé Inis Meáin** on Inis Meáin, and **Cé Inis Oírr** on Inis Oírr. Island-hopping tickets allow you to visit multiple islands. Ferries run between the islands, so you don't have to return to the mainland. Visiting all three islands in a day is possible, but you won't get enough time to explore each island.

Take Bus Éireann's Route 424 from multiple locations in Galway City to the ferry pier in Rossaveel (1 hour; €8 one-way). The Aran Island Ferries shuttle bus service from Merchants Road in Galway city center (1 hour) is another option. For a faster trip, taxis (40 minutes; €60-75) are available. If you drive, the journey takes about 40 minutes via the R336 road west from Galway to Rossaveel.

The Aran Islands

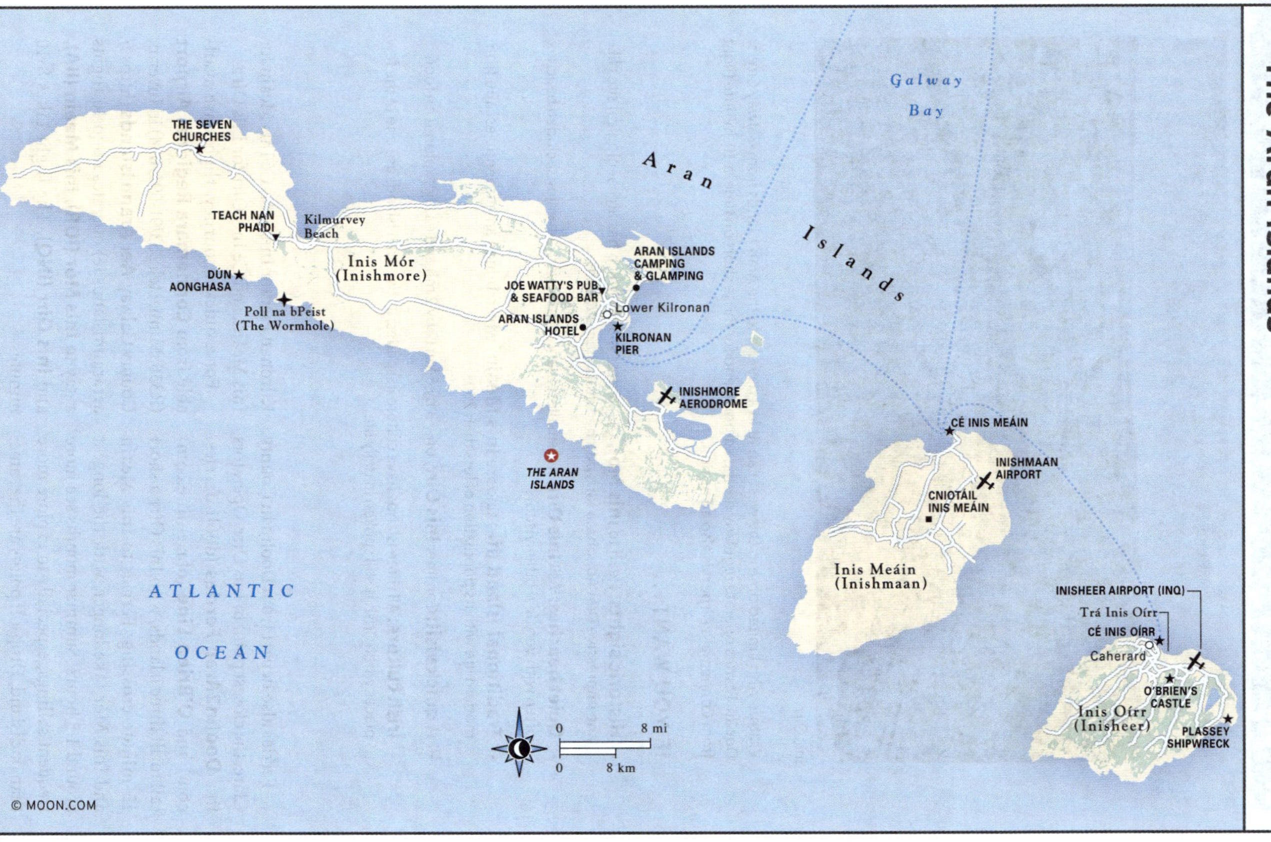

Which Aran Island?

Inis Oírr

Visitors with limited time in the west can fit in a day trip to the Aran Islands from Galway City or Doolin. Ferries operate regularly during summer, and for those short on time, a 10-minute flight from Connemara Airport is also an option.

IF YOU WANT...

- **Historic sights:** Head to **Inis Mór,** the largest island, which has archaeological sites like the impressive Dún Aonghasa fort, perched atop dramatic cliffs.
- **Quiet beaches:** Visit **Inis Oírr,** the smallest island, where you can enjoy secluded beaches, often with very few other visitors.
- **Traditional island life:** Choose **Inis Meáin,** which brings an authentic escape from modern life with its population of less than 200.
- **A quick visit:** Consider **Inis Oírr,** only 3 by 3 km (2 by 2 mi) and easily explored on foot.
- **Irish culture:** All three islands have culture in spades, as the Aran Islands are one of the few places where Irish is still spoken in daily life.

Ferries also depart from Doolin in County Clare, the closest point to Inis Oírr. Operators like **Doolin2Aran Ferries** (doolinferries.com) and **O'Brien Line** (obrienline.com) sail to all three islands, with Inis Oírr a short 15-minute crossing. Ferries to Inis Meáin and Inis Mór take longer, with the longest around 1.5 hours. Summer months see more frequent sailings, especially to explore more than one island. Drop-off points are the same: Kilronan Pier for Inis Mór, Cé Inis Meáin for Inis Meáin, and Cé Inis Oírr for Inis Oírr.

For a quicker journey, flights are available from **Connemara Regional Airport** (R336, Minna; tel. 353/91-593-034) in Inverin, County Galway. **Aer Arann Islands** (https://aerarannislands.ie) operates up to 10 flights a day to **Inis Mór (IOR), Inis Meáin (IIA),** and **Inis Oírr (INQ).** The flight takes 8-10 minutes.

INIS MÓR (INISHMORE)

Inis Mór is the largest of the Aran Islands and where most visitors first arrive. Its population is only 820, with most activity around the harbor, where you'll find places to eat, tourist info, and tour providers. The island is a tranquil spot ideal for wandering from secluded beaches to dramatic rural scenes along narrow country lanes. Away from the harbor, most of the major attractions, including Dún Aonghasa, Poll na bPeist, and the Seven Churches, are in the west part of the island.

Sights

TOP EXPERIENCE

Dún Aonghasa

tel. 353/99-61-008

Dún Aonghasa is a prehistoric stone fort on the edge of a dramatic 100-m (330-ft) cliff. The semicircular defensive structure, built with massive limestone blocks, backs onto the sheer cliffs, meaning it could only be attacked from one side. Believed to have been built as early as 1100 BCE, it is one of the most impressive archaeological sites in Ireland. The fort is free to enter but requires a walk down an uneven path across farmland, so it's not easily accessible. There are no safety rails whatsoever, so you need to be very careful approaching the edge or climbing the walls. It's about an hour's walk from the harbor.

Poll na bPeist (the Wormhole)

Poll na bPeist, also known as the Wormhole, is an otherworldly coastal formation. The rectangular pool looks entirely artificial, but it's a natural structure caused by the sea eroding the limestone cliffs. The pool is worth visiting for the views alone. During high tide, waves fill the pool, and some brave souls go swimming. The official line is don't swim, but if you decide to, extreme caution is required, and you do so at your own risk. Follow the red arrows from the settlement of Gort na gCapall, which is 80 percent of the total distance along the route to Poll na bPeist west of the harbor. It's a 20-minute walk in total.

The Seven Churches

Sruthán

Na Seacht Teampaill, also known as the Seven Churches, is an important monastic site. Despite its name, it comprises just two churches, but it's believed there were once more. The site was busy during the 800s CE, when pilgrims were encouraged to go to

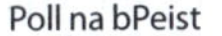

Poll na bPeist

far-flung, difficult-to-reach places for prayer. There are some rectangular buildings thought to date to the late medieval period that might be the earliest example of a hostel in Ireland. The main church, Teampall Bhreacáin, is dedicated to Saint Brecan, an important figure in early Irish Christianity who came from the islands. The smaller church is Teampall an Phoill. It's about a 90-minute walk (9 km/5.6 mi) from the port.

Beaches

Kilmurvey Beach

On the northern coast of Inis Mór, this stunning Blue Flag beach is renowned for its pristine white sand and crystal-clear turquoise water. Sheltered and crescent-shaped, it creates a peaceful atmosphere, perfect for relaxation.

Food and Accommodations

Teach Nan Phaidi

Kilmurvey; tel. 353/99-20-975; Instagram @teachnanphaidis; daily 11am-4pm; from €15

If you believe the saying "You eat with your eyes," you're going to love Teach Nan Phaidi before you step foot inside. This irresistible café is in a traditional whitewashed stone cottage complete with a thatched roof—you can't get more authentic. The menu is a mix of light bites like homemade vegetable soup and Aran Island goat cheese salad alongside heartier dishes like potato gratin and beef lasagna. The inside has a cozy atmosphere with a low ceiling and wooden beams, and the enormous fireplace catches the eye of everyone who pops in.

Joe Watty's Pub & Seafood Bar

Kilronan; tel. 353/99-20-892; www.joewattys.ie; Mon.-Thurs. noon-midnight, Fri.-Sun. noon-12:30am; from €18

There's always a good bit of craic agus ceol (music and fun) in Joe Watty's Pub & Seafood Bar, as it's the main point of socializing on the island. The large white building has a number of spaces for guests to escape from the elements, from a small bar to a dining area, and if the weather is good, there's a patio. The menu has plenty of seafood, and oysters on crushed ice is one of the more popular choices. Come in the evening and you'll likely hear live traditional music, a great excuse to order from the extensive Irish whiskey menu.

Aran Islands Camping & Glamping

Frenchman's Beach; tel. 353/99-61-104; www.irelandglamping.ie; €150

When you're in a place that's so connected with nature, it can be even more rewarding to sleep in nature. Aran Islands Camping & Glamping is tucked away on the eastern shore of Inis Mór and has 24 glamping units, including the 6-person Tigín Glamping Unit and 4-person Clochán Glamping Unit, both with showers, comfortable bedding, and outdoor seating. There's also a campground to pitch your own tent. The reception building has Wi-Fi, and there's a kitchen and a shower block.

Aran Islands Hotel

Killeany; tel. 353/99-61-104; https://aranislandshotel.com; €185

Just a short stroll from the harbor is the Aran Islands Hotel, with 22 en-suite rooms in the main building, some offering a patio overlooking the sea. The 23 chalets are great for families, and all come with sea views. **Madigans** is where you'll eat and drink; the space goes from hosting peaceful full Irish breakfasts in the morning to a hub of food and chat at night, when the restaurant and bar swing into action.

INIS MEÁIN (INISHMAAN)

Taking the slow pace of life on the Aran Islands even farther, Inis Meáin is an off-the-beaten-track destination for a tranquil break. Its isolation has allowed the Irish language to flourish and for traditions to deeply root themselves in the limestone landscape. Known across the country for its fantastic craftspeople, this island is where you'll find Aran jumpers (sweaters) made with patterns that have been passed down through the ages. The main village on Inis Meáin is Moore

The Gaeltacht and Irish Language Today

a traditional cottage common in the Gaeltacht

Irish, known as Gaelic in Irish, is a Celtic language of the Indo-European family. It is a struggling language with only about 70,000 speakers. The Gaeltacht refers to the parts of Ireland where Irish is the predominant language in daily life. These regions include parts of counties Donegal, Galway, Kerry, Cork, Waterford, and Meath.

Some regions popular with visitors are in the Gaeltacht, giving you a good chance of hearing people speak it. These include the Aran Islands and Connemara in County Galway and Dingle Peninsula in County Kerry. These areas preserve the language and other aspects of traditional Irish culture, including music, dance, and folklore. Ireland was under British rule for over 700 years, and Irish almost became extinct; under British rule, speaking Irish was illegal. Since independence, English has remained the most common language. Gaeltacht areas are mainly in the west, where Irish survived in the remote countryside, as the British stayed predominantly on the east coast.

There's a revival of the Irish language happening today, and you'll hear it in contemporary songs on the radio and even in towns and cities, with people dropping Irish words into English sentences. This contributes to the dialect of English spoken in Ireland, called Hiberno-English.

HIBERNO-ENGLISH PHRASES AND SAYINGS

Hiberno-English can be confusing to visitors, since Irish people tend to speak quickly and mix in Irish words. Some phrases and sayings:

- **Well:** Hello
- **What's the craic?:** How are things?
- **You won't have a cup of tea, would you?:** Would you like a cup of tea?
- **Grand:** OK.
- **Go raibh maith agat/Go raibh míle:** Thanks.
- **I will yeah!:** I will absolutely not.
- **Sláinte:** Cheers.

Irish Wool

Irish knitwear

In some parts of Ireland, you may see more sheep than people. We're a farming nation, and hardy sheep are fantastic livestock for the unforgiving landscapes in the west, where the animals and their wool are intertwined with our culture and heritage. In medieval times, monks spun wool to make clothes to survive the long, dark, wet winters. When trade with other countries became more common, Ireland gained a reputation for having fantastic wool.

The main breed in Ireland today is the native Galway sheep, but others include Suffolk, Texel, and Blackface, each creating wool with unique characteristics. Although many other wools are softer, Irish wool is known for being durable and versatile, which is vital in this part of the world. The residents of the Aran Islands noticed that the wool was also water resistant, so they began to make woolly jumpers (sweaters) with a cable knit for the fishermen. Each family had a unique cable pattern in case they needed to identify bodies found at sea.

Prices for a sweater are typically €120-150, though you can find more expensive pieces. A blanket will likely set you back around €100. Plenty of woolen mills are still active in Ireland producing knitwear and homewares:

- Pick up a sweater from any knitwear shop or at the original location on the Aran Islands, **Cniotáil Inis Meáin** (page 325).
- **Foxford Wolleen Mills** (Providence Rd., Foxford; tel. 353/94-925-6104; www.foxford.com; daily 10am-5pm) in Country Mayo has been selling woolen knitwear for over 130 years.
- On the east coast, stop into **Avoca** (The Mill, Avoca Village; tel. 353/402-35-105; www.avoca.com; daily 10am-5pm) in County Wicklow, which first opened in 1723.

Village, near the center of the island. When you arrive by ferry, you disembark at the small harbor on the eastern side of the island; from here, it's a 20-minute walk to Moore Village.

Shopping

There are only two shops on this tiny island of 200 people, both belonging to the Inis Meáin Knitting company. The one listed is a retail shop; the other is an occasional pop-up at the company's factory.

Cniotáil Inis Meáin-Inis Meáin Knitting Company

tel. 353/99-73-009; https://inismeain.ie/shop

The remote and sparse landscapes of Inis Meáin couldn't be farther from the glamour of Hollywood, but the knitwear made here is of such quality and style that they've been worn by movie stars in big productions. Chris Hemsworth wore one of their traditional sweaters in the movie *Knives Out,* and Patrick Dempsey has modeled for the brand. Each piece is made on the Aran Islands, and there are modern styles and designs alongside the classics. They're not cheap, but they're of incredibly high quality.

INIS OÍRR (INISHEER)

Small in size, just 3 by 3 km (2 by 2 mi), but with plenty to see, Inis Oírr is a surprising place. The beaches are beautiful, with unspoiled golden sand met by gentle turquoise water. From the southern shore, gaze across the ocean to the mighty Cliffs of Moher.

Sights

Plassey Shipwreck

Baile An Formna

Immortalized in the intro to the cult comedy TV series *Father Ted,* the rusted hull of the wrecked *Plassey* is one of the most visited and photographed parts of the Aran Islands. It ran aground in the 1960s during a brutal storm that forced it onto the rocks. Islanders were quick to react and saved all 11 crewmembers. Today, it sits as a reminder of the power of nature and the passage of time, and a testament to how the people of the Aran Islands are linked to the sea.

O'Brien's Castle

Oir

Standing on one of the highest points on the island, O'Brien's Castle is a formidable structure that brought shelter and safety to the Clann Teige, part of the O'Brien family, in the early 1400s. By 1652, Cromwell had invaded, captured the castle, and purposely damaged it, like he did many great Irish buildings. Now in ruins, there are no tours, but visitors can explore the hillsides and the many stone walls that lead up to the structure. Look out over the sea and imagine what it must have felt like to see the British invasion sailing to these shores.

Beaches

Trá Inis Oírr

An Trá

Trá Inis Oírr, also known as An Trá, is a beautiful white-sand beach on the northern coast of Inis Oírr. It's yet another award-winning beach with picturesque sandy shores and clear water.

Connemara

Connemara is wild Ireland. It's where the Twelve Bens Mountain Range folds into the sea, where narrow ribbon roads weave through glacial valleys, and where sheep and deer can bring traffic to a standstill. Maps don't do Connemara justice; it's hard to convey the beauty of the sparseness. Connemara is properly experienced when you're surrounded by its vastness and take in views that took nature millions of years to create.

Towns and villages dot the region, with Clifden and Oughterard the biggest, but the great outdoors can be momentarily forgotten in these places. Plenty of visitors choose instead to spend time in smaller places, like Leenaun and Roundstone, where it's impossible to forget where you are. Connemara National Park is at the heart of Connemara; although its borders are defined, natural landscapes spread across the region.

If Galway City is the cool cousin who studied abroad and came back with new style and outlook, Connemara is the one who stayed behind, knowing that what they have can't be

Connemara

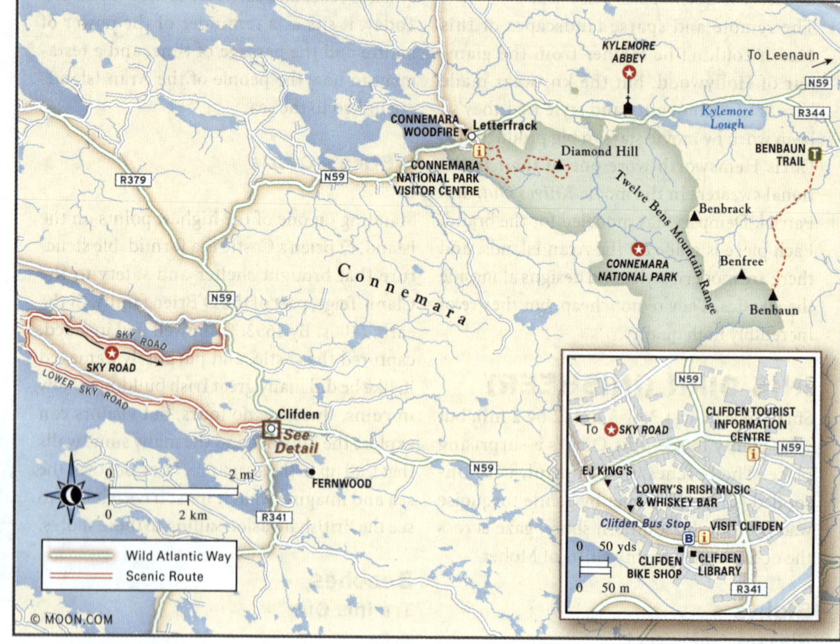

found anywhere else, and doubled down on learning Irish, playing trad music, and living in tune with the landscape.

ORIENTATION

Connemara's main road is the N59, a loop connecting Galway City, Clifden, and Leenaun. From Galway City, heading west on the N59 takes you to **Clifden,** one of the larger towns. Before Clifden you can divert southwest to **Roundstone** via smaller coastal roads to beaches like **Dogs Bay.** Continuing northwest from Roundstone leads back to the N59 toward Clifden, a base for trips to **Connemara National Park** and the **Sky Road** drive. From Clifden, northeast on the N59 is **Leenaun,** at Killary Harbour, a gateway to northern Connemara and County Mayo. The distances between the key hubs of Roundstone, Clifden, and Leenaun are 30-40 km (18-24 mi), making it easy to explore the area in short jaunts.

DOG'S BAY BEACH AND GURTEEN BEACH

If it weren't for the cattle walking the spine of land between the two beaches, you might think you were at the Indian Ocean. The turquoise water pops against the white sand as rocky cliffs crumble into the sea. The beaches are on either side of the spit. Dogs Bay is west and the more sheltered of the two. Gurteen is more open to the open sea, although both beaches are quite calm and great for swimming. There are no services except parking. Camping is prohibited, and the dunes are protected, so take extra care when exploring.

Getting There

Take the N59 road west from Galway City, following signs for Clifden. After about 55 km (34 mi), turn left onto the R341 toward Roundstone. Follow the road west, and turn left when you see the signs for the beach. The drive is 76 km (47 mi) and takes 1.25 hours. You'll be treated to amazing views of the Connemara landscape.

There's no easy way to get to these beaches by public transport. You can take the Route 419 bus to Clifden, then change for the Route 432 bus. This takes a minimum of 3 hours.

CLIFDEN

If Connemara had a capital, it would be Clifden. It's close to everything in Connemara, making it a great base. The streets are busy year-round with locals and visitors in the pubs and independent shops. Its size can detract from the beauty of the remoteness that many visitors seek. A short drive takes you to Connemara National Park, Kylemore Abbey, Sky Road, and other highlights.

Scenic Drives

★ Sky Road

Most drives in Connemara are scenic, but the Sky Road is one of the best, with views of the Atlantic, Inisbofin, and narrow country roads. It's a circular route of 16 km (10 mi) on the Kingston Peninsula and is well signposted from Clifden or from Letterfrack. It's split into the more popular Lower Road, which hugs the shore, and the Upper Road, which takes in more expansive views. You can drive, cycle, or walk, but keep in mind it's very narrow in places and many drivers are not familiar with these conditions. The drive takes just a few minutes, but factor in time to stop for the views; cycling takes roughly 1 hour, and walking the route can take 4 hours.

Cycling

Clifden Bike Shop

Market St.; tel. 353/95-22-630; www.clifdenbikeshop.ie; Mon.-Fri. 9:15am-5:30pm, Sat.-Sun. 10am-5:30pm

Bikes can be rented in town from Clifden Bike Shop. The Sky Road route is suitable for all levels of cyclists, particularly if you rent an e-bike.

Food and Nightlife

★ EJ Kings

Market Square; https://ejkings.com; Mon.-Thurs. 10am-11:30pm, Fri.-Sat. 10am-12:30am, Sun. 10am-11pm; from €17

I heard EJ Kings before I saw it. This well-placed traditional pub on the corner of Market Square is a natural meeting point, and the tables outside fill up on sunny days. Alongside wood-paneled walls and dark tiled floors, you'll find an international food menu with lots of local ingredients. Try the seafood chowder to start and a main course of duck confit served with braised red cabbage and fig jus. The pub kicks into gear when the live music starts or when there's a big football or rugby match.

Lowry's Irish Music and Whiskey Bar

Market St.; www.lowrysbar.ie; Sun.-Thurs. 12:30pm-11:30pm, Fri.-Sat. 12:30pm-12:30am; from €5

The name is a dead giveaway: They do two things very well, live music and whiskey. Both are available seven nights a week, and it's a brilliant place to let your hair down after a day exploring the national park. The music is traditional Irish, so expect the fiddle, bódhran (a small hand-held drum), tin whistle, accordion, concertina, and more. The 150 whiskeys include options from every part of Ireland and the world. It's the largest collection in Connemara, and the staff will help you find the right one for your tastes.

Accommodations

Fernwood

Killymongaun; tel. 353/87-640-7321; www.fernwood.eco; €250

The west of Ireland is closely linked with tradition and heritage, but there are some businesses bucking the trend with modern offerings. Fernwood is a working farm, 1 km (0.6 mi) from Clifden, that has lodging for couples in the Stilt House, the Studio, and the pick of the bunch, the Treehouse Dome. A dreamy escape to be immersed in nature, the dome sits 5 m (16 ft) off the ground in the

1

2

tree canopy. There's a sauna on-site where you can relax and unwind.

Information and Services

For visitor information, stop by the **Clifden Tourist Information Centre** (Galway Rd.; tel. 353/95-21-163; www.discoverireland.ie; typically Apr.-Oct. Mon.-Sat. 9am-5pm), **Visit Clifden** (Market St.; tel. 353/95-21-338; www.visitclifden.com; generally Mon.-Fri. 9:30am-5:30pm), or **Clifden Library** (Market St.; tel. 353/95-21-416; typically Mon., Wed., and Fri. 10am-1:30pm, Tues. and Thurs. 2:30pm-5pm).

Getting There and Around

To get to Clifden from Roundstone by car, take the R341 north for 15 km (9 mi) to the N59. Turn left and follow the N59 west for 20 km (12 mi) to Clifden. The drive is 35 km (22 mi) and takes 40 minutes. From Galway City, take the N59 west toward Oughterard. The road winds through picturesque landscapes directly to Clifden, a distance of 78 km (48 mi) that takes 1.5 hours by car.

You can take **Bus Éireann** (www.buseireann.ie) or **Citylink** (www.citylink.ie), which operate daily buses between Galway City and Clifden from the Galway Coach Station (Fairgreen Rd.). The journey takes 2 hours. Local Link operates bus service between Roundstone and Clifden, a journey of 30 minutes.

★ CONNEMARA NATIONAL PARK

Connemara National Park, in the wilds of County Galway, is one of Ireland's most stunning natural areas. Its otherworldly beauty is 2,957 ha (7,307 acres) of mountains, bogs, heaths, grasslands, and woodlands in deep green, brown, and orange tones. One of the park's most prominent features is the Twelve Bens mountain range, with several of the peaks within the park's boundaries, including the highest, Benbaun, at 729 m (2,392 ft). Fantastic mountain hikes for all fitness levels include the most popular, Diamond Hill, with two well-maintained trails.

Though it looks sparse, Connemara National Park is home to a rich variety of flora and fauna. The blanket bogs support heather, mosses, and orchids. Woodlands of oak and birch are home to meadow pipits, skylarks, and the rare red grouse. Golden eagles have been reintroduced to the region and can occasionally be spotted. Red deer and Connemara ponies graze in the grassy parts of the park.

Connemara National Park is also dotted with archaeological sites, including megalithic tombs that date back 4,000 years, remnants of ancient settlements, and 18th-century field systems that tell the story of early agriculture in the region. These aren't sights per se but are features of the landscape.

Visiting the Park

Gateway Towns

Unlike other national parks in Ireland, there is a formal entrance in Letterfrack, where the visitor center is. This small village has the closest lodging and dining to the park.

Fees and Regulations

Entry to the park is free. Dogs are welcome but must be kept on a leash.

Visitor Center

N59, Letterfrack; tel. 353/95-41-054; daily 9am-5:30pm

Stop by the visitor center in Letterfrack to get all the details before you head into the park. You'll learn about the park's ecology, history, and conservation efforts through exhibits and maps. There are also toilets and a small café.

Hiking and Walking

Lower Diamond Hill Trail

Distance: *3 km (2 mi) loop*
Duration: *1 hour*
Elevation gain: *112 m (367 ft)*
Effort: *Moderate*
Trailhead: *Connemara National Park Visitor Centre*

The best bang for your buck when it comes to trails for beginners in Connemara is Lower

1: Sky Road **2:** Connemara National Park

Diamond Hill. It's easily accessible from the visitor center and has plenty of parking. The trail is well signposted and is one of the most popular in the park thanks to its forgiving climb; all the ascent is in a 1-km (0.6-mi) stretch. Your effort is rewarded with views of the Atlantic Ocean and Diamond Hill from the foothills. Families with kids ages 10 or older should have no problem completing the loop.

Upper Diamond Hill Trail

Distance: *7.1 km (4.4 mi) round-trip*
Duration: *2.5 hours*
Elevation gain: *394 m (1,292 ft)*
Effort: *Moderate*
Trailhead: *Connemara National Park Visitor Centre*

Upper Diamond Hil is an extension of the lower loop and adds more distance and climbing. Once you hit the halfway point on the lower loop, the trail turns right and begins a 2-km (1.2-mi) climb to the summit of Diamond Hill, 442 m (1,450 ft) above sea level. The steep sections can become loose after heavy rainfall, so proper footwear is a must. The views from the top are an absolute treat, especially on a clear day when the sea is calm, where speckles of crumbling land dot the blue water of the bay. Once you round the summit, you return on the same path to join the rest of the lower loop.

Sruffaunboy Nature Trail

Distance: *8 km (5 mi) loop*
Duration: *2 hours*
Elevation gain: *133 m (436 ft)*
Effort: *Easy-Moderate*
Trailhead: *Sruffaunboy Nature Trail Car Park*

This gentle stroll immerses you in nature without going too far off the beaten track. The elevation is undulating throughout, making it a good choice to enjoy conversation as much as the view. The trail moves from wide gravel paths to narrow wooden boardwalks that can be slippery in the wet. You'll come across megalithic tombs dotting the blanket bogs, conifer forests, and rocky hills. The route returns to the small car park at the trailhead.

Benbaun Trail

Distance: *8.7 km (5.4 mi) round-trip*
Duration: *3-4 hours*
Elevation gain: *699 m (2,293 ft)*
Effort: *Difficult*
Trailhead: *Benbaun Trailhead Car Park*

At 729 m (2,392 ft), Benbaun is the highest of the Twelve Bens that dominate the park, and this out-and-back hike leads to the top. The trail starts gently along a winding stream for 2 km (1.2 mi) before the climb starts. The trail can be tricky to follow, so plan your route with a hiking map that you can buy in Clifden or Galway City; it's unlikely you'll have a phone signal out here. Another challenge is the weather, as heavy rain can make the small river crossings difficult. Hardy hikers are rewarded with views from the highest point in County Galway.

Food and Accommodations

The Country Shop

N59, Letterfrack; tel. 353/95-41-850; daily 8am-10pm

This rural shop sells a wide range of local produce and everyday essentials, making it a great place to stock up on snacks before going into the park. Try the homemade baked goods with a coffee.

Connemara Woodfire

Letterfrack Lodge, Letterfrack; www.connemarawoodfire.com; Tues.-Sun. 1pm-8:30pm; from €15

Near Kylemore Abbey, Connemara Woodfire is worth visiting. Most places in Connemara focus on seafood, but the team here, trained for two years by an Italian pizza chef with 40 years' experience, makes authentic pizzas. Toppings have some modern spins, but the classics like the pepperoni are hard to beat. Dining areas are inside the main building, where there's also lodging, and in the sweeping greenhouse among the leafy plants and DIY-style furnishings.

Letterfrack Lodge

Letterfrack Village; tel. 353/95-41-222; from €240

Letterfrack Lodge offers comfort and

convenience in a prime location a few minutes' stroll from Connemara National Park. The 12 clean and comfortable en suite rooms have timber floors and tiled baths. The fully equipped kitchen, dining area, and sitting room create a homely atmosphere. There's free Wi-Fi and breakfast served daily. June-September they also offer dinner.

Getting There and Around

Drive north from Clifden on the N59 toward Kylemore. After 10 km (6 mi), you come to a junction; continue on the N59 for 4 km (2.5 mi) to the park entrance in Letterfrack. The drive is 14 km (9 mi) and takes 15-20 minutes. **Citylink** (www.citylink.ie) operates the Route 923 bus four times daily between Clifden and Letterfrack, picking you up outside the library on Market Street and dropping you at the Country Shop, a journey of 30 minutes.

★ KYLEMORE ABBEY

Pollacappul; tel. 353/95-52-001; www.kylemoreabbey.com; daily 10am-5pm; €17

This outrageously grandiose building in the middle of nowhere rises from the gentle landscape, sheltered by mountains and reflected by lakes. Kylemore Abbey was built in 1867 and has hosted royalty and gentry from around the world, including Queen Salote of Tonga. A living piece of Irish history, it was built as a private residence for wealthy English politician Mitchell Henry. In 1920 Benedictine nuns who fled to Ireland from Europe during World War I bought the building. In 1923 they turned it into a school that ran until 2010. The nuns still live on the grounds, and you can sometimes hear their choir singing in the chapel. In the gift shop you can buy chocolates they make.

Sights and Tours

Touring the Abbey

Visitors can enter six of the nine rooms on the beautifully restored ground floor. Exhibits feature modern multimedia displays that tell the story of the abbey's evolution from a Victorian castle to a Benedictine abbey. The chapel is occasionally open to visits to hear the choir; ask about times when you arrive.

Victorian Walled Garden

In addition to the abbey, the other main attraction is the walled Victorian garden, a 1.8-km (1.1-mi) walk or short bus ride away. The picture-perfect symmetry and manicured lawns remain, and the greenhouses are home to exotic plants not normally found in Ireland. The entry fee to the abbey includes the gardens as well as the talks and shows that run about every two hours. These can be anything from a tour of the house to watching the pig and the ponies being fed. A tearoom next to the gardens has light refreshments, and the café at the exit has bigger meals. Two additional 1-km (0.6-mi) walks take you through the woods and along the nearby river.

Getting There

The N59 links Galway City, Clifden, and Letterfrack with Kylemore Abbey. Drive west along the N59 from Galway City for 1 hour to Clifden. Stay on the N59 for another 15 minutes to Letterfrack. Kylemore Abbey is a five-minute drive farther along the road. There is no public transport option, although you can get a bus to Letterfrack and a taxi from there.

LEENAUN

Leenaun, also known as Leenane and Lionán, is a small village on the edge of Killary Harbour. Even calling it a village might be a stretch; it's more a crossroads with some shops, pubs, and a café. Nature dominates, with mountains surrounding the shore. This is truly a spot for outdoorsy people. The raw, rich landscapes were the backdrop for the iconic Irish movie *The Field,* and nowadays it acts as a meeting point for adventurous visitors.

Sights

Killary Harbour

Leenaun looks onto 14-km-long (9-mi) Killary Harbour, one of the few fjords in Ireland. Glacial fjords are deep waterways where

1
2

seawater flows in and creates a lough. As the tide comes in and out, it brings nutrients to the abundant marine life. Killary Harbour is known for its mussels, farmed here and served in pubs and restaurants throughout the region. As you drive around the harbor from Leenaun, you'll see impressive mountains all around. To the north is Mweelrea, the highest peak in Connaught, and to the south is Maumturk. The roads in this area are narrow and twisty, so give yourself plenty of time.

Boating

Killary Fjord Boat Tours

Nancys Point; tel. 353/87-235-9136; www.killaryfjord.ie; daily 10:30am-6pm; €26

One of the best ways to experience the 14-km-long (9-mi) Killary Harbour is by getting on the water with Killary Fjord Boat Tours. The mountains and scenery are stunning from land, but it's hard to beat seeing them from the water. The 90-minute tour heads toward the mouth of the lough, where you have a good chance of seeing seals or dolphins, while the captain of the 21-m (69-ft) boat relates local folklore and how a German U-boat almost ran aground here.

Adventure Centers

Delphi Adventure Centre

Delphi Resort; tel. 353/95-42-208; www.delphiadventureresort.com; Mon.-Sat. 9am-6pm; from €20

The best way to experience Connemara is outdoors, and you can do that at Delphi Adventure Resort. Activities for all ages are on land and water. Family-friendly zip-lining and cycling are a strong focus, along with more advanced options like combat archery, sea kayaking, and mountain biking. The center is linked with the luxury resort on-site, so there's a great place to relax afterward.

1: Kylemore Abbey **2:** the gardens at Kylemore Abbey

Food and Accommodations

Misunderstood Heron

Derrynacleigh; www.misunderstoodheron.com; daily 11am-5pm; from €6

This glorified food truck has become one of the most sought-after places to eat for foodies across the country. Serving fresh fare with creative approaches in a jaw-droppingly gorgeous setting on the edge of the harbor, Misunderstood Heron is worth the five-minute drive from Leenaun. The wooden exterior and furniture give the place a rustic feel, but the food is incredibly refined, with items like a carrot, coconut, and green chili soup alongside Killary mussels served à la cholita for fans of spicy food. After eating on the large patio, you can walk on the trail along the water.

Delphi Resort

Delphi Resort; tel. 353/95-42-208; www.delphiadventureresort.com; €115

Like an oasis in remote Connemara, 45 minutes from Westport and 90 minutes from Galway City, Delphi Resort is an upmarket lodge with the comfort you need after a day outdoors. The 38 rooms have plush beds and views of valleys, mountains, and rivers, and trails start from the lodge. The adventure center has a bog obstacle course, a zip line, and kayaking. It's a great spot for fishing, and local guides are available. At the restaurant and bar (3 courses €39), the bangers and mash in a Yorkshire pudding is a highlight. Indulge at the spa with seaweed baths, facials, and massage treatments.

Getting There and Around

To get to Leenaun from Clifden, take the N59 north for 30 km (19 mi) and 40 minutes through sparse and beautiful countryside. Bus Éireann runs Route 423 five times daily from Clifden to Leenaun (50 minutes; €9.60 one-way, €15 round-trip). From Galway City, head northwest on the N59 for 75 km (47 mi), through Oughterard and Maam Cross to Leenaun, a drive of 1.25 hours.

Westport and Clew Bay

Like so many regions in the west of Ireland, Clew Bay is defined by the coast, anchored to the mainland in Westport, the drumlin-like micro islands in the bay, Clare Island to the west, and Achill Island to the north. The land has been inhabited since the Neolithic period and retains a sense of ceremony. Burial tombs mark the tops of mountains, like the Aillemore court tomb near Louisburgh. On Croagh Patrick, pilgrims journey to the church on the summit along the rocky trail, and on Reek Sunday walk it barefoot. The towns and villages feel isolated from one other but are often lively spots.

ORIENTATION

Westport, on the southeast corner of **Clew Bay,** is the hub for exploring the region. To the west, near the mouth of the bay, is **Clare Island,** 10 km (6 mi) away, accessible by ferry from **Roonagh Pier** near Louisburgh in County Mayo. Northwest of Westport, 50 km (30 mi) away and linked to the mainland by the Michael Davitt Bridge, is **Achill Island,** Ireland's largest.

WESTPORT

People come to Westport for its remote seaside location, and Croagh Patrick has become a beacon for outdoorsy types to paddle Clew Bay, climb the famous trail, and cycle the greenway. Others come for the atmosphere and the craic. Westport is well-known for talented musicians playing in pubs and small music festivals, which has given the town a slightly alternative feel. There's plenty of history, including Westport House and "the Curse of '51," which has prevented Yew County from winning the GAA football championship.

Sights

Westport House

Quay Rd.; tel. 353/98-27-766; www.westporthouse.ie; Mar.-Jan. daily 10am-5pm; €15

Within walking distance of the center of town, Westport House is a brilliant example of Georgian architecture. Built by the Browne family, who also founded the town, the house is on the site of a castle once owned by the fierce pirate queen Grace O'Malley. Access to the grounds is free, with three walking trails on the 160-ha (400-acre) property. To enter the house, you must be on a guided tour. The posh interiors feature period furniture, artwork, and historical artifacts. **Westport Adventure** is on-site for zip-lining, aerial trekking, and disc golf.

Beaches

Bertra Strand

Bertra Strand is a beautiful 1.5-km (1-mi) sand spit that reaches into Clew Bay from the foot of Croagh Patrick, creating striking places for a walk by the sea. Take in views of Clare Island and Achill Island and watch the windsurfers and kitesurfers on windy days. At low tide, an expansive beach makes a great stop along the Wild Atlantic Way or from Westport, 15 minutes away. There's plenty of parking at the nearby 50-space car park.

Hiking and Walking

★ Croagh Patrick

Distance: *7.1 km (4.4 mi) round-trip*
Duration: *3-4 hours*
Elevation gain: *764 m (2,506 ft)*
Effort: *Difficult*
Trailhead: *Croagh Patrick Visitor Centre*

No hike in Ireland has more cultural and historical importance than Croagh Patrick. The mountain is a 10-minute drive from Westport, near Bertra Strand, with a challenging hike to the top.

The mountain has been a pilgrimage site for over 5,000 years, dating to the pagan festival of Lughnasadh, which celebrated the beginning of the harvest season, but the connection to Ireland's patron, Saint Patrick, gave

Westport and Clew Bay

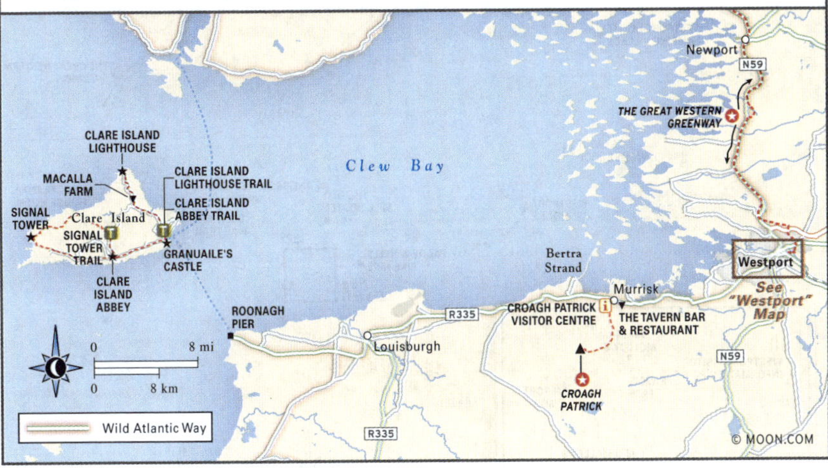

it its name and draws crowds. In 441 CE, Saint Patrick climbed the mountain and fasted for 40 days and nights, enshrining the mountain in Irish history. A church was built, now known as St. Patrick's Oratory, and pilgrims hike the trail on Reek Sunday, the last Sunday in July, with many doing it barefoot.

The route begins at the **Croagh Patrick Visitor Centre** (tel. 353/98-64-114; www.croagh-patrick.com) in Murrisk, where there is parking, a café, and information about the mountain, and of course fantastic views. The hike on the out-and-back trail gradually gets steeper, and it's rocky, with loose rocks underfoot, so pay attention to every step. Proper hiking footwear is a must, unless you're a pilgrim on Reek Sunday. At the summit, step inside the small church and join the thousands of pilgrims to look out over beautiful Clew Bay.

Westport House Loop

Distance: *2.4 km (1.5 mi) round-trip*
Duration: *45 minutes*
Elevation gain: *29 m (95 ft)*
Effort: *Easy*
Trailhead: *Westport House Car Park*

Starting at the main car park for Westport House, this walk is an easy stroll through the grounds of the estate and its parklands. Grab a coffee at the stables just steps into the walk and continue toward the Carrowbeg River. The river acts like a moat for Westport House, and it's not uncommon to see people kayaking. Gaze up at the fine house as the crushed gravel crunches underfoot, a common sound at stately homes like these. The parkland opens up with enormous beech trees and grazing horses. Continuing from the edge of the estate takes you back into town; otherwise, return along the same route, with a detour at the end into a quiet wooded area.

Cycling

★ The Great Western Greenway

Distance: *44 km (27 mi) one-way*
Duration: *3 hours*
Elevation gain: *82 m (269 ft)*
Effort: *Moderate*
Trailhead: *Mill Rd.*

The Great Western Greenway is Ireland's first greenway and one of the most popular in the country thanks to its amazing views, easy access from Westport, and flat profile from the town to Achill Island. The route is pedestrianized throughout and heads north

Westport

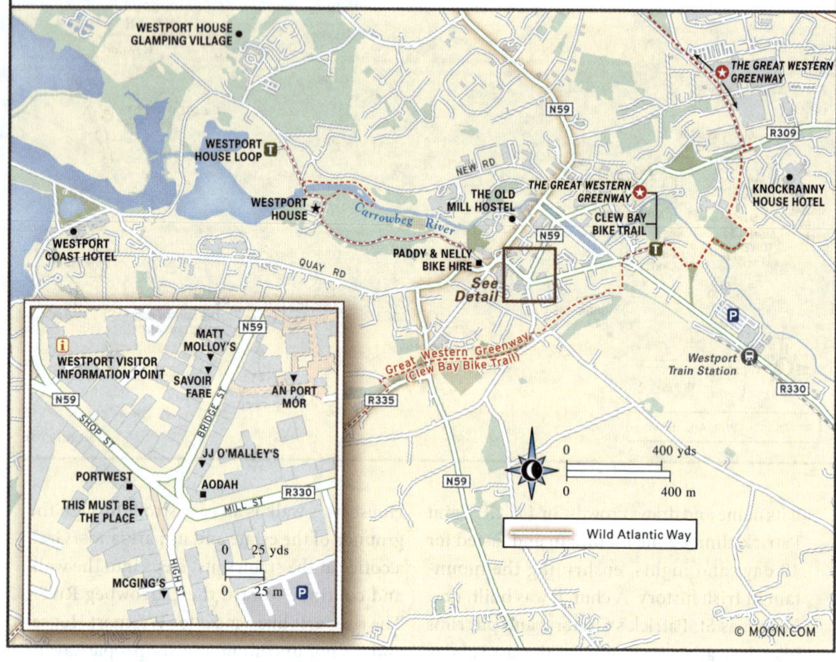

from Westport toward Clew Bay, where you'll see tiny islands in the water before reaching Newport and heading west for Achill. The greenway follows old railway lines, meaning they're quite flat and great for beginners, without the dangers of traffic or the challenge of big hills. As you reach Mulranny, you're within the last 15 km (9 mi) of the route; for most, this is time to refuel. Stop at **The Goat Café** (Main St.; tel. 353/98-36-106; www.mcloughlinsofmulranny.ie) for soup and a sandwich. Don't forget to refill your water bottle. From Mulranny, you cycle past Claggan Mountain before crossing the Michael Davitt Bridge to end on Achill Island. This is a popular route, so you'll see others enjoying the greenway and in cafés and pubs along the way.

Clew Bay Bike Trail

Distance: *105 km (65 mi) one-way*
Duration: *1-2 days*
Elevation gain: *1,164 m (3,819 ft)*
Effort: *Moderate-difficult*
Trailhead: *Westport*

This cycle route is for adventurous and experienced cyclists, with a bit of island hopping. Starting in Westport, the route heads west on the greenway to Murrisk, past the foot of Croagh Patrick, and on toward Louisburgh on winding country roads that can get quite busy. From here you'll cycle to Roonagh Pier, where the ferry to Clare Island sets sail. The loop around Clare Island is a tranquil, and you'll likely encounter more sheep than cars. Another ferry ride takes you north to Cloughmore on the southern tip of Achill Island. After a pedal along the coast, you arrive at the Michael Davitt Bridge to the mainland and the Great Western Greenway, which leads back to Westport. The challenge of this ride is the length, if you plan to do it in one day, and the logistics of timing the ferries. While the ferry to Clare Island runs daily year-round, the ferry to Achill only runs on Wednesday and Saturday-Sunday in July-August.

Paddy and Nelly Bike Hire

Church St.; tel. 353/83-882-5700; www.paddyandnelly.ie; Mon.-Sat. 9:30am-5:30pm, Sun. 10am-5pm; from €25

This bike shop in the center of town has a range of electric bikes to cycle the Great Western Greenway as well as Dutch tour bikes for a leisurely pedal through the grounds of Westport House or toward Croagh Patrick. Ask about family packages, which include bike seats and trailers.

Shopping

Aodah

Bridge St.; tel. 353/98-56-799; Instagram @aodha_westport; Tues.-Sat. 10am-6pm, Sun. 11am-4pm

This Irish craft and design shop is a great place to pick up a gift, with a wide selection for any budget. They don't focus on a particular craft or region; instead they've collected woodworking, photography, jewelry, and more from across the country. The bright and bold statement earrings from Culu Design are a big hit.

Portwest

Shop St.; tel. 353/98-51-729; www.theoutdoorshop.ie; daily 10am-6pm

This flagship outdoors store has a great choice of clothing and equipment, with its own designs alongside brands like Berghaus, Helly Hansen, Columbia, and Merrell. The staff are happy to give expert advice on rainwear, accessories, and wetsuits.

Food

This Must Be the Place

High St.; tel. 353/98-44-871; Instagram @thismustbetheplace_westport; Mon.-Sat. 8am-4pm, Sun. 9am-4pm; from €10

This 30-seat café feels like the center of town for 30-somethings. The pared-back furnishings are a mix of long wooden tables, enameled two-seaters, a collection of seats from primary schools, and bar seating along the window. The breakfast menu, served until 11:45am, is small but has trendy staples like shakshuka and poached eggs on toast. The changing lunch menu features arancini and poke bowls as the current top picks. The coffee is from Anam, a roastery in the Burren in County Clare, and it pairs brilliantly with the extensive choice of cookies, scones, cakes, and croissants. A small grocery section has Irish condiments and hot sauces.

Savoir Fare

Bridge St.; tel. 353/98-60-095; Instagram @savoir_fare; Tues.-Thurs. noon-5pm, Fri. noon-6pm, Sat. 11am-5pm; from €18

Using seasonal Irish produce to create French dishes, Savoir Fare has a reputation as a top-tier restaurant without the air of exclusivity. Open only during the day, it feels relaxed. The weekly special pâté en croûte (a loaf stuffed with pâté) uses local pork along with Mayo gooseberries and currants or pears with sage to create an unforgettable lunch. The low-intervention wines on offer improve the purity of the fruit while also being more environmentally friendly.

The Tavern Bar & Restaurant

Murrisk; tel. 353/98-64-060; www.tavernmurrisk.com; Wed.-Fri. 12:30pm-11:30pm, Sat.-Sun. 12:30pm-midnight; from €19

It's hard to miss the bright-pink exterior of The Tavern, in complete contrast to the muted natural tones of Croagh Patrick behind it. The sizeable menu uses local suppliers for vegetables, seafood, and pork and is a welcome sight for those who have just climbed the iconic peak. A mix of international cuisines

1
2

includes favorites like steamed Killary mussels, a feather blade of beef, and spiced Cajun chicken wraps. The decor is traditional, with rich wooden interiors, open fires, a pool table, and a bar stocked with Irish whiskey and beers.

An Port Mór

1 Brewery Place; tel. 353/98-26-730; www.anportmor.com; Tues.-Sat. 5pm-9:30pm, Fri. 4pm-9:30pm; from €39

Tucked away down a quiet lane is one of the nicest restaurants in Westport for an evening of fine Irish cuisine in a relaxed and unpretentious space. The staff are part of the welcoming feel as they crack a few jokes while they serve dishes like oxtail cottage pie and Atlantic plaice with a chicken butter sauce. The food is of high quality but the prices are reasonable—the three-course set menu costs €39. The dining area is a little unorthodox, as it snakes through the building, creating smaller spaces for more intimate meals.

Bars and Nightlife

★ Matt Molloy's

Bridge St.; tel. 353/98-26-655; www.mattmolloy.com; daily 12:30pm-midnight

Matt Molloy's is a trad music icon in Ireland for its lively sessions and famous owner. In 1989, Matt Molloy bought the pub, and his reputation as a member of Planxty and the Chieftains, both iconic Irish bands, saw the pub quickly become an important part of the music scene. There's live music seven nights a week, and the standard is always exceptional. The pub has a rich wooden interior that feels warm, with low ceilings and nooks that add to the coziness. The bar has a mix of craft beers alongside the more established breweries, but come for the craic more than anything else.

1: Croagh Patrick **2:** a bridge on the Great Western Greenway

McGing's

High St.; tel. 353/98-29-743; Facebook @mcgingsbar; daily 4pm-11:30pm, Fri. 4pm-12:30am, Sat. 2pm-12:30am

McGing's is a proper traditional pub that's slowly been brought into modern times. The bright yellow and blue exterior makes it hard to miss. Whether it's quiet or busy, the bare wooden furnishings and tiled floor create an atmosphere that's inviting and warm. The small room on the left side as you enter is the place to be. It feels like you've stepped back into the front room of a family member's house in the 1930s, which is fitting for the oldest pub in town. There's music regularly but it doesn't follow a schedule; they write their weekend music plans on the blackboard outside the pub.

JJ O'Malley's

Bridge St.; tel. 353/98-27-307; www.jjomalleys.com; Sun.-Wed. and Fri. 2pm-11:30pm, Thurs. 2pm-10pm, Sat. 2pm-12:30am

Decked floor-to-ceiling in wood, JJ O'Malley's is one of those spots that you might pop into for a quick bite and end up staying all night. Downstairs is the pub section and plenty of live music, but unlike most places in Westport, there's lots of contemporary and chart music played alongside the traditional. Upstairs is the restaurant, where things are a bit more relaxed, but it still has a good atmosphere. Hearty pub grub is on the menu, with tasty options like a blue cheese burger, surf and turf, and chicken parmigiana.

Accommodations

The Old Mill Hostel

Barracks Yard, James St.; tel. 353/98-27-045; www.oldmillhostel.com; €55

Most outdoorsy towns have a hostel that caters to hikers and walkers, and the Old Mill Hostel fills that role in Westport. The building has been here in the center of town for over 250 years; it was built as a warehouse and has served as a brewery, an animal shelter, and a forge before it was turned into a hostel in 1991. Catering to travelers on a budget, the nine rooms range from the smallest, with two bunk beds, through a 12-bed dorm. There are no single or private rooms, but breakfast is included.

Westport House Glamping Village

Quay Rd.; tel. 353/98-27-766; www.westporthouse.ie; €100

To live like the gentry without the cost, reserve a glamping stay at Westport House and wake to the beautiful parklands with the mountains in the distance. Each of the 17 bell tents comes with a double and two single beds, with nice touches like a picnic basket, a personal deck, and a barbecue. There are crisp cotton sheets, free Wi-Fi, and hot showers available. Taking a morning walk by the river is bliss.

Knockranny House Hotel

Knockranny; tel. 353/98-28-600; www.knockrannyhousehotel.ie; €150

This classically styled four-star hotel with 97 rooms is in the secluded foothills, yet just a 15-minute walk from the middle of Westport. Rooms are spacious regardless of the type; options include four-poster beds, two-bedroom suites, and a penthouse with a striking free-standing bath. There are US electric sockets in the rooms. While some hotel restaurants aren't worth shouting about, the dining options here are. Top of your list should be a sunset dinner reservation by the window in the **Fern Grill,** where the chef cooks an interesting mix of fowl and seafood alongside some vegetarian options. Afterward, stop by the **Brehon Bar** for the signature Brehon Cup, made with Southern Comfort, amaretto, Cointreau, Tito's vodka, grenadine, sour mix, and lemonade.

Westport Coast Hotel

The Quay; tel. 353/98-55-088; www.westportcoasthotel.ie; €180

This four-star hotel is on the waterfront at the pier in Westport, a five-minute drive from town, and feels like a quiet escape along the Wild Atlantic Way. The 12 room types include comfortable and recently renovated classic Queen rooms to the Experience rooms, with a balcony looking at Clew Bay or Croagh Patrick. Four self-catering apartments can sleep 2-9 people. Relax in the 17-m (56-ft) pool, jetted tub, and sauna. The **LuSeas Rooftop Restaurant** has unbeatable views of Croagh Patrick and Clew Bay and serves a seafood-heavy menu of traditional dishes.

Information and Services

Westport Visitor Information Point

The Octagon; tel. 353/98-28-459; Mon.-Sat. 9am-5:30pm

This small information point has local staff with plenty of knowledge and leaflets on local attractions. They also have information on other regions of Ireland.

Post Offices

The local **post office** (www.anpost.com) is on North Mall. There is an **AIB** (https://aib.ie) branch on Shop Street and a **Bank of Ireland** (www.bankofireland.com) on High Street.

Getting There and Around

The drive from Galway City to Westport is 80 km (50 mi) and takes about 1.25 hours. Follow the N84 north via Headford and Ballinrobe to Westport.

There are five direct buses to Westport daily with **Bus Éireann** (www.buseireann.ie) on Route 456 (1.5 hours; €14 one-way). Although Galway City and Westport both have train stations, they're not linked; instead you have to travel 85 km (53 mi) to Athlone and change trains. This option can take 3.5 hours, so it should be a last resort.

The drive from Clifden to Westport is 65 km (40 mi) and takes 1 hour. Follow the N59, which offers stunning views through the Connemara region, passing by Kylemore Abbey and Leenaun. The Bus Éireann Route 423 runs eight times daily from Clifden to Westport (1.25 hours; €13 one-way).

CLARE ISLAND

Don't let the name fool you; Clare Island is in County Mayo, not County Clare. It's a beautiful, tiny, remote island home to less than 150 people. Crossing on the ferry from Roonagh Pier, you're welcomed by stunning views of the harbor, guarded by Granuaile's Castle, home to the famous and feared pirate queen Gráinne Ní Mháille (Grace O'Malley). She guarded the waters of Clew Bay and charged sailors a toll to pass; if they didn't pay, she chased them down until they did. Thankfully, the island is far more welcoming these days, with most activity centered around the harbor, where you'll find a tiny café and two pubs. From here, walks, cycles, and hikes extend across the island to the Clare Island Lighthouse in the north, Clare Island Abbey in the south, and Signal Tower in the west.

Sights

Granuaile's Castle

Gráinne Ní Mháille, also known as Grace O'Malley, is a true Irish icon. In the late 1500s she defied gender roles, powerfully resisted English rule, and became one of the fiercest naval commanders Ireland has ever seen. Also known as the pirate queen, she became the head of her family's clan. Their castle is at the harbor on Clare Island, where she protected the waters. The impressive stone structure is closed to the public, but you can wander the grounds and look over the water, just as Gráinne Ní Mháille did 500 years ago.

Hiking and Walking

Clare Island Lighthouse

Distance: *8.8 km (5.5 mi) round-trip*
Duration: *2-3 hours*
Elevation gain: *72 m (236 ft)*
Effort: *Moderate*
Trailhead: *Clare Island Harbour*

This out-and-back trail begins at Clare Island Harbour and winds up to the lighthouse, built in 1806 by the Marquess of Sligo. It served for 159 years before being decommissioned in 1965. Today, it marks the island's maritime history and provides a lookout point. The walk to the lighthouse is beautiful and passes by Macalla Farm, where refreshments are available.

Clare Island Abbey

Distance: *3 km (2 mi) one-way*
Duration: *1 hour*
Elevation gain: *90 m (295 ft)*
Effort: *Easy*
Trailhead: *Clare Island Harbour*

Starting from Clare Island Harbour, the trail follows surfaced roads and easy tracks, passing through picturesque countryside. En route to the 13th-century abbey, hikers can enjoy panoramic views of Clew Bay and the landscape. This walk is suitable for most fitness levels and is an excellent opportunity to experience an even quieter side of this quiet island.

Signal Tower

Distance: *10.1 km (6.3 mi) loop*
Duration: *4 hours*
Elevation gain: *485 m (1,590 ft)*
Effort: *Moderate-challenging*
Trailhead: *Knockmore*

The Signal Tower walk on Clare Island is a challenging hike that leads to the ruins of a Napoleonic-era tower built in 1804. Starting at Knockmore, the loop begins with breathtaking views of Clew Bay and Achill Island before leading to the tower on the east coast of the island. Hikers should be prepared for changeable weather and varied terrain, including surfaced roads, tracks, and potentially boggy slopes. There is an alternative return route after you pass the signal tower, which offers a gentler but longer route back to the harbor along a dirt track and then road.

Food and Accommodations

Clare Island Oven

www.clareislandoven.com; Thurs.-Fri. 10am-3pm, Sat.-Sun. 10am-3pm and 6pm-8pm; from €10

Open for the season from May, Clare Island Oven is a food truck in a small courtyard that has some outdoor seating. The menu is tasty, with small freshly cooked pizzas and savory treats like sausage rolls. The owners are keen bakers, so treat yourself to something sweet. The coffee is from Java the Hut in Dublin.

1

2

Clare Island Community Centre Anchor Bar & Bistro

tel. 353/87-770-3976; www.clareislandcommunitycentre.com; daily 10am-8:15pm; from €15

In such small communities, businesses often have to wear multiple hats, so the community center is also the liveliest pub and the best place to get food in the evening. Most visitors to the island come here, and it's as much about meeting new people as food. The menu is pub grub with seafood featured prominently. The fish-and-chips with a pint of Guinness is hard to beat. The walls are decorated with photos of islanders throughout the ages, many celebrating their sporting successes.

Macalla Farm

tel. 353/87-250-4845; www.macallafarm.ie; Thurs.-Sun. 11:30am-4pm; from €17

Describing their ethos as "from seed to plate," Macalla Farm is a unique dining experience, as you're encouraged to learn about where your food comes from on their organic and regenerative farm. The food is all fresh, grown here, and focuses on seasonal ingredients. All dishes are vegetarian or vegan and of such high quality that even the most hardened carnivore will be won over. On weekends there's a six-course tasting menu in the evening. The café is small, and seating is limited, with eight tables inside the beautifully finished dining room, complete with a wood-paneled ceiling and whitewashed walls.

Getting There

Clare Island is only reached by boat from **Roonagh Pier** near Louisburgh in County Mayo. From Westport, drive west on the R335 for 30 minutes and follow signs to Louisburgh and then Roonagh Pier. **Clare Island Ferry Co** (www.clareislandferry.com) and **O'Malley Ferries** (www.clareislandfastferries.com) operate 4 crossings daily in winter and up to 10 in summer (20 minutes; €10 one-way).

1: Granuaile's Castle 2: Keem Bay

ACHILL ISLAND

John Lennon and Yoko Ono took a trip to Achill Island in 1967, as John wanted to buy an island in Clew Bay and live a quiet life away from the limelight. It's easy to imagine why he wanted to move here, as Achill Island is gorgeous, with idyllic spots like Keem Bay, just a short drive from Westport and connected to the mainland by bridge. This is Ireland's largest island, but it feels remote and sparsely populated. Achill is best experienced when you don't put too much importance on an itinerary. Instead, go at a slower pace and let the landscape and people direct your next move.

Orientation

The main areas on Achill Island are Achill Sound, near the bridge connecting the island to the mainland, and Keel, which stretches into Dooagh on the western tip.

Beaches

Keem Bay

Keem Bay is a long-standing favorite with Irish people, but the crystal-clear waters and white sand beach made people all over the world dream of coming to Ireland when it took center stage in the 2022 film *The Banshees of Inisherin.* The cottage that Brendan Gleeson's character lived in is here, but it's not an attraction; instead, people come for the natural beauty. Sheltered by steep hills, Keem Bay has unusually calm waters for the west coast, making it brilliant for a family dip in the sea, to try snorkeling, or to kayak. Wander the 1.5-km-long (1-mi) beach or venture uphill to the mass rock near the car park, where Catholic mass was held outdoors and in secret during British rule.

Hiking and Walking

Granuaile Loop Walk

Distance: *6.2 km (3.9 mi) loop*
Duration: *2.5 hours*
Elevation gain: *334 m (1,096 ft)*
Effort: *Moderate-difficult*
Trailhead: *Patten's Bar*

Pirate queen Gráinne Ní Mháille guarded

every inch of this part of the Irish coast, including a time she lived on Achill Island in Kildavnet Castle. This route can be done in either direction. Go counterclockwise from the trailhead for a shorter, steeper climb, or go clockwise for a gentler gradient over a longer distance. Whichever way you go, you'll see the castle to the south as well as cairns, which are prehistoric burial tombs for important people. The trail crosses bogland, and there's always the threat of rain in Ireland, so be prepared with waterproof footwear and a jacket. The trail ends back at **Patten's Bar** (Derreens; tel. 353/98-45-172; Facebook @pattenbar), as good an excuse for a drink as you're likely to find.

Food

One of the few downsides about remote parts of Ireland is that it can be difficult to find the upscale touches we get used to in the cities. But that's not the case on Achill Island.

Blásta at Ted's

Cashel; tel. 353/87-429-4994; Instagram @blastaatteds; Wed.-Sun. 11am-8pm; from €8

This seasonal food truck is well-known for cult Irish classics dialed up a notch. It's fast food made with proper ingredients to elevate it above the usual takeaway. Highlights on the menu are the chicken fillet roll and the curry chips. There are 10 colorful picnic tables to enjoy your grub with mountain views and fresh sea air. If indoor dining is a must, pop next door to Ted's Bar for some shelter and classic pub dishes.

Achill Island Kitchen

Dooagh Shop; tel. 353/85-760-2404; Instagram @achill_island_kitchen; Mon.-Sat. 9am-5pm, Sun. 9am-3pm; from €10

The Achill Island Kitchen is part café and part grocer, where they stock on-trend brands and serve delicious Colud Picker coffee. The menus are small but you'll find something to suit. In the morning, go with the breakfast bap, made with local sausages, rashers (similar to back bacon), and black pudding (blood sausage). For lunch, it's all about big sandwiches—the ham and cheese is hard to beat.

Bars and Nightlife

Lynott's Pub

Cashel; tel. 353/86-084-3137; Mon.-Thurs. 3pm-11:30pm, Fri. 3pm-12:30am, Sat. 2pm-12:30am, Sun. 2pm-11pm

Depending on who you ask, this is the smallest pub in Ireland, an old stone cottage with a thatched roof in what feels like the middle of nowhere along a country road. Inside, the lone room fills up unsurprisingly quickly with a surprising number of people. There's seating for 20 but more often squeeze in. This is definitely for those who like pubs with hustle and bustle and to chat with strangers. The odd tune is played too.

The Amethyst Bar

Keel; tel. 353/98-43-737; https://theamethystbar.com; summer daily 1pm-11:30pm; from €18

Once home to the famous landscape artist Paul Henry, the Amethyst Bar is now home to tasty pub grub served in a relaxed environment. Grab a seat at the circular bar or a table. On a sunny day, go for one of the four picnic tables outside. The menu is a throwback to classic pub fare, with deep-fried brie, poached salmon darns, and prawn cocktail. John Lennon and Yoko Ono had dinner here once. There's also regular live music, when the pub turns into a dance floor, but keep in mind that this seasonal pub closes once college starts in September.

Accommodations

Achill Cliff House Hotel

Keel; tel. 353/98-43-400; http://achillcliff.com; €160

This three-star hotel with 12 rooms is well located in Keel, making it easy to walk to Keel Beach and nearby pubs. The decor is dated, but the rooms are comfortable and come with all the amenities you'd expect. Choose between sea or countryside views. There's a restaurant in the hotel that is well-regarded in the area, particularly for its Clew Bay mussels.

Getting There

The drive from Westport to Achill Sound is 50 km (30 mi) and takes 50 minutes. The route is straightforward, on the N59 from Westport to Newport, then continuing through Mulranny. Shortly after Mulranny, turn onto the R319, which crosses the Michael Davitt Bridge to Achill.

The Route 450 direct bus, operated by **Bus Éireann** (www.buseireann.ie), departs from Westport six times daily for Achill Island (1 hour; €11 one-way). You can cycle the **Great Western Greenway** (page 335) the 44 km (27 mi) from Westport to Achill. It takes most cyclists about 3 hours.

Wild Nephin Ballycroy National Park

There's not much in Wild Nephin Ballycroy National Park, but that's what makes it so attractive. One of the least visited national parks, it covers 15,000 ha (37,000 acres) of mostly uninhabited land where flora and fauna thrive, giving an authentically wild feeling. The blanket bog system makes the landscape special: It's the biggest ecosystem of its type in Western Europe and creates a home for Greenland white-fronted geese, merlins, and otters.

The Nephin Beg Mountains in County Mayo form a rugged and remote range at the heart of Wild Nephin Ballycroy National Park. The highest peak, Nephin, at 806 m (2,644 ft), is the second-highest mountain in Connaught; Mweelrea beats it by 1 m (3 ft). The range runs north-south from Westport along Clew Bay into the Erris Peninsula. Hiking is the main outdoor activity, with plenty of options for all fitness levels, including short strolls and overnight hikes like the Bangor Trail. Try fishing for salmon and trout in the River Deel or look for red deer and pine martens.

VISITING THE PARK

Gateway Towns

For most visitors, Wild Nephin Ballycroy National Park is accessed via **Westport,** the largest tourism hub in the region. There are small towns closer to the park, like **Newport** and **Mulranny** in the south and **Crossmolina** in the north, but they have fewer services.

Visitor Centers

Ballycroy Visitor Centre

Ballycroy; www.nationalparks.ie/wild-nephin; daily 10am-5:30pm; free

In the western part of the park, the visitor center is a strikingly modern building that offers a welcome rest. Filled with natural light and exhibits, a visit is recommended, as there are no other services in the park. Stop by to ask about the trails and the best places to see wildlife. You can grab a bite at **Ginger & Wild Café** in the visitor center. There's also a short accessible trail on a raised boardwalk.

Tours

Wild Nephin doesn't have tours that you can book, but there are events throughout the year. These tend to be quite sporadic and ramp up in summer and around important dates like Heritage Week in August. They cover topics like guided walks to learn about plants, treasure hunts for kids, and talks with park rangers. These events are posted on the park's social media (@wildnephin_official).

HIKING AND WALKING

Claggan Mountain Boardwalk Trail

Distance: *2 km (1.2 mi) loop*
Duration: *30 minutes*
Elevation gain: *23 m (76 ft)*
Effort: *Easy*
Trailhead: *Coastal Trail Car Park*

This short, sweet walk by the shore and on a boardwalk is an easy way to experience the beautiful landscapes in Mayo. It's a loop

Mayo Dark Sky Park

Ballycroy Visitor Centre

There's a saying in Wild Nephin Ballycroy National Park that "half the park is after dark." When the sun sets on a clear evening, it is one of the best stargazing spots in Ireland thanks to the lack of light pollution. Mayo Dark Sky Park is free to access, and there are three main viewing points:

- **Brogan Carroll Bothy** (year-round daily 24 hours) is one of the very few bothies (mountain huts for shelter) in Ireland, 15 km (9 mi) from Newport, with lots of parking available. It often has hikers sleeping inside.
- **Claggan Mountain Boardwalk Trail** is 5 km (3 mi) from Mulranny on the Achill Island side of the park and is a smart choice for a walk under the night sky (page 345).
- **Ballycroy Visitor Centre** has a 2-km (1.2-mi) walk. To make the stars as visible as possible, there are no lights, so bring a torch or a headlamp (page 345).

walk with parking at the trailhead. Head south along the water and take in views of Bleanmore Island. This area of the park is covered in blanket bog, and you can see the remnants of ancient trees sticking out of the turf. There's very little elevation gain, and like most trails in Ireland, it's best enjoyed in summer.

Letterkeen Walking Loops

Distance: *6-12 km (3.7-7.5 mi) loops*
Duration: *3 hours for the red route*
Elevation gain: *382 m (1,253 ft)*
Effort: *Moderate-difficult*
Trailhead: *Letterkeen Trailhead at Brogan Carroll Bothy*

There are three loop walks that start at Brogan Carroll Bothy, with the 10-km (6-mi) **red route** being the pick of the bunch. The hike takes you from peaceful woodland trails to exposed and windswept sections of open mountain rambles across boggy ground. There's plenty of uphill on this route, but over the crest of every ridge is another beautifully sparse view across the Nephin Beg Mountains and Lough Aroher.

The **blue route** is shorter at 6 km (3.7 mi) and follows the path of an old cattle road, which farmers used to bring their livestock to market. For a longer and more challenging day out, try the 12 km (7.5 mi) **purple route,** which crosses a stream to reach the edge of remote forested land. This trail is difficult underfoot, so it's for experienced hikers.

Bangor Trail

Distance: *39 km (24 mi) one-way*
Duration: *10-12 hours*
Elevation gain: *985 m (3,232 ft)*
Effort: *Difficult*
Trailhead: *Mullet*

I can't imagine a better place to get away from it all than the Bangor Trail. An old route from Bangor Erris to Newport, parts of it have been used since the Iron Age. As well as enjoying views of the mountains and the peace of isolation, you'll also cross the Tarsaghaunmore River and wander down country roads and through boglands. It's a difficult hike with tricky terrain, and there are no shops along the way.

While fit hikers might complete the route in one long day, most will do it over two and sleep in **Lough Aroher Hut** or **Brogan Carroll Bothy,** both around the halfway mark, or dispersed camp. The north section of the trail is more difficult, so preserve enough supplies to make it the rest of the way.

GETTING THERE AND AROUND

To get to Wild Nephin Ballycroy National Park Visitor Centre from Westport, you have to drive, as there are no public transport options. Take the N59 north toward Newport, continuing through Mulranny, and follow the signs for Ballycroy. The journey is 45 km (28 mi) and takes 45-60 minutes.

The Northwest

In this wild and powerful part of Ireland, nature

is at its rawest. Frighteningly large waves rush in from the Atlantic Ocean, creating dramatic coastlines. The Sliabh Liag cliffs defy the waves and roaring winds. These conditions make Sligo and Donegal fantastic places for surfing, particularly in winter, when the waves are much bigger. The weather isn't always fantastic, but the views are. The powerful beauty of nature has also inspired delicate works of art.

Inland from the coast is Glenveagh National Park, in a sheltered valley in the Derryveagh Mountains. The grandeur of the landed gentry is on display, but scratch the surface and you'll hear stories of a wicked landlord and an eccentric archaeologist who went missing in suspicious circumstances.

Highlights

Look for ★ to find recommended sights, activities, dining, and lodging.

★ **National Surf Centre:** Learn to surf on Strandhill Beach at this facility dedicated to one of Sligo's favorite sports (page 360).

★ **Benbulben:** Discover this unearthly mountain shrouded in folklore and mysticism. Walk its forested foothills or make the tough hike to the top (page 362).

★ **Mullaghmore Head:** Walk this coastal beauty to see enormous waves thunder against the shore and the brave surfers who try to conquer them (page 364).

★ **Sliabh Liag:** Take in views of the Atlantic from the highest sea cliffs in Europe. Walk to the lookout point or take the grueling hike to the summit (page 376).

★ **Glenveagh National Park:** Explore this vast wild national park, interwoven with trails and shocking stories about some of the previous owners (page 378).

★ **Murder Hole Beach:** Gruesomely named but beautifully set, this might be the most stunning beach in a country that's home to many dramatic beaches (page 383).

★ **Fanad Lighthouse:** Stand on a remote part of the north coast of Ireland and drink in the views from this historic lighthouse that has protected sailors since 1817 (page 384).

The landscape has been an inspiration for generations, with mythological tales from Benbulben of unrelenting love and fearsome warriors. Sligo is called Yeats country, after the family of artists who drew inspiration here and gained worldwide fame for their paintings and poetry. In rural parts of Donegal, the local pub is the hub of the community, where stories are told and songs are sung, nurturing the talent of famous musicians like the band Clannad, which Enya was part of. "Powerful" is the only way to describe this region, for the views, the weather, and the lasting impact it has.

ORIENTATION

Northwestern Ireland is a beautiful, raw, and wild region with a dramatic coastline and remote mountain ranges in County Sligo and County Donegal. Starting in the south, Sligo is famed for its dramatic landscapes, like **Benbulben, Strandhill,** and **Mullaghmore,** all just a short drive from **Sligo Town,** the most populated place in this region.

North of Sligo lies Donegal, one of three counties in the traditional province of Ulster that are in the Republic of Ireland rather than Northern Ireland. Donegal begins with **Bundoran**, **Ballyshannon,** and **Donegal Town** in quick succession. West of Donegal Town are the towering cliffs of **Sliabh Liag,** with breathtaking views of the Atlantic. Following the coast, Donegal begins to feel remote, with **Árainn Mhór** and **Tory Island** to the west and **Glenveagh National Park** to the east. Continuing farther north are the scenic lookout points on **Fanad Head** before reaching the tip of mainland Ireland at **Malin Head.**

PLANNING YOUR TIME

Plan to spend at least three days in this part of Ireland. Sligo and its surroundings can be seen in a full day, splitting your time between Strandhill, Mullaghmore, and the town itself. Glenveagh National Park also warrants a full day, as it gets more and more beautiful the deeper you go into it. A full day by the coast is also recommended. Murder Hole Beach is the most picturesque; for remote landmarks, try Fanad Lighthouse or Malin Head. The adventurous can take the ferry to Árainn Mhór for the night, or spend the day in Derry.

Itinerary Ideas

Get as active or as leisurely as you like in the mountains and by the coast. The views are best enjoyed by getting onto the land, but you can also appreciate the landscapes from a distance.

DAY 1: SLIGO

1 Start your day with a 20-minute drive north to **Mullaghmore Head,** passing Benbulben en route. See Classiebawn Castle and drive the coastal road or walk the 4.5-km (2.8-mi) route.

2 Make your way over to Strandhill for breakfast at **Shells Café.**

3 Take a surf lesson with any of the surf schools at the **National Surf Centre.**

4 Pop into Sligo Town and tuck into the haddock tacos at **Hooked.**

Pervious: Sliabh Liag cliffs; Benbulben; National Surf Centre's surfing school.

The Northwest

THE NORTHWEST
ITINERARY IDEAS

Itinerary Ideas

5 Recover from your busy day with revitalizing evening at the Arabian-inspired Sólás Spa at the **Radisson Blu Hotel & Spa.**

DAY 2: SOUTH DONEGAL AND SLIABH LIAG

1 Begin the day in Bundoran with a barbecue breakfast burrito and coffee at **Foam.**

2 Enjoy a leisurely 20-minute walk to the **Fairy Bridge and Wishing Well,** where you cross the natural stone bridge above the sea.

3 Drive north and stop in Ballyshannon to see the **statue** of legendary guitarist **Rory Gallagher.**

4 Visit the **Donegal Craft Village** in Donegal Town for handmade gifts.

5 Drive to the **Sliabh Liag cliffs** and walk to the viewing platform for incredible views.

6 Stop at the **Killybegs Seafood Shack** in Killybegs for fish-and-chips by the pier.

7 Have a relaxing evening and book into **Harvey's Point** hotel. Enjoy a nightcap by Lough Eske.

DAY 3: GLENVEAGH NATIONAL PARK

1 Drive to Glenveagh National Park and get a good understanding of the park's history, landscapes, and animals at the **visitor center.**

2 Take the shuttle bus to **Glenveagh Castle** to learn about its history, infamous past owners, and famous visitors.

3 See the beauty on the **Bridle Path Walk,** which takes 3-4 hours, or stroll around the gardens for a shorter outing.

4 Book a table at **Fisk** in Downings for dinner. The prawn bánh mì is delicious.

5 After dinner, join a singsong in **The Singing Pub (An Sibín Ceoil).**

Sligo

Sligo feels like the forgotten middle child of the Wild Atlantic Way. Most visitors go south to Cork, Kerry, and Galway; some even venture north to Donegal, but few have Yeats country on their radar. They're missing out: While Sligo might not have big-name attractions, it's brimming with incredible coastal views and enough history to keep you enthralled. Sligo is a place to leave the crowds behind for a slower, more authentic experience.

ORIENTATION

In County Sligo, you'll spend most of your time close to the coast. **Sligo Town** is the main hub in the east of the county, surrounded by highlights like **Strandhill, Rosses Point,** and **W. B. Yeats's Grave.** To the north is **Benbulben** and the enormous waves of **Mullaghmore.**

SLIGO TOWN

Sligo Town (pop. 20,000) is where most people base themselves. It has a nice mix of traditional experiences and modern businesses, from pubs with fascinating backstories to surf shack-inspired seafood restaurants. From Sligo Town you can reach most highlights in 15-30 minutes.

Sligo

NATIONAL SURF CENTRE
THE STRAND BAR
SHORE RD
Strandhill Bus Stop
SURF N STAY
SHELLS CAFE
VOYA SEAWEED BATHS
Strandhill Beach
0 100 yds
0 100 m
MULLAGHMORE HEAD
MULLAGHMORE HEAD WALK
Mullaghmore
THE DONEGAL CYCLE ROUTE
CLASSIEBAWN CASTLE
N15
R279
ATLANTIC OCEAN
GORTAROWEY FOREST RECREATION CAR PARK
BENBULBEN
Benbulben Forest Walk
LEITRIM
SLIGO
The Devil's Chimney Waterfall
DEVIL'S CHIMNEY WATERFALL CAR PARK
N16
DRUMCLIFFE CHURCH & W. B YEAT'S GRAVE
0 2 mi
0 2 km
THE DRIFTWOOD
Rosses Point
R291
RADISSON BLU HOTEL & SPA
Wild Atlantic Way
Sligo Bay
See "Sligo Town" Map
See Detail
Strandhill
R292
KNOCKNAREA (QUEEN MEABH'S GRAVE)
Knocknarea
Sligo
STRANDHILL LODGE & SUITES
THE VENUE BAR & RESTAURANT
N4
SLIGO PARK HOTEL
© MOON.COM

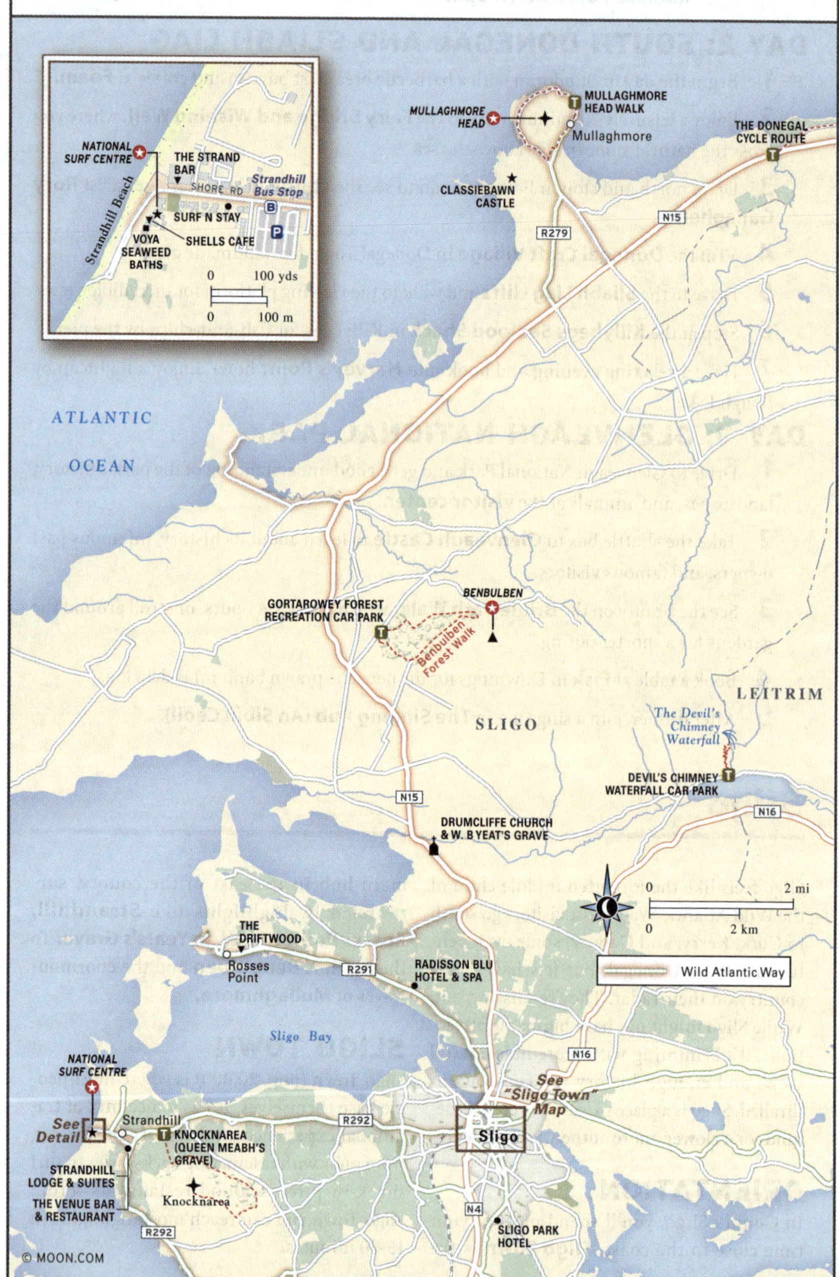

Sligo Town

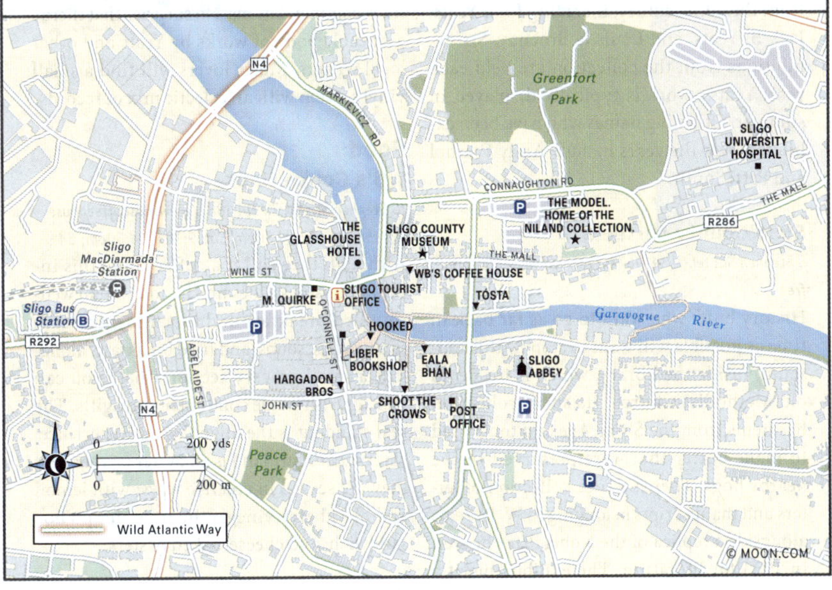

Sights

Drumcliffe Church and W. B. Yeats's Grave

Drumcliffe Church; tel. 71/914-3815; www.drumcliffechurch.ie; daily 9am-5pm; free

The Yeats family was an incredibly talented and creative bunch that has given Sligo an immense sense of pride. Of six children, William Butler (often called W. B.) and Jack were the most successful. Jack was a fantastic painter; he won Ireland's first ever Olympic gold in 1924 when painting was part of the games. Writer, poet, and Nobel laureate W. B. has the closest connection to the area, and you can visit his grave 10 minutes north of town at Drumcliffe Church. For such a celebrated individual, his grave is remarkably plain. The inscription reads, "Cast a cold eye on life, on death. Horseman, pass by!" Chosen for the views and because Yeats's great-grandfather was once rector, the church is still in use today.

Sligo Abbey

Abbey St.; tel. 71/914-6406; https://heritageireland.ie/places-to-visit/sligo-abbey; daily 10am-5:15pm; €5

This gem of Ireland's medieval Christian past is easy to spot and illustrates the story of the town. Architecturally, it is a mix of Romanesque and Gothic styles across the cloister arcade, the remains of the church, and the sculptures around the site, but what happened here over time makes it interesting. The wooden cross was once commandeered as a battering ram in a siege. It was severely damaged by a plantation landlord in 1642 and subsequently abandoned. The graveyard closed permanently in 1847 when it filled up with those who died in the famine.

The Model, Home of the Niland Collection

The Mall; tel. 71/914-1405; www.themodel.ie; Tues.-Sat. 11am-5pm; free

Offsetting the historic sights around Sligo is the Model, one of the most impressive contemporary art centers in the country. The focus is on visual and performing arts, with the Niland Collection comprising 300 works from the 20th century, including John Yeats, Jack B. Yeats, and Louis le Brocquy. Six exhibitions from the collection are held each year; Yeats's work is typically displayed in summer. Other big names who have been exhibited over the years include Andy Warhol and Patti Smith.

Sligo County Museum

3 Stephen St.; tel. 71/911-1679; Tues.-Sat. 9:30am-1pm; free

History buffs who want to go as far back in time as possible will want to stop by this museum, inside the library, which is inside an old Methodist Church. Its small collection has items from the Stone Age and tools used to make butter that were preserved in the nearby bogs. There's a nice collection of letters and manuscripts belonging to W. B. Yeats alongside a replica of the Nobel Prize he won in 1923 for literature. The exhibits merit a short visit.

Shopping

Sligo Town is a small, so shopping options aren't extensive, but the commercial parts of the town center are around John Street, O'Connell Street, and Lower Knox Street.

M. Quirke

23 O'Connell St.; tel.71/42624; hours vary

Michael Quirke is a local woodcarver whose works feature the mythology and stories of the area. He was trained as a butcher by his father and worked in this trade until 1988, when he converted the family storefront into his studio and shop. Inside are hand-carved figures of the Fianna warriors, Irish wolfhounds, and medieval Vikings. He's a local legend in Sligo, so even if you're just browsing, it's worthwhile dropping in for a chat with the artist.

Liber Bookshop

35 O'Connell St.; tel. 71/914-2219; www.liber.ie; Mon.-Sat. 9am-6pm

Find the antidote to impersonal online book shopping at Liber, with a homey feel that makes it comfortable to browse or ask staff for recommendations. No surprise that there's a sizeable body of works by Yeats and other local writers. Music lovers will find a small vinyl section with an eclectic mix of records.

Food

WB's Coffee House

10 Stephen St.; tel. 71/914-1883; www.wbscoffeehouse.ie; Mon.-Fri. 9am-4:30pm, Sat. 9:30am-4:30pm; €4

Although they call it a coffee shop, this inventive business does much more: Small well-rounded breakfast and lunch menus serve sandwiches, soups, and fried breakfasts alongside a small grocery section where you can pick up Irish-made condiments and gifts. The real standout is the Sligo Oyster Experience. The owner's husband is an oyster farmer, and they are served in creative ways: with lemon and blackberry vinegar, in an oyster po'boy sandwich, and cheese-baked oysters.

Tósta

Bridge St.; Instagram @tosta_sligo; Mon.-Fri. 8am-4pm, Sat. 9:30am-4pm; €9

Tósta has mastered toasted sandwiches. Toasties, as they're known in Ireland, are a people-pleasing favorite, and gourmet ones like these are becoming very popular. The slow-cooked pulled ham hock with Ballymaloe relish and their own signature cheese blend is the best of the bunch. It's also a good spot for vegetarians, with a triple-cheese option and one with sun-dried tomato, caramelized onion, and pesto. There's a small bar seating area by the window and a small table outside.

Hooked

Rockwood Parade; tel. 71/913-8591; http://hookedsligo.ie; Mon.-Thurs. noon-9pm, Fri.-Sun. 9:30am-9pm; €15

Restaurateurs in Sligo make the most of the sea, and at Hooked they've taken the nautical theme a step farther and designed the

---

1: W. B. Yeats's grave **2:** Sligo Abbey **3:** Drumcliffe Church

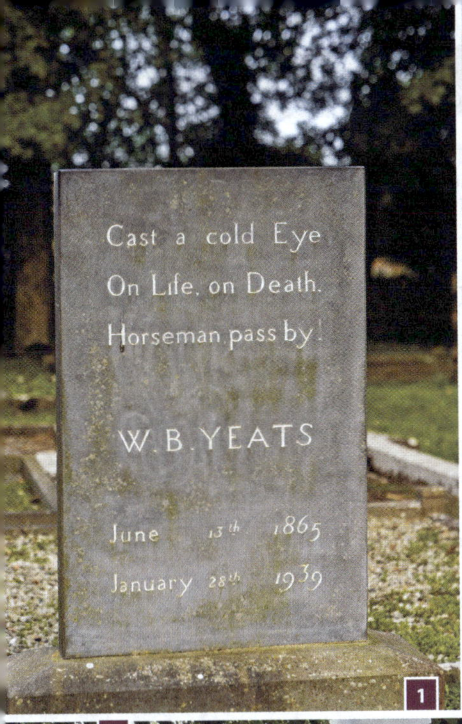
Cast a cold Eye
On Life, on Death.
Horseman pass by!
W. B. YEATS
June 13th 1865
January 28th 1939
1

2

Sligo Food Trail

oysters by the sea

The Sligo Food Trail (www.sligofoodtrail.ie) is a self-guided culinary route with over 70 food businesses from Enniscrone in the west to Mullaghmore in the east.

LOCAL SPECIALTIES

The aim is to promote local produce and sustainability. The Atlantic Ocean provides a healthy supply of seafood, and rivers, forests, and artisanal farms also contribute. The standouts to watch for are **Knocknarea honey, wild Mullaghmore lobster,** and **Lissadell oysters.**

BEST FOOD STOPS

A lot of the restaurants on the route are in the populous Sligo Town, but others are worth traveling for:

- At **WB's Coffee House,** try Lissadell oysters, farmed by the owner's husband (page 356).
- Check the social media pages for **Hooked** to see if the seasonal lobster rolls are on the menu—they're not to be missed (page 356).
- **The Driftwood** (Rosses Point Upper; tel. 71/931-7070; www.thedriftwood.ie; Thurs. 8am-9pm, Fri.-Sat. 8am-9:30pm, Sun. 8am-9pm; €18-34) in Rosses Point serves upmarket pub grub in a beautiful setting.
- **The Beach Bar** (Aughris Head; tel. 71/917-6465; www.thebeachbarsligo.com; daily noon-8pm; €14-28) in Aughris is a 300-year-old thatched pub with a traditional restaurant.

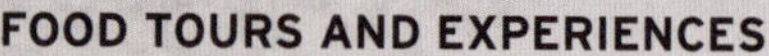

FOOD TOURS AND EXPERIENCES

For a more hands-on experience, join a tour along the trail:

- At the **Sligo Oyster Farm** (www.sligooysterexperience.ie; €45), learn how the oyster is forever linked with Sligo's heritage before watching them being professionally shucked and chowing down on the fresh shellfish, including Lissadell oysters.
- Meet up with chef and herbalist **Gaby Wieland** (neantog@gmail.com; €15) to go foraging in the woods for flowers, berries, and roots before learning how to cook them.

restaurant in the mixed-color wooden planks you'd see on old fishing boats. There's a good selection of seafood alongside meat options and a handful of choices for vegetarians and vegans. Hooked serves breakfast, brunch, and evening menus, with the smoked salmon shakshuka a standout for early risers, the pork belly Benedict a brunch highlight, and the beer-battered fish-and-chips a must in the evening.

Eala Bhán

5 Rockwood Parade; tel. 71/914-5823; www.ealabhan.ie; Mon.-Thurs. 5pm-9pm, Fri.-Sun. noon-9pm; €28

Local produce is front and center with 10 suppliers contributing to the menu at this fine-dining restaurant overlooking the Garvogre River. Among the six menus, the pre-theater menu has the best value, with three courses for €45; the braised feather blade of beef is a highlight. Foodies will want to reserve the eight-course tasting menu (€95 pp), where you'll try dishes like duck cooked three ways (liver pâté, smoked breast, and plum bonbon) and pan-seared lemon buttered scallops. During autumn and winter, they serve afternoon tea on weekends.

Bars and Nightlife

Shoot the Crows

Abbeyquarter South; tel. 71/914-2821; daily 5pm-11:30pm; €6

Most traditional pubs in Ireland are named after a family, making Shoot the Crows an outlier. The story goes that 150 years ago, the local landowner offered a reward for every crow shot on his land, paid weekly. The pub owner wanted his patrons to have money for beer every day, so he offered to pay a slightly lower rate, but paid daily. He then brought everyone's crows to the landowner, making a tidy profit. The pub is a real gem; it's dark, moody, and during winter when the fireplace in the back is blazing, warm. The drink offerings are straightforward, with the big-name brewers and some local craft beers on tap.

Hargadon Bros

The Canopy; tel. 71/915-3709; www.hargadons.com; Tues.-Thurs. noon-10pm, Fri.-Sat. noon-12:30am; €6

Hargadon Bros is one of those traditional Irish pubs that does everything. It has beautiful architectural touches, like the original stone floor and paneled snugs from 1864, and is a *Michelin Guide* recommended restaurant, where they delicately plate hearty modern pub grub like lamb stew, duck leg confit, and moules-frites. In the grocery section, pick up a fine wine, Irish whiskey, or champagne. The pub is worth a visit, but if you want to eat, book a table online in advance, especially on weekends in summer.

Accommodations

Sligo Park Hotel

Pearse Rd.; tel. 71/919-0400; www.sligoparkhotel.com; €140

Located 2 km (1.2 mi) south of Sligo Town, this spacious and luxurious four-star hotel has large parkland around it. There are 136 rooms, with the Innisfree Suite the top one with countryside views. There's a 16-m (53-ft) indoor pool, a jetted tub, and a gym. The food options are great: **The Hazelwood Restaurant** is a contemporary award-winning restaurant open for breakfast and dinner, and for casual meals, **Jack B's Bar** serves food from 10:45am daily.

Radisson Blu Hotel & Spa

Ballincar; tel. 71/914-0008; www.radissonhotels.com; €150

Wake to sea views in this 132-room hotel disguised as a manor house. The four-star rating and fantastic views toward Sligo Town and Rosses Point are big draws, along with the thermal suite at the **Sólás Spa** (tel. 71/919-2442; Sun.-Fri. 10am-6pm, Sat. 9:30am-6:30pm; €35 pp), the quartz crystal steam room, the herb sauna, and the ice fountain. Stop by the brasserie, where you'll find reimagined Irish dishes like roast chicken served with chestnut stuffing.

The Glasshouse Hotel

Swan Point; tel. 71/919-4300; www.theglasshouse.ie; €210

This four-star, 116-room hotel is in the middle of town and looks like a ship that's about to set sail. The modern exterior is reflected inside with extensive use of glass and metal, giving the hotel an up-to-date feel. **The Café Bar** is for casual bites, and for your evening meal, book a table overlooking the river at **The Kitchen Restaurant.** There's no pool or spa.

Information and Services

The **Sligo Tourist Office** (O'Connell St.; tel. 71/914-2821; Mon.-Sat. 10am-5pm, Sun. noon-5pm) is in the Old Bank Building. **Sligo University Hospital** (The Mall; tel. 71/917-1111; www.saolta.ie; daily 24 hours) is the main hospital for emergency care. There are multiple ATMs around town and an **AIB** (Stephen St.; www.aib.ie) branch. There are two **post offices** (www.anpost.ie): one on Knox Street and one on Castle Street.

Getting There and Around

You can walk between the main sights in just a few minutes, but to visit Benbulben and Yeats's grave outside town, the easiest solution is to rent a car. **Transport for Ireland** (www.transportforireland.ie) operates the Route 982 bus to this area, but there are only nine buses a day.

The 140-km (87-mi) drive from Galway City to Sligo Town takes 2 hours on the N83, N17, and N4 roads. **Expressway** (www.expressway.ie) operates Route 64 (2.5 hours; from €15 one-way), the most direct and frequent bus service. Buses depart from **Galway Coach Station** (Fairgreen Rd.) to **Sligo Bus Station** (Lord Edward St.) every 2 hours. **Bus Éireann** (www.buseireann.ie) also provides hourly buses on this route with similar fares. There are no trains between Galway and Sligo.

The drive from Dublin City to Sligo Town is 210 km (130 mi) and 2.75 hours on the M4 and N4. **Bus Éireann** (www.buseireann.ie) runs Route 23 (3.5 hours; from €15 one-way), departing from the Busáras central bus station in Dublin to Sligo Bus Station (Lord Edward St.). **Expressway** (www.expressway.ie) runs buses on this route with similar journey times and fares. **Irish Rail** (www.irishrail.ie) operates direct trains (3 hours; from €20 one-way) from Dublin Connolly Station (Amiens St.) to **Sligo MacDiarmada Station** (Knappagh Rd.). Both bus and train services operate multiple times daily.

STRANDHILL

Just a 15-minute drive from Sligo Town, Strandhill is a picturesque and exciting seaside town packed with great food and bars. It's a magnet for surfers with the newly opened National Surf Centre, which brings a youthful energy to the area. There's enough to keep you entertained for a full day even if you don't plan on getting in the water.

Sights

TOP EXPERIENCE

★ National Surf Centre

Shore Rd.; tel. 71/919-3550; www.nationalsurfcentre.ie; Mon.-Fri. 9am-5pm

Sligo is one of the main destinations for big-wave surfers in Ireland, but Strandhill is protected from the big swells, making it the ideal spot for the new National Surf Centre. This purpose-built facility has **Sligo Surf Experience** (www.sligosurfexperience.com) and **Atlantic Surf School Strandhill** (www.atlanticsurfschoolstrandhill.ie) schools, with beginner lessons on Strandhill Beach. More advanced surfers are brought to the bigger waves along the coast. Expect hot showers, spacious changing rooms, and a surf shop. They also host occasional community events that cover foraging, photography, and cooking by the coast.

Hiking and Walking

Knocknarea (Queen Medb's Cairn)

Distance: *10 km (6 mi) round-trip*
Duration: *2.5-3 hours*
Elevation gain: *327 m (1,072 ft)*
Effort: *Moderate*
Trailhead: *Sligo Rugby Club*

Queen Medb (anglicized as Maeve) was a legendary figure in Irish folklore. She led the famous **Táin Bó Cúailnge** (page 146) and battled with her foes in Ulster. When she died, she was buried on top of Knocknarea; some believe she was buried upright and facing Ulster. A wide natural track leads up the barren hillside to the stone monument, where you'll get fantastic views of Strandhill Beach and Benbulben. In summer you can join the **Warriors Run** (www.warriorsrun.ie), a race to the top from Strandhill.

Beaches

Strandhill Beach

Everything in Strandhill centers around the beach. Regardless of the weather, you'll see people walking on the beach or heading into

Big-Wave Surfing

big-wave surfing

Big-wave surfing is one of those extreme sports that goes under the radar, but when you see it, it stops you in your tracks.

WHAT IS BIG-WAVE SURFING?

Generally speaking, big-wave surfing is when waves are over 6 m (20 ft). Waves of this size require longer surfboards and Jet Skis to tow the surfers in—you can't paddle onto these waves. Big-wave surfing is only for experts, as you need a deep understanding of the sport and the waves.

WHY ARE THERE SO MANY BIG WAVES IN IRELAND?

A combination of the raw power of the Atlantic Ocean combined with the underwater reefs and shelves along the west coast creates big waves. The beautiful locations and remote beaches are another draw for adventurous surfers.

WHERE ARE THE BIGGEST WAVES?

Sligo is a key location in the big-wave scene in Ireland, with **Mullaghmore Head** considered legendary, where it's possible to get 15-m (50-ft) waves. When a big swell hits, try to see surfers taking on these almost unbelievable waves.

the waves on surfboards. Walkers can take in views of the nearby mountain Knocknarea and try to spot Queen Medb's cairn on top before stopping at one of the cafés along the beachfront. Join a surf lesson with one of the local schools, **Sligo Surf Experience** (www.sligosurfexperience.com) and **Atlantic Surf School Strandhill** (www.atlanticsurf-schoolstrandhill.ie), both at the National Surf Centre.

Spas and Saunas

VOYA Seaweed Baths

Shore Rd.; tel. 71/916-8686; www.voyaseaweedbaths.com; daily 10am-6pm; €45

The owners of VOYA Seaweed Baths make the most of their location, collecting local seaweed to create unique experiences. The most popular treatment is the seaweed bath (€45), where you lower yourself into a warm bath loaded with seaweed that rejuvenates skin and provides a natural detox. For a more traditional experience, there are massages (from €50) and facials (from €80).

Food

The Strand Bar

Shore Rd.; tel. 71/916-8140; www.thestrandbar.ie; Mon.-Thurs. noon-11:30pm, Fri.-Sat. noon-12:30am, Sun. noon-11pm; €6

The Strand Bar has been beside Strandhill Beach for over 100 years and still draws a big crowd of locals and visitors. The pub has retained its traditional feel, with blazing fireplaces, cozy snugs, and a hearty food menu, with the Guinness beef stew the recommended choice. There's also a more modern dining area up front with a pizza menu in a bright space decorated with leafy plants and light wood furniture.

The Venue Bar and Restaurant

Top Rd.; tel. 71/916-8167; www.venuestrandhill.ie; daily 12:30pm-9:30pm; €6

To avoid the hubbub along the beachfront, particularly during summer, make your way to the traditional Venue Bar and Restaurant on the edge of town. Quieter than others in town because of its location, it still attracts people with local seafood, steaks, and live music on the weekend. Spend an evening by booking a table and having the chargrilled salmon steak for dinner and then grab a seat and a drink beside the fireplace in the pub while you wait for the traditional music to start.

Shells Café

Seafront; tel. 71/912-2938; www.shellscafe.com; daily 9am-6pm; €7

Very busy Shells Café overlooks the beach and serves breakfast from 9am and lunch from noon. Local produce is in familiar favorites like eggs benny and more interesting dishes like beef rendang. When the weather is good, get a seat at the four outdoor tables for better views of the sea. Shells Café has a lifestyle store section with homewares and accessories like wooly hats and socks from Irish makers.

Accommodations

Surf N Stay

Shore Rd.; tel. 71/916-8313; €40

Catering to surfers, this cheap and cheerful lodging is mere meters from the action on Strandhill Beach. Twin rooms and rooms with two sets of bunk beds make it a good choice for groups on a budget. There's a surf school here and secure board storage inside. It's self-catering but close to cafés and restaurants if you don't want to cook.

Strandhill Lodge & Suites

Top Rd.; tel. 71/912-2122; https://strandhilllodgeandsuites.ie; €250

This recently built 22-room hotel is welcoming and personable, and if you book a room with a balcony, you'll wake up to sea views. Rooms are modern and serviceable for a short stay, with en suite baths, coffeemaking facilities, and flat-screen TVs. Upgrade to a suite for a king bed. There's no pool or spa, but the staff can book a session with the nearby **VOYA Seaweed Baths.** It's a 10-minute walk from Strandhill Beach for a dip in the sea.

Getting There and Around

Strandhill is less than 9 km (5.5 mi) from Sligo Town, a 15-minute drive on the R292 road. **Bus Eireann** (www.buseireann.ie) operates Route S2 from Markievicz Road in Sligo to Strandhill (40 minutes; €6 one-way), which runs twice per hour during the day. There are no cycle lanes separate from car traffic on this road; instead there's a cycle lane painted on the hard shoulder.

★ BENBULBEN

The striking flat-topped mountain Benbulben (also written as Benbulbin), with its scratch-like marks down its steep slopes, is an unforgettable sight, especially in winter, when the summit can be dusted in snow. This landmark gives the area a moody and atmospheric feel, Ireland's version of Table Mountain in South

1: Benbulben **2:** Devil's Chimney waterfall
3: Mullaghmore Head **4:** Classiebawn Castle

1
2
3
4

Africa. Glacial activity carved the slopes, leaving gorges where rare plants like alpine saxifrage and arctic meadow rue grow.

Benbulben has its share of myths and folklore. The Fianna, a guild of elite warriors, hunted on the mountain, and one of the soldiers, Diarmuid, fell in love with Gráinne, daughter of the High King of Ireland. Gráinne was betrothed to Fionn Mac Cumhaill, a much older man, so she fled to a cave on Benbulben with Diarmuid to escape her would-be warrior husband. The mountain also inspired W. B. Yeats, with the poem "Under Ben Bulben" his most famous work about it.

Climbing Benbulben is for experienced fit hikers; it's a 4-5-hour scramble with no defined trail or signage. Go with a local guide like **Northwest Adventure Tours** (www.northwestadventuretours.ie).

Hiking and Walking

Benbulben Forest Walk

Distance: *5.6 km (3.4 mi) loop*
Duration: *1.5 hours*
Elevation gain: *140 m (459 ft)*
Effort: *Easy-moderate*
Trailhead: *Gortarowey Forest Recreation Car Park*

Instead of taking the challenging ramble to the summit, this accessible family-friendly walk is a great way to see the mountain and views of the sea and Donegal, farther up the coast. The trail is wide gravel paths, and if the length is challenging, two turnoffs shorten the route. The majority of the climbing is in the first 500 m (0.3 mi) as you make your way up the foothills and onto a flat area with a view of the mountain. It's a loop route, and the section back toward the trailhead leads through forested countryside.

The Devil's Chimney Waterfall

Distance: *2.4 km (1.5 mi) round-trip*
Duration: *1.5 hours*
Elevation gain: *147 m (482 ft)*
Effort: *Moderate*
Trailhead: *Devil's Chimney Waterfall Car Park*

On the southern slopes of Benbulben, on the border with County Leitrim, this is one of the few hikes in Ireland where you'll be grateful for rainy weather. At 150 m (490 ft), Devil's Chimney is the country's largest waterfall. This out-and-back hike takes you to the top, where great views of the waterfall are even better if it's raining, along with views over Glencar Lough. The trail is wide gravel paths and wooden staircases that can be slippery.

Getting There

It's 12 km (7.5 mi) and 10-15 minutes to drive from Sligo Town to Benbulben. Take the N15 road north through Drumcliffe, and you'll begin to get views of the mountain. Turn right onto the L7402; this leads to the car park and Benbulben Forest Park. There is no public transport.

★ MULLAGHMORE HEAD

The small fishing village of Mullaghmore is one of the top spots along the Wild Atlantic Way to experience the power of the Atlantic Ocean, particularly on Mullaghmore Head, just a few minutes' drive along the coast.

Brave big-wave surfers are often seen at Mullaghmore Head in the 15-m (50-ft) waves. The best places to watch from are the Wild Atlantic Way Discovery Point and the Eire 69 sign on the coastal road, where you can park in the informal pullout.

There's more to do here besides watching the waves. On the northern edge of the headland is the ***Shadow V* Memorial,** remembering the IRA's bombing of Lord Mountbatten's boat, which also killed three civilians. On the western edge of the headland is the **Mullachgearr Memorial,** dedicated to the village that was destroyed to build Classiebawn Castle and the people who were displaced.

Sights and Scenic Drives

The sights of Mullaghmore Head are along the coast; see them all by driving the scenic 4.6-km (2.9-mi) loop around it. There's parking in Mullaghmore—a small car park on the north side and some spaces on the west side.

Wild Atlantic Way Discovery Point

Mullaghmore Head

There are 157 Discovery Points along the Wild Atlantic Way, including Mullaghmore Head. The Discovery Points are tall metal markers that indicate a notable attraction or a great view. The one here looks north toward the ocean, a fantastic spot to watch the big-wave surfers when the enormous winter swells roll in.

Eire 69 Sign

Mullaghmore Head

Ireland is a neutral country, so we didn't directly take part in World War II, but we did help guide Allied pilots with large signs on the ground made of stones. A lot of these signs have been lost, but this one was rediscovered in 2020. You can make out the outline of the text in the grass, but there isn't anything else to see.

Classiebawn Castle

Classiebawn Castle stands out in the landscape with Victorian-style chimneys and a tower in complete contrast to the rolling green landscape and the flat top Benbulben. The castle has a contentious past, as 300 locals were displaced to build it. Many of these people ended up homeless and hungry, with many forced to emigrate. The castle was completed in 1874 as a residence for the British gentry before being taken over by the Free State Army during the rebellion. Ultimately, the British regained control of the castle, and Lord Mountbatten was staying here when he was killed by the IRA in 1979. The castle is not open to visitors but is a joy to see from afar.

Hiking and Walking

Mullaghmore Head Walk

Distance: *4.5 km (2.8 mi) loop*

Duration: *1-1.5 hours*

Elevation gain: *77 m (252 ft)*

Effort: *Easy*

Trailhead: *Pier Head Car Park*

This loop walk is a great way to see Mullaghmore Head. It can be walked in either direction, but counterclockwise has better views of Classiebawn Castle. The route follows the road, with some short off-road sections; watch for traffic. Along the way, you'll pass the *Shadow V* Memorial, the swimming area at Bishop's Pool, and Wild Atlantic Way Discovery Point before you see Classiebawn Castle. The route then returns to Mullaghmore.

Sea Swimming

Bishop's Pool

Mullaghmore Head is known for ferocious waves and dangerous seas, but Bishop's Pool offers a rare slice of calm. The tide fills this natural rock pool and leaves a tranquil spot to swim when the tide retreats. It's very small, a place to experience sea swimming rather than a swimming pool. There are no changing facilities.

Getting There

Mullaghmore is 26 km (16 mi) from Sligo Town, a good option for a day trip. It takes 30 minutes to drive on the N15 and R279 roads. **Bus Eireann** (www.buseireann.ie) operates the Route 480 bus from Sligo Bus Station to Mullaghmore (45 minutes; €8 one-way), which runs three times daily.

South Donegal

Donegal was once a forgotten corner of Ireland, but word has gotten out about its world-class beaches, incredible cliffs, and lively rural towns filled with traditional music. The coast is the main draw, but the music scene is also worth seeking out. Singer-composer Enya and legendary guitarist Rory Gallagher hail from Donegal. There's also great short strolls and long-distance walks to explore.

ORIENTATION

Starting from **Donegal Town,** on the northeast shore of **Donegal Bay,** traveling south, you'll find **Ballyshannon** 20 km (12 mi) along the coast, with the surf village of **Bundoran** 15 km (9 mi) farther. West of Donegal Town are the towering cliffs of **Sliabh Liag** and the fishing village of **Killybegs.**

DONEGAL TOWN

Donegal Town lies in a protected corner of Donegal Bay at the mouth of the River Eske and near the Bluestack Mountains. It was first visited by the Gauls in the 9th century CE and soon got the name "Dún na nGall" in Irish, which translates to "Fort of the Foreigners." Today it's a busy market town with many layers of history, from the O'Donnell Dynasty to the time of the plantations.

Sights

The Diamond

The Diamond is a central square in Donegal Town, surrounded by pubs, restaurants, and lodging, making it feel like the hub. In the middle of the Diamond stands a stone obelisk dedicated to the Four Masters, Irish-speaking friars who wrote a detailed book on Irish history, *Annals of the Four Masters,* in 1616.

Donegal Castle

Castle St.; tel. 71/972-2405; https://heritageireland.ie; €5

Donegal Castle sits near the Diamond in the center of town and offers good insight into local history. Built in the 15th century by the O'Donnell clan, they held the building until 1607, when they fled Ireland for continental Europe. The castle fell into ruin but was restored in the 1990s; learn all about it on a guided tour in summer. Outside the busy periods, tours are self-guided. Expect to spend about an hour to see the courtyard, original stonework, and staircases.

Lough Eske

The 365-ha (900-acre) Lough Eske is 6 km (4 mi) northeast of Donegal Town at the base of the Blue Stack Mountains. Eske is an anglicization of the Irish word *iasc,* which means fish, an appropriate name, as the lake is known for its salmon and trout. The best views are from Harvey's Point and Lough Eske Castle.

Hiking and Walking

Donegal Town Trail

Distance: *3.2 km (2 mi) round-trip*
Duration: *45-60 minutes*
Elevation gain: *49 m (160 ft)*
Effort: *Easy*
Trailhead: *Donegal Methodist Church*

This easy walk brings you into the nature that surrounds Donegal Town on wide footpaths, making it great for families. Despite being quite short, you're likely to hear birds in the trees and in Donegal Harbour. The route leads to the bank of the Eske river and then along the harbor. The trail reaches its end on a small headland. Returning by the same route is recommended, but another option is to return via the GAA club; this route takes you away from the water.

The Bluestack Way: Donegal Town to Lough Eske

Distance: *6.3 km (3.9 mi) one-way*
Duration: *2 hours*
Elevation gain: *181 m (593 ft)*
Effort: *Moderate*
Trailhead: *The Diamond, Donegal Town*

Instead of hiking the full length of the 58-km (36-mi) Bluestack Way, this leg has the nature and sights of the trail in just a few hours. This section is the first of the long-distance trail. It begins at the Diamond and follows the River Eske for most of its length before turning to the ruins of the O'Donnell clan and ending at Harvey's Point. The route is country roads, footpaths, and some off-road trails.

South Donegal

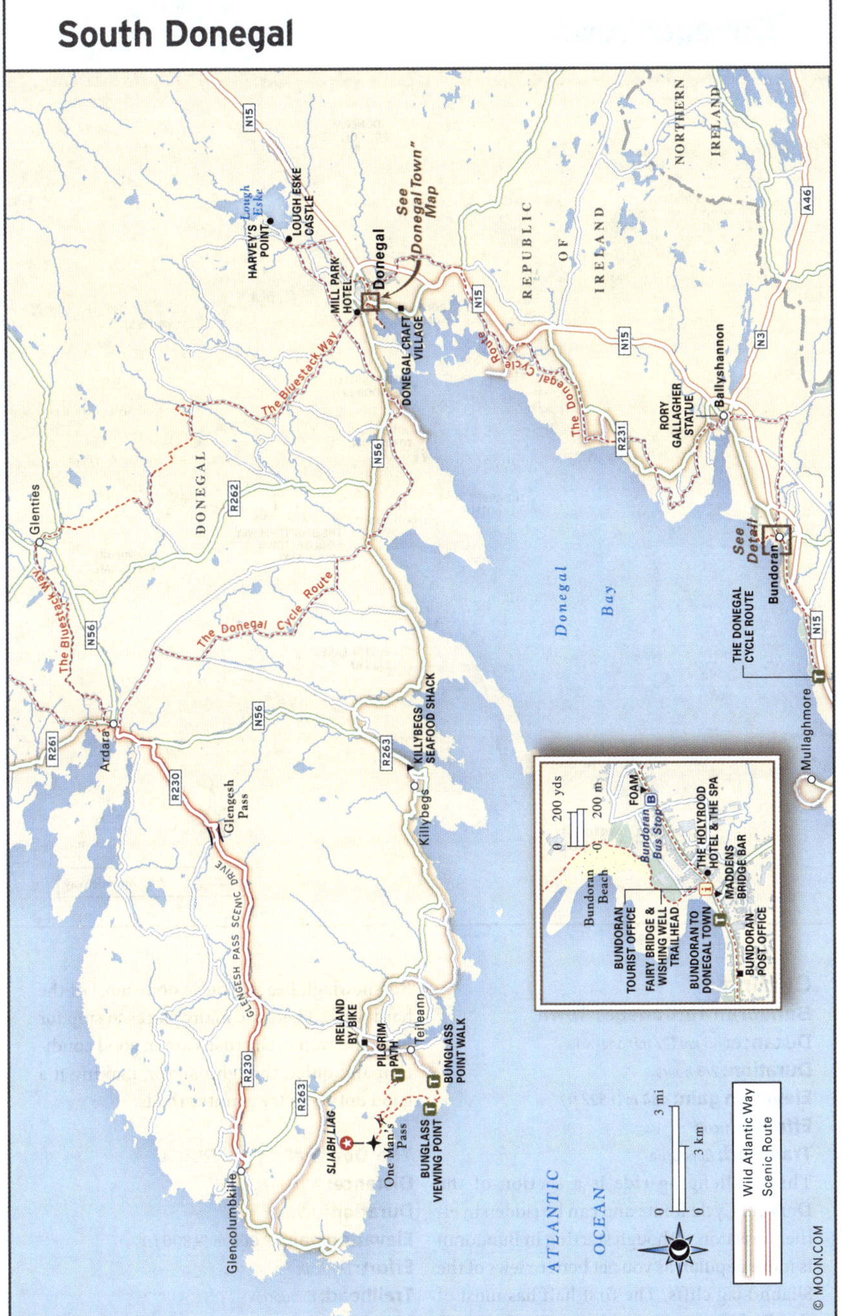

Donegal Town

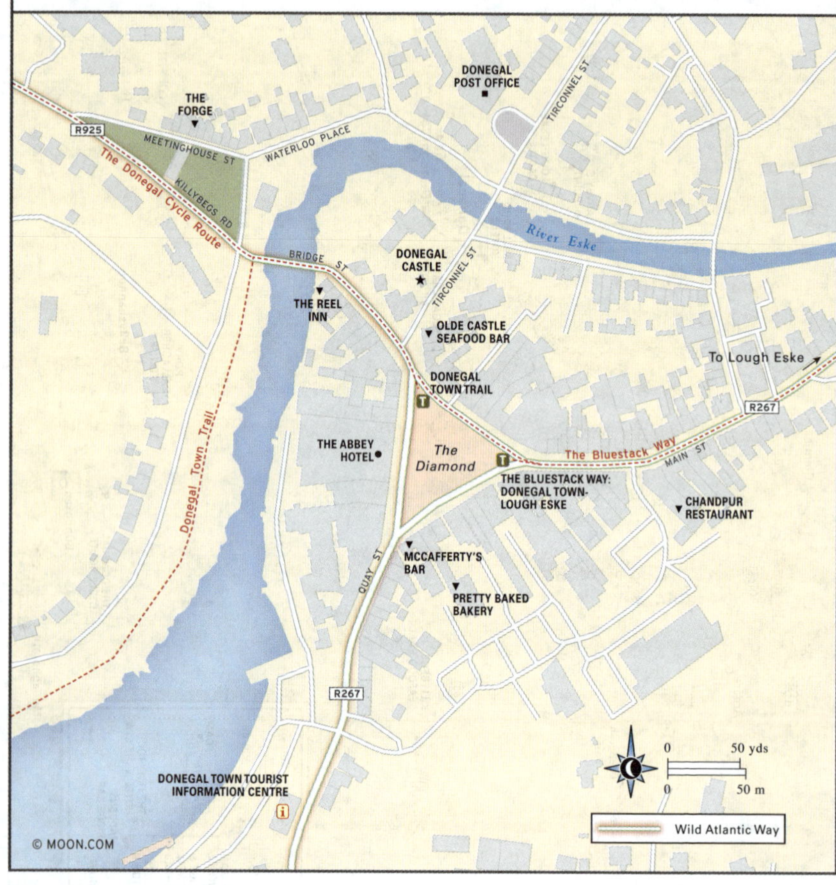

Cycling

Bundoran to Donegal Town

Distance: *43 km (27 mi) one-way*
Duration: *2-3 hours*
Elevation gain: *464 m (1,522 ft)*
Effort: *Difficult*
Trailhead: *Bundoran*

This challenging ride is a section of the Donegal Cycle Route and can be ridden in either direction, although starting in Bundoran is more popular, as you get better views of the Sliabh Liag cliffs. The first half has most of the climbing, so once you've reached beautiful Rossnowlagh Beach, you've done most of the hard work. There are many places to stop for food and water. The roads are in good condition and quiet, though narrow, making it a good option to try country roads.

The Donegal Cycle Route

Distance: *200 km (125 mi)*
Duration: *2-5 days*
Elevation gain: *3,000 m (9,800 ft)*
Effort: *Difficult*
Trailhead: *Bundoran*

This long cycle route runs from the border

Glengesh Pass Scenic Drive

Glengesh Pass

Distance: *28 km (17 mi) one-way*
Driving Time: *30 minutes*
Start: *Glencolumbkille*
End: *Ardara*

A stunning drive through unforgettable landscapes, Glengesh Pass, also called Donegal Pass, is a well-kept secret. It sees far less traffic year-round than the Ring of Kerry.

The name Glengesh comes from the Irish for "Glen of the Swans." The 28-km (17-mi) road traverses a breathtaking valley that links Glencolumbkille and Ardara. Named R230 on maps, the road snakes through the valley with uninterrupted views of remote mountains and isolated farms with sheep roaming the hillsides. There are small pullouts along the drive and a lookout at the highest point.

Watch for cyclists, especially around hairpin bends. These fit folk take 1.5-2 hours to cycle the road, climbing 345 m (1,130 ft) on the Glengesh Pass. Bus Éireann Route 991 runs between Glencolumbkille and Ardara, but it travels on the main roads instead of this scenic drive.

GETTING THERE

To get to the start of the Glengesh Pass, take the N56 west from Donegal Town, turn onto the R263 outside Killybegs, and continue to Glencolumbkille. The drive is 53 km (33 mi) and takes about an hour. Bus Éireann Route 490 runs from the Diamond to Glencolumbkille in 45 minutes, with buses running every 90 minutes during the day.

The route is most commonly driven from Glencolumbkille, but you can also start in Ardara. From Donegal Town, take the N56 west for 30 minutes to Ardara, 28 km (17 mi) away. Bus Éireann Route 492 runs from the Diamond to Ardara in 45 minutes.

of County Leitrim north to the border of County Derry and takes in the best sights of Donegal. The route has 14 one-way sections; advanced road cyclists aim to cover it all in two days. The sections along the coast, like those from Bundoran to Donegal Town and Ramelton to Letterkenny, are the flattest, while the mountainous sections around Glenveagh National Park reward with fantastic climbs and views.

The Bluestack Way

the Bluestack Way

The Bluestack Way is a 58-km (36-mi) long-distance hiking trail from the edge of Donegal Bay, along the edge of Lough Eske, and through the Bluestack Mountains before returning to the coast in Ardara. The sections from Donegal Town to Lough Eske and from Glenties to Ardara are flat and a mix of quiet country roads and boreens, those iconic country roads with grass growing in the middle. The real challenge is the mountainous 35-km (21-mi) section, with most of the climbing on single-track trails. Dispersed camping is allowed in the area, and there are also lodging and food options in Glenties, at the 46-km (29-mi) mark.

Shopping

Donegal Craft Village

Lurganboy; tel. 74/972-5928; www.donegalcraftvillage.com; summer Mon.-Sat. 10am-5pm, winter Tues.-Sat. 10am-5pm

This collection of six independently owned craft shops is a great place to stop for pottery, painting, and jewelry, with Kevin Callaghan's contemporary earthenware and Michelle McKee's felt artwork the standout choices. The shops surround a small courtyard that has some picnic tables, so you can get a coffee at Aroma Coffee Shop here and relax after all your shopping.

Food

Pretty Baked Bakery

Unit 7, Millcourt Mews, the Diamond; Instagram @prettybaked_donegal; Fri. 8:30am-2pm, Sat. 10am-2pm; €4

You'll be hard-pressed to find a more inviting exterior to a bakery than Pretty Baked's, with everything from the vintage hanging sign to the colorful flower arrangements drawing you in. The treats are just as tasty as the front, with a great selection of freshly baked cookies and brownies served alongside savory items like vegan sausage rolls and coffee. Seating is limited, but there is a bench out front.

Olde Castle Seafood Bar

Castle St.; tel. 74/972-1262; https://oldecastlebar.com; daily noon-9pm; €20

Enjoy locally caught seafood in this gastropub that has won a number of awards. The old stone building houses a familiar pub, but the food menu sets it apart, with favorites like salt-and-pepper calamari, sea bass with lemon sauce, a seafood platter, and lamb and chicken options.

Chandpur Restaurant

Main St.; tel. 74/972-5452; www.chandpurdonegal.com; Mon.-Sat. 4pm-10pm, Sun. 1pm-9pm; €18

The decor packs the same punch as the cuisine, with bright bold pink patterns floor to ceiling and across the furniture, setting the scene for an authentic Bangladeshi and Indian meal. The diverse menu features chicken Makhani and Indian railway curry. Chandpur has plenty for vegans and vegetarians.

Killybegs Seafood Shack

Main St., Killybegs; tel. 89/239-3094; Instagram @killybegseafoodshack; spring-Oct. daily 12:30pm-7:30pm; €10, cash only

Eating fish-and-chips on a pier is brilliant, especially when the fish was caught that morning. Killybegs Seafood Shack has a small menu of nine items, including battered haddock, breaded scampi, and battered mushrooms, along with chips. Everything is cooked to order, so expect to wait 10 minutes or so for your takeaway.

Bars and Nightlife

The Reel Inn

Bridge St.; tel. 85/841-6213; Instagram @thereelinndonegal; Mon.-Thurs. 10:30am-11:30pm, Fri.-Sat. 10:30am-1am, Sun. noon-11:30pm; €6

Some pubs in Ireland wind down in winter, but this recently renovated pub has live traditional music every night of the year. Cozy up beside the stove on wintery nights, and when the sun is shining, head for the small outdoor area that overlooks the River Eske. Guinness and Heineken are poured alongside local whiskeys.

The Forge

7 Meetinghouse St.; tel. 74/972-5578; Instagram @theforgebardonegal; Mon.-Thurs. 6pm-11:30pm, Fri.-Sat. 5pm-12:30am; €5

Irish pubs are loved because they're so welcoming, and the Forge is no different. The staff are friendly and the pub feels like somebody's house thanks to the small rooms with seating around a fire and newspaper clippings of milestones by local people. Craft beer is served alongside the big brands, and classics from the past five decades are played on weekends.

McCafferty's

The Diamond; tel. 74/974-2656; www.mccaffertysbars.com; Mon.-Thurs. 10:30am-11:30pm, Fri.-Sat. 10:30am-2:30am, Sun. noon-1:30am; €6

McCafferty's Bar is a recent addition to the pub scene in Donegal, and since opening in 2017, the owners have opened 16 more worldwide. Strong traditional elements like the exterior and the decor are augmented by refinements like a modern cocktail menu, pool, tables, and sports on the TVs.

Accommodations

The Abbey Hotel

The Diamond; tel. 74/972-1014; www.abbeyhoteldonegal.com; €150

The three-star Abbey Hotel is in the heart of town beside pubs and restaurants. The 234 guest rooms are tastefully decorated with rich wood furniture and soft lighting. The hotel is known for hosting country music events, with at least one each month. There are three dining options: the **Abbey Bar** for casual pub grub, the **Food Hall** for relaxed lunches, and the **Market House Restaurant** for fine dining with a focus on local ingredients.

Mill Park Hotel

The Mullins; tel. 74/972-2880; www.millparkhotel.com; €160

A classy four-star establishment set amid 3 ha (7 acres) of manicured lawns 1 km (0.6 mi) outside Donegal Town is the Mill Park Hotel. The 110 rooms include family rooms and suites, all with Wi-Fi included and flat-screen TVs. Leisure facilities include an indoor pool, a gym, and a spa along with the **Chapter Twenty** restaurant.

Harvey's Point

Lough Eske Rd.; tel. 74/972-2208; https://harveyspoint.com; €160

Harvey's Point is an impressive four-star, 88-room hotel in a brilliant setting on the edge of Lough Eske with the rolling Bluestack Mountains behind it. It feels like the sort of place you'd never want to leave. Activities include walking the shoreline and forest as well as hiking the hills behind the hotel. The helpful concierge can organize bike rides and water activities. For dinner, visit the **Lakeside Restaurant,** where the menu focuses on produce and flavors from Donegal, and watch the sun glisten on the water. Pop by **Harvey's Bar & Terrace** for a drink and watch night fall on Lough Eske.

Lough Eske Castle

Lough Eske; tel. 74/972-5100; www.lougheskecastlehotel.com; €335

On the shores of Lough Eske lies this five-star castle hotel, one of the most indulgent and luxurious in the country. This site was home to the O'Donnells in the 14th century and wealthy Edwardian landlords before the existing castle was built in the 1860s. The 96 rooms are elegant and classic, with four-poster beds and bay windows; for a more modern style, book the Garden Suite or Castle Suite. Surrounding the castle are 17 ha (43 acres) of parklands and woodlands with easy walking trails showing off the landscape and the castle. Reserve a table at **Cedars Restaurant** for fine dining, and visit the spa in the Victorian-style greenhouse.

Information and Services

Donegal Town Tourist Information Centre (The Quay; tel. 1/265-5634; www.govisitdonegal.com; Mon.-Sat. 9am-5pm) offers help to visitors. The closest major hospitals are **Letterkenny University Hospital** (Kilmacrennan Rd.; tel. 74/912-5888; www.saolta.ie) and **Sligo University Hospital** (The Mall; tel. 71/917-1111; www.saolta.ie). In emergencies, call 999 or 112.

All three towns have multiple ATMs in their town centers. **Bank of Ireland** and **AIB** have branches on the Diamond in Donegal Town.

The two main post offices are **Donegal Post Office** (The Castle Centre, Bridge St.; www.anpost.com) and **Bundoran Post Office** (West End; www.anpost.com).

Getting There and Around

The drive from Sligo Town to Donegal Town is a scenic 65 km (40 mi) and 1 hour along the coast on the N15 road. **Expressway** (www.expressway.ie) runs the Route 64 bus (1.25 hours; €19 one-way) from Sligo Bus Station (Lord Edward St.) to the **Abbey Hotel** (the Diamond).

Driving from Dublin is 225 km (139 mi) and 3.5 hours on the M3, N3, and N15. The **Expressway** (www.expressway.ie) Route 30 bus links Dublin with Donegal Town (4 hours; €24 one-way).

Much to the displeasure of everybody in Donegal, there are no train stations in the county. Your options to get around are driving or the **Local Link** (www.transportforireland.ie) bus service.

BALLYSHANNON AND BUNDORAN

A 10-minute drive separates these two very different towns. Bundoran is a surf town that's going through a resurgence, while Ballyshannon is all about music, especially the blues. Iconic Irish guitarist Rory Gallagher was born here and his love for music flows through the streets.

Sights

Rory Gallagher Statue

Main St., Ballyshannon; www.rorygallagherfestival.com

Often referred to as the greatest guitarist you've never heard of, Rory Gallagher was born in Ballyshannon and moved to Cork City, where he learned guitar as a child. He formed the blues band Taste and then launched a successful solo career, with "Bad Penny" his biggest commercial hit. He died in 1995 from complications from a liver transplant. A seven-foot bronze statue of the icon is visited by thousands of fans every

1: the Abbey Hotel **2:** Lough Eske Castle
3: Bundoran Beach **4:** Fairy Bridge

1
2
3
4
The

year, particularly during the Rory Gallagher International Tribute Festival, which runs over the June long weekend (1st Mon. in June). His estate was auctioned in 2024; his famous Fender Stratocaster was acquired and donated to the National Museum of Ireland.

Hiking and Walking

Fairy Bridge and Wishing Chair

Distance: *4 km (2.5 mi) round-trip*
Duration: *1 hour*
Elevation gain: *Negligible*
Effort: *Easy*
Trailhead: *Bundoran Tourist Office*

See two captivating geological features on this gentle stroll from the center of Bundoran. The Fairy Bridge is a short rock archway over the sea that's been an attraction since the 1700s, when locals said fairies haunted the bridge. The Wishing Chair is a natural rock formation that you can sit in and make a wish, but you have to keep it a secret for it to come true. It's less impressive but right beside the Fairy Bridge. The walk is along the road, which is quiet past Main Beach and Roguey Rock. Once you pass Aughrus Point, you'll see the bridge near Tullan Strand. There's a car park at the bottom of Tullan Strand Road, which cuts the walk to just 5 minutes.

Beaches

Bundoran Beach

This Blue Flag beach is the main draw of this seaside resort, once a big attraction. Bundoran has since declined in popularity, but things seem to be improving, and the beach is bringing people back. It's 500 m (0.3 mi) long and buzzes with families on hot summer days and with surfers when the waves roll in. Typical of seaside resorts, there are festival-style rides during school holidays in summer as well as the seasonal water park **Waterworld Bundoran** (www.waterworldbundoran.com; Easter-Sept.).

Performing Arts

Abbey Arts Centre

Tir Connell St., Ballyshannon; tel. 71/985-1375; http://abbeycentre.ie; from €10

Ballyshannon loves music and the arts, as seen in the three theaters at the Abbey Arts Centre. A range of performances includes theater and musicals, film clubs, and workshops with a focus on local acts. The biggest shows are in the 280-seat theater with the smaller shows using the 100-seat and 80-seat venues. Check for exhibitions at the Helen Allingham Gallery too.

Festivals and Events

Rory Gallagher Festival

Ballyshannon; www.rorygallagherfestival.com; June; free-€120

Held every year over the June holiday weekend (1st Mon. in June), the Rory Gallagher International Tribute Festival honors Ballyshannon's favorite son. Fans travel from all over to see headline acts like Uli Jon Roth from Scorpion play in the Big Top venue, a huge circus tent that serves as the main stage, while smaller acts play free concerts around town, including on the street. You're likely to find spontaneous music sessions in pubs that weekend. A festival ticket (€120) gives you access to all the gigs in the Big Top, or just enjoy the music on the streets for free. Book your lodging as far in advance as possible.

Ballyshannon Folk & Traditional Music Festival

Ballyshannon; http://ballyshannonfolkfestival.com; Aug.

This celebration of Irish music is the longest-running folk and traditional music festival in Ireland, first held in 1978. It takes place over the August holiday weekend (1st Mon. in Aug.) and draws thousands. Venues across town host ticketed events for big-name acts, and the pubs in town, including **McIntyre's Bar** (The Mall; Instagram @McIntyres-Saloon-Bar), host free live music and the chance to mix with fans.

Ballyshannon Rhythm & Blues

Ballyshannon; Instagram @BallyshannonBluesFest; Oct.

This music festival happens in late October over the holiday weekend (last Mon. in Oct.) and celebrates the style that made Rory Gallagher famous. Twelve venues host ticketed headline shows, and performances in the pubs on the Blues Trail are free. This season can feel sleepy, so it's a great way to perk things up.

Food

Foam

Main St., Bundoran; tel. 83/476-9823; www.foambundoran.com; daily 9am-4pm; €5

One of the main reasons for Bundoran's revival is young people setting up new businesses. Foam brings a slice of the specialty coffee world along with a short menu of seasonal dishes to be enjoyed post-surf. Their barbecue Buckfast burrito uses a sauce made from the tonic wine that's infamous with students, slow-cooked pulled pork, pickled zucchini, and cabbage. Enjoy coffee on the two benches and two tables out front, or inside at the two-seat tables under the surf photos.

Maddens Bridge Bar

Main St. W. End, Bundoran; tel. 71/984-2050; www.maddensbridgebar.ie; €6

Madden's is an old-world bar that overlooks the sea and has a beautifully aged wooden bar where the shelves are packed with Irish whiskeys and gins as well as European wines. A crowd-pleasing gastropub-style menu plays it safe with fish-and-chips, beef burgers, and veggie curry. Enjoy the view even when it's cold thanks to the covered and heated outdoor seating for 25. There's also a nine-bedroom guesthouse; two of the rooms have sea views.

Tête-à-Tête

Castle St., Ballyshannon; tel. 71/985-1889; Instagram @teteatete.ie; €9

Tête-à-Tête is a great spot for breakfast, brunch, or lunch, with a small international menu enhanced with daily specials. The full Irish breakfast served with potato bread is a fantastic choice, while lunch specials like the pan-fried chicken with mashed potato and tarragon sauce is hard to ignore. The restaurant is in a corner unit and has large windows for people-watching.

Nirvana Restaurant

The Mall, Ballyshannon; tel. 71/982-2369; Instagram @nirvanarestaurantfonegal; €20

It's hard to miss the colorful sign of this casual dining restaurant with a wide choice of well-known seafood, meat, and vegetarian dishes, including sirloin steak with peppercorn sauce, tempura-battered haddock, and roasted eggplant. The bartender will be happy to make you an after-dinner cocktail. Nirvana Restaurant regularly hosts groups, but call ahead to reserve.

Bars and Nightlife

The Thatch

Bishop St., Ballyshannon; tel. 71/985-1147; www.dorriansimperialhotel.com; Wed.-Sat. 8am-midnight; €6

If you'd never been to Ireland and imagined what a pub looks like, I'm guessing it's like the Thatch in Ballyshannon. The squat white cottage with a thatched roof looks like something from the days of horse-drawn carriages, and this historic feel continues inside. The exposed stone walls have been painted white, and all manner of vintage knickknacks hang from the ceiling, while a small fire crackles in the corner. Live music is common, but there's no schedule; sessions happen spontaneously. The best chance for music is on weekends in summer.

Accommodations

Dorrian's Imperial Hotel

Main St., Ballyshannon; tel. 71/985-1147; www.dorriansimperialhotel.com; €100

This historic hotel opened in 1781 and has been owned by the Dorrian family for over 70 years. The hotel doesn't shy away from its history, with antiques throughout. The 47 rooms feel dated but serviceable for a short stay. An on-site restaurant has a chef that serves locally sourced produce along with wines from an extensive list.

The Holyrood Hotel & The Spa

Main St., Bundoran; tel. 71/984-1232; www.holyroodhotel.com; €120

This 91-room kid-friendly hotel is on the waterfront with great sea views and only a short stroll from Bundoran Beach. A good fit for families with young kids, the family rooms can accommodate two adults and three kids; there's a kids club in July-August. The **Waterfront Bar & Grill** has a kid's menu with burgers and pizza, and later the adults can enjoy the **Watermelon Restaurant,** where locally sourced ingredients are served in plush surroundings.

Information and Services

Find information and recommendations at the **Bundoran Tourist Office** (The Bridge; tel. 71/984-1350; www.discoverbundoran.com; Wed.-Fri. 10am-4:30pm). **Bundoran Post Office** (West End; tel. 71/984-1224; www.anpost.com; Mon.-Fri.9am-5:30pm, Sat. 9am-1pm) sells stamps and ships parcels.

Getting There and Around

Bundoran is 9 km (5.6 mi) south of Ballyshannon along the coast. It takes 35 minutes to drive 35 km (22 mi) north from Sligo Town on the N15 road. A 10-minute drive on the N15 separates Bundoran and Ballyshannon, while Donegal Town is 22 km (13.6 mi) farther north, a 20-minute drive on the N15.

The **Expressway** (www.expressway.ie) Route 64 bus (from €12 one-way) links Donegal Town with Sligo Town and stops in both Bundoran and Ballyshannon. Buses depart Sligo Bus Station (Lord Edward St.) and outside the Abbey Hotel in Donegal Town, with stops at Ballyshannon Bus Station (Main St.) and outside the tourist office in Bundoran (The Bridge). There are six buses Monday-Saturday in each direction and four on Sunday and public holidays.

★ SLIABH LIAG

The Cliffs of Moher in County Clare get the limelight, but Sliabh Liag in Donegal is actually bigger, the tallest sea cliffs in Europe. Rather than a sheer drop, these 603-m (1,972-ft) cliffs gently cascade from the peak before dropping into the sea. The visitor center (www.sliabhliag.com) has information about the cliffs and the local area as well as toilets and a small café.

Hiking and Walking

Bunglass Point Walk

Distance: *2 km (1.2 mi) round-trip*
Duration: *45-60 minutes*
Elevation gain: *70 m (229 ft)*
Effort: *Easy*
Trailhead: *Sliabh Liag Car Park*

The easiest and quickest way to experience the cliffs is by walking the trail from the car park to the two viewing platforms, then returning along the same route. The drive cuts out most of the climb, eliminating the effort cyclists need to reach the same point. You can also drive beyond the car park to eliminate any walking. From the viewing point you'll see the rocky outcrops and the cliffs crumbling into the ocean below and feel the surging wind. This is the safest route in the area, suitable for most walkers, but don't get too close to the edge: It can get very windy and there are some unprotected edges.

Pilgrim Path

Distance: *3.2 km (2 mi) one-way*
Duration: *2-2.5 hours*
Elevation gain: *425 m (1,394 ft)*
Effort: *Difficult*
Trailhead: *Teelin*

Devout monks in the early Christian period traveled to the cliffs for solitude and to feel closer to God. Today you can walk the route of these monks on the Pilgrim's Path. This short but steep trail starts in Teelin and takes you to the ruins of McBric's Church and Well before you reach the lookout point's views from the cliff edge, where on a clear day you can see seven counties. The out-and-back trail is a mix of gravel paths, single track, and open mountain sections to the summit. This route is best for experienced hikers.

One Man's Pass

Distance: *9.5 km (5.9 mi) one-way*
Duration: *4 hours*
Elevation gain: *588 m (1,929 ft)*
Effort: *Extreme*
Trailhead: *Bunglass Viewing Point*

One Man's Pass is an extremely challenging hike on Sliabh Liag that can be done as an extension of the Pilgrim's Path. This is one of the most difficult hikes in the country and only for experts. One Man's Pass leads to the secondary peak of Sliabh Liag on a narrow scramble up a rocky ridge with room for only one person at a time. It gets more treacherous in bad weather. At the top is a rare view of the ocean and mountains.

Cycling

Ireland by Bike

Teelin Rd.; tel. 87/211-8638; www.irelandbybike.com; Tues.-Sat. 9:30am-6pm; from €45

This cycling tour company offers both guided and self-guided cycling tours in Donegal, Sligo, and the Causeway Coast, ranging from one-day e-bike adventures through a nine-night tour that covers the highlights of Donegal. You can rent bikes without booking a tour. Their shop is beside the Sliabh Liag cliffs, making it easy to see the cliffs by bike, especially if you rent an e-bike to ease the climb to the viewing platform.

Sliabh Liag and Teelin Pier Cycle

Distance: *17 km (11 mi) round-trip*
Duration: *1.5-2 hours*
Elevation gain: *164 m (538 ft)*
Effort: *Moderate*
Trailhead: *Teelin Rd., Carrick*

This cycle on country roads is short but has some steep sections as you make your way up to the viewing point at the Sliabh Liag cliffs. The first half of the outbound ride is quite flat as you follow the course of the river, but once you reach Teelin, the route turns uphill for roughly 4 km (2.5 mi). You'll return via the same way, so you get to enjoy freewheeling back down to Teelin.

Getting There

Head west from Donegal Town on the N26 road toward Killybegs, then follow the R263 to the cliffs. This drive is 46 km (29 mi) and takes 45-60 minutes. There is no direct bus route; take **Bus Éireann** (www.buseireann.ie) Route 492 to Killybegs, then change for Route 490 to Glencolumbkille, and get off at the Rock. This journey takes at least 2.5 hours.

view of Bunglass Point

★ Glenveagh National Park

Majestic and magical Glenveagh National Park, the second-largest in the country, is a 170-sq-km (65-sq-mi) expanse of wilderness, mountains, and lakes. The park centers around Glenveagh Castle, built by John George Adair, who has a contentious reputation. He made his fortune buying bankrupt estates after the famine and was hated by tenants when he forcibly evicted them from the land with the help of 200 police officers after he broke their tenancy agreement. Subsequent ownership saw celebrities like Marilyn Monroe and John Wayne visit. In 1983, Henry McIlhenny gifted the castle and gardens to Ireland.

The park is home to the largest herd of red deer in the country, which you might spot on the six walks that range from a 1-km (0.6-mi) stroll to a 16-km (10-mi) venture into the mountains. September-November is the best time of year to see the deer. You may also see golden eagles, reintroduced to the area a few years ago.

The park is free to visit with the option of paid tours, and there are accessible areas for wheelchair users. Dispersed camping is allowed in some sections of the park, and you can fish for your dinner in the rivers and lakes.

VISITING THE PARK

Gateway Towns

The largest town in the area is **Letterkenny,** a 20-minute drive east of the park. It doesn't have natural attractions but has plenty of food and lodging options. Another entry point is the Irish-speaking village of **Gweedore,** 25 minutes west of the park, the hometown of singer and composer Enya.

Slightly farther away is **Downings,** 30 minutes north of the park on the coast. It's a different setting by the sea, and you get the best of both worlds if you base yourself here.

Visitor Centers

Glenveagh National Park Visitor Centre

R251; tel. 1/539-3232; www.glenveaghnationalpark.ie; daily 9:15am-5:15pm; free

The visitor center is a cool circular building with a grassy green roof that blends into the landscape like a small hill. Inside are free exhibits on the conservation work in the park, including a display on the reintroduction of the eagles. The staff will help you choose a walk. The shuttle bus to the castle departs from here.

Tours

National parks in Ireland are good about running regular events year-round. They often cover guided walks in manicured gardens, Santa visits at Christmas, and educational hikes in the landscape. These events are announced on social media (Instagram @glenveaghofficial).

The tour of Glenveagh Castle (€7) is a self-guided walk through attentively preserved rooms with Victorian-era furnishings. Limited sporadic guided tours happen

Thursday-Tuesday but cannot be booked in advance. Contact glenveaghbookings@npws.gov.ie to find out when they're happening.

SIGHTS

Glenveagh Castle

This castle looks like it was plucked out of a fairy tale and dropped into this beautiful setting, surrounded by mountains by the edge of Lough Beagh. It's designed in the Scottish baronial style that was popular in the Victorian era, but inside, more creative license was taken; you'll see statues of Greek gods and Balinese temple guards. The castle has seen many owners, with Arthur Kingsley Porter the most interesting. Described as an Indiana Jones type, he went missing in mysterious circumstances in the 1930s. After your self-guided tour, give yourself time to wander the Garden Trail and sit by the water—the views are remarkable.

Glebe House and Gallery

Glebe; tel. 74/913-7071; http://glebegallery.ie; daily 11am-6:30pm; free-€5

This house turned art gallery lies outside the park's eastern boundary but is easily accessed by car. It's visually striking to walk through the regal rooms where owner and artist Derek Hill lived. Notice the impressive volume of Asian art and pieces by world-famous artists, including Picasso and Renoir. The gallery has a modern feel and hosts Hill's collection, which he donated to Ireland along with the house. The gallery is free to visit; entry to the house costs €5.

ACTIVITIES AND RECREATION

Hiking and Walking

The Lakeside Walk

Distance: *7.4 km (4.5 mi) round-trip*
Duration: *1.5-2 hours*
Elevation gain: *123 m (403 ft)*
Effort: *Easy*
Trailhead: *Glenveagh National Park Visitor Centre*

This out-and-back walk along the edge of Lough Beagh takes you from the visitor center to Glenveagh Castle. The crushed-gravel trail is wide throughout and has some wooden bridges. You'll see evergreen forests and brooding mountain peaks. You can walk one-way to the castle and then take the shuttle bus back to the visitor center. Dogs are allowed on the trail but must be on a leash.

The Garden Trail

Distance: *1 km (0.6 mi) round-trip*
Duration: *20-30 minutes*
Elevation gain: *Negligible*
Effort: *Easy*
Trailhead: *Glenveagh Castle*

This is a very easy amble around the beautiful castle gardens. Previous owners brought in a fantastic collection of ornamental plants, statement trees, and exotic plants to create a space in contrast with its surroundings. The walk is wheelchair-accessible with one somewhat steep section. Enjoy this leisurely stroll after a visit to the castle.

Bridle Path Walk

Distance: *15 km (9 mi) round-trip*
Duration: *3-4 hours*
Elevation gain: *385 m (1,263 ft)*
Effort: *Moderate*
Trailhead: *Glenveagh Castle*

Walk this peaceful trail from Glenveagh Castle to the top of the valley to take in the amazing views, worth seeing in both directions on this out-and-back trail. You'll also see the old houses the tenants lived in before the Derryveagh Evictions in 1861. From the castle, you can take the shuttle bus back to the car park at the visitor center.

Cycling

Glenveagh Gravel Loop

Distance: *33 km (20 mi) loop*
Duration: *2.5-3.5 hours*
Elevation gain: *460 m (1,509 ft)*
Effort: *Moderate*
Trailhead: *Glenveagh National Park Visitor Centre*

Cycle this scenic off-road route to quiet parts of the park where you'll likely be the only person around. Start at the visitor center and

1

2

pedal along the lakefront to Glenveagh Castle, then follow the route of the Bridle Trail, with a steep climb just before you reach the road. A long and fast descent on the road loops around the hills and to another gravel section that takes you back to the castle. Yield to walkers if you come across them.

Grass Routes Bike Hire

Glenveagh National Park Visitor Centre; tel. 86/868-3995; www.grassroutes.ie; from €15

This bike shop is inside the visitor center, making it easy to hop on a bike to explore. These bikes are best for beginners whose aim is leisurely exploration. Advanced riders will need their own bike for the serious routes in the area. Child buggies, e-bikes, and tandem bikes are available, and the staff will help you pick the most suitable route.

FOOD

Inside the Park

Glenveagh Tea Rooms

Glenveagh Castle; tel. 86/868-3995; www.glenveaghnationalpark.ie; daily 10am-4pm; €5

Unwind after a day in the park at this picturesque tea room inside an old stone building beside the gardens. Order tea and a baked treat to enjoy by the lake, or sit inside to feel like you're back in the 1800s. There's a small menu of toasted sandwiches and lasagna that's serviceable but not outstanding, especially when you're being charged a premium for the location.

Outside the Park

Brewery Bar & Restaurant

Market Square, Letterkenny; tel. 74/912-7330; www.thebrewerybar.ie; Sun.-Thurs. noon-11pm, Fri.-Sat. noon-1am; €18

Tuck into pub grub in this spacious traditional pub with modern elements where sports and live music take center stage. You'll find craft beer and excellently poured Guinness, and on the food menu the fish-and-chips are the standout. The menu has vegetarian options, light bites, and a range of chicken and beef. The Shack is a recent addition to the outdoor area to the rear; it's the place to be if there's an important match on TV.

Yellow Pepper

Main St., Letterkenny; tel. 74/912-6973; www.yellowpepperrestaurant.com; Mon.-Fri. 3pm-10pm, Sat.-Sun. 1pm-10pm; €24

The warm and inviting wood and exposed stone of the Yellow Pepper feels chic and complements the Irish-European fusion menu. Choose mains like sweet cured bacon with cabbage and mashed potatoes or sirloin jalfrezi with hot spices and sautéed vegetables. The Value Menu (Mon.-Fri. before 6pm, Sat.-Sun. before 5:30pm) has discounted starters, mains, sides, and desserts. Booking isn't always required, but reserve online in advance in summer and around holidays.

ACCOMMODATIONS

Outside the Park

The Birdbox

Glenleigham; www.hostunusual.com; €100; 2-night minimum

Stays in nature don't get more appealing than this singular wooden-clad treehouse hidden in the hills outside the national park. Wake to the sun illuminating the mountains and hear the birds. A small rope bridge takes you to the treehouse. Inside is a small living area with a wood-burning stove and a loft sleeping area for one or two people. The side that faces the park is mostly glass, with the light stirring you in the morning.

Station House Hotel

Main St., Letterkenny; tel. 74/912-3100; www.stationhouseletterkenny.com; €100

Expect 81 clean modern rooms at the three-star Station House Hotel in the heart of Letterkenny. Check the website for package deals, like the Romance Package, with a box of chocolates, a bottle of prosecco, and a bouquet of flowers. For dinner, the **Depot** in the lobby is a casual bar that serves an international menu.

1: Glenveagh Castle **2:** Lakeside Walk

GETTING THERE AND AROUND

Some park visitors base themselves in Letterkenny, the biggest town in the area, although it lacks that something special. The **TFI Local Link** (www.transportforireland.ie) Route 271 bus (40 minutes; €5 one-way) runs three times Sunday-Thursday and five times Friday-Saturday from Letterkenny to the Glenveagh National Park Visitor Centre. By car, take the N26 road to the R255 and the R251, which leads to the visitor center. The 23-km (14-mi) drive takes 25 minutes.

Downings is slightly farther away but has more for visitors to see and do. Take the R245 road south to the N26 and turn onto the R251 to enter the park. The 26-km (16-mi) drive takes 30 minutes. It's difficult to get to the park from Downings by public transport. **Patrick Gallagher Travel** (www.patrickgallaghertravel.com) runs three buses daily to Letterkenny (€5), where you change to the Route 271 bus to the park.

If you're staying farther away in Donegal Town, you can drive the 67 km (42 mi) to the park in just over an hour on the N15, N13, and R251. From Derry City, there are shorter routes, but the easiest drive is the A5 to Lifford, then the N14 and the N56 to the park. This drive is 72 km (45 mi) and takes just over an hour.

Once you're in the park, use the shuttle bus from the visitor center to reach Glenveagh Castle, leaving the rest of the park to be explored by bike or on foot.

North Donegal

Things are remote and wild in North Donegal, where rugged cliffs and mountains meet the beauty of secluded beaches and sheltered coves. The Wild Atlantic Way ends on the Inishowen Peninsula with welcoming villages and the golden eagles and wild deer in magnificent Glenveagh National Park. It takes effort to reach these remote parts of Donegal, but you'll soon see why it's worth making the journey.

ORIENTATION

The main attractions in North Donegal are along the coast. **Árainn Mhór,** the county's largest inhabited island, lies 5 km (3 mi) off the coast, with **Tory Island** to the north. On the mainland, the Ards Peninsula is home to Ards Forest Park, while farther along the coast are **Fanad Lighthouse** and then **Malin Head,** the northernmost part of the country.

DOWNINGS

Downings is a traditional Irish village in the Gaeltacht region, where you'll hear Irish spoken wherever you go. It's best known as a fishing village, but in recent years travelers have discovered the incredible beaches and scenery. The music and craic in the pubs has people coming back year after year, so pop into one of the welcoming pubs in town and wait for the tunes to start.

Parks

Ards Forest Park

Ards Forest Park is a peaceful 490-ha (1,200-acre) expanse of woodlands, sandy dunes, and picturesque beaches on Sheephaven Bay, a 20-minute drive from Downings. The seven walks include easy options like the 1-km (0.6-mi) **Sand Dune Trail,** on a boardwalk by the dunes, and strenuous walks like the 13-km (8-mi) **Red Trail.** History fans will want to seek out the standing stones and Mass Rock, where Catholics prayed in secret during the Penal Laws. There's ample parking at the park as well as toilets, a playground, and Ards Coffee Tree (Facebook @ardscoffeetree), with coffee, ice cream, and baked goods. To get to Ards Forest Park from Downings, drive 25 minutes south on the N56 road toward Creeslough.

The park is located between Creeslough and Dunfanaghy.

Beaches

★ Murder Hole Beach

It's fair to say that Ireland has some of the most beautiful beaches on the planet, and many think the gruesomely named Murder Hole Beach is the best of them all. Its official name is Boyeeghter Strand, but the reputation of the strong currents and stories of someone pushed to their death has seen its name change among locals.

The small golden beach is protected by gnarled headlands that reach into the sea; the views truly are astounding. The beach is not easily accessed. From the car park at the trailhead, walk down the gravel path for 20-30 minutes and 1 km (0.6 mi) to the sand. It's best at low tide, as there's more beach to walk on. Don't risk swimming here: The tides and currents are unforgiving. From Downings, it's a 10-minute drive north on the R248 to the new car park.

Food

Fisk

The Harbour Bar; http://fiskseafoodbar.com; Wed.-Thurs. 5pm-8pm, Fri.-Sat. 1pm-8pm, Sun. 1pm-5pm; €6

This fishing village has a love for seafood, and you'll find the charming Fisk in the whitewashed stone building overlooking Downings Bay Beach. The interior is welcoming and crisp, and clean wooden furnishings are warmed by soft glowing lights and a fire. Everything on the menu is locally sourced. Expect contemporary dishes like prawn bánh mì and fish tacos alongside seafood chowder and prawn cocktail. It's a relaxing place to dine and a great example of local traditions brought into the modern day.

Bars and Nightlife

The Singing Pub (An Sibín Ceoil)

Clontallagh; tel. 87/917-1950; Instagram @thesingingpub_; daily noon-midnight; €6

The thatched roof of this country pub is worth the 5-minute from Downings. The fantastic setting makes you feel like you've traveled back in time. Open the door and you're immersed in the friendly atmosphere, whether it's a quiet day or a lively music session. There's a small food menu alongside the usual Irish drinks. On a sunny day, sit outside with the view, or get a seat near the fire.

Accommodations

Downings Bay Hotel

Main St.; tel. 74/915-5586; www.downingsbayhotel.com; €140

Take a trip back to Victorian seaside grandeur at the three-star Downings Bay Hotel, just steps from the beach. The 40 en suite rooms have a strong emphasis on families, with interconnecting rooms, cots, and complimentary use of the nearby swimming pool. Your stay includes access to Kidz Kingdom, a soft-play facility with slides, ball pits, and trampolines, just a few minutes' drive from the hotel.

Rosapenna Hotel & Golf Resort

Sheephaven Bay; tel. 74/915-5301; www.rosapenna.ie; €200

Flanked by two stunning beaches and surrounded by natural beauty, the Rosapenna Hotel & Golf Resort makes for an unforgettable stay. The 66 rooms are decorated with a homey welcoming touch, and the suites have the best views of the beaches. Golfers will find three 18-hole courses: Old Tom Morris Links, Sandy Hills Links, and St. Patrick's Links. Greens fees are in addition to the room rates.

Getting There

There are two ways to drive to Downings from Donegal Town. The easiest and quickest is the N15 road north toward Letterkenny, then the N56 and Lough Salt Drive to Downings, a trip of 83 km (51 mi) that takes 1.25 hours. For a more scenic but challenging drive, head west from Donegal Town to Glenties on the N56 before turning onto the R250 through the mountains to Lough Salt Drive. The 99 km (61 mi) journey takes at least 1.5 hours.

The Islands of Donegal

Árainn Mhór (Arranmore)

Detour to the islands of Donegal for an even more remote escape in a remote part of the country. The islands are small and beautiful, rugged yet welcoming, and best suited to those traveling slowly and who want to discover every part of Donegal.

ÁRAINN MHÓR (ARRANMORE)

There are many islands off the coast of Donegal, and Árainn Mhór is the most populous, with 478 permanent residents. It's sparsely populated and has a particularly rugged west coast due to the unrelenting Atlantic. The island has a strong seafaring heritage, with many islanders working in fishing, and local folklore focusing on tales of great ships and legendary settlements. Árainn Mhór holds on to its heritage, and you're likely to hear people speaking Irish in shops and pubs.

★ FANAD LIGHTHOUSE

Cionn Fhánada Eara Thíre na Binne; tel. 74/911-6020; http://fanadlighthouse.com; Tues.-Sun. 10am-6pm; €12

Protecting ships and sailors, this towering white lighthouse stands defiant on a battered and gnarled part of the coast. It was built in 1817 by renowned lighthouse engineer George Halpin after a British Navy ship crashed during a storm, killing 200 people. Oil wick lamps were originally used, but nowadays it's fully automated.

The lighthouse is still an important navigation tool on Fanad Head, and the stunning setting has made it a tourist attraction. Book a tour (www.fanadlighthouse.com; 45 minutes; €12) to climb to the top of the tower and imagine what life was like for the first lightkeepers. You might spot dolphins in the water. The guided tour tells stories of the lightkeepers, and there's a vast collection of maps and logbooks. Explore the surrounding headland, as this is where you get the best views of the lighthouse.

Getting There

The only option to get to Fanad Lighthouse from Downings is to drive, as there are no bus routes. Take the R248 to Carrickart and then the R247 across the Harry Blaney Bridge. This 23-km (14-mi) drive takes 30 minutes.

Get a feel for the island on the 14-km (9-mi) walk that begins and ends at the Ol Pier at Leabgarrow. You'll see beautiful beaches and lakes and can detour to the lighthouse. Most food and drink options are on the eastern side of the island, with **Early's Bar** (www.earlys.bar) and **Teac Phil Ban** (Phil Ban's Pub) among the most popular.

Getting There

To get here, go to Bunport on the mainland and take the **Arranmore Ferry** (www.thearranmoreferry.com; 20 minutes; daily 8:30am-6:30pm; €15 one-way). More frequent crossings run during summer.

TORY ISLAND

Remote and isolated Tory Island is in the North Atlantic, 14 km (9 mi) off the coast, and home to 141 people. Despite its geographical challenges, the determined monks of the early Christian period made the crossing, and Saint Colmcille founded a monastery that was destroyed in the late 1500s, almost 1,000 years later. The remote location also allowed residents to preserve the Irish language.

A unique tradition is the Rí Thoraí (Tory King), where islanders vote for a person to act as an ambassador for the island—you might even see the Rí Thoraí greeting you at the port when you arrive. Experience the island's history at Tau Cross, a rare T-shaped cross that was used in the very early days of Christianity, and take the 9-km (5.6-mi) looped **Tory Island Walk** around the shore. Most of the socializing is around the port and the **Tory Island Hotel** (www.hoteltory.com), where you can eat, drink, or stay the night.

Getting There

The ferry to the island departs from Magheroarty Pier in Meenlaragh with **Tory Ferry** (www.toryferry.com; 45 minutes; daily 7:30am-6:30pm; €14 one-way). During peak summer months there are up to eight crossings a day. Most visitors use Downings as their base while exploring this part of the coast.

AN GRIANÁN OF AILEACH

Grianán of Aileach roughly translates to "Stone Temple of the Sun" and dates to the 6th century CE, though it's believed the area was in use as far back as 1700 BCE. The fort was the seat of the Kingdom of Aileach, and local folklore holds that members of the Tuatha Dé Danann are buried here. Walk up to the structure and touch the 5-m (16-ft) walls, laid with expert skill and without mortar or cement.

Technically, An Grianán of Aileach isn't on the Inishowen Peninsula, but it's a great place to see the peninsula; you get fantastic views of Lough Swilly and Lough Foyle to the north.

Getting There

You have to drive to An Grianán of Aileach from Derry. The 13-km (8-mi) drive takes 20 minutes. Take the Creggan Road northwest from the city before merging onto the Groarty Road, then follow the signs.

INISHOWEN PENINSULA

The Inishowen Peninsula is Ireland's largest and most northerly. It's a fantastic place to get away from it all and yet not be too far from Derry. The peninsula marks the end point of the Wild Atlantic Way.

Orientation

The Inishowen Peninsula, in the far northeast of Donegal, is almost completely surrounded

1
2
3
4

by water. A narrow stretch of land separates Lough Swilly and Lough Foyle before the peninsula swells in size into the Atlantic. This area feels truly remote, and in the right conditions, you can occasionally catch a glimpse of the northern lights. Malin Head, the country's northernmost point, is less than an hour's drive from Derry City. The main towns are Buncrana on the western side, Moville on the east, and Muff at the base, where actor Russell Crowe owns part of the local distillery. Most visitors use Derry as their base, as it's just a few minutes farther away but has more lodging and food options.

Sights

Inishowen Lighthouse

This historic lighthouse has been protecting ships near Stroove Beach since 1837. The lighthouse is not open to visitors, but you can explore the coast around it and take photos of the black-and-white structure.

Malin Head

Malin Head is the most northerly point of mainland Ireland. It's also where the 2,600-km (1,600-mi) Wild Atlantic Way ends, connecting towns, beaches, and experiences all along the west coast and into Kinsale, Couty Cork. This is a place to explore on foot, with the rocky headland home to hidden coves and tiny beaches. At the tip of the headland is a stout castle from 1805 named **Banba's Crown,** after the Irish goddess of war. You'll also find the **Eire 80 sign** used during World War II.

Hiking and Walking

Inishowen Head Loop

Distance: *9.3 km (5.8 mi) round-trip*
Duration: *2-3 hours*
Elevation gain: *333 m (1,092 ft)*
Effort: *Medium*
Trailhead: *Stroove Beach Car Park*

This hilly coastal walk explores lesser visited parts of the easternmost tip of the peninsula. The walk begins at Inishowen Lighthouse beside Stroove Beach and follows a quiet country road along the water. You'll get incredible sea views and on a clear day spot Scotland's Isle of Islay. The trail alternates between narrow country roads and gravel tracks throughout. Traffic is infrequent.

Malin Head Trail

Distance: *2.3 km (1.4 mi) round-trip*
Duration: *45 minutes*
Elevation gain: *64 m (209 ft)*
Effort: *Easy*
Trailhead: *Malin Head Car Park*

Malin Head Car Park is close to the edge of the headland, so you won't have to walk far for the amazing views. Start by walking along the road to Banba's Castle, where you'll also spot the Eire 80 sign, then begin the section along the coast. The trail is purpose-built with room for walking abreast, and it rolls up and down some short rocky sections until you reach the end just after Hell's Hole. The Atlantic Ocean surges into this opening in the headland, crashing with enormous power. The walk returns to the car park on the same route.

Spas and Relaxation

Sea View Sauna

Stroove Beach; tel. 86/441-9841; www.theseaviewsauna.ie; Mon.-Thurs. 4:30pm-5:30pm, Fri. 2:45pm-5pm, Sat.-Sun. 9am-5pm; €15

Treat yourself to a soothing sauna at Stroove Beach. Sea View Sauna has a large window with amazing views of the sea. If the tide is in, you can take a cold plunge in the sea. You can rent the sauna privately (€80 for 30 minutes).

Bars and Nightlife

Farren's Bar

Slievebawn; tel. 74/937-0128; daily 11am-1am; €6

After visiting the northernmost point on the mainland, stop by Farren's and have a drink at the northernmost pub in the country. The setting is cute, amid small cottages, creating a village feel. Inside the traditional pub,

1: Murder Hole Beach **2:** Ards Forest Park
3: An Grianán of Aileach **4:** Fanad Lighthouse

the barman can write your name in a pint of Guinness. There's a small menu of pub grub and pizzas.

Getting There

The Inishowen Peninsula begins a 15-minute drive north of Derry City when you cross the Foyle Bridge and reach the town of Muff. From here, the R238 loops around the peninsula, linking Moville, Malin Head, Ballyliffin, and Buncrana. A loop of the peninsula is a 100-km (60-mi) drive that takes 90 minutes or so. **TFI Local Link** (www.transportforireland.ie) and **Foyle Coaches** (www.northwestbusways.ie) operate buses between the more populated towns and villages.

Northern Ireland

Northern Ireland has been a contentious area since the country was first formed in 1921. It's one of the four countries that make up the United Kingdom and has a population of almost 2 million who consider themselves either British or Irish. The conflicts have been well documented, but these days there is very little tension between communities, and there is no danger to visitors.

It's unfortunate that an introduction to an entire country needs to be prefaced with this, but it's important to dispel any myths about this fantastic part of the island of Ireland. Ask anyone who has spent time here and they'll tell you that the thing that trumps the history and landscape is the people in the North, known to be extremely hospitable, especially if you venture into lesser-visited parts outside the main hubs.

Highlights

Look for ★ to find recommended sights, activities, dining, and lodging.

★ **The Cathedral Quarter:** Wander through this historic area, once full of warehouses but now home to art galleries, traditional pubs, and upscale restaurants (page 400).

★ **Titanic Belfast:** Learn all about the most famous ship of all time, built in Belfast, and take the Shipyard Ride through the hull (page 401).

★ **Belfast Murals:** See the famous murals that tell the story of both sides of the Troubles, covering everything from historical events, cultural messages, and solidarity with conflicts overseas (page 404).

★ **Carrick-a-Rede Rope Bridge:** Walk across the swaying wooden bridge to a small rocky island used for fishing since 1755 (page 417).

★ **Giant's Causeway:** See impressive rock formations that inspired legends that still live today. This collection of 40,000 hexagonal basalt columns is unlike anything else on the planet (page 424).

★ **Coleraine to Derry Scenic Train:** Lauded as one of the most scenic rail journeys in the world, the trip includes riverside views in the countryside and epic seascapes (page 431).

★ **Game of Thrones Studio Tour:** Relive the great TV show on this amazing studio tour with interactive exhibits, life-size models, and sets from the show (page 441).

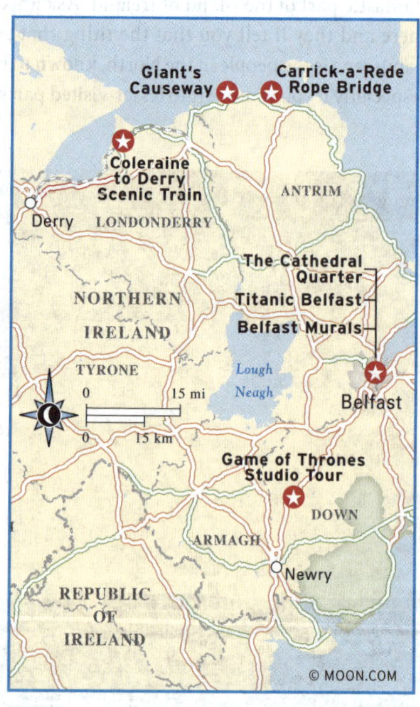

The two main cities in Northern Ireland are Belfast and Derry, both known for the ethno-nationalist conflicts in the 20th century, but nowadays they're up-and-coming cities with thriving creative and foodie scenes. Outside the cities, the landscape is a major draw. The magical Mourne Mountains call to hikers and walkers to explore endless trails, climb the highest peaks in the country, and discover local folklore. On the northern shores along the Causeway Coast are jaw-dropping beaches with golden sand and, of course, the world-famous Giant's Causeway, which needs to be seen to be believed.

ORIENTATION

Northern Ireland is a compact yet diverse country that makes it easy to experience city life, coastal beauty, and landscapes all in one day. **Belfast,** the capital, is at the center of Northern Ireland's east coast, at the end of Belfast Lough, divided by the **River Lagan.** The city center is walkable, with lots of hidden alleyways and side streets that add character. Venturing outside Belfast is easy and accessible thanks to the rail network, **NI Railways.**

Derry (also called Londonderry) is reachable by train from Belfast's **Lanyon Place Station.** The journey includes one of the world's most scenic railway routes, from Coleraine to Derry. The **Causeway Coast** runs from Ballycastle in the east to Portstewart in the west and is home to the **Giant's Causeway** and **Carrick-a-Rede Rope Bridge.** It's a rural area along the north coast that's best explored by car from Belfast but also accessible by train.

To the south, the **Mourne Mountains** have spectacular hiking trails and breathtaking views. While there's no direct train service to the Mournes, buses run from Belfast to **Newcastle,** the gateway to the mountains, but to fully experience the area, it's best to drive.

PLANNING YOUR TIME

Because Northern Ireland is part of the UK, it's no longer part of the European Union, which means non-European travelers must have an Electronic Travel Authorisation (ETA) when crossing the border. It can be a bit confusing, as there's no physical border on the island; you'll know you've crossed over when the road speed signs changed from km/h to mph.

Belfast will most likely be your hub in Northern Ireland and where you'll spend most of your time. Plan to spend at least one full day here, but two to three days is ideal. Book a tour in advance to learn about the *Titanic* or the Troubles, then spend the rest of the day wandering the Cathedral Quarter, city center, and Queen's Quarter. If you use Belfast as your base to visit the Mournes and Causeway Coast, you can enjoy more of the city's nightlife.

The Mournes and Causeway Coast are often visited on day trips from Belfast or Derry, which allows time to see main attractions like the Bushmills Distillery or to go surfing in Portrush. If you prefer the countryside, there's enough for two to three days exploring both areas. Derry is much smaller than Belfast and can be experienced with a one- to two-day visit.

Previous: the Northern Irish coast; Titanic Belfast; Giant's Causeway.

Northern Ireland

Itinerary Ideas

A busy three-day itinerary is a great way to see the best of Northern Ireland, but if you have more time, there are plenty of ways to add more great days. It's best done by car to see all the coastal highlights, but if you'd rather focus on the cities and big towns, it's possible to travel by rail.

DAY 1: BELFAST

1 Start your day in East Belfast with a coffee at **Root & Branch Coffee Roastery.**

2 Walk to **Titanic Belfast** and see the Loyalist murals on the Newtownards Road before going on a self-guided tour and the Shipyard Ride.

3 Learn about the impact of the Troubles on a **Black Taxi Tour** and see more of the murals that mean so much to the city. Book in advance and the driver can pick you up from Titanic Belfast.

4 Get dropped off at **Ryan's Bar & Restaurant** and have their bangers and mash for lunch.

5 Spend the rest of the day strolling around the **Botanic Gardens,** where the ornate glass Palm House is a real highlight.

6 Have a cheap but tasty dinner of fish-and-chips at **John Long's.**

7 After dinner, make your way over to the **Sunflower Public House** for a local craft beer and live music.

DAY 2: THE CAUSEWAY COAST SCENIC DRIVE

1 From Belfast, drive 89 km (55 mi) north to Ballycastle on the Causeway Coast and enjoy your first stop at **Ballycastle Beach** with views out to Rathlin Island from the golden sand.

2 Hop back in your car and head 10 km (6 mi) west to your reservation at the **Carrick-a-Rede Rope Bridge.** Walk across the bridge to the viewpoint on the rocky island.

3 Continue for 14 km (9 mi) along the coast to the **Giant's Causeway** and marvel at this incredible geological wonder.

4 Pop into nearby Bushmills for a spot of lunch at **The Nook.** They're known for their seafood, and the fish pie is fantastic.

5 After lunch, join a tour at the **Old Bushmills Distillery** where you can taste some of their creations.

6 Back on the road, drive 14 km (9 mi) to Coleraine and finish your day with a riverside dinner at **Lir.**

7 Head to your overnight stay at **Burrenmore Nest** and sleep under the treetops in these luxury treehouses.

DAY 3: DERRY

1 Wake up in the forest and grab a coffee at **The Surf Shack.**

Itinerary Ideas

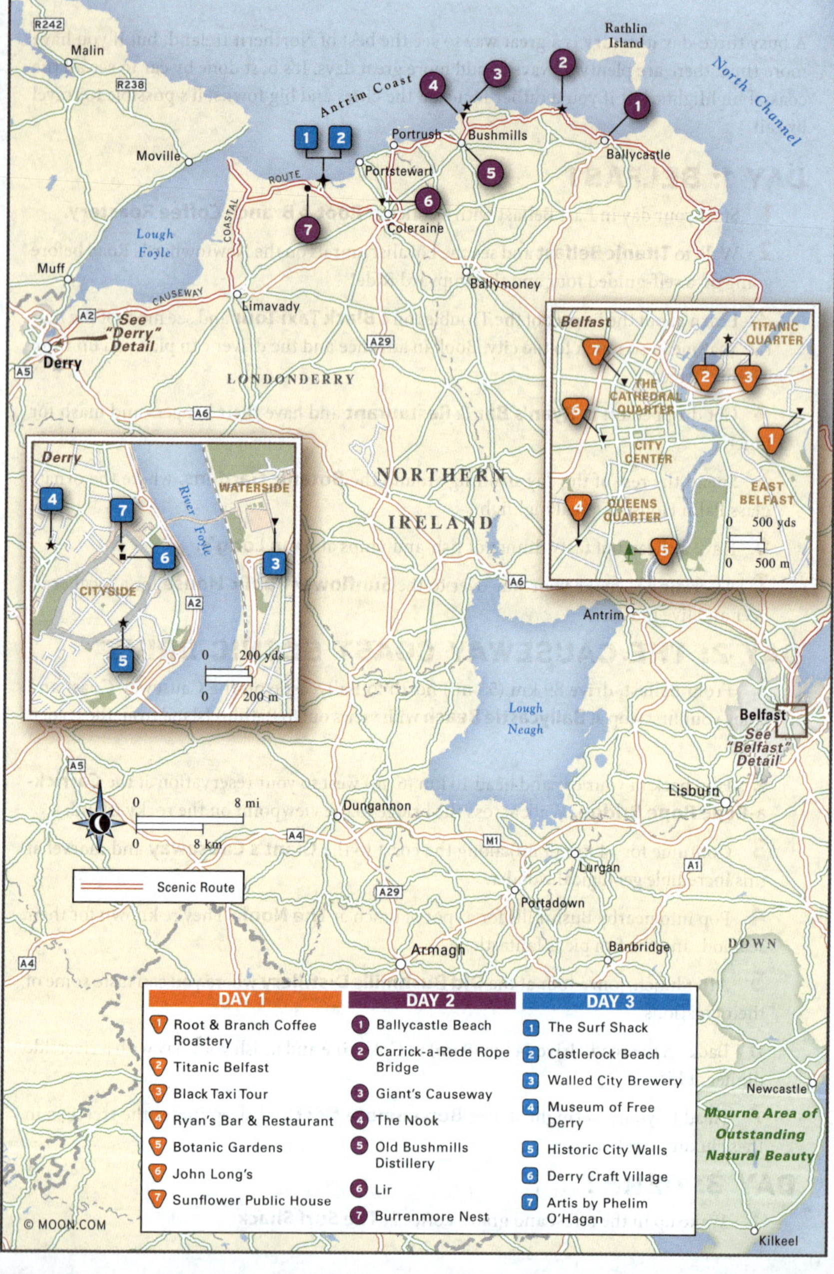

2 Stop at **Castlerock Beach** for a morning stroll before driving along the coast to Derry, with great views throughout.

3 In Derry, grab a quick lunch at the **Walled City Brewery.** The salt and chili squid makes for a great light bite. Wash it down with a glass of their oyster stout.

4 Book a walking tour with Bogside History Tours and visit the **Museum of Free Derry** to learn all about the Troubles.

5 After your tour, enjoy a more leisurely walk around the **historic city walls.**

6 Finish your day at the shops in **Derry Craft Village** and treat yourself to some handmade jewelry and homewares.

7 For dinner, indulge in some fine dining at **Artis by Phelim O'Hagan.**

Belfast

Belfast is an incredible small city full of wit, craic, and charm. It's going through a period of regeneration that's seen a wave of trendy coffee shops and fine eateries open in recent years. The outdoors are on its doorstep, and it's quite easy to get to the sea or the mountains from the city center. Of course, the recent past can't be ignored. Thankfully, the Troubles are over and there are countless opportunities to learn about history.

ORIENTATION

Belfast is a compact city with distinct areas and quarters, known by their general location or main roads. Metro buses serve the city, and the Glider rapid transit system connects East and West Belfast.

City Center

The city center, divided by the **River Lagan,** is the busiest area. Use Royal Avenue as your guide to reach **Victoria Square** and **City Hall.** The city center runs roughly from City Hall in the south to the Cathedral Quarter in the north.

Cathedral Quarter

North of the city center, the Cathedral Quarter is home to **St. Anne's Cathedral** and numerous art galleries. The area is known for its nightlife and cultural scene with cobblestone streets and historic warehouses creating a trendy atmosphere. It centers around Donegall Street, Hill Street, Waring Street, and Talbot Street.

Queen's Quarter

South of the city center, Queen's Quarter is defined by highly regarded **Queen's University** and has a neighborhood feel with youthful energy. There are great museums, including the **Ulster Museum,** and the **Botanic Gardens,** great to explore on a relaxing day.

East Belfast and Titanic Quarter

East of the city center is the rejuvenated Titanic Quarter, home to the **Titanic Museum.** This area of Belfast might be its most fascinating, firmly rooted in the past, with Harland and Wolff's mighty **Samson and Goliath cranes** harking back to its shipbuilding heritage. Farther into East Belfast is an area going through major changes to become Belfast's hip capital thanks to trendy shops and purist coffee shops.

North Belfast

North Belfast, north of the city center and the Cathedral Quarter, has a residential feel and

Belfast

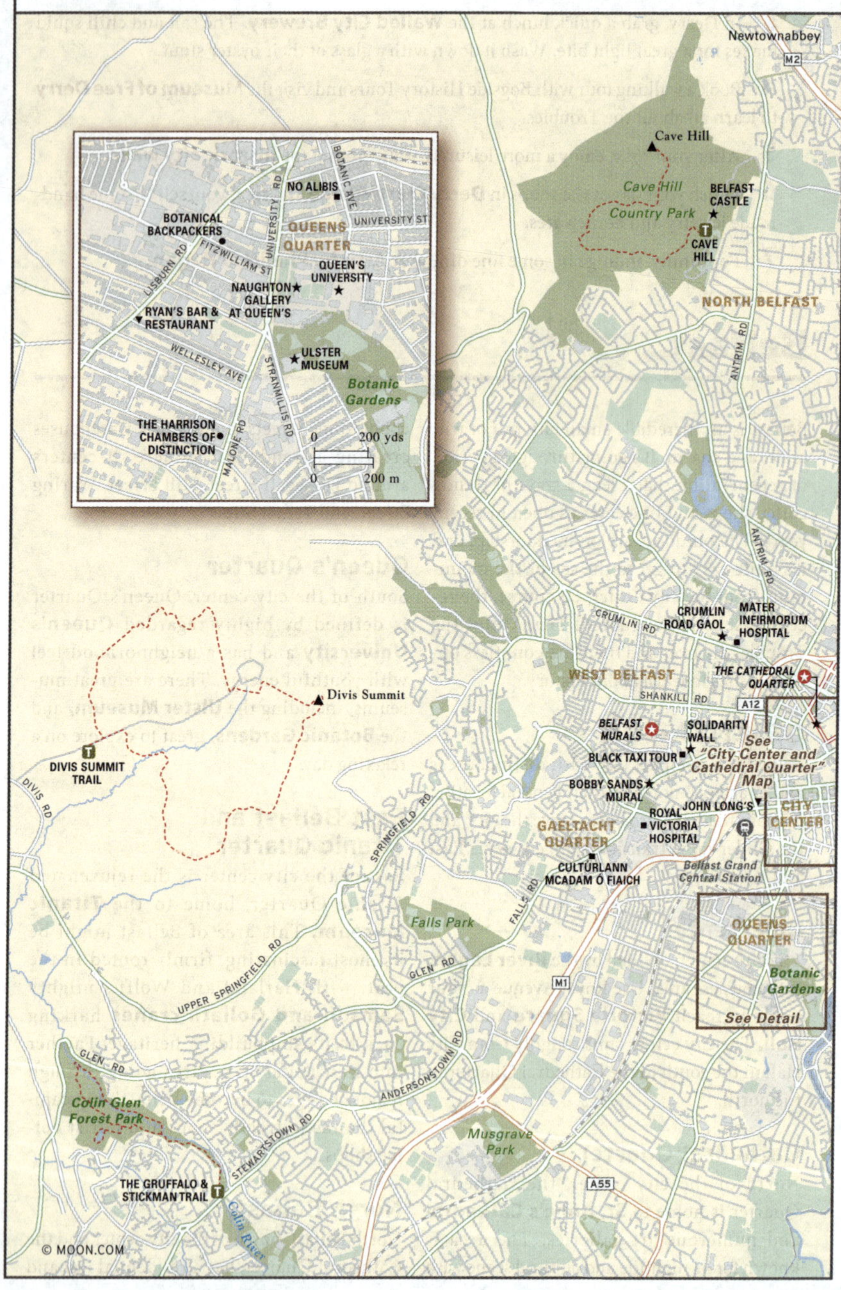

Newtownabbey
M2
Cave Hill
Cave Hill
Country Park
BELFAST CASTLE
CAVE HILL
NORTH BELFAST
ANTRIM RD
NO ALIBIS
BOTANIC AVE
UNIVERSITY ST
BOTANICAL BACKPACKERS
QUEENS QUARTER
UNIVERSITY RD
FITZWILLIAM ST
LISBURN RD
QUEEN'S UNIVERSITY
NAUGHTON GALLERY AT QUEEN'S
RYAN'S BAR & RESTAURANT
ULSTER MUSEUM
WELLESLEY AVE
STRANMILLIS RD
Botanic Gardens
THE HARRISON CHAMBERS OF DISTINCTION
MALONE RD
0 200 yds
0 200 m
CRUMLIN RD
CRUMLIN ROAD GAOL
MATER INFIRMORUM HOSPITAL
WEST BELFAST
THE CATHEDRAL QUARTER
SHANKILL RD
A12
Divis Summit
BELFAST MURALS
SOLIDARITY WALL
DIVIS SUMMIT TRAIL
BLACK TAXI TOUR
See "City Center and Cathedral Quarter" Map
BOBBY SANDS MURAL
DIVIS RD
SPRINGFIELD RD
GAELTACHT QUARTER
ROYAL VICTORIA HOSPITAL
JOHN LONG'S
CITY CENTER
CULTÚRLANN MCADAM Ó FIAICH
Belfast Grand Central Station
FALLS RD
Falls Park
QUEENS QUARTER
UPPER SPRINGFIELD RD
GLEN RD
M1
Botanic Gardens
See Detail
GLEN RD
ANDERSONSTOWN RD
Colin Glen Forest Park
STEWARTSTOWN RD
Musgrave Park
THE GRUFFALO & STICKMAN TRAIL
A55
Colin River

M5
M2
CAUSEWAY COASTAL ROUTE
Belfast Harbour
ANTRIM
DOWN
QUEENS RD
GEORGE BEST BELFAST CITY AIRPORT
Holywood
A2
A55
TITANIC BELFAST
BARGE AT TITANIC
TITANIC QUARTER
W5
THE SAMSON & GOLIATH CRANES
Victoria Park
CONNSWATER COMMUNITY GREENWAY
M3
COMBER GREENWAY
CS Lewis Square
ULSTER FREEDOM CORNER
FLOUT!
ROOT & BRANCH COFFEE ROASTERY
THE BUREAU
A20
UPPER NEWTOWNARDS RD
Stormont Estate
Comber Greenway
River Lagan
Connswater River
EAST BELFAST
LATE CAFÉ
Knock River
Loop River
Orangefield Park
Ormeau Park
GENERAL MERCHANTS
Castlereagh
0
0.75 mi
0.75 km
Scenic Route

features landmarks like **Belfast Castle** and **Crumlin Road Gaol.**

West Belfast and Gaeltacht Quarter

West Belfast is home to well-known Falls Road and Shankill Road and the **Gaeltacht Quarter,** the hub of Irish language and culture around the Falls Road.

SIGHTS

City Center

Belfast City Hall

Donegall Square N.; tel. 28/9032-0202; www.belfastcity.gov.uk; Mon.-Fri. 9am-5pm

The magnificent baroque style of Belfast City Hall has made it a landmark in the center of the city since 1906. It still operates as an administrative building, and the architecture draws visitors to see its stone facade and copper-domed roof in tranquil Donegall Square, a respite from the city around it. Inside, grand styling includes tall stained-glass windows, marble pillars, and decorative staircases. **Tours** (Mon.-Fri. 11am, 2pm, 3pm, Sat.-Sun. noon, 2pm, 3pm; £6) run three times per day.

Titanic Memorial Garden

20 Donegall Square E.; tel. 28/9027-0456; www.belfastcity.gov.uk; daily 10am-5pm; free

On the grounds of Belfast City Hall is the Titanic Memorial Garden, a tribute to those who died on the infamous ship in 1912. The 9-m-long (30-ft) plinth is engraved with 1,512 names. The garden opened in 2012 on the 100th anniversary of the incident with a 7-m-tall (22-ft) statue of a person holding a wreath over a drowned sailor as the focal point. The gardens are not extensive; you can walk the area in just a few minutes, but there's plenty for plant lovers, including Himalayan birch trees, blue forget-me-nots, and the *Magnolia × soulangeana* 'Alba Superba'.

Cathedral Quarter

St. Anne's Cathedral

Donegall St.; tel. 28/9032-8332; www.belfastcathedral.org; Mon.-Sat. 10:30am-2:30pm; £4

St. Anne's Cathedral, the centerpiece of the Cathedral Quarter, is a fine example of Romanesque architecture. Built in the early 20th century, its striking facade and lofty ceilings make it memorable. Intricate details include mosaics and the black-and-white marble floor alongside major architectural works of art like the Spire of Hope, a 40-m (130-ft) stainless steel spire added in 2007.

Golden Thread Gallery

23-29 Queen St.; tel. 28/9033-0920; www.goldenthreadgallery.co.uk; Tues.-Fri. 11am-5pm, Sat. 11am-4pm

Belfast was once one of the biggest linen producers in the world, giving it the nickname Linenopolis. While that industry is long gone, its influence is still seen today. Golden Thread Gallery, in a converted linen mill in the city's Cathedral Quarter, has one of the best collections of contemporary art in Northern Ireland, with the robust permanent collection from local artists alongside temporary exhibits from international artists across digital and physical mediums.

Queen's Quarter

Queen's University

University Rd.; tel. 28/9024-5133; www.qub.ac.uk

Educating students for over 175 years, this prestigious university attracts visitors to see the magnificent grounds and galleries. The main Lanyon Building was designed by Sir Charles Lanyon in Gothic Tudor style. Other architectural highlights include the Ruskinian-style Lynn Building and the Great Hall, restored in 2000. The university is a cultural hub thanks to **Queens Film Theatre,** a two-screen cinema that shows art-house and big-budget films. Art lovers come for the **Naughton Gallery.**

City Center and Cathedral Quarter

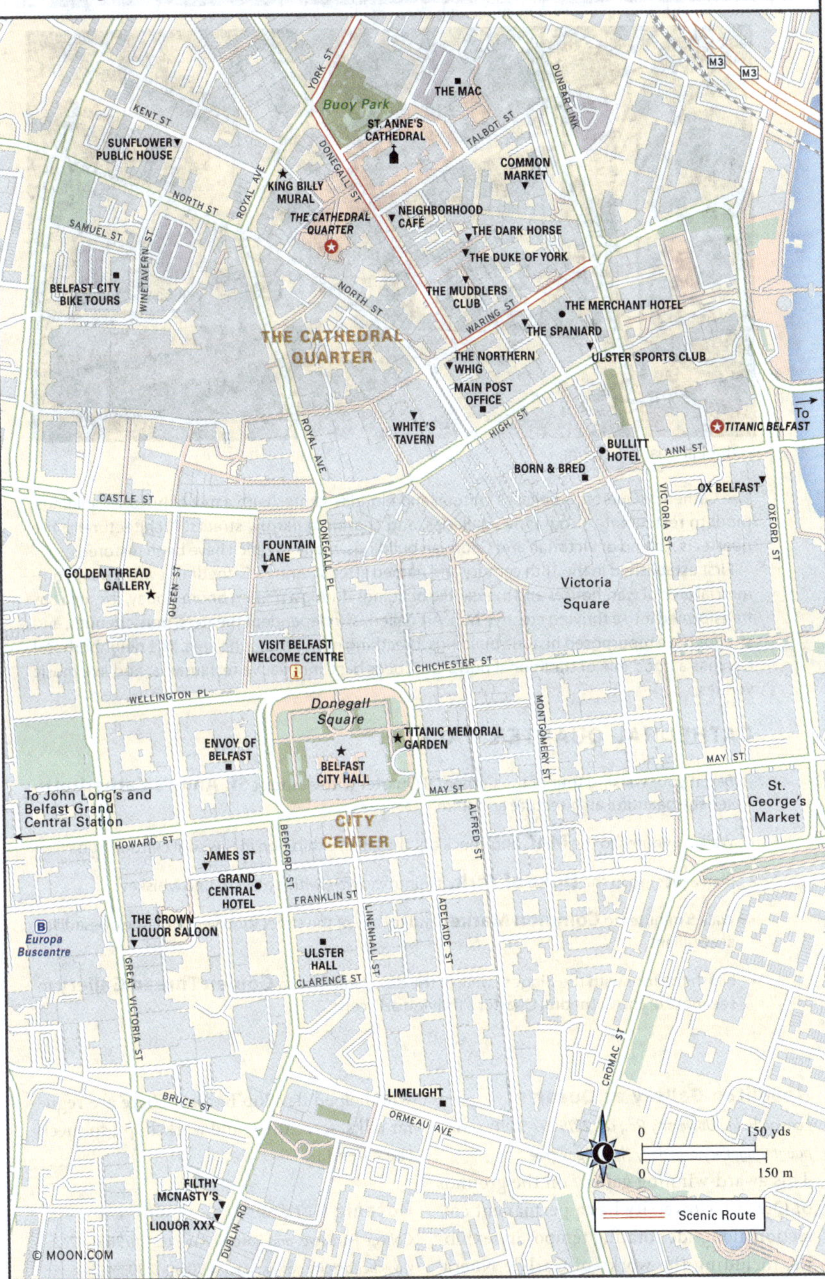

☆ The Cathedral Quarter

Cathedral Quarter at night

The Cathedral Quarter is Belfast's cultural and nightlife center, with a mix of historic buildings, modern restaurants, progressive galleries, and charming narrow streets. Architecturally, the quarter is a blend of Victorian and Georgian buildings, many of which have been restored.

First established in the 18th century and named after St. Anne's Cathedral, it was a busy commercial area of warehouses and mercantile buildings during a trading boom. Today, the area has transformed into a thriving creative hub. Art galleries, independent theaters, music venues, and studios have repurposed historic buildings, breathing new life into the area. The neighborhood also has a good mix of traditional pubs, craft beer bars, innovative restaurants, and live music venues.

CATHEDRAL QUARTER WALK

- Begin your walking tour of the Cathedral Quarter with a stop at **St. Anne's Cathedral** to see the beautiful architecture and spire.
- Walk 2 minutes to the **MAC** and check out the latest exhibition in this cool cultural hub.
- Plan a pit stop in the **Duke of York,** 3 minutes away, with a glass of fine whiskey.
- Walk 5 minutes to **Common Market** and try any of the street food vendors. The quesadillas are brilliant.
- Finish the tour with the biggest walk of the day, 7 minutes to **Golden Thread Gallery** to see more of the Cathedral Quarter's thriving art scene.

Naughton Gallery at Queen's

Lanyon Bldg., University Rd.; tel. 28/9097-3580; www.naughtongallery.org; daily 11am-4pm; free

This award-winning gallery on the grounds of Queen's University has a permanent collection alongside rotating temporary exhibits, including the works of Carlyle Nuera, who helped develop Barbie. There are regular talks, screenings, and workshops, so check the calendar.

Botanic Gardens

College Park Ave. and Botanic Ave.; tel. 28/9031-4762; www.belfastcity.gov.uk; daily 7:30am-8:30pm; free

First opened in 1852, the Botanic Gardens have become a key part of the city with extensive insight into tropical plants, native species, and colorful flowers. The **Palm House** greenhouse is the most important building on the 11 ha (28 acres). Built in the Victorian style by Charles Lanyon, it uses curved iron and glass to create a habitat for tropical and rare plants. Banana trees and orchids also grow in the Tropical Ravine, where you can tread the treetops on a suspended walkway. Outside is a rose garden, an alpine garden, and manicured flower beds.

Ulster Museum

Botanic Gardens; tel. 28/9044-0000; www.ulstermuseum.org; Tues.-Sun. 10am-5pm; free

The brutalist design of the Ulster Museum is at odds with its green surroundings in the Botanic Gardens, but it's undeniably a magnificent building. Five floors have exhibits that cover history, nature, and art. The museum's collections include remnants of the last ice age, a full-scale model of Muiredach's High Cross from the early Christian period, and works of art from the Renaissance. The variety makes the museum stand out; with so many topics and eras covered, there's bound to be something for you.

East Belfast and Titanic Quarter

★ Titanic Belfast

1 Olympic Way; tel. 28/9076-6386; www.titanicbelfast.com; Sun.-Wed. 9am-6pm, Thurs.-Sat. 9am-7:30pm; £25

The shimmering behemoth of a building is a landmark that brings the story of the most famous ship ever built into the modern day. Describing itself as an experience rather than a museum, this attraction stands on the site where the *Titanic* was built and covers the history of the shipyard, the ship, the passengers, and its infamous end. The **Titanic Experience** is nine interactive galleries with a self-guided tour. You'll get fascinating insight into the construction of the ship with a fully re-created cabin and the **Shipyard Ride**—a suspended car that feels like you're moving through the hull of the ship. Give yourself two hours to soak it all up. And yes, the bow of the ship is here too, so you can channel your inner Leonardo DiCaprio and shout, "I'm on top of the world!" There's also the 1-hour **Discovery Tour** (£15), a guided walk that runs 2-3 times daily around the old shipyard, showing you where the ships were launched and giving insights into the new building.

The Samson and Goliath Cranes

West Bank Dr.; tel. 28/9045-8456; www.harland-wolff.com

There's no structure more synonymous with the city than the enormous yellow Harland and Wolff cranes that stand tall over East Belfast. Called Samson and Goliath, these giants are 96 m (315 ft) and 106 m (348 ft) tall and have been building ships here since 1969. Some think they were used to build the *Titanic*, but that ship was built in 1911. The cranes are worth visiting to get an understanding of the scale of the industry that once operated here. The shipyard has struggled in recent years, and the cranes are rarely used. Photographers may want to visit at night, as the cranes are often lit up.

W5

The Odyssey, 2 Queens Quay; https://w5online.co.uk; Thurs. 10am-4pm, Fri.-Sat. 10am-6pm, Sun. 1pm-6pm; from £10

Families with inquisitive kids who ask "why" all the time should visit W5, an award-winning science center in a modern building by the water with 250 interactive exhibits to answer all the who, what, when, where, and why questions your little ones might have. Optical illusions capture the imagination, climbing structures exercise the body and mind, and the Skull Cave transports them to the age of the dinosaurs. The cherry on top is the MED-Lab, a series of futuristic and interactive displays that teach kids about the human body.

North Belfast

Crumlin Road Gaol

53-55 Crumlin Rd.; tel. 28/9074-1500; www.crumlinroadgaol.com; daily 10am-4pm; £14

Most of what's documented about the North's turbulent history revolves around the Troubles in the late 20th century, but at Crumlin Road Gaol you journey back to the Victorian era. "The Crum" has stood since 1845 and over the years held 25,000 political prisoners, suffragettes, and even poor families. There's a self-guided tour, but the guided 90-minute guided tour, which only runs occasionally and is announced one week in advance on their website, brings you to more areas, with the walk through the underground tunnel that connects the jail to the courthouse and the execution chamber the most chilling aspects.

Belfast Castle

Antrim Rd.; tel. 28/9077-6925; www.belfastcastle.co.uk; Tues.-Sat. 9am-9pm, Sun.-Mon. 9am-6pm; free

Tucked into the lower slopes of Cave Hill in a strategic location that looks over Belfast Lough is the impressive Belfast Castle. Finished in 1870, the sandstone building is a highlight of Victorian architecture thanks to its Scottish Baronial style and the whimsical **Cat Garden,** with its resident white cat. It's believed that if you see it, you'll have good luck. Nine other cats are hidden in the garden in the form of statues, topiaries, and mosaics. Inside the castle is the **Cave Hill Visitor Centre** as well as opulent rooms with the finest furnishings of the time.

ACTIVITIES AND RECREATION

Parks

The Victorian era saw the development of outdoor leisure and parks, with Belfast still benefitting from them today, including wide-open parks like Stormont Estate and small, modern, urban parks like C. S. Lewis Square.

Ormeau Park

Ormeau Rd.; tel. 28/9032-0202; www.belfastcity.gov.uk; daily 7:30am-8:30pm

The classic Victorian Ormeau Park is the oldest in the city, opened in 1871. It covers 40 ha (100 acres) and features winding paths through mature woodlands, seasonal flowerbeds that bring a pop of color, and the meticulously manicured lawns that the Victorians loved. The park isn't stuck in the past, however, with modern amenities that include a public BMX track and the Belfast City BMX Club.

C. S. Lewis Square

402 Newtownards Rd.; daily 24 hours

C. S. Lewis Square is a modern public space with seven bronze sculptures of characters from Lewis's beloved *The Lion, the Witch and the Wardrobe,* including Aslan, the White Witch, and Mr. Tumnus. Opened in 2016, the square is linked to the wider area via the pedestrian Comber Greenways. The square is fully illuminated at night.

Victoria Park

4 Kyle St.

Historic municipal Victoria Park, in East Belfast, opened in 1906. The centerpiece is a large lake, originally used for boating and now a sanctuary for swans, ducks, and herring gulls. There are short walking trails and a BMX track.

Stormont Estate

Stormont Court

The Northern Irish government's Parliament Buildings are on the outskirts of Belfast, surrounded by the 91-ha (224-acre) Stormont Estate, which includes manicured lawns and natural woodlands. A wide gentle trail, surfaced in crushed gravel, asphalt, and boardwalks, loops around the estate on a 4-km (2.5-mi) walk that shows off the beauty of the park as well as interesting leftovers from

1: City Hall **2:** Palm House at the Botanic Gardens **3:** Belfast Castle **4:** Titanic Memorial Garden

1
2
3
4
In Memory of those who died on the 15th April 1912

TOP EXPERIENCE

☆ Belfast Murals

mural of Bobby Sands on the Falls Road

The Troubles were a 30-year conflict between republicans, who wanted to separate from the United Kingdom and join the Republic of Ireland, and loyalists, who wanted to remain part of the UK.

The Troubles were an awful time that is thankfully over. There were no winners, only losers: At least 3,600 people died, families were torn apart, and communities were destroyed. With the Good Friday Agreement in 1998, the paramilitary groups agreed to a ceasefire, and slowly Northern Ireland has left these horrors behind. The mark of this time can be seen in Belfast's murals, a reminder of the history, the people lost, and the culture on both sides.

The most prolific time for mural painting was from the 1960s to the Good Friday Agreement in 1998, when both loyalists and republicans used the art form. Due to the controversial nature of the murals, most of the painters remained anonymous so as to not make themselves a target.

REPUBLICAN MURALS

The republican murals are centered around the Falls Road and West Belfast and tell the story of republican leaders, the Easter risings, and the hunger strikers who demanded the British govern-

World War II, like the barrage balloon anchors. For families with little ones, head to the Mo Mowlam Play Park, with 40 pieces of play equipment, including climbing frames, rubber surfaces, and wheelchair-friendly areas. The easiest way to get here from the city is the Glider G1 route.

Hiking and Walking

Cave Hill

Distance: *6.2 km (3.8 mi) round-trip*

Duration: *2-3 hours*

Elevation gain: *289 m (948 ft)*

Effort: *Moderate*

Trailhead: *Belfast Castle*

From the splendor of Belfast Castle begins the hike up Cave Hill, the striking peak that stands above the city. The trail starts gently

ment treat them as prisoners of war. More recent murals show support for overseas liberation movements.

- The Falls Road, a republican Catholic area, has some of the better-known murals, including the portrait of **Bobby Sands,** one of the hunger strikers who died in the Maze Prison in County Down.
- The republican movement in Ireland has had a brotherhood with other oppressed nations, seen at the **Solidarity Wall** on the Falls Road. The artwork is in support of the Palestinians and the Basque people.
- Another mural in support of struggles overseas is the **Nelson Mandela** mural on Northumberland Street.

LOYALIST MURALS

The loyalist murals are mainly in and around the Shankill Road. These tend to focus on the history of Protestants in Ireland, loyalist culture, and people who died in the conflict.

- Marching bands are extremely important to this community, seen on Cultra Street with a mural that honors the **Tigers Bay First Flute band.**
- On the Newtownards Road is the **Ulster Freedom Corner,** with a strong image of the red hand of Ulster.
- On Linfield Street, referring to the Battle of the Boyne in 1690, is the mural of **King Billy,** a Protestant, who waged war on the Catholics in Ireland.

LEARNING MORE

Black Taxi Tour (155 Northumberland St.; tel. 28/9032-1912; https://blacktaxitourbelfast.com; £32 pp) is one of the best ways to learn about the Troubles. This forward-thinking and healing tour company uses black cabs you'd normally associate with London, and they hire drivers from republican and loyalist backgrounds who were either involved in the conflict or who have been impacted by it. It's a first-hand historical account of the city. The **tour of the murals** is the most popular, and the guides bring the artwork to life by explaining the cultural importance of each piece and the climate in Belfast when it was painted. If you do one guided tour in Ireland, this is it. The taxi will pick you up anywhere in the city center or outside for an extra fee. The tours are private.

with winding sections through woodlands for 1.6 km (1 mi) before the path becomes steeper as it heads toward the ridge, known as Napoleon's Nose. As you hike through the trees, the trail emerges into an open green landscape with views across Belfast Lough and the city below. Continuing to the cave on top that gives this hill its name, you'll also see McArt's Fort, the remnants of an Iron Age fortification. This is a great option for a challenging hike without going far from the city.

The Gruffalo and Stickman Trail

Distance: *2 km (1.2 mi) loop*
Duration: *30-60 minutes*
Elevation gain: *Negligible*
Effort: *Easy*
Trailhead: *Colin Glen Forest Park*

This family-friendly walk is aimed at the little

ones thanks to the Gruffalo and Stickman, children's book characters created by Julia Donaldson. The easy and wide natural path is dotted with sculptures from the books. The short trail can be walked in half an hour, but most will go much slower to take pictures with the sculptures. After your walk, stop by Mona's Café in the park for a hot drink and visit the gift shop to pick up a Gruffalo gift. Guided tours of the trail (www.colinglen.org) can be booked for weekends.

Divis Summit Trail

Distance: *4.5 km (2.8 mi) loop*
Duration: *1-1.5 hours*
Elevation gain: *166 m (544 ft)*
Effort: *Moderate*
Trailhead: *The Barn Coffee Shop*

Some of my favorite hikes start and end with coffee, and that's why this is one of the best in Belfast. Leaving the stone Barn Coffee Shop, the circular route begins on a crushed gravel path. As the trail gets steeper toward the summit, you'll navigate large rock slabs on the trail, but these are manageable. At the top you can see the Harland and Wolff cranes, and on a clear day, the Mourne Mountains. The route down follows the same style of trail back to the Barn Coffee Shop.

Cycling

Cycling in Belfast feels a few steps ahead of other cities in Ireland thanks to the number of bike-friendly paths and greenways. It also feels quite safe to cycle the city streets in the bike lanes.

Comber Greenway

Distance: *11 km (7 mi) one-way*
Duration: *1-2 hours*
Elevation gain: *Negligible*
Effort: *Easy*
Trailhead: *Dee St.*

This traffic-free route runs from the port in East Belfast to Comber in the countryside. The greenway is made of smooth asphalt, which makes it great for cyclists who want to get more confident before cycling on the street. The route passes through C. S. Lewis Square and the bronze statues from Narnia before reaching the grounds of Stormont Estate and the Parliament Buildings. It's an easy route to Comber and back.

Connswater Community Greenway

Distance: *16 km (10 mi) one-way*
Duration: *1-2 hours*
Elevation gain: *Negligible*
Effort: *Easy*
Trailhead: *Victoria Park*

While the Comber Greenway follows one single route, the Connswater Community Greenway branches out to follow the route of three rivers. The greenway starts in the Titanic Quarter at Victoria Park, where you'll see the famous yellow Harland and Wolff cranes. Cycling south along the Connswater River, you reach C. S. Lewis Square, a modern urban park that celebrates the work of the writer. Once you reach the Conn O'Neill Bridge, the greenway splits, with one route following the Knock River to the east and the other following the Loop River to the west. The western route has highlights like the Cregagh Estate and the home of Belfast's favorite son, George Best. The Knock River side is great for families, as you visit Orangefield Park, which has playgrounds and playing fields.

Belfast City Bike Tours

18 Winetavern St.; tel. 7780-496969; https://belfastcitybiketours.com; daily 10am-5pm; from £20

Belfast Bike Tours offers one all-encompassing cycling tour through the city. Lasting around three hours, this tour hits major attractions, including Titanic Belfast, the Harland and Wolff cranes, and the Cathedral Quarter. The pace is relaxed, so there's no need to be super fit, and there are even toddler seats available for kids up to age 3. Bike rental is included in the tour cost, and they use a modern style of city bike that anyone age 12 and up can ride.

ENTERTAINMENT AND EVENTS

Performing Arts

The MAC

10 Exchange St.; tel. 28/9023-5053; http://themaclive.com; Tues.-Sun. 9am-5pm; from £10

The Metropolitan Arts Centre, known in Belfast as the MAC, is a state-of-the-art venue with two modern theaters, three galleries, and smaller spaces that facilitate the arts. All manner of events include gripping photography exhibitions, local theater group performances, and even pantomimes at Christmas. The exhibitions run for a few months at a time. After your visit, stop by the **MAC CaféBar** (daily 9am-3:30pm), with hot dishes like chorizo hash.

Cultúrlann McAdam Ó Fiaich

216 Falls Rd.; tel. 28/9096-4180; www.culturlann.ie; Mon.-Sat. 9am-6pm, Sun. 11am-4pm; free

Cultúrlann McAdam Ó Fiaich is an Irish language arts and cultural center that aims to revive the struggling language. Opened in 1991 in a former Presbyterian church, it has become the heart of the Gaeltacht Quarter. The host of activities includes Irish language classes, art workshops, dances, concerts, and exhibitions. It houses the Gerard Dillon art gallery, a theater, a restaurant, and a bookshop.

Live Music

Ulster Hall

34 Bedford St.; tel. 28/9033-4455; www.ulsterhall.co.uk; Mon.-Fri. noon-6pm; from £25

Part of Belfast's Victorian heritage is the Ulster Hall, which has stood for over 150 years. During World War II American soldiers blew off steam here, even during the bombings of the Belfast Blitz. Some impressive names have taken to the stage over the years, including Charles Dickens, Led Zepplin, and local icon Van Morrisson. These days there are events almost daily in music, theater, and comedy.

Limelight

17 Ormeau Ave.; tel. 28/9032-7007; www.limelightbelfast.com; Mon. and Wed.-Thurs. 10pm-2am, Fri.-Sat. 5pm-2am; from £5

Limelight is one of those places where you visit to see live music and end up staying for the whole night. Most live performances are at Limelight 2, a dimly lit space that's seen rock heavyweights like the Strokes and Joe Strummer. On a summer evening, the outdoor space, the Rock Garden, fills up after the show, and to keep the party going into the wee hours, Limelight 1 is the club venue, where cheesy pop is the focus on Thursday.

Festivals and Events

Belfast City Marathon

https://belfastcitymarathon.com; May

Runners from across the country and abroad run the 42-km (26-mi) Belfast City Marathon, through the heart of the city and past the River Lagan and Titanic Belfast. The race ends in Ormeau Park with crowds at the finish line. The whole city shuts down for this enormous event that often has 18,000 entrants. It fills quickly, so if you're planning on running, plan ahead.

Belfast Film Festival

https://belfastfilmfestival.org; early Nov.

Belfast Film Festival stands out because it incorporates so many local filmmakers, giving them a chance to be seen alongside films that have screened at the film festivals in Cannes and Venice. For 10 days at seven venues, including the majestic Waterfront Hall and the intimate Beanbag Cinema, visitors can see big-name performers as well as art-house flicks. There are also Q&A events with directors.

C. S. Lewis Festival

late Nov.; free

The magical world of Narnia was conjured by Belfast native C. S. Lewis in the 1950s, and now the city celebrates their famous writer over a weekend. The thick of the action focuses on C. S. Lewis Square in East Belfast, where attendees step through the wardrobe and into a square with statues of Aslan and Mr. Tumnus, Narnia-themed market stalls, and mulled wine. Other events in the area are run by local businesses to celebrate the writer.

SHOPPING

City Center

Victoria Square

1 Victoria Square; tel. 28/9032-2277; www.victoriasquare.com; Mon.-Wed. and Sat. 9am-6pm, Thurs.-Fri. 9am-9pm, Sun. 1pm-6pm

It's hard to miss the glass dome of Victoria Square in the heart of Belfast. This modern shopping center spans four floors and 70 shops that include big names like the House of Fraser, Flannels, and M.A.C. Make time to go up to the viewing platform in the glass dome, with incredible views of the city and the mountains. The impressive list of restaurants is on the smarter end of fast food, with the likes of Nando's, Five Guys, and Pizza Express.

St. George's Market

12 East Bridge St.; tel. 28/9043-5704; www.belfastcity.gov.uk; Fri. 8am-2pm, Sat. 9am-3pm, Sun. 10am-4pm

St. George's Market has been operating in this redbrick building since 1896 and continues to draw people with brilliant stalls selling everything from artisanal food to antique furniture. Friday sees 200 sellers open stalls, making it a great day to visit. Saturday is all about food, with cheese, coffee beans, and fresh fish. On Sunday, the crafts shine; expect to find handmade furniture and decorations by local makers.

Envoy of Belfast

4 Wellington St.; tel. 28/9031-1110; https://envoyofbelfast.com; Tues.-Sat. 10am-5:30pm

This womenswear shop focuses on modern clean styles heavily influenced by Japanese fashion. They stock well-known on-trend brands like Simone Rocha, Acne Studios, and Dries Van Noten. The prices are definitely on the luxury end, but the high-quality pieces will stand the test of time.

Cathedral Quarter

Born & Bred

62 Ann St.; tel. 28/9023-0475; https://wearebornandbred.com; Mon.-Sat. 10am-6pm, Sun. 1pm-6pm

Born & Bred is all about promoting Northern Irish makers and designers, selling a large cross-section of gifts and homewares with a modern and sleek feel. Find Irish-language

viewing platform at Victoria Square

prints, their in-house range of clothing and accessories, and conversation-starting homewares.

Queen's Quarter

No Alibis

83 Botanic Ave.; tel. 28/9031-9601; https://noalibis.com; Mon.-Sat. 9am-5:30pm

No Alibis is a specialist bookshop that focuses on mystery fiction as well as some kids books, Irish literature, and history. The tables are stacked high with books, and there's a real bookworm feel thanks to the reading nooks and very knowledgeable staff. Serious book fans will want to check out the rare books section, which has some collectible first editions.

East Belfast and Titanic Quarter

The Bureau

310 Newtownards Rd., B2 Portview; tel. 28/9046-0190; www.thebureaubelfast.com; Mon.-Fri. 10am-5:30pm, Sat. 10am-12:30pm

The Bureau is a surprising menswear shop in a renovated industrial area in East Belfast. Inside the unassuming facade is an extensive collection of Japanese menswear from brands that are hard to find outside Asia. Expect stylish workwear made with heavy-duty materials and über-fashionable cuts. Prices aren't cheap, but the quality is top-notch.

FOOD

Belfast's foodie scene is one of the most exciting on the island. The cheaper rents and fewer multinational chain restaurants have attracted incredible chefs and creative entrepreneurs. Locals have welcomed them with open arms and are always seeking the newest, coolest spot. From vibrant street food to perfectly executed fine dining, Belfast has it all.

City Center

John Long's

39 Athol St.; tel. 28/9032-1848; www.johnlongs.com; Tues.-Fri. noon-6:30pm, Sat. noon-6pm; from £4

A short walk from the upmarket Europa Hotel is a famous eatery that's been feeding workers in Belfast for over 100 years. The decor looks like it was last updated decades ago. John Long's fish-and-chips are famous (*The Times* named it the best fish-and-chip shop in the UK in 2024) along with friendly service.

Fountain Lane

16 Fountain St.; tel. 28/9032-4769; www.fountainlanebelfast.com; Mon.-Sat. noon-1am, Sun. noon-midnight; from £8

Fountain Lane has been a stronghold of the Belfast pub grub scene since 1901, and the atmosphere here is hard to beat. Serving both lunch and evening menus that focus on meat, this traditional pub has been updated with modern furnishings. Come on Sunday noon-4pm for the roast dinner, with kids eating for free. If you're in Belfast on Monday, stop by for their quiz night from 9pm.

James St.

19 James St. S.; tel. 28/9560-0700; www.jamesst.co.uk; Mon. and Wed.-Thurs. 5pm-9:30pm, Fri.-Sat. 1pm-9:30pm, Sun. 1pm-8pm; from £20

This elegant steak house shuns the usual macho approach to opt for a fine-dining feel with contemporary artwork and a brightly lit space. The steak is sourced locally and makes up most of the menu, with sharing options available. The best value is the set menu with two (£27) or three (£30) courses. Vegetarian options are available, and look for menu items that are listed in chef Niall McKenna's cookbook.

OX Belfast

1 Oxford St.; tel. 28/9031-4121; www.oxbelfast.com; Wed. 6pm-9:30pm, Thurs.-Sat. noon-2pm and 6pm-9:30pm; from £55

This Michelin-starred restaurant on the banks of the River Lagan merges French cuisine and Irish hospitality. Highlights of the fine-dining menu are scallops served with autumn truffles as well as venison from Wicklow finished with fig. If the evening menu prices are too rich, book a table for lunch, where three courses cost £55. The OX Cave is their wine bar next door, where you'll see framed knives from the TV show *Game of Thrones*.

Cathedral Quarter

Common Market

16-20 Dunbar St.; https://commonmarketbelfast.com; Thurs.-Sun. noon-midnight; from £5

Common Market is Belfast's answer to the famous TimeOut Market in Lisbon, except with a more industrial feel. Various food vendors inside a warehouse offer a range of cuisines, from the Canadian favorite poutine to Mexican street food. The relaxed vibe makes it a good spot to catch up with friends, take the family to eat, and even bring your dog for a walk, as the market is dog-friendly. It can get chilly inside when the temperatures drop, so treat it like eating outdoors.

Neighbourhood Café

33 Donegall St.; www.neighbourhood.cafe; Mon.-Fri. 7:30am-4pm, Sat.-Sun. 8:30am-5pm; from £7

As one of the many cafés at the forefront of Belfast's brunch charge, Neighbourhood Café is a consistently busy spot that's popular with a younger crowd. Like something you'd expect to find in New York rather than Belfast, the exposed redbrick wall and floor-to-ceiling windows set the scene for a great coffee and late breakfast. The Turkish eggs with chili butter and sourdough toast are the standout. Pick up merch that matches the trendy vibe of the place.

The Northern Whig

2, Northern Whig Bldg., 2-10 Bridge St.; tel. 28/9050-9888; www.thenorthernwhig.com; Mon.-Wed. noon-11pm, Thurs. noon-midnight, Fri.-Sat. noon-1am, Sun. 1pm-midnight; from £15

The Northern Whig is a classy gastropub in a historic building in the Cathedral Quarter serving cosmopolitan and contemporary dishes. The all-day menu has pub classics like roast beef and Yorkshire pudding, pork loin with caramelized apples, and beer-battered fish-and-chips. The interior is spacious, and in the evening fills with people dropping by for a drink. The Northern Whig is known for high-quality cocktails that use premium liquors, which you can learn to make at their cocktail masterclasses.

The Muddlers Club

1 Warehouse Lane; tel. 28/9031-3199; www.themuddlersclubbelfast.com; Wed.-Thurs. 5pm-9:30pm, Fri.-Sat. 12:30pm-1pm and 5pm-9:30pm; from £90

The Muddler's Club is another of Belfast's Michelin-starred restaurants that opts for modern fine-dining with a focus on local produce. Diners can choose the tasting menu or the vegetarian tasting menu; both have eight courses and cost £90. The restaurant is named after a secret society that met here 200 years ago, but the atmosphere is more contemporary thanks to dishes like celeriac and pea consommé and lamb carpaccio with eggplant.

Queen's Quarter

Ryan's Bar & Restaurant

116-118 Lisburn Rd.; tel. 28/9050-9850; www.ryansbelfast.com/menus; Mon.-Tues. noon-11pm, Wed.-Thurs. noon-midnight, Sat. noon-1am, Sun. 12:30pm-11pm; from £9

Part bar, part restaurant, Ryan's is a relaxing spot in Belfast to enjoy Irish produce. Known for chicken wings with sriracha and honey hot sauce as well as their steaks, Ryan's is all about unpretentious food and good value, with two courses for as little as £14. When the kitchen closes, the dining area turns into an extension of the bar, and on Saturday night live music starts around 10pm.

East Belfast and Titanic Quarter

Root & Branch Coffee Roastery

Portview Trade Centre, 310 Newtownards Rd., Unit A3; Mon.-Fri. 8:30am-3pm; http://rootandbranch.coffee; Mon.-Fri. 8:30am-3pm; from £3

If you're a coffee nerd, Root & Branch Coffee Roastery should be top of your list. Coffee is treated as both a science and an art in this rejuvenated industrial space that acts as an active microroaster. It's more a coffee bar that seats 10 than a café; there are no couches or spaces to work. Instead, it's a place for purists who put the sourcing, roasting, and flavor of their coffee first. Each cup is served on a small wooden board along with a glass of water—a sign that you're in a serious coffee shop.

Late Café

4 Orangefield Lane; Instagram @latecafe__; Mon.-Wed. and Sat. 8am-4pm, Thurs.-Fri. 8am-8pm, Sun. 8am-2pm; from £3

Set in a neighborhood in East Belfast beside Greenville Park, Late Café caters to people who see coffee as a lifestyle rather than just a drink. The café has a gallery-like feel, with clean white walls, Scandi-chic minimalist furnishings, and a rotating collection of art from local artists. The coffee is front and center, with a choice of beans from different roasters and a small selection of baked goods.

Flout!

Portview Trade Centre, 310 Newtownards Rd., Unit D5; www.flout.pizza; Wed.-Sat. noon-2pm; from £5

To say that Flout! is popular is a massive understatement. This pizza place has limited open hours and fans line up before it opens. Be prompt, as the chef only has a limited amount of dough each day, and when they sell out, he shuts the doors. There isn't one style of pizza; they flout the rules and make their own creations. The menu changes often, but previous pies have included mushroom and bechamel, slow-cooked anchovy with spiked tomato sauce, and creamed spinach with Irish mozzarella.

General Merchants

361 Ormeau Rd.; tel. 28/9029-1007; http://generalmerchants.co.uk; Mon.-Fri. 8am-5pm; from £11

This buzzing neighborhood café has a menu of twists on café favorites, like triple-cooked potatoes served with grilled chorizo, fried eggs, and local relish. There are three locations in Belfast, but this is the original and can be enjoyed at a slower pace. Dark furnishings and soft lighting give it a cozy feel, and leafy hanging plants give the space a pop of life. Seating comprises a large communal table for 10 with bar seating by the window, two-seaters along the wall, and outdoor seating for 10 when the weather is good.

BARS AND NIGHTLIFE

Belfast's nightlife is an extension of its food scene, with a wide choice of great venues. Cozy up with a pint in a traditional pub or sip a craft beer in a trendy bar. Friday-Saturday nights are the busiest.

City Center

The Crown Liquor Saloon

46 Great Victoria St.; tel. 28/9024-3187; www.nicholsonspubs.co.uk; Mon.-Sat. 11:30am-midnight, Sun. 12:30pm-midnight; from £6

If you like your beer with a side serving of architectural history, the beautifully crafted Crown Liquor Saloon is a must. Striking shimmering tiles on the exterior catch your eye as you approach, and inside are mosaic tiles, stained glass, and hand-painted signage. Given the city center location of the pub, there's always a crowd, but if you have the chance to sit in one of the 10 snugs, you'll feel as if you have the place to yourself.

Filthy McNasty's

45 Dublin Rd.; www.filthysbelfast.co.uk; Mon. and Wed. 5pm-1am, Tues. and Thurs. 5pm-3am, Fri.-Sat. 1pm-3am, Sun. 1pm-midnight; from £5

Don't let the name put you off; Filthy McNasty's is a welcoming venue that has live music seven nights a week, including a country special Thursday, as well as regular quiz nights. The front bar, suitably called the Front Bar, is for a quiet drink and sports on the TVs before the live music starts and the party begins. The nightclub area opens four nights a week with a top-quality sound system and strobe lights into the early morning. Rounding off this multifaceted venue is Filthy's Garden, a beer garden with covered tables and string lights.

Liquor XXX

49 Dublin Rd.; www.liquorxxxbelfast.com; Mon.-Thurs. 5pm-1am, Fri. 4pm-1am, Sat. 2pm-1am, Sun. 6pm-midnight; from £10

Cocktail lovers will feel as if they've been transported to a trendy underground venue in Los Angeles when they step through the doors of Liquor XXX. The rich velvet interiors, exposed brick walls, and comfortable seats make it easy to spend a whole night. The drinks match the appeal, with the bar voted Ulster's best cocktail bar. Their signature cocktail, Rainfall, is made with gin, green Chartreuse, lime cordial, sour apple, and makrut lime.

Cathedral Quarter

White's Tavern

2-4 Winecellar Entry; tel. 28/9031-2582; www.whitestavernbelfast.com; Mon. 11:30am-midnight, Tues.-Fri. 12:30pm-1am, Sat. 11:30am-midnight, Sun. 12:30pm-2am; from £6

Belfast has a lot of historic buildings, but only one has been operating as a tavern since 1630. The centuries of history can be seen on the worn exterior, and the interior has been carefully restored and renovated with modern amenities without losing the old-world charm. White's Tavern is a cozy pub with low ceilings, fireplaces, and exposed beams, a perfect shelter on a wintery day. The extensive food menu covers gastropub favorites, including beer-battered haddock and chips.

Sunflower Public House

65 Union St.; tel. 28/9023-2474; www.sunflowerbelfast.com; Mon.-Wed. noon-midnight, Thurs.-Sat. noon-1am, Sun. 1pm-midnight; from £6

The first thing you'll notice is the cage on the door, a remnant of more turbulent times. Describing itself as a "simple pub," the Sunflower has gained a reputation for its no-fuss approach to having a pint. Not worrying about opulent interiors, the focus is on local craft beers, with the taps pouring brews from Belfast and across Northern Ireland. On a sunny day, the south-facing beer garden is the place to be, as the chefs cook wood-fired pizzas. When night draws in, pop upstairs to the music venue, where live tunes play every night.

The Duke of York

7-11 Commercial Court; tel. 28/9024-1062; www.dukeofyorkbelfast.com; Mon. 11:30am-midnight, Tues.-Sat. 12:30pm-1am, Sun. 1pm-9pm; from £6

There are so many pieces of Belfast memorabilia decorating the walls of the Duke of York that they have taken over the ceiling. Many pubs in Belfast date back centuries, but the Duke only dates to 1972, when the building was accidentally blown up in the Troubles. Behind the bar, expect perfectly poured pints of Guinness and a seriously impressive whiskey collection featuring some bottles thought to be the only ones of their kind in existence. These whiskeys aren't for sale, but lots of other rare creations are available.

The Dark Horse

30 Hill St.; tel. 28/9023-7807; www.dukeofyorkbelfast.com; Mon.-Fri. 9am-5pm, Sat. 10am-6pm; £4

If you want the atmosphere of a classy bar but without the alcohol, stop by the Dark Horse, a classic European-style coffee house down a cobblestone street decorated with vintage decor and memorabilia that harks back to the Victorian era. It's also home to one of the iconic doors from the TV show *Game of Thrones,* intricately carved from wood salvaged from the Dark Hedges and a must-visit for fans of the series. They serve beer and wine, but the focus is on loose-leaf teas and coffees beautifully presented.

Ulster Sports Club

96-98 High St.; tel. 28/9023-0771; www.ulstersportsclub.com; Mon.-Thurs. 5pm-1am, Fri.-Sat. noon-2am, Sun. noon-midnight; from £5

Ulster Sports Club is not a sports bar; it's an electronic music venue. The space has a retro feel with wood paneling and a tiled floor harking back to the 1970s along with contemporary art that shows the witty humor of Belfast. Upstairs, you'll find the nightclub area and a brewery called Out of Office, with their Dark Mode stout rivalling Guinness.

The Spaniard

3 Skipper St.; tel. 28/9023-2448; Mon.-Sat. noon-1am, Sun. noon-midnight; from £5

If you're looking for an eccentric bar in Belfast, you've found it with the Spaniard. Spread over two floors and decorated with religious memorabilia, it provides the rare opportunity to have a late-night caipirinha while gazing up at paintings of Jesus. Downstairs has comfortable seating for having a chat, while upstairs is more bar-like and the place to go to dance.

ACCOMMODATIONS

Stay in the city center to be in the thick of the action, where hotels tend to be in modern buildings. The Cathedral Quarter is best to make the most of Belfast's restaurants and pubs, although it may be too busy if you want an early night. Queen's Quarter is a relaxed area that has a residential feel. East Belfast is a good choice to stay somewhere quieter but farther away from the main attractions.

City Center

Grand Central Hotel

9-15 Bedford St.; tel. 28/9023-1066; www.grandcentralhotelbelfast.com; £250

In contrast to Belfast's Victorian heritage is the contemporary sleek styling of the Grand Central Hotel. This 23-floor, 300-room hotel has marble surfaces, chic lighting, and straight lines throughout. Even though it's in the heart of the city, there are many links to the landscape, particularly at **The Observatory**—Ireland's highest bar, with 360-degree views of the mountains and the sea. Breakfast and brunch are served at **The Grand Café** on the ground floor in a relaxed atmosphere with large windows.

Cathedral Quarter

Bullitt Hotel

40a Church Lane; tel. 28/9590-0600; www.bullitthotel.com; £120

As a self-proclaimed "no-nonsense hotel," Bullitt Hotel is a pleasant stay without breaking the bank. It's clean, modern, and cheap, but the rooms are very small. The three room types are dinky, comfy, and roomy, with the last being close to what you'd expect in a standard hotel. All rooms come with king beds, smart TVs, and Wi-Fi, but this hotel is really best if you spend the majority of your time exploring the city rather than lounging in the hotel. On sunny weekend days, pop up to the roof garden, where you'll find DJs playing.

The Merchant Hotel

16 Skipper St.; tel. 28/9023-4888; www.themerchanthotel.com; £240

Live the life of luxury in this five-star hotel in a Grade A historic building that was once a bank. The 63 rooms are in Victorian or art

the Duke of York

deco style, all lavishly decorated and dotted with antiques. It is hard to walk past the hotel's **Great Room Restaurant** and its fine-dining menu, awarded a 2 AA Rosette distinction. The on-site luxury spa, complete with five treatment rooms and a hydrotherapy area, is perfect for unwinding.

Queen's Quarter

Botanical Backpackers

63 Fitzwilliam St.; www.botanicalbackpackers.co.uk; £35

The Botanical Backpackers is a house on a suburban street in the Botanical Quarter that prides itself on being friendly, well-located, and a great place to meet other travelers. The dorms are bright and clean but quite basic with simple bunk beds without sockets or reading lights. Botanical Backpackers offers a homey experience, with guests sharing meals in communal areas and feeding the birds outside.

The Harrison Chambers of Distinction

45 Malone Rd.; tel. 28/9460-0123; www.chambersofdistinction.com; £220

For a quirky stay, the Harrison Chambers of Distinction boasts an eclectic bohemian feel in 16 individually designed rooms, some equipped with four-poster beds, glistening chandeliers, and leafy green plants. There is no on-site restaurant, but breakfast is delivered hot and fresh to your room. Modern touches include rainfall showers, free Wi-Fi, and vegan toiletries from a local maker, and when it comes time to venture outside, you're less than 0.8 km (0.5 mi) from the Botanic Gardens.

East Belfast and Titanic Quarter

Barge at Titanic

Corporation Square; tel. 7801-594445; www.bargeattitanic.com; £150

Barge at Titanic is one of the most unique stays in the city and a must for anyone who wants to connect with the city's shipbuilding past. The two barges on the water, *Harland* and *Wolff*, are named after the famous shipbuilding cranes. Both can accommodate four guests in two bedrooms with three beds and one shower. *Harland* has better views of the city and *Wolff* has a nice outdoor area where you can relax by the water. The barges came from Scotland and have been meticulously restored into fine vessels by a talented and passionate team.

INFORMATION AND SERVICES

Visitor Information

Visit Belfast Welcome Centre

Donegall Square N.; tel. 28/9024-6609; https://visitbelfast.com; daily 9am-5pm

The Visit Belfast Welcome Centre is a great first stop. Knowledgeable staff can help you plan attractions, tours, or events and offers free maps and brochures. Check the website for seasonal hours.

Hospitals and Pharmacies

For emergencies, Belfast is served by the **Royal Victoria Hospital** (Grosvenor Rd.; www.belfasttrust.hscni.net) and the **Mater Infirmorum Hospital** (Crumlin Rd.; www.belfasttrust.hscni.net).

Pharmacies are abundant, from well-known chains like Boots to independent shops. For a late-night option, try **Clear Pharmacy** (Shankill Rd.), typically open until 8pm.

Banks and ATMs

ATMs are easy to find, and major banks like Ulster Bank and HSBC have branches throughout the city. Most grocery stores and petrol stations also have cash machines.

Post Offices

The main **post office** (www.postoffice.co.uk) is at 12-16 Bridge Street in the city center. You can send parcels and buy stamps.

GETTING THERE

Air

With two main airports, Belfast is well-connected. **George Best Belfast City Airport** (BHD) is just 5 km (3 mi) from the city center and primarily serves UK destinations with Aer Lingus, British Airways, and Flybe. **Belfast International Airport** (BFS), 29 km (18 mi) from the city, offers European routes and trans-atlantic flights, including connections with easyJet, Ryanair, and Virgin Atlantic. Both airports are compact and easy to navigate.

To get to the city from Belfast City Airport, take a taxi (10 minutes; £10-12) or the **Airport Express** Route 600 bus (Translink; £2.50) that runs regularly into the city center. From Belfast International Airport, take the Airport Express Route 300 bus (40 minutes; £8). Taxis (£30-35) are available but are more expensive.

Car

Belfast is easily accessible by car via the A1/M1 motorway, which connects to Dublin in about two hours, depending on traffic. The city is compact, but drivers should note that parking in the center can be limited. The M2 and M3 motorways connect Belfast to the northern and eastern regions of Northern Ireland. Driving from the UK mainland, ferry services to Belfast operate from ports like Cairnryan in Scotland, arriving at Belfast Harbour.

Bus

Aircoach (www.aircoach.ie) provides hourly bus connections from Dublin City (O'Connell St.) and Dublin Airport to Upper Queen Street (2.5 hours; €14/£13 one-way).

Dublin Express (www.dublinexpress.ie) buses depart from multiple locations in Dublin, including Pearse Street and Custom House Quay to the Europa Bus Centre. The journey time is slightly longer, but they offer flexible departure options and 16 departures daily.

Train

The *Enterprise* train service departs from the new **Belfast Grand Central Station** (Durham St.), a £340 million transport hub that opened in 2024. Trains run hourly between Belfast Grand Central Station and Dublin Connolly Station (2.25 hours; €14/£13 one-way), with stops in Dundalk and Drogheda. The timetable offers 15 daily trains Monday-Saturday and 8 on Sunday. Trains to Coleraine or Derry depart from Lanyon Place Station.

GETTING AROUND

On Foot

Belfast is compact and walkable, with popular landmarks like City Hall, St. George's Market, the Titanic Quarter, and the Cathedral Quarter near the center and all within 15-20 minutes' walk of each other. The city is pedestrian-friendly, with wide footpaths and clearly marked crossings.

Public Transport

Belfast's buses, operated by **Translink Metro** (www.translink.co.uk), are the backbone of the city's public transportation. Most routes depart the city center and cover East Belfast, West Belfast, and the Titanic Quarter. Buses run frequently, and day tickets or Smartlink cards are cost-effective for multiple journeys.

A standout service is the **Glider** (www.translink.co.uk), a rapid transit system that connects East Belfast, West Belfast, and the Titanic Quarter via the city center. Glider buses are sleek, modern, and offer reliable frequent service.

While Belfast lacks a local rapid-transit rail network, it is served by a robust train network operated by **Translink NI Railways** (www.translink.co.uk). Key lines include routes to Bangor, Portadown, Derry, and Larne, with frequent stops along the way.

Cycling

Belfast has invested in improving its cycling infrastructure, with several bike lanes running through the city. These are often shared with bus lanes, which can be intimidating for new cyclists. For safer cycling, look for dedicated bike paths in areas like the Lagan Towpath and Comber Greenway. **Belfast**

Bikes (www.belfastbikes.co.uk) is an affordable bike-sharing scheme with docking stations across the city.

Taxis

You can hail black taxis on the street, or use apps like **FonaCAB** (www.fonacab.com) and **Value Cabs** (www.valuecabs.co.uk) to book a taxi. Standard taxis are metered, but confirm the fare if booking by phone or app. Card payments are widely accepted, though it's still advisable to carry some cash.

Uber (www.uber.com) operates in Belfast, but unlike in the United States, the app connects you with licensed taxi drivers.

Car

Driving in Belfast is more manageable than in larger cities, but expect congestion during peak hours. Parking is available through on-street pay-and-display zones and in multistory car parks near key areas like Victoria Square and CastleCourt Shopping Centre.

STRANGFORD LOUGH

Strangford Lough, a 150-sq-km (58-sq-mi) coastal lake, has the impressive accolades of being a UNESCO Global Geopark, Area of Outstanding Natural Beauty, and Area of Special Scientific Interest. Newtownards marks the northern most point of Strangford Lough, and at the southernmost point are Strangford and Portaferry, which face each other across the inlet. Most of the sights are in these areas, but a short distance away on the edge of the Quoile River is Downpatrick, where you'll find others.

Sights

Exploris Aquarium

1 The Rope Walk, Newtownards; tel. 28/4272-8062; www.explorisni.com; daily 10am-5pm; £15

There are 2,000 types of marine creatures in the lough, and the best way to learn about them is at Exploris Aquarium. The seal sanctuary is the main draw, and you can touch starfish and rays in the pools.

Strangford Lough Activity Centre

40 Whiterock Rd., Newtownards; tel. 7909-721898; www.strangfordloughactivitycentre.com; daily 9am-9pm; from £45

For an exciting way to see the lough with the family, hop on a rib boat with Strangford Lough Activity Centre and zip across the water to see historic castles and picturesque villages.

Winterfell Castle & Demesne

Park Rd., Downpatrick; tel. 28/4372-3933; www.winterfell-tours.com; daily 9am-5pm; from £33

Fans of the TV show *Game of Thrones* will want to visit Winterfell Castle & Demesne, outside the village of Strangford, to visit filming locations and meet the direwolf dogs you saw on screen. Spend the day and join one of four tours.

Hiking and Walking

Kearney Coastal Walk

Distance: *5.8 km (3.6 mi) round-trip*
Duration: *1 hour*
Elevation gain: *36 m (118 ft)*
Effort: *Easy*
Trailhead: *Kearney Rd.*

Make your way to Kearney on the tip of the Ards Peninsula and hike the Kearney Coastal Walk, which takes you to isolated lookout points over the sea.

Getting There

From Belfast, you can reach Newtownards by car in 20 minutes via the A20, or by Translink bus from Laganside Bus Centre in 30 minutes. To get to Portaferry, drive southeast through Newtownards and follow the A20 for 1 hour, or take a bus from Belfast (1.5 hours). For Strangford, drive south on the A24 to Downpatrick, then follow the A25, about 1 hour, or by bus to Downpatrick and connect to a bus to Strangford, a total of 1.5 hours. A ferry links Portaferry and Strangford across the mouth of Strangford Lough, operating frequently with a crossing time of 8 minutes.

The Causeway Coast

The Causeway Coast is a spectacular section of Northern Ireland lined with seaside villages in harmony with the coast and incredible landscapes, including the world-famous Giant's Causeway, which you can explore in short stints or multiday hikes. It's a rural area with no town larger than 25,000.

This area is popular with whiskey lovers for the legendary Bushmills distillery. Tourism is evolving, with established tourist towns like Portrush joined by small villages with new businesses. The surf scene is also taking hold, with surfers coming for the predictable waves and cheaper prices than in the republic. These factors give the region a nice mix, and there's no domineering type; instead you'll find all sorts of people who come to enjoy the coast.

ORIENTATION

The Causeway Coast covers the northern coast of County Antrim and into County Derry. **Ballycastle** lies at the eastern end, a gateway to the region 88 km (55 mi) north of Belfast. Moving westward, **Bushmills** is 20 km (12 mi) away and close to the **Giant's Causeway.** Farther west, **Portrush,** known for its beaches and **Royal Portrush Golf Club,** is 9.5 km (6 mi) from Bushmills, with **Portstewart,** a quiet seaside town, just 5.5 km (3 mi) beyond Portrush.

BALLYCASTLE

Ballycastle is a small town with big views thanks to **Fair Head,** a mountain cliff nearby, and the sea. There's a busy marina that sees sailors from Rathlin Island, Scotland, and the Isle of Man. Most of the socializing happens around the waterfront, but you're never far from peace and quiet if you walk down Ballycastle Strand. The town is both a hub to explore the Causeway Coast and a stopping-off point for food and drink on the way to Carrick-a-Rede Rope Bridge.

Sights

★ Carrick-a-Rede Rope Bridge

Ballintoy; tel. 28/2076-9839; www.nationaltrust.co.uk; daily 9am-4:30pm; £16

This swaying rope bridge has become an unlikely hit with visitors, who love to walk across

Carrick-a-Rede Rope Bridge

The Causeway Coast

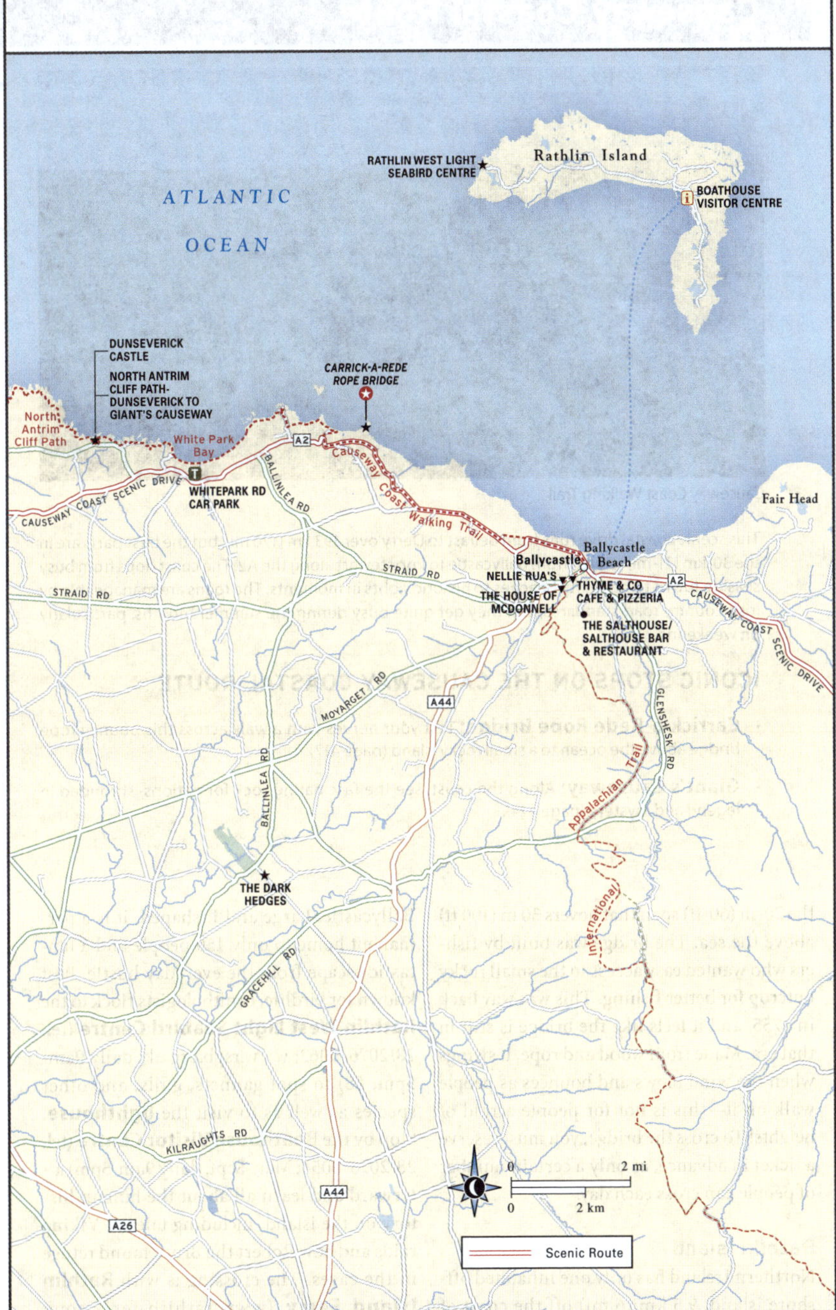
ATLANTIC
OCEAN
Rathlin Island
RATHLIN WEST LIGHT
SEABIRD CENTRE
BOATHOUSE
VISITOR CENTRE
DUNSEVERICK
CASTLE
NORTH ANTRIM
CLIFF PATH-
DUNSEVERICK TO
GIANT'S CAUSEWAY
CARRICK-A-REDE
ROPE BRIDGE
North
Antrim
Cliff Path
White Park
Bay
A2
Causeway Coast Walking Trail
WHITEPARK RD
CAR PARK
CAUSEWAY COAST SCENIC DRIVE
BALLINLEA RD
Fair Head
Ballycastle
Beach
Ballycastle
NELLIE RUA'S
THE HOUSE OF
MCDONNELL
THYME & CO
CAFE & PIZZERIA
THE SALTHOUSE/
SALTHOUSE BAR
& RESTAURANT
STRAID RD
STRAID RD
A2
CAUSEWAY COAST SCENIC DRIVE
GLENSHESK RD
A44
MOYARGET RD
International Appalachian Trail
BALLINLEA RD
THE DARK
HEDGES
GRACEHILL RD
KILRAUGHTS RD
A44
A26
0
2 mi
0
2 km
Scenic Route

Causeway Coastal Route

Causeway Coast Walking Trail

This scenic coastal drive runs from Belfast to Derry over 193 km (120 mi), but the best parts are in the 30-km (21-mi) stretch from Ballycastle to Portstewart along the A2. The coast hops from busy seaside towns to beautiful beaches to historic sights in moments. The roads are manageable by Irish country road standards, but they get quite busy during the summer months, particularly on weekends.

ICONIC STOPS ON THE CAUSEWAY COASTAL ROUTE

- **Carrick-a-Rede Rope Bridge:** Test your nerves with a walk across this bouncy rope bridge above the ocean to a small rocky island (page 417).
- **Giant's Causeway:** Along the coast, see the fascinating rock formations, shrouded in legend and mystery (page 424).

the 20-m (60-ft) span that hovers 30 m (100 ft) above the sea. The bridge was built by fishers who wanted easy access to the small rocky outcrop for better fishing. This was way back in 1755, and it feels like the bridge is still in that era. Made from wood and rope, it swings when the wind blows and bounces as people walk on it—this is not for people afraid of heights! To cross the bridge, you must reserve a ticket in advance, as only a certain number of people can cross each day.

Rathlin Island

Northern Ireland has only one inhabited offshore island, 9.5 km (6 mi) off the coast of Ballycastle. Large and L-shaped, it is a permanent home to only 150 people and a fantastic escape from the everyday hustle. Best known for birdlife, ornithologists flock to the **Rathlin West Light Seabird Centre** (tel. 28/2076-0062; www.rspb.org.uk; daily 9am-5pm; £8) to spot gannets, gulls, and other species as well as to visit the **lighthouse.** Stop by the **Boathouse Visitor Centre** (tel. 28/2076-0054; Mar.-Sept. daily 9am-5pm) afterward and learn all about the human history on the island, including tales of Viking raids and how Robert the Bruce found refuge in the caves. The crossing is with **Rathlin Island Ferry** (www.rathlin-ferry.com;

- **Old Bushmills Distillery:** Raise a glass to the famous whiskey at this world-class distillery (page 424).
- **Dunluce Castle:** Look over the sea from the ruins of this medieval castle, once owned by the MacDonnell clan (page 424).
- **Portstewart Strand:** Explore 3 km (2 mi) of golden sandy shoreline at this gorgeous beach. Keep an eye out for birds nesting in the dunes (page 427).

CAUSEWAY COAST WALKING TRAIL

To explore the Causeway Coast on foot, on the Causeway Coast Walking Trail you can avoid the crowds and see some of the popular attractions without driving. Like the scenic drive, this long-distance trail can be started anywhere, with the end points at Portstewart in the west and Ballycastle in the east.

Distance: *54 km (34 mi) one-way*
Duration: *2-3 days*
Elevation gain: *1,427 m (4,681 ft)*
Effort: *Difficult*
Trailhead: *Ballycastle Harbour or Portstewart Strand*

The route is long, but that shouldn't put you off, as it can be broken into segments, with many opportunities to join the trail along the coast. One of the many highlights is the 18-km (11-mi) section from Portballintree to Dunseverick, where you'll hike along the incredible Giant's Causeway and experience it in a way that many dream of. You'll meet people in the villages along the way and are bound to have unplanned adventures.

The trail is a mix of country roads shared with cars, crushed gravel, and single track, so proper hiking footwear is advised. Given that it runs along the coast for its entirety, you can expect wind and quickly changing weather. Plan to stay in Ballycastle and a choice of Bushmills, Portrush, and Portstewart along the trail.

25-45 minutes; £8 one-way) from Ballycastle Marina.

Hiking and Walking

White Park Bay

Distance: *4.5 km (2.8 mi) round-trip*
Duration: *1 hour*
Elevation gain: *None*
Effort: *Easy*
Trailhead: *Whitepark Rd. car park*

This gentle walk runs the length of White Park Bay along the beach. The sand is pristine and the water shimmers in the sunshine. You'll see large sand dunes and rocks crumbling into the sea. The car park at the trailhead can fill early on sunny summer days, so get here early if possible.

Beaches

Ballycastle Beach

Ballycastle Beach begins in town and runs 1.2 km (0.7 mi) toward **Fair Head,** with magnificent views of the coast and cliffs. As you walk the sandy shore, you'll spot people having picnics on sunny days and swimmers taking a dip; the sea remains chilly year-round. You can see Rathlin Island, and on a very clear day the view stretches as far as the Mull of Kintyre in Scotland. There are public toilets along with parking, and during summer (July-Aug.) lifeguards are on duty.

Food and Accommodations

Nellie Rua's

Ann St.; tel. 28/2005-4217; Instagram @nellieruasballycastle; Fri.-Sat. noon-midnight, Sun.-Thurs. noon-11pm; £5

Nellie Rua's is a popular local bar with a lively and authentic atmosphere even though it's a 15-minute walk from the seafront and marina. Come on the weekend when there's often live music. The weekend's big sports matches are on the TV.

Thyme & Co Café & Pizzeria

5 Quay Rd.; tel. 28/2076-9851; Instagram @thymeandco; Mon.-Tues. and Thurs.-Sat. 9:30am-3:30pm; from £7

Award-winning Thyme & Co Café & Pizzeria serves delicious homemade food from breakfast to late lunch. Their bread is a highlight, and you'll see locals popping by to pick up a fresh loaf. They use local ingredients to make menu favorites like the breakfast frittata and pulled-pork burger. If you just fancy a sweet treat, there's a fantastic selection—the lemon meringue tarts are a must.

Bars and Nightlife

The House of McDonnell

71 Castle St.; tel. 28/9027-0456; http://houseofmcdonnell.blogspot.com; daily 10am-5pm; from £6

Having first swung its doors open 280 years ago, the House of McDonnell served as a place for travelers to stop with their horses. Part of that legacy is seen today with historical fixtures like the original bar and diamond-pattern floor tiles that date to the 1920s. Nowadays, this pub is popular on the traditional music scene, with trad sessions every Friday night. Pop by on Saturday for folk songs from singer-songwriters.

Accommodations

The Salthouse

39 Dunamallaght Rd.; tel. 28/9045-8456; www.thesalthousehotel.com; £150

This eco-friendly luxury hotel is a 5-minute drive from Ballycastle, yet it feels like you're in the countryside. Offering 24 rooms around a central courtyard, visitors can disconnect from the world and unwind at the outdoor thermal journey, which includes two hot tubs, a sauna with landscape views, and a cold shower. Reserve dinner at the **Salthouse Bar & Restaurant,** with an incredible view out over the sea as you dine on seasonal locally caught seafood.

Marine Hotel

1-3 North St.; tel. 28/9032-0202; www.marinehotelballycastle.com; £160

Wake up and open the curtains to views of Ballycastle Beach and Fair Head with a stay at the four-star Marine Hotel, beside the marina in Ballycastle. The 51 recently renovated rooms have modern standards with a clean aesthetic. The on-site restaurant, **Marconi's Bar & Bistro,** serves food daily from noon, with plenty of seafood. The Strangford Lough mussels with white wine and mustard cream are the top pick. The hotel has some interesting free activities every week, with an Irish coffee-making class on Thursday evening and bread-making demonstrations every Wednesday morning.

Getting There

By car from Belfast, the journey to Ballycastle takes 1.25 hours heading north on the M2 motorway. Take the exit for the A26 toward Ballymena and Coleraine. Continue past Ballymena and follow the signposted right turn for Ballycastle. There are no direct public transport links between Belfast and Ballycastle, but you can get a train from Lanyon Place in Belfast to Ballymena and change to a bus operated by **Translink** (www.translink.co.uk).

International Appalachian Trail

hiking on the International Appalachian Trail

Distance: *449 km (279 mi) one-way*
Duration: *20-25 days*
Elevation gain: *8,066 m (26,463 ft)*
Effort: *Difficult*
Trailhead: *Larne or Sliabh Liag*

Most hikers have heard about the iconic Appalachian Trail in the United States in movies, books, and songs; it's a bucket-list through-hike. A US biologist realized that the mountains don't end in Katahdin, Maine; they were actually much longer when the continents were joined. His theory is that the same mountain range ended up in other parts of North America, North Africa, and Europe, including here in Northern Ireland, where the International Appalachian Trail (IAT) exists.

The IAT in Northern Ireland is a monstrous long-distance hike that begins or ends in Larne, County Antrim, and Sliabh Liag in County Donegal. The route is through landscapes of mature woodlands alive with nature, thunderous coastlines with enormous waves, and idyllic towns that you'll remember forever.

Hiking the full route is a rare achievement, mainly due to the time commitment, so the trail builders have split the IAT into 11 sections, including the Causeway Coast. Not all of the sections are recommended for a shorter hike, as some are mainly transfer days. The section from Dungiven to Castlerock brings you through the natural beauty of the Sperrin Mountains on a 60-km (37-mi) hike that'll keep you busy for a few days.

From Derry by car, the journey to Ballycastle is 1.5 hours. Take the A2 coastal road east, passing through Coleraine. Follow the signs for Ballycastle on the A2 and then the A44. There are no direct public transport links between Derry and Ballycastle. Buses run between Derry and Coleraine, where you can change to another bus to Ballycastle.

BUSHMILLS

Bushmills is famous for two things: world-class whiskey and the Giant's Causeway. Named after the River Bush, used to make the famous liquor, Bushmills is a quaint small town with old-fashioned shops that mostly serve visitors. For a town of its size, there are ample places to eat, drink, and stay.

Sights

★ Giant's Causeway

free

The Giant's Causeway is more than just a landmark; it's a part of the landscape so revered that it's spawned legends and shaped our folklore over the centuries. It's a UNESCO World Heritage Site made up of 40,000 interlocking basalt columns that formed millions of years ago due to volcanic activity. Legend has it that a giant named Fionn Mac Cumhaill threw the rocks into the sea as a way to reach Scotland. Look for the Giant's Boot, a large basalt boulder eroded into a boot shape, and the towering Chimney Stacks, the tallest of the basalt columns.

To get here, drive north from Bushmills to the visitor center. The way the car park is set up, you might feel you have to go through the visitor center and pay to see the Giant's Causeway, but you don't; it's free. Look for the trail beside the car park that leads to the coast and walk that way to avoid the visitor center, which charges a £14 entrance fee.

The visitor center is hit and miss, to be honest. It opened with some controversy, as local politicians insisted that their Creationist beliefs be acknowledged despite being at complete odds with scientific fact. These mentions have been removed now, but overall it still feels like an expensive fee for not a whole lot of benefit. If you do choose to pay and go in, there are toilets as well as a gift shop and café.

Old Bushmills Distillery

2 Distillery Rd.; tel. 28/2051-0000; www.bushmills.eu; Mon.-Sat. 10am-5pm, Sun. 11am-5pm; from £15

Bushmills has been making whiskey here for over 400 years, the oldest licensed whiskey distillery in the world, so they know a thing or two about fine drink. The tradition of distilling has been passed down through generations using water from the river to make triple-distilled whiskey with malted barley and copper pot stills. On the tours you'll learn about the stills, meet the people behind the whiskey, and of course sample some of the creations. For most, the **1-hour tour** (£15) is enough insight into the history and the distillery; there's also a **tasting tour** (£35) to learn about the flavors and notes, and finally, the **premium tour** (£35) to discover the stories of Bushmills through the ages.

Dunluce Castle

87 Dunluce Rd.; tel. 28/2073-1938; www.discovernorthernireland.com; daily 9am-4pm; £6

This medieval castle sits atop rocky crumbling cliffs overlooking the sea. It's in ruins, but in the Middle Ages it was home to the McDonnell clan and the seat of the Earls of Antrim. You'll see an exhibit about the archaeological work at the site, watch a video on the history of the castle, and go on a self-guided tour of the structure.

Hiking and Walking

North Antrim Cliff Path: Dunseverick to Giant's Causeway

Distance: *7.5 km (4.6 mi) one-way*
Duration: *2.5 hours*
Elevation gain: *375 m (1,230 ft)*
Effort: *Moderate*
Trailhead: *Dunseverick Castle or Giant's Causeway*

This scenic coastal trail follows the natural ebb and flow of the cliffs along a well-maintained trail that amazes with outstanding views. There's a bus route between Dunluce Castle and Giant's Causeway, so you can park at either end, hike the trail one-way, and catch the bus back. Or make it an out-and-back hike following the same trail on your return.

Shopping

Maegden

119 Main St.; tel. 7834-346708; https://cheesemaegden.com; Wed.-Sun. 9:30am-5:30pm

This specialty shop is all about top-quality cheese. The owners have gone from serving toasted cheese sandwiches from a food truck to stocking amazing cheese made with fresh Irish produce. Grab a coffee while you browse the premade hampers. The cheese makes great

1: Giant's Causeway **2:** Old Bushmills Distillery

1
2
OLD BUSHMILLS DISTILLERY CO LIMITED
SINGLE MALT
1608

Ulster Way

Ulster Way

Distance: *1,024 km (636 mi) round-trip*
Duration: *3-4 weeks*
Elevation gain: *11,745 m (38,533 ft)*
Effort: *Difficult*
Trailhead: *Various points*

This multiday loop trail is one of the longest waymarked trails in the UK. Like the IAT, it is most often hiked in sections rather than in its entirety. The trail winds through all six counties in Northern Ireland, with no official trailheads, giving you lots of chances to hop on and off at will. Some of the most popular sections include the **Moyle Way** from Dungiven to Waterfoot, the **North Down Coastal Path** from Hollywood to Groomsport, and the **Lecale Way** at Strangford Lough.

gifts, but it'll be hard to stop yourself from eating it before you get home.

The Designerie

75 Main St.; tel. 28/2073-2606; https://thedesignerie.co.uk; Mon.-Sat. 10am-5pm

Find tasteful touches to furnish your home or pick up thoughtful gifts for friends and family. They stock Irish-made candles and handmade pottery, and if the weather is colder than you expected, pick up a cozy scarf by McNutt.

Food and Accommodations

The Nook

48 Causeway Rd.; tel. 28/7083-2015; daily 8:30am-11pm; from £17

This old schoolhouse has been carefully brought into the modern era and now exists as a small pub that has managed not to lose its historic charm. Wooden furniture and a wooden bar are inside, heated in winter by the open fire. In summer, an outdoor terrace provides a view along with the Taste of Ulster menu that champions local produce. Highlights of the unpretentious offerings are the steak and Guinness pie and deep-fried scampi.

Tartine at the Distillers Arms

140 Main St.; tel. 28/2073-2993; www.distillersarms.com; daily 11am-5pm; from £22

Serving modern brasserie-style dishes at

affordable prices, Tartine at the Distillers Arms is worth a visit. The building is the original home of the owners of the Bushmills Distillery, and you can see its age in the exposed rock walls in the dining room, which can accommodate 85. The chef prides himself on simple dishes that let the quality of Northern Irish ingredients shine. The slow-roasted lamb with braised root vegetables, champ (mashed potatoes and green onions), and capers is a popular choice.

Bushmills Inn

9 Dunluce Rd.; tel. 7894-854791; www.bushmillsinn.com; £200

First built as a coach inn in the 1600s, the Bushmills Inn is now a 41-room, four-star hotel that still has many original and historic features, like the striking tower-like entrance and sash windows. Each day, two flags are flown outside from their collection of 300, which you can see in the Flag Room. The rooms have simple traditional style with crisp white bed linens and heavy curtains, but there are modern amenities too, with flat-screen TVs and Wi-Fi in each room. There's a restaurant on-site, and the bar is a standout thanks to the roaring open fireplace and old-world furniture.

Getting There

It's a simple 20-minute journey from Ballycastle to nearby Bushmills by car. Head west on the A2 toward Bushmills Road and continue for 18 km (11 mi), following signs for Bushmills. A more scenic route is to detour off the main A2 just outside Ballycastle and drive along the cliffs by Torr Head.

Using public transport, you can take the Ulsterbus Route 402, operated by Translink (www.translink.co.uk). The bus departs from **Ballycastle Marine Corner** and stops at **Bushmills Old Tram Stop** (30-35 minutes). Buses run about every 30 minutes throughout the day.

PORTRUSH AND PORTSTEWART

These neighboring towns along the Causeway Coast have both embraced their seaside location, making them good stop-off spots. Portrush is the livelier of the two, with a busy main street that leads to the water and **Ramore Head.** The **Royal Portrush Golf Club** has put the town on the map, with many calling it a bucket-list golf course. Portstewart is quieter, with **Portstewart Strand** being the big draw. The two towns are just 6.5 km (4 mi) apart, so visiting both is feasible.

Sights

Ramore Head is a rocky headland formed by volcanic activity 60 million years ago. It gives you panoramic views of the coastline along short walking paths flanked by grasses. On your way back toward Portrush, you'll see White Strand Beach and Portstewart farther along the coast.

Beaches

Whiterocks Beach

This beautiful beach has been awarded Blue Flag status for its clear swimming water and pristine sand that runs 5 km (3 mi). Tall cliffs of white limestone have been carved away by the sea, creating caves and coves to explore. The beach also draws surfers, particularly during winter, when the waves are clean and consistent. It's free to park here, dogs are allowed, and lifeguards are on duty in July-August.

Portstewart Strand

This 3.2-km (2-mi) stretch of sandy shoreline runs from Portstewart to the mouth of the River Bann, creating a wide expanse for picnicking and exploring the beach and the dunes behind it. This inclusive beach has accessible toilets and parking, as well as beach equipment that you can borrow through the **Mae Murray Foundation** (www.maemurrayfoundation.org). Surf lessons are available here with **Sub 6** (118 Strand Rd.; www.sub6life.com; £40), or for a more relaxing experience, reserve a sauna and cold plunge with **Sauna and Sea** (www.saunaandsea.co.uk; £20).

Surfing

The west coast of Ireland gets the plaudits when it comes to surfing, and the enormous waves are a serious challenge for the skilled, but for ordinary folk, the waves can be too big. Surfing on the Causeway Coast is a great choice to learn the basics, as the waves are often gentle, clean, and predictable.

Portrush Surf School

Harbour Rd.; tel. 345/744-0088; www.portrushsurfschool.com; daily 10am-6:30pm; £43

There aren't many more qualified people to teach you how to surf than Martin "TK" Kelly, the longest-serving surfing coach in Ireland and an 11-time Irish National Surf Champion. He runs Portrush Surf School from the Portrush Yacht Club, where there are hot showers, changing rooms, and a café. Two slots are available each day (10am-1pm and 2pm-5pm), where they guarantee two hours in the water. Get a place in a group lesson (£43), a private lesson (£100 pp), or a lesson for a family of four (£160). Lessons can sell out during summer holidays. Other reputable surf schools in the area include **Sub 6** (118 Strand Rd.; www.sub6life.com; £40) and **Troggs** (East Strand Watersports Centre; tel. 7719-315372; www.troggs.com; £37).

Golf

Royal Portrush Golf Club

Dunluce Rd.; tel. 28/4372-1066; www.royalportrushgolfclub.com; from £185

Ireland is held in high regard in the golfing world, and Royal Portrush Golf Club is one of the jewels. Two links courses, Dunluce Links and Valley Links, take advantage of the coastal location to create 36 challenging holes. Open since 1888, it first hosted the Irish Open in 1951, and it returned in 2019, when Irishman Shane Lowry won, and again in 2025. Visitors can play a round, but advance reservations are essential. Peak season fees during summer are £385 per person for Dunluce Links and £185 for Valley Links, with lower greens fees in winter.

Portstewart Golf Club

117 Strand Rd.; tel. 28/4372-5620; www.portstewartgc.co.uk; daily 9am-5pm; £275

The Portstewart Golf Club is in the shadow of Royal Portrush, but it's still an exceptional course that has hosted the Irish Open and the Irish Amateur Championship. There are three 18-hole courses: the Strand Course, where competitions are played; the Riverside Course; and the Old Course. Greens fees for a round in peak season are £275 and drop as low as £70 in the depths of winter. Advanced booking is required.

Shopping

The White House

45 Main St.; tel. 28/7082-2244; www.whitehouseportrush.com; Mon.-Fri. 10am-5:30pm, Sat. 9:30am-5:30pm, Sun. 1pm-5pm

This large independently owned department store has been here since 1891 and is a destination for many in Northern Ireland. The building has been historically preserved, so it feels like you're back in Victorian times as you browse the shelves. Queen Victoria herself shopped once by mail order. There's a wide range of products across womenswear, menswear, homewares, and furniture, with a mix of famous international brands like Crew, O'Neill, and Samsonite along with Irish brands. The **Trocadero Restaurant** is a nice place to grab a coffee and pastry; it also has a wide choice of substantial mains and light bites.

Food and Accommodations

The Harbour Bar & Bistro

6 Harbour Rd.; tel. 28/7126-7266; www.ramorerestaurant.com; daily 5:30pm-late; from £10

First opened in the mid-1800s, the Harbour Bar is one of the oldest on the Causeway Coast, quite a feat considering how many Victorian pubs there are here. Overlooking the water, it's a fantastic spot for an outdoor

Golfing In Ireland

links golfing in Ireland

Ireland punches above its weight in many sports on the world stage; we're great boxers, rugby players, horse trainers, and golfers. The development of courses along the coast created difficult challenges and raised the standard across the board. Today there are 350-plus 18-hole golf courses in Ireland.

THE TOP COURSES

- Around Dublin, **The K Club** (www.kclub.ie) is popular with people who prioritize a luxury experience, and **Portmarnock Golf Club** (www.portmarnockgolfclub.ie) sticks with tradition, where they haven't altered the course routing in over 100 years.
- In Kerry, **Waterville Golf Links** (www.watervillegolflinks.ie) stands out for its bumpy course among sand dunes, while **Killarney Golf Club** (www.killarneygolfclub.ie) has hosted the Irish Open six times.
- In Northern Ireland, the standout courses are **Royal Portrush** (page 428) and **Royal County Down** (page 443), considered a very difficult course.

GOLFING TOURS

Not all courses are public, but the members-only ones often have open days. Expect to pay a minimum of €100 greens fees and much more at the more sought-after courses. If you're planning a golfing visit, tour companies like **Golf Tours Ireland** (www.golftoursireland.ie) and **Irish Golf Tours** (www.irishgolftours.com) have packages with tee times at some of the most exclusive courses.

drink on a summer day, and it has a cozy rich wooden interior with historic photos and a blazing fire on cold days. Pints are the order of the day, but there's also a nice selection of gins. The food offering is small, with choices like salt and chili prawns and a steak sandwich.

Harry's Shack

118 Strand Rd.; tel. 28/7083-1783; https://harrysshack.app; daily 12:30pm-3:15pm and 4:45pm-8:45pm; £15

This casual but polished eatery has an incredible view of Portstewart Strand and uses the coastline as the inspiration for its brunch, lunch, and dinner menus. The chef uses local produce to make classic dishes like fish-and-chips, crab salad, and plaice served with baby potatoes. The dining area leans into the nautical theme with wooden furniture and worn paint, but if it isn't raining, you'll want to be outside on the partly covered deck, right on the beach, where there's seating for 50.

Elephant Rock

17 Landsdowne Crescent; tel. 28/7087-8787; www.elephantrockhotel.co.uk; £135

It's hard to miss the black and bright-pink exterior of this boutique hotel on the waterfront in Portrush. Offering 18 individually designed rooms in a renovated building on a Victorian terrace, it has a home-away-from-home feel with decor that's full of character. As a boutique hotel in an old residential property, amenities and services are not extensive, but there is a trendy 30-seat restaurant and an art deco-inspired cocktail lounge.

Getting There

It's a straightforward 15-20-minute journey from Bushmills to nearby Portstewart and Portrush by car. Head north on the A2 toward Portrush Road and continue 8 km (5 mi) to Portrush. For Portstewart, continue on the A2 for 3 km (2 mi) past Portrush.

Using public transport, take the Ulsterbus Route 402, operated by Translink (www.translink.co.uk). The bus departs from Bushmills Old Tram Stop and stops at both Portrush and Portstewart. Buses run about every 30 minutes throughout the day. The journey to Portrush is 20-25 minutes, and to Portstewart 30-35 minutes.

COLERAINE

If you tell people in Northern Ireland that you're planning to visit Coleraine, they might look at you a bit funny, but in recent years new businesses have brought young exciting energy to this old plantation town that spans the River Bann. A visit to Coleraine is a chance to try great seafood, sleep in the forest, and get ahead of the travel trend curve.

Hiking and Walking

Mountsandel Wood

Distance: *3.7 km (2.3 mi) round-trip*
Duration: *45 minutes*
Elevation gain: *Negligible*
Effort: *Easy*
Trailhead: *Mountsandel Rd.*

This wooded walk along the River Bann provides a bit of fresh air on a visit to Coleraine. The trail slopes slightly, and if it's been raining, expect it to be slippery. The highlight is the large green mound of Mountsandel Fort, which has been reclaimed by nature.

Beaches

Castlerock Beach

Castlerock Beach is a stunning 1.6-km (1-mi) Blue Flag stretch of golden sand just outside Castlerock with 360-degree views of the Atlantic and the coast. It's popular for swimming, surfing, and family outings, with amenities like parking, toilets, and seasonal lifeguards.

Downhill Beach

Downhill Beach is an 11-km (7-mi) sandy stretch with Mussenden Temple perched on the cliffs above. It's a good spot for swimming, scenic walks, and bird-watching. The beach also featured as a set in the TV show *Game of Thrones,* where it was home to Dragonstone.

☆ Coleraine to Derry Scenic Train

the scenic train ride from Coleraine to Derry

World-famous travel writer Michael Palin has described the train journey from Derry to Coleraine as "one of the most beautiful rail journeys in the world," but even with this praise, it still goes under the radar. The 44-km (27-mi) trip takes 40-50 minutes and stops in Bellarena and Castlerock.

Trains run hourly in each direction Monday-Saturday and half as often on Sunday. The trains are modern, wheelchair accessible, and have toilets on board.

COLERAINE TO DERRY

If you take the train from Coleraine, you leave the riverside setting alongside the River Bann before reaching the coast. Pass through Victorian Castlerock Station, designed by John Lanyon, on the way to Derry. Natural beauty reveals itself past Benone Strand, and there are uninterrupted views of Lough Foyle before the green farmland beside the River Foyle. The train then arrives in Derry, the end of the scenic route.

DERRY TO COLERAINE

If you take the train from Derry, you meander alongside the River Foyle through green farmland before reaching the coast and the uninterrupted views of Lough Foyle, with Benone Strand out one window and Downhill out the other. Castlerock Station, designed by John Lanyon, is a quintessential Victorian. At the end of the journey in Coleraine, the coastal and cliff views are replaced with the banks of the River Bann.

Food and Accommodations

The Surf Shack

11 Main St.; tel. 7849-992383; www.thesurfshack-castlerock.com; Mon.-Thurs. noon-11pm, Fri.-Sat. 11:30am-11pm, Sun. noon-10pm; from £3

Some people surf for the waves, some for the surf culture. You can experience both at the Surf Shack on Castlerock Beach just outside Coleraine. Part surf school, part café, they have a brilliant lookout point over the beach and the waves. Most days the menu is limited to hot drinks, but on weekends there's toasted sandwiches and specials like a spicy tuna rice bowl. This place is all about the view, however, so order your coffee, sit in the covered outdoor seating area, and watch the waves roll in.

Lir

66 Portstewart Rd.; tel. 7740-858426; https://lirseafood.com; Thurs.-Sun. 10am-4pm; tasting menu £90

In 2023, seafood restaurant Lir opened in the old yacht club building on the banks of the River Bann, shaped by its location and serving native seafood alongside sustainable produce. The menu changes constantly based on what is in season; expect innovative dishes like the miso-glazed monkfish with barley and mushroom risotto and a carbonara made with dogfish instead of pork. If the weather is good, try to reserve a table outside, where a small seating area overlooks the river and boats.

Burrenmore Nest

5 Burrenmore Rd.; tel. 28/7082-4313; http://burrenmore-nest.com; daily noon-midnight; 2-night minimum; £265

This stunning treehouse is like reliving your youth but with the comforts you want as an adult. Tucked away in a small forest, less than 1.6 km (1 mi) from Downhill Beach and beside the International Appalachian Trail, Burrenmore Nest is about being in touch with nature. Three luxury lodges have floor-to-ceiling windows, private hot tubs, and king beds. Most of the year has a two-night minimum, but the ground-level lodge is sometimes available for one night. A breakfast basket is served in the morning, and if you're still hungry, **Sea Shed Coffee** (Instagram @seashedcoffee) is a one-minute walk away, with hot drinks and light bites.

Getting There

Coleraine is a 15-minute drive from Portrush on the Atlantic Road. A train runs hourly during peak times from **Portrush Train Station** to **Coleraine Train Station** (20 minutes; £4 one-way). Route 104 and Route 402 buses from Dunluce Avenue stop at **Coleraine Buscentre** (£3.10 one-way) as frequently as every 15 minutes.

From Belfast, take the M2 north toward Ballymena, then the A26 to Coleraine, a drive of 1 hour and 88 km (55 mi). Hourly trains depart from Lanyon Place Train Station to Coleraine Train Station (1.25 hours; £16 one-way). The Route 218 bus also runs hourly from Laganside Buscentre to Coleraine Buscentre (1.75 hours; £13 one-way).

Driving from Derry to Coleraine is a 48-km (30-mi) journey on the A2 to Limavady and the A37 to Derry. Because of the coastal views, taking the train is the best way to get to Coleraine from Derry. Services run hourly from Derry Train Station to Coleraine Train Station (40 minutes; £13 one-way).

Derry City

Derry, also called Londonderry (a prefix added by King James I in 1613), is a historic walled city that was fortified in the 17th century. Derry's turbulent past dates to British rule with the Siege of Derry in 1689 and the Battle of the Bogside in 1969. Derry doesn't shy away from its past and tells the stories of these events. Today the city has a burgeoning contemporary feel thanks to its craft beer breweries, art galleries, and festivals.

ORIENTATION

Derry's historic walled city center, called **Cityside,** is on the west bank of the **River Foyle.** The **Bogside** neighborhood lies just outside the city walls to the south. The 17th-century walls surround the old city center and its Renaissance-style street plan, with four main streets radiating from the central Diamond. The **Peace Bridge** spans the River Foyle, connecting the walled city center on the west bank to the **Waterside** area on the east bank. This bridge symbolizes unity between

Derry City

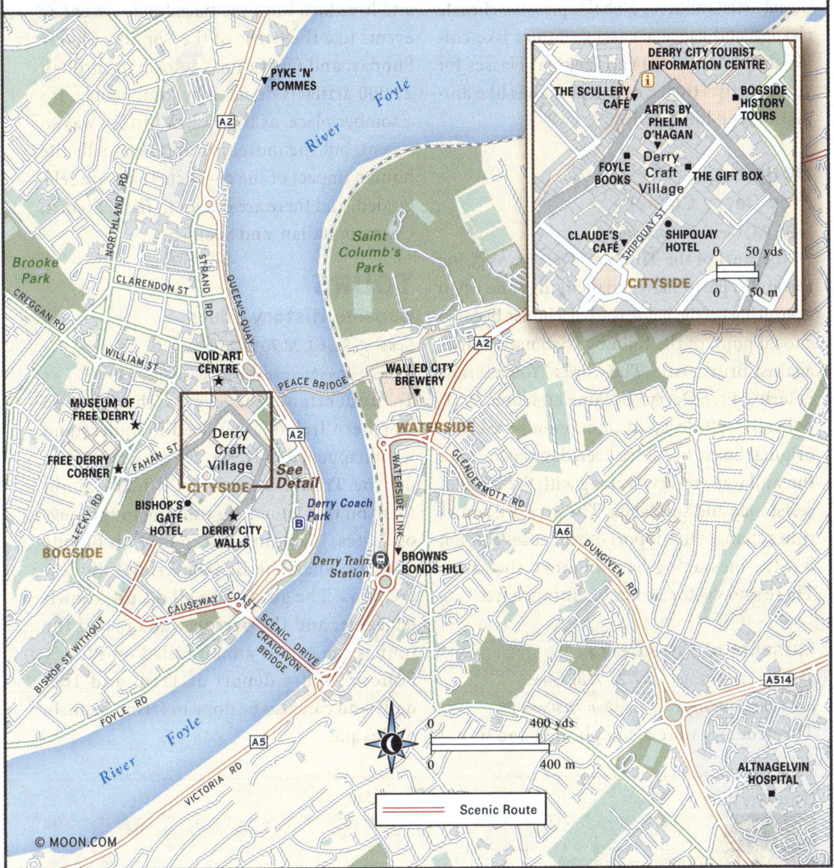

the predominantly unionist Waterside and the largely nationalist Cityside.

SIGHTS

Cityside

Derry City Walls

The Diamond; tel. 7894-534553; www.thederrywalls.com; free

The Derry City Walls, completed in 1619, are a remarkable historical landmark that surround the old city center. About 1.5 km (0.9 mi) in length, they are the only complete city walls in Ireland and played a pivotal role in the Siege of Derry in 1689, when they withstood 105 days of attacks from the Jacobites. A lot of this success was due to the walls' scale, 8 m (26 ft) high and 9 m (29 ft) thick. Nowadays you can walk their entirety, see cannons lined up on top, and take in views over the city and the river.

Void Art Centre

10 Waterloo Place; tel. 28/8676-0681; www.derryvoid.com; Sun.-Thurs. 11am-7pm, Fri.-Sat. 11am-9pm; free

The Void Art Centre is one of the driving forces behind Derry's contemporary feel, as it brings a diverse range of visual arts exhibitions to the city. Works by Irish and international artists address global topics like climate change and more accessible topics like coffee shops. Void also runs regular classes for young artists to discover techniques like animation and life drawing.

Bogside

Free Derry Corner

Lecky Rd., Glenfada Park; free

At the start of the Troubles, Derry was going through a particularly challenging time when a painting on the gable wall of a house became a focal point of the fight by Irish nationalists against British rule. The words "You are now entering Free Derry" became an iconic symbol of the self-declared autonomous area. The original house has since been demolished, but the wall was preserved along with the ethos of resistance and solidarity. The artwork sometimes changes to support other causes abroad, but the messaging has remained the same. There's no visitor center or entrance fee.

Museum of Free Derry

55 Glenfada Park; tel. 28/7122-9081; www.museumoffreederry.org; daily 8am-3:30pm; £8

The Troubles were a complicated and brutal time in Derry's history, and the Museum of Free Derry acts as an archive of the battles and lives lost. Multimedia exhibits cover key events like the Battle of the Bogside, Bloody Sunday, and Operation Motorman through 25,000 artifacts donated by local people. It's a somber place, as the violent history was so recent, but the museum's approach tells the human impact of the conflict. Tours are self-guided, and there are guides in Irish, French, German, Italian, and Spanish.

TOURS

Bogside History Tours

Guildhall St.; tel. 28/7082-2311; www.bogsidehistorytours.com; daily 8am-4pm; £10

To understand the events that shaped Northern Ireland, you need to understand what happened in Derry. Events here kicked off the Troubles, and you'll learn about them on this hour-long walking tour to pivotal sites, including a deep dive on Bloody Sunday, when the British Army killed 13 civilians. The guides are all deeply knowledgeable, and the person who created the tour is the son of a man killed on Bloody Sunday. Tours depart at 11am and 1pm daily and can also be done in Irish, Spanish, or Basque.

Derry City Walls

The Emigrant's Walk Tour

Tirkane Rd.; tel. 28/7134-5180; www.theemigrantswalk.com; Tues. 5pm-9pm, Wed.-Thurs. noon-2:30pm and 5pm-9pm, Fri.-Sat. noon-2:30pm and 5pm-10pm; £35

The Emigrant's Walk re-creates part of the journey taken by Irish people during the famine as they left this country in search of a better life overseas, mainly to the United States, Australia, and Britain. This 3-hour guided hike is along the Old Coach Road and up **Carntogher Mountain,** where you'll see views of the Sperrin Mountains and Mourne Mountains. At the top, you can leave a stone, which many visitors with Irish heritage say connects them with their past. On the way back down, the tour stops at **Friel's Bar & Restaurant** (4 Kilrea Rd.; tel. 28/7940-1206; https://friels.ie; Thurs.-Mon. 11:30am-11pm; from £17) where they cook nettle stew in an authentic famine pot.

PARKS

OM Dark Sky Park and Observatory

155 Davagh Rd.; tel. 28/4372-1066; www.omdarksky.com; free

Away from light pollution, spectacular OM Dark Sky Park and Observatory comes to life when the sun sets. The best place to see the stars is at the modern observatory, where you can gaze up at the Milky Way and learn about the planets and the telescope at the OM Exhibition (£5). During the daytime there are numerous family-friendly walks through Davagh Forest; the 2.8-km (1.8-mi) loop walk from the car park is the most accessible. Stay overnight at **Sperrin View Glamping** (www.sperrinviewglamping.com; £105) and look up at the stars from your luxury pod with a window to the stars.

FESTIVALS AND EVENTS

Oyster & Stout Festival

www.walledcitybrewery.com/oysterandstoutfestival; Feb.

It's well-known on these shores that oysters and stout pair beautifully, with the oyster's subtle sweetness bringing out roasted flavors in the stout. The legendary combo is celebrated at the Oyster & Stout Festival, held at the Walled City Brewery's taproom in Ebrington Square. Watch as local seafood experts shuck fresh oysters, taste a range of dishes cooked by local chefs, and try the brewery's stouts. The brewers have a reputation for creative drinks, so don't be surprised to see a Tabasco stout and a chocolate chipotle stout on the menu.

City of Derry Jazz and Big Band Festival

https://cityofderryjazzfestival.com; May

The City of Derry Jazz and Big Band Festival transforms Derry into a musical hub, with 200 live performances at 70 venues, and world-renowned jazz artists and fans from around the country and the world. The diverse range of jazz styles, from traditional to contemporary, includes free outdoor concerts, workshops, and master classes.

Foyle Maritime Festival

www.foylemaritime.com; June in even-numbered years

The Foyle Maritime Festival is a biennial celebration of Derry's rich maritime heritage. An array of tall ships and boats line the shore of the River Foyle. For visitors the festival is a way to experience sailing, kayaking, and other water sports. On land there's live music performances, street theater, artisanal markets, and food stalls showcasing local produce. The event finishes with a big fireworks display over the Foyle, attracting crowds to the city's waterfront.

Derry Halloween

www.derryhalloween.com; Oct. 28-31

Derry Halloween, Europe's largest Halloween festival, takes place in the Walled City. The four-day event transforms Derry into a spooky playground, celebrating the ancient Celtic festival of Samhain that created the Halloween that we know today. Visitors can experience the Awakening the Walled City Trail, with illuminations, aerial performances, and light shows. The

The Troubles

Bloody Sunday mural in Derry

It's impossible to cover the complexity and brutality of the Troubles in a few words without glossing over key topics, so take this as a very brief rundown.

THE BEGINNINGS

In the Easter Rising of 1916, the Irish Republican Army (IRA) fought the British Army, resulting in the independent Republic of Ireland, with the British keeping six counties as Northern Ireland. Tensions grew in Northern Ireland between republicans (mainly Catholic and Irish) and loyalists

festival includes family-friendly activities, ghostly tours, and a grand carnival parade on Halloween night. The celebration culminates with a spectacular fireworks display that attracts thousands.

SHOPPING

Cityside

Derry Craft Village

Shipquay St.; tel. 28/7127-9379; daily 9am-4pm

The village square, thatched cottages, and shops in this period village have been faithfully re-created in late-18th-century style. More than just a time machine to the Georgian period, it is full of modern shops that sell everything from homewares to books. **The Sacred Tree** and **Derry Designer Makers** are the standouts for gifts. Stop by **Oui Bakery** for a freshly made pastry, and book a table to dine at **Artis by Phelim O'Hagan** (page 438).

Foyle Books

12 Magazine Place; tel. 28/7137-2530; Instagram @FoyleBooks; Mon.-Sat. 11am-5pm

For die-hard book lovers, charming Foyle Bookshop specializes in Irish literature and Irish language. Things get interesting with the secondhand and antique books, with a dazzling collection of volumes hard to find anywhere else. The staff here are knowledgeable and can answer any questions.

The Gift Box

32 Shipquay St.; tel. 28/7126-4462; www.thegiftboxderry.com; Mon.-Sat. 9:30am-5:30pm

The Gift Box is a cute gift shop open for over 30 years. The vast selection of thoughtful and

(mainly Protestant and British), who lived in different neighborhoods of Derry and Belfast. Under British rule, Catholics faced discrimination in employment, public housing, and elections.

THE EVENTS

In August 1969, this tension boiled over when residents in Derry's Catholic Bogside neighborhood clashed with loyalists and the Royal Ulster Constabulary (RUC), the British police force. This riot lasted three days and is often seen as the starting point of the Troubles. The euphemism "Troubles" understates the conflict; depending on who you ask, it was more like a civil war or an uprising.

Other major events of the period include Bloody Sunday in 1972, when the British Army Parachute Regiment opened fire on a crowd of protesting civilians in Derry, killing 13 people. The IRA fought using impactful but often horrific methods, including car bombs. In 1998 a splinter group of the IRA, the Real IRA, exploded a bomb on the main street in Omagh, killing 29 people, including Breda Devine, who was less than two years old.

THE RESOLUTION

The Troubles technically ended in 1998 with the Good Friday Agreement, which established power-sharing in government and the ability for citizens to legally self-identify as Irish or British. The agreement was spearheaded by Irish Taoiseach (Prime Minister) Bertie Ahern, British Prime Minister Tony Blair, US President Bill Clinton, and the leaders of the main unionist and nationalist parties in Northern Ireland, David Trimble and John Hume. Because it's such a recent conflict, with victims still living in these communities, local people have rare insights into this pivotal historical event. Keep this in mind if you're speaking with locals, as they might be victims themselves. And please, for the love of God, do not try to order an "Irish car bomb" in a bar. It will not be well received.

unique gifts includes local jewelry, lovely homewares, and greeting cards for every occasion imaginable.

FOOD

Cityside

Claude's Café

4 Shipquay St.; tel. 7828-127739; www.claudescafe.com; Wed.-Sat. 9am-11pm; from £9

Claude's Café is a popular local spot with good food at good prices. The variety on offer includes breakfast, daily specials, stews, and sandwiches. Standout menu items are the full Irish breakfast with coffee (£10), beef lasagna and chips (£8), and beef stew (£6). The café is spacious, with plenty of seating for solo diners, couples, and families. The bar seating by the window is the best option to people-watch.

The Scullery Café

48 Waterloo St.; tel. 28/7122-9081; Instagram @the_scullery_derry; daily 8am-3.45pm; from £9

The Scullery Café brings a more on-trend café to the city, mixing traditional offerings with dishes like avocado toast with fried eggs, granola bowls, and tomato and mozzarella salad. The interior matches this approach, with colorful metal chairs around tables for two or four with large pendant lights overhead. This place is dog friendly; they'll even make your dog a puppycino to go along with your coffee.

Pyke 'N' Pommes

53-55 Strand Rd.; tel. 28/7130-8080; http://pykenpommes.ie; Tues.-Sat. 11am-5pm; from £14

Pyke 'N' Pommes started as a food truck and quickly became a hit; the owners opened a permanent restaurant in 2019. The warehouse styling, with polished concrete floors and brick walls, gives the space an industrial feel. The team makes everything from scratch, with the menu focusing on burgers, tacos, and charcoal-cooked dishes. The standout and what most diners order is the Legenderry Burger, made with Wagyu beef. Seafood lovers will want to try the squid taco. There's also a small selection of vegetarian options.

Artis by Phelim O'Hagan

29-31 Craft Village; 28/7126-1212; www.artisatcraftvillagederry.com; Wed.-Thurs. 5pm-9pm, Fri.-Sat. noon-2:30pm and 5pm-9pm; 2 courses £32

Head chef Phelim O'Hagan rose to fame on the TV show *The Great British Menu,* where he championed the use of local Irish ingredients. This is the ethos at his restaurant in the Craft Village, where diners can choose à la carte or the seven-course tasting menu, a journey through the country's top producers and produce. Dishes include scallops with summer squash, free-range pork topped with smoked almonds and carrots, and wild venison with beetroot and broccoli. Artis is a popular restaurant, so reserve in advance.

Waterside

Browns Bonds Hill

1 Bonds Hill; tel. 28/7134-3336; www.brownsbondshill.com; Mon.-Thurs. 5pm-8:30pm, Fri.-Sat. 1pm-3pm and 5pm-9:30pm, Sun. 1pm-5pm; from £24

Browns Bonds Hill is one of the top fine-dining restaurants in Northern Ireland, with a focus on using Irish produce in international dishes. Seven menus cover lunch, early bird, and dinner for meat eaters, vegetarians, and vegans, and all change regularly with the seasons. Previous top dishes have included roasted monkfish with tamarind curry and crispy rice, pear salad with celery, grape, and blue cheese, and a butternut squash risotto. While other fine-dining restaurants have more contemporary dining rooms, it's hard to compete with the artful plating here.

Walled City Brewery

70 Ebrington St.; tel. 7731-450088; www.walledcitybrewery.com; daily 9am-5pm; 2 courses £28

This modern brewery was the first to open in Derry in over 100 years, and it brings a contemporary industrial touch. The craft beers all reflect the city's past, with Stitch IPA a nod to Derry's shirt-making industry, and the Sister Michael Stout named after a character from the TV show *Derry Girls.* The food menu is more ambitious and refined than what you'd normally find in a brewery, with salt and chili squid and miso-glazed chicken wings, and mains like the Donegal sea bass with nduja sausage a standout choice.

ACCOMMODATIONS

Cityside

Shipquay Hotel

15-17 Shipquay St.; tel. 28/7167-2691; www.shipquayhotel.com; £120

Look out over the old city walls from this four-star boutique hotel surrounded by landmarks. The 21 rooms are finished to a modern standard, and family rooms are available. **Shipquay Restaurant** serves contemporary Irish cuisine for your evening meal and a bottomless brunch Saturday-Sunday. For a late-night drink, the **Lock & Quay Bar** makes cocktails and pours craft beers.

Bishop's Gate Hotel

24 Bishop St.; tel. 28/7136-0880; www.bishopsgatehotelderry.com; £175

For a hearty dose of luxury, book a stay at this historic boutique hotel with 31 rooms that reflect its Edwardian heritage. The luxury suites have four-poster beds, Egyptian cotton sheets, and a walk-in monsoon shower. For more space, there are two apartments on London Street and Palace Street. Also with high-end atmosphere are the on-site restaurant **The Gown** and **The Wig Champagne Bar,** where food and drink are served all day. There's no pool or spa but there is a small fitness area.

INFORMATION AND SERVICES

Visitor Information

Derry City Tourist Information Centre

1 Waterloo Place; www.visitderry.com

The Derry City Tourist Information Centre is a valuable resource that provides a good overview as well as maps, guides, and expert advice on local attractions, events, and accommodations. Visitors can purchase tickets for various tours, attractions, and transportation as well as reserve lodging.

Hospitals

For emergency medical services, **Altnagelvin Hospital** (Glenshane Rd.; www.westerntrust.hscni.net) is the main hospital in Derry.

GETTING THERE AND AROUND

To drive from Dublin to Derry, take the M1 north to Drogheda, then the N2 to Aughnacloy, merging with the A5, which leads to Derry. This drive is 240 km (150 mi) and 3.5 hours. From Belfast to Derry is 112 km (70 mi) and a 1.5-hour drive along the M2 and A6 roads.

Translink operates hourly direct trains from Coleraine to Derry (45 minutes). From Belfast, trains depart from Belfast Grand Central Station and Lanyon Place Station (2 hours) with hourly departures daily 6am-10pm.

By bus, Route 705X with **Aircoach** (www.aircoach.ie; from £12 one-way) departs O'Connell Street in Dublin 17 times a day and stops at Dublin Airport, Queen Street in Belfast, Belfast International Airport, and **Derry Coach Park.** From Dublin, the journey takes 4 hours, and from Belfast 2 hours.

In Derry, walking is the best way to explore, especially within the historic walls, as the compact nature of the city center makes it ideal for pedestrians.

The Mournes

Most visitors who want to spend time in Ireland's mountains head to Wicklow or Kerry to get their outdoor fix, leaving the Mournes unfairly overlooked. The granite mountains define the area, with rolling peaks calling hikers to the summits, but there's a strong coastal influence too with the Irish Sea and Carlingford Lough. It's a rural area of small towns and villages that were involved in local textiles and fishing. You're likely to see wildlife, particularly buzzards and falcons in the sky. Failing that, you're certain to see sheep in the fields.

The Mourne Area of Outstanding Natural Beauty unfolds into a network of scenic trails and coastal views. Its title recognizes its significantly beautiful and diverse landscapes. Get on the hiking trails or surround yourself with nature in a part of the country that many drive past.

ORIENTATION

The Mournes region spans the southeastern corner of County Down and is defined by the dramatic **Mourne Mountains,** surrounded by soft green countryside and rural villages. **Banbridge,** north of the range, is a gateway from Belfast, 40 km (25 mi) away. Heading southeast, **Newcastle** is 30 km (19 mi) from Banbridge, at the foot of the mountains, and is loved for its sweeping promenade along **Dundrum Bay** and its proximity to **Slieve Donard,** the highest peak in Northern Ireland.

The **Mourne Area of Outstanding Natural Beauty** is 32 km (20 mi) south of Belfast and stretches across 570 sq km (220 sq mi). It covers the Mourne Mountains, the promenade in Newcastle, **Tollymore Forest,** and as far south as the shores of Carlingford Lough, where the Mourne Mountains meet the Cooley Mountains.

The Mournes

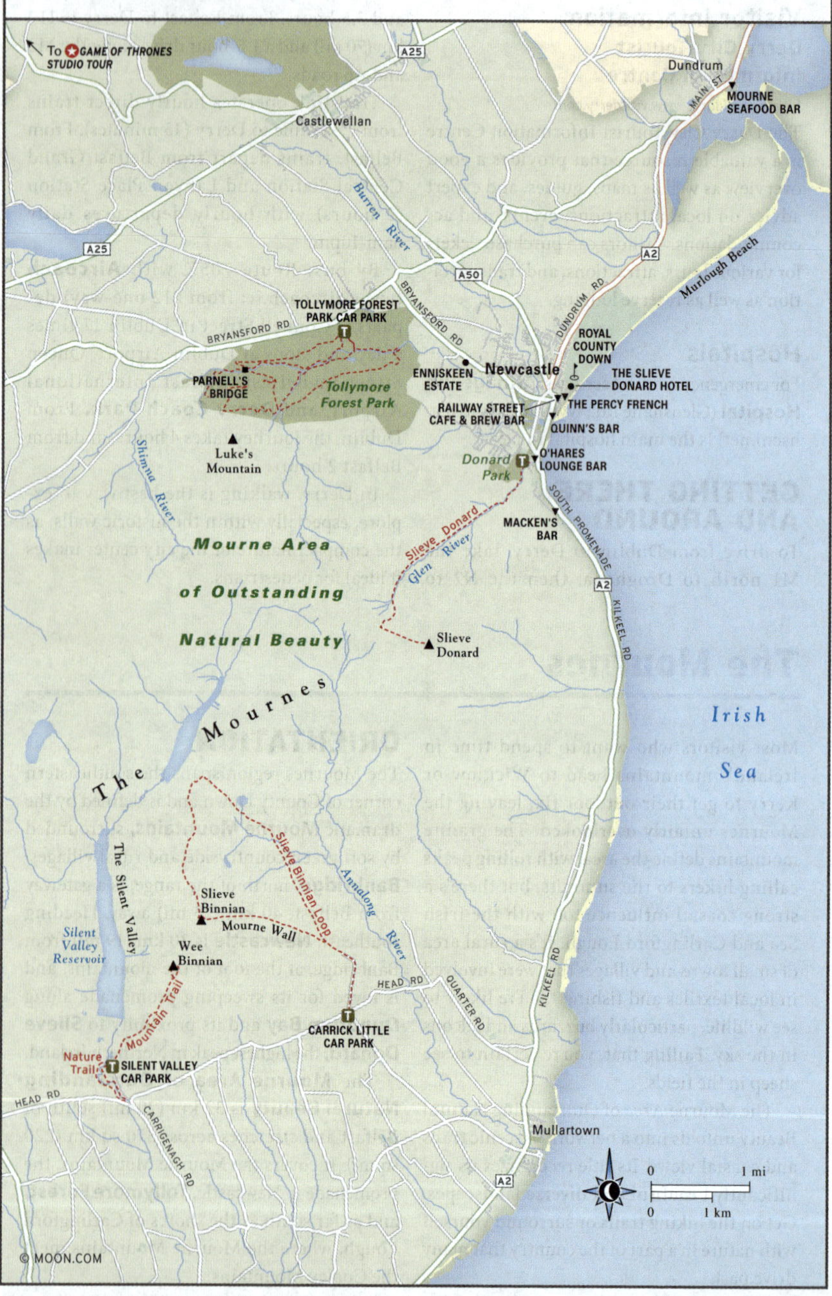

To GAME OF THRONES STUDIO TOUR
A25
Castlewellan
Dundrum
MAIN ST
MOURNE SEAFOOD BAR
Burren River
A25
A50
A2
Murlough Beach
TOLLYMORE FOREST PARK CAR PARK
BRYANSFORD RD
BRYANSFORD RD
DUNDRUM RD
ROYAL COUNTY DOWN
PARNELL'S BRIDGE
Tollymore Forest Park
ENNISKEEN ESTATE
Newcastle
THE SLIEVE DONARD HOTEL
THE PERCY FRENCH
RAILWAY STREET CAFE & BREW BAR
QUINN'S BAR
Luke's Mountain
Shimna River
Donard Park
O'HARES LOUNGE BAR
MACKEN'S BAR
SOUTH PROMENADE
Slieve Donard
Glen River
Mourne Area of Outstanding Natural Beauty
A2
KILKEEL RD
Slieve Donard
The Mournes
Irish Sea
Slieve Binnian Loop
Annalong River
The Silent Valley
Slieve Binnian
Mourne Wall
Silent Valley Reservoir
Wee Binnian
Mountain Trail
HEAD RD
QUARTER RD
KILKEEL RD
CARRICK LITTLE CAR PARK
Nature Trail
SILENT VALLEY CAR PARK
HEAD RD
CARRIGENAGH RD
Mullartown
A2
0 1 mi
0 1 km
© MOON.COM

BANBRIDGE

In the late 1700s Banbridge was built on the linen industry, which brought employment to the area and lasted 200 years until the sectarian violence of the Troubles marred the town. This area isn't on the must-see list of many visitors, unless you're a fan of the TV show *Game of Thrones,* as it's where you'll find the studio from the show.

Sights

F. E. McWilliam Gallery and Studio

200 Newry Rd.; tel. 28/9044-0000; www.femcwilliamcom; Tues.-Sun. 10am-5pm; free

Frederick Edward McWilliam was a talented surrealist sculptor from Banbridge whose work focused on the human form, including a collection called Women of Belfast, which he made in response to the Troubles. The F. E. McWilliam Gallery and Studio opened in 2008, a celebration of the life and work of this local hero and home to a permanent collection of his work as well as insights into his creative process. After seeing the gallery, visit the garden outside, where his sculptures stand atop granite plinths. Stop by the craft shop and the on-site café for light refreshments.

★ Game of Thrones Studio Tour

The Boulevard, Cascum Rd.; tel. 28/9024-5133; www.gameofthronesstudiotour.com; £30

Take a journey into the fantasy world of Westeros on the Game of Thrones Studio Tour. This is where 30 percent of the show's filming took place. Impressive authentic sets include the Stark's Great Hall at Winterfell and the Targaryen's Dragonstone, complete with dragon skull sculptures. The Beyond the Wall exhibit is a powerful display of the craft and expertise of the show's crew, with full-scale models of the giants and Wildlings as they fought the White Walkers and Night King beyond the Wall. The tour is a must for fans of the show thanks to the enormous amount of memorabilia, including costumes, weapons, and props.

The self-guided tour takes 2-3 hours, with plenty of time to soak up the details. See how iconic sets like King's Landing, Castle Black, and Winterfell came to life from initial sketches to fully built environments. Although the show was for adults, the tour is family-friendly. There's a studio shop with licensed merchandise, including T-shirts, tote bags, and maps. Grab a seat at the **Studio Restaurant** for a sit-down meal or a quick bite at the **Lobby Café.**

Getting There

To drive from Belfast to Banbridge, take the A1 south toward Newry and the A26 for Banbridge, a journey of 43 km (27 mi) and 40 minutes.

By bus, **Translink** (www.translink.co.uk) operates regular buses from Belfast to Banbridge. Route X1 and Route X2 Goldline Express buses depart the **Europa Buscentre** in Belfast city center and stop at **Banbridge Bus Station** (50-60 minutes; from £8.50 one-way). Multiple departures throughout the day are as frequent as every 30 minutes at peak times. The studio is a 30-minute walk from the bus station, so a taxi from the street outside is the best option. The F. E. McWilliam Gallery is 10 minutes' walk from the studio, farther from Banbridge.

NEWCASTLE

The coastal town of Newcastle is a magnet to explore the outdoors. Its beachfront location and proximity to Tollymore Forest Park make it great for walks, and if you want to challenge yourself, the trailhead to Northern Ireland's tallest mountain is at the edge of town. That's not to say that Newcastle is full of mucky hikers; it also has a luxury side with the Slieve Donard Hotel and Royal County Down Golf Club.

Parks

Tollymore Forest Park

Bryansford Rd.; tel. 28/7126-1212; www.nidirect.gov.uk; daily 24 hours; free

Game of Thrones

It's safe to say that *Game of Thrones* was one of the biggest TV shows in recent memory (despite that ending—yikes!), and Northern Ireland is proud of its connection. Over 25 locations here were used to create the fantasy world of Westeros.

GAME OF THRONES LOCATIONS

The landscape and architecture of Northern Ireland lend themselves well to recreating the north of Westeros:

- **Tollymore Forest Park** (Newcastle, County Down) is where Ned Stark found the direwolf pups.
- Though damaged by a storm, the **Dark Hedges** (Bregagh Rd., County Antrim) is visited by people who want to see Kingsroad. Drive southwest for 10 minutes from Ballycastle.
- Along the coast are the **Cushendun Caves** (Cushendun, County Antrim) where Melisandre had some key scenes. Drive 20 minutes east to Cushendun from Ballycastle to reach the caves.
- **Fair Head** (Ballycastle, County Antrim) was used as parts of Dragonstone.

GAME OF THRONES DOORS

When the famous beech trees of the Dark Hedges fell in 2016, the wood was saved and used to create 10 decorative doors that tell the stories in the books. These doors hang in pubs and hotels in Northern Ireland. Some of the most accessible ones for visitors are:

- **The Dark Horse** (page 412): This door focuses on the Lannisters, with the family lion above the Great Sept of Balor.
- A little farther from the main sights is the door in **Ballygally Castle** (Coast Road, Ballygally; tel. 28/2858-1066; www.ballygallycastlehotel.com), which depicts the Battle of the Bastards.
- Just outside Derry is **Owens in Limavady** (50 Main Street, Limavady; tel. 28/7772-2328; Facebook @frankowensbar), whose door features an intricate carving of the Night King and his White Walkers.

This 630-ha (1,560-acre) forest park is less than a 10-minute drive outside Newcastle and home to incredible mature trees that line the trails and pathways at the base of the Mourne Mountains. TV fans will recognize the park from *Game of Thrones,* where it was used as the set for the Haunted Forest. For a quick walk in the park, try the 0.8-km (0.5-mi) Arboretum Path, which leads to some of the best examples of mature trees in the park. For a longer walk, the 8.5-km (5.3-mi) Mountain Trail leads into the foothills of the mountains.

Donard Park

www.visitmournemountains.co.uk; daily 24 hours; free

If you prefer an open parkland feel to your parks, take a short stroll from the center of town to Donard Park, beside the Glen River. From here you can see the peak of Slieve Donard and the forests in the foothills. Families come for picnics and to play football on the fields, while serious hikers use the trailhead in the park to climb to the summit of Slieve Donard, 850 m (2,800 ft) above sea level. There's on-site parking.

Hiking and Walking

Arboretum Path

Distance: *650 m (0.4 mi) loop*
Duration: *15 minutes*
Elevation gain: *19 m (62 ft)*
Effort: *Easy*
Trailhead: *Tollymore Forest Park Car Park*

This short easy walk is a good choice with young kids. It's a loop trail under mature trees with plenty of sights and sounds of nature to keep the little ones engaged. The draw is the trees from around the world, including a cork tree and the remains of a giant redwood.

Tollymore River Trail

Distance: *6.3 km (3.9 mi) loop*
Duration: *1.5-2 hours*
Elevation gain: *196 m (6443 ft)*
Effort: *Easy*
Trailhead: *Tollymore Forest Park Car Park*

This gentle easy walk along the Shimna River in the forest park is good for families, with lots of trailside attractions. Leaving the car park, you can follow the red signs in either direction, but the best views are if you head toward Parnell's Bridge first. After this, a short detour takes you to the ruins of White Fort, a farmstead from around 500 CE. In summer, there's no need for hiking-specific gear, but areas like the stepping stones become slippery when wet.

Tollymore Mountain Trail

Distance: *8.5 km (5.3 mi) loop*
Duration: *3 hours*
Elevation gain: *343 m (1,125 ft)*
Effort: *Moderate*
Trailhead: *Tollymore Forest Park Car Park*

For a more challenging route in Tollymore Forest, hike the mountain loop trail that begins and ends in the car park and climbs toward Luke's Mountain before descending. You'll see White Fort and cross Shimna River on an old stone bridge before returning to the starting point. The trail is signposted throughout and well maintained.

Beaches

Murlough Beach

A2

Murlough Beach is 8 km (5 mi) long, on the edge of Dundrum Bay, which runs from Newcastle to the south and Dundrum to the north. You'll get spectacular views of the Mourne Mountains, including Slieve Donard, the Irish Sea, and 6,000-year-old sand dunes.

Golf

Royal County Down

36 Golf Links Rd.; tel. 28/4372-3314; www.royalcountydown.org; May-Sept. £425, winter £150

Royal County Down Golf Club is one of the world's most prestigious and has hosted the Irish Open, the Walker Cup, and many more big events. The draws are the challenging 18-hole courses, the renowned Championship Links and the shorter Annesley Links, made even more difficult by the windy weather. Tee times for nonmembers are limited and should be booked well in advance.

Food

Railway Street Café & Brew Bar

2 Railway St.; Instagram @railwaystcoffee; Wed.-Mon. 9am-5pm; from £4

A modern café in Newcastle is Railway Street Café & Brew Bar, just across the street from the historic train station. Floor-to-ceiling windows draw you in, and bright wooden furniture and clean lines tell you this place knows its flat whites from its cortados. The food menu includes breakfast and brunch items, with the Railway Fry (sausage, bacon, poached eggs, soda bread, potato bread, black pudding, and beans) being a fresh take on the classic full Irish.

Mourne Seafood Bar

10 Main St.; tel. 28/4046-4777; www.mourneseafood.com; daily 10am-6:30pm; from £15

Less than a 10-minute drive north of Newcastle is this cute yet refined seafood restaurant that uses hand-picked shellfish from their own beds and other locally sourced produce. The dining room has a slight round-around-the-edge feel that's common in seaside towns and makes it feel welcoming. Oysters feature prominently, with Japanese-style (soy, pickled ginger, and cucumber) the most interesting choice. For mains, it's hard to ignore the whole roasted seabream served with polenta fries.

Quinn's Bar

62-64 Main St.; tel. 28/4062-3322; www.quinnsbarnewcastle.com; Mon.-Sat. 9am-5pm; from £16

Quinn's Bar opened over 100 years ago as a pub and grocer. The grocer is gone but the furnishings and atmosphere have been preserved by the current owners; the walls are decorated with vintage signage. The pub grub menu plays the hits with steak and burger offerings, and some international dishes include the Moroccan-style butternut squash and chickpea curry. Expect live music on weekend nights.

The Percy French

Downs Rd.; tel. 28/4375-1377; www.thepercyfrench.com; Wed.-Fri. 12:30pm-3pm and 5pm-9pm, Sat. 12:30pm-9pm, Sun. 12:30pm-6pm; from £18

Gastropubs don't come much classier than the Percy French. Named after the songwriter, poet, and author, this establishment carries that air of class to its space, which feels like a hunting lodge thanks to the exposed wooden beams, leather seating, and hunting trophy above the fire. The menu is gastropub, but it elevates its dishes by using local and Irish produce like mussels from Strangford Lough. The children's menu is quite good value; a three-course meal can cost as little as £15. For the adults, the cheese board uses an Irish cheddar, brie, and blue and shouldn't be missed.

Bars and Nightlife

O'Hares Lounge Bar

121 Central Promenade; tel. 28/4372-6622; www.hughmccanns.com; daily 11am-1am; £15

O'Hares Lounge Bar is dog-friendly, which makes it popular with locals who spend their weekends on the trails with their pets. Expect a warm atmosphere with a roaring log fire, great food like beef burgers, lasagna, and fish-and-chips, and a wide selection of drinks. The bar is known for its welcoming staff, always quick to provide water bowls and treats for dogs.

Macken's Bar

73 South Promenade; tel. 28/4372-3430; Facebook @mackensnewcastle; Wed.-Sun. noon-midnight; £15

Macken's Bar is a traditional cozy pub that's the oldest in Newcastle and central to the town's music scene, with jam sessions every Wednesday night, traditional Irish music the last Friday of the month, and live music every weekend. The bar also hosts popular open mic nights, welcoming musicians of all abilities. The kitchen has recently reopened and serves typical pub grub like pies, fish-and-chips, and steaks.

Accommodations

The Slieve Donard Hotel

Downs Rd.; tel. 28/4372-2428; https://marineandlawn.com; £270

The hotel was first built in the late 1890s to attract holidaymakers who visited Newcastle by train on the now-defunct Great Northern Railway. The rail line is gone but the luxury 180-room hotel remains, with views over the water and mountains. Its Victorian heritage is kept alive through design choices and displays of mementos of bygone eras. On-site dining options are the upmarket gastropub the **Percy French** and the old-world luxury feel of the locally sourced dishes at **J. J. Farrall's.** The 20-m (60-ft) pool is a must, as the view toward the mountains is incredible as you swim.

Enniskeen Estate

98 Bryansford Rd.; tel. 28/7114-0300; www.enniskeen.com; £330

The luxury glamping cabins at Enniskeen Estate make for a magical countryside stay, as the wood-clad cabins are decorated with

1: Slieve Donard, Northern Ireland's tallest mountain 2: Silent Valley

1

2

festoon lights and surrounded by trees. Interiors feature sweeping curves and large windows that draw nature inside, but best of all is that each cabin has a private hot tub—perfect for couples. Book a slot at the **WILD forestSPA** for a traditional Finnish massage, a wood-fired sauna, an outdoor waterfall shower, and a foot spa. There are also seasonal spa experiences like Twilight Spa & S'Mores in autumn and a cycling and spa package during summer.

Getting There and Around

From Banbridge, drive on the A50 southeast toward Newcastle for 32 km (20 mi) and 45 minutes. By bus, **Translink** (www.translink.co.uk) operates the regular Route 240 Ulsterbus from **Banbridge Bus Station** to **Newcastle Bus Station** (1.25 hours; £8 one-way). Multiple buses throughout the day depart every 1-2 hours.

From Belfast, take the A24 south toward Newcastle and then the A2, a journey of 45 km (31 mi) and 1 hour. The route offers scenic views as you approach the Mourne Mountains. By bus, the Route 237 Goldline Express departs **Belfast Europa Buscentre** and stops at Newcastle Bus Station (1.25 hours; from £12 one-way). Multiple departures throughout the day included buses every hour during peak times.

SLIEVE DONARD

Distance: *9.5 km (5.9 mi) round-trip*
Duration: *5-6 hours*
Elevation gain: *840 m (2,755 ft)*
Effort: *Difficult*
Trailhead: *Donard Park*

Climbing to the top of the highest peak in the country is a fantastic achievement for any hiker, and the route from Donard Park is sometimes steep but always rewarding. The trail crosses the River Glen and becomes a single track with rocky sections and open mountain stretches across uneven ground. Toward the top, you'll hike alongside the 35-km (22-mi) Mourne Wall, built in the early 1900s to keep livestock out of water supplies. The sheer effort required to build the wall is astounding. From the peak, hikers are rewarded with panoramic views in every direction, and on a clear day, the Isle of Man and Scotland are visible. The hike then returns on the same route back to the park.

Getting There

Follow the A2 south of Newcastle to O'Hare's Lounge Bar. Turn right and you'll see the car park for Donard Park. It's a 5-minute drive or a 25-minute walk on the same route.

SLIEVE BINNIAN LOOP

Distance: *11 km (7 mi) loop*
Duration: *3-4 hours*
Elevation gain: *603 m (1,978 ft)*
Effort: *Difficult*
Trailhead: *Carrick Little car park*

Slieve Binnian is the third-highest mountain in Northern Ireland, and its name means "mountain of the little peaks," which you'll experience on this hike as you reach the summit and another peak 30 minutes later. The trail leads up a rocky single-track trail to the Mourne Wall. You follow the wall to the summit, but watch for uneven ground, as part of this route is a stretch of open mountain. From the top, you'll have brilliant views of the Silent Valley to the west and the Irish Sea to the east.

Getting There

Take the Ballagh Road south from Newcastle along the coast. It turns into the Glassdrumman Road. Turn right after 15 minutes onto Quarter Road, which leads to the car park.

THE SILENT VALLEY

Head Rd.; tel. 7713-642427; https://discovernorthernireland.com; free

The Silent Valley is a reservoir between two barren peaks in the beautiful Mourne Mountains where sheep roam the mountainsides and the Mourne Wall runs across the ridge. The reservoir was created in 1923 to provide drinking water for Belfast; a 100-m-high (330-ft) dam holds 13 million cubic m (11,000 acre-ft). You can see part of the Silent Valley by driving through it, but the real experience is when you get onto any of the seven walking trails.

Hiking and Walking

Nature Trail

Distance: *1.8 km (1.1 mi) loop*
Duration: *20 minutes*
Elevation gain: *42 m (137 ft)*
Effort: *Easy*
Trailhead: *Silent Valley car park*
The Nature Trail (marked green) is the easiest trail, with no hiking gear required.

Mountain Trail

Distance: *3.4 km (2.1 mi) loop*
Duration: *1 hour*
Elevation gain: *214 m (702 ft)*
Effort: *Moderate*
Trailhead: *Silent Valley car park*
The most challenging is the Mountain Trail, which rewards hikers who climb the steep slopes with fantastic views.

Getting There

Take the Ballagh Road south from Newcastle along the coast. It turns into the Glassdrumman Road. Turn right after 15 minutes onto Quarter Road, which leads to Carrick Little car park. Continue past it for another 10 minutes. When you reach the T-junction at the end of the road, turn right, and you'll arrive at the car park.

Background

The Landscape

GEOGRAPHY

Ireland's landscape is an ever-present character in the history and folklore of the island and has shaped the people who have lived here over thousands of years. Rolling green fields, dramatic coastlines, and moody mountains have been created by ice, wind, and water. The small island has diversity in lush valleys, rugged peninsulas, and some of Europe's highest sea cliffs.

Varying Landscapes

The country is divided into four provinces, Leinster, Munster, Connacht, and Ulster, each with its own scenery. The east is gentler, with low-lying farmland, river valleys, and the Wicklow Mountains breaking up the terrain south of Dublin. To the west the land becomes wilder, giving way to the karst limestone of the Burren in County Clare, the wide open expanses of Connemara, and the unforgiving mountains of Kerry, with Carrauntoohil, Ireland's tallest mountain at 1,038 m (3,406 ft). Ireland's longest river, the Shannon, flows through the heart of the country, while lakes such as Strangford Lough and Lough Hyne add to the island's watery landscape.

The Coast

Ireland's Atlantic coastline is its most defining feature, stretching 2,500 km (1,550 mi) with jagged cliffs, sandy beaches, and offshore islands. The Atlantic Ocean carves out dramatic features like the Cliffs of Moher, Skellig Michael, and Murder Hole Beach. On the opposite side of the country, the Irish Sea offers a sheltered contrast, with gentle bays and historic port towns.

CLIMATE

Ireland is often painted as a place where it never stops raining, and while it does get more precipitation than most, the weather is more nuanced. Thanks to the warming effects of the North Atlantic Drift, Ireland enjoys a temperate maritime climate, meaning winters are mild and summers are cool.

Rain, Rain, and More Rain

You'll still want to pack your rain gear, as rainfall is frequent but varies significantly by region. The west, particularly Kerry, Galway, and Mayo, gets the most rain, while the east is relatively drier. The drizzling rain, also known as soft rain, is often more of a mist than a downpour, while Atlantic storms bring heavy showers and strong winds.

Long Summer Nights

Summers are pleasantly mild, rarely exceeding 25°C (77°F), and daylight can last until as late as 10:30pm, ideal for outdoor activities. Winters, on the other hand, are cool but rarely extreme, with temperatures typically ranging from 0-8°C (32-46°F) and daylight disappearing as early as 3pm. Snow is rare and usually confined to the mountains.

ENVIRONMENTAL ISSUES

Like much of the world, Ireland faces environmental challenges, particularly concerning climate change, biodiversity loss, and pollution. Rising sea levels and coastal erosion pose a significant threat, especially to communities in the west, where storm surges are becoming more frequent. Efforts are being made to preserve sand dunes and protect vulnerable cliffside areas from further degradation.

Peatlands

Peatlands, also known as bogs, once a key part of the rural economy, have suffered from extensive harvesting for fuel. Today, conservation efforts are underway to restore these vital carbon sinks, particularly in the Midlands. Using peat for fuel has cultural ties to this region, so despite efforts to protect the bogs, people still harvest them to burn. Rewilding initiatives have also gained momentum, with projects aimed at reintroducing native species and protecting remaining old-growth forests.

Water Quality

Water quality remains a concern in some areas due to agricultural runoff and wastewater pollution, but tap water is safe to drink. Significant improvements have been made in recent years, with stricter environmental

Previous: Monasterboice.

policies and local cleanup initiatives making a tangible difference. Sustainability is increasingly a focus, with more farmers adopting eco-friendly practices and tourism operators emphasizing responsible travel.

PLANTS AND ANIMALS

Despite its small size, Ireland has a surprising range of plant and animal life, much of it shaped by the mild climate and isolation from mainland Europe. Ireland was once covered in dense forests, but centuries of deforestation have left only pockets of ancient woodland, such as Killarney National Park and the oak woods of Glengarriff.

Ireland's Plants

The most common trees today include oak, ash, birch, and holly, with wildflowers like primroses, bluebells, and foxgloves adding bursts of color to the countryside. In the Burren, a unique mix of alpine, Mediterranean, and Arctic plants thrive on the limestone, creating one of Europe's most unusual botanical landscapes. Coillte manages most of the forests in Ireland, but the vast majority are commercial mono-growth forests that bring very few positives to the natural environment.

Diverse Wildlife

The wildlife is less varied compared to continental Europe, but there are a number of standout animals. Red deer, the country's only native deer species, roam freely in the southwest, while pine martens, foxes, and badgers are among the more elusive forest creatures. Birds include the peregrine falcon, barn owl, and buzzard, while the cliffs of the west coast provide nesting grounds for puffins, razorbills, and gannets.

Marine life is rich, with dolphins, porpoises, and even humpback whales frequently spotted off the coast. Seals bask on the rocks along the Wild Atlantic Way, and the cold nutrient-rich water support a thriving seafood industry, from oysters in Carlingford Lough to lobsters off the coast of Sligo.

Ireland doesn't have any large predators, but its landscapes have been shaped by nature and time and remain wild in their own unique way.

History

PREHISTORY

Long before Ireland became an island of rolling green hills and rugged coastlines, it was a land covered by ice. The last ice age sculpted the landscape, carving valleys and creating loughs, leaving behind a terrain that would later be home to some of Europe's earliest settlers. The first known inhabitants arrived around 10,000 years ago, drawn to the forests, rivers, and fertile land.

By the Neolithic period, around 4,000 BCE, early farmers had begun clearing land, building homes, and leaving behind mysterious megalithic tombs. Newgrange in County Meath, older than both Stonehenge and the Great Pyramids, makes up part of the Boyne Valley and stands as one of the world's most significant prehistoric structures. Built to align with the winter solstice, it shows an advanced understanding of astronomy and the cycles of nature. Knocknarea in Sligo and Knowth in Meath are also fascinating remnants of Ireland's ancient past.

THE CELTS AND PAGANISM

The Celts arrived in Ireland around 500 BCE, bringing with them iron tools, new farming techniques, and a system of governance. They formed tribal kingdoms, each ruled by a rí (king), with druids serving as religious leaders, the law, and keepers of knowledge. Pagan Ireland thrived on storytelling, where tales of warrior queens, shape-shifting gods, and epic battles were passed down through generations.

Celtic Ireland had no single ruler but instead consisted of numerous tuatha (tribes), often at war with each other. The Hill of Tara in County Meath, considered the seat of the High Kings, held symbolic importance, but true power was spread across the island. The pagans also gave birth to a holiday celebrated around the world today, Halloween.

EARLY CHRISTIAN IRELAND

With the arrival of Christianity in the 5th century, Ireland underwent one of the most profound transformations in its history. Saint Patrick, though not the first Christian missionary, became the most famous, credited with converting the island. It's said that he drove the snakes out of Ireland, but the snake is a metaphor for paganism.

Monasteries sprang up across the country and became centers of learning and preserving knowledge through beautifully crafted manuscripts such as the Book of Kells, on display in Trinity College in Dublin. Monasterboice in Louth and Glendalough in Wicklow are among the best-preserved examples of early Christian monastic sites, with their iconic round towers, Celtic crosses, and ancient churches.

THE VIKINGS

The 9th century saw the arrival of a new force—the Vikings. These Scandinavian raiders targeted Ireland's monasteries, as many held precious items and wealth. Over time, the Vikings transitioned from pillagers to settlers, establishing trading ports that would evolve into cities like Dublin, Waterford, and Limerick.

Temple Bar in Dublin was built as a Viking stronghold, and though it's a tourist trap these days, you can still feel the Viking history. Reginald's Tower in Waterford, the oldest civic building in the country, was originally built by the Vikings and is now a museum dedicated to their story.

THE NORMANS

In 1169, yet another invader arrived, this time from across the Irish Sea, marking England's first involvement in Ireland. The Anglo-Normans, led by Richard "Strongbow" de Clare, Earl of Pembroke, landed in the southeast at the invitation of an exiled Irish king, Dermot MacMurrough. What began as a small force quickly grew, and within a few years, much of Ireland had fallen under Norman control.

Norman rule introduced castles, walled towns, and feudalism, changing Ireland's political and social structure. Kilkenny Castle, built in 1195, remains one of the most impressive examples of Norman architecture. Trim Castle, the largest Norman castle in Ireland, is one of the many highlights in the Boyne Valley.

COLONIZATION AND OLIVER CROMWELL

By the 16th century, England sought tighter control over Ireland, leading to centuries of conflict. The Tudor and Stuart monarchs imposed plantations, seizing land from Irish lords and redistributing it to English and Scottish settlers. This resulted in violent resistance, including the Nine Years' War (1594-1603) and the Flight of the Earls in 1607.

The most brutal phase of colonization came under Oliver Cromwell in the 1650s. His army devastated Ireland, with massacres at Drogheda and Wexford. Thousands of Irish were executed and many more were banished to the poor farmlands in Connaught or sent to the Caribbean as indentured servants. Their land was confiscated, leaving native Irish people landless in their own country. Derry's walls were built decades before Cromwell but were put to the test when he arrived, now standing as a reminder to the era's turbulence.

FAMINE AND EMIGRATION

One of the darkest chapters in Irish history, the Great Famine (1845-1852) saw the population decimated by starvation and disease.

Historical Timeline

10,000 BCE	Arrival of first known inhabitants, drawn to the forests, rivers, and fertile land.
4000 BCE	Early farmers cleared land, built homes, and left behind megalithic tombs like Newgrange in the Boyne Valley.
500 BCE	Celts arrived, bringing with them iron tools, new farming techniques, and a system of governance; tribal kingdoms formed, ruled by rís (kings) with druids as religious leaders. Pagans originated Halloween.
400-800 CE	Arrival of Christianity, with monasteries springing up across the country. Manuscripts such as the Book of Kells, housed at Trinity College in Dublin, are created and preserved.
800-900 CE	Arrival of the Vikings, who raided Ireland's monasteries. Over time the Vikings settled and established cities like Dublin, Waterford, and Limerick.
1169	Norman invasion, led by Strongbow. Norman rule introduced castles, walled towns, and feudalism, changing Ireland's political and social structure.
1500-1700	England sought tighter control over Ireland, leading to centuries of conflict and violent resistance, including the Nine Years War (1594-1603) and the Flight of the Earls in 1607. The most brutal phase of colonization came under Oliver Cromwell in the 1650s.

The failure of the potato crop, combined with harsh British policies in which massive amounts of grain were exported and aid from other nations was prohibited, led to the deaths of over 1 million people and the emigration of millions more.

Ireland's population never fully recovered. Those who left spread Irish culture across the world, particularly in the United States, Canada, and Australia. The diaspora remains a defining feature of Irish identity. EPIC The Irish Emigration Museum in Dublin tells the detailed stories of those who left these shores.

EASTER RISING AND WAR OF INDEPENDENCE

The 20th century saw Ireland's fight for independence from British rule boil over. The Easter Rising of 1916 was a military failure but reignited nationalism among the public. Led by figures like Michael Collins, Pádraig Pearse, and James Connolly, the rebellion's suppression and subsequent executions and killings of the leaders turned public opinion against British rule.

This led to the War of Independence (1919-1921), fought between the Irish Republican Army (IRA) and British forces. The conflict ended with the Anglo-Irish Treaty, creating the Irish Free State in 1922. The GPO, where the Easter Rising was centered, and Kilmainham Gaol in Dublin, where many revolutionaries were imprisoned and executed, are some of the most significant historical sites from this time.

THE TROUBLES

While most of Ireland gained independence, six counties in the north remained under British rule, creating Northern Ireland. This

1845-1852	The Great Famine saw the population decimated by starvation and disease. The failure of the potato crop, combined with harsh British policies, led to the deaths of over 1 million people and the emigration of millions more.
1870-1921	Ireland's fight for independence from British rule boiled over; the Easter Rising of 1916 was a military failure but reignited nationalism among the public. The War of Independence (1919-1921) was fought between the Irish Republican Army (IRA) and British forces.
1922	The War of Independence ended with the Anglo-Irish Treaty in December 1921, creating the Irish Free State in 1922.
1969-1998	Six counties in the north remained under British rule, creating Northern Ireland. This division led to decades of sectarian conflict known as the Troubles (1969-1998). Nationalists (mainly Catholic) sought reunification with Ireland, while Unionists (mainly Protestant) wanted to remain part of the UK.
2013-present	As the country's recession came to an end, Ireland transformed into a global tech and financial titan, leading to skyrocketing costs of living and a painful housing crisis.

division led to decades of sectarian conflict known as the Troubles (1969-1998). Nationalists (mainly Catholic) sought reunification with Ireland, while Unionists (mainly Protestant) wanted to remain part of the UK.

Bombings, assassinations, and violent clashes between the IRA, British forces, and loyalist paramilitaries defined the era. The Museum of Free Derry and Crumlin Road Gaol in Belfast provide in-depth perspectives on this brutal time. The murals in Belfast, still standing today, serve as reminders of what happened.

THE CELTIC TIGER

In the late 20th and early 21st century, Ireland transformed from economic recession into a global tech and financial titan. The "Celtic Tiger" era saw huge economic growth driven by foreign investment and a booming property market. However, the financial crash of 2008 hit hard, leading to years of austerity and emigration.

THE TECH BOOM

Ireland's recession officially ended in 2013, and since then there's been a booming tech industry in the country with major companies like Meta, LinkedIn, and Airbnb all headquartered in Dublin. While this has brought much needed funds into the country, it's also seen the cost of living sky rocket. Ireland is also going through a very painful housing crisis that began in 2007.

Folklore

Irish folklore holds deep cultural and historical significance, preserving the myths, beliefs, and traditions of Ireland's past. It reflects our country's ancient Celtic roots, oral storytelling traditions, and connection to nature and the supernatural. Even today, Irish folklore influences literature, music, and popular culture, keeping the spirit of Ireland's storytelling heritage alive.

TÁIN BÓ CÚAILNGE (CATTLE RAID OF COOLEY)

Often referred to as Ireland's epic of epics, the Táin Bó Cúailnge is one of the most famous tales from Irish mythology. It follows the warrior Cú Chulainn as he single-handedly defends Ulster against the armies of Queen Medb of Connacht, who seeks to steal the prized bull Donn Cúailnge.

The story begins with Queen Medb and her husband, Ailill, arguing over who has more wealth. When Queen Medb finds out that Ailill owns a magnificent white-horned bull that surpasses anything in her herd, she becomes determined to find an equal or better bull for herself. She learns of Donn Cúailnge, the Brown Bull of Cooley, a mighty beast residing in Ulster, and sets out to claim it.

However, Ulster is under a curse that renders its warriors weak and defenseless, leaving only the young hero Cú Chulainn to stand against Medb's forces. Armed with supernatural strength and the ability to perform the terrifying ríastrad (warp spasm), where his body contorts into an unrecognizable monstrous form, Cú Chulainn engages in a series of legendary battles. His greatest fight is against his foster brother and closest friend, Ferdiad, in a brutal four-day battle that ends with Ferdiad's death. Though victorious, Cú Chulainn is heartbroken over killing his friend.

The battle rages on, but when Ulster's warriors finally recover, they join the fight and drive Medb's army back to Connacht. The Brown Bull of Cooley, having been taken by Medb, fights Ailill's bull to the death, only to return to Ulster and collapse from exhaustion. The tale is filled with themes of loyalty, betrayal, and the devastating consequences of pride.

THE CHILDREN OF LIR

A tragic tale of transformation and loss, the Children of Lir is one of the most heartbreaking stories in Irish folklore. Lir, a powerful chieftain of the Tuatha Dé Danann, had four beloved children, Fionnuala, Aodh, Fiachra, and Conn. Their mother died when they were young, and after a time, their father remarried to a woman named Aoife. At first, Aoife treated the children well, but soon she became jealous of the love Lir had for them.

Overwhelmed by envy, Aoife came up with a cruel plan. She lured the children to a secluded lake and used her dark magic to transform them into swans. They would spend 300 years on Lough Derravaragh, 300 years on the Sea of Moyle, and 300 years on the waters around Inishglora. Though cursed, they retained their voices and spent their centuries singing sorrowful songs across the waves.

During their time on the Sea of Moyle, the swans endured relentless storms and bitter cold, suffering immense hardship. They found momentary relief when they were reunited with each other after long periods of separation, but their suffering didn't stop. As the centuries passed, the world changed, and the Tuatha Dé Danann faded into legend.

Finally, after 900 years, the children heard the first Christian bells ringing from a monastery on the shore. Seeking refuge, they found a monk who baptized them, and when they touched the land, they transformed back into their human forms—aged, frail, and moments from death. They died soon after, their souls finally at peace, and were buried together in a single grave, forever united in their suffering and love for one another.

THE SALMON OF KNOWLEDGE

The story of the Salmon of Knowledge is one of the best-known myths in Ireland and revolves around Fionn Mac Cumhaill, the legendary warrior and leader of the Fianna. As a boy, he unknowingly gained all the wisdom of the world by tasting a magical salmon that had been prophesied to give immense knowledge to the first person who ate it.

According to legend, the salmon lived in the River Boyne and had eaten nine hazelnuts that fell from a sacred tree, making it the most intelligent creature in existence. A wise poet and druid named Finegas spent years trying to catch the salmon, believing that eating it would grant him unlimited wisdom. One day he finally succeeded, and instructed his young apprentice, Fionn, to cook the fish for him, but warned him not to taste it.

As Fionn cooked the salmon over an open fire, he noticed a blister forming on its skin. Instinctively, he pressed his thumb against it to stop the fish from burning, but in doing so, he burned himself. Without thinking, he put his thumb in his mouth to soothe the pain. At that moment, all the knowledge of the salmon was transferred to him.

When Finegas saw the light of wisdom in Fionn's eyes, he realized what had happened. Accepting that destiny had chosen Fionn instead of him, he told the boy to eat the entire fish. From that day on, whenever Fionn needed guidance or insight, he would place his thumb in his mouth, unlocking the vast wisdom contained within him. This knowledge allowed him to become the greatest leader of the Fianna and one of Ireland's best-known heroes.

Government and Economy

GOVERNMENT

Comprising the Republic of Ireland and Northern Ireland, the island has a complex government and economic landscape that a lot of the population aren't even fully aware of.

The Republic of Ireland is a parliamentary democracy with a president as head of state and a taoiseach (prime minister) leading the government with TDs (members of parliament). The Oireachtas, consisting of the Dáil and Seanad, forms the legislative body. As of March 2025, the government is a coalition of Fianna Fáil, Fine Gael, and independent TDs.

Northern Ireland operates under a power-sharing arrangement, with the Northern Ireland Assembly comprising 90 MLAs elected by proportional representation. The executive includes a first minister and deputy first minister, who must come from different political designations, ensuring representation of both unionist and nationalist communities. As of March 2025, Sinn Féin is the largest party in Northern Ireland.

ECONOMY

Ireland's economy is known for its openness to international trade and strong focus on attracting foreign direct investment (FDI) with a low corporate tax rate of 12.5 percent. The technology sector is particularly prominent, with Ireland hosting major tech companies like Apple, Meta, and Airbnb. Pharmaceuticals and life sciences are also big contributors to exports.

Northern Ireland's economy lags behind the republic, but the region benefits from its unique position, with special access to the EU single market and the UK after Brexit. The main sectors include business services, manufacturing, and construction, but some say there is an overreliance on public-sector employment. Cross-border trade with the republic is crucial, with over 50 percent of Northern Ireland's exports going to the republic.

ECONOMIC CHALLENGES

Both regions face serious challenges. The Republic of Ireland must navigate global economic uncertainties while being reliant on US trade; in 2024 Ireland exported €72.6 billion worth of goods and services to the United States. There's also a crippling housing crisis in the country that has been ongoing since 2007. Northern Ireland's economy is vulnerable to Brexit-related trade complexities, but its unique position creates opportunities for growth through cross-border deals.

People and Culture

DEMOGRAPHICS

Ireland's population has grown steadily in recent years, with the Republic of Ireland now home to nearly 5 million people and Northern Ireland with just over 1.9 million. While the republic has seen consistent growth fueled by immigration and economic development, Northern Ireland's population is expected to have the slowest growth of any region in the UK over the next 20 years. In both regions, urban centers like Dublin, Cork, Belfast, and Galway dominate in terms of population density, while rural areas retain their charm with close-knit communities and slower-paced lifestyles.

Life expectancy across the island is high, with people in both countries living into their late 70s and early 80s. Ireland's age profile shows a youthful country, with a significant portion of the population under age 35. However, an aging demographic is beginning to emerge in some areas, partly due to young people being unable to buy their own homes and raise families, which is creating challenges for health care and social services.

IMMIGRATION

Ireland has become increasingly diverse in recent decades. Once known as a country of emigration due to famine and economic hardship, the tide has turned, and Ireland is now a destination for people from all over the world. The Republic of Ireland has seen significant immigration from Eastern Europe, Africa, and Asia, particularly since joining the European Union in 1973. Polish, Lithuanian, and Indian communities have grown substantially, adding new layers to Irish society.

Asylum seekers arriving in Ireland are put into a system called Direct Provision, which provides housing, meals, and basic services while their applications are processed, but it has faced criticism for its poor living conditions and restrictions on asylum seekers' movements.

Northern Ireland has also experienced rising immigration, though it remains less diverse than other parts of the UK. The influx of newcomers has diversified local culture but also posed challenges in terms of integration and education.

RELIGION

Religion has long been intertwined with Irish identity but is undergoing profound changes in both parts of the island. Despite multiple child abuse scandals in the republic, Catholicism remains dominant but has seen a steady decline in younger generations. The most recent census revealed that around 69 percent of people identify as Roman Catholic—a sharp drop from previous decades—while those claiming no religion have risen to 14 percent. Other faiths like Islam and Hinduism are growing steadily due to immigration.

Northern Ireland is quite different due to its historical sectarian divide between Catholics and Protestants. For the first time in history, Catholics now outnumber Protestants in Northern Ireland (45.7 percent to 43.48

percent), according to the 2021 census. This shift reflects broader trends that could reshape the region's political landscape in years to come.

Despite declining church attendance across the island, religion still plays an important cultural role. Traditional festivals like Christmas, St. Patrick's Day, and Easter remain widely celebrated.

LANGUAGE

Language is central to Irish identity and culture. In the Republic of Ireland, Irish (Gaelic) is recognized as the first official language alongside English. While English is the one you'll hear spoken in daily life, Irish remains an important symbol of national pride and is taught in schools throughout the country. Around 40 percent of people claim some ability to speak Irish, though fluency is less common outside Gaeltacht regions such as Connemara and Kerry. Generally speaking, Irish people have cúpla focail (a few words) of Irish, but few have a conversational level of Irish.

In Northern Ireland, English is overwhelmingly dominant, but recent legislative changes have elevated the status of Irish as a minority language. The Identity and Language Act (2022) formally recognized Irish as an official language for public use in Northern Ireland, a significant event given its historical suppression during British rule.

Irish is often described as a dying language, but with Ireland going through an era of being cool, the Irish language is seeing a resurgence, helped by Northern Irish group Kneecap, who rap in Irish.

CULTURAL IDENTITY

Ireland's cultural identity is deeply rooted in its history and conflicts, but it is evolving in the modern day. In Northern Ireland especially, identity often means political and religious affiliation, as many Catholics identify as Irish while Protestants tend toward British or unionist identities—people from Northern Ireland can choose to have an Irish passport, a British one, or both.

The legacy of emigration has left a huge mark on Irish culture worldwide. Today there are more people claiming Irish ancestry abroad than there are living on the island itself—particularly in countries like the United States, Canada, Australia, and the UK.

THE ARTS

Handicrafts

The Aran sweater is one of the most iconic symbols of Irish craft. Originally designed for fishermen and farmers, these woolen garments have become synonymous with Ireland's textile tradition. The intricate stitch patterns of the Aran sweater show off the skill of Irish knitters, the quality of the materials, and the cultural significance of knitting. In recent years, there has been a resurgence of interest in woolen crafts, with contemporary brands working to preserve these techniques.

One craft that might surprise you is Irish crystal. Known for its intricate cuts and high-quality glass, crystal from studios like Waterford Crystal has become a luxury good worldwide. Each piece reflects centuries of tradition and skill, often passed down through family lines, to create both timeless and contemporary designs.

Music and Dance

Traditional Irish music is popular in Ireland, and it's hard to not be drawn in by the lively tunes and powerful rhythms that can often spring up out of nowhere in a pub or at a celebration. These sessions quite often have an open mic approach, where you can join in with whatever instrument you have and can sing as well.

Traditional Irish instruments such as the bodhrán (a handheld drum), fiddle, and tin whistle create the distinctive melodic sounds that are associated with Irish folk music. These instruments, along with others like the accordion, concertina, and even the spoons, form part of the colorful tapestry of Irish traditional music.

Dancing is never too far away when music is being played, with popular dances like the jig and reel matching up harmoniously with the styles of music. The success of shows like Riverdance has brought Irish dancing to global audiences on a theatrical stage.

Literature

Ireland and writing seem to go hand in hand throughout the centuries, with acclaimed works ranging from ancient myths and legends to modern masterpieces. Some of the most famous Irish writers include Samuel Beckett, known for his bleak outlook and black humor; W. B. Yeats, a driving force behind the Irish Literary Revival; Edna O'Brien, renowned for her frank depiction of women's inner lives; and Brendan Behan, celebrated for his plays.

Television and Cinema

Ireland's storytelling craft has seen it punch well above its weight on the global movie and TV scene with some fabulous works of art and actors coming from these shores. On the silver screen, Irish films have gained international acclaim. Movies like *The Wind That Shakes the Barley, My Left Foot,* and *Brooklyn* have showcased Irish storytelling on the global stage. Irish actors such as Saoirse Ronan, Michael Fassbender, and Colin Farrell have become Hollywood household names.

Irish television has also made its mark, with series like *Normal People* and *Derry Girls* gaining international popularity and cult shows like *Father Ted* remaining relevant decades later.

SPORTS

Ireland is a sports-mad country, with four main team sports played, and a host of individual sports too. On any given weekend you're likely to see sports on the TV in pubs and bars, and lengthy discussions on radio and TV.

Gaelic Games

Gaelic sports, governed by the Gaelic Athletic Association (GAA), are deeply embedded in the cultural fabric of Ireland and include the sports of Gaelic football and hurling. Everyone from small kids through to adults can play at varying levels, from underage games at club level through senior intercounty level.

Gaelic football, which can loosely be described as a mix of soccer and rugby, is the most widely played of all Gaelic sports. Played with a football, teams use both their hands and feet to score points by scoring goals or putting the ball over the crossbar. It's a very physical game with big hits and very fit players. Hurling, one of the oldest field games in the world, is played with a wooden stick called a hurl and a small ball known as a sliotar. It's an extremely fast-paced and powerful game that requires incredible skill and the deftest of touches.

Football

Internationally, Ireland's national football (soccer) team has enjoyed moments of success, particularly during the World Cups of Italia '90, USA '94, and South Korea & Japan '02, with notable players like Packie Bonner, Ray Houghton, and Robbie becoming national heroes. Most Irish football fans support teams in England, with most of our top players playing there, but support for the League of Ireland has grown rapidly in recent years with teams like Dundalk, Shamrock Rovers, and Bohemians drawing big crowds.

Rugby

Rugby tends to be played in more affluent parts of the country and by students in fee-paying schools. There's a well-embedded system where the best school players go on and play interprovincial club rugby for Leinster, Munster, Connaught, or Ulster, with the best then going on and playing international rugby for Ireland. The Republic of Ireland and Northern Ireland come together to play as Ireland and have been hugely successful in recent years.

Boxing

Ireland has always produced good boxers, but when Katie Taylor exploded onto the scene in 2005 and became the with World Amateur Champion, it started almost 20 years of domination in the sport. She has won one Olympic gold medal, five World Championships, and six European Championships. Fighting as an amateur boxer in Ireland is a huge source of pride, but having won everything, she turned professional in 2016 and went on to become the undisputed champion of the world and two-weight world champion.

Horse Racing

Ireland is regarded as one of the best countries in the world for breeding horses and training them, with some famous horse owners winning the biggest races on the planet, like the Grand National, Melbourne Cup, and key races at the Cheltenham Festival.

Golf

Ireland's location by the sea has seen people build challenging links courses, which has created a steady flow of top-quality golfers. Padraic Harrington was the big name in the sport for years, but Rory McIlroy and Shane Lowry are the current cream of the crop.

Essentials

Transportation

GETTING THERE

Air

Dublin Airport (DUB) is the main international hub, as it has the widest range of flight options from North America, Europe, and beyond. Shannon Airport (SNN) in County Clare and Ireland West Airport Knock (NOC) in County Mayo are excellent alternatives if you want to begin your trip on the Wild Atlantic Way. Cork Airport (ORK), while smaller, has efficient services to European destinations and some UK cities. Belfast International (BFS) and Belfast City (BHD)

airports offer numerous connections from UK and European cities for those starting in Northern Ireland.

From North America

There are year-round direct flights from New York City (JFK and EWR), Boston (BOS), Chicago (ORD), Toronto (YYZ), and other cities to Dublin, many of which are operated by **Aer Lingus** (www.aerlingus.com). United, Delta, and American Airlines also serve these routes. Shannon Airport (SNN) has seasonal summer flights from New York and Boston, with the added advantage of US preclearance facilities, meaning you clear immigration before departure and arrive as a domestic passenger.

From the UK and Europe

From the United Kingdom and continental Europe, there are frequent and affordable connections to Ireland. Dublin Airport alone handles over 150 flights a day, with carriers like Aer Lingus and **Ryanair** (www.ryanair.com) operating routes as short as 1 hour from London. Budget airlines provide crazy cheap fares, sometimes under €50 round-trip, from dozens of European cities, including Paris, Amsterdam, Berlin, and Barcelona to Dublin, Cork, Shannon, and Belfast.

From Australia and New Zealand

Travelers from Australia and New Zealand typically connect through major Asian or Middle Eastern hubs. The most popular connections are via Dubai with **Emirates** (www.emirates.com) or via Doha with **Qatar Airways** (www.qatarairways.com), with some of the flight legs taking longer than 12 hours and often lengthy layovers.

From South Africa

South African travelers have excellent connections to Ireland through London, with multiple daily flight options. **British Airways** (www.britishairways.com) and **Virgin Atlantic** (www.virginatlantic.com) operate direct flights from both Johannesburg and Cape Town to London's Heathrow Airport, where you can easily connect to Dublin, Cork, or Belfast.

Sea

Regular ferry crossings connect Ireland with the UK and continental Europe. **Irish Ferries** (www.irishferries.com) operates multiple daily sailings from Holyhead to Dublin Port (2 hours) and from Pembroke to Rosslare (4 hours), while **Stena Line** (www.stenaline.com) operates crossings from Liverpool to Belfast (8 hours overnight).

You can board these ferries as a foot passenger or with your vehicle. Services on board include restaurants, lounges, and sleeping cabins for overnight journeys.

GETTING AROUND

Ireland is small, but getting around requires some planning. The public transport network connects major towns and cities well, but nowhere nearly as well as in other countries in Europe. To explore those picture-perfect country lanes and coastal routes, you'll need a car.

Air

For long jumps across the island, **Aer Lingus** (www.aerlingus.com) operates handy flights between Dublin and regional airports like Kerry and Donegal. These tiny prop planes give you stunning aerial views of the countryside, though with just a few flights daily, you'll need to time it right. **Aer Arann** (www.aerarannislands.ie) operates short flights between the Aran Islands and Galway on the mainland.

Bus

Bus Éireann (www.buseireann.ie) runs an extensive network reaching most of the country, even remote areas with infrequent

Previous: Irish sheep.

routes. The buses have comfortable seats and free Wi-Fi on most direct routes. Private regional operators often provide alternative services between major cities. Don't be surprised if buses in rural areas are late or make unscheduled stops. Buses in the cities are more likely to be on time but are still not 100 percent reliable.

Train

Irish Rail (www.irishrail.ie) runs the train services, connecting most major cities, but there are some gaps in the coverage. Dublin is the best connected, and you can reach other major cities from Dublin by rail. The DART commuter rail around Dublin Bay offers a scenic way to travel, while the Luas in Dublin is a light-rail option to get around the city.

Car

To see the best of Ireland, you'll need a car to reach remote parts of the country, but be prepared for narrow country lanes where two cars can barely squeeze past each other. Rural roads often lack space, with hedgerows or stone walls right up to the edge. The M50 around Dublin and the M1 are the busiest motorways, while there's a good network of other motorways and national roads (marked with a N). Beyond this are regional roads (R) which can be narrow and winding, then at the bottom of the pack are local roads (L), which can be even narrower and windier.

Car Rentals

Major international car rental companies operate in Ireland, with desks at every airport and in major cities, where **Europcar** (www.europcar.ie) and **Hertz** (www.hertz.ie) offer a wider selection. Manual transmissions are standard in Ireland; automatics are available but normally come with a surcharge. Full insurance coverage is strongly advised given Ireland's narrow roads. Rental companies offer excess car insurance, but you'll get a better deal by finding a third-party insurer online before your trip starts.

Traffic Regulations and Navigation

Remember, we drive on the left in Ireland. Roundabouts (traffic circles) circulate clockwise, and priority goes to vehicles coming from your right unless marked otherwise. Speed limits are posted in kilometers: 120 km/h (75 mph) on motorways, 100 km/h (60 mph) on national roads, 80 km/h (50 mph) on regional roads, and 50 km/h (30 mph) or lower in urban areas.

Maps and Directions

Google Maps and Waze work well for navigation, but make sure you download your maps to use offline or carry a paper map in case you don't have phone signal in rural parts of the country. The **Ordnance Survey** (https://store.osi.ie) produces excellent detailed maps for walkers and drivers that can be bought online or in big bookshops. If in doubt, ask a local, and they'll be more than happy to help you, but keep in mind that directions are often based on landmarks that you might not know, and might include vague descriptions like "a country mile."

Safety

Ireland is a safe country to drive in, but as a visitor, you should pay extra attention, as the roads can be difficult to navigate. Watch for quickly changing weather conditions, particularly in coastal and mountainous areas. Sheep are known to wander onto country roads, and night can fall quite early in winter.

Parking

Presume that all parking in towns and cities is paid. There are payment terminals dotted along the streets where you can pay by contactless or coins, then display your ticket on your dashboard. Parking in rural areas is generally free unless signs indicate otherwise. Failure to pay in cities will often result in your car being clamped, which is costly to get removed. Expect paid parking at busy attractions, and expect parking in rural towns to fill up early during summer.

Taxi and Rideshare

FreeNow (www.freenow.com), **Bolt** (www.bolt.eu), and **Uber** (www.uber.com) all operate in Ireland, with FreeNow the most used. Traditional taxis are plentiful and safe, with regulated meters, and they can be hailed on the street or found at taxi ranks. In country areas, you'll often need to call local cab companies in advance; your lodging host, pub, or restaurant can help arrange this. All taxis must accept card payments, though many try to tell visitors otherwise. This is illegal, and you are well within your rights to insist that they take card payments.

Cycling

Ireland is becoming more friendly to cyclists, but our roads are not very bike-friendly. Cities are the best prepared, but many bike lanes are part of bus lanes, which can be quite intimidating. Cycling is best suited to remote, quiet areas with less traffic on the roads.

Tours

Guided tours solve many transport headaches. **Paddywagon** (www.paddywagontours.com) offers single-day and multiple-day trips across the country, but the day trips from Dublin to the west coast have been criticized lately by tourism groups, who would prefer visitors to spend time in the west rather than making brief visits. For deeper experiences, try a bespoke tour company like **Spud** (www.spudxp.com), which focuses on culturally rich trips away from the usual hot spots.

Visas and Officialdom

PASSPORTS AND VISAS

Entry requirements to Ireland vary depending on your nationality. Citizens of the European Union, the United Kingdom, the United States, Canada, Australia, and New Zealand only need a valid passport for stays up to 90 days, and no visa is required. Your passport should be valid for at least six months beyond your planned departure date.

Visitors from other countries should check with the **Irish Naturalisation and Immigration Service** (www.irishimmigration.ie) well in advance, as some nationalities must apply for a visa before travel. While Ireland is part of the European Union, it's not in the Schengen Area, so Schengen visas don't apply.

BORDER CROSSINGS

Traveling between Ireland and Northern Ireland, which is part of the UK, is seamless, with no border checks thanks to the Common Travel Area agreement. You might notice the road signs changing from kilometers to miles and the currency switches to pounds, but there are no physical border posts.

However, travelers from Ireland to Northern Ireland need an **Electronic Travel Authorisation (ETA)** unless they are British or Irish citizens. The ETA, which costs £16, is required for entry into Northern Ireland and is valid for multiple journeys over a two-year period. Find out more at www.homeoffice.gov.uk.

If you're renting a car, check with your rental company about cross-border policies, as some have restrictions. When flying into Northern Ireland first, you'll clear UK immigration, but there are no further checks when continuing to Ireland by land.

CUSTOMS

Ireland's customs allowances follow standard EU regulations, where visitors arriving from non-EU countries can bring in 200 cigarettes, 1 liter of spirits or 2 liters of wine, and other goods up to €430 in value without paying duty. There are strict prohibitions on bringing meat, dairy, or plants from outside the European Union. Ireland has particularly rigorous checks on illegal drugs, with severe penalties that include lengthy prison sentences.

For Northern Ireland, different rules apply. Travelers from EU countries to Northern Ireland do not need to declare or pay tax or duty on goods for personal use. For those arriving from outside the European Union, allowances include 200 cigarettes, 1 liter of spirits, 4 liters of still wine, and other goods worth up to £390.

FOREIGN EMBASSIES AND CONSULATES IN IRELAND

Dublin is home to embassies from over 50 countries, with many more nations represented through consulates. The **US Embassy** (www.ie.usembassy.gov) is one of the largest, offering full services to US citizens. Most EU countries maintain embassies in Dublin, while some smaller nations share representation. For countries without local representation, visitors may need to contact embassies in London or other European capitals. Take note of your embassy's contact information before traveling in case of emergencies.

Food and Accommodations

FOOD AND DRINK

Ireland's food scene has become impressive in recent years, distancing itself from stereotypes of potatoes and stew. Today you'll find Michelin-starred restaurants and international street-food markets showcasing Ireland's incredible local produce. The seafood is particularly outstanding—think plump oysters, sweet crab, and succulent scallops. Traditional dishes have been reinvented with modern flair, often billed as modern Irish or contemporary Irish cuisine, where chefs use seasonal local ingredients to elevate well-known dishes.

Irish Delicacies

There are a number of Irish delicacies, and you're sure to come across a few. Start your day with a proper Irish breakfast of bacon and eggs along with black or white pudding (made with blood and grains), grilled tomatoes, and potato bread. Or have a breakfast sandwich made with blaa, a type of bread. For lunch, you can't beat vegetable soup with hearty brown soda bread in a pub.

In Dublin, you have to try coddle, a warming sausage and potato stew that's been feeding Dubliners for generations. There are modern additions, like chicken fillet rolls, served in most convenience shops, and spice bags are the top tier on the Irish takeaway scene.

Ireland's Craft Beer Scene

While Guinness is still undoubtedly the biggest name in Irish beer, Ireland's craft beer revolution has brought exciting new brewers to the pub scene. Small breweries like **Tom Crean Brewery** (www.tomcreanbrewerykenmare.ie) in Kenmare and **Walled City Brewery** (www.walledcitybrewery.com) are creating innovative ales and lagers that go far beyond the standard stout. Look for citrusy IPAs, rich porters, and even barrel-aged specialties in pubs.

Many breweries offer tours and tastings—the Guinness Storehouse in Dublin is the most famous, but smaller operations like the **Treaty City Brewery** (www.treatycitybrewery.ie) in Limerick give a more intimate experience.

Vegetarian and Vegan Options

Vegetarians and vegans will find Ireland surprisingly accommodating. Nearly every restaurant offers solid meat-free options, and dedicated vegan spots are popping up everywhere. Foodie hubs like Dublin, Galway, Belfast, and Kenmare have plenty of options. It's not uncommon to find that traditional pubs in rural areas have a vegetarian option on the menu.

Tipping

Tipping is not expected but is appreciated, with most people choosing to tip 10 percent on top of the bill in restaurants after good service. We don't tip in bars or pubs, and you pay for your drinks each time you get them. Tipping culture is creeping in, but don't feel bad whatsoever for choosing the "no tip" option on the machine, as you're not expected to tip for coffee, casual meals, or taxis.

ACCOMMODATIONS

Expect to find a whole host of places to stay, from historic castles to cozy countryside bed-and-breakfasts, but don't expect any stay to be cheap, as Ireland has some of the most expensive room rates in Europe. Rates soar when there's a big-name act playing a concert in one of the cities. Many of the best properties showcase heritage and design, letting you experience part of Ireland's story. The quality has improved dramatically in recent years, with even the cheapest options offering acceptable facilities and service.

Hostels

Ireland's hostel scene has evolved beyond basic backpacker digs. Modern hostels like **Generator Dublin** (www.generatorhostels.com) offer stylish design and hotel-quality amenities at budget prices. Independent hostels in smaller towns often have more character, with features like traditional music sessions or homemade breakfasts. Many now provide private rooms alongside dorms, perfect for travelers wanting a social atmosphere without shared sleeping quarters. In summer, book well ahead, as demand often outstrips supply.

Bed-and-Breakfasts

Family-run guesthouses and bed-and-breakfasts dot almost every town and village, offering comfortable rooms and generous breakfast spreads in a homey environment. Standards vary from simple homes to luxurious country houses. Look for the Fáilte Ireland approval symbol for quality assurance; The **Irish Tourist Board** (www.ireland.com) has a comprehensive listing. Remember that most bed-and-breakfasts have limited reception hours, so let them know if you'll be arriving late.

Hotels

Irish hotels can be anything from historic city-center landmarks to sleek modern escapes. Dublin's **Shelbourne Hotel** (www.theshelbourne.com) has hosted presidents and celebrities since 1824, while newer properties like **Wren Urban Nest** (www.wrenhotel.ie) cater to eco-conscious travelers. Outside the cities, country house hotels have golf, spa treatments, and fine dining in stunning settings. Many historic buildings like lighthouses and manor houses have been converted into unique accommodations. Room rates fluctuate dramatically by season, with winter discounts, except at Christmas and the New Year's, often making luxury properties more affordable.

Camping and Glamping

Ireland's campgrounds are often in spectacular settings and come at budget prices, but you roll the dice with the weather. Official campsites like those run by **Camping Ireland** (www.campingireland.ie) offer good facilities, while dispersed camping is permitted in many remote areas, but it's essential to be considerate and camp out of view of people. If the landowner asks you to move on, do it.

Glamping options have exploded in popularity, with everything from geodesic domes to chic tiny homes available. Places like **Oaklane Glamping** (www.oaklaneglamping.com) in County Kerry combine style with stunning views.

Castle Stays

Fulfil your fairy-tale fantasies by sleeping in an authentic Irish castle. Properties like **Lough Eske Castle Hotel** (www.lougheskecastlehotel.com) in County Donegal offer luxury stays in historic settings, complete with afternoon tea. More affordable options include castle self-catering apartments or bed-and-breakfasts in converted tower houses.

Practical Details

HEALTH AND SAFETY

Ireland is generally a safe and healthy destination for travelers, with excellent medical facilities and low crime rates. The health care system meets high European standards, though visitors should still take basic precautions. Emergency services can be reached by dialing 112 or 999, with operators trained to handle everything from injuries to coastal emergencies.

Pharmacies are widely available and can provide advice for nonemergency issues. For more serious issues, public hospitals provide free emergency treatment to EU citizens with an EHIC (European Health Insurance Card), while others may need travel insurance coverage. Road safety requires special attention, as narrow country lanes can be hazardous for unfamiliar drivers. Petty theft does occur in tourist areas, so keep valuables secure, especially in crowded places like Dublin's Temple Bar.

MONEY

Currency and Exchange Rages

Ireland uses the euro (€) as its currency, while Northern Ireland uses the UK pound sterling (£). Euro notes come in denominations of 5, 10, 20, 50, 100, 200, and 500, though 200 and 500 notes are rarely seen. Coins range from 1 cent to 2 euros, with the distinctive Irish harp design on one side. Exchange rates fluctuate daily, but at time of writing €1 equals about US$1.10 or £0.85. ATMs, called cash machines or cashpoints, are widely available, even in small towns, and generally offer the best exchange rates.

Credit cards are accepted almost everywhere, though not every business accepts American Express. Some rural businesses may only take cash. Contactless payments up to €50 are now standard across the country. When exchanging money, avoid airport kiosks, which typically have poor rates; banks and post offices offer better deals.

Taxes

Ireland's VAT (value-added tax) rate stands at 23 percent for most goods and services, though reduced rates apply to certain items. Visitors from outside the EU can claim VAT refunds on purchases over €75 when exported from the country. Look for "Tax Free Shopping" stickers in stores and ask for the proper forms. Hotel accommodations include a 13.5 percent tourism VAT rate. Restaurant meals and alcohol carry the standard 23 percent rate. The price you see posted is the price you pay, as all taxes are included.

OPENING HOURS

Irish business hours might surprise visitors used to 24-7 services or the limited hours found in places like Spain and Italy. Most shops are open 9am-6pm Monday-Saturday, with shorter Sunday hours. Banks typically operate 10am-4pm Monday-Friday only. Pubs serve alcohol until 11:30pm Sunday-Thursday and until 12:30am Friday-Saturday, although many have licenses to serve later. Outside the cities, restaurants often stop serving food by 9:30pm.

Public Holidays

Ireland celebrates 10 annual public holidays, called bank holidays, when most businesses close. Major ones include St. Patrick's Day (Mar. 17) and Christmas (Dec. 25), which shuts down the country for several days. Other holidays like Bloomsday (June 16) in Dublin or Galway's Oyster Festival create great atmospheres but can lead to scarce hotel rooms. On Good Friday (Mar. or Apr.), pubs traditionally remain closed, though you can drink at the resident's bar in your hotel on that day. If a holiday falls on a weekend, the following Monday becomes the day off. Public transport runs reduced schedules on holidays, so plan accordingly.

LAUNDRY

Finding laundry services in Ireland is straightforward in cities but harder in rural areas. Most hotels offer expensive wash-and-fold services, while budget travelers can use self-service launderettes. Many bed-and-breakfasts and hostels have washing machines for guest use. A recent addition to Ireland has been self-service washing machines and dryers in the car parks of large grocery stores like Tesco.

TOILETS

Public toilet facilities in Ireland range from challenging to nonexistent, forcing you to nip into a coffee shop or pub, where you'll be expected to buy something in return. Many tourist sites have good accessible toilets, but not all are well maintained and lack supplies.

COMMUNICATIONS

Phones and Cell Phones

Expect excellent mobile phone coverage across most of the country, with some dead spots in very remote areas. The main providers are **Vodafone** (www.vodafone.ie), **Three** (www.three.ie), and **Eir** (www.eir.ie), all offering prepaid SIM cards that can be purchased at airports or in town centers. For short visits, consider an international plan from your home provider, while longer stays may warrant a local pay-as-you-go SIM. Public pay phones are mostly a thing of the past, but there's a chance that you'll spot one in a transport hub. When dialing within Ireland from your cell phone, use the +353 prefix and drop the first 0, even for local calls.

Internet Access

Wi-Fi is widely available across Ireland, with most hotels, cafés, and public spaces offering free connections. Internet speeds are generally good across the island. For constant connectivity, pick up a local SIM card on a pay-as-you-go basis, where €20 will get you enough data for a visit—often 40 GB or unlimited data. Internet cafés are mostly a thing of the past, but some print shops and tourist centers still offer paid computer access.

Media

Catch up on the latest news during your visit with quality newspapers like the ***Irish Independent*** (www.independent.ie) and independent radio stations covering everything from traditional music to current affairs. **RTÉ** (www.rte.ie) operates national television and radio services, while Virgin Media and Sky provide additional channels. International newspapers and magazines are widely available in cities, though selection may be limited in smaller towns. Irish podcasts have gained global popularity in recent years, particularly those discussing history, culture, and true crime.

Shipping and Postal Services

An Post (www.anpost.com) operates the postal service in Ireland, while **Royal Mail** (www.royalmail.com) manages the service in Northern Ireland, with generally reliable mail delivery island-wide. Standard postcards and letters to Europe typically take 3-5 days, while international mail may require a week or more. For important documents or packages, there's the option of registered post or private couriers like **DHL** (www.dhl.ie) or **UPS** (www.ups.com). Many shops offer international shipping for purchases, though VAT and customs fees may apply depending on the destination. Some hotels will hold packages for arriving guests if arranged in advance.

MAPS AND VISITOR INFORMATION

Get to where you want to go with the help of the many excellent visitor information services across the country. **Fáilte Ireland** (www.ireland.com) runs tourist offices nationwide, staffed by knowledgeable locals who are happy to provide personalized advice.

Free maps and brochures are widely available, though more detailed **Ordnance Survey** (https://store.osi.ie) maps are worth purchasing for serious hikers. Many towns have self-guided walking-tour maps available at tourist offices or as signage on the street.

Digital options include the excellent Discover Ireland app and Google Maps, which provides reliable directions for most of the country, while the Irish-owned **Hiiker** (www.hiiker.app) is a good option for phone navigation on the trails.

WEIGHTS, MEASURES, AND TIME

The metric system is used in Ireland, with distances in kilometers, weights in grams and kilograms, and temperatures in Celsius. However, you'll still encounter some people using "old money" imperial measurements, particularly in pubs, where beer is served in pints and people talk about weight in stones and height in feet. When you cross the border to the north, you'll see road signs in miles per hour. Clothing follows UK sizes, though many stores also display EU and US equivalents.

Ireland is in the western European time zone (UTC+0) and observes daylight saving late March-late October. The Irish weekend traditionally runs from Friday evening to Sunday night, with many businesses closed or operating with reduced hours on Sunday.

ELECTRICITY

Ireland uses Type G electrical outlets, with three rectangular pins, the same as in the UK, with 230V at 50Hz. Visitors from outside the UK and Ireland will need a plug adapter and possibly a voltage adapter.

Most hotels provide blow-dryers, and some offer universal outlets, but it's wise to bring your own adapters. Power surges are rare but sensitive electronics may benefit from surge protection. Modern chargers for phones and laptops handle 100-240V automatically (check the small print on the device), meaning only the physical plug adapter is needed. Camping sites typically provide electrical hookups compatible with standard European camping plugs.

Traveler Advice

CONDUCT AND CUSTOMS

The Irish are famously welcoming, but understanding local etiquette helps. Pubs are social hubs where striking up conversations with strangers is normal, and so is them offering to buy you a drink. When you're out in a group in a pub, drinks are bought in rounds, where one person goes and orders and pays for a drink for everyone in the group. If you're in a round, don't leave before you've bought a round, and don't ask for fancy cocktails when everyone else is having cheaper drinks. When ordering at the bar, order Guinness first, then the other drinks, as it takes longer to pour.

When visiting someone's home, it's polite to bring a small gift like chocolates or wine, and if you're offered a cup of tea or coffee, accept it.

People who lived through the Troubles are still around, so keep that in mind when asking about certain events or groups.

SIGHTSEEING PASSES AND DISCOUNTS

Ireland isn't an inexpensive country, but some money-saving passes can cut costs for travelers. The **Heritage Ireland Card** (www.heritageireland.ie; €40) gets you unlimited access to all Office of Public Works sites for one year. Students should always carry **ISIC cards** (www.isic.org) for discounts, while families can save with group tickets at many attractions. Always check if your hotel offers guest discount cards for local attractions.

ACCESS FOR TRAVELERS WITH DISABILITIES

Ireland is improving accessibility, but challenges remain, particularly outside the main cities. Modern hotels and attractions meet good standards, but historic sites and towns often have limited access due to preservation laws. Dublin's public transport is mostly accessible with ramp access, though some rural buses don't have this feature. Many coastal paths and nature areas have accessible routes, particularly recently built greenways that have accessible surfaces.

TRAVELING WITH CHILDREN

Traveling with kids is manageable, with some hotels offering free stays for kids under age 12. Restaurants commonly provide children's menus and high chairs, and major attractions sell family tickets. The narrow footpaths in cities and access to historic sites can be challenging with a stroller.

WOMEN TRAVELING ALONE

Ireland is generally safe for solo female travelers, with low, but not nonexistent, violent crime rates. Normal precautions apply in cities at night: Stick to well-lit areas and licensed taxis, and don't leave your drink unattended. Rural Ireland is very safe, though remote areas may lack public transport options. Many hostels offer female-only dorms.

LGBTQ+ TRAVELERS

Given the grip the Catholic Church had on the country, you might be surprised to hear that Ireland is LGBTQ-friendly and marriage equality was legalized by a public vote in 2015. Dublin's **LGBTQ+ Pride festival** (www.dublinpride.ie) draws huge crowds each June. Most urban areas are openly welcoming, though some rural communities remain conservative, but any danger or risk is small. Many hotels proudly display their inclusivity, and gay bars thrive in Dublin, Cork, and Galway.

SENIOR TRAVELERS

There are some great deals and discounts to be had if you're a senior traveler. Many attractions and transport services offer senior discounts or free access to people over age 60. You might have to ask, as these aren't always advertised. Historic houses and gardens often have seating areas and gentle walking routes. Pharmacies provide great advice for minor ailments, and EU health cards cover emergency care for European seniors.

TRAVELERS OF COLOR

Thanks to more diversity in recent decades, travelers of color will generally feel welcome. Racist incidents are rare but do occur, and support organizations like the **Irish Network Against Racism** (www.inar.ie) can advise if needed. There is a small anti-immigrant movement in Ireland, but by and large, Irish people are welcoming regardless of where you come from—even if it's England.

Resources

Glossary

This compilation includes slang and common cultural and historical references in both Irish and English.

Anglo-Irish Treaty: the 1921 agreement that divided Ireland into British-controlled Northern Ireland and the independent republic

Anglo-Irish: a land-owning Protestant family of English descent, or any descendants thereof

***ard rí* (ard REE):** high king

bank holiday: an official three-day weekend when banks close and everyone's off work on Monday; expect crowds at pubs, restaurants, and accommodations

bap: a lunch roll, like a seedless hamburger bun

Black and Tans: a brutal and violent British auxiliary force sent to Ireland in 1920-1921 to suppress rebels, especially the IRA

black/white pudding: sausage made with dried pigs' blood

Blue Flag: an "eco-label" awarded by an independent group, the Foundation for Environmental Education, that indicates the beach in question is very clean and safe

bodhrán (boh-RAWN): a handheld drum used in traditional Irish music

bog: wet terrain with thick, spongy layers of moss and other plant matter; also slang for toilet

bothy: a simple shelter, sometimes found in remote areas

bridleway: path for walkers, cyclists, and horseback riders

camogie: the women's version of hurling

caravan: a trailer or mobile home

***céad míle fáilte* (kayd MEE-leh FAWL-cheh):** traditional greeting, meaning "a hundred thousand welcomes"

ceilidh (KAY-lee): a session of traditional dance and music

champ: mashed potatoes and spring onions

chemist: pharmacist

chipper: a fish-and-chips shop

cider: alcoholic apple cider

coach: long-distance charter bus, usually for large tourist groups

coddle: a traditional Dublin stew made with sausage, bacon, and potatoes

concession: discounted admission

Connaught: one of the four Irish provinces, encompassing counties Galway, Mayo, Sligo, Roscommon, and Leitrim

***craic* (crack):** a fun time, good music, and conversation; sometimes used in greeting, as in "What's the craic?"

***culchie* (CULL-chee):** an urbanite's derogatory term for a person from the country; a country bumpkin

curragh: a rowboat covered with tarred canvas, traditionally used for fishing

DART: Dublin Area Rapid Transit, the commuter train line running from Howth through Dublin south to Bray in County Wicklow

drink: alcohol (often called "the drink")

dual carriageway: a divided four-lane highway with two lanes in each direction

Dubs: short for Dubliners

Éire (air): the Irish name for the Republic of Ireland

***eolas* (OH-lahs):** information

***feis* (fesh):** a gathering

***feis ceoil* (fesh kyohl):** a festival of music

Fenians: originated as a nickname for members of the Irish Republican Brotherhood (IRB), a militant nationalist group founded in 1858; predecessors of the IRA, now a derogatory term for Catholics

***fir* (fihr):** men; used on toilet doors (singular *fear*)

freephone number: toll-free telephone number

GAA: Gaelic Athletic Association, the organization founded in 1884 to promote the native pastimes of hurling, Gaelic football, and other sports

Gaeltacht (GALE-tahkt or GWALE-tahkt): a region where Irish is the primary language spoken (plural Gaeltachtaí)

gangway: aisle

***garda, gardaí* (GAR-da, gar-DEE):** the Irish police, the full name being An Garda Síochána, "Guardian of the Peace"

***geansaí* (gaan-zee):** sweater

homely: cozy, homey, homelike; never means "ugly"

hooker: a traditional Galway sailing ship, from the Irish *húicéir*

hurling: a traditional Irish sport, one of the fastest games in the world; a cross between hockey, lacrosse, and soccer

IHH: Independent Holiday Hostels of Ireland; a hostel's membership in this organization is indicative of high standards in safety, cleanliness, and hospitality

interval: intermission

IRA: the Irish Republican Army, the largest republican paramilitary group, founded in 1919 with the aim of a reunited Ireland, achieved by force if necessary

Irish mammy: a strong, caring, and often humorously overprotective mother

jacks: toilet

jars: alcoholic drinks

jumper: sweater

kerb: another spelling of *curb*

***leabharlann* (lau-er-lahn):** library

Leinster: one of the four Irish provinces, encompassing 12 southeastern counties from Louth to Kilkenny and Wexford

loo: toilet

lough (lock): a lake or narrow sea inlet

loyalist: usually a Protestant who supports Northern Ireland's continued existence as part of Great Britain; another word for unionist

Luas: the light-rail system through suburban and downtown Dublin

marching season: between Easter and mid-June, when loyalist marches in Northern Ireland celebrate the victory of William of Orange at the Battle of the Boyne in 1690

minced meat: hamburger

***mná* (meh-naw):** women; used on toilet door (singular *bean*)

mobile (MOH-bile): cell phone

MP: member of Parliament (British)

Munster: one of the four Irish provinces, encompassing counties Clare, Limerick, Kerry, Cork, Tipperary, and Waterford

***naomh* (nave):** saint

nationalism: the belief that Ireland should be reunited; its proponents are called nationalists

off-license: liquor store

Oireachtas: the bicameral parliament of the Irish Republic, consisting of the Dáil (lower house) and the Seanad Éireann (upper house or senate)

OPW: Office of Public Works, the republic's governmental agency for town planning as well as conservation and restoration efforts

Orange Order: the largest Protestant fraternal order in Northern Ireland, established in 1795

OS: Ordnance Survey, Britain's national mapping agency; Ordnance Survey Ireland (OSI) issues detailed region maps for all Ireland

partition of Ireland: the division of Ireland into Northern Ireland and the Irish Republic in 1921

pay-and-display parking: the paid hourly parking system in most Irish towns, whereby motorists are required to purchase a ticket to display in their windscreens

peat: partially carbonized plant matter, found in bogs, which has traditionally been dried and used for fuel

petrol: gasoline

plaster: adhesive bandage

poitín (putch-een): illegal whiskey, potent enough to kill in large quantities, usually brewed by dispossessed Irish farmers to make extra money

Prod: a derogatory word for Northern Irish Protestant

quay (key): a street along a river or harbor

queue (cue): a line at the bank, supermarket, etc.

quid: slang for pounds; now refers to euros

rashers: bacon

republicanism: the belief in a reunited Ireland

return ticket: a round-trip fare

roundabout: traffic circle

RTÉ: Ireland's broadcast network, the acronym for Radio Telefís Éireann

rubber: eraser

SDLP: Social Democratic and Labour Party, the largest nationalist political party in the Northern Ireland assembly

***sean nós* (shan-NOS):** a style of traditional song with three primary characteristics: the songs are unaccompanied, performed solo, and always sung in the Irish language; literally, "in the old way"

***séipéal* (SHAY-pail):** church

***seisún*:** a traditional music session

***síbín* (shuh-BEAN):** an illicit tavern or speakeasy; anglicized as *shebeen*

single ticket: a one-way fare

Sinn Féin: a republican political party whose longstanding goal is a reunited Ireland

slagging (off): making fun of someone

***sláinte* (SLAWN-cha):** a common Irish toast meaning "health"

***slí* (shlee):** literally "way," a hiking trail

slieve (sleeve): a mountain, from the Irish *sliabh*

snug: a booth tucked away in a pub, meant for a bit of privacy

strand: beach

takeaway: takeout food

taking the piss: making fun of someone

Tánaiste (TAHN-iss-teh): deputy prime minister of the Irish Republic

Taoiseach (TEE-shock): prime minister of the Republic of Ireland; literally, a chieftain

***teach, tí, tigh* (tchock, tchee):** house; often used as in a public house, meaning a pub

Teachta Dála (TCHOCK-tah DOLL-ah): a member of the Irish parliament, abbreviated TD

top up: to fill up a drink, or to add credit to your mobile phone account

trad: short for traditional music

traveller: the politically correct term for one of a group of nomadic Irish people who travel in caravans and have traditional values and their own unique culture; the full term is *member of the travelling community*

Tricolour: the green, white, and orange Irish flag symbolizing peace between the (green) Catholic Irish and the (orange) Protestant Irish

turf: another word for peat

***uisce* (ISH-keh):** water

***uisce beatha* (ISH-keh BAH-hah):** whiskey; literally, "water of life"

Ulster: one of the four Irish provinces, encompassing the six counties of Northern Ireland (Antrim, Armagh, Derry, Down, Fermanagh, and Tyrone) along with three counties in the republic (Cavan, Monaghan, and Donegal)

unionist: usually a Protestant who supports Northern Ireland's continued existence as part of Great Britain; synonym for loyalist

UVF: Ulster Volunteer Force, a unionist paramilitary group established in 1966

Wellingtons: knee-high rubber boots, also known as wellies

PLACE-NAMES

Irish words that form place-names in English:

***ard*:** high

***ath* (awth):** fort

***baile* (BAL-ee or BALL-yuh):** village; town

***beag* (beg):** small

***bothár* (BOH-hir):** road

***caislean* (CASH-lin):** castle

***carraig* (KAR-rig):** rock

***cath* (kah):** battle

***ceann* (kyown):** headland

***cill* (kill):** church

***coill* (kwill):** wood; forest

***droichead* (drick-ed):** bridge
***dún* (doon):** fort
***gort*:** field
***inis* (inish):** island; river meadow
***knock* (nok):** hill
***lough* (lock):** lake
***mór* (more):** big
***ráth* (raw):** ringfort, enclosure
***slí* (shlee):** path, way
***teach* (tchock):** house

Suggested Reading

CLASSIC NOVELS

Joyce, James. *Ulysses*. Shakespeare and Company, 1922. This celebrated masterpiece follows Leopold Bloom through Dublin on June 16, 1904, paralleling Homer's *Odyssey*. It's a challenging but rewarding read that revolutionized the novel form with its stream-of-consciousness style and intricate structure.

Lewis, C. S. *The Lion, the Witch and the Wardrobe*. Geoffrey Bles, 1950. This beloved fantasy novel transports four siblings to the magical world of Narnia, where they join forces with the lion Aslan to defeat the evil White Witch. It's a timeless tale of good versus evil that has been loved by generations thanks to its imaginative storytelling.

Stoker, Bram. *Dracula*. Archibald Constable and Company, 1897. This iconic horror novel follows Count Dracula's attempt to move from Transylvania to England and the battle between the vampire and a group led by Professor Abraham Van Helsing.

Swift, Jonathan. *Gulliver's Travels*. Benjamin Motte, 1726. This satirical novel follows Lemuel Gulliver on four extraordinary voyages, including his encounters with the tiny Lilliputians and the noble Houyhnhnms. It's a biting critique of human nature and society, cleverly disguised as a fantastical adventure story.

Wilde, Oscar. *The Picture of Dorian Gray*. Ward, Lock and Company, 1891. This Gothic and philosophical novel tells the story of a young man who sells his soul for eternal youth while his portrait ages instead. It's a fascinating exploration of beauty, morality, and the dangers of hedonism.

MODERN FAVORITES

Blindboy Boatclub. *The Gospel According to Blindboy*. Gill Books, 2017. This collection of satirical short stories critiques contemporary Irish society with humor and absurdity while delving into themes like masculinity and mental health. It's a bold and inventive work that challenges societal norms.

Doyle, Roddy. *The Van*. Secker & Warburg, 1991. Set during Ireland's 1990 World Cup euphoria, this novel follows two unemployed friends who start a fish-and-chips van business, testing their friendship along the way. It's a humorous yet touching exploration of male camaraderie and midlife struggles.

Feeney, Elaine. *How to Build a Boat*. Harvill Secker, 2023. This heartwarming novel follows Jamie, a neurodivergent teenager building a traditional Irish boat to connect with his late mother, alongside his teachers Tess and Tadhg. It's a beautifully crafted story about grief, community, and the healing power of creativity.

McCourt, Frank. *Angela's Ashes*. Scribner, 1996. This memoir recounts McCourt's impoverished childhood in Limerick, marked by his father's alcoholism and his family's resilience. It's a poignant, darkly humorous story of survival and hope, offering an unforgettable portrait of Irish life.

Rooney, Sally. *Normal People*. Faber & Faber, 2018. This novel explores the complex relationship between Connell and Marianne as they navigate love, class differences, and personal growth from their small Irish town to Trinity College. It's a tender and insightful portrayal of modern relationships and emotional intimacy.

Suggested Watching

TV SHOWS

Comedy

Bad Sisters: Based in Dublin, this black comedy series revolves around five sisters entangled in a life insurance investigation following the death of one sister's abusive husband.

Derry Girls: Set in Derry during the 1990s, this comedy explores the lives of five teenagers navigating adolescence amidst the backdrop of the Troubles.

Father Ted: A cult classic set on the fictional Craggy Island off Ireland's west coast, this 1990s sitcom follows the misadventures of three Catholic priests and their housekeeper. It was way ahead of its time.

The Hardy Bucks: Filmed in Mayo, this comedy series depicts the lives of four friends living in the fictional hamlet of Castletown, often seeking pints, women, and the craic.

The Young Offenders: Showcasing Cork City, this series follows the adventures of two delinquent teenagers and their mother as they navigate life and trouble.

Drama

The Fall: Filmed and set in Belfast, Northern Ireland, this psychological thriller follows DSI Stella Gibson as she hunts for a serial killer targeting young women in the city.

Kin: Set in Dublin, this crime drama revolves around the fictional Kinsella family embroiled in a gangland war against a powerful drug cartel.

Love/Hate: Set in Dublin's criminal underworld, this gritty crime drama follows the lives of gangsters and drug dealers, centering on Darren Treacy as he gets pulled back into a life of crime.

Normal People: Based in County Sligo and Dublin, this series explores the complex relationship between Marianne and Connell as they navigate adolescence and young adulthood.

Say Nothing: Based on true events, this historical drama explores the Troubles in Northern Ireland, focusing on the disappearance of Jean McConville and the involvement of IRA members in the conflict.

MOVIES

Comedy

The Commitments: Based in Dublin, this musical comedy follows Jimmy Rabbitte as he forms a soul band with a group of misfits from the city's northside, leading to a journey of fame, friendship, and musical discovery.

The Guard: Set in the Connemara region of Galway, this dark comedy follows Sergeant Gerry Boyle, a quirky and unconventional Garda officer, as he teams up with an FBI agent to take down a group of drug smugglers.

In Bruges: Although not an Irish film per se, it features Irish actors and is often associated with Irish cinema. The story follows two hitmen hiding in Bruges, Belgium, after a botched job, exploring themes of guilt and redemption.

Intermission: Set in Dublin, this film explores the interconnected lives of various characters, including petty criminals and a detective, as they navigate love, crime, and redemption in a chaotic urban landscape.

The Van: Located in the fictional Dublin suburb of Barrytown, this comedy tells the story of Bimbo, a baker who loses his job and starts a successful burger van with his friend Larry, but their partnership leads to tension and conflict.

Drama

The Butcher Boy: Set in a small Irish town in the 1960s, this dark comedy-drama follows Francie Brady, a troubled boy whose disturbing behavior escalates as he loses touch with reality.

The Crying Game: This film explores complex themes against the backdrop of the Troubles, following an IRA member who becomes involved with his captive's lover, leading to unexpected revelations.

The General: This film tells the story of Martin Cahill, a notorious Dublin thief known as the General, who orchestrated daring heists and attracted attention from the police and the IRA. The movie explores his rise and fall in Dublin's underworld.

Hunger: Depicting the 1981 Irish hunger strike, this intense drama focuses on Bobby Sands and the events in the Maze Prison, highlighting the conflict between IRA prisoners and British authorities.

In the Name of the Father: Based on a true story, this drama depicts the wrongful conviction of the Guildford Four for an IRA bombing, focusing on Gerry Conlon's fight to clear his name and that of his father.

The Wind That Shakes the Barley: Set in County Cork during the Irish War of Independence and Civil War, this film follows two brothers who join the IRA but end up on opposing sides of the conflict.

COMEDIANS

Peter McGann: McGann gained popularity during the pandemic with his humorous social media videos (Instagram @peterjmcgann) and has since performed successful stand-up tours and written for TV series.

Joanne McNally: A stand-up comedian and writer, McNally cohosts the *My Therapist Ghosted Me* podcast and has appeared in various Irish TV shows.

Dylan Moran: Renowned for his observational comedy and starring in *Black Books,* Moran is a versatile comedian and actor.

Pat Shortt: Famous for his stand up shows and work in D'Unbelieveables and *Killinaskully,* Shortt is a writer, producer, and performer known for his comedic roles.

Tommy Tiernan: Known for his energetic stand-up comedy and hosting The Tommy Tiernan Show, he also played Gerry in *Derry Girls.*

Suggested Listening

TRADITIONAL IRISH SONGS

"The Fields of Athenry": This iconic Irish folk ballad, written by Pete St. John, tells the story of a man from Athenry who is deported to Australia for stealing food during the Great Famine. It has become a powerful anthem for Irish sports supporters.

"Lisdoonvarna": Written by Christy Moore, this upbeat song celebrates the town's famous matchmaking festival, capturing the essence of Irish culture and romance.

"The Old Triangle": Associated with Brendan Behan, this song reflects life in Mountjoy Prison, Dublin, with themes of love and hardship.

"On Raglan Road": Based on a poem by Patrick Kavanagh, this song recounts a past love affair on Raglan Road in Dublin, exploring themes of heartache and longing.

"Theme from Harry's Game": Clannad's haunting song, written for a TV series about the Troubles, features Irish-language lyrics and ancient mouth music, conveying the futility of violence.

BEST IRISH ALBUMS

The Cranberries, *No Need to Argue* (1994): Their most popular and consistent album, featuring the iconic hit "Zombie" and other beloved tracks in their signature alternative rock style.

The Dubliners, *A Drop of the Hard Stuff* (1967): Their breakthrough album, reaching number 1 in Ireland and number 5 in the UK, featuring their iconic hit "Seven Drunken Nights."

Fontaines D.C., *Dogrel* (2019): Their debut album, blending post-punk with indie rock, marked by catchy, head-bopping tunes and socially conscious lyrics reflecting Dublin's working-class life.

Kneecap, *Fine Art* (2024): The Irish hip-hop trio's second studio album, featuring guest appearances and debuting at number 2 on the Irish albums chart, showcasing their unique blend of Irish language and hip-hop.

Lankum, *The Livelong Day* (2019): A haunting and innovative album that reimagines traditional Irish folk music with experimental elements.

Christy Moore, *Ride On* (1984): A classic album in Moore's folk career, featuring socially conscious songs that highlight his storytelling ability and musical depth.

Van Morrison, *Astral Weeks* (1968): A timeless masterpiece combining folk, jazz, and soul, showing off Morrison's poetic lyricism and unique vocal style.

My Bloody Valentine, *Loveless* (1991): A groundbreaking shoegaze masterpiece, featuring innovative guitar techniques and ethereal soundscapes.

Sinead O'Connor, *I Do Not Want What I Haven't Got* (1990): Her critically acclaimed second album, featuring the unforgettable hit "Nothing Compares 2 U," which catapulted her to international fame.

The Pogues, *If I Should Fall from Grace with God* (1988): Their magnum opus, blending Celtic folk with punk energy and featuring their Christmas hit "Fairytale of New York."

Thin Lizzy, *Jailbreak* (1976): Their breakthrough album featuring the famous "The Boys Are Back in Town" and Phil Lynott's exceptional songwriting in their signature hard rock style.

Whipping Boy, *Heartworm* (1995): A cult classic of Irish alternative rock, known for its raw emotion and powerful songwriting.

BEST IRISH PODCASTS

The Blindboy Podcast: Hosted by Blindboy Boatclub, this podcast explores a wide range of topics including arts, society, culture, and mental health through engaging monologues and interviews.

My Therapist Ghosted Me: Cohosted by Joanne McNally and Vogue Williams, this podcast offers candid advice and humor, born from the ideas that their friendship can replace therapy.

Tea with Me: Hosted by comedian Shane Todd, this podcast features weekly chats with various guests, blending humor and local culture.

Three Castles Burning: A social history podcast focused on Dublin, sharing lesser-known stories of the city's past.

Young Hot Guys: A comedy podcast featuring Shane Daniel Byrne, Tony Cantwell, and Killian Sundermann, known for their funny discussions on a variety of daily topics.

Internet Resources

SIGHTSEEING AND TOURIST INFORMATION

www.discoverireland.ie
Discover Ireland: Official tourism site with information on attractions, itineraries, and events.

www.heritageireland.ie
Heritage Ireland: Details on Ireland's historic sites, castles, and monuments.

www.discovernorthernireland.com
Discover Northern Ireland: Information on sights and attractions in Northern Ireland.

ACTIVITIES AND RECREATION

www.coillte.ie/our-forests/recreation-map
Coillte Outdoors: Interactive map of Ireland's forests, trails, and outdoor activities.

www.sportireland.ie/outdoors/find-your-trails
Sport Ireland: National trail directory for hiking and walking routes.

www.trailforks.com/region/ireland
Mountain Biking Ireland: A trail guide for mountain biking across Ireland.

www.waterwaysireland.org
Waterways Ireland: Information on kayaking, boating, and canal routes.

ENTERTAINMENT

www.entertainment.ie
Entertainment.ie: Listings for concerts, festivals, theater, and nightlife across Ireland.

www.ticketmaster.ie
Ticketmaster Ireland: Ticket booking for major concerts, sports, and theater.

www.visitdublin.com
Visit Dublin: Events calendar for the capital's music, arts, and cultural happenings.

TRANSPORTATION

www.buseireann.ie
Bus Éireann: National and regional bus service schedules.

www.dublinbus.ie
Dublin Bus: Timetables and route maps for public transport in Dublin.

www.irishrail.ie
Irish Rail: Train schedules, ticket booking, and route maps.

www.transportforireland.ie
Transport for Ireland: Journey planner for buses, trains, and trams across the country.

NEWS AND PUBLICATIONS

www.independent.ie
Irish Independent: Coverage of Irish politics, business, and lifestyle.

www.irishtimes.com
The Irish Times: National newspaper covering news, culture, and travel.

www.rte.ie
RTÉ News: Ireland's state broadcaster with daily news and weather updates.

www.thejournal.ie
The Journal: Digital-first Irish news and opinion site.

Index

C

D

E

P

QR

S

T

UV

WXYZ

List of Maps

Photo Credits

All photos © Cían Byrne except for title page; © Boarding1now | Dreamstime.com; page 5 (top) © Gergo Kazsimer | Dreamstime.com; (middle top) © Romrodinka | Dreamstime.com; (middle bottom) © Hecke01 | Dreamstime.com; page 6–7 © Patryk Kosmider | Dreamstime.com; page 8–9 © Irimaxim | Dreamstime.com; page 10 (top) © VanderWolfImages | Dreamstime.com; (bottom) © Pablo Escuder Cano | Dreamstime.com; page 11 © Pablo Escuder Cano | Dreamstime.com; page 11 © Attila Tatár | Dreamstime.com; page 12 (top) © MNStudio | Dreamstime.com; (bottom) © Meunierd | Dreamstime.com; page 13 © MNStudio | Dreamstime.com; page 14–15 © Dawid Kalisinski | Dreamstime.com; page 16 © Mark Gusev | Dreamstime.com; page 17 (top) © Bhofack2 | Dreamstime.com; (bottom) © Schager/shutterstock; page 18 (bottom) © MNStudio | Dreamstime.com; page 21 (top) © Ddkg | Dreamstime.com; page 22 (top) © Robert Mullan | Dreamstime.com; (middle) © Frank Bach | Dreamstime.com (bottom) © Paulmccabe1 | Dreamstime.com; page 24 © Vladislav Mavrin | Dreamstime.com; page 25 © Pajda83 | Dreamstime.com; page 26 © Michael McMahon; page 28 © Volodymyr Semeniuk | Dreamstime.com; page 29 © Debra Reschoff Ahearn | Dreamstime.com; page 30 © MNStudio | Dreamstime.com; page 31 © Stbernardstudio | Dreamstime.com; page 33 (top) © Andrei Dzemidzenka | Dreamstime.com; (middle) © Radovan Mlatec | Dreamstime.com; (bottom) © Dprog05 | Dreamstime.com; Abdone | Dreamstime.com; page 34 © Abdone | Dreamstime.com; page 35 © Marion Horan | Dreamstime.com; page 36 © Markcus Greber; page 37 © Ihervas | Dreamstime.com; page 38 (top) © Marco Regalia | Dreamstime.com; (bottom) © Pilar Martín | Dreamstime.com; page 40 (bottom left) © Glitterd | Dreamstime.com (bottom right) © VanderWolfImages | Dreamstime.com; page 41 © Shahid Khan | Dreamstime.com; page 42 (top left) © Daniel M. Cisilino | Dreamstime.com; (top right) © VanderWolfImages | Dreamstime.com; page 46 © Maros Galgoci | Dreamstime.com; page 51 (top) © Chon Kit Leong | Dreamstime.com; (bottom) © Chon Kit Leong | Dreamstime.com; page 54 © Attila Tatár | Dreamstime.com; page 57 © Clement Mantion Pierre Olivier | Dreamstime.com; page 58 © Miruna Niculescu | Dreamstime.com; page 62 © Irina Pislari | Dreamstime.com; page 67 (top left) © Attila Jandi | Dreamstime.com; (top right) © Dublinuser | Dreamstime.com; (bottom) © Abdone | Dreamstime.com; page 71 (top) © John A Megaw, Jr | Dreamstime.com; (bottom) © Faithiecannoise | Dreamstime.com; page 81 © Michael Harper | Dreamstime.com; page 88 © Daniel M. Cisilino | Dreamstime.com; page 89 © Spiroview Inc. | Dreamstime.com; page 95 © Clive Stapleton | Dreamstime.com; page 102 (top) © Dawid Kalisinski | Dreamstime.com; (bottom) © Wirestock | Dreamstime.com; page 105 (top left) © Daniel M. Cisilino | Dreamstime.com; (top right) © Eg004713 | Dreamstime.com; page 112 (top) © Wirestock | Dreamstime.com; (left middle) © Les Palenik | Dreamstime.com; (right middle) © Robert Grim | Dreamstime.com; (bottom) © Daniel M. Cisilino | Dreamstime.com; page 118 (bottom) © Boris Breytman | Dreamstime.com; page 123 (top) © Daniel M. Cisilino | Dreamstime.com; (bottom) © Stephenkiernan | Dreamstime.com; page 135 © Chris Moncrieff | Dreamstime.com; page 136 © Karl M | Dreamstime.com; page 149 © Tamas Karpati | Dreamstime.com; page 150 (top left) © Patryk Kosmider | Dreamstime.com; (top right) © Algirdas Gelazius | Dreamstime.com; page 159 (top left) © Chris Dorne | Dreamstime.com; (top right) © Rudolf Ernst | Dreamstime.com; (bottom) © Yykkaa | Dreamstime.com; page 160 © David Ribeiro | Dreamstime.com; page 163 © David Morrison | Dreamstime.com; page 166 (top) © Daniel M. Cisilino | Dreamstime.com; (left middle) © Emanuele Leoni | Dreamstime.com; (right middle) © Daniel M. Cisilino | Dreamstime.com; (bottom) © Robert Grim | Dreamstime.com; page 172 (top left) © Chris Dorney | Dreamstime.com; (top right) © Chris Dorney | Dreamstime.com; (bottom) © Emma Moloney | Dreamstime.com; page 174 © | Wikimedia Commons; page 176 © I L | Dreamstime.com; page 177 (top left) © David Ribeiro | Dreamstime.com; (top right) Stephen Smith | Dreamstime.com; page 183 © David Ribeiro | Dreamstime.com; page 188 (top) © Shawn Williams | Dreamstime.com; (left middle) © Brett Andersen | Dreamstime.com; (bottom) © Jjfarq | Dreamstime.com; page 197 © David Morrison | Dreamstime.com; page 199 (top) © MNStudio | Dreamstime.com; (right middle) © 2darrenleeming | Dreamstime.com; (bottom) © David Ribeiro | Dreamstime.com; page 201 (top left) © Linda Williams | Dreamstime.com; (bottom) © Jenifoto406 | Dreamstime.com; page 207 (bottom) © Patryk Kosmider | Dreamstime.com; page 211 (top) © Matthias Grlich | Dreamstime.com; page 213 © Altezza | Dreamstime.com; page 215 © Fotoab | Dreamstime.com; page 216 © Algirdas Gelazius | Dreamstime.com; page 219 (top left) © Peghess07 | Dreamstime.com; (top right) © Tupungato | Dreamstime.com; page 229 © © Peewam | Dreamstime.com; page 230 (top right) © Paop | Dreamstime.com; page 236 (top) © Jenifoto406 | Dreamstime.com; (bottom) © E55evu |

Dreamstime.com; page 238 © Michel Dreher | Dreamstime.com; page 240 © Gabe9000c | Dreamstime.com; page 243 (top) © Oleksii Kononenko | Dreamstime.com; (bottom) © Igor Igdal | Dreamstime.com; page 246 © Christian Mueringer | Dreamstime.com; page 249 (top) © ShutterUpIreland | Dreamstime.com; (bottom) © Frank Bach | Dreamstime.com; page 252 © Dawid Kalisinski | Dreamstime.com; page 257 © Radomír Režný | Dreamstime.com; page 260 © Michel Dreher | Dreamstime.com; page 262 © Michel Dreher | Dreamstime.com; page 263 (top) © Pajda83 | Dreamstime.com; page 266 (top left) © Pajda83 | Dreamstime.com; (top right) © Mark Gusev | Dreamstime.com; page 276 © Joe Ormonde | Dreamstime.com; page 279 (top) © Bartkowski | Dreamstime.com; page 284 (top) © Bertgphotography | Dreamstime.com; (bottom) © John Holmes | Dreamstime.com; page 288 © Makasanaphoto | Dreamstime.com; page 293 © Michael Walsh | Dreamstime.com; page 299 © Michel Dreher | Dreamstime.com; page 300 (top left) © Helen Hotson | Dreamstime.com; (top right) © Albertoloyo | Dreamstime.com; page 309 (top left) © Frank Bach | Dreamstime.com; (top right) © Stephen Smith | Dreamstime.com; (bottom) © Elzbieta Sekowska | Dreamstime.com; page 310 (top) © Mark Gusev | Dreamstime.com; (bottom) © Mark Gusev | Dreamstime.com; page 314 © Louis Michel Desert | Dreamstime.com; page 320 © Joe Ormonde | Dreamstime.com; page 321 © E55evu | Dreamstime.com; page 323 © Pniesen | Dreamstime.com; page 324 © Whpics | Dreamstime.com; page 328 (top) © Mark Gusev | Dreamstime.com; (bottom) © Elena Schweitzer | Dreamstime.com; page 332 (top) © Romrodinka | Dreamstime.com; (bottom) © Irimaxim | Dreamstime.com; page 338 (top) © Karlo Curis | Dreamstime.com; (bottom) © Lisandrotrarbach | Dreamstime.com; page 342 (top) © Debra Reschoff Ahearn | Dreamstime.com; (bottom) © Mark Gusev | Dreamstime.com; page 346 © Shawn Williams | Dreamstime.com; page 348 © Paul Shiels | Dreamstime.com; page 349 (top left) © MNStudio | Dreamstime.com; (top right) © Mark Gusev | Dreamstime.com; page 357 (top left) © Mark Gusev | Dreamstime.com; (top right) © Eva Jimenez | Dreamstime.com; (bottom) © Debra Reschoff Ahearn | Dreamstime.com; page 361 © Sean O' Dwyer | Dreamstime.com; page 363 (left middle) © Mark Gusev | Dreamstime.com; (right middle) © MNStudio | Dreamstime.com; (bottom) © MNStudio | Dreamstime.com; page 369 © Romrodinka | Dreamstime.com; page 370 © Thomas Lukassek | Dreamstime.com; page 373 (top) © Daniel M. Cisilino | Dreamstime.com; (left middle) © Gareth Cosgrove | Dreamstime.com; (right middle) © Sergejus Lamanosovas | Dreamstime.com; (bottom) © Thomas Lukassek | Dreamstime.com; page 377 © Davide Devecchi | Dreamstime.com; page 380 (top) © Romrodinka | Dreamstime.com; (bottom) © Ihervas | Dreamstime.com; page 384 © Thomas Lukassek | Dreamstime.com; page 386 (top) © Agnieszka Glowala | Dreamstime.com; (left middle) © Shawn Williams | Dreamstime.com; (right middle) © 4kclips | Dreamstime.com; (bottom) © Agnieszka Glowala | Dreamstime.com; page 389 © Agnieszka Glowala | Dreamstime.com; page 390 (top left) © Atmosphere1 | Dreamstime.com; (top right) © Phillip Gray | Dreamstime.com; page 400 © Nataliya Hora | Dreamstime.com; page 403 (top) © Meunierd | Dreamstime.com; (left middle) © Tupungato | Dreamstime.com; (right middle) © Krzysztof Nahlik | Dreamstime.com; (bottom) © Chusnie Mubarok | Dreamstime.com; page 404 © Andrea La Corte | Dreamstime.com; page 408 © 4kclips | Dreamstime.com; page 413 © Michael Harper | Dreamstime.com; page 417 © Luca Bergami | Dreamstime.com; page 420 © Tupungato | Dreamstime.com; page 423 © Daniel Nagy | Dreamstime.com; page 425 (top) © Muzzyco | Dreamstime.com; (bottom) © Marco Sardi | Dreamstime.com; page 426 © Nigel Hoy | Dreamstime.com; page 429 © Petr Doubek | Dreamstime.com; page 431 © Pfeifferv | Dreamstime.com; page 433 © Daniel M. Cisilino | Dreamstime.com; page 436 © Graphicjet | Dreamstime.com; page 445 (top) © Dawid Kalisinski | Dreamstime.com

MOON IRELAND

Avalon Travel
Hachette Book Group, Inc.
555 12th Street, Suite 1850
Oakland, CA 94607, USA
www.moon.com

Editor: Vy Tran
Managing Editor: Hannah Brezack
Copy Editor: Christopher Church
Graphics and Production Coordinator: Suzanne Albertson
Cover Design: Toni Tajima
Interior Design: Avalon Travel
Map Editor: John Culp
Cartographer: John Culp
Proofreader: Callie Stoker-Graham
Indexer: Greg Jewett

ISBN-13: 979-8-88647-142-7

Printing History
1st Edition — December 2025
5 4 3 2 1

Front cover photo: Mourne Mountains © Cían Bryne
Back cover photo: Ross Castle, Killarney National Park © Jenifoto406 | Dreamstime.com

Printed in China by RRD Dongguan

MAP SYMBOLS

Highway
Primary Road
Secondary Road
Unpaved Road
Walkway
Stairs
Featured Trail
Trail
Ferry
Railroad

City/Town
State Capital
National Capital
Highlight
Sight
Accommodation
Restaurant/Bar
Other Location

Information Center
International Airport
Regional Airport
Train Station
Metro
Bus Stop
Parking
Trailhead
Camping

Park
Golf Course
Place of Worship
Mountain
Unique Feature
Hydro Feature
Waterfall
Winery/Vineyard
Glacier

CONVERSION TABLES

°C = (°F - 32) / 1.8
°F = (°C x 1.8) + 32
1 inch = 2.54 centimeters (cm)
1 foot = 0.304 meters (m)
1 yard = 0.914 meters
1 mile = 1.6093 kilometers (km)
1 km = 0.6214 miles
1 fathom = 1.8288 m
1 chain = 20.1168 m
1 furlong = 201.168 m
1 acre = 0.4047 hectares
1 sq km = 100 hectares
1 sq mile = 2.59 square km
1 ounce = 28.35 grams
1 pound = 0.4536 kilograms
1 short ton = 0.90718 metric ton
1 short ton = 2,000 pounds
1 long ton = 1.016 metric tons
1 long ton = 2,240 pounds
1 metric ton = 1,000 kilograms
1 quart = 0.94635 liters
1 US gallon = 3.7854 liters
1 Imperial gallon = 4.5459 liters
1 nautical mile = 1.852 km

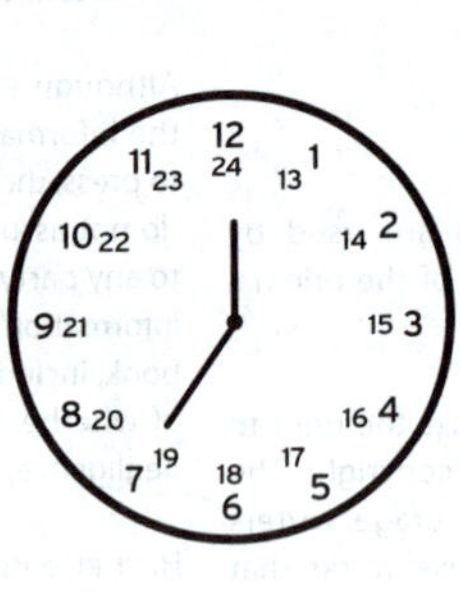

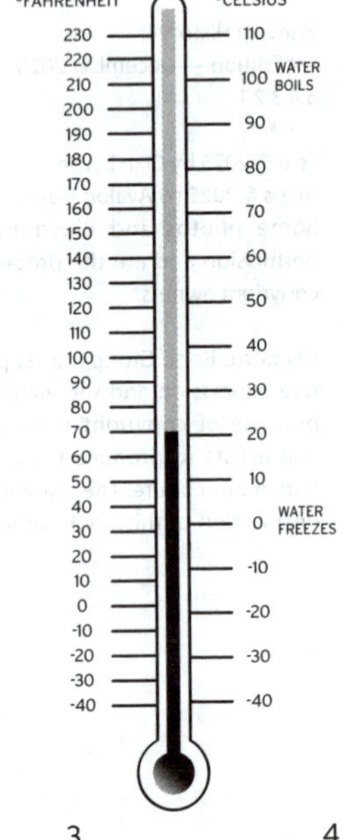

Cities

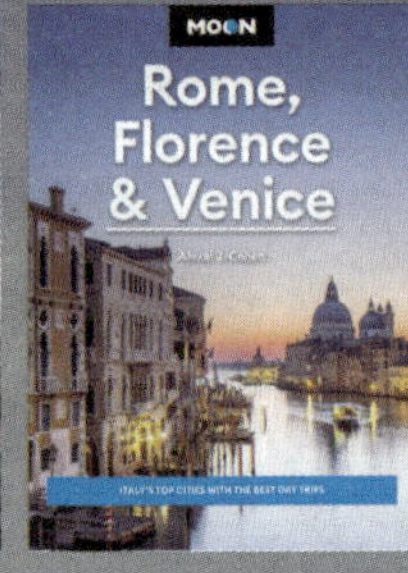

Europe, Middle East & Africa

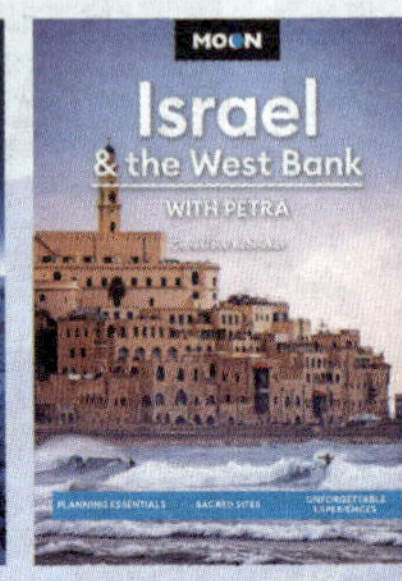

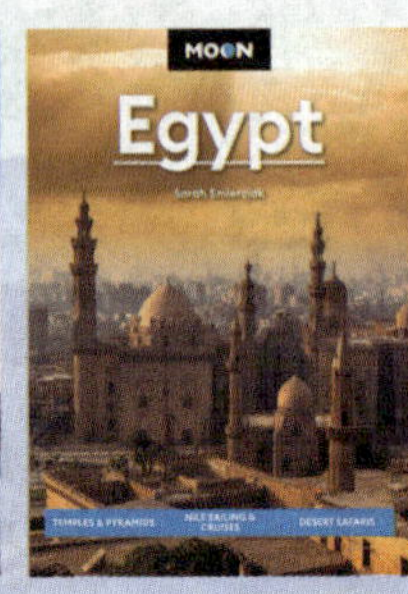

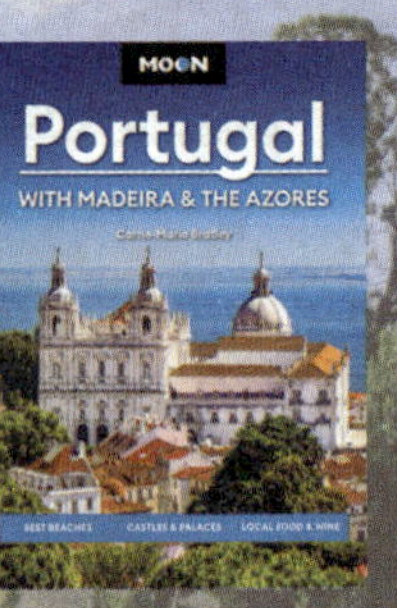

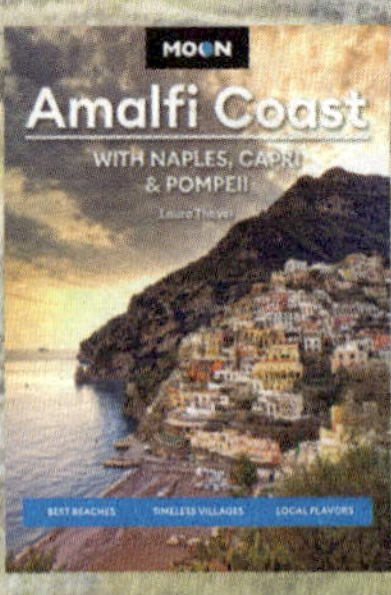

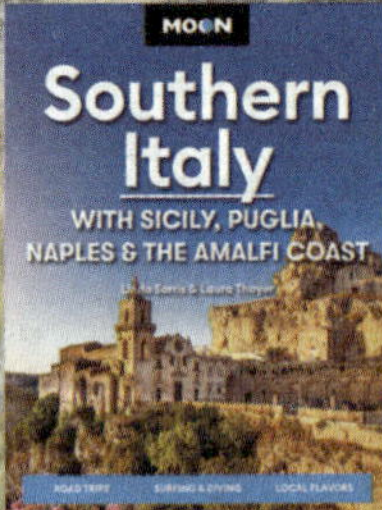

Latin America

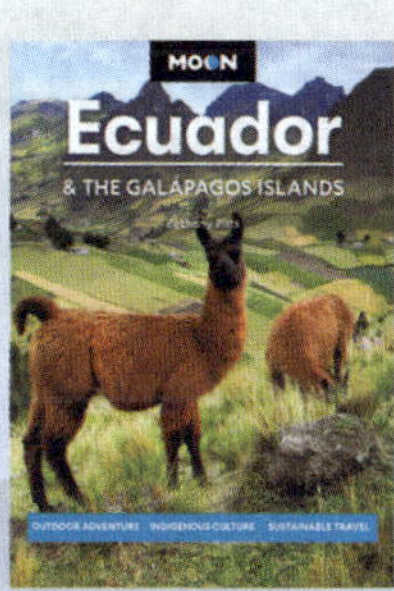

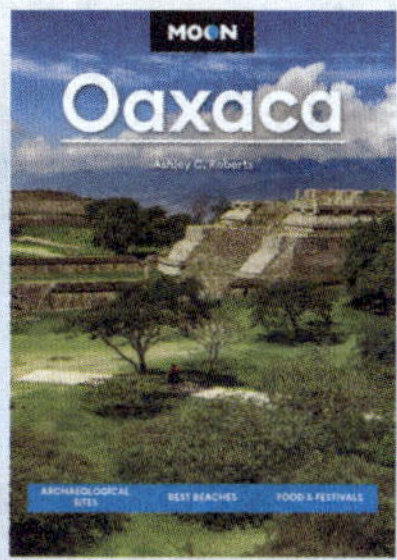

United States

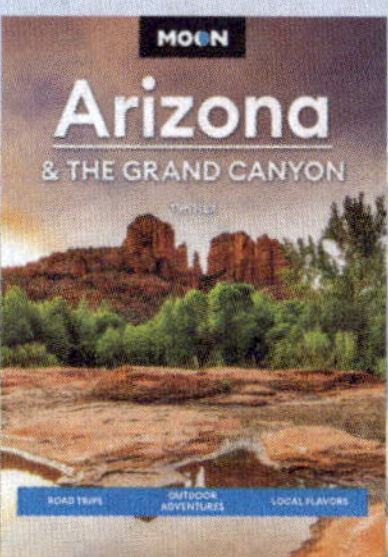

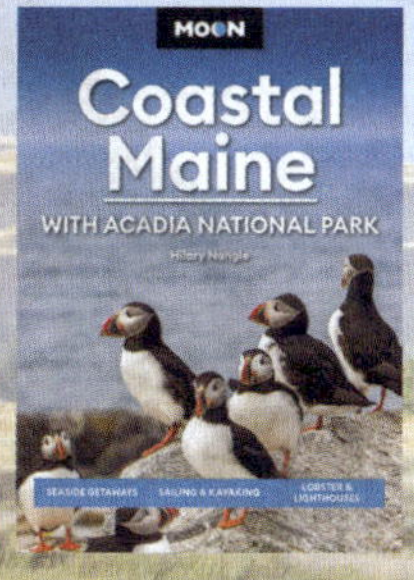

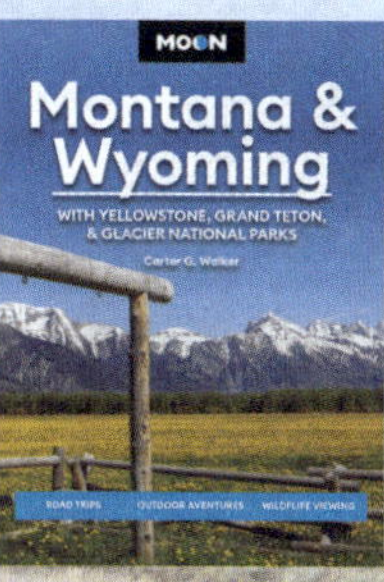

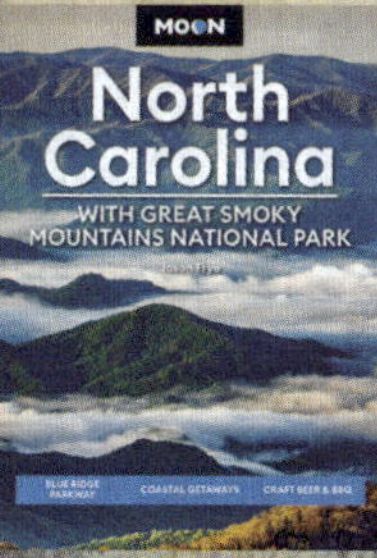

MOON.COM | @MOONGUIDES